PASO DOBLE

A second stage Spanish course on BBC radio

Course writer
Clare Mar Molinero
University of Southampton

Language consultants
Salvador Ortiz-Carboneres
University of Warwick

Hugh O'Shaughnessy
Latin American correspondent of the *Observer*

Production assistant
Jacqui Shields

Editor and series producer
Carol Stanley

PASO DOBLE

BBC BOOKS

Paso Doble is a second stage Spanish course on BBC Radio, first broadcast in January 1989.

The course consists of 10 radio programmes.

This book covers all the programmes.

Two audio cassettes are also available.

This book accompanies the BBC Radio series **Paso Doble**
first broadcast on Radio 4 VHF in January 1989
(produced by Carol Stanley),
and is prepared in consultation with the
BBC Educational Broadcasting Council.

Published by BBC Books
a division of BBC Enterprises Limited,
Woodlands, 80 Wood Lane, London W12 0TT.

First published 1989.

© The author & BBC Enterprises Ltd 1989

ISBN 0 563 21453 8

Set in 10/12 pt Univers and
printed and bound in Great Britain by
Butler & Tanner Limited Frome and London
cover printed by Fletchers of Norwich

CONTENTS

ACKNOWLEDGEMENTS

ALL-SPORT pages 108–9 (Vandystad) & 110 (David Cannon); ASSOCIATED PRESS page 131; J. ALLAN CASH PHOTOLIBRARY pages 45 & 119; JAIME SUAREZ GARCIA pages 28 *right*, 46 *inset*, 102 & 128; GRABACIONES ACCIDENTALES, S.A. page 98; HULTON page 82 (UPI/Bettmann Newsphotos); STEPHEN MOSS page 84; MUSEUM OF MODERN ART, NY pages 58–9; HUGH O'SHAUGHNESSY page 7 *centre right*; POPPERFOTO pages 70–1 & 91; TOMAS SUAREZ SHUTTE page 32; FERNANDO SUAREZ page 104; MICK WEBB pages 7 *far right*, 21, 56, 69, 94 *both* & 107.

All other photographs were taken for BBC Enterprises by David Gee.

Jacket and Book Design: Annette Peppis
Cover illustration: Melanie Bowles
Inside a/w and maps: Shirley Walker

INTRODUCTION

THE COURSE

Paso Doble is the second step to take if you already know some Spanish. It's a follow-up to the BBC beginners' course **España Viva**, and is designed to increase your understanding of Spanish and your ability to take part in conversations on all sorts of subjects: yourself and your family, things that have happened, and the important – and trivial – topics of the day. **Paso Doble** also introduces the varieties of Spanish spoken in many of the countries of Latin America.

The three elements of **Paso Doble** are ten radio programmes, a pack of two cassettes, and this book, and they're based on recorded interviews and conversations.

THE RECORDINGS

In Spain, the recordings were all made in Madrid, and they centre on a typical building just off the Plaza Mayor in the heart of the old part of the city. The building is a mixture of flats and commercial premises, and our interviewers Isabel Soto and Julia Bueno talked to some of the people who live and work there. From what they have to say you'll get a picture of Spain today, and in particular of what it's like to live in the capital.

By contrast, the Latin America recordings cover a huge geographical area and a wide cross-section of people. The interviewers were Hugh O'Shaughnessy and BBC producer Mick Webb, who visited many of the countries of Central and South America in the course of making several series for Radio 4. The interviews touch on a wide variety of subjects, including early South American civilisations, how to change money in Peru, Mexico City after the 1985 earthquake, and the future of the Panama Canal.

From left to right: Julia Bueno, Isabel Soto, Mick Webb, Hugh O'Shaughnessy

THE PROGRAMMES

Each programme uses the recorded interviews and conversations to highlight different areas of the language and give insights into life in both Spain and Latin America. There are also opportunities to practise using Spanish and to test your understanding.

THE CASSETTES

The cassettes have a separate section for each of the ten units, which contain the recordings from Spain and a short exercise. The Latin America recordings are all grouped together on one side of cassette 2. The interviews printed in the *Suplemento* section of the book are also included.

THE BOOK

The book has ten units, each divided into sections:

First comes the text of the interviews and conversations recorded in Spain. Unusual or difficult words and phrases are translated alongside, and each interview is followed by one or two *Preguntas* – questions in Spanish to check you've understood. Answers to the *Preguntas* are in the *Clave* at the back of the book.

Lengua explains the main language points of each unit.

América Latina features interviews from all over Central and South America, and highlights some of the *americanismos* in them.

España Actual contains short articles on aspects of Spain and Spanish life today.

Prácticas are exercises to get you to use the language. Answers are in the *Clave* at the back of the book.

The ten units are followed by a reference section (on the tinted pages):

Suplemento is a selection of extra interviews from both Spain and Latin America – the recordings are on the cassettes.

Gramática is a more formal summary of the language in the course, including lists of the verb forms.

Pronunciación is a guide to standard Spanish pronunciation, with notes on Latin American variations.

Clave contains answers to the *Preguntas* and *Prácticas*.

Vocabulario is a list of all the Spanish words that appear in the book, with English translations.

USING THE COURSE

Paso Doble is designed to be flexible. It's best if you use all the elements of the course – book, cassettes and radio programmes, but you can decide for yourself how much work you want to do. As a basis though, you should concentrate on the main interviews and language points of each unit. The Latin American recordings can be an optional extra – the *americanismos* highlight the kinds of words and phrases that may catch you out if you go to the region.

You'll get more out of the programmes if you look at the appropriate unit in the book beforehand. Read through the interviews and answer the *Preguntas*, and read the *Lengua* section. Go through the *Amèrica Latina* interviews too – and be prepared for the very different accents when you hear them. Don't try to follow the interviews in print while listening to the programmes. Concentrate instead on understanding what's being said and how it's being said. You can use the cassettes to link the spoken language with how it's written, though the more you listen without looking, the more your ear will become attuned to the sounds of the language – essential when you have to put what you've learnt into practice.

The *España Actual* sections are written in the kind of language you'll encounter in Spanish newspapers and magazines – that's to say, it's a bit more complex than ordinary conversational Spanish. When you first read the articles, concentrate on understanding the gist – don't stop and look up every word (though all the words are in the *Vocabulario* at the back).

If you want further practice, the *Suplemento* at the back has a further selection of interviews, all of which are on the cassettes.

Take advantage of any opportunities you get to practise speaking Spanish – with friends or family, at an adult education class, or on visits to Spanish-speaking countries.

THE SPANISH LANGUAGE

This course concentrates on teaching 'standard' Spanish, which will enable you to communicate with Spanish speakers anywhere in the world. However, Spanish (like English, another world-wide language) comes in a large number of varieties. Even within Spain, the language varies from one region to another, but in other countries the differences are even more marked.

Latin American Spanish, for instance, has many features in common with the language of southern Spain, because that's where many of the early settlers came from, but it's also been subjected to a whole range of other influences: the language of native Indian peoples, other European languages brought by immigrants, African languages and, especially in Mexico, the English of the USA.

Among the varieties of Spanish you'll find differences of vocabulary and, to a much lesser extent, grammar, but the most noticeable feature is regional accents. When you listen to the **Paso Doble** recordings you'll hear accents from different parts of Spain among the people interviewed in Madrid, though the differences between them pale into insignificance when you compare them with, say, a Chilean or Venezuelan accent.

Notes on the Spanish that you should concentrate on learning are in the *Lengua* section of each unit, and in *Gramática* on page **145**, but it's worth remembering a few general points:

1   Spanish verb forms hold the key to a number of things. The different verb endings show who the subject of the verb is: for instance, *hablo* means 'I speak' and *hablas* is 'you speak' – contrast that with English where just saying 'speak' would be meaningless.

The endings also show the tense, or time, of the verb – past, present or future: *hablé* is 'I spoke' (past), *hablaré* is 'I will speak' (future).

Spanish verbs fall into one of three groups according to whether their infinitive ends in *-ar*, *-er* or *-ir*, e.g. *hablar*, *comer*, *vivir*. Verb endings vary for the different groups.

Whether you learn them in lists or by gradually absorbing them as you go along, it's important to become familiar with the different verb endings and how to use them.

2   The Spanish words for 'I', 'you', 'he', 'we' and so on are not used as much as their English equivalents. In English they're essential – 'I speak', 'we speak' – but in Spanish the verb on its own is enough: *hablo*, *hablamos*. *Yo, tú, nosotros*, etc. are only used for emphasis, e.g. *yo soy de Valencia pero él es de Granada*.

3   As explained in unit 1, Spanish has different ways of saying 'you'. **Paso Doble** mainly uses the informal *tú* form, which is more common in Spain nowadays, but it's as well to be aware of the *usted* form as well.

4   Every noun in Spanish is either masculine or feminine, so remember that the words for 'a' and 'the', and adjectives, have to agree with this gender.

5   Word order is quite flexible in Spanish, and changing the order can cause a subtle change of emphasis. Tone of voice and intonation often tell you whether something is a statement or a question, rather than the order of the words.

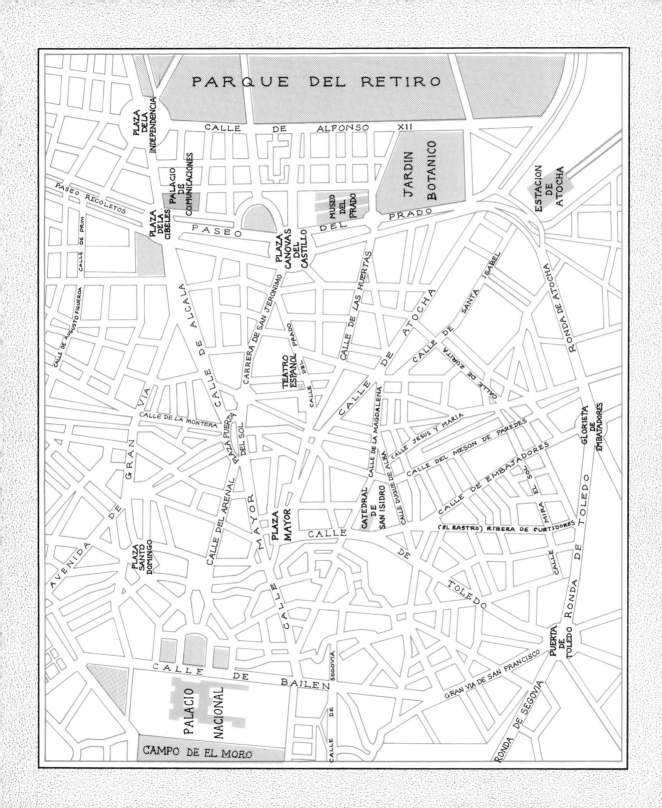

¿QUIÉN ERES?

Talking about yourself

Calle Toledo is in the heart of old Madrid: at the Plaza Mayor end, the 17th-century buildings are divided into apartments; below, at street level, are arcades with shops, bars and restaurants.

1

Isabel Soto, one of the *Paso Doble* interviewers, lives with her husband, Jaime, in one of the flats in number 4 Calle Toledo. Her friend and co-interviewer, Julia Bueno, came to talk to some of the other people who live or work in the building. On the left of the street door of number 4 is a draper's shop . . .

Julia	Estoy en la tienda que hay en el número cuatro de la calle Toledo. Es una pañería, una tienda muy antigua, y estoy con ¿el señor . . . ?
Sr Angulo	José Fernández, exactamente el mismo nombre que lleva la sociedad, porque la sociedad es *Fernández Angulo SA*, y yo soy José Fernández Angulo.
Julia	O sea, esto es una sociedad.
Sr Angulo	Esto es una sociedad anónima.
Julia	¿Y hay muchos socios?
Sr Angulo	Solamente tres hermanos.
Julia	¿Y usted está casado?
Sr Angulo	Yo estoy soltero.
Julia	¿De dónde es usted?
Sr Angulo	De Madrid.
Julia	¿Y toda su familia también?
Sr Angulo	No. Mi madre es de Madrid, sí, pero mi padre es de Burgos, y mi abuelo es de Burgos. O sea, los Angulos, cuando vea un apellido Angulo en España, provienen la mayoría de ellos de la provincia de Burgos.

Fernández is a very common surname so he's generally known as Sr Angulo

o sea *that's to say, in other words*
sociedad anónima (SA) *limited company*
estoy soltero *I'm unmarried (it's more usual to say* **soy soltero***)*
cuando vea *whenever you see*

PREGUNTAS
1   ¿Tiene mujer el Sr Angulo?
2   ¿Es el Sr Angulo de Madrid?

2

On the other side of the street door of number 4 is a restaurant.

Julia	Estamos en el restaurante *El Cuchi*, que se encuentra en la calle Toledo número cuatro, justo debajo de la casa de Isabel y Jaime. Y vamos a hablar con . . .
Sergio	Sergio Durazo.
Julia	Muy bien. ¿Tú eres el propietario o eres un . . . sólo un camarero aquí?
Sergio	Soy el propietario del restaurante. Tengo varios socios, pero yo soy el . . . el que tiene que trabajar.
Julia	Y tú no tienes acento de ser madrileño, ¿de dónde eres?
Sergio	Yo soy de Méjico, de la ciudad de Méjico.

se encuentra *is (situated)*
justo debajo de *right underneath*
el que tiene que *the one who has to*
tú no tienes acento de ser *you don't sound as though you are*

PREGUNTAS
1   ¿Es español el propietario de *El Cuchi*?
2   ¿Es Sergio el único propietario?

in Mexico, Méjico is also written 'México'

Sergio da un servicio con una sonrisa

3

Meanwhile, Isabel went to talk to one of the owners of the *Hostal Los Gallegos* on the first floor. Like thousands of people living in Madrid, Mercedes Arias Sánchez wasn't born there.

Isabel	Mercedes, eres una de las propietarias del *Hostal Gallegos*, ¿no es así?
Mercedes	Pues sí.
Isabel	¿Eres gallega?
Mercedes	Sí, gallega, de la provincia de Lugo.
Isabel	¿Tienes hijos?
Mercedes	Dos chicas.
Isabel	¿Sí? ¿Viven contigo?
Mercedes	No, casadas, ya casadas las dos.
Isabel	¿Tienes nietos?
Mercedes	Ninguno de momento.
Isabel	¿Cuánto tiempo hace que tenéis el hostal?
Mercedes	Pues mira, exactamente desde el sesenta y nueve, me parece.
Isabel	O sea, casi veinte años.
Mercedes	Mmm . . .

¿no es así? *isn't that so?*
contigo *with you*
las dos *both of them*
de momento *at the moment*
¿cuánto tiempo hace que tenéis . . .? *how long is it that you've had . . .?*
pues mira *well now*
me parece *I think*

PREGUNTAS
1 ¿De dónde es Mercedes?
2 ¿Tiene hijos o hijas Mercedes?

4

Ana and Antonio are a married couple who live up on the fourth floor.

Isabel	Ana, ¿cómo te apellidas?
Ana	Recio Beladiez.
Isabel	¿Y de dónde son esos apellidos?
Ana	Recio es extremeño . . . yo soy de Cáceres. Y Beladiez es de Almazán y Soria.
Isabel	¿Y tú te consideras extremeña o . . .?
Ana	No, de Madrid. Llevo treinta años en Madrid.

¿cómo te apellidas? *what is your surname?* (*a rather formal way of asking*)
llevo *I've spent*

Isabel	Antonio, ¿cómo te apellidas?
Antonio	Pueche, de primer apellido, y Cervera de segundo apellido.
Isabel	¿Y tú de dónde eres?
Antonio	Yo soy de Madrid, de Chamberí.
Isabel	¿De Chamberí?
Antonio	Chamberí.

Isabel	O sea, lo más castizo ...
Antonio	De lo más castizo, sí, sí.

lo más castizo *the most typical/authentic*

PREGUNTAS

1 ¿Son Ana y Antonio los dos madrileños?

5

Rosa García Rodero is Isabel and Jaime's next-door neighbour.

Julia	Rosa, ¿tú de dónde eres?
Rosa	Soy de un pueblo minero del sur de Ciudad Real, Puertollano.
Julia	¿Y cuánto tiempo llevas viviendo en Madrid?
Rosa	Desde los once años, y tengo cuarenta y dos, casi toda mi vida.
Julia	¿En qué trabajas?
Rosa	Doy clases de griego en enseñanza media.
Julia	¿Tú estás casada, Rosa?
Rosa	No, no.
Julia	¿Soltera o divorciada?
Rosa	Sí, soltera.

desde los once años *since I was eleven*
doy clases de / *teach*
en enseñanza media *at secondary school level*

PREGUNTAS

1 ¿Cuántos años lleva Rosa viviendo en Madrid?
2 ¿Qué hace Rosa?

6

On the top floor live the Espada family, and Isabel talked to them about their origins and their daily routines. First, Tere, whose full name is María Teresa Santalla Padín. Like all Spanish wives, Tere uses her maiden name . . .

Isabel	Tere, ¿cómo te apellidas?
Tere	Santalla Padín.
Isabel	Santalla Padín. ¿De dónde eres?
Tere	De Madrid.
Isabel	¿Y llevas toda tu vida viviendo en Madrid?
Tere	En Madrid, sí.
Isabel	¿Vives sola?
Tere	Vivo con mi marido, mi hija, y una perrita que tengo.
Isabel	¿A qué te dedicas?
Tere	¡Ay, a muchas cosas, hija! Mira, me levanto por la mañana, me voy a la plaza, a la compra, saco mi perrito a hacer sus cositas. Luego después traigo la compra, preparo la comida, y me pongo a coser. Luego después viene Almudena a comer, preparo la comida, friego los cacharros, me pongo a ver *Los Colbys*, que no la pierdo por nada del mundo. Entonces, luego ya me siento en mi taller a coser. Siempre viene alguna clienta por la tarde y . . . en fin.

perrita *little dog*
¿a qué te dedicas? *what do you do?*
'hija' *'my dear'*
sus cositas *its 'business'*
traigo / *bring (back)*
me pongo a / *settle down to, I begin to*
friego los cacharros *I do the washing-up*
que no la pierdo por nada del mundo *because I wouldn't miss it for the world*
en fin *there you are*

Next, Tere's husband, Isidoro, who jokes about his name . . .

Isabel	Isidoro, ¿cómo te apellidas?
Isidoro	Espada Moreno.
Isabel	¿De dónde son esos apellidos?
Isidoro	Espada, creo que tiene un origen italiano. Y Moreno, pues no sé de dónde vendrá porque yo soy rubio, y mi familia, ¡pues todos han sido rubios!
Isabel	¿De dónde sois?
Isidoro	Yo de Madrid, mi padre de Zaragoza, mi madre de un pueblo de la provincia de Madrid, mi abuelo paterno también de Madrid, y el resto de mis abuelos, pues, de distintos puntos de la geografía de España.
Isabel	¿A qué te dedicas?
Isidoro	En este momento, al dulce no hacer nada. Los italianos lo expresan diciendo *'il dolce far niente'*.

de dónde vendrá *where it can come from*

todos han sido *they've all been*

al dulce no hacer nada *to the delights of doing nothing*

lo expresan diciendo *say, express it as*

Isidoro, Tere y Pola, la perra

And lastly, Tere and Isidoro's daughter, Almudena . . .

Isabel	Almudena, ¿cuál es tu apellido?
Almudena	Almudena Espada Santalla.
Isabel	Háblame un poco de lo que haces, a qué te dedicas. ¿Trabajas o . . .?
Almudena	Bueno, yo vivo con mis padres, y trabajo. Trabajo en una oficina, como secretaria, y normalmente, bueno, pues salgo con los amigos, amigas.

Spaniards take their first surname from their father and the second from their mother

salgo / go out

PREGUNTAS

1 ¿Quién vive en la casa de la familia Espada?
2 ¿Trabaja Isidoro?

LENGUA

Important: If you haven't already done so, read the section on **The Spanish Language**, page 9.

TO BE: *SER* OR *ESTAR*?

Ser is mostly used to say who or what you are:
Yo **soy** José Fernández Angulo.
Soy el propietario del restaurante.

or where you're from:
Soy de Méjico.   **Soy** gallega.

or what something is:
Es una pañería.   Recio **es** extremeño.

Estar is mostly used to say where someone or something is located:
Estoy en la tienda del Sr Angulo.
Cáceres **está** en Extremadura.

or with words describing states or moods that are changeable, e.g. *enfermo* (ill), *contento* (happy).

One exception is talking about marital status:
Soy soltero/a.   **Soy** viudo/a.
but
Estoy casado/a.   **Estoy** divorciado/a.

(For the formation of *ser* and *estar*, see **Gramática**, pages 153 and 154.)

HOW TO SAY 'YOU'

Remember there are different ways of saying 'you' in Spanish:
tú   vosotros   usted   ustedes
which are used with different forms of the verb (see **Gramática**, page 146).

Use the *tú* form (or *vosotros* with more than one person):
● when you're on first-name terms with the person (like Isabel with her neighbours)
● when talking to a child
● with a person of the same age and background as you (e.g. Julia with Sergio)
● with anyone very close to you (family etc.)

Use *usted* (*ustedes* with more than one person):
● when you want to be respectful (e.g. Julia with Sr Angulo, whom she doesn't know and who's older)
● in very formal situations
● when in doubt (e.g. if you've just met)

In Spain you'll find increasingly that people prefer to use *tú* almost immediately to establish a friendly, equal relationship. In southern Spain, *vosotros* isn't used at all, only *ustedes*. (For Latin American variations see page 146.)

Remember also to use the correct word for 'your': *tu, vuestro* or *su* (see **Gramática**, page 146).

LLEVAR

The verb *llevar* has several meanings, including 'to have', 'to carry', 'to take', 'to wear', and 'to spend (time)':

... el mismo nombre que lleva la sociedad.	... the same name that the company has.
Lleva el pelo corto.	She has short hair.
Lleva una camisa azul.	He's wearing a blue shirt.
Llevo treinta años en Madrid.	I've spent thirty years in Madrid.

¿CUANTO TIEMPO ...?

'How long have you been ...?'. To ask this kind of question, use the phrase *¿Cuánto tiempo ...?*, followed by a verb in the **present** tense:

¿Cuánto tiempo **llevas** *viviendo* en Madrid?	How long have you been ...?
¿Cuánto tiempo **hace** que **tenéis** el hostal?	How long is it that ...?

There are various ways of answering:

Desde el sesenta y nueve.	Since 1969.
Desde hace veinte años.	For twenty years.
Hace veinte años **que** lo tenemos.	We've had it for twenty years.

AMÉRICA LATINA

As you read or listen to these interviews and conversations from Latin America, you'll notice words and phrases that are peculiar to Latin American Spanish. Some are words you'll hear in Spain but used with different meanings; some are words you'll hear a lot in Latin America but hardly ever in Spain. We've highlighted some of these 'Americanisms' – though if you're going to Latin America, you'll soon get a feel for the Spanish around you, and find yourself picking up local phrases.

1   ARGENTINA

On his travels round Latin America, Mick Webb met Tomás (Tommy) Suárez Shutte, who lives and works in Bahía Blanca. Mick asked him about his job and about the area.

Mick	¿Vos qué haces actualmente?
Tommy	Actualmente yo pertenezco … estoy en la actividad financiera, soy subgerente general de un banco de características regionales, un banco que abarca siete provincias, siete estados provinciales. Es el banco número uno del interior del país.
Mick	¿Mucha riqueza hay por esta zona?
Tommy	Tenemos fruticultura, ganadería, cereales. Tenemos pesca, tenemos, este, lana, o sea, hay ovejas. Tenemos las mejores ciudades turísticas del país. Además la ciudad de Bahía Blanca, en la que vivo yo con mi familia, se le llama 'la puerta de la Patagonia'. Es la ciudad más importante del sur argentino, desde Buenos Aires hacia Ushuaia. Fuera de Buenos Aires es la más importante, desde el punto de vista económico.

vos *you*
yo pertenezco *I belong*
este *'um', 'well'*
en la que *in which*
se le llama *they call it*
punto de vista *point of view*

Tommy's wife, Zulema, is a teacher.

Zulema	Yo, este, ya hace muchos años soy docente, soy maestra de escuela primaria, o sea de los niños más chicos, este, que acá en la Argentina, es una carrera que se desempeña con mucho amor, ¿no es cierto?, porque gratificado económicamente, es muy poco. O sea, que por lo general, los maestros tenemos más vocación, ¿no es cierto?
Mick	Y menos pago …
Zulema	Y muy mal pago, sí.

los niños más chicos *the youngest children*
se desempeña *we do*
¿no es cierto? *right?*

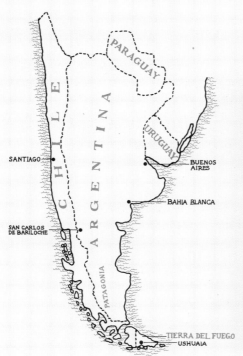

2 CHILE

Elizabeth Subercaseaux lives in Santiago de Chile. Hugh O'Shaughnessy, who's Irish, asked her to guess where he was from.

Hugh	¿De dónde soy yo, por mi acento?
Elizabeth	Es bien curioso tu acento, porque los norteamericanos que hablan español no hablan como tú, tienen un acento completamente distinto. Ellos siempre tienen como una patata dentro de la boca, ¿no? Estoy dudando entre dos cosas, o que tú eres de origen español y te educaste en Inglaterra y aprendiste muy bien el inglés, o que tú eres un inglés que aprendiste muy bien el español, pero muy influenciado por el acento más bien centroamericano.

bien curioso *very strange*
estoy dudando *I'm hestitating*
te educaste *you were brought up*
aprendiste *you learnt*

americanismos
vos *used instead of* tú *in Argentina and some other countries*
este *is very commonly used in Latin America to mean 'well' or 'um'*
chico *young, small* (*'boy' in Spain*)
acá *used much more than* aquí
¿no es cierto? ¿verdad? *in Spain*

ESPAÑA ACTUAL

LAS VARIEDADES DEL ESPAÑOL

Al pasearse por las calles de Madrid, al igual que todas las ciudades grandes de España, no se oye a la gente hablar con un acento único. Siendo la capital de España allí está representada gente de todas las partes de España y hasta de todas las partes de habla española. Los acentos varían mucho de región en región, de país a país donde se habla español, o, mejor dicho, castellano.

El acento local de Madrid tiene las características de los acentos que se encuentran en el centro de España, en las dos Castillas. Se identifica por los rasgos más típicos de la pronunciación castellana tal como se enseña en los libros de texto. Sobre todo la 's' es muy fuerte y nos parece a los ingleses casi como 'sh'; y la 'd' del final de la palabra suena más como la 'th' inglesa de la palabra 'thin'. Escuchen por ejemplo la pronunciación del Sr Angulo, de Tere e Isidoro cuando dicen 'Madrid'.

Los aragoneses hacia el norte y los andaluces hacia el sur, en cambio, hablan de una manera muy distinta los unos de los otros. Los aragoneses se caracterizan por su manera muy suya de dar un énfasis muy fuerte a la última sílaba de cada frase, y por su afán por añadir '–ico' o '–ica' a cada palabra. (Y por lo tanto se conocen como los mañicos.)

Por otra parte los andaluces comparten varias características de su habla con ciertos acentos latinoamericanos. A un andaluz, como a un chileno, le resulta difícil emitir la 's', sobre todo al final de la palabra o después de una 'e'. Hay muchos ejemplos de esto en la conversación con la chilena, Elizabeth. Además el famoso ceceo, es decir el modo de pronunciar ciertas 'c's y la 'z' como el 'th' del inglés, que nos parece tan típicamente español, no existe en la pronunciación andaluza ni latinoamericana. Otro rasgo de estos castellanoparlantes es el incluir un sonido casi como la 'h' inglesa delante de la 'e' o la 'i' iniciales. Otro sonido que se pronuncia distintamente en Latinoamérica y partes del sur de España que en el resto de España, es la 'y' y 'll'. En casi todas partes ya se pronuncian igual estas dos letras, pero en España normalmente suena a la 'y' de 'you' del inglés, mientras que en partes de Latinoamérica, sobre todo la Argentina y el Uruguay, se parece al sonido de la 's' en medio de 'measure'. Se puede apreciar esta pronunciación con el acento de Zulema, sobre todo cuando dice 'yo'.

A estas variaciones regionales y geográficas de los acentos y preferencias españoles hay que añadir el hecho de que el castellano no es el único idioma oficial de España. Dentro de los territorios donde se conserva otro idioma indígena, según la Constitución de 1978, este idioma puede ser co-oficial con el castellano. Este es el caso para el catalán en Cataluña, el euskera en Euskadi (el País Vasco), y el gallego en Galicia.

Y por lo tanto se entiende que España ya es una nación multilingüe con una riqueza de variedades lingüísticas.

El mundo hispanoparlante

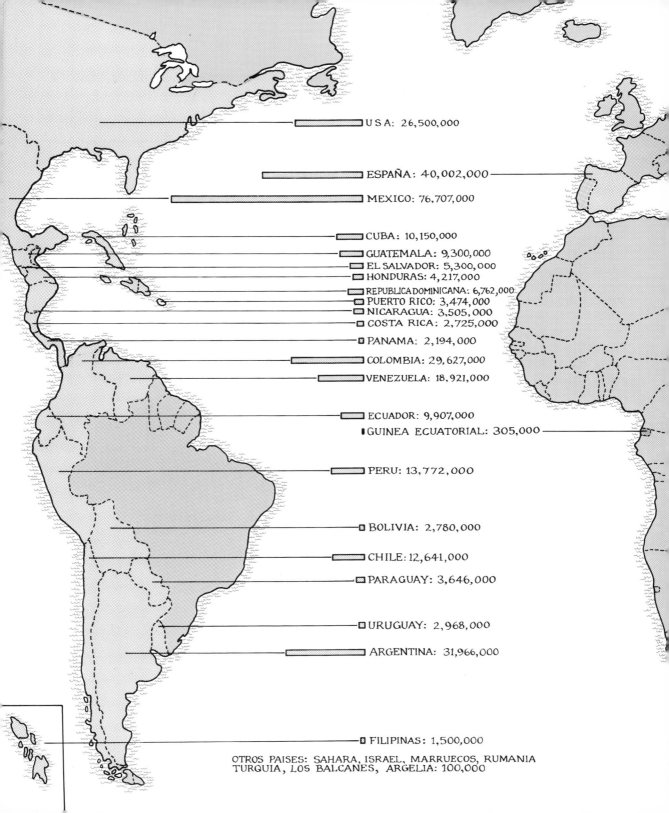

USA: 26,500,000

ESPAÑA: 40,002,000

MEXICO: 76,707,000

CUBA: 10,150,000

GUATEMALA: 9,300,000

EL SALVADOR: 5,300,000

HONDURAS: 4,217,000

REPUBLICA DOMINICANA: 6,762,000

PUERTO RICO: 3,474,000

NICARAGUA: 3,505,000

COSTA RICA: 2,725,000

PANAMA: 2,194,000

COLOMBIA: 29,627,000

VENEZUELA: 18,921,000

ECUADOR: 9,907,000

GUINEA ECUATORIAL: 305,000

PERU: 13,772,000

BOLIVIA: 2,780,000

CHILE: 12,641,000

PARAGUAY: 3,646,000

URUGUAY: 2,968,000

ARGENTINA: 31,966,000

FILIPINAS: 1,500,000

OTROS PAISES: SAHARA, ISRAEL, MARRUECOS, RUMANIA
TURQUIA, LOS BALCANES, ARGELIA: 100,000

PRÁCTICAS

1

Encuentro

You're staying in Madrid with some Spanish friends, and they've just introduced you to María, who's about the same age as you. You want to ask her a bit about herself. Put your questions into Spanish.

You	(*Ask her where she's from.*)
María	Yo soy de Albacete.
You	(*Where's Albacete?*)
María	Pues está en La Mancha, al sudeste de Madrid, a unos 250 kilómetros.
You	(*But now you live in Madrid.*)
María	Sí, ahora vivo en Chamberí.
You	(*How long have you been living in Madrid?*)
María	Desde hace un año y medio.
You´	(*What job do you do?*)
María	Soy recepcionista de hotel aquí en el centro.

2

Los vecinos de calle Toledo 4

Work out the answers to these questions from information in the interviews.

a De las personas entrevistadas por Isabel y Julia, ¿cuántas son españolas?

b ¿Cuáles son de Madrid?

c ¿Cuántas de las mujeres cree usted que están casadas?

d ¿De qué región es Ana?

e ¿Dónde vive la perra?

f ¿Qué hace Tere después de comer?

3

¿Dónde viven?

Look at the diagram opposite and say where these couples live in relation to each other. Use *debajo de, encima de, con* or *enfrente de* as appropriate.

Example: Ana – Antonio. Ana vive con Antonio.

	izquierda	*derecha*
5º	Isidoro Espada Moreno Tere Santalla Padín Almudena Espada Santalla (y la perra)	
4º	Antonio Pueche Cervera Ana Recio Beladiez	
3º		
2º	Rosa García Rodero	Isabel Soto García Jaime Suárez García
1º	*Hostal Los Gallegos* José Fernández Rajo Mercedes Arias Sánchez	
	Fernández Angulo SA prop. José Fernández Angulo y hermanos	*Restaurante El Cuchi* prop. Sergio Durazo y socios

a Mercedes – Isabel

b Rosa – Jaime

c Mercedes – *El Cuchi*

d Ana – Almudena

e Isidoro – Tere

4

¿Quién soy?

Here are some people describing themselves. Match what each one says with the appropriate picture below.

a   Estamos casados.
b   Trabajo en una oficina.
c   Soy andaluza.
d   Vivo en un piso moderno.
e   Soy profesor.
f   Tengo tres hijos.
g   Soy del Perú.
h   Estoy en Londres.

5

Así es mi vida

Here's Ana Recio talking about herself and her husband. Fill in the gaps with the appropriate parts of the verbs *ser*, *estar* or *tener*.

Yo .... casada con Antonio. No .... hijos. Vivimos en una casa de la calle Toledo, que .... en la parte antigua de Madrid. Los dos trabajamos en casa. Yo hago tapices, entonces .... un taller textil. Y Antonio .... fotógrafo. .... su estudio y su laboratorio también en casa. Nos gusta mucho esta casa, sin embargo .... pensando en buscar otra, porque aquí .... muy poco espacio.

6

Arbol genealógico

Unravel the information below to put names in the family tree in place of the numbers.

Loli González está casada con Juan Gómez. Tienen dos hijas y un hijo: María, Dolores, y Tomás. Tienen cuatro nietos: los dos niños de Tomás se llaman Diego y Roberto. María tiene una niña, Marisa, y Dolores otra, que se llama Mercedes. El marido de Dolores es Jorge Fernández. Tomás está casado con Montse Suárez.

Now answer these questions:

a ¿Cuántos hermanos tiene Dolores?
b ¿Quién es el abuelo de Diego?
c ¿Cuáles son los apellidos de Mercedes?

7

¿De dónde son?

Jaime es de Madrid; es madrileño.
Complete the sentences below along the same lines, choosing the right adjective for each town from this list (and making it masculine or feminine as appropriate):

granadino	valenciano
coruñés	zaragozano
bilbaíno	salmantino
barcelonés	malagueño
conquense	madrileño

a Begoña es de Bilbao; es ....
b Pilar es de Zaragoza; es ....
c Jordi es de Barcelona; es ....
d Juan es de Valencia; es ....
e Miguel es de Cuenca; es ....
f Luz es de Salamanca; es ....
g Carmen es de Granada; es ....
h Pepe es de La Coruña; es ....
i Ramón es de Málaga; es ....

8

Curriculum vitae

Now try introducing and describing yourself by answering the following questions. Use complete sentences if you can. (There is no key to this exercise.)

a ¿Cómo te llamas?
b ¿Cuál es tu nacionalidad?
c ¿Cuántos años tienes?
d ¿De dónde eres?
e ¿Dónde vives ahora?
f ¿Cuánto tiempo hace que vives allí?
g ¿Estás casado/casada?
h ¿Tienes hijos?

¿CÓMO ES?

Describing people and places

1

There are nine households in *calle Toledo 4*, and Isabel asked Almudena (who lives on the top floor) to describe some of the neighbours downstairs on the first floor.

Isabel	Almudena, ¿me puedes describir cómo son los vecinos?
Almudena	Pues son simpáticos, son gente muy maja.
Isabel	¿Cuántos sois?
Almudena	Somos . . . bueno, somos nueve vecinos, porque hay un piso, el primer piso, es una pensión.
Isabel	¿Y quién vive en esa pensión?
Almudena	Los dueños y los huéspedes.
Isabel	¿Y cómo son los dueños?
Almudena	Los dueños son simpáticos, son gallegos . . .
Isabel	¿Cómo se llaman?
Almudena	Mercedes y José.
Isabel	Muy bien. ¿Y Mercedes cómo es? ¿Es alta, baja, flaca, gorda?
Almudena	Mercedes es normal, es . . es una señora de mediana edad, es más bien delgadita, muy simpática.
Isabel	¿Y José cómo es?
Almudena	Y José es un señor grande, fuerte, bastante alto, también simpático, y siempre va fumando puros.
Isabel	¿Es rubio, como tú?
Almudena	No, es . . es moreno.

maja *nice*
de mediana edad
  middle-aged
más bien delgadita
  rather thinnish
va fumando puros *he*
  goes around smoking
  cigars

PREGUNTAS
1 ¿Cómo encuentra Almudena a sus vecinos?
2 ¿Es gorda Mercedes?
3 ¿De qué color es el pelo de José?

2

Mercedes has lived by the Plaza Mayor for twenty years. What are the pros and cons of the area?

Isabel	Mercedes, estamos en plena Plaza Mayor.
Mercedes	Sí.
Isabel	¿Os gusta la zona?
Mercedes	Sí, mucho.
Isabel	¿Cuáles son las ventajas y desventajas de vivir en esta zona?
Mercedes	Bueno, pues ventajas tiene muchas, porque es una zona muy bonita, muy . . muy turística, es una plaza muy hermosa, de recreo, y . . . en fin.
Isabel	¿Y hay alguna desventaja?
Mercedes	Bueno, no, no muchas, que tal vez un poco de ruido de los coches de la calle, pero nada más. No, no hay desventajas. Más ventajas que desventajas.

en plena Plaza Mayor
right in the Plaza Mayor
tal vez *maybe*

PREGUNTAS

1 ¿Le gusta a Mercedes vivir en plena Plaza Mayor?
2 ¿Qué desventaja puede tener vivir allí?

a la izquierda: Mercedes y su marido, José a la derecha: Adeline y sus padres

3

Rosa hasn't lived in the area for very long – how does she get on with her neighbours?

Julia	¿Tienes mucha relación con tus vecinos?
Rosa	Sí, y te puedo decir que es con la gente que me encuentro mejor, en cuanto a las relaciones humanas, en cuanto al barrio.
Julia	¿Y tienes especial amistad con alguno de ellos?
Rosa	Me llevo bien, son relaciones muy agradables y muy educadas, gente muy amable y muy cariñosa.

me encuentro mejor *I feel happiest/best*
en cuanto a *as regards*
me llevo bien *I get on well (with them)*
educadas *polite, civilised*

PREGUNTAS

1   ¿Qué tal se lleva Rosa con sus vecinos?

4

Isabel went to visit some friends in a Madrid suburb, and talked to their eight-year-old daughter Adeline.

Isabel	Adeline, descríbeme cómo son papá y mamá, físicamente. ¿Son altos, son bajos, son gordos, son feos? ¿Cómo son?
Adeline	Son los dos flacos, guapos, altos . . . aunque mamá es un poco baja.
Isabel	¿Y es morena mamá?
Adeline	No. Ah, sí, era de pequeña pero se ha . . . se lo ha . . .
Isabel	¿Teñido?
Adeline	Sí, teñido . . . teñido.
Isabel	¿De qué color?
Adeline	De rubio, o de amarillo, no sé.
Isabel	¿Y yo cómo soy?
Adeline	Un poco baja, guapa, con los ojos marrones, y con el pelo medio marrón y medio negro.
Isabel	¿Y lo llevo largo o corto?
Adeline	Corto.
Isabel	¿Y cómo me llamo?
Adeline	Isabel.
Isabel	Isabel, ¡sí, señora!

Adeline's father is American, hence her un-Spanish name

era de pequeña *she was when she was little*
se lo ha teñido *she's dyed it*
¡sí, señora! *yes, indeed!*

PREGUNTAS

1   ¿Cómo es la madre de Adeline?
2   ¿Cómo es el pelo de Isabel?

5

The Plaza Mayor is a focal point for both tourists and *madrileños*, and it's full of activity at all hours of the day and night. Julia, who's from a quieter part of the city, wondered what it was like to live there.

Julia   ¿No te parece un poco ruidosa la zona con la Plaza Mayor? Me imagino que hasta la una o las dos de la madrugada hay mucho ruido.

Isabel   Bueno, esto es inevitable en Madrid, o en cualquier capital, el ruido. Es ineludible. Desventajas sí, desde luego tiene desventajas: ruido, contaminación … y nada más. Ruido y contaminación, que claro que son desventajas gordísimas, pero aparte de eso a mí la zona me encanta, es auténtica, es algo rufianesca, te metes por esas calles del Madrid de los Austrias y te pierdes … Es una zona muy hermosa en ese sentido, tiene una carga histórica fuerte …

Julia   Y además es el Madrid castizo.

Isabel   Efectivamente. Hay otras zonas muy castizas también de Madrid, Chamberí, por ejemplo, pero yo me conformo con esta zona … es hermosa, la Plaza Mayor es una belleza. Tienes todo muy cerquita, desde una alpargatería hasta el Rastro, pasando por el Teatro Español, cines … en fin, tienes todo, ¿eh?, a un tiro de piedra. Puedes llegar andando a todas partes. Por ejemplo, el coche es innecesario viviendo en esta zona.

Julia   Sí, eso es verdad.

Isabel   Y para mí hay una ventaja casi sin precio, que es que puedo ir andando al trabajo. Tardo diez minutos.

el Madrid de los Austrias (see page 34)

the Rastro is Madrid's flea market

desde luego, claro que *of course*
algo rufianesca *a bit rough*
te metes por *you go into*
te pierdes *you lose your way*
carga histórica fuerte *great historical tradition*
yo me conformo con *I'm happy with*
pasando por *including*
a un tiro de piedra *within a stone's throw*
tardo diez minutos *it takes me ten minutes*

PREGUNTAS

1   ¿Cuáles son las dos desventajas inevitables de vivir en esta zona?
2   ¿Por qué le gusta a Isabel esta zona?
3   ¿Va Isabel en coche al trabajo?

LENGUA

DESCRIPTIONS

Remember that, in Spanish, words used to describe people and things (adjectives) change their endings according to whether the word they're describing is singular or plural:
un vecino simpático   vecinos simpáticos
and, in most cases, whether it's masculine or feminine:
un señor simpático   una señora simpática

Many adjectives have four forms: *bonito, bonita, bonitos, bonitas.* Some have only singular and plural: *grande, grandes; marrón, marrones.* (For more details, see **Gramática**, page 145.)

Adjectives usually come after the word they're describing; *un señor grande, ojos marrones,* and words like *muy* (very) or *bastante* (quite) come in between:
gente muy amable   un señor bastante alto

Some very common adjectives normally come before the word, e.g. *mucho, poco, otro, todo, alguno, ninguno,* and words for 'first', 'second' – *primero, segundo,* and so on.

A few lose their endings when they come before the word, e.g. *primer(o), tercer(o), algun(o), ningun(o), buen(o), mal(o), gran(de)*:
el primer piso   ningún problema

MORE, MOST

To say 'more' or 'most', or the equivalent of adding '–er' or '–est' in English, just use **más**:
*El hombre chileno es **más bajo**.* (shorter)
*La zona **más hermosa**...*   (most beautiful)

An exception is the word for 'better' or 'best':
*Esta zona es **mejor**.   Son mis **mejores** amigos.*

When you're comparing one thing with another (saying 'more than' or 'less than'), use *más ... que* or *menos ... que*:

*Los argentinos son **más** altos **que** los chilenos.*
*Esta zona es **menos** ruidosa **que** el centro.*
*Madrid me gusta **más que** Barcelona.*

But notice that, when numbers or quantities are involved, it is *más ... de* or *menos ... de*:
más de *cien*   **menos de** *un kilo*

VERY...

Sometimes Spanish speakers add endings to words to give the idea of 'very' or 'little', or to seem friendly or affectionate. For instance, Isabel says that the noise and pollution are *'desventajas gordísimas'.* The *–ísimo* ending means 'very', as in *muchísimas gracias.* The commonest ending for 'little' is *–ito,* which can also be affectionate. For instance, Tere calls her dog *perrita,* and Almudena describes Mercedes as *delgadita,* which could mean 'very slim' or just be a friendly way of describing her. You'll hear other endings like this in different parts of the Spanish-speaking world, e.g. *–ico* in Aragón, or *–illo* in parts of South America.

GUSTAR

Remember that to say you like something in Spanish you can't do a word-for-word translation of the English. Instead of 'I like Madrid', you say the equivalent of 'Madrid is pleasing to me':
Me gusta Madrid.   ¿Os gusta la zona?
Me gustan los argentinos.

Encantar works in the same way:
Me encanta la zona.   I love the area.

TIENE LOS OJOS MARRONES

When referring to parts of people or things, remember to include the definite article *el, la, los* or *las,* as appropriate:
*Tiene el pelo negro y los   She has black hair and
ojos marrones.   brown eyes.*

AMÉRICA LATINA

1 ARGENTINA

Tommy showed Mick a couple of photos of his family, taken at Christmas.

Tommy	Esta es mi hija mayor, Nora.
Mick	Es muy linda.
Tommy	Es muy bonita, sí. ¡Igual al papá!
Mick	Exactamente...
Zulema	Sí, igualita.
Tommy	Yo no lo conozco el papá, ¿eh?
	(*Todos ríen*)
Tommy	Ese es Alejandro, Nora, María Fernanda, Santiago, éste soy yo, Zulema, Naho el perro, Santiago ... eh, perdón, este...
Zulema	Benito...
Tommy	Benito, el gato, Benito, y Jack, es el perro viejo.
Mick	¿Y qué están haciendo actualmente la ... los miembros de la familia?
Tommy	La mayor está trabajando, es bioquímica, es doctora en bioquímica. Está en Buenos Aires, está en un hospital, además es jefa de trabajos prácticos de la universidad. Mi hija, la más chica, la que tiene veinticinco años, es abogada, *'lawyer'*, ¿no? ¿Está bien dicho, *'lawyer'*?

¡igual al papá! *just like her father!*

yo no lo conozco el papá *I don't know the father*

¿está bien dicho? *is that the right way to say it?*

Mick	Perfectamente.
Tommy	Está en Bariloche, San Carlos de Bariloche. Y los varones, los dos hijos varones, el mayor y el menor, que son Santiago el menor y Alejandro el mayor, están en la playa en Monte Hermoso, en estos momentos.

2 CHILE

What differences are there between Argentinians and Chileans? And where men are concerned which nationality does Elizabeth prefer?

Hugh	¿Cómo se distingue lingüísticamente el argentino del chileno? Cuando los argentinos turistas vienen acá, ¿cómo se distinguen?
Elizabeth	Mira, en muy pocas palabras, yo te diría que el argentino habla español y el chileno canta. El argentino habla español y habla fuerte, que a mí personalmente me gusta mucho, ¿ah? El pueblo argentino es un pueblo muy potente, ¿no es cierto?, y eso lo...
Hugh	¿Prepotente?
Elizabeth	No, ¡potente!
Hugh	¿Pero a veces prepotente?
Elizabeth	Yo no lo encuentro prepotente. Mira, la mayoría de los chilenos lo .. lo encuentra muy prepotente y aquí existe, yo percibo, un cierto complejo, ¿no es cierto? Por ejemplo, los hombres chilenos les tienen un poco como de envidia a los hombres argentinos, porque los hombres argentinos hablan más fuerte, son buenmocísimos, yo los encuentro francamente una delicia de hombres, ¿no es cierto? Son mucho más altos que los chilenos, en general el hombre chileno es más bajo, el hombre chileno es un hombre que siente complejo frente al hombre argentino, ¿no es cierto?, porque aquí vienen mucho los argentinos a veranear, ¿no es cierto?, y las 'lolitas' chilenas se vuelven pero locas con los argentinos y con justa razón, porque tienen mucha más personalidad, hablan más fuerte, son muy varoniles, ¿no es cierto? ...

yo te diría *I'd say*
les tienen un poco de envidia a *are a bit envious of*
buenmocísimos (*from* **buenmozo**) *very good-looking men*
una delicia de hombres *delightful men*
frente a *towards*
'lolitas' *Chilean slang for 'girls'*
se vuelven pero locas *they go quite crazy*
con justa razón *with good reason*

americanismos
linda *pretty – more used in Latin America than Spain*
no lo conozco *in Spain you would hear* no le conozco
  (*see* **Gramática**, page 147)
buenmozo (buenmocísimo) *more common in Latin America*

ESPAÑA ACTUAL

LA CIUDAD DE MADRID

Los orígenes de Madrid son romanos, pero de esto
sólo quedan palabras: por ejemplo, su nombre
propio, que según una teoría viene del latín *matrice*,
es decir 'madre' o 'matriz', refiriéndose al agua. Se
piensa que los castellanos lo llamaron entonces
Magerit, y luego los árabes Mayrit. Y de ahí viene
Madrid. El símbolo de esta villa todavía muy rural y
aislada es ahora el escudo de la capital: el oso
apoyado en el madroño, árbol entonces muy
corriente por estas partes. Madrid pasó a ser un
pueblo árabe, y el nombre de su plaza más conocida,
la Puerta del Sol, viene de un castillo de la época
de los musulmanes, que ya no existe.

Como capital de España, Madrid es
relativamente joven, con sólo unos cuatrocientos
años. El honor de ser la capital se lo debe a su
situación céntrica y al deseo del rey Felipe II de
tener una sede permanente para la corte, símbolo ya
de la reunión de los distintos reinos bajo una corona.

El Madrid de hoy es una ciudad de contrastes,
con partes tradicionales y folklóricas, barrios
elegantes con calles arboladas, edificios
supermodernos y caserones antiguos. No es
especialmente grande ni por su población ni por su
tamaño, aunque ofrece una variedad impresionante
tanto en su aspecto físico como social. Madrid se ve
a sí misma como el escaparate de España hacia el
mundo, y le gustaría ser aceptada como el foco de
la nación española.

En otras capitales regionales, tales como
Barcelona o Sevilla, se habla de Madrid como de
una ciudad sin tradición o historia. Pero lo
tradicional, lo folklórico, lo castizo de Madrid se
encuentra fácilmente en su zona antigua, el Madrid
de los Austrias. Se llama así porque se refiere a la
corona que era por parte de la familia real austriaca.
En esta parte antigua y tradicional están las calles
estrechas, los edificios históricos con sus escudos,
y, como atracción principal, la Plaza Mayor con sus
soportales. Esta plaza fue proyectada originalmente

arriba: En la Puerta del Sol, el oso y el madroño, que
figuran en el escudo de Madrid
a la derecha: La Plaza Mayor desde la calle Toledo

en el siglo XVI, pero fue reconstruida en el siglo XVIII después de un incendio. En esta plaza se celebran muchas fiestas, y la más conocida es la de San Isidro, el santo patrón de Madrid. En Navidades hay una feria de artículos navideños en el centro de la plaza. Alrededor, por los soportales, concurre mucha gente, madrileños, españoles de fuera de Madrid, extranjeros. Algunos venden sellos, otros, artículos turísticos. En esta zona, más que en ninguna otra, siente Madrid su identidad y su orgullo, el sentido especial de ser 'castiza'.

Madrid es una capital como tantas otras: es el origen de la red de carreteras; es el centro administrativo; es la sede del gobierno y del parlamento, las Cortes; es el centro diplomático. A todo esto hay que añadir un cinturón industrial que

La Plaza Mayor, a las seis de la madrugada

ha atraído un gran número de inmigrantes, muchos de ellos venidos de otras partes más pobres del país en busca de trabajo o fortuna; una alta proporción de los que viven en Madrid no han nacido allí. No todos tienen la misma suerte; hay muchos que no encuentran trabajo y tienen que vivir del paro o dedicarse a la mendicidad.

Madrid tiene que luchar contra su imagen de centralismo dominante, su imagen de opresor de las regiones y pozo en donde desaparecen los recursos económicos de las regiones. Cierto es que Madrid es hoy en día un centro donde se busca una vida movida y emocionante, tanto a nivel social como económico.

PRÁCTICAS

1

La ciudad de Madrid

When you come back from your first visit to Madrid, you're asked by your Spanish teacher to say something about the city in Spanish.

Profesora	¿Te gusta Madrid?
You	(*I love it; it's a beautiful city.*)
Profesora	¿Es una ciudad grande? ¿Cuántos habitantes tiene?
You	(*Yes, it's quite big. It has a population of nearly four million.*)
Profesora	¿Es una ciudad con mucho sentido histórico?
You	(*Yes, some parts of the city are very old and pretty. There are also lots of modern areas.*)
Profesora	¿Qué parte te parece a ti la más atractiva?
You	(*The most attractive part is the Plaza Mayor.*)

2

Descríbeme

Below María describes herself. Now you give this same description to a friend, changing words to the 'she' or 'her' form as appropriate.

Soy alta y delgada. Tengo veinte años. El pelo lo llevo corto. Soy morena con el pelo teñido de rubio. Me gusta llevar ropa elegante. Me encanta salir con los amigos. Me llevo muy bien con todos.

3

La familia Ramírez

Look at the pictures and finish the sentences describing this family, by using *más* or *menos*.

a   Carmen es . . . . baja que José.
b   José tiene . . . . pelo que Carmen.
c   El pelo de Teresa es . . . . largo que el de Carmen.
d   Jesús es . . . . joven que Teresa.
e   Carmen es . . . . gorda que José.
f   El pantalón de José es . . . . corto que el de Jesús.
g   Carmen es . . . . vieja que Jesús.

4

La casa

In this description of a block of flats in a typical Madrid street, put the adjective in brackets in the correct form so that it agrees with the word it is describing.

Es una casa (*viejo*) y (*alto*) con (*mucho*) pisos. En el (*primero*) piso vive una familia de origen (*gallego*). Son personas muy (*amable*) pero un poco (*ruidoso*). En los (*otro*) pisos hay una (*grande*) variedad de gente: un matrimonio (*joven*), una familia (*aragonés*) con diez niños, un señor (*silencioso*) con dos perros (*enorme*). En el (*último*) piso vive una pareja (*anciano*) y (*solitario*). A esta pareja le gusta poner unas plantas (*precioso*) en las ventanas (*grande*) de la casa.

5

Los Juegos Olímpicos

When it comes to deciding where to hold the Olympic Games, every city has its advantages or disadvantages. Read the descriptions of some possible candidates, and then fill in the table showing one or two of the pros and cons for each.

París es muy accesible y muy bonita, pero carísima. Nueva York es ruidosa y congestionada, pero bien organizada. El Cairo es muy exótica y demasiado caliente. Sydney es muy lejana y muy tranquila. Atenas es tradicional, folklórica e ineficaz. Río es húmeda, un poco peligrosa y bastante barata.

6

Mi familia y otros animales

You're swapping personal details with a Spanish woman you've met in your hotel. Put your part of the conversation into Spanish.

Señora	¿Tú tienes hijos?
You	(*No, only a dog.*)
Señora	¿Qué tipo es?
You	(*I don't know what it's called in Spanish, but in English it's a spaniel.*)
Señora	¡Suena como 'español'!
You	(*Yes, that's true, but it's English.*)
Señora	¿Cómo es?
You	(*It's quite small and it has fairly long hair and very long ears. It's very intelligent.*)
Señora	¿De qué color es?
You	(*Brown.*)
Señora	Debe ser un perro de aguas.

7

¿Cómo es?

Now describe your next-door neighbour by answering these questions. (If your neighbour's female, remember to use feminine forms of words as appropriate.)

a   ¿Es alto o bajo?
b   ¿De qué color es su pelo?
c   ¿Tiene barba?
d   ¿Lleva gafas?
e   ¿Tú le consideras delgado, gordo o regular?

ciudad	ventajas	desventajas
París		
Nueva York		
El Cairo		
Sydney		
Atenas		
Río de Janeiro		

¿CÓMO SE HACE?

Information and instructions

1

In Spanish towns and cities, most people live in flats, and by law every block of flats has to have a residents' association, *una comunidad de vecinos*. It's Isabel's turn to chair the *comunidad* in her building, but she's not sure what is involved.

Isabel	Jaime, como sabes, me acaban de nombrar presidenta de la comunidad. Estoy un poco asustada.
Jaime	Bueno, se trata de una cosa muy sencilla. En la casa hay una serie de gastos comunes, como pueden ser la luz de la escalera, la limpieza de la escalera, y entonces lo que se hace es que cada año uno de los vecinos por turno se encarga de llevar las cuentas y de hacer los arreglos necesarios.
Isabel	Y, vamos a ver, lo primero que yo voy a tener que hacer, ¿qué va a ser?
Jaime	Bueno, pues el trabajo más peliagudo es el hacer los recibos de final de mes. Cada mes hay que pasarle un recibo a cada uno de los inquilinos en el que le … se le cobra lo que le corresponda durante ese mes.

me acaban de nombrar *they've just made me*
se trata de *it's a question of*
como pueden ser *such as*
lo que se hace es *what happens is*
vamos a ver *let's see*
yo voy a tener que hacer *I'm going to have to do.*

PREGUNTAS
1 ¿Qué cargo acaba de ocupar Isabel?
2 ¿Cuáles van a ser sus primeras responsibilidades?

2

There are of course rules and regulations connected with running hotels and guest houses, but are there any particular house rules in the *Hostal Los Gallegos*?

Isabel	En el hostal, ¿qué normas tenéis? ¿Qué es lo que se puede hacer y qué es lo que no se puede hacer?
Mercedes	Bueno, normas … ningunas, o sea normas, las de los hoteles y hostales. No hay normas específicas.

¿qué es lo que se puede hacer? *what are you allowed to do?*

Isabel	¿Tenéis algún horario de comidas, por ejemplo?
Mercedes	No damos comidas, porque es hostal-residencia. Al ser hostal-residencia, no entran comidas, ni desayuno ni nada … no damos nada. Solamente dormir.
Isabel	¿Hay una hora de entrada por la noche, o la gente puede entrar a la hora que quiera?
Mercedes	Normalmente hay hora de entrada, pero bueno, si alguno va al teatro o va a algún espéctaculo que sea de noche, pues también se permite que entre a cualquier hora. O por cuestión de trabajo, si una persona trabaja de noche, pues claro, tiene que regresar a la hora que termina su trabajo.
Isabel	¿Y cuál es esa hora de entrada general?
Mercedes	Normalmente a las doce, doce y media, una.
Isabel	O sea, bastante tarde.

al ser *being, as it is*
a la hora que quiera *whenever they like*
que sea de noche *that's on at night*
tiene que *he/she has to*

PREGUNTAS

1 ¿Por qué no dan comidas en el hostal de Mercedes?
2 ¿En qué circunstancias se vuelve después de la hora de entrada general?

La carta de *El Cuchi* **con platos mejicanos y españoles – está presentada en un pizarrón**

3

The menu at *El Cuchi* includes Spanish dishes, along with some concoctions invented by the management, but the emphasis is on Mexican cuisine.

Julia Sergio, ¿me puedes explicar cómo se prepara un plato típico mejicano, por ejemplo los frijoles?

Sergio Sí, los frijoles son ... pues aquí les llaman judías negras. Pues básicamente se hierven, se hierven a presión durante alrededor de veinte a treinta minutos. Posteriormente se pasan a una sartén con un poco de aceite, aceite de girasol, y manteca de cerdo, para darle un cierto sabor. Allí se fríen con un poco de chorizo y bacon y cebolla. Todo esto se fríe, y posteriormente nada más, un agregarle sal al gusto de la persona. Es un plato que, pues se utiliza mucho. En Méjico es muy popular, ¿no?

se hierven a presión *they're pressure-cooked*
un agregarle sal *adding salt*

PREGUNTAS
1 ¿Cómo se llaman los frijoles en España?
2 ¿Qué se hace con los frijoles antes de freírlos?

4

Isabel has a computer at home that she uses for word processing (and that Jaime uses for computer games!). Not surprisingly, the language of computer technology is English.

Julia Isabel, ahora que estamos aquí sentadas las dos delante del ordenador, ¿por qué no me cuentas cómo funciona?

Isabel Bueno, pues tiene la pantalla, el teclado y la impresora.

Un juego en el ordenador

Vamos a ver ... te enseño cómo funciona esto. Primero, lo pongo *'on'*, es decir, se da a un interruptor que hay aquí detrás.

Julia   Aha, y hace un ruidito que indica ...

Isabel   Hace un 'clin', eso indica que ya está en marcha. Ahora se enciende la pantalla, el icono que sale con la interrogación indica que se tiene que poner un diskette, un programa.

Julia   Sí.

Isabel   Aquí tengo uno, que dice ... que es un diskette de procesamiento de textos. Se mete en la ranura. Entonces, la flecha se lleva a este cuadrado, ¿eh?, y se hace 'click' dos veces. Y esto te enseña todas las carpetas, es decir, todo lo que está guardado en el programa.

Julia   Sí, ¿y qué ... qué queremos hacer?

Isabel   Pues, vamos a crear un nuevo documento, ¿te parece?

Julia   Sí, muy bien.

Isabel   Em ... *'New'*. Entonces te enseña una hoja en blanco.

Julia   Sí.

Isabel   Primero tenemos que guardarlo, el nuevo documento.

Julia   ¿Se guarda primero?

Isabel   Sí, porque le tienes que dar un título, de momento no lleva título. Vamos a ver. Vamos a llamarle 'Julia'. Entonces, en el teclado se tecla 'Julia'. Y esto se vuelve a guardar. (*Isabel guarda el documento*) Podemos escribir lo que queramos, ¿verdad? Voy a escribir: 'Hace mucho calor. No parece invierno, sino verano'. Bueno, el teclado es idéntico a cualquier teclado de un ordenador o incluso ...

Julia   ¿De una máquina de escribir?

Isabel   Sí, sí, sí ... bueno, con la ventaja de que puedes retroceder y borrar y rectificar, en el momento, ¿verdad?

Julia   Sí.

Isabel   Y luego para guardar esto, claro, lo que se hace es lo siguiente: se aprieta el *'Save'* ...

Julia   Y se guarda en el diskette.

Isabel   Eso es. Y ahora para cerrarlo todo, es decir, para acabar, porque ahora creo que vamos a cenar ... *'Quit'*. *'Eject'* ... Ahora verás ...

Julia   Un poco de música, 'clin' ...

Isabel   Y ahora *'Shutdown'*.

es decir *that is*
se da a *you press*
está en marcha *it's working*
procesamiento de textos *word processing*
hoja en blanco *blank page*
se vuelve a guardar *you save it again*
lo que queramos *whatever we like*
máquina de escribir *typewriter*
en el momento *instantly*
lo siguiente *the following*
verás *you'll see*

PREGUNTAS

1   ¿En qué parte del ordenador se escriben las frases de Isabel?
2   ¿Qué ventajas tiene un ordenador cuando se compara con una máquina de escribir normal?

LENGUA

ASKING FOR INFORMATION

¿Cómo?, ¿qué?, ¿a qué hora?, ¿dónde? These are the sorts of question words that are used when asking for information:

*¿**Cómo** funciona?*	How does it work?
*¿**A qué** hora sale?*	When does it leave?
*¿**Qué** se hace?*	What do you do?

To be polite when asking these questions you can begin with a simple *por favor*, or with:

¿Me puede(s) decir …?	Can you tell me …?
¿Me puede(s) explicar …?	Can you explain …?

THIS IS WHAT YOU DO …

You can explain how to do something by using the 'you' form of the verb:

***Aprietas** el botón.*	You push the button.
*Usted **baja** por esa calle.*	You go down that street.

Or you can turn it into an instruction by using the imperative or command form of the verb (see **Gramática**, page 150):

***Aprieta** el botón.*	Press the button.
***Baje** usted por esa calle.*	Go down that street.

Or you can use what's called an impersonal form of the verb (see below):

*Se **aprieta** el botón.*	You press the button.
*Lo que **se hace** es …*	What you do is …

There are also several ways of saying 'you have to' or 'you must': *tener que, hay que, deber, hace falta*. All of these are followed by another verb in the infinitive form (*–ar, –er*, or *–ir* ending). *Hay que* and *hace falta* never change but *tener* and *deber* do in the normal way:

*Usted **tiene que** tomar un avión.*	You have to catch a plane.
***Tenemos que** guardarlo.*	We have to save it.
*No **debes** ir.*	You shouldn't go.
***Hay que** comprar un billete.*	You must buy a ticket.
***Hace falta** lavarlo.*	You have to wash it.

SE HACE, SE PUEDE …

There are many examples in this unit of verbs being used with the word *se*. Isabel uses the impersonal form of the verb a lot when explaining to Julia how to use her computer:

***Se enciende** la pantalla.*	You turn on the screen.
***Se mete** en la ranura.*	You put it in the slot.
***Se aprieta** el 'Save'.*	You press 'Save'.

Sergio, when talking about *frijoles*, uses *se* in a slightly different way – with verbs in the plural as well as the singular:

*Los frijoles **se hierven**.*	The beans are boiled.
*Todo esto **se fríe**.*	All this is fried.

Se is also a part of reflexive verbs, which you will find listed in dictionaries with *se* on the end of the infinitive, e.g. *llamarse* (to be called), *levantarse* (to get up). (See unit 10, and **Gramática**, page 147.)

ENCIENDE, APRIETA …

Some verbs may mislead you if you want to look them up in a dictionary (where they are listed in their infinitive form), because the middle of the word is different:

*pu**e**de* (*p**o**der*)	*enci**e**nde* (*enc**e**nder*)
*apri**e**ta* (*apr**e**tar*)	*qui**e**ro* (*qu**e**rer*)

The change only applies to some of the verb, but the most common patterns are that *e* becomes *ie* (*tener – tiene*), and *u* becomes *ue* (*poder – puede*). (See **Gramática**, page 151.)

VOLVER A

Followed by another verb, *volver a* means 'again':
Se vuelve a guardar.
Las tiendas vuelven a abrir a las seis.

ACABAR DE

Acabar de followed by another verb means 'to have just' done something: *Me acaban de nombrar presidenta de la comunidad.*

AMÉRICA LATINA

1 PERU

In Lima, Hugh asked Milagros from the tourist office about official – and unofficial – ways of changing foreign money.

Hugh	¿Cómo puedo cambiar dinero aquí en Lima?
Milagros	Tenemos dos sistemas de cambio. Uno es a través del Banco de la Nación, que es el banco oficial, y el otro es a través de agencias de cambio.
Hugh	¿Dónde dan el mejor cambio?
Milagros	En las agencias, puesto que allí le pueden dar desde cien intis por dólar. En cambio, en el Banco de la Nación tiene usted setenta y cinco intis por dólar.
Hugh	¿Yo puedo cambiar en la calle sin problema, sin peligro?
Milagros	Yo diría que sin peligro no, porque muchos de los cambistas de la calle son ladrones, y cuando usted le entrega los dólares simplemente no le entregan los intis. O también puede ser que le puedan entregar menos o también dinero falso.
Hugh	¿Me cuido entonces?
Milagros	¡Claro!

the inti is now the official currency in Peru

a través de *through*
puesto que *since, because*
en cambio *on the other hand*
puede ser que le puedan entregar *it's possible that they may give you*
¿me cuido? *I must be careful?*

2 PERU

The ruins of the Inca city of Machu Picchu lie high up in the Andes, and getting there from Lima involves several forms of transport.

Hugh	¿Cómo llego a Machu Picchu?
Milagros	Bueno, para ir a Machu Picchu necesariamente tiene que tomar un avión hacia la ciudad de Cuzco. El vuelo dura aproximadamente una hora y siempre salen en las mañanas.
Hugh	¿Luego para seguir a Machu Picchu?
Milagros	Después de haber llegado a Cuzco y después de haber dormido en la ciudad de Cuzco, en la mañana siguiente se tiene uno que levantar muy temprano para ir a la estación y hacer su cola y comprar el boleto de tren.
Hugh	¿Y a qué distancia está Machu Picchu de Cuzco?
Milagros	El viaje en tren dura tres horas y media aproximadamente, y allí salen unos buses que los llevan hacia las ruinas.

haber llegado/dormido *having arrived/slept*
se tiene uno que levantar *you have to get up*
hacer cola *to queue up*

3   ARGENTINA

Tommy phones up to check on the departure time of a flight to the capital – earlier he
was told it might be late.

Tommy	Señor, buenas tardes. Quiero tomar información sobre el vuelo que debe salir a Buenos Aires a las veintidós cero cinco. ¿A qué hora se estima la salida? . . . ¡Ah! ¿Ha recuperado el tiempo perdido? . . . Fabuloso, gracias, hasta luego. (*cuelga el teléfono*) (*a Zulema*) Recuperó el tiempo. O sea, va a salir a horario.
Zulema	¿Sí?
Tommy	Sí.

¿ha recuperado . . .? *it
has made up . . .?*
a horario *on time*

americanismos
tomar *never use* coger *in Latin America to talk about taking
a train etc.* (*it has a sexual meaning*)
en las mañanas (*also* a la mañana) por las mañanas *in
Spain*
boleto billete *in Spain*

Machu Picchu

ESPAÑA ACTUAL

LA CIUDAD DEL FUTURO

En Madrid, al igual que en muchas otras grandes ciudades, o más aun, se siente el crecimiento aplastante de los nuevos edificios. Tanto que, según las estadísticas, en el barrio del Pilar, uno de los barrios de Madrid, el número de habitantes por metro cuadrado es el más alto de Europa. Esto produce un sentido de claustrofobia que podría empeorar a medida que Madrid acrecenta su importancia como capital europea, sirviendo los intereses comerciales y políticos de la comunidad europea.

La intensidad de edificación e industrialización ha propiciado una toma de conciencia general sobre el tema del medio ambiente. A esto hay que añadir el disgusto por el humo de las fábricas y la circulación de vehículos, y el ruido de la gente, los coches, y sobre todo, las motos.

Las soluciones son varias: hay quienes deciden, y cada día hay más, ir a vivir a las afueras de Madrid, cosa, sin embargo, que ha hecho subir los precios de las viviendas en la periferia y ha contribuido a aumentar la congestión en las carreteras o transportes públicos de entrada y salida a la ciudad. El gran afán de vivir en el mismo centro de las ciudades, rasgo tan típicamente español, está verdaderamente cambiando.

Otra solución, por supuesto, es una planificación a nivel municipal de las viviendas e infraestructura urbana. Más control sobre qué se deja construir y dónde. Más atención a los servicios necesarios para cualquier expansión de viviendas; es decir, hospitales, escuelas, limpieza de las calles, etc. En fin: más dinero para las necesidades de la población urbana.

Los planes que existen sobre el futuro de la ciudad se dirigen, por un lado, a aumentar la oferta de viviendas con mejores servicios públicos, y por otro, a ampliar la cantidad de oficinas con buen acceso para los directivos españoles y europeos que quieren establecerse en la capital.

En este contexto vale la pena citar el plan de

ampliación de la Casa de Campo en Madrid, ampliación que dará lugar a una expansión residencial con zonas verdes, acceso fácil igualmente a la sierra como a la ciudad, y contará con los mejores servicios urbanísticos.

Es de esperar que todos estos cambios en la configuración física de la ciudad no hagan desaparecer las relaciones sociales de barrio, a nivel local. En España, típicamente, se vive en la calle, en los bares locales, en las plazas de al lado de casa. Cada edificio tiene su comunidad de vecinos y la gente se conoce y se apoya. A medida que los individuos pasan más tiempo en sus coches, en sus chalets aislados, y viendo sus televisiones, se aislan de la comunidad, y se podría perder el sentido de identidad local.

Es justamente este espíritu de comunidad el que ha ayudado a los nuevos madrileños, los emigrantes pobres, que tuvieron que empezar su vida en Madrid en 'chabolas' miserables e intolerables. Juntos lucharon por mejorar sus viviendas y hacer valer sus derechos.

PRÁCTICAS

1

Hervir un huevo

Here's a pictorial explanation of how to boil an egg. Describe the process in words by putting the sentences below in the right order.

a   Se quita el huevo del agua.

b   Y ahora se come el huevo caliente.

c   Después, se mete el huevo en el agua.

d   Se llena una cacerola con agua.

e   Hay que decidir si se quiere duro o no.

f   Se deja hervir el agua.

g   Si se quiere poco duro, se tiene que sacar el huevo del agua después de tres minutos.

h   Y se deja más tiempo antes de sacar el huevo del agua.

i   Una vez fuera del agua, se rompe la cáscara.

j   Pero si le gusta duro, no hay que tocarlo.

2

Se puede ...

Match the symbols above with the appropriate wording from the list below.

a   Se prohibe el paso de bicicletas.

b   Se lava a mano.

c   No se debe fumar.

d   No se permite la entrada a los perros.

e   Se puede planchar.

f   No se puede doblar a la izquierda.

3

Cambios

In the following passage put the verbs in brackets in the correct form.

Un buen domingo

Mi marido (*pensar*) ir a ver un partido de fútbol. Yo no (*querer*) ir porque me (*sentir*) mal hoy. (*Preferir*) quedarme en la cama y dormir. Si (*dormir*) todo el día, me (*encontrar*) mucho mejor. En los partidos hay mucho ruido, y se (*tener*) que estar de pie. Después, siempre se (*venir*) muy cansado a casa con ganas de sentarse. Me gusta mucho el fútbol, pero hoy (*quedarse*) en casa.

4

Se hace así

A number of people are asking you questions. Give them the information they want.

Julio	¿Sabes cómo funciona esto?
You	(*You have to press the red button.*)
Señora	Por favor, ¿dónde se puede aparcar?
You	(*You can park in front of the hotel.*)
Concha	¿A qué hora empieza la película?
You	(*It starts at eight o'clock.*)
Señor	¿Me puede decir usted cómo se llega a la estación de Atocha?
You	(*You go down this street and turn left; it's on the right.*)
Manuel	¿Cómo se prepara una tortilla española?
You	(*You fry an onion and some potatoes, then you add the eggs.*)
Señor	¿Puedo ir a Machu Picchu en avión?
You	(*No, you have to get the train from Cuzco and then the bus.*)

5

Habas a la catalana

Below are the ingredients for another bean dish (for broad beans this time) which is very popular in Cataluñã. First, you fry the onion and *tocino* in the lard with the garlic and herbs, next you add the beans, the *butifarra* and tomatoes. Add salt, pepper and a little sugar, and then leave it all to simmer for at least two hours. Finally you add the wine and *anís*.

Write the instructions for this recipe using the *tú* form of the verb. ('To add' is *añadir*, and 'to simmer' is *hervir a fuego lento*.)

6

Te toca a ti

Work out some instructions which you might need to give a Spanish friend staying with you. Tell them how to use the public telephone, or how to get from your home to the nearest shops.

Habas a la catalana

Ingredientes

4kg de habas
300 gr de butifarra negra
100 gr de tocino
2 cucharadas de
manteca de cerdo
1 cebolla
ajo
3 tomates maduros
1 vaso de vino rancio
1 copita de anís seco
hierbas, perejil
pimienta, sal
azúcar

4 ¿TE GUSTARÍA...?

Invitations and arrangements

1

Julia asks Isabel if she'd like to go to see *La Malquerida*, a play by the Nobel Prize-winning writer, Jacinto Benavente.

Julia	Oye, Isabel, ¿te gustaría venir un día de éstos al teatro?
Isabel	Sí, me encantaría, hace mucho tiempo que no voy al teatro.
Julia	Estoy pensando que podríamos ir a ver *La Malquerida*.
Isabel	¿*La Malquerida*? ¿Dónde la hacen?
Julia	Sí, en el Teatro Español.
Isabel	Ah, estupendo, porque me pilla muy cerca del trabajo. Entonces, ¿qué día te vendría bien? Yo podría el viernes.
Julia	El viernes... bueno, sí, creo que está bien.
Isabel	Muy bien. Entonces, ¿a qué hora quedamos?
Julia	Bueno, la obra empieza a las ocho...
Isabel	Aha.
Julia	Entonces podemos quedar a las siete y media, o las ocho menos cuarto.
Isabel	Mejor las ocho menos cuarto, y así me da tiempo de llegar del trabajo.
Julia	Bueno, muy bien, pues nos juntamos en la puerta del teatro, si te parece.
Isabel	Muy bien, perfecto. Entonces, quedamos en eso, que... el viernes hemos dicho, ¿no?
Julia	Sí, el viernes a las ocho menos cuarto en la puerta del Teatro Español.
Isabel	Estupendo.

¿te gustaría...? *would you like...?*
un día de éstos *one of these days*
podríamos ir *we could go*
me pilla muy cerca de *it happens to be very close to*
¿...te vendría bien? *...would suit you?*
yo podría *I could (go)*
¿a qué hora quedamos? *what time shall we meet?*
hemos dicho *we said*

PREGUNTAS
1 ¿Va mucho al teatro Isabel?
2 ¿Dónde van a encontrarse las dos?

2

Julia visited the *Instituto* where Rosa teaches and asked a couple of her students what they usually did at weekends.

Julia	Los domingos y . . . los fines de semana, ¿qué sueles hacer?
Clara Isabel	Los fines de semana suelo salir sólo un día, y esos días o voy al cine o a la discoteca o al teatro.
Julia	¿Y qué tipo de cine te gusta?
Clara Isabel	Hombre, me gustan las películas románticas, películas musicales también.
Julia	¿Qué haces normalmente los fines de semana? ¿Cómo te diviertes?
Héctor	Bueno, salgo con los amigos y procuramos pasárnoslo bien.
Julia	¿Y por qué zona de Madrid soléis ir?
Héctor	Empezamos por el centro, y cuando ya estamos algo felices y tal, pues nos vamos a . . . al norte de Madrid, a Moncloa.

¿qué sueles hacer? *what do you usually do?*
hombre *well*

¿cómo te diviertes? *what do you do to enjoy yourself?*
pasárnoslo bien *to have a good time*
estamos algo felices y tal *we're fairly happy and so on, i.e. we've had a few drinks*

PREGUNTAS

1   ¿Los dos se quedan en casa los fines de semana?

3

Another student, Beatriz, has discovered there's a special Picasso exhibition on in Madrid and asks her friend Paloma if she'd like to go.

Beatriz	Oye, Paloma, me he enterado que mañana hay una exposición de Picasso en el Centro de Arte Reina Sofía, ¿te apetece venir?
Paloma	Ay sí, claro, sí me gusta mucho Picasso. ¿Cuándo quedamos?
Beatriz	Pues, es mañana y está todo el día, ¿no? Podemos ir por la mañana, quedamos a las once o así.
Paloma	Bueno, es que por la mañana tengo que estudiar. Si pudiera ser por la tarde, que la tengo libre.
Beatriz	Bueno, ¿y qué hora te viene bien?
Paloma	Pues, ¿a eso de las siete podría ser?
Beatriz	Vale, estupendo.
Paloma	De todos modos te llamo si no puedo, ¿vale?
Beatriz	Vale, llámame, mañana.

me he enterado *I've found out*
¿te apetece venir? *do you fancy coming?*
si pudiera ser *if it could be*
la tengo libre *I'm free*
a eso de *about*
vale *all right*
de todos modos *anyway*
llámame *call me*

PREGUNTAS

1   ¿Por qué no puede ir Paloma a la exposición a las once?

El Instituto San Isidro

4

Julia went to a travel agent's, *Viajes Torija*, to find out about coach tours to Andalucía.

Julia	Hola, buenos días.
Sr Torija	Buenos días, señorita.
Julia	Mire, quería enterarme si tienen viajes para Andalucía, porque tengo unos amigos ingleses que están aquí y querrían hacer algún pequeño viaje, un circuito o algo de esto.
Sr Torija	Pues sí, en concretamente Andalucía tiene circuitos saliendo de Madrid prácticamente todos los días de la semana, y tiene de muy diversos días. Los tiene de tres días, de cuatro días, de cinco, de seis, de siete combinado con estancia en la Costa del Sol, y combinado con Marruecos, en fin la variedad es grande.
Julia	¿Y, eh, a qué hora salen estos circuitos?
Sr Torija	Estos circuitos salen a las ocho y media de la mañana.
Julia	¿Y de dónde?
Sr Torija	Bueno, pueden salir desde San Bernardo número 23, desde Gran Vía 68, o desde Plaza Oriente número 8.

quería enterarme / *wanted to find out*
querrían *they'd like*
algo de esto *something like that*
de muy diversos días *(lasting) for various numbers of days*

PREGUNTAS

1 ¿Por qué necesita Julia detalles sobre los viajes a Andalucía?

5

Rosa teaches Classical Greek at the *Instituto San Isidro*, but she also has a strong interest in the theatre and puts on plays with her students.

Julia Oye, creo que tienes una gran afición por el teatro.

Rosa Sí, es que el teatro me parece la manifestación artística más interesante, una de ellas. Y dentro de mis posibilidades lo procuro hacer con mis alumnos, y con teatro griego.

Julia O sea, que eres profesora de teatro también.

Rosa No, el instituto tiene profesores de teatro, de asignatura teatro. Yo lo intento como práctica y como comprensión de mi asignatura de una forma viva.

Julia ¿Y esto cuándo lo haces, en las horas de clase o fuera del horario de clase?

Rosa No, fuera de mi horario, en las horas que tengo libres los fines de semana, y con grupos muy grandes, y hacemos tragedia y comedia.

Julia ¿Y podéis practicar aquí en el instituto, tenéis alguna sala para practicar, o dónde lo hacéis?

Rosa Sí, el instituto tiene el mejor teatro de la zona. Entonces normalmente ensayamos allí, si no en los parques, en El Retiro por ejemplo, si hace buen día, pues vamos a ensayar en El Retiro.

Julia ¿Y tú crees que la gente joven va a los teatros?

Rosa Sí, sí, claro que va. Les encanta el teatro.

Julia ¿Pero no crees que a veces son bastante caros?

Rosa Sí. Y yo te podría contar que los alumnos, a partir de doscientas pesetas, supone un gasto extremo para ellos.

Julia Claro, y prácticamente no pueden ir a ningún teatro por ese dinero.

Rosa No, no.

El Retiro – a large park in the centre of Madrid

oye *tell me*
como práctica *as a practical exercise*
de una forma viva *in a real live way*
si hace buen día *if the weather's fine*
te podría contar *I could tell you*
a partir de *anything more than*
supone un gasto extremo *it means an enormous expense*

PREGUNTAS

1 ¿Qué tipo de teatro practica Rosa?
2 ¿Por qué encuentran difícil los estudiantes el ir al teatro?

LENGUA

INVITING

The most informal ways of asking if someone wants to do something are with the verbs *querer* and *apetecer*, followed by an infinitive:

¿**Quieres** ir al cine?	Do you want to go to the cinema?
¿**Te apetece** venir al teatro?	Do you fancy/feel like going to the theatre?

Notice that *apetecer* works in the same way as *gustar* and *encantar*:

¿**Te apetece** venir?	(literally, 'Does it appeal to you to come?')
Sí, **me apetece.**	

You can use *gustar* for a more polite or tentative way of inviting someone:

¿**Te gustaría** venir al teatro?	Would you like to come to the theatre?

Remember that if you are using the *usted* form, it's ¿**Le gustaría** ... ? *Gustaría* is the conditional tense of the verb (see below).

ACCEPTING AND DECLINING

To accept an invitation you can say:

Me gustaría mucho.	I'd like to very much.
Me encantaría.	I'd love to.

To turn down an invitation:

No puedo.	I can't.
Lo siento, pero ...	I'm sorry, but ... followed by your reason (or excuse).

MAKING ARRANGEMENTS

You may need to discuss what's convenient:

¿*Te viene bien?*	Does it suit you?
¿*Te vendría bien?*	Would it suit you?
Yo puedo/podría ir el jueves.	I can/could go on Thursday.
Podemos/Podríamos ir mañana.	We can/could go tomorrow.

If it's not convenient, you can say:
No me viene/vendría bien.
Me viene/vendría mal.

If it is, one of these phrases is enough:

vale	*de acuerdo*	*muy bien*
estupendo	*perfecto*	

You'll want to decide where and when to meet:

¿*Dónde nos encontramos?*	Where shall we meet?
¿*A qué hora ...?*	¿*Cuándo ...?*

Nos encontramos a las ocho menos cuarto en la puerta del teatro.
Nos vemos en el parque a eso de las cuatro.

The most common way of agreeing to an arrangement is by using the verb *quedar*:

¿*A qué hora quedamos?*	What time shall we decide on?
Podemos quedar a las siete y media.	We can make it half past seven.
Quedamos en eso.	Let's agree on that.

THE CONDITIONAL

The conditional form of the verb gives the idea of 'would':

¿*Te* **gustaría** venir al teatro?	Would you like to go to the theatre?
¿*Qué día te* **vendría** bien?	Which day would suit you?
Yo **podría** el viernes.	I could (would be able to) on Friday.

(For more details, see **Gramática**, page 148.)

SOLER

To talk about things you usually do or are in the habit of doing, you can use *soler* followed by another verb in the infinitive:
¿*Qué sueles hacer los fines de semana?*
Suelo salir todos los domingos.
Solemos ir al norte de Madrid, a Moncloa.

AMÉRICA LATINA

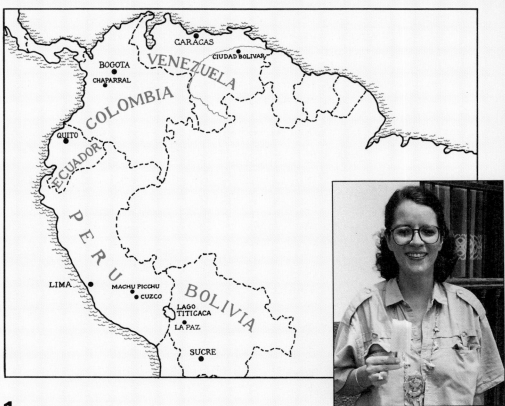

1 COLOMBIA

Journalist Patricia Lara needs to talk to a sociologist friend for a newspaper article she is writing about violence in Colombia. She phones to arrange to meet him.

Patricia ¿Haló? ¿Eduardo Pizarro, por favor? ... Eduardo, habla Patricia, ¿cómo estás? ... Te llamo por lo siguiente. Estoy escribiendo un artículo sobre violencia, el porqué la violencia en Colombia, para lecturas dominicales de *El Tiempo*, y me gustaría conversar contigo como sociólogo. ¿Podemos almorzar hoy a la una en *Casa Vieja*? ... Bueno, te veré, pues allá. Adiós.

el porqué *why, the reason for*
te veré *I'll see you*

2 ARGENTINA

Tommy is phoning a friend, Elena, in London, but it's not a convenient time to call, so he arranges to phone back later.

Tommy	Bueno, vamos a hacer algo, si a usted le parece bien. ¿En cuántas horas le parece que yo la puedo llamar a usted? ... ¿Qué hora es allí, las tres de la tarde? ... Tres menos veinte. Por eso, ¿en qué tiempo llamo, en cuántas horas? ... O sea, a las seis horas, sí, está bien, a las dieciocho horas de la Argentina.

si a usted le parece bien *if it's all right with you*

Before ringing off, Elena asks Tommy for his phone number and address as she may be visiting Buenos Aires soon.

Tommy	Elena, un gusto de escucharla, luego llamamos ... Ah, ¡se lo doy yo! La característica es cero nueve uno, de Bahía Blanca ... Y el número de mi casa es *****. Y el domicilio es ********, que por otra parte, nos encantaría que vengan. ... Me gustaría sacarle el compromiso ... O a lo mejor, este, como yo viajo bastante, de pronto puedo viajar yo a Buenos Aires ... ¡Bárbaro, bárbaro! Un cariño y hasta luego, Elena. Hasta luego, hasta luego.

se lo doy yo *I'll give it to you*
nos encantaría que vengan *we'd love you to come*
sacarle el compromiso *to get you to promise*
de pronto *perhaps*

3 BOLIVIA

Bolivian general Gary Prado has been trying to phone a fellow officer, but there is no answer from his office.

General Prado	Haló, Rodolfo. Buenos días, ¿cómo le va?, ¿cómo está? ... ¿Qué dice, cómo andan esas actividades? ... ¿Todo bien? Dígame, ¿qué es del General Cordero?, porque no me contesta en su oficina. ... ¡Ah!, está con el Presidente. Bueno, entonces lo voy a llamar a Cordero yo más tarde a la .. a su oficina ... Sí. Ya, está muy bien, Rodolfo, gracias. Un abrazo, hasta luego.

¿cómo le va? *how are things with you?*
¿qué es de ...? *what's happened to ...?*

americanismos
haló *the usual way to start a phone conversation*
habla Patricia soy Patricia *in Spain*
conversar *often used instead of* hablar
¿en cuántas horas? ¿dentro de cuántas horas? *in Spain*
un gusto de escucharla *great to hear you – very Latin American style of speaking*
la característica *dialling code* (el prefijo *in Spain*)
de pronto quizá(s) *in Spain*
¡bárbaro! *terrific! – more common in Latin America*
¿qué dice? *common way to open a conversation*

ESPAÑA ACTUAL

ESPAÑA CULTURAL

Madrid es indudablemente un centro muy importante en el mundo artístico, cosa que ha sido reconocida al ser elegida Madrid como Capital Europea de la Cultura para el año 1992.

El museo del Prado tiene una de las mayores colecciones del mundo de obras maestras, sobre todo, desde luego, de pintores españoles: El Greco, Velázquez, Murillo, Goya, … Y ahora incluso, con el fin del régimen franquista, el famoso cuadro de Picasso, *Guernica*, está colocado en una sala madrileña después de muchos años fuera del país.

La obra de Picasso, en su mayoría, sin embargo, se encuentra en un museo dedicado únicamente a este gran artista en Barcelona. Esta ciudad también tiene salas de arte de gran interés. Y al norte de Barcelona, también en Cataluña, en la pequeña ciudad de Figueras se ha construido un museo para exponer la obra de Salvador Dalí, quien junto a artistas tales como Miró y Tàpies simboliza la actividad productiva del arte moderno en España.

Aunque en el mundo se conoce a España de modo especial por sus pintores, no hay que olvidar la actividad artística en los demás campos culturales. Hay que señalar, sin embargo, que esta actividad pasó una etapa difícil durante el régimen franquista cuando regía una censura muy estricta contra las artes.

El cine español es otra forma artística que ya está teniendo éxito dentro y fuera de España. Los

nombres de directores como Buñuel, Berlanga y Saura han sido conocidos desde hace tiempo, pero también han aparecido nuevos talentos como es José Luis Garci, ganador de un Oscar en 1983, como Pedro Almodóvar, y películas que han tenido éxito universal como *El espíritu de la colmena* o *Los santos inocentes.*

El mayor problema, tal vez, para el cine español es el de la falta de fondos, cosa que también se observa en la promoción tanto de la música como del teatro en España. El teatro español ha progresado mucho desde la muerte de Franco, y ahora incluso fuera de España se puede ver teatro español, como por ejemplo las obras que trae a Londres la actriz y directora Nuria Espert. Pero la escasez de recursos económicos hace que el precio de las entradas sea alto, cosa que pasa con todos los actos culturales en general, lo que suele excluir a mucha gente de estas actividades. Sin duda donde más oferta teatral hay es en Madrid, y se encuentran algunos sitios, como el Teatro Español, donde hay cierta ayuda a nivel estatal, con subvenciones de parte del gobierno, cosa que hace más accesible el asistir. Por otro lado, en Barcelona hay una nueva ola de teatro experimental y de la calle, realizado por grupos como La Fura dels Baus.

En cambio, la música clásica probablemente tiene más facilidades en Barcelona, con su famoso Liceo para la ópera, y el *Palau de la Música.* Y en este campo hay algunos nombres verdaderamente bien conocidos: Plácido Domingo, Montserrat Caballé, Victoria de los Angeles, José Carreras. También fueron los catalanes quienes más promocionaban la música folk como protesta política y social en los años sesenta y setenta, a través de un movimiento conocido en catalán como *la nova cançó.* Pero la música indígena, la música 'de raíces', se ve en todas las regiones de España, siendo el flamenco la más conocida y popular fuera de sus territorios de origen.

Es en la palabra escrita – la novela, la poesía – donde España ha sufrido más la represión de cuatro décadas. La rehabilitación en este campo es lenta pero visible, sobre todo con la vuelta a España de escritores que durante muchos años tuvieron que vivir en el exilio. El novelista Juan Goytisolo es un ejemplo. Otros escritores que destacan hoy son Manuel Vázquez Montalbán, Justo Jorge Padrón y Camilo José Cela. El hecho de que compartan el mismo idioma que los lectores de América Latina significa que potencialmente hay un mercado enorme y entusiasta para su obra. Este entusiasmo ya se nota con la enorme popularidad del grupo de escritores latinoamericanos tales como García Márquez (autor de *Cien años de soledad*), Borges, Vargas Llosa, Carpentier, Neruda o Asturias, y muchos otros, algunos de los cuales han ganado premios literarios internacionales, y cuya obra se ha traducido a muchos idiomas.

Guernica, la famosa obra de Picasso está colocada en El Casón del Buen Retiro en Madrid

PRÁCTICAS

1

Una invitación

Invite a friend to go to the cinema with you.

You	(*What do you usually do at the weekends?*)
Carmen	Pues, suelo salir con los amigos a tomar unas copas y charlar.
You	(*Would you like to go to the cinema with me* (conmigo) *this Sunday?*)
Carmen	Sí, me encantaría. ¿Qué ponen?
You	(*They're showing* El Dorado. *Do you fancy seeing it?*)
Carmen	Sí, me gustaría mucho verla. ¿Cuándo quedamos?
You	(*Would seven o'clock suit you?*)
Carmen	Vale. Entonces, nos encontramos a las siete en la puerta del cine.

2

Quedamos en eso

When you arrange to meet someone, you need to be sure where it is you're expected to be and when. Decide in each case which rendezvous matches the arrangement being made.

a Nos encontramos a las siete y cuarto de la tarde en la Puerta del Sol, en la entrada del metro.
7.15 in the Puerta del Sol.
7.15 at the entrance to the underground station in the Puerta del Sol.
7.15 in the middle of the Puerta del Sol.

b Quedamos a las dos menos cuarto de la tarde en el restaurante enfrente del hotel.
2.15 in the restaurant in front of the hotel.
1.45 in the hotel restaurant.
1.45 in the restaurant opposite the hotel.

c Nos encontramos el domingo por la tarde en El Retiro.
Sunday afternoon in the park.
Sunday evening in the main square.
Sunday afternoon at the football stadium.

d Nos vemos mañana después del trabajo. Tomamos unas cañas en la cervecería, y luego vamos al teatro, que está a dos pasos.
Tomorrow evening at the theatre.
Tomorrow after work in the bar near the theatre.
Tomorrow evening in the theatre bar.

e La excursión sale a las nueve menos cuarto de la mañana, entonces nos encontramos un cuarto de hora antes delante de la agencia de viajes.
8.30 outside the travel agency.
8.45 in front of the travel agency.
8.30 opposite the travel agency.

3

¿Jugamos al tenis?

Four friends are trying to arrange a mixed doubles match on a weekday. They all have certain times when they're free:

Juan	Yo puedo el lunes o el miércoles, después de las siete de la tarde, o el viernes después de comer.
Inés	Yo podría el martes por la mañana, el miércoles, o el jueves.
Miguel	Para mí es imposible antes de las seis de la tarde, aparte del viernes.
Laura	Me vendría bien el martes por la mañana o el miércoles por la tarde.

Some sessions are already booked up:

Hora	L	M	M	J	V
1000					
1300	X				
1500					
1900					X

Are they going to be able to book a session, and if so, when?

4

Excursiones

It's June and you've just arrived in Madrid. You want to go on a couple of guided tours and have got a brochure about them.

a Which days can you visit the Escorial?

b Can you go on an excursion to Cuenca?

c You'd like to go on an all-day trip on a Tuesday – where can you go?

d How much is the flamenco night (including dinner)?

e What time does the afternoon visit to Toledo leave?

f If you only have a morning free, which excursions are available?

EXCURSIONES RADIALES MADRID

EXCURSIONES		Salida	PTS.	Frecuencia
M	**Artístico** (mañana)	09:45	2.950	
	Panorámica (tarde)	15:30	1.950	
A	**Noche Flamenca (cena en Tablao)**	20:30	7.800	
D				
R	**Noche de Gala (cena en Sala)**	20:30	8.800	
I				
D	**Show**	20:30	5.900	
	Show Flamenco	20:30	4.900	DIARIAS
T	Todo el día	09:45	4.800	
O	Medio día (mañana)	08:30	3.000	TODO
L				
E	Medio día (tarde)	1/4 a 15/9 15:30 16/9 a 31/3 15:00	3.000	EL
D				
O				AÑO
	Toledo - Aranjuez *	08:30	5.700	
	Toledo - Escorial - Valle de los Caídos *	08:30	6.400	
	Aranjuez Medio día (tarde)	1/4 a 31/10 15:00	2.600	
	Escorial y Valle mañana	08:30	3.100	
		tarde	1/4 a 15/9 15:30 16/9 a 31/3 15:00	3.100	
	Avila, Segovia y La Granja *	08:30	6.300	
	Salamanca, Alba de Tormes *	1/5 a 30/9 07:45	7.800	lunes, miércoles, viernes
	Toros y Panorámica	a confirmar	4.200	domingos y días de corrida; en temporada
	Cuenca *	1/5 a 31/10 08:00	7.800	martes, jueves, sábados

* día completo

NO OPERAN	
LUNES	MARTES
Escorial - medio día Escorial - día completo Toledo - Escorial - Valle	Toledo - Aranjuez Aranjuez - medio día

TEATRO LOPE
BODAS DE SANGRE
de Federico García Lorca

domingo 9 marzo
tarde, a las 8.30

ENTRADAS: 1500pts

números limitados

5
Obra de teatro
Fill in the gaps in the conversation below with the appropriate information from this advertisement.

Pedro	A mí me gustaría ir al teatro un día de éstos. ¿Sabes qué ponen ahora?
Luis	Sí, me parece que ponen ....
Pedro	¿Es de un autor famoso?
Luis	¡Hombre! ....
Pedro	¿Y dónde la ponen?
Luis	En ....
Pedro	Bien, si te apetece ir, ¿en qué día quedamos?
Luis	Sólo la ponen ....
Pedro	Vale. ¿A qué hora?
Luis	....
Pedro	Y las entradas, ¿hay que sacarlas antes?
Luis	Sí, porque ....
Pedro	¿Y cuánto cuestan?
Luis	....
Pedro	Es mucho, pero ¡vamos!, ya es normal.

6
¿Qué sueles hacer?
Answer these questions about what you usually do in your free time.

a   ¿Qué sueles hacer los domingos?
b   ¿Dónde sueles pasar las Navidades?
c   ¿Vas más frecuentemente al cine o al teatro, o a ninguno de los dos?
d   ¿Sales más con los amigos o con tu familia?
e   ¿Cómo sueles ocupar tus ratos libres?

¿QUÉ PASÓ?

Past events

1

Fernández Angulo SA is a long-established business but when did Sr Angulo himself start working in the shop?

Sr Angulo	Esta casa se fundó por un tío de mi abuelo. Luego pasó a mi abuelo, luego pasó a mis padres, y por último ha pasado a mis hermanos y a mí. Son desde el año 1870.
Julia	¡Más de un siglo!
Sr Angulo	Más de un siglo tiene esta tienda.
Julia	¿A qué edad empezó usted a trabajar aquí, era muy niño?
Sr Angulo	Pues no, verá usted. Estuve haciendo las oposiciones de notario, pero cuando murió mi padre, se quedó mi madre al frente de este negocio, y claro, yo dejé la carrera y le ayudé a mi madre y a mis hermanos. O sea, que yo estoy aquí desde la muerte de mi padre hace veintitantos años, 1965, que murió. O sea, que no son muchos años.

esta casa se fundó por *this business was founded by*
ha pasado *it has passed*
¿era muy niño? *were you very young?*
estuve *I was*
oposiciones *public examinations*
murió mi padre *my father died*
al frente de *in charge of*
hace veintitantos años *twenty-odd years ago*

PREGUNTAS

1 ¿Este negocio es de la familia del Sr Angulo desde hace cuántas generaciones?
2 ¿Por qué empezó el Sr Angulo a trabajar en el negocio?

2

How did Sergio, a Mexican, come to be running a restaurant in Madrid?

Julia	¿Qué hace un mejicano aquí en Madrid?
Sergio	Pues, tratando de sacar adelante este restaurante. En Méjico hemos … tenemos algunos restaurantes, surgió la idea de venir a poner algo aquí a Madrid y pues, pensé que era una buena experiencia, una buena oportunidad, y aquí estamos.
Julia	¿Y cuánto tiempo hace que has abierto el restaurante?
Sergio	Lo abrimos hace dos años y medio.
Julia	Y una cosa que me sorprendió cuando entré en el restaurante fue ver a estos personajes que tenéis sentados en las mesas.

sacar adelante *to run, make work*
era, eran *was, were*
has abierto *you've opened*
fue *was*

Unos clientes (dos de algodón) en el restaurante *El Cuchi*

Sergio	Sí, este, son pues nuestros amigos de algodón. La idea de esto surgió porque, pues al principio cuando abrimos, pues teníamos muchos días con muy poca gente, y pensamos que si poníamos a los muñecos aquí en las mesas sentados como personas, pues la gente desde afuera pensaría que eran gentes verdaderas, porque muchas veces, al ver un sitio vacío, pues no nos llama la atención para entrar, ¿no? Entonces, fue . . fue más bien para eso.

si poníamos *if we were to put*
pensaría *would think*
gentes *people (Mexican usage* – gente *is normally singular)*
no nos llama la atención *doesn't attract our attention*

PREGUNTAS
1 ¿Es *El Cuchi* el único restaurante que tiene Sergio?
2 ¿Qué reacción le dio a Julia ver los muñecos?

3

Among the crowds of people who flock to the Plaza Mayor there are unfortunately some less well-behaved elements, as Isidoro found to his cost one day when he was involved in an incident in the street.

Isabel	Explícame cómo ocurrió.
Isidoro	Pues, tenía en casa pintores, y la verdad, por quitarme un poco de ese jaleo, pues me bajé al . . . la perrilla que tengo a la calle. Y en la calle, pues inopinadamente un grupo de . . de hinchas de fútbol debían ser, porque llevaban banderines, pues me arrollaron y me tiraron al suelo.
Isabel	¿Y qué pasó luego?
Isidoro	Me recogieron, me llevaron a una clínica cercana y de allí, pues en una ambulancia al sanatorio.

hinchas de fútbol debían ser *football supporters they must have been*
llevaban *they were carrying*
me tiraron al suelo *they knocked me to the ground*

Here's Tere's version of events.

Isabel	¿Qué pasó exactamente?
Tere	Bueno, pues le tiraron y le tuvieron que llevar a la clínica de la Plaza Mayor, chorreando sangre. Nos tuvieron que avisar por el automático a nosotros. ¡Tú fíjate! Bajamos, ya bajó mi hija primero, y en seguida le llevaron a la clínica esta. Le tuvimos que ingresar en el sanatorio, le dieron cinco puntos, dijeron que tenía una fisura de cadera, que le tuviéramos dos meses en la cama sin moverse, y allí ha estado hasta hace cosa de unos días que se levantó. Eso pasó.

tuvieron que *they had to*
chorreando sangre *streaming with blood*
¡tú fíjate! *imagine it!*
le dieron *they gave him*
tenía *he had*
fisura de cadera *fractured hip*
le tuviéramos *we should keep him*

PREGUNTAS
1 ¿Por qué salió Isidoro de casa?
2 ¿Qué le hicieron en el sanatorio?

4

As Isabel explains to Julia, she's lived most of her life outside Spain, as a consequence of the situation following the Spanish Civil War.

Julia	Isabel, ¿tú hace mucho tiempo que vives en Madrid? No, ¿verdad?
Isabel	No, vivo en Madrid desde hace cuatro años y pico.
Julia	Sí, ya sé que vivías en Londres, pero tú no has nacido en Londres.
Isabel	No, nací en Madrid, pero me marché a Londres de muy pequeñita … Claro, me fui con mis padres.
Julia	¿Y por qué tu familia se fue a Londres?
Isabel	Pues, por razones políticas mayormente. Habíamos perdido la guerra, y la vida era extremadamente difícil. Entonces nos marchamos en busca de una vida mejor. No nos fuimos muy lejos, nos fuimos a Londres.
Julia	¿Y por qué Londres exactamente? Porque parece que la mayoría de la gente se fue a Francia, incluso a Latinoamérica muchos, a Méjico sobre todo, pero lo de Londres es .. es un poco nuevo para mí.
Isabel	Hubo algunos exiliados que fueron a Londres, mayormente intelectuales, pero tienes razón, las olas grandes fueron a Latinoamérica o a países europeos más cercanos. La verdad es que no lo sé muy bien por qué fuimos a Londres. Creo que la idea inicial era de ir primero a un país cuyas condiciones de vida en aquellos momentos realmente eran óptimas, eran inigualables en Europa, y de allí dar el salto a Argentina donde mi padre tenía familia.
Julia	¿Pero no llegasteis a ir a Argentina?
Isabel	No. Nos quedamos en Londres … gracias a Dios.

y pico *and a bit*
vivías *you used to live*
me fui, nos fuimos *I went, we went*
habíamos perdido *we had lost*
sobre todo *especially*
lo de Londres *as for London*
hubo *there were*
tienes razón *you're right*
cuyas condiciones de vida *whose living conditions*
dar el salto *to make the move*
no llegasteis a ir *you didn't end up going*

PREGUNTAS

1 ¿Cuándo fue Isabel a Londres y cuándo volvió a España?
2 ¿En general qué tipo de exiliado español fue a Inglaterra?

LENGUA

THE PAST

Talking about the past (what happened, how things used to be and so on) in Spanish involves using different forms of verbs. There are three main forms, which we will cover in this and the next two units. The difference between them is roughly the same as that between the English 'I went', 'I used to go' and 'I have been'.

WHAT HAPPENED?

The first of these forms is called the preterite tense. It's used when you're talking about specific events in the past – what you did, things that happened on one particular occasion:

*¿Qué **pasó**?*	What happened?
*Mi padre **murió**.*	My father died.
***Fuimos** a Londres.*	We went to London.
*Me **llevaron** a una clínica.*	They took me to a clinic.

Sometimes a specific date or time may be mentioned:

*Lo **abrimos** hace dos años y medio.*	We opened it two and a half years ago.
*Colón **llegó** a las Américas en 1492.*	Columbus reached America in 1492.
*El avión **salió** a las seis.*	The plane left at six.

These are all events that happened and are over and finished – they are past history.

FORMING THE PRETERITE

There are two sets of verb endings in the preterite, one for verbs whose infinitive ends in –*ar*, and one for those ending in –*er* or –*ir*:

	–ar	**–er** and **–ir**
(*yo*)	habl**é**	com**í**
(*tú*)	habl**aste**	com**iste**
(*usted, él, ella*)	habl**ó**	com**ió**
(*nosotros*)	habl**amos**	com**imos**
(*vosotros*)	habl**asteis**	com**isteis**
(*ustedes, ellos, ellas*)	habl**aron**	com**ieron**

There are some exceptions, e.g.:

estar	estuve, estuviste, estuvo, estuvimos, estuvisteis, estuvieron
hacer	hice, hiciste, hizo, hicimos, hicisteis, hicieron
tener	tuve, tuviste, tuvo, tuvimos, tuvisteis, tuvieron

Ser and **ir** have the same preterite forms:
fui, fuiste, fue, fuimos, fuisteis, fueron

(For other exceptions, see **Gramática**, page 152.)

IR, IRSE

Irse, the reflexive form of *ir*, is more forceful, meaning 'to leave' or 'to go away' rather than just 'to go':
***Fuimos** a Londres el mes pasado.*
***Nos fuimos** a Londres en busca de una vida mejor.*

DATES

Except for the first of the month, dates in Spanish are ordinary numbers. The names of days and months are written with a small first letter:

el primero de octubre	1 October
el veintitrés de febrero	23 February
el treinta y uno de agosto	31 August

Years are expressed slightly differently:

mil novecientos ochenta y nueve	1989
mil cuatrocientos noventa y dos	1492

HACE

Hace can also mean 'ago':

Hace veinte años.	Twenty years ago.
Hace dos años y medio.	Two and a half years ago.

AMÉRICA LATINA

1 VENEZUELA

The whole of Latin America is a melting pot for people from all over the world – not just Europe, but Africa, Japan and China as well.

Hugh	¿Cómo se llama usted?
Oliver	Mi nombre es Oliver Luis Guerrero Wong, descendiente de chinos.
Hugh	¿Y dónde nació?
Oliver	Nací aquí en Venezuela.
Hugh	¿En qué ciudad de Venezuela nació?
Oliver	Nací en Guayana, Ciudad Bolívar.
Hugh	¿Su mamá era de ascendencia china?
Oliver	Es de ascendencia china.
Hugh	¿De dónde provino la familia de su mamá?
Oliver	Mi abuelo proviene de Cantón, cantonés. Mi abuela es hija de mi bisabuela que era martiniqueña, casada con mi bisabuelo que era francés.

¿de dónde provino ...? *where did ... come from?*
martiniqueña *from Martinique*

2 PERU

A number of advanced cultures existed in Latin America long before the arrival of the Spanish *conquistadores*, among them the Mayas, the Aztecs and the Incas. Ruined buildings from these cultures can be found all over the region, and some of the best-known are in Peru.

Hugh	Las ruinas de Cuzco y de Machu Picchu, ¿de qué cultura son?
Milagros	Bueno, las ruinas de Machu Picchu y las de Cuzco son de la cultura incaica o del imperio incaico.
Hugh	¿De qué fecha?
Milagros	Cuando los españoles llegaron aquí al Perú en 1535, ya habían existido doce Incas antes de la llegada de los españoles. Para la época en la que llegaron los españoles, habían dos Incas, dos emperadores incaicos, que se disputaban el trono. Ellos eran hermanos, y uno de los hermanos se quedó en Quito, y el otro se quedó en Cuzco.
Hugh	¿Cómo se llamaban?
Milagros	Bueno, los hermanos se llamaban Huáscar y Atahualpa.

incaica/o *Inca*
habían existido *had existed*
se llamaban *were called*

3 HONDURAS

The Mayan city of Copán was lost in the jungle of Honduras for hundreds of years, until it was rediscovered in 1839 by an enterprising traveller and writer from New York. Hugh was shown round the ruins by Napoleón Guerra, a local guide.

Hugh	Este sitio fue olvidado por muchos siglos, ¿quiénes fueron que lo descubrieron de nuevo?
Napoleón	Lo es ... descubrió John Stephens, comprándolo por cincuenta dólares al dueño local acá en Copán ruinas.
Hugh	¿Qué se hizo de Copán después de la venta de Copán?
Napoleón	Después, se empezaron las excavaciones, cuando el gobierno de nuestro país firmó un contrato con la universidad de Harvard, de los Estados Unidos, para obtener fondos para el inicio de las excavaciones.
Hugh	¿Los monumentos principales quedan aquí o han sido expatriados algunos ejemplos?
Napoleón	El fin de los fondos que se obtuvieron fue, con el contrato firmado, que toda escultura duplicada, tomaban una y dejaban otra en el país.
Hugh	¿Pero fueron saqueados algunos originales de estelas?
Napoleón	Exactamente. En 1880 un inglés visitó las ruinas y fue el primero que tomó fotografías y hizo esquemas de los monumentos. Fue el primero también en informar que existían las ruinas de Copán en el occidente de Honduras, pero el problema que surgió él, fue llevarse varias esculturas de las cuales encontró en el abandono de las ruinas de Copán.

Una estela en Copán

de nuevo *again*
han sido expatriados
have been taken out of the country
se obtuvieron *were obtained*
tomaban *they would take*
dejaban *they would leave*
estelas *stelae, large carved stones*
el problema que surgió él, fue llevarse ... *the problem with him was that he took with him ...*

americanismos
mamá *normally used in Latin América instead of* madre
habían dos Incas *the plural* habían *is common in Latin America* (*instead of* había)
inicio comienzo *or* principio *in Spain*

ESPAÑA ACTUAL

LA HISTORIA RECIENTE DE ESPAÑA

Durante muchos años la propaganda turística española repetía el slogan 'España es diferente', refiriéndose a las diferencias entre España y el resto de la Europa Occidental. Ahora se debe reinterpretar esta frase en un sentido: 'La España de hoy es diferente a la España de ayer'.

España ha cambiado profundamente en los últimos quince a veinte años, y ya no es el país casi subdesarrollado que encontraron los primeros turistas ingleses de los años sesenta. Desde luego sólo se puede apreciar esta transformación después de repasar los hechos importantes de la reciente historia española: su guerra civil, que duró tres terribles años, desde julio de 1936 hasta abril de 1939, después de una sublevación en contra del entonces gobierno legítimo. Y el resultado: una larga dictadura con recriminaciones, mucha

represión, y muchos exiliados, sobre todo entre los políticos de la izquierda e intelectuales.

Los vencedores y algunos de los vencidos coexistieron durante los treinta y seis años del régimen franquista en una atmosfera de resentimiento. Fue una época de censura, de aislamiento internacional, donde destacaban los valores tradicionales y católicos. La primera parte de este régimen se caracterizó por una migración masiva de población del sur rural hacia el norte relativamente más próspero e industrializado. Fue una época de mucha pobreza y sufrimiento. Sin embargo, en la segunda mitad la situación económica experimentó una gran mejora gracias a los pactos con los Estados Unidos y a la llegada del turismo con todos los recursos monetarios que ambos trajeron. La censura cedió un poco, pero la represión policíaca contra cualquier oposición al régimen no se alteró mucho.

A la muerte del General Franco en noviembre de 1975, la nación esperaba con anticipación e incertidumbre la reinstauración de la monarquía con el rey Juan Carlos. Este sorprendió a todos con la rapidez con la que inició cambios tanto políticos como sociales. Los que le habían calificado como nada más que una continuación fiel de los deseos de El Caudillo, pronto tuvieron que aceptar la nueva realidad. El rey promocionó la introducción de una verdadera democracia, con una constitución que ha dado muchos más poderes a las regiones y ha fomentado la libertad de expresión en general. El primer presidente del gobierno en la nueva democracia, Adolfo Suárez, fue escogido personalmente por el rey. Casi desconocido por el público, pudo empezar un régimen democrático sin demasiados lazos con el régimen anterior.

Desde 1975 España ya ha conocido gobiernos libremente elegidos tanto del centro como de la izquierda. Pero no siempre ha sido un proceso sin problemas. En 1981 hubo un intento fracasado de golpe de estado. El 23 de febrero, conocido ya como el 23-F, entró en las Cortes un tal Tejero, teniente coronel de la Guardia Civil, y mantuvo como rehenes a todos los diputados durante muchas horas. La intervención personal del rey para solucionar este secuestro fue decisiva para conservar el régimen democrático.

Luego, bajo el gobierno socialista de Felipe González, España entró en la Comunidad Europea. También estrechó sus relaciones con la OTAN. Sobre todo, España ha permitido florecer a una sociedad libre y abierta donde caben todos los extremos en cuanto a cultura, prensa, movimientos políticos, modos de vestir, y comportamiento sexual, como sucede en cualquier país tolerante.

El 23-F

PRÁCTICAS

1

¿Verdad o mentira?

Which of these statements are true and which are false?

a El Sr Angulo empezó a trabajar en la pañería después de la muerte de su madre.

b Los padres de Isabel la llevaron a Inglaterra de bebé.

c A Isidoro unos gamberros le tiraron al suelo y le rompieron la cadera.

d Después de abrir el restaurante Sergio invitó a unos amigos a cenar allí.

e El negocio de *Fernández Angulo SA* se fundó hace más de cien años.

f Hubo muchos españoles que dejaron su país para buscar unas condiciones mejores de vida después de la Guerra Civil.

g Almudena se quedó en casa cuando su madre bajó a la calle para ayudar a su padre.

h El restaurante de Sergio no tuvo mucho éxito al principio porque hubo pocos clientes.

2

Testigo presencial

A couple of days ago you witnessed a minor road accident, and below is your statement about what happened. Put the verbs in brackets into the correct form.

Yo (*ver*) un coche blanco acercarse desde la izquierda. De repente un coche azul (*salir*) de la callecita de enfrente. El conductor del primer coche (*tener*) que torcer violentamente para evitarlo y (*acabar*) en el otro lado de la calle, donde (*chocar*) con un árbol. El coche azul no (*pararse*), al contrario (*irse*) a toda prisa hacia el centro de la ciudad. Yo (*correr*) hacia el coche blanco y les (*ayudar*) al conductor y a su compañera a salir.

3

Historia de España

Here are some notes about some events in Spanish history. Turn each one into a proper sentence and supply the missing dates.

a Moros – invadir España (711)

b Cristóbal Colón – descubrir América (?)

c Felipe II – mandar Armada Invencible contra Inglaterra (?)

d Miguel de Cervantes (autor de *Don Quijote*) – morir (?)

e Guerra Civil española – estallar (?), terminar (?)

f Juan Carlos – subir al trono (?)

4

Un encuentro

Fill in the gaps in this conversation between María and Loli.

María Hola, Loli, ¿qué tal? ¿Qué hiciste ayer?

Loli Pues, ayer ....

María ¿Sí? Fuiste al cine. ¿Qué película viste?

Loli .... *Bodas de sangre*.

María ¿Y te gustó?

Loli Sí, ... mucho.

María ¿A qué hora terminó la sesión?

Loli .... a las once.

María ¿Volviste directamente después a casa, o tomaste algo por ahí?

Loli Primero me .... unas cañas con los amigos, y luego .... a casa.

María Pues, me alegro, tengo que irme. ¡Hasta luego!

Loli ....

El descubrimiento de América por Cristóbal Colón

5

Una receta

Here's the recipe Pedro used to make *sangría* for his party. Alongside he explains what he did – fill in the gaps in what he's saying.

Sangría

Ingredientes
2 litros vino tinto
½ litro coñac
1 litro gaseosa
canela
fruta, por ejemplo:
½ kilo naranjas
½ kilo limones
½ kilo manzanas
½ kilo melocotones

Método
lavar y cortar la fruta
meterla toda en un recipiente grande
añadir el vino
mezclarlo todo
echar el coñac
añadir una cucharada de canela
dejarlo doce horas
echar la gaseosa
servir frío

'Pues, compré la bebida y la fruta en el mercado. En casa primero .... y luego .... la fruta. La .... en un recipiente grande, y .... el vino. Después, ... todos los ingredientes y .... el coñac también. Finalmente .... una cucharada de canela. .... la mezcla en la nevera durante doce horas. Por la noche .... la gaseosa. Es mejor servirla muy fría.'

6

Tiempos pasados

Look at Isidoro and Tere's accounts of Isidoro's encounter with the football supporters. Now spot all the preterite forms, and list them with the infinitive form of the verbs that they come from.

7

Momentos en tu vida

Answer these questions in Spanish.

a   ¿Dónde estuviste el último primero de enero?
b   ¿Qué hiciste el sábado pasado?
c   ¿En qué año naciste?
d   ¿A qué hora cenaste anoche?
e   ¿Adónde fuiste de vacaciones el año pasado?

6 ¿QUÉ HACÍAS?

The way things used to be

1

Isidoro tells Isabel about the job he used to do before he retired.

El Palacio de Comunicaciones

Isabel	Antes de dedicarte al *dolce far niente*, ¿qué hacías?
Isidoro	Pues, trabajaba en Correos.
Isabel	¿Me puedes hablar un poco de tu trabajo, en qué consistía?
Isidoro	Pues en Correos he desempeñado yo creo que casi todos los .. las labores, desde empezar repartiendo cartas por la calle a . . . ya dentro de la oficina, pues desde operaciones de caja postal en ventanilla hasta clasificación de paquetes.
Isabel	¿Y dónde trabajabas exactamente? ¿En el Palacio de Comunicaciones?
Isidoro	En el Palacio de Comunicaciones.
Isabel	¿Te gustaba?
Isidoro	¡Hombre!, como gustarme, . . . la verdad, hubiera preferido mi profesión actual, jubilado.

he desempeñado *I've done*

como gustarme *as for liking it*

la verdad, hubiera preferido *the truth is, I'd have preferred*

PREGUNTAS
1 ¿Trabajaba Isidoro como cartero?
2 ¿Cuál es la profesión preferida de Isidoro?

2

Tere and Isidoro's next-door neighbour, Salud, has lived in the building for a long time but, as Tere explains, not always on the same floor.

Isabel	¿Cuánto tiempo llevas viviendo aquí?
Tere	Pues mira, vamos a ver ... ¿en qué año llegamos? En el ...
Isidoro	Sesenta ...
Tere	Sesenta, sí, en el sesenta.
Isabel	O sea, desde hace veintiocho años estáis aquí, ¿no?
Tere	Sí.
Isabel	¿Y Salud también lleva tanto tiempo?
Tere	No, Salud no. Salud llevará aquí, pues veintidós años.
Isabel	¿Y siempre habéis vivido en esta planta?
Tere	Bueno, no, en esta planta ella no vivía, vivía sí en las guardillas.
Isabel	¿Y por qué vivía en las guardillas?
Tere	Porque entonces tenía la portería abajo y era portera, y el chiscón era para estar de día, y la guardilla era para dormir de noche.
Isabel	¿Y qué era el chiscón?
Tere	Una casita, o sea una habitación chiquitita, que había en el portal, con un cristal que se podía mirar y ver quién subía, quién bajaba, y estar la portera atenta de todos los inquilinos o gentes extraños que pudieran subir por la escalera y bajar.

llevará aquí *she must have been here*
habéis vivido *you've all lived*
guardillas *attic*
chiquitita *tiny little*
que pudieran subir *who might go up*

PREGUNTAS
1   ¿A qué se dedicaba Salud antes?
2   ¿Y dónde vivía?

3

Mercedes remembers what used to happen when the *portera* had gone off duty and there were *serenos* (night watchmen) patrolling the streets.

Isabel	¿Tú te acuerdas de la época de los serenos?
Mercedes	Sí, perfectamente.
Isabel	Cuéntame un poco esa época.
Mercedes	Pues mira, que normalmente la puerta ... entonces las puertas estaban abiertas todo el día. Estaba la puerta abierta todo el día, a partir de las diez y media de la noche entraba el sereno, se cerraba la puerta, y luego la gente para entrar tocaba las palmas, el sereno ya acudía al .. al toque de las palmas, y venía corriendo a abrir las puertas de cada portal,

¿tú te acuerdas de ... ?
do you remember ... ?
cuéntame *tell me about*
tocaba las palmas
clapped their hands
él sentía *he heard*

Mercedes y un
huésped

y luego todo el mundo le daba una propina.

Isabel ¿Y el sereno dónde estaba?

Mercedes Pues por la calle, y la gente, como las palmas tocaba fuerte,
pues él sentía y ya iba al portal que .. que le llamaban.

PREGUNTAS

1 ¿Por qué la gente no podía entrar en casa después de las
diez y media de la noche?

2 ¿Qué hacía el sereno cuando sentía un toque de palmas?

4

Julia has a degree in sociology, but at the moment she doesn't have a full-time job.

Isabel ¿Has podido poner en práctica tu título, tu carrera, de alguna
forma?

Julia No, hasta el momento no. Quizá un poco también porque
cuando terminé la universidad, empecé a trabajar muy
rápido pero no en un trabajo relacionado con la sociología,
sino en algo que no tenía nada que ver, como era una
escuela de idiomas, de inglés concretamente, que dependía
de la Embajada de Estados Unidos. Y entonces, bueno,
como dedicaba ocho horas del día a este trabajo, quizá
abandoné un poco todo el tema de la sociología.

¿has podido ... ? *have
you been able to ... ?*

no tenía nada que ver
*had nothing to do with
it*

PREGUNTAS

1 ¿Dónde trabajaba Julia?

2 ¿Cuántas horas trabajaba al día?

5

What was life like in London for Isabel, and why did she return to Spain?

Julia   Cuando estabas allí en .. en Londres, cuando eras niña, ¿tenías algún contacto con España? O sea ... mantenías el español me imagino también, porque lo hablas perfectamente.

Isabel   Sí. Bueno, el contacto se mantuvo sobre todo en casa. Hablábamos español en casa, y eso unido a la determinación de mis padres de no romper los lazos con España ... y por tanto volvíamos todos los años; eso hizo que yo me criara en un ambiente bicultural, bilingüe, ¿verdad?

Julia   ¿Y tenías ganas de vivir en España, o por qué volviste?

Isabel   En aquellos momentos yo tenía muchas ganas de vivir en España. Siempre me ha atraído, por razones románticas a lo mejor, y en aquel momento ... es decir, me vine concretamente a Madrid porque me ofrecieron un contrato de trabajo.

Julia   Y ¿para trabajar dónde? ¿En el periódico que estás ahora?

Isabel   No, no, no, no. Mi vida profesional ha dado muchos tumbos. En Londres yo era lo que se dice una académica. Yo quería cambiar esa rutina, y me ofrecieron un contrato como traductora profesional en la OMT, la Organización Mundial del Turismo. Entonces, me convertí en funcionaria internacional, durante casi un año.

Julia   ¿Aquí en Madrid hacías este trabajo?

Isabel   Aquí en Madrid, sí.

se mantuvo *was kept up*
por tanto *so, therefore*
eso hizo que yo me criara *that meant that I was brought up*
¿tenías ganas ... ? *were you wanting ... ?*
me ha atraído *has appealed to me*
ha dado muchos tumbos *has had many ups and downs*

PREGUNTAS
1 ¿Cómo mantenía los lazos con España la familia de Isabel?
2 ¿A qué se dedicaba Isabel en Inglaterra?

LENGUA

WHAT USED TO HAPPEN?

Talking about the past often involves describing things that happened not just once but repeatedly, or that continued over a period of time. In English there are various ways of doing this, but in Spanish they're all conveyed by the imperfect tense:

Trabajaba en Correos.	I **used to work** in the Post Office.
*Las puertas **estaban** abiertas todo el día.*	The doors **were** open all day.
*En aquella época, yo **vivía en Londres**.*	At that time, I **was living** in London.
***Salía** todos los días a las nueve.*	He **would go out** every day at nine o'clock.

Remember that the important difference between the imperfect and preterite tenses is that the imperfect is continuous or repeated, while the preterite is completed and one-off:

*Antes **trabajaba** en Correos, pero hace seis años **me jubilé**.*

***Tenía** ganas de vivir en España, y **me vine** concretamente a Madrid.*

*Nosotros **llegamos** en el sesenta; entonces Salud **vivía** en las guardillas.*

If you're telling a story, for instance, you use the imperfect to set the scene (describing what things were like, what the time was, what people were doing and so on); and the preterite for the events that happened:

*La casa **era** blanca, **había** flores alrededor de la puerta, **eran** las doce en punto, Miguel **estaba** en la cocina, el teléfono **sonó**, yo lo **contesté**…*

You also use the imperfect when you're reporting what someone said:

*Dijo que **se iba** a Barcelona.*	He said he was going to Barcelona.

FORMING THE IMPERFECT

There are two sets of verb endings, one for –ar verbs and one for –er and –ir types:

	–ar	**–er** and **–ir**
(*yo*)	habl**aba**	com**ía**
(*tú*)	habl**abas**	com**ías**
(*usted, él, ella*)	habl**aba**	com**ía**
(*nosotros*)	habl**ábamos**	com**íamos**
(*vosotros*)	habl**abais**	com**íais**
(*ustedes, ellos, ellas*)	habl**aban**	com**ían**

Notice that *ver* (to see) keeps the e – *veía, veías, veía*, etc. Otherwise, there are only two exceptions:

ser era, eras, era, éramos, erais, eran

ir iba, ibas, iba, íbamos, ibais, iban

HAY

The past tense forms of *hay* are *había* (imperfect) and *hubo* (preterite):

Había una habitación chiquitita.	There was a tiny little room.
Hubo algunos exiliados que fueron a Londres.	There were some exiles who went to London.

TENER

As well as meaning 'to have', *tener* is also part of lots of common Spanish phrases:

***Tiene** diez años.*	She's ten years old.
*¿**Tenías ganas** de vivir en España?*	Were you wanting to live in Spain?
*Sí, **tienes razón**.*	Yes, you're right.

Others are:

tener hambre/sed	to be hungry/thirsty
tener calor/frío	to be hot/cold
tener miedo	to be afraid
tener sueño	to be sleepy
tener la culpa	to be guilty

AMÉRICA LATINA

1   NICARAGUA

César Augusto Sandino (pictured overleaf) was the Nicaraguan guerrilla leader of the 1920s and 30s who fought against the Samoza dictatorship, and from whom the present-day Sandinistas take their name. Doña María Borjas, now in her eighties, vividly remembers seeing Sandino.

Doña María   Era más bajo que el señor éste. Blanco. Como estaba joven . . joven en ese tiempo, era bonito. Ahora después, ya estaba más viejo, más trabajado, más sufrido, y entonces ya estaba más viejo. Pero cuando yo lo conocí . . . bonito, joven, de treinta y cinco años. Yo estaba joven también, de veintiséis años. Yo salía corriendo cuando decían 'viene Sandino'. Yo salía corriendo a verlo cerquita, para conocerlo. El montaba en un . . . su machito viejo, raspado, y los soldaditos atrás, de caitillos. Entonces, él pasaba para acá, arengando gente.

Hugh   ¿Cómo fue muerto Sandino?

Doña María   Bueno, aquí lo mataron en Managua. El se de– . . él se dejó engañar, se engañó. El creyó que el Presidente que estaba era compadre de él, y creyó que era buen amigo. El lo mandó matar, por . . por órdenes de Somoza.

estaba joven/viejo *found in spoken Spanish but it's more correct to say* era . . .
machito *mule*
de caitillos *in sandals*
¿cómo fue muerto Sandino? *how did Sandino die?*
él se dejó engañar *he let himself be deceived*
él lo mandó matar *he had him killed*

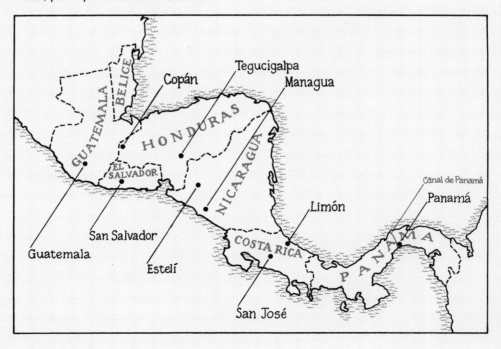

2 CHILE

Elizabeth remembers, equally vividly, her first visit to her somewhat eccentric English grandparents.

Elizabeth Mi primer recuerdo de Inglaterra se remonta a cuando yo era una niña. A los nueve años me enviaron a Inglaterra a aprender inglés. Esto te digo, mi abuela, una señora perfectamente inglesa y perfectamente extraña para mí, se casó tres veces: la primera vez con un alemán que murió, la segunda vez con un inglés que también murió, y la tercera vez con otro inglés que era un coronel inglés, un perfecto coronel inglés de película, de película de las colonias inglesas, ¿no?

Hugh ¿Con bigote?

Elizabeth Con bigote, naturalmente. Entonces, yo llegué a un 'cottage' inglés en la Isle of Wight a enfrentarme con este coronel, ¿no es cierto?, y con esta dama inglesa, que se tenía que cambiar tres veces al día, porque ella se cambiaba para el 'breakfast', para el 'lunch', para el 'five o'clock tea', que era toda una ceremonia a mi juicio perfectamente ridícula e innecesaria, y por último se volvía a cambiar para la comida. Pues yo la encontraba una loca a mi abuela, y muy poco simpática. Mi abuela era bastante pesada, digamos, ¿no? No así mi abuelo, 'el coronel', como le decimos nosotros. Este era un hombre muy dulce, le gustaban mucho las flores, era un hombre extraordinariamente fino. Pero era un hombre que le gustaban mucho los niños. Entonces, yo quería mucho más a mi abuelo que a esta señora extraña, que entre paréntesis las veces que venía a Chile nos miraba a nosotros como verdaderos 'Indians', como nos decía: 'ustedes son unos indios'. Y, bueno, allí yo enfoco mis primeros recuerdos de Inglaterra, y la persona que está en mi memoria con ternura, digamos, es el coronel, mi abuelo.

se remonta a *goes back to (a rather formal word)*
se tenía que cambiar *had to change her clothes*
a mi juicio *to my mind*
por último *lastly*
yo la encontraba una loca a mi abuela *I thought my grandmother was a crazy woman*
no así *not so*
como lo decimos nosotros *as we called him*
entre paréntesis *by the way*
las veces que *whenever*

americanismos
bonito, dulce *describing a man, Latin American usage*
¿cómo fue muerto? *in Spain would be ¿cómo murió?*
compadre *friend, comrade – common Latin American usage*
como le decimos llamamos *more usual in Spain in this sense*
ustedes *'you' in the plural, formal and informal –* vosotros *is not used in Latin America*

a la vuelta:
César Augusto Sandino

ESPAÑA ACTUAL

LA MUJER ESPAÑOLA

Todas las mujeres entrevistadas en este curso trabajan de un modo o de otro. La situación de la mujer en España ha cambiado muchísimo en los últimos diez años. Durante el régimen franquista sólo se consideraba a la mujer como ama de casa y madre. Su deber era quedarse en el hogar, cuidar a los niños, y hacer las faenas domésticas. Actualmente la mujer está empezando a adquirir derechos de igualdad con el hombre, como está, en teoría, aceptado en la constitución democrática de 1978.

Cada día hay más mujeres que trabajan fuera de casa; en 1988 lo hacían el 42% de las mujeres españolas en edad de trabajar. Otro 18% hacía estudios, y un 7% buscaba trabajo. Y, además, lo importante es que las mujeres ya no sólo ocupan empleos típicamente designados como femeninos.

Ahora, aunque pocas, se encuentran mujeres que son ingenieras, arquitectas, aviadoras, mineras, etcétera. Hay las que practican la medicina y administran la justicia, pero es significativo que la lengua española todavía no reconoce este hecho: no existen en el vocabulario español ni 'juezas' ni 'bomberas' ni 'carteras' (trabajo que hacía Almudena), ni muchas otras versiones femeninas de las ocupaciones.

A parte del principio básico de la nueva constitución, que reconoce absoluta igualdad para todos los ciudadanos, otras leyes recientes, y para algunos controversiales, han afectado a la mujer española y la han librado del papel tradicional. Hoy en día son legales en España el divorcio, el aborto dentro de ciertos límites, el uso de anticonceptivos y el matrimonio civil. Además, los sindicatos han conseguido mejoras importantes en las normas de trabajo que refuerzan, y a veces extienden, la ley en cuanto afecta a las mujeres trabajadoras. Estas tienen derechos claros en lo que respecta a la baja por maternidad, y al derecho a trabajar a tiempo parcial para poder cuidar a los niños de menos de seis años. Obviamente estas normas no sirven de nada si las mujeres no consiguen puestos de trabajo en competencia con los hombres. En este sentido, desde luego, hay las que dudan de que realmente exista ya igualdad de oportunidades.

Para mejorar la situación, por lo tanto, los partidos socialistas y comunistas han resuelto dedicar una cuota mínima de 25% de los puestos de sus órganos directivos a las mujeres. Este gesto de mejorar la imagen de las mujeres como líderes es imprescindible. Se encuentran muy pocas mujeres en cargos de responsabilidad, tanto en el mundo político como en el comercial o el industrial. De las pocas que hay podemos señalar Matilde Fernández y Rosa Conde, ambas nombradas miembros del gabinete de Felipe González en 1988. Otras españolas en la cumbre de sus profesiones son la jefa de la Radio Televisión Española, Pilar Miró, que también es directora de cine, y Agatha Ruiz de la Prada, famosa diseñadora de moda.

La inauguración de un Instituto de la Mujer debe mejorar la situación. Más de la mitad de la población española son mujeres. Sólo muy lentamente se está progresando hacia un nivel que reflejará esta cifra en las actividades públicas y profesionales que ejercen las mujeres fuera del hogar.

arriba: Agatha Ruiz de la Prada
a la derecha: La Asociación de Mujeres Jóvenes da
información sobre cuestiones de la salud y del
trabajo

MUJERES JOVENES
MUJERES JOVENES
YO YA TENGO PLAN
PLAN DE ACCION
PARA LA IGUALDAD
DE OPORTUNIDADES DE LAS MUJERES.

PRÁCTICAS

1

¿Cómo pasabas los veranos?

You're reminiscing with a Spanish friend about summer holidays in the past. Put your part of the conversation into Spanish.

Manuela	Yo de pequeña pasaba los veranos en la playa, cerca de San Sebastián. ¿Tú qué hacías?
You	(*I used to go to Wales with my parents. We would spend a fortnight in the mountains and then a week on the coast.*)
Manuela	¿Y qué hacías durante el resto del verano?
You	(*I stayed at home.*)
Manuela	¿Pero no salías nunca?
You	(*Yes, I used to play tennis with my friends, or sometimes we went to the swimming pool.*)
Manuela	A mí me gustaba bañarme y tomar el sol.
You	(*We couldn't sunbathe much; it was always raining.*)

2

Cuando sonó el teléfono...

When the phone rang you were having supper. Answer this question: *¿Qué hacías cuando sonó el teléfono?*, and then say what these other people were doing.

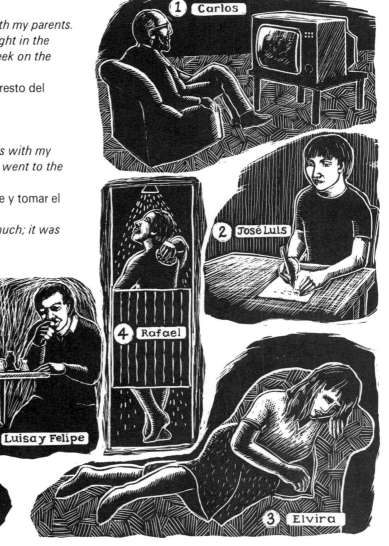

Muy Señor mío:

Me interesa el puesto que anunció su compañía en el periódico de este domingo. Me gustaría explicar mi experiencia profesional.

Durante dos años **(trabajar)** de secretaria para una editorial bien conocida. **(Tener)** que escribir muchas cartas. También **(traducir)** muchos reportes del inglés al español. **(Solicitar)** un puesto con más responsabilidad con la empresa, que me **(dar)** los jefes en seguida. Mi nuevo cargo **(consistir)** en seleccionar los mejores libros que nosotros **(ir)** a publicar.

(Dejar) este trabajo el año pasado para hacer un curso avanzado de informática. Ahora otra vez estoy buscando trabajo y su empresa me parece muy atractiva.

Le saluda muy atentamente,

Loli González

LOLI GONZALEZ

3
Una carta
In the letter Loli is applying for a job, giving details of her past experience. Put the verbs in brackets in the imperfect or the preterite, as appropriate.

4
¿Qué tal día?
Read the following account, and then answer the questions.

Era un domingo muy oscuro. Hacía frío y llovía. Fuimos a dar una vuelta por la mañana y luego volvimos a comer a casa con los abuelos. Durante la comida la gente charlaba sobre su trabajo y comentaba el partido de fútbol. De repente hubo una llamada en la puerta y apareció nuestro vecino. Tomó café con nosotros y nos explicó que su hija tenía un trabajo nuevo. Parecía muy orgulloso de su hija.

a   ¿Qué día de la semana era?
b   ¿Qué tiempo hacía?
c   ¿Qué hicieron antes de comer?
d   ¿Sobre qué temas hablaron durante la comida?
e   ¿Para qué vino el vecino?
f   ¿Comió también el vecino?
g   ¿Por qué estaba orgulloso el vecino?

5

¿Qué tiene?

Describe the state of each of the people in the pictures, using phrases made up with *tener*.

6

¿Cómo eras?

Describe yourself when you were ten – what you looked like, the colour and length of your hair, where you lived, what you liked doing, and so on.

¿QUÉ HAS HECHO?

What you've done recently

1

One of Julia's interests is women writers, but it turns out she's also an enthusiastic filmgoer.

Isabel Supongo que una de tus aficiones será la lectura, ¿pero tienes otro tipo de afición?

Julia Sí, el cine, fundamentalmente. Yo creo que el cine incluso por delante de la lectura.

Isabel ¿De verdad?

Julia Sí, sí.

Isabel ¿Por qué te gusta tanto el cine?

Julia Bueno, no lo sé. Es una cosa desde muy niña, desde muy, muy pequeña. A mis padres les gusta mucho y siempre me llevaban de niña, lógicamente a ver películas para niños, pero siempre me ha gustado mucho el cine, no sé por qué es.

Isabel ¿Qué películas has visto últimamente que te han gustado?

Julia Pues últimamente ... La última que he visto y que me ha gustado mucho, es la película de Wim Wenders, se llama *El cielo sobre Berlín*, y es una película que te recomiendo si no has visto. Y también es muy buena *Ojos negros* ...

Isabel Ah sí, la vi el otro día.

Julia Que está muy, muy bien. Y bueno, creo que éstas son las dos mejores que he visto últimamente.

será la lectura *must be reading*
por delante de *more than*
***El cielo sobre Berlín,
Ojos negros*** English *titles*: Wings of Desire, Dark Eyes

PREGUNTAS

1 ¿Qué explicaciones da Julia por su afición por el cine?

2

Isabel has been very busy lately, but she has managed to have an evening out.

Julia	¿Qué has hecho estos días, Isabel?
Isabel	Pues mira, he hecho muchas cosas: trabajar desde luego todos los días, he tenido que hacer algunas entrevistas, he tenido que salir fuera de Madrid algunas veces también. Y he procurado compaginar esas obligaciones, pues con un poco de relax. Por ejemplo, el otro día hemos estado en . . en esta sala rociera, no sé si la conoces, *Las Marismas del Rocío*.
Julia	No, no lo conozco. Ahora está de mucha moda esto de las sevillanas y las salas rocieras, ¿no?
Isabel	Sí, desde luego ha sido un 'boom'. En Madrid el flamenco siempre ha tenido muchísimo auge, pero yo creo que en la última época, durante los últimos tres o cuatro años, las sevillanas realmente se han puesto de moda como se ha puesto de moda, pues hacer 'aerobic', ¿verdad? La gente va a clase de sevillanas o a clase de aerobic . . .
Julia	Sí, yo conozco . . . En mi anterior trabajo tenía compañeras que estaban yendo a clase de sevillanas como podía ser clase de francés, de inglés o de . . .
Isabel	Yo he ido a clases de sevillanas.
Julia	¡No me digas!
Isabel	Sí, y me gusta mucho, francamente.

sevillanas are a type of folk song and dance from Seville; salas rocieras are nightclubs and bars where they're performed

estos días *these past few days*

está de mucha moda *it's very fashionable*

ha tenido muchísimo auge *it's been very popular*

se han puesto *have become*

yendo *going*

como podía ser *as if it was*

¡no me digas! *you don't say!*

PREGUNTAS

1   ¿Qué obligaciones ha tenido Isabel como parte de su trabajo?
2   Además de las sevillanas, ¿qué otra cosa se ha hecho popular recientemente?

3

Ana and Antonio have just come back from a week in London.

Isabel	Creo que habéis estado en Londres hace poco, ¿no?
Ana	Sí, hemos estado una semana de vacaciones, esta semana sí.
Isabel	Pero ¿por qué Londres? ¿Por qué os habéis ido a Londres en pleno mes de marzo?
Ana	Porque Londres está muy bien para cualquier época del año.
Isabel	¿Dónde habéis estado?

en pleno mes de marzo *in the middle of March*

Ana	Enfrente de Hyde Park. Me parece que los jardines eran Kensington.
Isabel	Buena zona, es una zona muy hermosa de Londres.
Ana	¡Preciosa, preciosa!

PREGUNTAS

1 ¿Por qué estuvieron Ana y su marido en Londres?

4

Tere has seen many changes in the Plaza Mayor during the years she's lived there.

Isabel	Tere, tú llevas viviendo aquí muchos años.
Tere	Sí.
Isabel	¿Ha cambiado mucho la zona?
Tere	¡Uy!, bastante.
Isabel	¿En qué ha cambiado?
Tere	Pues, ha cambiado en que cuando yo vine aquí no había tanto gamberro, ni tanta delincuencia en la Plaza Mayor. Era extraordinaria. Había en la Plaza Mayor unos setos con verde, jardines, había bancos, unas fuentes estupendas para sentarse y tomar el fresco, y sin embargo ahora todo eso se ha convertido en .. en 'kinkis' con las botellas, bebiendo. Y no se puede uno sentar, han quitado los bancos y ha cambiado muchísimo, horrible. Podías antes salir al fresco y sentarte a las dos de la mañana, a las tres, a la hora que fuera, había una tranquilidad bárbara, y además estaba hasta más bonita la Plaza Mayor. Ahora la han puesto con adoquines y está feísima, pero antes estaba extraordinaria.

tanto gamberro *so many hooligans*

para sentarse *where you could sit down*

tomar el fresco *get some fresh air*

a la hora que fuera *at any hour*

la han puesto con adoquines *they've paved it over*

PREGUNTAS

1 ¿Qué cosas había antes en la Plaza Mayor que ya no hay?

La Plaza Mayor en tiempos pasados

5

Sr Angulo was actually born in Calle Toledo, though he now lives on the other side of the Plaza Mayor. He agrees that things aren't what they used to be – but there is one good thing . . .

Sr Angulo	Tiene una ventaja muy grande, que es el estar cerca del negocio. Yo realmente salgo de mi casa, vengo por debajo de los soportales, y aún en el día de lluvia, sin paraguas no me mojo, porque voy a cubierto de los soportales.
Julia	Claro. ¿Pero la vida normalmente en este barrio le parece cómoda?
Sr Angulo	Era, era antes, ahora se ha deteriorado muchísimo.
Julia	¿Por qué?
Sr Angulo	Pues, la droga, los parados, las mujeres de mala vida, que andan por ahí, eso se ha deteriorado mucho. Antes era un barrio muy castizo, como se decía aquí en Madrid.
Julia	¿Entonces usted cree que ha cambiado mucho el barrio desde que usted era niño o joven hasta ahora?
Sr Angulo	Sí, sí, sí, indudablemente. Y sin remontarnos a la edad de cuando yo era niño, sino concretamente a la edad de hace veinte años. Hace veinte años esto era un barrio tranquilo, había más orden y había más autoridad.
Julia	Pero a pesar de todo, le gusta el barrio.
Sr Angulo	Sí, sí, a pesar de todo yo sigo siendo del barrio.

no me mojo *I don't get wet*

a cubierto de *under cover of*

mujeres de mala vida *prostitutes*

como se decía *as we used to say*

a pesar de todo *despite everything*

yo sigo siendo *I still belong to*

PREGUNTAS

1   ¿Quiénes son los que se encuentran ahora en la Plaza Mayor que a Tere y al Sr Angulo no les gustan?

LENGUA

WHAT HAVE YOU DONE?
The third way of talking about the past in Spanish is by using the perfect tense, which is very similar both in the way it's formed and the way it's used to the English 'I have been', 'I have done', etc.

It's used to talk about things that have happened recently (and which may still be happening) e.g.:

¿Qué **has hecho** estos días?	What have you done these past few days?
Hemos estado en Londres.	We've been to London.
Siempre me **ha gustado** el cine.	I've always liked the cinema.

FORMING THE PERFECT
To form the Spanish perfect tense, you use part of the verb *haber* – the equivalent of 'I have', 'he has', and so on – followed by the *–ado* or *–ido* part of the verb (the past participle) e.g.:

He tenido que salir.
Hemos estado en una sala rociera.
He ido a clases de sevillanas.

The forms of *haber* to use are:
he, has, ha, hemos, habéis, han

Past participles are formed as follows:
–ar verbs become *–ado*:

estar – estado	cambiar – cambiado
gustar – gustado	quitar – quitado

–er and *–ir* verbs become *–ido*:

ser – sido	tener – tenido
ir – ido	venir – venido

and *ha habido* is the perfect form of *hay*.

There are a few exceptions such as:

hacer – hecho	ver – visto
decir – dicho	poner – puesto

(See also **Gramática**, page 149.)

THE PAST TENSES
In units 5–7 we've given guidelines about using the Spanish past tenses, preterite, imperfect and perfect, and if you stick to these you'll have few problems, but there are some things to notice. For instance, the difference between the preterite and the perfect is not always so clear. In particular you'll discover that the perfect is used far less in Latin America – instead everything is put into the preterite.

On the other hand, in parts of Spain, especially the centre and the north, it's the preterite which is heard less, with the perfect being used instead.

You'll also find that, in general, the perfect is used more in Spanish than its English equivalent if what has happened is very recent, e.g.:

¿A qué hora has llegado esta mañana?	What time did you arrive this morning?
¿Has dormido bien?	Did you sleep well?

In one or two cases there isn't any logical reason why one form or the other is preferred. For example:
¿Has nacido en Inglaterra?
No, nací en Madrid.

SIGO SIENDO ...
The verbs *seguir* and *continuar* can both mean 'to continue', 'to go on', or 'to be still doing something'. In this case, they're followed by a verb in the *–ando* or *–iendo* form:

Sigo siendo del barrio.	I still belong to the area.
Voy a continuar trabajando aquí.	I'm going to go on working here.

The *–ando/–iendo* form is also used with *estar* to say what you are doing – emphasising what you're in the process of doing:
Estoy preparando la cena.
Tenía compañeras que estaban yendo a clases de sevillanas.

AMÉRICA LATINA

1   COLOMBIA

March 1988 saw the first ever local elections held in Colombia. Doña Esperanza was one of the independent judges appointed by the government to see fair play in the small town of Chaparral, five hours' drive from the capital, Bogota.

Hugh   ¿A qué hora se abrió el acto electoral esta mañana, doña Esperanza?

Doña Esperanza   Sí, a las siete y media de la mañana los jurados debían estar en las mesas. A las ocho de la mañana ya todo estaba completo, se iniciaron las votaciones normalmente. Nosotras las dos delegadas, los jueces de instrucción, y las autoridades militares, han estado permanentemente dentro del área escogida para las votaciones, y todo ha trascurrido normalmente.

Hugh   ¿Ha habido alguna irregularidad hasta el momento, por ejemplo en las mesas de votación, que han sido tal vez corregidas?

acto electoral *electoral process*

jueces de instrucción *examining magistrates*

Las elecciones municipales de Chaparral, Colombia a la derecha: Otilia y su marido, Anastasio

Doña Esperanza	Sí, se presentaron dos pequeños incidentes en dos mesas, y hubo de cambiarse algunos de los jurados de votación. Pero ya se corrigió.
Hugh	Sí. ¿Y por qué se separaron?
Doña Esperanza	Porque dos de los jurados tenían en sus mesas votos y no debían tenerlos allí.
Hugh	¿Y se cambiaron y todo está bien?
Doña Esperanza	Sí, perfectamente en este momento, ya hay nuevos jurados para garantizar la pureza del voto y para garantizar la imparcialidad.

hubo de cambiarse *had to be changed*

¿por qué se separaron? *why did they leave?*

2   NICARAGUA

The Sandinista revolution in 1979, when the Somoza dictatorship was overthrown, brought about sweeping changes in people's lives. Otilia, a Sandinista *militante*, lives with her husband Anastasio in a village near Estelí, where she's a health worker.

Hugh	¿Cómo ha cambiado tu vida desde el triunfo de la revolución?
Otilia	Bueno, en gran manera, porque en la dictadura somocista muchas mujeres no tenían derecho a tener relaciones, tanto internacionales como nacionales, y ahora toda aquella mujer organizada o no organizada tiene un gran derecho a tener relaciones, a prepararse cada día mejor, y a escoger el campo que más le gusta, o sea, puede ser que sea educadora de adultos, si a ella le gusta ser profesora puede ser profesora dentro de prescolar, y así sucesivamente va avanzando hasta ser una profesora titulada de . . . para primario. Si le gusta el campo de salud, cada día nos preparamos mejor y entonces bien podemos ser unas enfermeras tituladas.
Hugh	Y tu vida personalmente, ¿cómo ha cambiado?
Otilia	Bueno, ha cambiado en el sistema. Yo cuando era muy niña quise siempre estudiar, pero nunca pude porque mis padres todo el tiempo vivieron escasos de recursos, no tuve ese derecho. Ahora con el proceso revolucionario yo he tenido un gran derecho de estudiar lo que a mí me guste, y he escogido el campo de salud, y ése es el que estoy estudiando, y lo estoy ejerciendo dentro de mi comunidad. Entonces, para mí ha cambiado en gran . . en gran parte.

en gran manera/parte *greatly*

somocista *of Somoza*

tener relaciones *to have contact (also often used in sense of sexual relations, though not here)*

toda aquella mujer *any woman*

organizada *belonging to a (political) organisation*

va avanzando *goes on, progresses*

vivieron escasos de recursos *were short of money*

americanismos
comunidad *commonly used, as here, to mean 'village'*
  (pueblo *in Spain*)

ESPAÑA ACTUAL

EL 'BOOM' DE LA MUSICA TRADICIONAL

El impresionante resurgimiento de la popularidad de las sevillanas, y las salas rocieras donde se ven estos bailes, son ejemplos de un rasgo general que es el renacimiento de interés y entusiasmo por los bailes tradicionales y música popular, como el flamenco, en todas partes de España.

Las sevillanas son bailes que tienen sus raíces en la ciudad de Sevilla y los nombres asociados con ellas, como los nombres de los distintos bailes, proceden de Sevilla. También 'rociera' se refiere al barrio del Rocío de Sevilla. Y aunque ya españoles de todas partes y todas clases sociales del país se entusiasman por bailar sevillanas, desde las infantas Elena y Cristina hasta la mujer de Felipe González, siguen siendo una expresión fundamentalmente de Andalucía y el sur de España.

No obstante, se han establecido en Madrid, y en muchas otras ciudades de España, salas donde se puede ir a bailar o ver bailar sevillanas. Además, han proliferado los sitios que ofrecen clases de enseñanza sobre estos bailes, que se han puesto muy de moda. En las tiendas de discos se encuentran zonas enteras dedicadas exclusivamente a las sevillanas. Parte de esta popularidad fuera de Andalucía se debe a la gran cantidad de andaluces que se marcharon de sus pueblos en busca de trabajo a vivir en las ciudades industriales del centro y norte.

El flamenco y las sevillanas tienen sus orígenes en la música gitana: 'flamenco' significa 'gitano' en el argot gitano. A estos orígenes también se añadieron influencias árabes adquiridas durante los ocho siglos de dominación musulmana. El arte flamenco abarca tanto la música, como el baile, como la canción. Sufrió mala publicidad durante gran parte de los últimos años al ser incorrectamente interpretado como un símbolo barato y cursi de 'lo

Bailando sevillanas

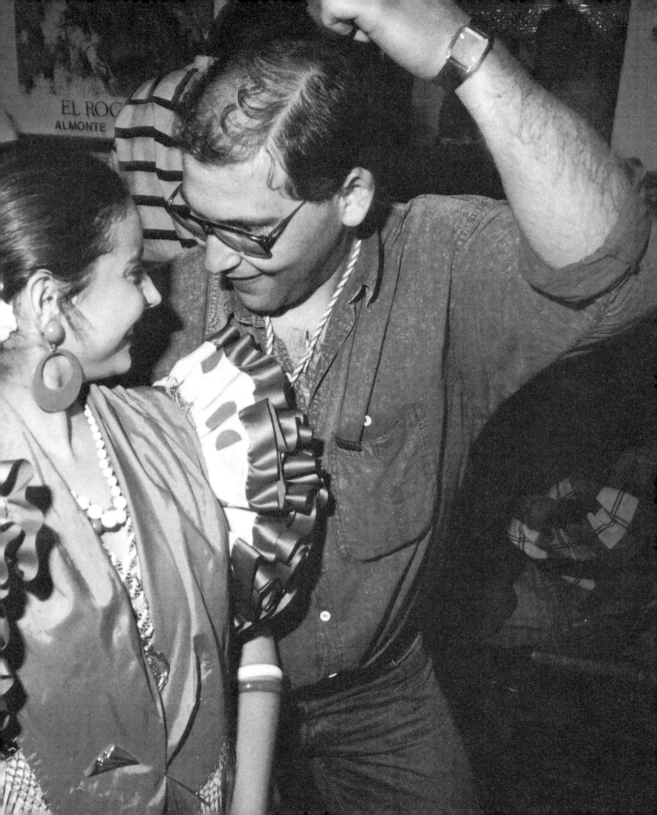

español típico'. Pero la nueva moda ha conseguido que la gente reconozca su verdadera profundidad, tratándolo como un fenómeno serio y como una fuente de inspiración. Cantantes, o mejor dicho 'cantaores' del flamenco se han hecho muy populares, como es Antonio Mairena y Vicente Soto 'El Sordera'. Y también se nota este 'boom' con los compositores y guitarristas del flamenco, como por ejemplo Gerardo Núñez. Algunos cantantes de música pop también mezclan su música con características del flamenco. Conjuntos musicales como Triana iniciaron este movimiento de flamenco-rock que actualmente se encuentra en la música de grupos como Los Chichos y Los Gitanos.

No son sólo los andaluces y los aficionados al flamenco los que están volviendo a las raíces de la cultura regional para enriquecer la música popular. Esta mezcla de lo moderno y lo tradicional también se observa en sitios como Galicia y Cataluña. Y en general el orgullo por la música y bailes locales regionales se ha generalizado ahora por toda España, desde el flamenco en Andalucía hasta las sardanas en Cataluña. Ya no se consideran estos bailes como cosas para entretener a los turistas extranjeros; ahora los aprecian los mismos españoles, y sobre todo los españoles jóvenes.

PRÁCTICAS

1

En la Aduana

Answer the questions you're asked when you arrive at a Spanish airport.

Oficial ¿De dónde viene usted ahora?
You (*I've arrived from London.*)
Oficial ¿Ha estado antes en España?
You (*No, I've never been here before.*)
Oficial ¿Ha recogido su equipaje?
You (*Yes, I've got my three suitcases.*)
Oficial ¿Ha leído esta lista de regulaciones? ¿Tiene algo que declarar?
You (*Nothing, I'm here on holiday.*)
Oficial Muy bien. Puede pasar.

2

Preparaciones para un viaje

Match the sentences to the pictures to say what each person has just done before going away on holiday.

a Ha hecho la maleta.
b Se ha lavado los dientes.
c Ha cerrado la puerta con llave.
d Se ha levantado temprano.
e Ha llamado por un taxi.
f Ha desayunado.

3

¿Qué has hecho esta semana?
You've taken a week off work and are asked by a friend what you've been up to. Look at your diary (above) and say what you've been doing.

4

En busca de trabajo
While visiting friends in Spain you want to persuade them to have your sister as their new au pair. Here's a summary of her qualifications for the job. Try convincing your friends by adding verbs to make sentences.

17 años – mucha experiencia con niños – canguro (*babysitter*) para los hermanos pequeños – tres veranos en Escocia con una familia con muchos niños – aprobado los exámenes – trabaja los sábados en un bar – ayuda en la casa – familia simpática y buena gente.

5

Recuerdos
Here's someone talking about travel and holidays. Make sense of what they're saying by putting the verbs in brackets into the appropriate past tenses.

Siempre me (*gustar*) viajar al extranjero. (*Estar*) varias veces en España, en Portugal y en Grecia, pero no (*estar*) nunca fuera de Europa. El año pasado (*pasar*) quince días en un pequeño pueblo en Andalucía, que me (*encantar*). El pueblo (*ser*) muy tranquilo, (*hay*) muy pocos turistas. Yo (*pasar*) los días dando paseos por el campo. Después de comer, como (*hacer*) mucho calor, (*soler*) dormir la siesta. Por la tarde (*tomar*) unos finos y unas tapas y (*charlar*) con la gente en el bar. (*Ser*) unas vacaciones estupendas. Ultimamente (*tener*) que trabajar mucho y (*estar*) pensando en volver a España en busca de la tranquilidad.

6

¿Qué has hecho hoy?
Say what you've done today in as much detail as you can.

¿QUÉ OPINAS?

Discussions and opinions

1

Isabel's husband, Jaime, plays volleyball every weekend with a whole crowd of friends. Isabel talked to some of them, as they waited for their turn to play, about the general state of sport in Spain.

Isabel	¿En España se practica mucho deporte?
Aurelio	No. En España se practica muy poco deporte. La gente en general no .. no lo practica, no se practica desde pequeños, y luego ya sin tener hábito la gente no empieza.
Isabel	¿Qué piensas tú del nivel ... la categoría deportiva de España, respecto a otros países?
Aurelio	¡Hombre!, si lo comparamos con Tanzania o con Libia, algo se puede hacer, pero vamos, en general no. Los dirigentes del deporte en España tienen una suerte, y es que salen de vez en cuando algunos genios y les mantienen el .. el medallero.
Isabel	Javier, ¿tú crees que España puede competir a nivel mundial?
Javier	¿Voleibol?
Isabel	Sí.
Javier	No, nunca.
Isabel	¿Nunca?
Javier	O sea, de momento no. No es un deporte nada nada nada promocionado en España.
Isabel	¿Crees que España tiene alguna posibilidad de ganar medallas en el noventa y dos?
Javier	Muy pocas, muy pocas.

luego ya sin tener hábito *then not being in the habit*

tienen una suerte *are lucky*

de vez en cuando *from time to time*

les mantienen el medallero *they keep the medals coming in*

el noventa y dos *1992, the Barcelona Olympics*

PREGUNTAS

1 Según Aurelio y Javier, ¿hay muchos españoles que destacan en el deporte a nivel mundial?

2

Isabel asked two more of the volleyball players whether they thought Spaniards were taking more interest in sport.

Isabel	¿Creéis que se practica más deporte en España ahora que hace unos años?
Patricia	Sí.
Olga	Mucho más.
Patricia	Sí. Se ha puesto de moda, además, está de moda hacer deporte ahora.
Isabel	¿Por qué?
Patricia	No lo sé, no lo sé, pero hace años ir de . . . vestido en chándal por la calle era algo raro, ¿no?, algo extraño, y ahora no, ahora está de moda hacer deporte, no sé por qué ha sido. Quizá por la influencia de países extranjeros, o no lo sé. Es una moda buena yo pienso, ¿no?
Isabel	¿Tú estás de acuerdo, Olga?
Olga	Yo no sé si es moda o no es moda, pero desde luego en los colegios se le da importancia al deporte, cosa que antes no se le daba. Yo creo que han . . se han dado cuenta que es necesario el deporte, que no sólo la educación intelectual sino también la física, es importante ya desde muy pequeños los niños.

vestido en chandal *wearing a tracksuit*
¿tú estás de acuerdo? *do you agree?*
se le da importancia *they attach importance*
se han dado cuenta *they've realised*

PREGUNTAS

1 ¿Han cambiado las actitudes en España hacia el deporte recientemente?

3

At the *Instituto*, Julia asked Rosa her opinion of education in Spain.

Julia	¿Qué opinas del sistema educativo en España ahora mismo?
Rosa	Necesita una . . una revisión profunda, en total. Tiene un planteamiento que no es correcto, me parece a mí. Unos programas muy densos, de un nivel superior a su . . a su edad, demasiada información y poca práctica, los profesores no pueden dar abasto con el programa que impone el Ministerio, y no se investiga, no hay a sus . . a sus niveles un medio de investigación.

planteamiento *set-up*
no pueden dar abasto *can't cope*
no se investiga *there's no research done*

PREGUNTAS

1 ¿Está satisfecha Rosa con el actual sistema educativo?

4

Julia also spoke to a couple of Rosa's students. The syllabus for the pre-university course they're doing includes Classics – Greek or Latin.

Julia	¿Qué opinas de la .. de la enseñanza en España?
Héctor	Bueno, se va reformando, pero le falta mucho por .. por avanzar, según mi . . . o sea, según lo que yo quisiera.
Julia	Creo que estás estudiando griego, ¿no?
Héctor	Sí.
Julia	¿Y te parece útil?
Héctor	Sí, porque muchas palabras del griego son la raíz de muchas españolas, incluso inglesas también.
Julia	¿Qué piensas de estudiar latín y griego, que son lenguas muertas?
Beatriz	Me parece interesante porque te ayuda a comprender muy bien el lenguaje actual y los orígenes de .. de nuestro idioma.
Julia	¿Y te parece difícil?
Beatriz	Sí, sobre todo al principio. Es más difícil porque se cambia el alfabeto, todas las letras pero, bueno, luego te acostumbras y .. y es más fácil.

se va reformando *it's being reformed*
le falta mucho *it needs a lot*
según lo que yo quisiera *as regards what I'd like*

PREGUNTAS

1 ¿Qué ventajas tiene el aprender una lengua muerta como el griego clásico, según Héctor y Beatriz?

5

Julia, Isabel and Jaime have been to see the play *La Malquerida*. One of the *Paso Doble* team asked them what they thought of it.

Carol	Bueno, y ¿qué tal la obra, os ha gustado?
Julia	Sí, a mí me ha gustado mucho. Me parece muy interesante, aunque pienso que es un poco melodramática, ¿no crees, Isabel?
Isabel	Sí, tiene un final terriblemente dramático, que yo confieso que a mí no .. no me molestó. El montaje me parece muy bueno, el argumento es muy bueno, te mantiene en vilo hasta el final. ¿Tú qué piensas?
Jaime	Sí, a mí la verdad es que me gustó mucho la obra. Lo mejor de la obra me ha resultado la puesta en escena y la escenografía. Quizá la actuación, para mi gusto, ha estado

no me molestó *didn't bother me*
te mantiene en vilo *it keeps you in suspense*
puesta en escena *staging*

Una escena de
La Malquerida

un poco por debajo del resto, ¿no?, pero me ha parecido correcta.

Julia   Sí. No, yo también pienso lo mismo, está bien, la obra está bien, y en conjunto los actores son bastante buenos.

Isabel   Sí, sí, sí, está bien dirigida la obra. Y francamente la actuación de la Ana Marzoa y de la criada . . . me parecieron más que correctas, me parecieron muy buenas. Y la Ana Marzoa ya la vimos, acuérdate Jaime, hace un par de años en *El castigo sin venganza*, y también me impresionó en los momentos tranquilos de la obra. Y también me parece una lástima que en cuando se llegaba un momento dramático elevara el tono de voz y pusiera a dar gritos. En esta obra lo hace menos.

Jaime   Sí, yo creo que es una característica casi del . . del teatro español, ¿no?

Isabel   Sí, pero de todas formas esta chica es muy buena como actriz (*sí*), ya lo creo.

Jaime   Sí, sí, sí.

Julia   Yo creo que es una de las . . de las mejores ahora mismo.

Isabel   Sin duda. Sin duda.

correcta *OK, all right*
en conjunto *all in all*
acuérdate *remember*
en cuando *whenever*
elevara el tono de voz
   she should raise her voice
(se) pusiera a dar gritos
   should start to shout
de todas formas *anyway*

PREGUNTAS

1   ¿Están los tres de acuerdo en sus opiniones sobre la obra?

2   ¿Creen que han destacado algunos actores?

LENGUA

WHAT DO YOU THINK . . . ?

If you want to ask someone's opinion of something, you can say *¿Qué piensas de . . . ?* or *¿Qué opinas de . . . ?* (*opinar* is more appropriate to interviews and more organised discussions):

¿Qué piensas de estudiar latín y griego?
¿Qué opinas de la enseñanza en España?

Parecer (literally 'to seem') works in the same way as verbs like *gustar* and *apetecer*:

*¿Qué **te parece** esto?*	What do you think of this?
***Me parece** muy interesante.*	I think it's very interesting.

To ask 'do you think/believe that . . . ?', or to give your opinion, you can use *pensar* or *creer*, followed by *que*:

*¿**Piensas que** es difícil?*
*¿**Crees que** se practica más deporte ahora?*
***Pienso que** es un poco melodramática.*
***Creo que** el deporte es necesario.*

To stress that it's **your** opinion:
***En mi opinión**, es muy bonito.*
***Para mí**, es maravilloso.*
*No es correcto, **me parece a mí**.*

DISCUSSING

To give your reasons for thinking the way you do, start with *porque*:
Porque te ayuda a comprender.
Porque es muy difícil.

Various words and phrases can help you link your reasons and develop your argument:

en cambio, por otra parte	on the other hand
por un lado, por otro lado	on the one hand, on the other hand
sin embargo	however
no sólo . . . sino también	not only . . . but also
o sea, es decir	in other words

You can show how one thing follows another:

primero, en primer lugar	firstly
entonces, luego, después	then, next
además	besides, what's more
por (lo) tanto	therefore
por eso, es por eso que	that's why
al fin y al cabo	when all's said and done

AGREEING AND DISAGREEING

Estar de acuerdo means 'to agree':

¿Tú estás de acuerdo?	Do you agree?
No estoy de acuerdo contigo.	I don't agree with you.

Other ways of showing that you do or don't share someone's opinion:

tienes razón	you're right
pienso lo mismo	I think the same
¡claro!, desde luego, por supuesto	of course
exactamente, efectivamente	exactly
no, en absoluto	no, not at all
al contrario	on the contrary
¡qué va!	no way!, far from it!

REACTIONS

Use past tenses to express your reactions to something you've seen or done, e.g.:
No me ha gustado mucho.
Me impresionó muchísimo.
La actuación me pareció muy interesante.

Instant reactions, in the form of exclamations, begin with *¡qué!*:

¡Qué bonito!	How pretty!
¡Qué ruido!	What a noise!
¡Qué calor!	Phew, it's hot!

You can emphasise this by adding *más*:

¡Qué película más extraña!	What a very strange film!

AMÉRICA LATINA

1 ARGENTINA

Nacha Guevara is one of Argentina's top stars – a singer, dancer and actress who's appeared in films as well as in many stage musicals. Hugo Gómez is her choreographer, and Hugh O'Shaughnessy spoke to him about Nacha during rehearsals for a production of *Cabaret* in Buenos Aires.

Hugh ¿Cómo es trabajar con la Nacha?

Hugo Maravilloso, para mí, maravilloso. Es por eso que quiero hablar de Nacha, porque hay opiniones muy disímiles, gracias a Dios, de todos nosotros en este rubro, en este ambiente, en este trabajo. Para mí, trabajar con Nacha es una de las experiencias mejores que me ha sucedido.

Hugh Muy .. muy agresiva, ella ...

Hugo No sé si es muy agresiva. Es muy exigente, que es distinto.

Hugh ¿Violenta, a veces?

Hugo Sí. Si se le llama violento a una forma directa y incisiva de decir las cosas, sí, es violenta. Pero si vamos a llamarle así, gracias a Dios que lo es, porque los resultados son maravillosos. Los resultados son lo que deben ser.

Hugh ¿Ella es actriz, cantante, bailarina ... ? ¿Qué .. qué es?

Hugo Creo que es un artista, y eso engloba todo, no sé si se entiende lo que quiero decir. Es un artista que se preocupa por hacer clases de canto. Es un artista que se preocupa por hacer clases de teatro, o por teatralizar todo lo que vive a menudo y .. y en el día. Creo que su vida es un poco el teatro, y el teatro es la vida, o sea, viceversa. Yo, por ejemplo ... Ella ha estudiado baile en Estados Unidos, en Europa, en muchos lados y, sin embargo, se pone a mis órdenes, y con todo su carácter, digamos, fuerte, es maravilloso tenerla como alumna, porque aprende de una forma impresionante. Yo no lo puedo creer, yo no lo puedo creer, porque se preocupa por cada momento, por cada indicación que un profesor le da. Y lo que Nacha ha adelantado desde dos meses a ahora, ninguna estrella en Sudamérica lo hace, creo, o muy poca gente. He conocido muy poca gente que lo haga, y eso es valiosísimo, porque claro, se llega a *'star'*, ¿no? – *'I am a star, a great star'*, y allí se quedó todo el mundo. Nunca nadie más estudió nada.

si se le llama violento a ... *if you call ... violent*

lo que quiero decir *what I mean*

se preocupa por *is concerned about*

a menudo *often*

en muchos lados *in lots of places*

se pone a *she puts herself under*

lo que Nacha ha adelantado *the progress Nacha has made*

he conocido muy poca gente que lo haga *I've known very few people do it*

allí se quedó todo el mundo *that's where everyone else stopped*

nunca nadie más estudió nada *no one else ever did any more studying*

Talking about Nacha's character, Hugo also sees her as cat-like.

Hugo Nacha es tímida, por ejemplo. Nacha es perspicaz, no sé si se entiende eso. Es fuerte, y es felino. Un felino se defiende solamente porque se siente acorralado, ¿eh? Eso es muy chino. El felino, es muy difícil que ataque, sobre todo un gato, pongamos, a menos que cuatro o cinco personas, o perros ... Corre, y cuando siente que nada más ... Ahí lo conocemos.

Hugh ¿Se siente muy acorralada ...?

Hugo No, no, no, no, no, no, te digo que ... No sé si Nacha es así, pero pienso, esto es una apreciación mía, ¿eh?, que puedo equivocarme si pienso que, este ... ¡Cuidado!, uno si ... se ha sentido muy tocado muchas veces en la vida, y la gente ... y Nacha es una mujer muy sensible, muy, muy sensible.

es muy difícil que ataque *it's very unlikely to attack*
pongamos *let's say*
a menos que *unless*
ahí lo conocemos *that's how we recognise it*
puedo equivocarme *I may be wrong*
¡cuidado! *look out!*
sensible *sensitive*

americanismos
disímiles distintas *or* diferentes *in Spain*
rubro *area, business – a word only found in Latin America*
chino *funny – used in River Plate area; has different meanings in different parts of Latin America; in Spain it means only 'Chinese'*

Hugo Gómez y Nacha Guevara

ESPAÑA ACTUAL

LOS DEPORTES EN ESPAÑA

En España se observa hoy un nuevo fenómeno social: el aumento de interés y la participación activa en el mundo de los deportes. La participación en el deporte se considera tanto como un desafío competitivo como una parte integrante de un modo de vivir basado en ocupar el ocio y mantenerse en forma físicamente. El deporte aún no tiene suficiente apoyo económico por parte de los organismos públicos, ni está aún bien establecido como elemento educativo en los colegios. No obstante, una señal de progreso es el hecho de que desde enero de 1987 hay un Secretario de Estado responsable del deporte.

Es de notar, en particular, que quienes participan en algún tipo de deporte proceden de diversas capas sociales. Ya no se da el caso de que sólo son deportistas quienes son muy fuertes o muy machos. Ahora a todo el mundo le resulta atractivo el deporte. Tampoco se quiere prolongar la imagen de que la mayoría de las actividades deportivas son para la elite, los que tienen bastante dinero como para ser miembros de los clubs privados y caros. Hacer accesible todo tipo de deporte al público en general requiere fondos, y todavía no hay muchos, pero la situación va cambiando.

Se puede confirmar que el fútbol sigue siendo el rey del deporte español, pero no tanto como antes. Los toros y las corridas que tanto se asocian con España son cada día más una atracción principalmente para turistas, sin negar que siempre habrá un fiel grupo fanático indígena de seguidores de este espectáculo nacional. Aunque el fútbol es el deporte más popular, el footing, el ciclismo, el tenis, el baloncesto, el golf y la natación tienen muchos aficionados. En general se ve una mentalidad nacional de querer hacer algún tipo de ejercicio.

El famoso 'estrés' de los ejecutivos – pero también de la secretaria y el ama de casa – empuja

Pedro Delgado en el Tour de Francia de 1987

a la gente a matricularse no sólo en clases de tenis y natación, sino también en clases de yoga, de aeróbica, y de sevillanas.

Cada obsesión o moda tiene su cara menos simpática, y esto pasa también con los deportes. Algo de la violencia que se asocia con los aficionados al fútbol en Gran Bretaña o Holanda ya se detecta en ciertos grupos que son entusiastas de deportes y equipos populares. No es, no obstante, un problema social de las dimensiones a que se llega en estos otros países.

El papel de España en el mundo deportivo ha sido reconocido por la comunidad internacional: basta recordar que la Copa Mundial de fútbol tuvo lugar en España en 1982, y tener en cuenta, sobre todo, la manera tan competitiva en que la ciudad de Barcelona llegó a ser nombrada huésped de las Olimpíadas de 1992. Si antes sólo se conocían fuera de España ciertos nombres de españoles que destacaban individualmente en su deporte, como el tenista Santana, el jugador de golf Ballesteros, y los equipos de fútbol del Real Madrid y del Barcelona, ahora la presencia española en ciertos deportes se deja sentir de forma más colectiva. Al examinar la lista de jugadores del campeonato de Wimbledon se encuentran varios nombres españoles; con Seve Ballesteros ya se han juntado otros jugadores españoles de nivel internacional, como José María Cañizares y Manuel Piñero; el otro equipo barcelonés de fútbol, el Español, llegó a la final de una de las copas de Europa en 1988; y el ciclista Pedro Delgado cumplió un sueño cuando ganó el Tour de Francia en 1988.

Severiano Ballesteros en el Open Británico de 1988

PRÁCTICAS

1

¿Qué te parece nuestro país?

When you visit Spain, Spaniards always want to know what you think of their country. Put your part of the conversation into Spanish.

Cristina Bueno, ¿qué te parece España, y Madrid en particular?

You (*I think that Spain's a marvellous country, I like it very much. And for me, Madrid is a very beautiful and very interesting city.*)

Cristina ¿No piensas que Barcelona es más interesante en cuanto a la vida cultural?

You (*Perhaps, but there are lots of theatres and cinemas in Madrid, and besides I love the whole Plaza Mayor area.*)

Cristina ¿Has estado también en otras regiones?

You (*Yes, last year I went by train from Bilbao to Granada.*)

Cristina ¡Caramba! ¡Qué viaje más largo! Te gusta viajar entonces.

You (*In my opinion, it's the only way to see the country.*)

2

Reacciones

Match each reaction to the appropriate picture:

a ¡Qué gol más bonito!

b Creo que es imposible.

c Me parece asqueroso.

d ¡Qué valiente, con el frío que hace!

e Nos ha gustado mucho.

f ¡Qué ruido!

En su opinion, ¿cuál de estas cosas es más importante para la salud?			
No fumar	33	Evitar tensiones	19
Comer bien	23	Hacer ejercicios	25

¿Cuál de estas características valora usted más en su marido/mujer?			
Inteligente	59	Simpático/a	37
Trabajador/a	45	Sincero/a	62
Cariñoso/a	40	Enérgico/a	5

¿Está usted satisfecho/a con su trabajo?			
Muy	20	Poco	13
Bastante	55	Nada	11

¿Piensa usted que las mujeres tienen más, igual o menos oportunidades de trabajo que hace diez años?				
	Más	Igual	Menos	No sabe
Varones	10	46	41	3
Mujeres	8	41	45	8

3
Discusiones
You're sitting in a noisy bar and can only hear the first words of each of the exchanges between the people sitting next to you. Look at the list of these words and then say whether this means they're agreeing or disagreeing with each other.

a   De acuerdo ...
b   ¡Qué va! ...
c   Obviamente ...
d   ¡Qué razón tienes ... !
e   Y además ...
f   De ninguna manera ...
g   Claro ...
h   Al contrario ...

4
Problemas
Fill in the appropriate word or phrase from the list below to link the sentences so that they make sense.

por un lado   al principio
sin embargo   pero
por otro lado   al final

.... nos gustó el hotel .... entonces empezaron los problemas. .... el director dimitió, y .... los otros clientes hacían mucho ruido. Era insoportable. Cuando nos quejamos, el nuevo director nos prometió cambios. .... el ruido y la ineficacia seguían. .... nos marchamos hartos sin pagar los últimos días de nuestra estancia.

5
En su opinión
Look at these opinion poll results, and then decide whether the statements below are true or false.
¿Verdad o mentira?

a   La mayoría de la gente está satisfecha con el trabajo que hace.
b   Para mucha gente es importante casarse con una persona muy enérgica.
c   Un cincuenta por ciento piensa que es importante mantenerse en forma.
d   En general, la gente da más importancia a la sinceridad que a la inteligencia.
e   Más hombres que mujeres piensan que las mujeres tienen las mismas oportunidades de trabajo que los hombres.
f   Según un gran número de personas, es más importante comer bien que no fumar.

6
¿Tú qué piensas?
Say what you think about something you've seen or heard recently: a film, play, concert, sports event, television programme – even *Paso Doble* on the radio!

¿QUÉ PIENSAS HACER?

Plans for the future

1

At the *Instituto*, Julia asked a couple of Rosa's students what they were planning to do when they finished there.

Julia	¿Qué estás estudiando?
Beatriz	Estoy estudiando COU, que es un curso de preparación antes de ir a la universidad.
Julia	Y cuando vayas a la universidad, ¿qué te gustaría estudiar?
Beatriz	Lo que más me gustaría estudiar es derecho.
Julia	¿Y cuántos años son la carrera de derecho?
Beatriz	Son cinco años, y después iré a oposiciones y . . . a ver lo que pasa.

COU Curso de Orientación Universitaria

cuando vayas *when you go*

lo que más me gustaría *what I'd like most*

a ver lo que pasa *let's see what happens*

Julia	¿Qué curso estás estudiando?
Mari Carmen	Estoy estudiando COU.
Julia	Y cuando acabes COU, ¿qué piensas estudiar?
Mari Carmen	No . . no estoy muy segura. Quizá periodismo.

cuando acabes, cuando termines *when you finish*

Julia	Y cuando termines periodismo, en el futuro, ¿en qué te gustaría trabajar?
Mari Carmen	Me gustaría trabajar con la gente, preguntando, haciendo entrevistas. No me gusta la redacción.
Julia	¿Pero en televisión, radio, prensa?
Mari Carmen	Prensa.

PREGUNTAS

1 ¿Quieren seguir estudiando las dos chicas?
2 ¿Cuál de las dos quiere ser periodista?

2

Isabel asked two of the volleyball players, both of them university students, about their job prospects.

Isabel	¿Estudias o trabajas, Olga?
Olga	Las dos cosas.
Isabel	Explícame, ¿qué es lo que haces?
Olga	Estoy trabajando en el Banco de España, y al mismo tiempo terminando mi carrera universitaria.
Isabel	¿Que es . . .?
Olga	Ciencias empresariales.
Isabel	¿Te gusta tu trabajo?
Olga	Sí, aunque llevo poco tiempo.
Isabel	¿Cuánto tiempo llevas?
Olga	Seis meses.
Isabel	Seis meses. ¿Y vas a continuar mucho tiempo?
Olga	El contrato es temporal, entonces ya depende de si te lo renuevan o no te lo renuevan.
Isabel	¿Te gustaría?
Olga	Sí, claro.
Isabel	Y tú, Patricia, ¿qué es lo que haces?
Patricia	Yo estoy estudiando farmacia.
Isabel	¿Y por qué curso vas de tu carrera?
Patricia	Estoy haciendo cuarto, y ya el año que viene acabo.
Isabel	Ya tendrás ganas, ¿no?
Patricia	¡Muchísimas! Cada día más, cada día tengo más ganas.
Isabel	¿Qué perspectivas de trabajo tienes?
Patricia	Pues, yo creo que muchas, quiero creer que tengo muchas salidas, ya veremos dentro de un año qué pasa.
Isabel	Y tú, Olga, ¿qué piensas hacer después? ¿Qué salidas crees que tienes?

ciencias empresariales *business studies*
llevo poco tiempo *I've not been there long*
si **te lo renuevan** *if they renew it*
¿por qué curso vas? *what year are you in?*
el año que viene *next year*
tendrás ganas *you'll be wanting to*
muchísimas (ganas) *very much so*
ya veremos *we'll see*

Olga   Yo creo que al estar trabajando ahora, me da posibilidad para continuar trabajando, no .. no quedarme sin trabajo.

quedarme sin trabajo *to find myself without a job*

PREGUNTAS

1   ¿Son optimistas respecto a su futuro profesional estas dos chicas?
2   ¿Cuántos años son la carrera de farmacia?

3

Sr Angulo has only a few years to go until he retires. What does he plan to do afterwards?

Julia   ¿Piensa continuar mucho tiempo aquí?
Sr Angulo   Pienso continuar, pues si Dios me da salud, hasta que me jubile.
Julia   ¿Y tiene algunos planes para después de jubilarse?
Sr Angulo   No, ya después de jubilado, a descansar. Creo que es lo justo, ¿no le parece a usted?
Julia   Sí, por supuesto. ¿Y seguirá viviendo en Madrid?
Sr Angulo   Sí, desde luego, y seguiré viviendo en el barrio.
Julia   Porque le gusta mucho este barrio.
Sr Angulo   Me gusta.

si Dios me da salud *God willing* (literally 'if God gives me health')
hasta que me jubile *until I retire*

PREGUNTAS

1   ¿Dónde pasará su jubilación el Sr Angulo?

4

Isabel is expecting a baby, and Julia asks her what she's planning to do when the baby's born.

Julia	Supongo que llevas un control con el ginecólogo, ¿cada cuánto tiempo vas a verle?	**llevas un control** *you have check-ups*
Isabel	Pues una vez cada mes, y además me están viendo médicos en Londres, porque yo voy a Londres a dar a luz.	**¿cada cuánto tiempo?** *how often?*
Julia	Y entonces, ¿cuándo te irás a Londres? ¿Un mes antes de lo que se supone que es el parto?	**dar a luz** *to give birth* **¿cuándo te irás?** *when will you go?*
Isabel	Más o menos.	**antes de lo que se**
Julia	¿Y qué piensas hacer cuando tengas el niño o niña?	**supone que es el**
Isabel	¿Te refieres a si voy a seguir trabajando?	**parto** *before the baby's*
Julia	Sí, si vas a continuar trabajando, o ¿quién va a cuidar el bebé? ¿Lo vas a llevar a una guardería, o va a venir una mujer a tu casa a cuidarlo?	*due* **cuando tengas** *when you have*
Isabel	Pues, la verdad es que no lo sé. Hemos pensado en muchas cosas. Yo desde luego seguiré trabajando. Entonces, pues habrá que buscar o bien una guardería muy buena, o bien contratar a una persona que venga a casa … En suma, que no lo sé, no sé lo que voy a hacer.	**habrá que** *we'll have to* **o bien … o bien** *either … or* **que venga** *who'll come*

PREGUNTAS

1 ¿Dónde nacerá el niño de Isabel y Jaime?
2 ¿Piensa Isabel volver al trabajo después del parto?

5

What sort of father is Jaime planning to be?

Julia	¿Estás ilusionado con el futuro hijo o hija que vais a tener?	**¿estás ilusionado con …?** *are you excited*
Jaime	Hombre, pues claro, ¿no?	*about …?*
Julia	¿Y vas a ser un padre moderno, digamos, o vas a ser el típico padre español que dice que cuidar al niño y limpiarle y darle biberón, eso que lo haga la madre?	**eso que lo haga la madre** *that's the mother's job*
Jaime	Ah no, no, no, yo quiero … yo quiero jugar también con él, ¿no? Isabel trabaja y entonces tendremos que participar al cincuenta por ciento.	**tendremos que** *we'll have to*

LENGUA

THE FUTURE

There are many ways of talking about the future, from things that will definitely happen to what you want or hope to do.

WHAT YOU PLAN OR WANT TO DO

To talk about what you're thinking of doing, you can use *pensar* followed by a verb in the infinitive:
*¿Qué **piensas hacer** después?*
***Pienso estudiar** periodismo.*

To say what you want or hope to do, again use the appropriate word followed by an infinitive:
***Quiero hacer** una carrera universitaria.*
***Me apetece trabajar** en una farmacia.*
***Espero ir** a la universidad de Salamanca.*

Or for what you would like to do, you can use the conditional form of *gustar*:
*¿Qué **te gustaría** estudiar?*
***Me gustaría** trabajar con la gente.*

WHAT YOU'RE GOING TO DO

For more definite plans, you can use part of *ir*, plus *a*, followed by an infinitive – it's the Spanish equivalent of the English 'I'm going to . . .', 'are you going to . . .?', and so on:
***Voy a seguir** trabajando.*
*¿**Vas a ser** un padre moderno?*
*¿Quién **va a cuidar** el bebé?*
*No sé lo que **voy a hacer**.*

THE FUTURE TENSE

Spanish also has a form of the verb called the future tense, equivalent to saying 'shall' or 'will' in English, e.g.:

***Veremos** qué pasa.*	We'll see what happens.
*¿**Te irás** a Londres?*	Will you go to London?
***Seguiré** viviendo en el barrio.*	I'll go on living in the area.

The future tense is formed by adding one set of endings (the same for all types of verb, *–ar, –er* and *–ir*) to the infinitive:

(*yo*)	hablar**é**	(*nosotros*)	hablar**emos**
(*tú*)	hablar**ás**	(*vosotros*)	hablar**éis**
(*usted, él, ella*)	hablar**á**	(*ustedes, ellos, ellas*)	hablar**án**

There are a few exceptions where it's not exactly the infinitive, e.g.: *tener – tendré, tendrás*, etc; and the future of *hay* is *habrá*. (See **Gramática**, page 152.)

Sometimes Spanish uses the present tense where English uses the future, e.g. when the doorbell goes you say *voy*, but in English it's 'I'll go'.

WHEN YOU GO . . .

English uses the present tense after 'when', but Spanish uses a different form of the verb:
*Cuando **acabes** COU, ¿qué piensas estudiar?*
*¿Qué te gustaría ser cuando **seas** mayor?*

It's also used with the phrase *hasta que* (until):
*Pienso continuar hasta que **me jubile**.*

This form is called the subjunctive, which is used quite a lot in Spanish but doesn't exist in English. It's formed rather like the present tense, but with the verb endings changed to swap the vowels from *a* to *e* and *e* to *a*, e.g.:

	present	subjunctive
terminar	*termin**as***	*termin**es***
acabar	*acab**as***	*acab**es***
seguir	*sig**ues***	*sig**as***

Some commonly-used exceptions are:

ir	*vaya, vayas, etc.*
ser	*sea, seas*
tener	*tenga, tengas*

(For more on the formation and use of the subjunctive, see **Gramática**, page 150.)

AMÉRICA LATINA

1 VENEZUELA

Oliver Guerrero Wong, a Venezuelan of mixed Chinese, French and Martinique descent, is already doing a couple of jobs, and is about to begin a computing course – but he'd like to do something quite different eventually.

Hugh ¿Cuál es su profesión?

Oliver Estudio, trabajo.

Hugh ¿Pero en qué trabaja en este momento?

Oliver En este momento trabajo como oficinista, y a la vez como chofer, que digamos, para una compañía contratista que presta su servicio a una filial de Petróleos muy importante aquí en Venezuela.

Petróleos is Petróleos de Venezuela (state oil company)

Hugh Pero también usted estudia, ¿qué estudia?

Oliver Yo saqué el bachillerato de . . . Voy a empezar ahora a estudiar, ¿cómo va a ser?, el técnico superior en computación. O también una cosa, me gusta mucho la carrera de derecho, o sea, abogado.

Hugh ¿Y se piensa hacer abogado?

Oliver Si Dios quiere, sí.

Hugh ¿Y por qué abogado?

Oliver Una carrera muy interesante en este país.

Hugh ¿Y qué se hace como abogado?

Oliver Se pueden hacer muchas cosas buenas y malas. Es como quien dice 'una arma de doble filo'.

Hugh Una arma de doble filo.

Oliver Sí.

Hugh ¿Y usted va a utilizar los dos filos del arma?

Oliver Tal vez, tal vez.

Hugh Y si no se hace abogado, ¿a qué se va a dedicar?

Oliver No, primero pienso hacer el técnico superior en computación. Me gusta mucho también, pienso hacer ahora . . . no tardará más de dos meses, voy a hacer el curso de inglés, que me .. me gusta mucho, o sea aparte de gustarme es algo ahorita básico, algo muy importante, muy .. muy primordial.

a la vez *at the same time*

como chofer, que digamos *as a sort of driver*

presta su servicio a *services*

bachillerato *a school-leaving examination*

¿cómo va a ser? *what's it called?*

técnico superior *an advanced technical qualification*

si Dios quiere *God willing*

una arma de doble filo *a double-edged weapon*

no tardará más de dos meses *there won't be more than two months to wait*

americanismos

chofer *written with an accent and stressed differently in Spain:* chófer

ahorita *right now – this kind of diminutive word is generally more common in the northern part of Latin America*

2 PANAMA

The Panama Canal is a marvel of engineering: built above sea level, it has a series of locks through which ships pass on their way between the Atlantic and Pacific Oceans. But ships are getting ever bigger, and the canal locks use huge quantities of fresh water from two nearby lakes. There has long been talk of building a sea-level canal, and in the course of an interview in 1985 with General Noriega, head of the armed forces of Panama, Hugh asked him when he thought this would happen.

Hugh	Panamá, ¿cuándo va a tener un canal a nivel?
Gral Noriega	Ahora mismo se encuentra la etapa de los estudios del canal a nivel. Podemos avanzar que ya hay común acuerdo, en principio, de Japón, Estados Unidos y Panamá en este gran trabajo futuro.
Hugh	¿Usted desea un canal a nivel?
Gral Noriega	Un canal a nivel es la evolución de la tecnología. Un canal a nivel es el ajuste a la realidad de .. del calado y la dimensión de los barcos que puedan transitar, como también es el balance y el ahorro de las aguas que, por esclusas, utiliza el actual canal. Así que las cosas se van ajustando a medida que históricamente se van desarrollando. Nosotros consideramos que ya este canal se va quedando viejo para las nuevas tecnologías de construcción de las naves que transitan los océanos.

avanzar *announce*
común acuerdo *joint agreement*
calado *draught*
puedan transitar *may be travelling*
esclusas *locks*
así que *so that*
a medida que *as*
se va quedando viejo *is getting old*

ESPAÑA ACTUAL

LA ENSEÑANZA

El sistema educativo español es bastante distinto del sistema británico, aunque los cambios que han tenido lugar recientemente los han hecho parecerse más. Posiblemente esto tiene que ver con el hecho de que el Ministro de Educación, José María Maravall, que introdujo una reforma importante del sistema después de la llegada del gobierno socialista en 1982, había pasado bastante tiempo en la universidad inglesa.

Los niños españoles tienen que empezar a asistir a la escuela obligatoriamente a los seis años. Las posibilidades de ir a alguna guardería o lugar parecido antes de esta edad dependen del sitio donde se vive, a no ser que se tenga bastante dinero como para mandar a los niños a un centro privado. A pesar de un gran esfuerzo destinado a aumentar la red escolar pública a partir de 1982, sigue habiendo más centros escolares privados que públicos a todos los niveles.

Para entender la educación española hay que empezar por aprender muchos nombres especiales que se refieren a los distintos niveles y distintos centros. En primer lugar, el niño sigue la Educación General Básica, conocido como EGB, hasta los catorce años. Al terminar este nivel, se puede seguir haciendo estudios o bien académicos, o bien del tipo más bien práctico y profesional.

Los que siguen el camino más práctico tienen la opción de hacer FP, Formación Profesional, que consta de tres ciclos, y cuyo nivel máximo es equivalente a una carrera universitaria. Pero en general, los estudiantes sólo completan el primer nivel de FP.

Los que continúan haciendo estudios muy académicos, aspirando muchos a entrar en la universidad, hacen unos estudios que se conocen como BUP, Bachillerato Unificado Polivalente. Este nivel se llama Enseñanza Media, porque se considera como el puente entre la EGB y la enseñanza superior de la universidad. La selección de asignaturas que

uno puede escoger a este nivel es mucho más amplia que en Inglaterra, sin el énfasis en una concentrada especialidad.

A los dieciocho años, los que quieren seguir estudiando deben hacer COU, Curso de Orientación Universitaria, y quienes aprueban este curso pasan

a la universidad donde hacen cinco cursos, cada uno de un año, dos más que en Inglaterra.

El rasgo típico de la educación española es el ser un sistema mucho menos especializado, insistiendo en una elección más amplia de asignaturas en, por lo menos, los niveles más bajos.

Desgraciadamente, el sistema sufre de una gran falta de recursos. Por lo tanto, existen todavía escuelas mal provistas y profesores con una preparación insuficiente. Sobre todo, a nivel universitario no hay suficiente dinero para apoyar la investigación. Por ello, a veces se ve la falta de confianza entre los que ejercen la profesión. Se sienten mal pagados y mal vistos por el público.

Las reformas de Maravall pretendían mejorar esta situación, pero se trata de un problema muy hondo que se tardará en solucionar; mientras tanto, la gente se impacienta.

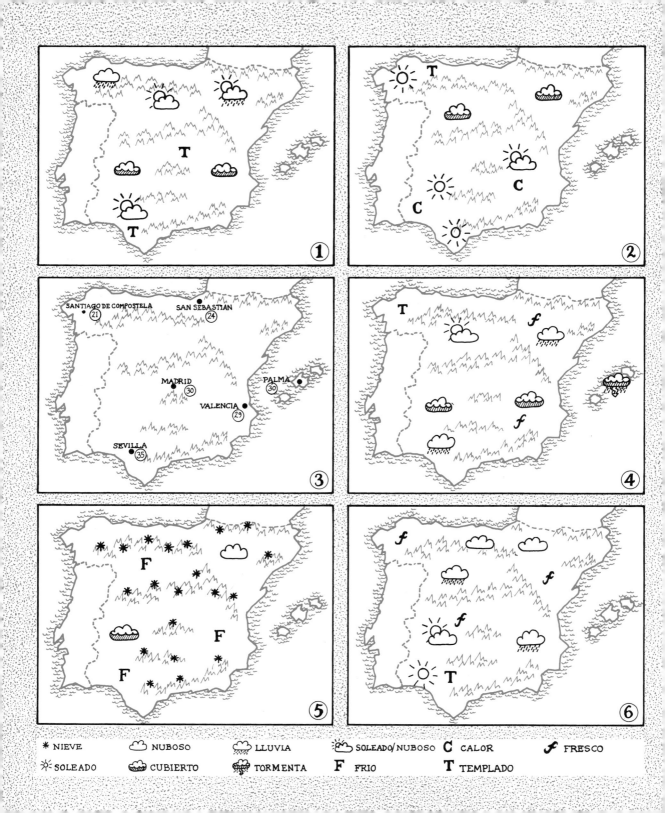

1

2

3

SANTIAGO DE COMPOSTELA 21   SAN SEBASTIAN 24

MADRID 30

VALENCIA 29   PALMA 30

SEVILLA 35

4

5

6

| ❉ NIEVE | ☁ NUBOSO | 🌧 LLUVIA | ⛅ SOLEADO/NUBOSO | C CALOR | ℱ FRESCO |
| ☀ SOLEADO | ☁ CUBIERTO | ⛈ TORMENTA | F FRIO | T TEMPLADO | |

PRÁCTICAS

1

Proyectos

You're explaining to a Spanish friend why you're learning Spanish. Put your part of the conversation into Spanish.

Salvador	¿Por qué estás estudiando español?
You	(*I'm planning to live in Spain for a few years.*)
Salvador	¿Piensas trabajar aquí?
You	(*Yes, my company is going to send me to Madrid.*)
Salvador	¿Ah sí? ¿En qué trabajas?
You	(*I sell computers. I'll have an office in Madrid, but I'll have to travel all over Spain.*)
Salvador	¿Vas a vivir en la capital?
You	(*I'm not sure. I'd prefer to live outside Madrid, but I'll decide when I get there.*)

2

El tiempo

Match each weather forecast with the appropriate map on the opposite page.

a   La temperatura más alta será en Sevilla.

b   Habrá cielos nubosos en Cantabria y el País Vasco.

c   Se encontrará algo de nieve en los puertos de montaña.

d   Lloverá en Galicia.

e   Andalucía disfrutará del sol todo el día.

f   Habrá chubascos tormentosos en Baleares, más probables por la tarde.

3

¿Qué vas a hacer cuando venga tu amigo español?

Your Spanish friend is coming to stay and you're writing to tell him what you're going to do. Put the verbs in brackets into the right form.

Querido Miguel:

Cuando (llegar), yo (estar) en el aeropuerto. Te (poder) llevar a casa en seguida, o podremos dar un paseo por la ciudad. (Pensar) presentarte a mis amigos, e (ir) todos juntos a ver un partido de fútbol. Y luego, si te (gustar) la cerveza, te (invitar) yo a tomar algo en un típico pub inglés.

¡Hasta pronto!

Un abrazo,

4

Cuando les toque la lotería . . .

Here are some people dreaming of what they'll do when they win the lottery. Match the pictures to the sentences.

a   Organizará una gran fiesta para sus amigos.
b   Viajará a Nueva York.
c   Se pondrá a cultivar su jardín.
d   Se comprará un coche muy grande.
e   Pasará todo el día en su propia piscina.
f   Se levantará tarde.

5

Ambiciones

Here are various people saying what they intend to do in the future. Finish each sentence with the most appropriate ambition or aspiration from this list.

a   A mí me gusta mucho viajar, y tengo muchas ganas de ir a Sudamérica. El año que viene espero ....

b   Acabo de terminar la carrera de periodismo, y dentro de poco voy a ....

c   Soy muy aficionada al atletismo, y estoy ahorrando todo el dinero que pueda porque en el 1992 quiero ....

d   Cuando nos jubilemos, pensamos ....

e   Tengo que hacer un viaje largo y pesado en autobús para ir al trabajo. Es por eso que quiero ....

f   Me ha gustado siempre escribir cuentos y poesías, y un día espero ....

1   .... ir a los Juegos Olímpicos, que tendrán lugar en Barcelona.
2   .... comprarme un pequeño coche.
3   .... explorar las ruinas de Cuzco y Machu Picchu.
4   .... ser novelista y escribir un best-seller.
5   .... trabajar en un periódico regional en Asturias.
6   .... ir a vivir en un pueblo en la costa valenciana.

6

Te toca el premio

You've won a week's holiday in Spain. Say where you'll go, what you're intending to do when you get there, what you'd like to see, and so on.

¿CÓMO TE SIENTES?

Your state of health

1

Running a restaurant means working very long hours, as Sergio can testify.

Julia   Sergio, ¿te sientes muy cansado después de una jornada tan larga de trabajo?

Sergio   Pues sí, después de tantas horas de trabajo, sí, se siente uno con ganas de descansar. Es mucho tiempo y seguido.

una jornada tan larga
such a long day

2

It's some time since Isidoro was knocked down and suffered a fractured hip. Is he fully recovered?

Isidoro	Me ha tenido tres meses en la cama porque me produjeron una fisura en la cadera izquierda . . . bueno, una brecha en la cabeza que se me curó rápidamente.
Isabel	¿Y ahora cómo te sientes?
Isidoro	Pues resentido todavía de la pierna, y tengo que andar con un bastón.
Isabel	¿Para mucho tiempo todavía?
Isidoro	Pues, no lo sé. Lo que tarde en recuperarme, pero vamos, ya salgo a la calle y puedo bajar inclusive las escaleras que son bastante altitas.
Isabel	Y son muchas, ¿no?
Isidoro	110 escalones.
Isabel	¡Caramba!

me ha tenido *it's kept me*
me produjeron *they gave me*
se me curó *healed up*
resentido todavía *still feeling the effect*
lo que tarde en *as long as it takes*

PREGUNTAS

1   ¿Ha vuelto Isidoro a utilizar la pierna herida?

3

Isabel has noticed that Jaime isn't looking very well.

Isabel	¿Qué tal te sientes? Tienes mala cara.
Jaime	Sí. No, no estoy muy bien. Tengo un pequeño resfriado.
Isabel	¿Tienes fiebre?
Jaime	No, fiebre no creo que tenga, pero me molesta la garganta y tengo un poco de dolor de cabeza. Me duelen todas las articulaciones.
Isabel	Eso es gripe.
Jaime	Pues sí, tiene todos los síntomas, sí.
Isabel	Bueno, pues nada. Te metes en la cama pronto esta noche, te llevo una leche caliente, te tomas una aspirina, sudas, y mañana bueno, ya verás.
Jaime	Sí, esperemos.

tienes mala cara *you don't look well*
un pequeño resfriado *a bit of a cold*
te metes en la cama *you'll go to bed*
esperemos *let's hope so*

PREGUNTAS

1   ¿Qué consejo le da Isabel a Jaime para mejorarse?

4

Volleyball involves a lot of leaping in the air after the ball and, inevitably, falling down. What's more, Jaime and his friends play on a cement surface. Do the players get hurt, and what sort of protective clothing do they wear?

Isabel	¿Es peligroso este deporte?
Chema	Todos los deportes tienen su peligro. Te puedes hacer daño en un tobillo, en un dedo . . .
Isabel	¿Tú te has hecho daño alguna vez?
Chema	Sí, muchas veces.
Isabel	¿Qué te has hecho?
Chema	¡Uy! Pues luxaciones de hombro, esguinces . . . bueno, esguinces de dedo, de tobillo, muchas cosas.

Chema is a common nickname for people called José Manuel

te puedes hacer daño *you can hurt yourself*

Isabel	Aurelio, veo que llevas unas cosas muy extrañas en las piernas, ¿me las puedes describir?
Aurelio	Pues son unas tobilleras, para prevenir lesiones en los tobillos.
Isabel	Y esto, ¿qué es?
Aurelio	Estos son rodilleras. Pues nada, se ponen en la rodilla y evitan que al tirarte al suelo a por un balón te . . . pues no sé, te roces contra el suelo o te golpees, esto es más que nada por golpearse.
Isabel	¿El voleibol es un deporte peligroso?
Aurelio	¡Yo cuando empecé a jugar al voleibol creía que no! Pero desde que juego al voleibol me he sacado el hombro, me he fastidiado los tobillos, los dedos y una rodilla. ¡Sí, debe ser peligroso, sí!

a por un balón *to get a ball*

te golpees *you bump yourself*

más que nada *more than anything*

creía que no *I didn't think so*

me he sacado *I've dislocated*

me he fastidiado *I've hurt*

PREGUNTAS

1 ¿En qué partes del cuerpo puede uno hacerse daño al jugar al voleibol?
2 ¿Qué cosas llevan los jugadores para protegerse?

5

How is Isabel coping with being pregnant and leading a normal working life at the same time?

Julia	¿Cómo va tu embarazo?
Isabel	Pues, hasta aquí bien, creo.
Julia	¿Y cómo te sientes, estás cansada, o todavía no sientes demasiadas cosas?

Isabel	Bueno, al principio me sentía muy, muy cansada, y ahora poco a poco, pues me voy sintiendo más normal, aunque cada vez me muevo con menos agilidad, claro.
Julia	Y por ejemplo, ¿notas que tienes más sueño que antes de estar embarazada, es decir, necesitas dormir más horas para sentirte bien?
Isabel	¡Sí! Yo siempre estoy cansada. Yo no sé si es porque tengo la tensión baja o ... no sé. Desde luego me siento algo más cansada al terminar el trabajo, pues me meto en la cama, cosa que no es muy normal en mí porque no me gusta estar en la cama, pero me esfuerzo en reposar más de lo normal.
Julia	¿Y estás haciendo algún régimen de comidas especial o puedes comer cualquier tipo de comida?
Isabel	No, yo no he seguido ningún régimen especial. Sí, procuro tomar muchas vitaminas, algún suplemento de hierro, pero aparte de eso, hasta aquí no he tenido que cambiar mi alimentación.
Julia	¿Y tienes algún antojo?
Isabel	No, no exactamente. Sí te puedo decir que la pasta, es decir los espaguetis, desde que estoy embarazada me gustan más, pero no se puede llegar a describir como un antojo.
Julia	¿Y estás haciendo mucho reposo, o puedes hacer una vida normal en cuanto a ejercicios pesados o cargar con mucho peso ...?
Isabel	No puedo cargar con mucho peso. No hago ningún tipo de ejercicio. Llevo, en la medida que me es posible, una vida bastante normal, procurando descansar lo que pueda, aunque es difícil, pero creo que todo marcha bien.

hasta aquí *up to now*
poco a poco *bit by bit*
me voy sintiendo *I'm beginning to feel*
tienes más sueño *you're more sleepy*
me esfuerzo en *I make an effort to*
no se puede llegar a describir *I can't go so far as to describe it*
cargar con mucho peso *pick up heavy weights*
en la medida que *as far as*
lo que pueda *as much as I can*

PREGUNTAS

1   ¿De qué manera se siente Isabel distinta ahora que está embarazada?
2   ¿Hasta qué punto ha tenido que cambiar su vida?

Jaime, Isabel y
Clara
¡Todo marchó
bien!

LENGUA

HOW DO YOU FEEL?
As a general 'How are you?' you can say:
¿Cómo estás?   *¿Qué tal?*

If you're genuinely interested in someone's health and want to ask 'How do you feel?':
¿Cómo te sientes?   *¿Qué tal te sientes?*
¿Cómo te encuentras?   *¿Qué tal te encuentras?*
¿Estás mal?   *¿Estás enfermo/a?*

If the person is looking unwell, you might say:
Tienes mala cara.   *¡Qué mala cara tienes!*

And to ask what the matter is:
¿Qué tienes?   *¿Qué te pasa?*

SAYING HOW YOU FEEL
To say how you are or how you feel, use *estoy* or *me siento* (from *sentirse*):
No estoy muy bien.   I'm not very well.
Me siento mal.   I feel unwell.
Me siento cansado/a.   I feel tired.
Estoy resfriado/a.   )
Estoy constipado/a.   )   I've got a cold.

Some other symptoms:
Tengo gripe.   I've got flu.
Tengo fiebre.   I've got a temperature.
Tengo dolor de   I've got a headache/
cabeza/estómago.   stomach ache.

To say that some part of you aches or hurts, start with *me duele* or *me duelen*:
Me duele la cabeza.   *Me duelen los ojos.*

If something hurts or upsets you, you can use the expression *hacer daño*:
Me hacen daño los zapatos.
La aspirina me hace daño.

If you've injured yourself, use the reflexive form *hacerse daño*:
*Me he hecho daño en el   I've injured my foot.
pie.*

Notice that you don't refer to parts of the body as '**my** head', '**your** hands', etc.; instead you use the word for 'the':
Me duele la cabeza.
Tienes las manos muy pequeñas.

The pronoun (*me*) or verb (*tienes*) shows whose head/hands are being referred to.

REFLEXIVES
Many words to do with how you feel, the state of your health, or things that you do to yourself, are what are known as reflexive verbs, e.g.:
***Me siento** muy cansada.*
*¿**Te has hecho** daño alguna vez?*
***Se llama** Carlos.*

These verbs are listed in dictionaries with the pronoun *se* on the end of the infinitive, e.g. *sentirse, levantarse, llamarse*, and you need to remember to use the right pronoun with each part of the verb. (See **Gramática**, page 147.)

PRONOUNS
Me, te, le, lo, nos, etc., are object pronouns. They're the Spanish equivalents of saying 'me', 'to me' or 'for me', 'you', 'to you', and so on, and they generally come before the verb:
***Lo** abrimos hace dos años y medio.*
***Te** enseño cómo funciona.*
*No **me** gusta estar en la cama.*

When used with an infinitive, they're generally tacked on the end:
*Es importante reparar**las**.*

Though if there are two verbs together, they often come before:
*No **lo** puedo creer.*
*¿**Lo** vas a llevar a una guardería?*

(For a complete list of pronouns: subject, object and reflexive, see **Gramática**, pages 146 and 147.)

AMÉRICA LATINA

1   MEXICO

The *barrio* of Tepito in Mexico City has existed for centuries, since before the Spanish *conquistadores* arrived. Its inhabitants, the *tepiteños*, want to preserve its special characteristics, and have set up their own organisations to do this, inviting in experts from outside to help them plan their future, Alfonso Hernández works in a community centre in Tepito, helping to coordinate these activities.

Hugh	Alfonso, ¿cómo es el espíritu del barrio de Tepito?
Alfonso	El espíritu tepiteño es ser solidario, muy trabajador, y tener sus propias formas de trabajo y de vida dentro de este barrio.
Hugh	¿Y cómo se manifiesta la solidaridad de los tepiteños?
Alfonso	A nivel trabajo, el barrio no nada más da chamba a los habitantes del barrio sino a una población flotante que viene de la periferia, y que desde siempre ha prendido en los oficios de este barrio. La otra es ofreciendo para la población flotante que viene a Tepito a adquirir cosas baratas, y que sólo aquí las encuentra. La población flotante que viene a Tepito son gentes de bajo poder adquisitivo, que encuentra aquí objetos usados, sin el precio del aparador, objetos reparados en Tepito, reciclados, mucho más baratos que en cualquier otro lugar y, este . . . y este servicio social que presta además, hay muchos prestadores de servicio en Tepito, ¿no?, que ofrecen la especialidad de un oficio que ya no se encuentra en otra parte de la ciudad, que pueden ser hojalateros, este, sastres, que hacen modificaciones o un traje en unas horas, este, cosas rápidas y que la formalidad de otros, este, centros de artesanos no tienen. Aquí se puede conseguir algo muy rápido, un servicio de un soldador, de un plomero, de un albañil, de un hojalatero, de un . . . hasta de un relojero, que los tenemos hasta algunos graduados en Suiza.

a nivel trabajo *as regards work*
no nada más *not only*
ha prendido en *has taken root in*
bajo poder adquisitivo *low purchasing power*
usados *second-hand*
aparador *showcase*
prestadores de servicio *people in service industries*
los tenemos hasta algunos *we even have some*

Hugh's visit to Tepito came in January 1986, a few months after the earthquake that devastated parts of Mexico City. Tepito was not as badly hit as some areas, and was better able to recover afterwards.

Hugh	¿Cómo fue el proceso de reconstrucción popular después del sismo del año pasado?
Alfonso	La pérdida de vidas en Tepito fue, gracias a Dios, casi nula, ¿no?, cinco personas perdieron la vida. Hubo una gran

cobertura porque la altura de la mayoría de las viviendas es de un nivel. Las casas son de tierra, son de adobe, y tienen muros muy anchos. Se cayeron muy pocas, pero todas tienen fracturados sus muros. Es importante repararlas lo más pronto posible.

Hugh   ¿Pero hubo un esfuerzo popular de reconstrucción, de autoayuda?

Alfonso   Claro. Nosotros hemos visto que en otros lugares la gente permaneció muy estática, esperando la ayuda, las primeras veces de la comida, las casas. En el caso de nosotros fue diferente porque la misma dinámica artesanal y comercial del barrio nos obligaba a retomar inmediatamente los talleres, salvar materiales, y sobre todo seguir abasteciendo a gentes de bajo poder adquisitivo que en ese momento habían perdido muchas cosas. Y la ayuda de ropa o de cosas no llegó a toda la gente. Entonces el único lugar de abasto, inclusive a nivel comida, fue Tepito. Entonces, pues mucha gente vino aquí. El cuarto artículo de consumo en la zona comercial de Tepito es la comida hecha. Entonces, era importante tener comida hecha y caliente, si no para dar, para vender a muy bajos precios durante todo ese proceso inicial de recuperación de la normalidad.

hubo una gran cobertura *people were well protected (literally 'there was a great covering')*
lo más pronto posible *as quickly as possible*
las primeras veces *in the first instance*
la misma dinámica artesanal y comercial del barrio *the way the* barrio *is geared to craft industries and business*
habían perdido *had lost*
comida hecha *ready-cooked food*

americanismos
no nada más *would be* no sólo *in Spain*
chamba *work – Mexican usage*
aparador *showcase – generally means 'sideboard' in Spain*
plomero fontanero *more usual in Spain*
claro *more like* sí *here (NB: in Chile, regularly means 'yes')*
las primeras veces *would be* en primer lugar *in Spain*
retomar *to take up again – not used in Spain in this sense*
inclusive incluso *more common in Spain*

ESPAÑA ACTUAL

LA SALUD

En España los que trabajan pagan una cuota, un porcentaje de su sueldo, a la Seguridad Social. Esta cantidad cubre un seguro de paro (el paro se cobra durante un tiempo limitado en caso de perder el trabajo), la pensión y la asistencia sanitaria. De esta manera se financia gran parte de la sanidad pública.

Una pequeña parte de la sanidad pública la organizan los municipios y las comunidades autónomas, pero la mayor parte corresponde al Instituto Nacional de la Salud, el llamado INSALUD. La gran parte del presupuesto de INSALUD proviene de la Seguridad Social, y por lo tanto este instituto depende tanto del Ministerio de Sanidad como del Ministerio del Trabajo y Seguridad Social.

El sector privado es todavía responsable de una gran parte de la oferta en cuanto a asistencia médica, oferta que es mayor que la pública. Pero se están haciendo grandes esfuerzos para mejorar y ampliar los servicios públicos. A partir de ahora incluso se dará tratamiento en ciertas instituciones privadas a pacientes pagados por la Seguridad Social. Este será el caso, por ejemplo, de los hospitales de la Cruz Roja.

INSALUD tiene 165 hospitales y 800 ambulatorios. Pero inevitablemente no están igualmente distribuidos por el país. Las listas de espera suelen hacerse largas, y un problema muy grande es el de la modernización. Muchos hospitales necesitan renovarse, y, sobre todo, hace mucha falta aumentar la provisión de alta tecnología médica en estos centros sanitarios. Otro problema es el de la preparación de los médicos, muchos de los cuales aspiran a pasar una época en el extranjero, en países con mejores recursos económicos para ampliar sus conocimientos. No cabe duda de que el estado español debe gastar más dinero en salud. Si se compara con otros países europeos, España queda atrás en su gasto público en la asistencia sanitaria.

Lo que sí que se aprecia ahora es más énfasis a nivel educativo en lo que puede mejorar la salud de

la nación: instruir a los niños desde pequeños en la escuela para que se cuiden mejor. Se ven campañas contra el abuso del alcohol, y la lucha contra el tabaco ha recibido una prioridad especial a través de nuevas leyes realmente severas en contra de los fumadores. El cuidado de la mujer embarazada y la atención a la nueva madre también han hecho progresos, aunque todavía falta bastante para que los beneficios lleguen a toda la población. También empieza a manifestarse un grado más alto de concienciación con respecto a la dieta.

Sin embargo, como sucede con tantos otros aspectos de la sociedad española hasta que se inviertan los necesarios fondos públicos no se puede esperar una salud pública de la más alta calidad.

Cirugía general

Comprende tratamiento médico-quirúrgico y asistencia farmacéutica completa con internamiento clínico, en todas las especialidades quirúrgicas.

Prestaciones del Seguro Escolar

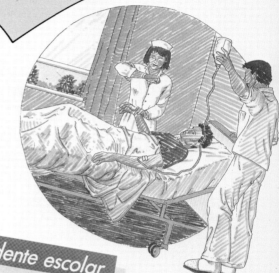

Accidente escolar

Ofreciéndote asistencia médico-farmacéutica, incluido internamiento sanatorial e intervenciones quirúrgicas, por toda lesión corporal que sufras con ocasión de actividades directa o indirectamente relacionadas con tus estudios e indemnización económica en los casos de incapacidad permanente absoluta [para] los estudios iniciados, pensión vitalícia en casos de gran invalidez. También [habrá] indemnización si el accidente [provoca] la muerte del estudiante.

¡Estudiante!
Conoce
las ventajas
del Seguro
Escolar...

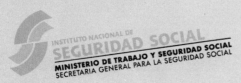

INSTITUTO NACIONAL DE
SEGURIDAD SOCIAL
MINISTERIO DE TRABAJO Y SEGURIDAD SOCIAL
SECRETARIA GENERAL PARA LA SEGURIDAD SOCIAL

PRÁCTICAS

1

¡Qué mal genio!

You were out late last night, and are feeling pretty rough this morning. Your Spanish host has noticed this. Put your grumpy retorts into Spanish.

Mario ¡Qué mala cara tienes! ¿Qué te pasa?

You (*I don't feel very well. My head aches.*)

Mario ¿Tienes resaca?

You (*No, I didn't drink much. But I'm very tired.*)

Mario ¿Por qué llevas esas gafas de sol?

You (*Because my eyes hurt. Do you have any aspirins?*)

Mario Sí, están en el cuarto de baño.

You (*Thanks. I'll have to go to bed very early tonight.*)

2

¿Qué le pasa?

What's the matter with these people? Match each sentence to the appropriate picture.

a Le duele el oído.

b Se ha roto la pierna.

c Se ha quemado con agua caliente.

d Tiene dolor de cabeza.

e Le duele el estómago.

f Tiene fiebre.

3

¿Qué remedio?

Here are some diagnoses of people's problems or state of health. Match each one with the appropriate prescription.

a   Tiene los músculos muy fláccidos.
b   Está muy gordo.
c   Tiene mucho sueño.
d   Le hacen daño los zapatos.
e   Le duele mucho la cabeza.
f   Está embarazada.

1   Debe acostarse.
2   Puede ir a clases de culturismo.
3   Tendrá que hacer régimen.
4   Debe quitarse los zapatos.
5   Tiene que cuidarse mucho.
6   Puede tomar una aspirina.

4

¿Te gusta?

Fill in the missing word in these sentences.

a   A mí ... gusta la música.
b   ¿ ... conformas con este coche?
c   ¿Cómo ... llaman tus hermanos?
d   ¿Qué ... parecen a usted estos precios?
e   ¿ ... gustan los niños a Blanca?
f   ¿Has visto las llaves del coche? ... dejé en la mesa.

5

Vestidos protectores

Which of these people would wear which set of protective clothing?

a   un torero
b   un cirujano
c   un jinete
d   un ciclista
e   un caballero
f   un bombero

6

¿Quién? ¿Cómo? ¿Dónde?

See how much you can remember about the people you've encountered in *Paso Doble*. Answer these questions in Spanish.

a   ¿Quién trabaja como costurera?

b   ¿Cómo se llama el marido de la propietaria del *Hostal Los Gallegos*?

c   ¿Dónde nació Isabel?

d   ¿Dónde ponían *La Malquerida*?

e   ¿En qué ciudad argentina viven Tommy y Zulema?

f   ¿Cómo se llama el negocio del Sr Angulo?

g   ¿Dónde vivían los abuelos de la chilena Elizabeth?

h   Los estudiantes que aprenden el griego con Rosa, ¿qué curso están haciendo?

7

Una consulta médica

You're having a medical examination in order to get your Spanish driving licence. Answer the following questions about yourself.

a   ¿A qué hora se levanta usted?

b   ¿Duerme bien?

c   ¿Tiene sueño durante el día?

d   ¿Le duele la cabeza después de ver la televisión?

e   ¿Se cansa fácilmente? (¿Y por qué?)

f   ¿Se ha roto algún hueso alguna vez?

g   ¿Sufre de dolor de espalda?

h   ¿Reacciona mal a las aspirinas?

i   ¿Cuándo fue la última vez que tuvo usted fiebre alta?

SUPLEMENTO

This is a further selection of interviews from both Spain and Latin America. The recordings are included on the cassettes but not in the radio programmes.

ESPAÑA

1

Julia doesn't have a full-time job, but she's devoting some of her time to compiling a dictionary of contemporary women authors – women writing in Spanish, from both Spain and Latin America. Isabel asks her what stage the project has reached.

Isabel ¿En qué fase está el proyecto?

Julia Pues, ahora mismo está en manos de una editorial, y estamos esperando que de un momento a otro nos den una respuesta, y esperamos que sea afirmativa.

Isabel Hablas en plural, dices 'esperamos' . . .

Julia Sí, sí, sí . . .

Isabel ¿Trabajas en equipo?

Julia No, es . . . bueno, es un equipo de dos, o sea, una pareja. Es un amigo alemán, que es hispanista y está muy interesado en literatura femenina, y sabe mucho, y entonces . . . bueno, la idea surgió conjuntamente, y vamos a ver qué .. qué pasa.

Isabel Dices literatura femenina, ¿quieres decir literatura escrita por mujeres o literatura feminista, es decir, con una carga ideológica determinada, o ambas cosas? . . . no sé.

Julia Sí, te explico. Pensamos que literatura femenina es la literatura escrita por mujeres, bueno, pueden ser escritoras feministas o no feministas, pero no vamos a hacer mucho hincapié en sólo las feministas, porque hay muchas mujeres escritoras muy buenas, y queremos con este diccionario que se conozca lo que es la literatura que está escribiendo la mujer.

Isabel Sí. Este grupo de escritoras, dos preguntas: primero, ¿es muy amplio? Y segundo, ¿qué época abarcáis? Es decir, ¿os

estamos esperando que . . . nos den *we're waiting for them to give us*

esperamos que sea afirmativa *we hope it's positive*

una carga ideológica determinada *a particular ideological focus*

hacer hincapié *to emphasise*

queremos . . . que se conozca *we want people to get to know*

extendéis hasta el siglo pasado, o remontáis simplemente, yo qué sé, a los años treinta? ¿Cómo lo hacéis? ¿Qué limites os habéis marcado?

yo qué sé *I don't know*
¡qué bárbaro! *how amazing!*

Julia   Sí, sí, por supuesto, hay unos límites. Para España, partimos de la Guerra Civil española, entonces hasta la actualidad. Y para Latinoamérica hemos tomado como límite 1950, que es más o menos cuando empieza todo el 'boom' de literatura latinoamericana.

Isabel   Ya, ya, ya. Y la otra pregunta era que si es un grupo muy extenso.

Julia   Sí, bueno, el número de escritoras no sabemos cuál va a ser, ¿no? Calculamos unas cuatrocientas.

Isabel   ¡Qué bárbaro! ¡Qué bárbaro!

Julia   Sí, sí, parece que hay pocas mujeres escritoras en España y en Latinoamérica, pero realmente hay muchas.

Isabel   ¿Me puedes dar algunos nombres?

Julia   Sí, bueno … españolas, conoces seguramente a Ester Tusquets, Monserrat Roig, Carmen Riera, que ya son del área catalanoparlante. Luego, madrileñas, pues está Rosa Montero, que es una de las más jóvenes … Lourdes Ortiz. Está también Carmen Gómez Ojea, que es muy interesante, es asturiana … Y bueno, éstas son novelistas pero, por ejemplo, vamos a incluir también autoras teatrales y poetas. Y en Latinoamérica, pues desde el caso de Isabel Allende, que es muy famosa, actualmente, no sólo en los países de habla castellana sino también está traducida a otros idiomas. Pues, hay muchas autoras argentinas, muchas escritoras argentinas muy buenas. Recuerdo una que me gusta mucho que se llama Marta Lynch. Mejicanas también, hay una que se llama Elena Poniatowska, que es una mejicana de origen polaco, y Elena Garro, también es mejicana … Bueno, hay montones.

a female poet in Spanish is generally called una poetisa

2

Ana's main occupation is weaving *tapices*, tapestries, which she shows in exhibitions. It's a fairly long and complicated process as Ana not only designs and weaves the tapestries, but dyes her own yarns as well. The first step is to make a sketch …

Ana   Bueno, pues yo parto de un boceto. Primero hago con lápiz, luego ya lo paso a las acuarelas. Entonces de allí ya saco un poco las tintadas que yo quiero para luego hacerlo en las lanas. Entonces, si por ejemplo hago un paisaje, pues las nubes azules, grises, una serie de cosas, entonces

lo paso a las acuarelas *I transfer it to watercolours*

procuro que tenga más o menos la misma calidad la acuarela, y luego intento . . . no siempre sale igual porque es imposible, pero intento, que esto, luego hacerlo, repetirlo con las lanas o con las telas. Entonces a partir del boceto, luego ya hago una maqueta, o sea, cómo va a quedar en pequeño. Y luego ya lo traslado a grande, que lo hago con un telar que tengo, de alto lizo que se llama. El telar de alto lizo es un telar de unas barras, con lo cual yo monto una urdimbre, y entonces en esa urdimbre luego yo tejo. Y entonces es un poco mi trabajo de tapices.

Isabel ¿Dónde consigues los tintes?

Ana Los tintes, bueno, los consigo . . . tiñe todo, o sea, las cascas de cebolla tiñe, las hojas de zanahoria tiñe, las fresas tiñe. ¡Lo que pasa que son más buenas y me las como!

Isabel O sea, que tú misma te haces tus propios tintes.

Ana Claro, claro, claro, yo me hago mis propios tintes.

Isabel ¡Ah, pues eso es fantástico!

Ana Sí, es muy interesante, es muy apetecible. ¡Hombre!, están muy bien los tintes también sintéticos, que ya son los que te venden. Pero lo que pasa es que es más interesante el jugar un poco y el empezar a experimentar, ¿no?, con . . . La henna tiñe, la cáscara de nuez, cuando está verde, tiñe a negros, entonces, bueno, es como muy . . . como muy divertido, ¿no?, hacer potingues.

Isabel ¿Y qué te puede llevar hacer un tapiz normal?

Ana Pues, un tapiz normal, entre boceto, diseño, maqueta, un mes más o menos. Un mes trabajando, trabajando relajadamente, o sea, unas seis horas o siete horas diarias.

procuro que tenga . . . la acuarela I try to make the watercolour have
maqueta model
cómo va a quedar en pequeño how it's going to turn out in miniature
lo traslado a grande I transfer it to full size
telar de alto lizo upright loom
urdimbre warp
¡lo que pasa que son más buenas y me las como! the trouble is that they're really good and I eat them!
te haces tus propios tintes you make your own dyes
potingues concoctions
¿qué te puede llevar . . . ? how long can it take you . . . ?

'henna' is English; the Spanish word is la alheña

3

Being at the heart of the city, the Plaza Mayor is the focus of many of the festivals celebrated throughout the year in Madrid. For Tere, one *fiesta* has a special significance.

Isabel ¿Qué fiestas se celebran en la Plaza Mayor?

Tere Pues mira, aquí casi todas. Aquí celebran los carnavales, celebran las fiestas de enero, celebran las fiestas de San Isidro el quince de mayo . . .

Isabel ¿Para ti cuál es la fiesta más bonita o más simpática de todas las que se celebran aquí?

Tere La de mayo, la de San Isidro.

Isabel ¿Por que?

Tere Lo primero porque mi hijo nació el día quince, por eso le puse Isidro, Carlos Isidro. Y lo segundo porque es la

January (enero) *means not just New Year festivities but (more importantly)* el día de Reyes *on the 5th, when* los Reyes Magos (*the Three Wise Men) bring children their Christmas presents*

le puse I called him

primavera y es más bonita. Hacen la procesión de San Isidro, sacan a San Isidro, le sacan en una carroza, hacen una procesión, y está muy bien. Así que la que más me gusta es la de mayo.

San Isidro is the patron saint of Madrid

4

The *fiesta de San Isidro* lasts from 15th to 26th May, and is famous for its bullfights. The main celebrations are centred on the area around the cathedral of San Isidro and the Plaza Mayor nearby. The *Instituto* where Rosa works is right in the middle of it all …

Julia Este Instituto está al lado de la catedral de San Isidro, ¿no?

Rosa Sí. No es la catedral de Madrid, pero sí es la más popular, porque es la catedral del santo patrón de la villa.

Julia ¿Y en San Isidro se hacen muchas fiestas en Madrid?

Rosa Sí, la procesión del santo sale de aquí hacia la … hacia la pradera de San Isidro. Y hay fiestas en el Instituto también para celebrar, y se celebra también la semana cultural en el Instituto.

Julia ¿Y normalmente qué tipo de .. de festejos se hacen para estas fiestas?

Rosa Pues, comienza una procesión del santo, después hay festejos populares de meriendas, bailes, concursos de disfraces.

Julia ¿Y hay alguna verbena como antiguamente, que eran tan típicas en Madrid?

Rosa Sí, por toda esta zona. Generalmente los vecinos se agrupan y hacen una peña, entonces ponen un puesto de bebidas, y unas farolitas adornan la calle, y por la tarde hay concursos de bailes, y que duran hasta la noche. Venden aperitivos, bebidas, y se baila hasta la una de la noche o hasta las dos.

Julia ¿Y tú vas frecuentemente a estas fiestas?

Rosa Las veo, y a veces he bailado en alguna verbena.

Julia ¿Y te gusta?

Rosa Sí, mucho. Me gusta mucho bailar el pasodoble en las verbenas.

concursos de disfraces *fancy dress competitions*
verbena *open-air fair*
peña *group*

AMÉRICA LATINA

1 BOLIVIA

In La Paz, Hugh spoke to Ramiro Paz, son of the Bolivian president, and asked him about some of the different accents of Latin America, starting with that of La Paz itself.

Hugh ¿Cómo se distingue el hablar del paceño?

Ramiro Bueno, yo creo que es más enunciado, con una pronunciación de las eses, y de la PS, es el 'psss'. Se dice, por ejemplo, '¿cómo estás, puesss?'. Y la PS tiene una gran gravitación en el acento paceño. Y hay otra cosa en el acento paceño que viene más de ... se da más en el aymara, que hay una transgresión entre el 'usted' y el 'tú'. En ciertos estratos que recién llegan a la ciudad, o que están entrando en la lengua castellana, pueden decirte: 'Señor, ¿cómo estás, pues? Usted me va a dar, pues, mañana para mi sueldo, y después contigo vamos a ir a pasear.' Entonces, hay un tuteo y un ustedo que se da simultáneamente, que también es interesante.

Aymara and Quechua are two of the languages of the Indian peoples

Hugh ¿Que proviene del aymara?

Ramiro Yo creo que es más aymara que quechua.

Hugh Y se habla de 'tú' y no de 'vos' acá.

Ramiro Aquí el 'tú' es más acentuado que el 'vos'. Ahora, en ciertas partes como Santa Cruz, el oriente y Tarija, el 'vos', y inclusive el 'vos' que viene de la influencia argentina, no necesariamente hispánica, se usa bastante. Entonces, hay una diferenciación dentro del país entre el 'tú' y el 'vos'.

Hugh Tú has viajado mucho por América Latina, ¿cuál acento te complace más?

Ramiro Bueno, no es cuestión de complacencia, sino de articulación y de capacidad de expresión, yo creo. Existe, por ejemplo, en Venezuela ... grandes sectores de la población venezolana tienen una gran capacidad de expresión, y eso creo que también viene porque no pronuncian muy severamente la ese, se la saltan. Entonces, pueden ir mucho más rápidamente a través de eso. En la Argentina también hay una gran capacidad de expresión. Los modismos en el hablar argentinos son muy interesantes, y tienen mucha vitalidad, quizás eso es un poco la vitalidad de gesticulación que viene de Italia y de la influencia italiana.

la ese *letter 's'*
tiene una gran gravitación *is heavily emphasised*
se da *occurs*
un tuteo y un ustedo *a use of* tú *and* usted
se la saltan *they miss it out*
a través de *through*
modismos en el hablar *speech idioms*

americanismos
recién *just, recently – Latin American usage; in Spain it would be* recientemente

2 CHILE

In cities all over Latin America, there are children without homes and families who live in the streets and survive by doing any job they can find or invent. Hugh spoke to social worker Marta Cortés about the street children of Santiago.

Hugh   Aquí en la ciudad de Santiago, hay muchos niños que están tratando de hacer labores precarias en la calle. ¿Qué tipo de labores realmente hacen estos pobres y desamparados niños?

Marta   Por ejemplo, son vendedores ambulantes. Venden galletas, dulces, son lustrabotas, venden periódicos. Eso es lo que normalmente uno los ve, y algún sector de niños que a veces ... bueno, cantan en la micro, que es un ... algo bien típico que se está viendo, ¿no?, en este momento, desde hace algunos años se está viendo el cantante de micro.

Hugh   ¿Y van a la escuela, estos cantantes de micro?

Marta   Los cantantes de micro, los vendedores de chocolate o de pastillas, algunos van a la escuela, no todos. Pero algunos son el sustento para toda la familia.

Hugh   Y cuando se le acerca un menor o una chica desamparada, ¿usted siempre da una moneda, o se resiste a dar limosna?

Marta   ¡Eso estaría en contra de los principios del trabajo social!

Hugh   ¿Dar limosna?

Marta   ¡Ya sé para dónde va su debut! Como madre, me duele el alma, me duele el alma saber que hay un niño que me está pidiendo un pedazo de pan. Pero allí salta inmediatamente el profesional.

Hugh   Pero entre la mujer y la profesional, ¿quién gana? Cuando uno se le acerca pidiendo, limosneando ...

Marta   La mujer.

Hugh   Y da una moneda.

Marta   A veces, sí. Sí, porque da pena. Y yo le voy a dar el caso de esta mañana, una niña en la estación del metro lloraba – ¡Por favor! – porque no tenía qué comer. Y entonces me dijo – Mire, yo llevo varios días sin comer –. Yo creo que el hambre es una cosa bien seria, y me lo dijo en una forma tan triste, que allí venció la mujer.

Hugh   ¿Qué edad tenía la niña esa?

Marta   La niña tenía unos doce años.

Hugh   Doce años, y no tenía qué comer.

Marta   No tenía qué comer. Y me pidió. Claro, que algunos son vagos y acostumbrados a hacerlo, pero uno nota bien cuando realmente son profesionales en la materia.

---

vendedores ambulantes *pedlars*

uno los ve *one sees them (doing)*

se le acerca *comes up to you*

dar limosna *to give money/alms*

eso estaría en contra de *that would be against*

¡ya sé para dónde va su debut! *I know what you're getting at!*

me duele el alma *it hurts me deeply*

salta el profesional *the professional (in me) comes out*

da pena *it's distressing, it makes you feel sorry*

yo le voy a dar el caso *I'll give you the example*

no tenía qué comer *she didn't have anything to eat*

uno nota bien *one can easily tell*

en la materia *in the subject*

americanismos
lustrabotas *in Spain, bootblacks are usually called* limpiabotas
micro *bus, in Chile and Peru*

3 COSTA RICA

Costa Rica is famous for its exotic plants and wildlife, which aren't confined to the rural and jungle areas. When Hugh visited the port of Limón, on the Caribbean coast, he discovered that the local park had some unusual residents, as the man working in the nearby bar explained:

Barman	En el Parque Vargas, aquí en Puerto Limón, tenemos como ocho perezosos. Son animales que viven en estos árboles, que son ... tienen bastante tiempo de estar en este parque.
Hugh	¿Y se los puede ver?
Barman	Pues, no señor, no se les puede ver, porque el color que ellos tienen, son gris oscuro, un verde claro, un verde amarillo, y se les confunde totalmente con la vegetación. No se les puede ver de noche, a poco de día.
Hugh	¿Y son muy camuflados entonces?
Barman	Sí, sí, sí, son muy camuflados, en verdad que sí. Así como son de callados son camuflados, porque no tienen ni grito ni voz.
Hugh	¿No hacen ningún ...?
Barman	Yo que sepa, yo que sepa. Yo he tocado un oso ... un perezoso de éstos, lo he tocado, y lo único que hacen es como un gruñido, pero como enojado, como ... (*imita el sonido*)
Hugh	¿Pero no gritan?
Barman	No gritan, tono de voz no tienen, y se ponen histéricos, pero ...
Hugh	¿Rígidos?
Barman	Rígidos, sí, fuertes, pero nada más de ahí. Son mansitos, mansitos.
Hugh	¿Son grandes?
Barman	No, pues no, no son muy grandes, es un animalito que puede pesar unos siete u ocho kilos, y puede medir unos quince centímetros de largo, y el alcance de las patas puede tener unos diez ... ocho centímetros. Los machos son más grandes y las hembras son más pequeñitas. Los dos son iguales, no se diferencian. Son ñaticos y casi no tienen nariz. La cara es ojos negros, grandes, redondos, y son mansos, mansos, mansos.
Hugh	Y se mueven muy lentamente.

perezosos *sloths;* perezoso *also means lazy*

tienen bastante tiempo de estar en este parque *they've been in this park for quite a long time*

a poco de día *nor in the daytime*

en verdad que sí *that's quite right*

así como son de callados *in the same way as they're silent*

yo que sepa, que yo sepa *as far as I know*

ñatico *snub-nosed*

Barman	Lentamente, lentamente, sí, señor, como la marea.
Hugh	¿Y de estos árboles bajan de vez en cuando?
Barman	Sí, casi siempre se les ve abajo, pero depende, porque si, digamos, hay poca gente y está lloviendo, ellos bajan. Que yo sepa, no creo que les tengan miedo, ellos no distinguen quién es gente, quién es ... No, no, ellos andan solos, y parece que no tuvieran miedo de nada, porque como son tan perezosos no les importa nada.

americanismos

tienen tiempo de ... *Latin American usage; in Spain
you'd hear* hace tiempo que ...

ñatico (ñato) *only found in Latin America* (chato *in
Spain*); *the ending* -ico *is more common in Latin America*

de vez en cuando *from
time to time*

**no creo que les tengan
miedo** *I don't think
they're afraid* (*of them*)

**parece que no tuvieran
miedo de nada** *they
don't seem to be afraid
of anything*

no les importa nada *they
don't care about
anything*

GRAMÁTICA

This is a more detailed and systematic summary of the grammar introduced in the *Lengua* sections. It doesn't include some very basic points covered in beginners' courses, or more complex points that don't arise in **Paso Doble**.

NOUNS AND ADJECTIVES
Gender and agreement
All Spanish nouns are masculine or feminine. Often the ending of a noun will show which, but, if not, you should try to learn it with the definite article, *el* or *la*. (With male and female people and animals, the gender is obvious.)

Nouns ending in *-o* are mostly masculine. The very few exceptions include: *la mano, la radio*. Nouns ending in *-a, -dad, -ción* are generally feminine. Exceptions mostly end in *-a*: *el día, el mapa, el clima, el telegrama*.

Some nouns can be both genders, but with different meanings: *el guía* (guide), *la guía* (guidebook); *el capital* (financial capital), *la capital* (capital city). Some feminine words are used with *el* rather than *la* because it's easier to pronounce – they're ones that begin with a stressed *a*, e.g. *el agua, el águila* (the plural is *las aguas, las águilas*).

As a general guideline, nouns change in the plural by adding *-s* when they end in a vowel, or *-es* when they end in a consonant: *calle, calles; rey, reyes*.

The endings of adjectives change to agree with the noun they're describing, according to whether it's masculine or feminine, singular or plural. If used with two or more singular nouns, the adjective becomes plural, e.g. *el rey y el príncipe españoles*. If it's with a mixture of masculine and feminine nouns, it takes the masculine plural form, e.g. *hombres* (m) *y mujeres* (f) *españoles* (m).

Many adjectives end in *-o* in the masculine and *-a* in the feminine; add *-s* to make them plural: *vino blanco, casa blanca; vinos blancos, casas blancas*.

Adjectives ending in *-e* are the same for masculine and feminine, and add *-s* for the plural: *hombre fuerte, hombres fuertes; mano fuerte, manos fuertes*.

Adjectives ending in a consonant are the same for masculine and feminine, and add *-es* for the plural: *coche azul, coches azules, compañía internacional, compañías internacionales*.

An exception to this is adjectives of nationality ending in a consonant. They add *-a* for the feminine: *hombre español, mujer española*.

Position of adjectives
Spanish adjectives usually come directly after the noun they're describing: *hombres argentinos, zona antigua, judías negras*.

Some very common adjectives are generally used before the noun: *mucho, poco, bastante, demasiado, otro, todo, alguno, ninguno, cuanto, cada, demás, tal*, and numerals such as *primero, segundo, tercero*, etc. For example: *mucha gente, otras personas, cada año, segundo apellido*.

Other adjectives can be used before the noun to give a slightly different emphasis. A few actually have different meanings when they come before. For instance, *un hombre grande* means 'a big man', but *un gran hombre* is 'a great man'; *una familia pobre* is 'a poor/needy family', but *una pobre familia* is 'a wretched/miserable family'; *varios libros* means 'several books', but *libros varios* would be 'various/different books'.

Notice that some adjectives drop their final -*o* when used before a singular noun, e.g. *alguno, ninguno* (both of which then need a written accent), *bueno, malo, primero, tercero*:

algún hombre   *ningún problema*
un buen día   *el primer piso*

Grande becomes *gran* when used before any singular noun: *un gran hombre, en gran parte*.

Possessive Adjectives

These are the words meaning 'my', 'your', 'his', etc. They also change to agree with the noun they're describing, e.g. *nuestra casa, nuestro coche*.

	singular	plural
my	**mi**	**mis**
your (*tú*)	**tu**	**tus**
(*usted*)	**su**	**sus**
his, her, its	**su**	**sus**
our	**nuestro/a**	**nuestros/as**
your (*vosotros*)	**vuestro/a**	**vuestros/as**
(*ustedes*)	**su**	**sus**
their	**su**	**sus**

Remember to use the correct word for 'your': *tu* with *tú*; *su* with *usted* and *ustedes*; *vuestro/a* with *vosotros/as*.

Su has several meanings – 'your', 'his', 'her', 'its', 'their'. To avoid confusion it may be necessary to replace it with *de usted, de él, de ella*, etc.:
el coche de usted   *el amigo de él*

Possessive adjectives are not used as much in Spanish as in English, particularly with parts of the body or clothing:
Me duele la cabeza.   My head aches.
Se quitó el sombrero.   He took off his hat.

PRONOUNS
Subject pronouns
These are the subjects of the verb, the equivalent of 'I', 'you', 'we', and so on. Remember that Spanish verb endings show who or what the subject is, so subject pronouns are used only for emphasis or clarity – though *usted* and *ustedes* are used more generally, to show politeness:
Yo soy inglés, pero él es español.
¿Es usted de aquí?

Spanish subject pronouns are:

I	**yo**	we	**nosotros/as**
you (informal)	**tú**	you (informal)	**vosotros/as**
(formal)	**usted**	(formal)	**ustedes**
he	**él**	they	**ellos/as**
she	**ella**		

Notice that 'it' and 'they', when referring to things, are not translated:
Es verdad.   It's true.
Son bastante caros.   They're quite expensive.

Unit 1 explains the differences between the words for 'you' – *tú, vosotros, usted, ustedes. Tú* and *vosotros* are used with the 2nd person forms of verbs (singular and plural respectively). *Usted* and *ustedes* are used with the 3rd person forms. In writing they're often abbreviated to *Vd* and *Vds*, or (particularly in Latin America) to *Ud* and *Uds*.

There are variations in usage in different parts of the Spanish-speaking world. In Latin America, and also in southern Spain and the Canary Islands, *vosotros/as* is not used at all – *ustedes* is used for 'you' in the plural for everyone. In some parts of Latin America, such as Argentina, Ecuador and Costa Rica, *vos* is used rather than *tú* – and it has a separate verb form (see below).

Object pronouns
These are the objects of the verb, the equivalent of 'me', 'you', 'him', 'her', 'it', 'us', 'them', e.g. 'I saw her', 'we drank it'. Object pronouns can be direct (as in those examples) or indirect. To identify an indirect object pronoun, think of it as having 'to' or 'for'

before it, e.g. 'I gave him the book' (i.e. 'to him'). In practice, Spanish mostly uses the same word for both types, except in the 3rd person:

	direct	indirect
me	**me**	**me**
you (*tú*)	**te**	**te**
you (*usted*)	**le**	**le**
him	**le**	
her	**la**	**le**
it	**lo, la**	
us	**nos**	**nos**
you (*vosotros*)	**os**	**os**
you (*ustedes*)	**les**	**les**
them (things)	**los, las**	**les**
them (people)	**les, las**	

Notice that in Latin America *lo* is generally used as the direct object pronoun for 'him'; and in areas where *vos* is used, *te* is used as the object pronoun.

With verbs like *gustar*, *encantar*, *apetecer*, *parecer*, you use the indirect object pronouns:
***Les** encanta el teatro.*
*¿**Te** apetece venir al teatro?*

Remember that when a person is the direct object of a verb, you put *a* before the noun, or use an indirect object pronoun:
*Vi **a María** esta mañana.*
***Le** vi esta mañana.*

Le and *les* can both have several meanings, so to avoid confusion you can add *a él*, *a ella*, *a usted* and so on, as appropriate:
*A él no **le** gusta.*
*A ellos **les** parece maravilloso.*

Object pronouns generally come before the verb:
***La** vi el otro día.*
*Todo el mundo **le** daba una propina.*
***Me** tiraron al suelo.*

When an infinitive or present participle follows another verb, the pronoun can come before the first verb or attached to the end of the second:
Los** quiero ver.*   or *Quiero ver**los.
Lo** estoy haciendo.*   or *Estoy haciéndo**lo.

When the infinitive or present participle is on its own, or when the verb is a command (imperative), the pronoun is attached to the end:
*Para cerrar**lo** todo ...*
*Haciéndo**lo** de esta manera ...*
*Lláma**me** mañana.*

If there are two pronouns, the indirect object always comes before the direct object. In this case *le* and *les* change to *se* if the second pronoun is *lo*, *la*, *los*, or *las*:
***Te lo** llevaré.*
*¿Puedes pasár**melo**?*
***Se lo** daré mañana.*

Notice that after prepositions (words like *a*, *de*, *para*), you mostly use the subject pronouns, except for *mí* (me) and *ti* (you):
*A **mí** no me gusta.*
*Lo compré para **él**.*

Reflexive pronouns

These are used to make reflexive verbs, and in Spanish they are **me, te, se, nos, os, se**:

me llamo	*nos llamamos*
te llamas	*os llamáis*
se llama	*se llaman*

Sometimes the reflexive pronoun can be translated as 'myself', 'yourself' etc., though there are many cases where the pronoun has no equivalent in English:

¿Cómo se llaman?	What are they called?
No me siento bien.	I don't feel well.
Me tomé unas cañas.	I had a few beers.
¿Te acuerdas de ...?	Do you remember ...?

Reflexive verbs are listed in dictionaries with *se* attached to the infinitive, e.g. *llamarse*, *sentirse*.

Se is also used to make a verb passive, when the verb has no subject, as in these examples:

Aquí se habla español.	Spanish is spoken here.
Los frijoles se hierven.	The beans are boiled.
El museo se abre a las diez.	The museum opens at ten.

In each case there is no indication of who 'speaks' Spanish, 'boils' the beans or 'opens' the museum. Notice that the verb agrees with what is now the subject of the verb, i.e. *español* (singular, so the verb is singular), *los frijoles* (plural), *el museo* (singular).

In a slightly different type of impersonal construction *se* is always used with a 3rd person singular verb. It may help to think of *se* as meaning 'you' or 'one' or even 'people', as in these examples:

Se aprieta el botón.	You push the button.
En España se cena tarde.	In Spain people dine late.
Se dice que es muy interesante.	People/They say that it's very interesting.

VERBS

Spanish verbs are characterised by different endings that tell you who or what the subject is (who's doing the action), and when (past, present or future). They are listed in dictionaries in the infinitive form, and can be divided into three groups according to whether their infinitive ends in *-ar*, *-er* or *-ir*. In the tables on page 152 an example of each group is given, with the endings for the tenses highlighted in bold type. There are also a number of verbs that don't follow the patterns exactly, and the most common of these are listed, with the irregular parts highlighted.

The present tense

As well as the irregular forms listed, some verbs ending in *-cer* and *-cir* have *zc* in the 1st person singular, e.g. *conozco* (*conocer*), *produzco* (*producir*).

The Spanish present tense is used in much the same way as the English, but it can translate both the English simple present and the present continuous, e.g. *escribo una carta* can mean 'I write a letter' or 'I'm writing a letter'. (See **Continuous tenses** below.)

Spanish also uses the present tense to refer to the immediate future, e.g. when the phone rings a Spaniard says *voy* where in English you'd say 'I'll go'.

Vos, the word for 'you' found in parts of Latin America, is used with a different present tense form, e.g. *vos hablás*, *vos comés*, *vos vivís*. You can work out what the form should be by replacing the final *-r* of an infinitive with an *-s*, and adding an accent in writing. An exception is *sos*, from ser.

The future tense

This is the equivalent of the English 'will' or 'shall'. Forming the future tense is easy – take the infinitive form and add the following endings: **-é, -ás, -á, -emos, -éis, -án**. The endings are always regular though the first part of the verb sometimes isn't, e.g. *decir – diré, dirás*, etc.; *hacer – haré, tener – tendré*. (Irregular forms are listed.)

Spanish also uses *ir a* followed by an infinitive to express future ideas, as in the English 'going to':

Voy a estudiar derecho.	I'm going to study law.

The conditional

This is the equivalent of the English 'would' or 'should'. It's used to express speculative plans or to be especially polite:

¿Te gustaría venir al cine?	Would you like to come to the cinema?
Me gustaría estudiar derecho.	I'd like to study law.
Yo podría ir el viernes.	I'd be able to go on Friday.

It is formed in the same way as the future, by adding a set of endings to the infinitive. The conditional endings are: **-ía, -ías, -ía, -íamos, -íais, -ían**. For example, *yo hablaría, comería, viviría*. Irregularities are the same as for the future tense, e.g. *decir – diría, hacer – haría*.

Past tenses

These are the preterite, the imperfect, the perfect and the pluperfect. The first three are explained in some detail in units 5, 6 and 7. The notes below concentrate on some irregular forms and uses.

The preterite

Irregular forms are listed in the verb tables; notice how the stress on the endings differs between regular and irregular forms. It's worth mentioning that a few verbs have a slight change of meaning when used in the preterite, e.g.:

conocer (to know)	conocí	I met, got to know
saber (to know)	supe	I found out
querer (to want)	quise	I intended

To use these verbs in the past tense with their original meanings, you use the imperfect: *conocía* (I knew), *sabía* (I knew), *quería* (I wanted).

The imperfect

There are two sets of endings for the imperfect:

-ar verbs: **-aba, -abas, -aba, -ábamos, -abais, -aban**

-er and *-ir* verbs: **-ía, -ías, -ía, -íamos, -íais, -ían**

There are only two irregular verbs (*ser* and *ir*); *ver* keeps the e to give *veía, veías*, etc.

The imperfect can be used to translate both the English simple past and the past continuous, e.g. *yo vivía* can mean 'I lived' or 'I was living'. It can also be 'I used to live'.

Remember that you need to decide whether the imperfect or the preterite is the appropriate way to translate the English past tense.

The perfect and the pluperfect

These are the equivalents of the English 'has/have done' and 'had done'. They are both compound tenses, formed by using the appropriate part of *haber*, plus the past participle of the verb (see below). The perfect uses the present tense of *haber*, and the pluperfect uses the imperfect, e.g. *he hablado* – 'I have spoken', *había hablado* – 'I had spoken'; *ha ido* – 'he has gone', *había ido* – 'he had gone'. (For the formation of *haber*, see the verb list.)

The past participle

This is formed as follows:

-ar verbs:	habl**ado**	
-er and *-ir* verbs:	com**ido**	viv**ido**

There are various irregular past participles, including *abierto* (*abrir*), *dicho* (*decir*), *escrito* (*escribir*), *hecho* (*hacer*), *puesto* (*poner*), *visto* (*ver*), *vuelto* (*volver*).

When used to form the perfect and pluperfect, past participles never change to agree with anything. However, they can also be used as adjectives, in which case they change just like other adjectives, e.g. *están sentados, mi abuela era bastante pesada*.

The present participle

This is the equivalent of '-ing' in English. It is formed as follows:

-ar verbs:	habl**ando**	
-er and *-ir* verbs:	com**iendo**	viv**iendo**

A notable exception is *yendo*, from *ir*, and there are a few verbs where y replaces the i to avoid three vowels in a row, e.g. *leyendo* (*leer*). The ending never changes to agree with anything.

The present participle is used for continuous tenses (see below). It can also be used with *seguir* and *continuar* to mean 'to go on/be still doing':

Sigo viviendo aquí.	I'm still living here.
Voy a continuar trabajando.	I'm going to go on working.

Continuous tenses

These are formed by using the appropriate part of *estar* followed by the present participle. They emphasise that an action is or was going on at a precise moment in time, e.g.:

¿Qué estás haciendo?
Estoy preparando la cena.
Estaban jugando al voleibol.

These tenses are used far less in Spanish than in English.

The subjunctive

This is hardly noticed in English and is not important (though for instance 'if I were a rich man' is a subjunctive). However, it is widely used in Spanish when speaking about uncertain and hypothetical events and actions.

The present subjunctive is the one used most, and it is easy to form. It is similar to the ordinary present tense, except that the endings of the groups are swopped over. They are added to the 1st person singular, minus the final -o:

	present	subjunctive
hablar	hablo	hable, hables, hable, hablemos, habléis, hablen
comer	como	coma, comas, coma, comamos, comáis, coman
vivir	vivo	viva, vivas, viva, vivamos, viváis, vivan

The same rule applies to most irregular verbs:

hacer	hago	haga, hagas, etc.
decir	digo	diga, digas
poder	puedo	pueda, puedas

Completely irregular are:

ir	vaya, vayas, vaya, vayamos, vayáis, vayan
saber	sepa, sepas, sepa, sepamos, sepáis, sepan
ser	sea, seas, sea, seamos, seáis, sean
haber	haya, hayas, haya, hayamos, hayáis, hayan

Rather than trying to learn all the ins and outs of using the subjunctive, start by aiming to recognise it when you hear or see it. In that way you'll gradually become familiar with some of the common uses.

One main feature is that the subjunctive often occurs as the second verb in a sentence, where the two verbs have different subjects – that is, in a dependent or subordinate clause, introduced by the word *que*:

*Quiero que **vayas** ahora.*	I want you to go now.
*Dígale que **venga** hoy.*	Tell him to come today.

You'll find it after words expressing emotion:

*Siento que **estés** mal.*	I'm sorry you're unwell.
*Me alegro que **puedas** venir.*	I'm glad that you can come.

After impersonal expressions:

*Es importante que **llegues** a tiempo.*	It's important that you arrive on time.
*Es una lástima que no **puedas** venir.*	It's a pity that you can't come.

And after phrases like *cuando* (when), *mientras que* (while), *en caso de que* (if, in the event that), when no fixed point in time is mentioned:

*Cuando **termines**, ¿qué piensas hacer?*	When you finish, what do you plan to do?
*¿Qué vas a hacer en caso de que **sigas** trabajando?*	What are you going to do if you go on working?

The imperative

This is the command form of the verb, which is used to tell someone to do something. (Other ways of giving instructions are covered in unit 3).

The *tú* form is the same as the 3rd person singular of the present tense. For *vosotros*, take the infinitive and replace the final -r with a -d. For *usted*, *ustedes* and *nosotros*, use the present subjunctive forms. For example:

sing!	¡canta! (tú)
	¡cantad! (vosotros)
	¡cante usted!
	¡canten ustedes!
let's sing!	¡cantemos! (nosotros)

A few exceptions in the *tú* imperative are: *haz* (*hacer*), *di* (*decir*), *pon* (*poner*), *ve* (*ir*), *ten* (*tener*).

Object pronouns (including reflexives) are joined to the end of the verb. Note that the reflexive form of *nosotros* drops the final -s before the pronoun, and *vosotros* drops the final -d:

Cántalo.	Sing it.
Acuérdate.	Remember.
Vámonos.	Let's go.
Sentémonos.	Let's sit down.
Sentaos.	Sit down.

To tell someone not to do something (a negative command), use *no* plus the present subjunctive in all cases. Pronouns come before the verb:

No vayas.	Don't go.
No corráis.	Don't run.
No lo creas.	Don't believe it.

Imperatives appear in some set expressions:

¿Diga?/¿Dígame?	Yes, can I help you? (said by shop assistant)
	Hello. (said by person answering phone)
Oiga.	Excuse me. (to waiter etc. to attract attention)
Tenga.	Here you are. (as you hand something over)
¡No me digas!	You don't say!
¡Fíjese!/¡Fíjate!	Imagine it! Good heavens!

Radical-changing verbs

These are also known as root-changing or stem-changing verbs. They are verbs which make a change to the vowel in the first part of the verb, the root – the endings remain regular. The changes mainly affect the present tense.

There are three main patterns of change. In the present tense they affect all the singular persons and the 3rd person plural:

1 *e* changes to *ie*

pensar: pi**e**nso, pi**e**nsas, pi**e**nsa,
pensamos, pensáis, pi**e**nsan

Other examples are *cerrar, perder, empezar, preferir.*

2 *o* or *u* changes to *ue*

poder: p**ue**do, p**ue**des, p**ue**de,
podemos, podéis, p**ue**den

Other examples are *dormir, costar, encontrar, jugar.*

3 *e* changes to *i*

pedir: pido, pides, pide,
pedimos, pedís, piden.

Other examples are *decir, seguir, freír, elegir.*

The same sort of change also happens in the present subjunctive, except that the third group has the *i* in the 1st and 2nd persons plural as well:

pensar: pi**e**nse, pi**e**nses, pi**e**nse,
pensemos, penséis, pi**e**nsen

pedir: pida, pidas, pida,
pidamos, pidáis, pidan

Radical-changing verbs ending in *-ir* also make changes in the present participle and in the preterite, in the 3rd person singular and plural. The *e* changes to *i*, and *o* changes to *u*:

sentir	*present participle:* sintiendo
	preterite: sentí, sentiste, sintió, sentimos, sentisteis, sintieron
dormir	*present participle:* durmiendo
	preterite: dormí, dormiste, durmió, dormimos, dormisteis, durmieron

You'll get used to recognising the sort of verb where these sort of changes happen. You can get a clue if you know a noun related to the verb, e.g.:

comenzar	to begin	*comienzo*	beginning
encontrar	to find	*encuentro*	meeting
jugar	to play	*juego*	game

Spelling changes

Some Spanish words undergo spelling changes in some of their forms – the sound remains the same but is written differently, e.g.:

*co**g**er, co**j**o, co**g**es,* etc.
*po**c**o, po**qu**ito*
*jue**z**, jue**c**es*
*pa**g**ar, pa**gu**é*
*creer, creí, cre**y**ó*

REGULAR VERBS

	Present	*Future*	*Preterite*	*Imperfect*
-ar type: **hablar**	Past participle: habl**ado**		Present participle: habl**ando**	
yo	habl**o**	hablar**é**	habl**é**	habl**aba**
tú	habl**as**	hablar**ás**	habl**aste**	habl**abas**
usted, él, ella	habl**a**	hablar**á**	habl**ó**	habl**aba**
nosotros/as	habl**amos**	hablar**emos**	habl**amos**	habl**ábamos**
vosotros/as	habl**áis**	hablar**éis**	habl**asteis**	habl**abais**
ustedes, ellos/as	habl**an**	hablar**án**	habl**aron**	habl**aban**
-er type: **comer**	Past participle: com**ido**		Present participle: com**iendo**	
yo	com**o**	comer**é**	com**í**	com**ía**
tú	com**es**	comer**ás**	com**iste**	com**ías**
usted, él, ella	com**e**	comer**á**	com**ió**	com**ía**
nosotros/as	com**emos**	comer**emos**	com**imos**	com**íamos**
vosotros/as	com**éis**	comer**éis**	com**isteis**	com**íais**
ustedes, ellos/as	com**en**	comer**án**	com**ieron**	com**ían**
-ir type: **vivir**	Past participle: viv**ido**		Present participle: viv**iendo**	
yo	viv**o**	vivir**é**	viv**í**	viv**ía**
tú	viv**es**	vivir**ás**	viv**iste**	viv**ías**
usted, él, ella	viv**e**	vivir**á**	viv**ió**	viv**ía**
nosotros/as	viv**imos**	vivir**emos**	viv**imos**	viv**íamos**
vosotros/as	viv**ís**	vivir**éis**	viv**isteis**	viv**íais**
ustedes, ellos/as	viv**en**	vivir**án**	viv**ieron**	viv**ían**

IRREGULAR VERBS (irregular forms in **bold** type)

	Present	*Future*	*Preterite*	*Imperfect*
dar	**doy**	daré	**di**	daba
	das	etc.	**diste**	etc.
	da		**dio**	
	damos		**dimos**	
	dais		**disteis**	
	dan		**dieron**	
decir	**digo**	**diré**	**dije**	decía
Past participle:	dices	**dirás**	**dijiste**	etc.
dicho	dice	**dirá**	**dijo**	
	decimos	**diremos**	**dijimos**	
	decís	**diréis**	**dijisteis**	
	dicen	**dirán**	**dijeron**	

	Present	*Future*	*Preterite*	*Imperfect*
estar	**estoy**	estaré	**estuve**	estaba
	estás	etc.	**estuviste**	etc.
	está		**estuvo**	
	estamos		**estuvimos**	
	estáis		**estuvisteis**	
	están		**estuvieron**	
haber	he	habré	hube	había
	has	habrás	hubiste	etc.
	ha	habrá	hubo	
	hemos	habremos	hubimos	
	habéis	habréis	hubisteis	
	han	habrán	hubieron	
hacer	**hago**	**haré**	**hice**	hacía
Past participle:	haces	**harás**	**hiciste**	etc.
hecho	hace	**hará**	**hizo**	
	hacemos	**haremos**	**hicimos**	
	hacéis	**haréis**	**hicisteis**	
	hacen	**harán**	**hicieron**	
ir	**voy**	iré	**fui**	**iba**
Present participle:	**vas**	etc.	**fuiste**	**ibas**
yendo	**va**		**fue**	**iba**
	vamos		**fuimos**	**íbamos**
	vais		**fuisteis**	**ibais**
	van		**fueron**	**iban**
oír	**oigo**	oiré	oí	oía
Present participle:	**oyes**	etc.	oíste	etc.
oyendo	**oye**		**oyó**	
	oímos		oímos	
	oís		**oísteis**	
	oyen		**oyeron**	
poder	**puedo**	**podré**	**pude**	podía
Present participle:	**puedes**	**podrás**	**pudiste**	etc.
pudiendo	**puede**	**podrá**	**pudo**	
	podemos	**podremos**	**pudimos**	
	podéis	**podréis**	**pudisteis**	
	pueden	**podrán**	**pudieron**	

	Present	*Future*	*Preterite*	*Imperfect*
poner	**pongo**	**pondré**	**puse**	ponía
Past participle:	pones	**pondrás**	**pusiste**	etc.
puesto	pone	**pondrá**	**puso**	
	ponemos	**pondremos**	**pusimos**	
	ponéis	**pondréis**	**pusisteis**	
	ponen	**pondrán**	**pusieron**	
querer	**quiero**	**querré**	**quise**	quería
	quieres	**querrás**	**quisiste**	etc.
	quiere	**querrá**	**quiso**	
	queremos	**querremos**	**quisimos**	
	queréis	**querréis**	**quisisteis**	
	quieren	**querrán**	**quisieron**	
reír	**río**	reiré	reí	reía
Present participle:	**ríes**	etc.	reíste	etc.
riendo	**ríe**		**rio**	
	reímos		reímos	
	reís		reísteis	
	ríen		**rieron**	
saber	**sé**	**sabré**	**supe**	sabía
	sabes	**sabrás**	**supiste**	etc.
	sabe	**sabrá**	**supo**	
	sabemos	**sabremos**	**supimos**	
	sabéis	**sabréis**	**supisteis**	
	saben	**sabrán**	**supieron**	
salir	**salgo**	**saldré**	salí	salía
	sales	**saldrás**	etc.	etc.
	sale	**saldrá**		
	salimos	**saldremos**		
	salís	**saldréis**		
	salen	**saldrán**		
ser	**soy**	seré	**fui**	**era**
	eres	etc.	**fuiste**	**eras**
	es		**fue**	**era**
	somos		**fuimos**	**éramos**
	sois		**fuisteis**	**erais**
	son		**fueron**	**eran**

	Present	*Future*	*Preterite*	*Imperfect*
tener	**tengo**	**tendré**	**tuve**	tenía
	tienes	**tendrás**	**tuviste**	etc.
	tiene	**tendrá**	**tuvo**	
	tenemos	**tendremos**	**tuvimos**	
	tenéis	**tendréis**	**tuvisteis**	
	tienen	**tendrán**	**tuvieron**	

traer	**traigo**	traeré	**traje**	traía
Present participle:	traes	etc.	**trajiste**	etc.
trayendo	trae		**trajo**	
Past participle:	traemos		**trajimos**	
traído	traéis		**trajisteis**	
	traen		**trajeron**	

venir	**vengo**	**vendré**	**vine**	venía
Present participle:	**vienes**	**vendrás**	**viniste**	etc.
viniendo	**viene**	**vendrá**	**vino**	
	venimos	**vendremos**	**vinimos**	
	venís	**vendréis**	**vinisteis**	
	vienen	**vendrán**	**vinieron**	

ver	**veo**	veré	vi	**veía**
Past participle:	ves	etc.	etc.	**veías**
visto	ve			**veía**
	vemos			**veíamos**
	veis			**veíais**
	ven			**veían**

The Spanish alphabet

a	a	**h**	hache	**ñ**	eñe	**v**	ve, uve
b	be	**i**	i	**o**	o	**w**	ve doble, doble v
c	ce	**j**	jota	**p**	pe		doble u in Latin America
ch	che	**k**	ka	**q**	cu	**x**	equis
d	de	**l**	ele	**r**	erre	**y**	i griega
e	e	**ll**	elle	**s**	ese	**z**	zeta
f	efe	**m**	eme	**t**	te		
g	ge	**n**	ene	**u**	u		

PRONUNCIACIÓN

Many letters are pronounced as in English. Exceptions are:

Vowels

Letters(s) Rough equivalent	Example
a 'a' as in northern English 'cat' (between southern English 'cat' and 'cut')	hablar
e 'e' as in 'hen'	tres
i 'ee' as in 'seek'	vivo
o 'o' as in 'rob'	nombre
u 'oo' as in 'boot' not pronounced after **q** or in **gue** or **gui**	numero

Consonants

b except at beginning of word or after **m** or **n**
lightly pronounced, between 'b' and 'v' — trabajar, hablar

c followed by **e** or **i**, and **z**
'th' as in 'thin' — acento, ciudad
in Latin America:
's' as in 'sing'

d except at beginning of word
lightly pronounced, — Madrid
'th' as in 'other'

g followed by **e** or **i**; and **j**
'ch' as in Scottish 'loch' — gente, trabajo

h always silent — hablar

ll 'lli' as in 'million' — llevar, llamo
in Latin America: 'y' as in 'yet' (in Argentina: 's' as in 'measure')

ñ 'ni' as in 'onion' — mañana

q 'k' as in 'key' — quien

r at beginning of word, and **rr**
like Scottish **r**, strongly rolled — restaurante, arrollar

r between vowels
only slightly rolled — eres

s before **b,d,g,l,m,n**
's' as in 'prism' — desde, mismo

v pronounced same as **b**

x as English, or can be 's' as in 'best' — exacto

y in Argentina, 's' as in 'measure' — yo, mayor

Stress

In words of more than one syllable, one syllable is emphasised more strongly than the other(s):

1 If the word has a written accent, the accented vowel is stressed: aquí; afición; básico.

2 If the word ends in a vowel, an **n** or an **s**, the stress falls on the next to last syllable: **pla**za, **vi**ven, espa**ño**les.

3 If the word ends in any other consonant, the stress falls on the last syllable: ma**yor**; Ma**drid**; **fi**nal.

Punctuation

1 In written Spanish, upside-down question marks and exclamation marks are used at the beginning of a question or exclamation: ¿de dónde eres?, ¡qué calor!

2 Capital letters are not used for yo (I), days of the week and months of the year, adjectives of nationality, and titles: sábado, el dos de agosto; soy mejicano, el señor Fernández.

CLAVE: PREGUNTAS

UNIT 1

1
1   No, no tiene mujer.
2   Sí, es de Madrid.

2
1   No, no es español, es mejicano.
2   No, no es el único propietario, tiene varios socios.

3
1   Es de Galicia, de la provincia de Lugo.
2   Tiene dos hijas.

4
1   Antonio sí es de Madrid, pero Ana es de Cáceres, en Extremadura.

5
1   Lleva treinta y un años viviendo en Madrid.
2   Es profesora de griego. (Da clases de griego.)

6
1   Tere, Isidoro, Almudena y la perra viven en la casa.
2   No, Isidoro no trabaja.

UNIT 2

1
1   Les encuentra muy simpáticos.
2   No, no es gorda, es delgada.
3   José tiene el pelo moreno.

2
1   Sí, le gusta mucho.
2   El ruido de los coches puede ser una desventaja.

3
1   Rosa se lleva bien con sus vecinos.

4
1   La madre de Adeline es flaca, guapa y un poco baja.
2   Isabel tiene el pelo medio marrón y medio negro, y lo lleva corto.

5
1   Las desventajas son el ruido y la contaminación.
2   Le gusta esta zona porque lo tiene todo a mano, todo está muy cerca.
3   No, va andando al trabajo.

UNIT 3

1
1   Acaba de ocupar el cargo de presidenta de la comunidad.
2   Va a tener que hacer los recibos de final de mes, y pasarle un recibo a cada uno de los inquilinos.

2
1   No dan comidas porque es hostal-residencia y sólo se puede dormir allí.
2   Si alguien va al teatro o a un espéctaculo puede volver después de la hora de entrada general.

3
1   En España los frijoles se llaman judías negras.
2   Antes de freír los frijoles hay que hervirlos a presión durante veinte a treinta minutos.

4
1   Las frases se escriben en la pantalla.
2   Con un ordenador se puede retrodecer y borrar y rectificar en el momento.

UNIT 4

1
1   No, Isabel no va mucho al teatro.
2   Se van a encontrar en la puerta del teatro.

2
1   No, los fines de semana suelen salir los dos.

3
1   Paloma no puede ir a las once porque tiene que estudiar.

4
1   Porque tiene unos amigos ingleses que están de vacaciones en España y quieren hacer un circuito por Andalucía.

5
1   Rosa practica teatro griego.
2   Porque los teatros son bastante caros.

UNIT 5

1
1   El negocio es de la familia del Sr Angulo desde hace tres generaciones.
2   Empezó a trabajar en el negocio porque su padre murió y él tuvo que ayudar a su familia.

2
1   No, no es el único. Tiene otros restaurantes en Méjico.
2   Le sorprendió a Julia ver los muñecos.

3
1   Porque tenía pintores en casa, y quería quitarse del jaleo.
2   Le dieron cinco puntos.

4
1   Isabel fue a Londres de muy pequeña, y volvió a España hace cuatro años y pico.
2   Los exiliados que se fueron a Londres eran intelectuales.

UNIT 6

1
1   Sí, trabajaba de cartero, y trabajaba también en la oficina en el Palacio de Comunicaciones.
2   Su profesión preferida es la de jubilado.

2
1   Antes Salud era portera.
2   Vivía en las guardillas.

3
1   Porque la puerta de la casa estaba cerrada.
2   Cuando sentía un toque de palmas acudía a abrir la puerta.

4
1   Julia trabajaba en una escuela de idiomas.
2   Trabajaba ocho horas al día.

5
1   La familia mantenía los lazos con España hablando español en casa, y también volvían a España todos los años.
2   En Inglaterra Isabel era una académica.

UNIT 7

1
1   Cuando era joven sus padres la llevaban al cine y desde entonces siempre le ha gustado mucho.

2
1   Isabel ha tenido que hacer unas entrevistas, y también salir fuera de Madrid algunas veces.
2   Hacer clases de 'aerobic' se ha puesto de moda también.

3
1   Estuvieron de vacaciones.

4
1   Antes había setos con verde, jardines, bancos y fuentes en la Plaza Mayor.

5
1   Los que no les gustan a Tere y al Sr Angulo son los parados, las mujeres de mala vida y los 'kinkis'.

UNIT 8
1

1   No, según ellos hay pocos españoles que destacan en el deporte a nivel mundial.

2

1   Sí, ahora el deporte está de moda, y se le da más importancia que antes.

3

1   No, no está satisfecha con el sistema educativo en España.

4

1   Ayuda a comprender el lenguaje actual y las raíces de muchas palabras españolas.

5

1   Sí, están de acuerdo.
2   Creen que ha destacado la actriz Ana Marzoa.

UNIT 9
1

1   Sí, las dos quieren seguir estudiando.
2   Mari Carmen quiere ser periodista.

2

1   Sí, las dos son optimistas respecto a su futuro profesional.
2   Son cinco años.

3

1   Después de jubilarse el Sr Angulo seguirá viviendo en Madrid, en el mismo barrio.

4

1   Nacerá en Londres.
2   Sí, Isabel va a volver al trabajo después del parto.

5

(no *Preguntas*)

UNIT 10
1

(no *Preguntas*)

2

1   Sí, Isidoro ha vuelto a utilizar la pierna, aunque tiene que andar con un bastón.

3

1   Jaime debe meterse en la cama, y tomar una leche caliente y una aspirina.

4

1   Al jugar al voleibol, uno puede hacerse daño en los tobillos, los dedos y las rodillas.
2   Para protegerse llevan tobilleras y rodilleras.

5

1   Se siente muy cansada y se mueve con menos agilidad.
2   Procura llevar una vida normal aunque tiene que descansar más.

CLAVE: PRÁCTICAS

UNIT 1

1 Encuentro

Your part of the conversation:

¿De dónde eres?

¿Dónde está Albacete?

Pero ahora vives en Madrid.

¿Cuánto tiempo llevas viviendo en Madrid?

or ¿Cuánto tiempo hace que vives en Madrid?

¿En qué trabajas? *or* ¿A qué te dedicas?

2 Los vecinos de calle Toledo 4

a   Ocho de las nueve personas entrevistadas por Isabel y Julia son españolas. Sergio, el propietario del restaurante *El Cuchi*, es mejicano.

b   El Sr Angulo, Antonio, Tere, Isidoro y Almudena son de Madrid, y también Ana se considera madrileña.

c   Tres de las mujeres están casadas: Mercedes, Ana y Tere.

d   Ana es de Extremadura.

e   La perra vive con Tere, Isidoro y Almudena.

f   Después de comer, Tere friega los cacharros, se pone a ver *Los Colbys*, y luego se sienta en su taller a coser.

3 ¿Dónde viven?

a   Mercedes vive debajo de Isabel.

b   Rosa vive enfrente de Jaime.

c   Mercedes vive encima de *El Cuchi*.

d   Ana vive debajo de Almudena.

e   Isidoro vive con Tere.

4 ¿Quién soy?

a – 4   b – 3   c – 6   d – 7   e – 1
f – 8   g – 2   h – 5

5 Así es mi vida

Yo *estoy* casada con Antonio. No *tenemos* (or *tengo*) hijos. Vivimos en una casa de la calle Toledo, que *está* en la parte antigua de Madrid. Los dos trabajamos en casa. Yo hago tapices, entonces *tengo* un taller textil. Y Antonio *es* fotógrafo. *Tiene* su estudio y su laboratorio también en casa. Nos gusta mucho esta casa, sin embargo *estamos* pensando en buscar otra, porque aquí *tenemos* muy poco espacio.

6 Arbol genealógico

On the family tree:

1   Loli González   2   María
3   Jorge Fernández   4   Dolores
5   Tomás   6   Montse Suárez
7   Marisa   8   Diego
9   Roberto

a   Dolores tiene dos hermanos. Es decir, tiene una hermana, María, y un hermano, Tomás.

b   El abuelo de Diego es Juan Gómez.

c   Los apellidos de Mercedes son Fernández Gómez.

7 ¿De dónde son?

a   Begoña es bilbaína.

b   Pilar es zaragozana.

c   Jordi es barcelonés.

d   Juan es valenciano.

e   Miguel es conquense.

f   Luz es salmantina.

g   Carmen es granadina.

h   Pepe es coruñés.

i   Ramón es malagueño.

UNIT 2

1   La ciudad de Madrid
Your part of the conversation:
Me encanta; es una ciudad hermosa.
Sí, es bastante grande. Tiene una población de casi cuatro millones.
Sí, algunas partes de la ciudad son muy antiguas y muy bonitas. Hay también muchas zonas modernas.
La parte más atractiva es la Plaza Mayor.

2   Descríbeme
Es alta y delgada. *Tiene* veinte años. El pelo lo *lleva* corto. *Es* morena con el pelo teñido de rubio. *Le* gusta llevar ropa elegante. *Le* encanta salir con los amigos. *Se lleva* muy bien con todos.

3   La familia Ramírez
a   más
b   menos
c   más
d   más
e   más
f   menos
g   más

4   La casa
Es una casa *vieja y alta* con *muchos* pisos. En el *primer* piso vive una familia de origen *gallego*. Son personas muy *amables* pero un poco *ruidosas*. En los *otros* pisos hay una *gran* variedad de gente: un matrimonio *joven*, una familia *aragonesa* con diez niños, un señor *silencioso* con dos perros *enormes*. En el *último* piso vive una pareja *anciana* y *solitaria*. A esta pareja le gusta poner unas plantas *preciosas* en las ventanas *grandes* de la casa.

5   Los Juegos Olímpicos
Ventajas:
París – accesible, bonita
Nueva York – bien organizada
El Cairo – exótica
Sydney – tranquila
Atenas – tradicional, folklórica
Río de Janeiro – barata

Desventajas:
París – carísima
Nueva York – ruidosa, congestionada
El Cairo – caliente
Sydney – lejana
Atenas – ineficaz
Río de Janeiro – húmeda, peligrosa

6   Mi familia y otros animales
Your part of the conversation:
No, sólo un perro.
No sé cómo se llama en español, pero en inglés es un 'spaniel'.
Sí, es verdad, pero es inglés.
Es bastante pequeño y tiene el pelo bastante largo y las orejas muy largas. Es muy inteligente.
Marrón.

UNIT 3

1   Hervir un huevo
The correct order of the sentences is:
d – f – c – e – g – j – h – a – i – b

2   Se puede . . .
a – 4   b – 3   c – 6   d – 1   e – 5   f – 2

3   Cambios
Mi marido *piensa* ir a ver un partido de fútbol. Yo no *quiero* ir porque me *siento* mal hoy. *Prefiero* quedarme en la cama y dormir. Si *duermo* todo el día, me *encuentro* mucho mejor. En los partidos hay mucho ruido, y se *tiene* que estar de pie. Después, siempre se *viene* muy cansado a casa con ganas de sentarse. Me gusta mucho el fútbol, pero hoy *me quedo* en casa.

4   Se hace así
Tienes (*or* Hay) que apretar el botón rojo.
Se puede aparcar delante del hotel.
Empieza a las ocho.
Usted baja (*or* Baje usted) por esta calle y gira (*or* gire) a la izquierda; está a mano derecha.
Fríes (*or* Se fríen) una cebolla y unas patatas, luego añades (*or* se añaden) los huevos.
No, tienes (*or* hay) que tomar el tren desde Cuzco y luego el autobús.

5 Habas a la catalana
Primero, fríes la cebolla y el tocino en la manteca con el ajo y las hierbas, después (or luego) añades las habas, la butifarra y los tomates. Añades sal, pimienta y un poco de azúcar, y luego lo dejas hervir todo a fuego lento durante al menos dos horas. Finalmente, añades el vino y el anís.

UNIT 4
1 Una invitación
¿Qué sueles hacer los fines de semana?
¿Te gustaría ir al cine conmigo este domingo?
Ponen *El Dorado*. ¿Te apetece verla?
A las siete, ¿te vendría bien? or ¿Te vendría bien a las siete?

2 Quedamos en eso
a 7.15 at the entrance to the underground station in the Puerta del Sol.
b 1.45 in the restaurant opposite the hotel.
c Sunday afternoon in the park.
d Tomorrow after work in the bar near the theatre.
e 8.30 outside the travel agency.

3 ¿Jugamos al tenis?
Yes, Wednesday at 1900.

4 Excursiones
a Any day except Monday.
b Yes.
c Toledo; Toledo – Escorial – Valle de los Caídos; Avila, Segovia y La Granja; or Cuenca.
d 7,800 pesetas.
e 15.30 (3.30 pm).
f Madrid (artística); Toledo; Escorial y Valle de los Caídos.

5 Obra de teatro
Pedro A mí me gustaría ir al teatro un día de éstos. ¿Sabes qué ponen ahora?
Luis Sí, me parece que ponen *Bodas de sangre*.
Pedro ¿Es de un autor famoso?
Luis ¡Hombre! *Es de Federico García Lorca*.
Pedro ¿Y dónde la ponen?
Luis En *el Teatro Lope*.
Pedro Bien, si te apetece ir, ¿en qué día quedamos?

Luis Sólo la ponen *el domingo*.
Pedro Vale. ¿A qué hora?
Luis *A las ocho y media de la tarde*.
Pedro Y las entradas, ¿hay qué sacarlas antes?
Luis Sí, porque *los números son limitados* (or *son números limitados*).
Pedro ¿Y cuánto cuestan?
Luis Mil quinientas pesetas.
Pedro Es mucho, pero ¡vamos!, ya es normal.

UNIT 5
1 ¿Verdad o mentira?
a Mentira.
b Verdad.
c Verdad.
d Mentira.
e Verdad.
f Verdad.
g Mentira.
h Verdad.

2 Testigo presencial
Yo *vi* un coche blanco acercarse desde la izquierda. De repente un coche azul *salió* de la callecita de enfrente. El conductor del primer coche *tuvo* que torcer violentamente para evitarlo y *acabó* en el otro lado de la calle, donde *chocó* con un árbol. El coche azul no *se paró*, al contrario *se fue* a toda prisa hacia el centro de la ciudad. Yo *corrí* hacia el coche blanco y les *ayudé* al conductor y a su compañera a salir.

3 Historia de España
a Los moros invadieron España en 711.
b Cristóbal Colón descubrió América en 1492.
c Felipe II mandó la Armada Invencible contra Inglaterra en 1588.
d Miguel de Cervantes, autor de *Don Quijote*, murió en 1616.
e La Guerra Civil española estalló en 1936 y terminó en 1939.
f Juan Carlos subió al trono en 1975.

4 Un encuentro
María Hola, Loli, ¿qué tal? ¿Qué hiciste ayer?
Loli Pues, ayer *fui al cine*.

María	¿Sí? Fuiste al cine. ¿Qué película viste?
Loli	*Vi* Bodas de sangre.
María	¿Y te gustó?
Loli	Sí, *me gustó* mucho.
María	¿A qué hora terminó la sesión?
Loli	*Terminó* a las once.
María	¿Volviste directamente después a casa, o tomaste algo por ahí?
Loli	Primero me *tomé* unas cañas con los amigos, y luego *volví* a casa.
María	Pues, me alegro, tengo que irme. ¡Hasta luego!
Loli	¡Hasta luego!

5 Una receta

Pues, compré la bebida y la fruta en el mercado. En casa primero *lavé* y luego *corté* la fruta. La *metí* en un recipiente grande, y *añadí* el vino. Después, *mezclé* todos los ingredientes y *eché* el coñac también. Finalmente *añadí* una cucharada de canela. *Dejé* la mezcla en la nevera durante doce horas. Por la noche *eché* la gaseosa. Es mejor servirla muy fría.

6 Tiempos pasados

ocurrió – ocurrir
me bajé – bajarse
arrollaron – arrollar
tiraron – tirar
pasó – pasar
recogieron – recoger
llevaron – llevar
pasó – pasar
tiraron – tirar
tuvieron – tener
bajamos – bajar
bajó – bajar
llevaron – llevar
tuvimos – tener
dieron – dar
dijeron – decir
se levantó – levantarse
pasó – pasar

UNIT 6

1 ¿Cómo pasabas los veranos?

Yo iba (*or* solía ir) a Gales con mis padres.
Pasábamos quince días en la montaña y luego una semana en la costa.
Me quedaba en casa.
Sí, jugaba (*or* solía jugar) al tenis con mis amigos, o a veces íbamos a la piscina.
No podíamos tomar el sol mucho; siempre llovía.

2 Cuando sonó el teléfono . . .

Yo cenaba (*or* estaba cenando).
1 Carlos veía (*or* estaba viendo) la televisión.
2 José Luis escribía (*or* estaba escribiendo) una carta.
3 Elvira dormía (*or* estaba durmiendo).
4 Rafael se duchaba (*or* se estaba duchando).
5 Luisa y Felipe jugaban (*or* estaban jugando) al ajedrez.
6 Teresa leía (*or* estaba leyendo) un libro.

3 Una carta

Muy Señor mío:
Me interesa el puesto que anunció su compañía en el periódico de este domingo. Me gustaría explicar mi experiencia profesional.
Durante dos años *trabajé* de secretaria para una editorial bien conocida. *Tenía* que escribir muchas cartas. También *traducía* muchos reportes del inglés al español. *Solicité* un puesto con más responsabilidad con la empresa, que me *dieron* los jefes en seguida. Mi nuevo cargo *consistía* en seleccionar los mejores libros que nosotros *íbamos* a publicar. *Dejé* este trabajo el año pasado para hacer un curso avanzado de informática. Ahora otra vez estoy buscando trabajo y su empresa me parece muy atractiva.
Le saluda muy atentamente,
Loli González

4 ¿Qué tal día?

a Era domingo.
b Hacía frío y llovía.

c Fueron a dar una vuelta.

d Hablaron sobre el trabajo y el fútbol.

e El vecino vino para hablar con ellos (*or* para decirles que su hija tenía un trabajo nuevo).

f No, no comió, sólo tomó un café.

g Porque su hija tenía un trabajo nuevo.

5 ¿Qué tiene?

1 Tiene sed. (*also* Tiene calor.)

2 Tienen miedo.

3 Tiene calor.

4 Tiene cinco años.

5 Tiene sueño.

6 Tienen hambre.

UNIT 7

1 En la Aduana

Vengo de Londres.

No, no he estado aquí nunca. (*or* No, nunca he estado aquí antes.)

Sí, he recogido mis tres maletas.

Nada, estoy aquí de vacaciones.

2 Preparaciones para un viaje

a – 2   b – 3   c – 5   d – 6   e – 1   f – 4

3 ¿Qué has hecho esta semana?

He comido con el tío Ramón, he visitado al médico, he hecho las compras en el supermercado, he ido a la piscina, he arreglado el coche, he jugado al fútbol, y he asistido a un concierto.

4 En busca de trabajo

Tiene diecisiete años. Ha tenido mucha experiencia con los niños. Ha sido (*or* Ha hecho de) canguro para sus hermanos pequeños. Ha pasado tres veranos en Escocia con una familia con muchos niños. Ha aprobado los exámenes. Trabaja los sábados en un bar y ayuda en la casa. Su familia es simpática y buena gente.

5 Recuerdos

Siempre me *ha gustado* viajar al extranjero. *He estado* varias veces en España, en Portugal y en Grecia, pero no *he estado* nunca fuera de Europa. El año pasado *pasé* quince días en un pequeño pueblo en Andalucía, que me *encantó*. El pueblo *era* muy tranquilo, *había* muy pocos turistas. Yo *pasaba* (*or pasé*) los días dando paseos por el campo. Después de comer, como *hacía* mucho calor, *solía* dormir la siesta. Por la tarde *tomaba* unos finos y unas tapas y *charlaba* con la gente en el bar. *Fueron* unas vacaciones estupendas. Ultimamente *he tenido* que trabajar mucho y *he estado* (*or estoy*) pensando en volver a España en busca de la tranquilidad.

UNIT 8

1 ¿Qué te parece nuestro país?

Pienso (*or* Creo) que España es un país maravilloso, me gusta muchísimo. Y para mí, Madrid es una ciudad muy hermosa y muy interesante.

Quizá(s), pero hay muchos teatros y cines en Madrid, y además me encanta toda la zona de la Plaza Mayor.

Sí, el año pasado fui en tren desde Bilbao a Granada. En mi opinión, es el único modo de ver el país.

2 Reacciones

a – 4   b – 6   c – 2   d – 5   e – 1   f – 3

3 Discusiones

a, c, d, e, g – agreeing

b, f, h – disagreeing

4 Problemas

Al principio nos gustó el hotel *pero* entonces empezaron los problemas. *Por un lado* el director dimitió, y *por otro lado* los otros clientes hacían mucho ruido. Era insoportable. Cuando nos quejamos, el nuevo director nos prometió cambios. *Sin embargo* el ruido y la ineficacia seguían. *Al final* nos marchamos hartos sin pagar los últimos días de nuestra estancia.

5 En su opinión

a Verdad.

b Mentira.

c Mentira.

d Verdad.

e Verdad.

f Mentira.

UNIT 9
1 Proyectos
Pienso vivir en España durante algunos (*or* unos) años.

Sí, mi compañía va a enviarme (*or* mandarme) a Madrid.

Vendo ordenadores. Tendré una oficina en Madrid, pero tendré que viajar por toda España.

No estoy seguro/a. Preferiría vivir fuera de Madrid, pero lo decidiré cuando llegue allí.

2 El tiempo
a – 3   b – 6   c – 5   d – 1   e – 2   f – 4

3 ¿Qué vas a hacer cuando venga tu amigo español?
Querido Miguel:

Cuando *llegues*, yo *estaré* en al aeropuerto. Te *podré* llevar a casa en seguida, o podremos dar un paseo por la ciudad. *Pienso* presentarte a mis amigos, e *iremos* todos juntos a ver un partido de fútbol. Y luego, si te *gusta* la cerveza, te *invitaré* yo a tomar algo en un típico pub inglés.

¡Hasta pronto!

Un abrazo

4 Cuando les toque la lotería . . .
a – 4   b – 2   c – 5   d – 1   e – 6   f – 3

5 Ambiciones
a – 3   b – 5   c – 1   d – 6   e – 2   f – 4

UNIT 10
1 ¡Qué mal genio!
No me siento bien. Me duele la cabeza.

No, no bebí mucho. Pero estoy muy cansado/a.

Porque me duelen los ojos. ¿Tienes aspirinas?

Gracias. Tendré que acostarme muy temprano esta noche.

2 ¿Qué le pasa?
a – 6   b – 1   c – 4   d – 5   e – 2   f – 3

3 ¿Qué remedio?
a – 2   b – 3   c – 1   d – 4   e – 6   f – 5

4 ¿Te gusta?
a   me
b   Te
c   se
d   le
e   le
f   las

5 Vestidos protectores
a – 3   b – 5   c – 2   d – 6   e – 1   f – 4

6 ¿Quién? ¿Cómo? ¿Dónde?
a   Tere.
b   José.
c   En Madrid.
d   En el Teatro Español.
e   Bahía Blanca.
f   *Fernández Angulo SA*.
g   En la Isle of Wight.
h   COU.

VOCABULARIO

Notes

1 The English translations apply to the words as they are used in this book.

2 Words or usages that don't apply to Spain are followed by (*LA*) – Latin America, (*CA*) – Central America, (*Mex*) – Mexico, and so on.

3 Adjectives which have different endings for masculine and feminine are shown thus: **bueno/a.**

4 Verbs: regular verbs follow the patterns shown on page 152. Irregular verbs are marked * (see page 152); those followed by **(i), (ie)** or **(ue)** are radical-changing verbs (see page 151). Verbs followed by **(zc)** are irregular in the 1st person singular, e.g. **conocer – (yo) conozco.**

5 Remember that **ch, ll,** and **ñ** are separate letters in the Spanish alphabet, following **c, l** and **n** respectively.

6 Abbreviations: *adj* – adjective, *f* – feminine, *inf* – infinitive, *m* – masculine, *pl* – plural, *pp* – past participle (see page 149).

A

a   *to; at*
abajo   *down below*
abandonar   *to abandon*
el abandono   *abandonment*
abarcar   *to cover, include*
abastecer (zc)   *to supply*
el abasto   *supply*
la abogada, el abogado   *lawyer*
el aborto   *abortion*
un abrazo   *all the best, regards*
abril (*m*)   *April*
abrir (*pp* abierto)   *to open*
absoluto/a   *absolute*
la abuela   *grandmother*
el abuelo   *grandfather*   los abuelos   *grandparents*
el abuso   *abuse*
acá   *here*
acabar   *to finish, to end up*   acabar de + *inf*
   to have just

académico/a   *academic*
accesible   *accessible*
el acceso   *access*
la acción   *action*
el aceite   *oil*
el acento   *accent*
acentuado/a   *accentuated*
aceptado/a   *accepted*
aceptar   *to accept*
acercarse a   *to approach, come up to*
acordarse (ue) de   *to remember*
acorralado/a   *cornered*
acostarse (ue)   *to go to bed*
acostumbrado/a (a)   *used to*
acostumbrarse (a)   *to get used to*
acrecentar   *to increase*
la actitud   *attitude*
la actividad   *activity*
activo/a   *active*
el acto   *event*   acto electoral   *voting*
el actor   *actor*
la actriz   *actress*
la actuación   *acting*
actual   *present, present-day*
la actualidad   *the present*
actualmente   *at present, at the moment*
la acuarela   *watercolour*
acudir a   *to come (to), answer*
el acuerdo   *agreement*   de acuerdo   *agreed, fine*   estar de acuerdo   *to agree*
adelantar   *to (make) progress*
adelante   *forward*
además   *besides, also, what's more*   además de   *besides*
adiós   *goodbye*
administrar   *to administer*
administrativo/a   *administrative*
el adobe   *adobe, sun-dried brick*
el adoquín   *paving-stone*
adornar   *to decorate*

adquirir *to acquire*
adquisitivo: el poder adquisitivo
  purchasing power
el adulto *adult*
la aeróbica *aerobics*
el aeropuerto *airport*
el afán *desire, urge*
afectar *to affect*
la afición *liking, interest*
el aficionado *fan, enthusiast*
aficionado/a a *keen on*
afirmativo/a *positive*
afuera *outside*
las afueras *outskirts*
la agencia *agency*
la agilidad *agility*
agradable *pleasant*
agregar *to add*
agresivo/a *aggressive*
agruparse *to get together*
el agua (*f*) *water*
el águila (*f*) *eagle*
ahí *there*
ahora *now*   ahora mismo *right now*
ahorita (*LA*) *right now*
el ahorro *saving*
aislado/a *isolated*
el aislamiento *isolation*
aislarse *to cut oneself off*
ajustarse *to adjust/adapt oneself*
el ajuste *adjustment*
al = a + el
el albañil *bricklayer, mason*
el alcance *reach, span*
el alcohol *alcohol*
alemán/ana *German*
el alfabeto *alphabet*
algo *something, anything; a bit, rather*
el algodón *cotton*
alguno/a (algún) *some, any*
la alimentación *food*
el alma (*f*) *soul*
almorzar (ue) *to have lunch*
la alpargatería *shoe shop*
alrededor (*all*) *around*   alrededor de *around,*
  about
alterarse *to alter, to change*
alto/a *high, tall*
la altura *height*
la alumna, el alumno *pupil, student*

allá *there, over there*
allí *there*
el ama (*f*) de casa *housewife*
amable *nice, friendly*
amarillo/a *yellow*
ambiente: el medio ambiente *environment*
el ambiente *atmosphere; field, business*
ambos/as *both*
la ambulancia *ambulance*
ambulante: el vendedor ambulante *pedlar*
el ambulatorio *health clinic*
América Latina (*f*) *Latin America*
la amiga, el amigo *friend*
la amistad *friendship*
el amor *love*
la ampliación *expansion, enlargement*
ampliar *to increase*
amplio/a *extensive*
anciano/a *old, elderly*
ancho/a *wide*
andaluz/uza *Andalucian*
andar *to walk, to go*
el animal *animal*
el anís *anis, aniseed liqueur*
anónima: la sociedad anónima *limited company*
anterior *previous*
antes (de) *before*
la anticipación *anticipation*
el anticonceptivo *contraceptive*
antiguamente *in the old days*
antiguo/a *old*
el antojo *whim, craving*
anunciar *to announce, advertise*
añadir *to add*
el año *year*   tener ... años *to be ... years old*
el aparador (*LA*) *showcase*
aparcar *to park*
aparecer (zc) *to appear*
aparte de *apart from*
apellidarse *to be called (surname)*
el apellido *surname*
el aperitivo *aperitive*
apetecer: ¿te apetece ...? *do you fancy...?*
apetecible *appealing*
aplastante *overwhelming*
apoyado/a en *leaning on*
apoyar *to support*
el apoyo *support*
la apreciación *estimation*
apreciar *to appreciate, to notice*

aprender *to learn*
apretar (ie) *to press*
aprobar (ue) *to pass*
aproximadamente *approximately*
aquello/a (aquel) *that*
aquí *here*
árabe *Arab(ic)*
aragonés/esa *Aragonese*
el árbol *tree*
arbolado/a *tree-lined*
el área (*f*) *area*
arengar *to harangue, shout at*
Argelia (*f*) *Algeria*
argentino/a *Argentinian*
el argot *slang*
el argumento *plot*
el arma (*f*) *weapon*
la arquitecta, el arquitecto *architect*
arreglar *to fix*
el arreglo *arrangement*
arriba *above*
arrollar *to knock down*
el arte (*m*) *art*   las artes (*fpl*) *the arts*
artesanal *craft*
el artesano *craftsman*
la articulación *articulation; joint*
el artículo *article*
el artista *artist*
artístico/a *artistic*
la ascendencia *descent, origin*
así *so, in that way, like that*   así como *in the
    same way as*   así que *so that*   o así *or
    so*   y así sucesivamente *and so on*
la asignatura *subject, course*
la asistencia *assistance*
asistir *to attend*
la asociación *association*
asociado/a *associated*
asociar *to associate*
el aspecto *aspect*
aspirar *to aspire, hope*
la aspirina *aspirin*
asustado/a *scared, alarmed*
atacar *to attack*
Atenas *Athens*
la atención *attention*
atento/a *aware*
el atletismo *athletics*
la atmosfera *atmosphere*
la atracción *attraction*

atractivo/a *attractive*
atraer* (*like* traer) *to attract*
atrás *behind*
el auge *success, boom*
aumentar *to increase*
el aumento *increase*
aun *even*   más aun *even more*
aún *still, yet*
aunque *although*
austriaco/a *Austrian*
auténtico/a *authentic*
la autoayuda *self-help*
el autobús *bus*
el automático *entrance phone*
autónomo/a *autonomous*
el autor *author*
la autoridad *authority*
avanzado/a *advanced*
avanzar *to advance, make progress; to put forward*
el aviador *pilot*
el avión *aeroplane*
avisar *to tell, let someone know*
ayer *yesterday*
la ayuda *help*
ayudar *to help*
el azúcar *sugar*
azul *blue*

B

el bacon *bacon*
el bachillerato *school-leaving examination*
bailar *to dance*
la bailarina *dancer*
el baile *dance*
la baja por maternidad *maternity leave*
bajar *to come down, go down; to take down*
bajo *under*
bajo/a *low; short*
el balance *balance*
los Balcanes *Balkans*
el balón *ball*
el baloncesto *basketball*
el banco *bench, seat; bank*
el banderín *banner*
el bar *bar*
barato/a *cheap*
la barba *beard*
bárbaro/a *terrific, amazing*
barcelonés/esa *of/from Barcelona*

el barco *boat, ship*
la barra *bar*
el barrio *neighbourhood, district*
basado/a *based*
básicamente *basically*
básico/a *basic*
bastante *enough; quite a lot (of); quite, fairly, rather*
bastar *to be enough*
el bastón *(walking) stick*
el bebé *baby*
beber *to drink*
la bebida *drink*
la belleza *beauty, lovely thing*
el beneficio *benefit*
el biberón *(baby's) bottle*
la bicicleta *bicycle*
bicultural *bicultural*
bien *well; very* muy bien *very well, fine*
   más bien *rather* o bien … o bien
   either … or else
el bigote *moustache*
bilingüe *bilingual*
la bioquímica *biochemistry; biochemist*
el bisabuelo *great-grandfather*
blanco/a *white*
la boca *mouth*
el boceto *sketch*
el boleto *(LA) ticket*
el bombero *firefighter*
bonito/a *pretty, good-looking*
borrar *erase*
la botella *bottle*
la brecha *gash*
británico/a *British*
buenmozo *good-looking man*
bueno *well; right, OK*
bueno/a (buen) *good*
el bus *(LA) bus*
busca: en busca de *in search of*
buscar *to look for*
la butaca *stalls seat*
la butifarra *Catalan sausage*

C

el caballero *knight*
caber *to fit in, to be room for* no cabe
   duda *there's no doubt*
la cabeza *head*
la cacerola *saucepan*

los cacharros *pots and pans*
cada *each, every*
la cadera *hip*
caerse *to fall down*
el café *coffee*
el caite (*CA*) *rough leather sandal*
la caja postal (de ahorros) *post office savings bank*
el calado *draught*
calcular *to calculate*
la calidad *quality*
caliente *hot*
calificar *to label*
calor: hace calor *it's hot (weather)*
callado/a *silent*
la calle *street*
la cama *bed*
el camarero *waiter*
cambiar *to change*
cambiarse *to change round; to change (one's clothes)*
el cambio *change; exchange* en cambio *on the other hand*
el cambista *moneychanger*
el camino *path, road*
la campaña *campaign*
el campeonato *championship*
el campo *countryside; field, area*
camuflado/a *camouflaged*
el canal *canal*
la canción *song*
la canço (*Catalan word*) *song*
la canela *cinnamon*
cansado/a *tired*
cansarse *to get tired*
el/la cantante *singer*
el cantaor *flamenco singer*
cantar *to sing*
la cantidad *amount, number*
el canto *singing*
cantonés/esa *Cantonese*
la caña *glass of beer*
la capa *level, stratum*
la capacidad *capacity*
la capital *capital*
la cara *face* tener mala cara *to look ill*
el carácter *character*
la característica *characteristic; (LA) dialling code*
característico/a *characteristic*
caracterizar *to characterise*
¡caramba! *good heavens!*

la carga *charge*
cargar con *to lift, pick up*
el cargo *position, duty*
un cariño *love from …, best wishes*
cariñoso/a *affectionate*
el carnaval *carnival*
caro/a *expensive*
la carpeta *file*
la carrera *career, profession; (university) course*
la carretera *(main) road*
la carroza *float, cart*
la carta *letter; menu*
el cartero *postman*
la casa *house, home* en casa *at home*
casado/a *married*
casarse *to get married*
la casca *skin*
la cáscara *shell*
el caserón *large house*
casi *almost, nearly*
el caso *case; instance*
castellano/a *Castilian*
castellanoparlante *Castilian-speaking*
el castillo *castle*
castizo/a *authentic, pure, typical*
catalán/ana *Catalan*
la catedral *cathedral*
la categoría *standing, rank*
católico/a *Catholic*
catorce *fourteen*
el Caudillo *leader (title given to Franco)*
la cebolla *onion*
el ceceo *pronunciation of c and z as 'th'*
ceder *to relax, yield*
celebrar *to celebrate*
celebrarse *to take place, be celebrated*
cenar *to have dinner*
la censura *censorship*
el centímetro *centimetre*
el centralismo *centralism*
céntrico/a *central*
el centro *centre, middle*
centroamericano/a *Central American*
cerca (de) *near (to), close (to)*
cercano/a *nearby*
el cerdo *pork*
los cereales *cereals*
la ceremonia *ceremony*
cero *zero*
cerrar (ie) *to close, to close down*

la cervecería *bar, pub*
el ciclismo *cycling*
el ciclista *cyclist*
el ciclo *course*
cien, ciento *a hundred* por ciento *per cent*
las ciencias empresariales *business studies*
cierto/a *certain; some* ¿no es cierto? *right?*
la cifra *figure*
cinco *five*
cincuenta *fifty*
el cine *cinema*
el cinturón *belt*
el circuito *tour*
la circulación *traffic*
la circunstancia *circumstance*
el cirujano *surgeon*
citar *to mention, cite*
la ciudad *city, town*
el ciudadano *citizen*
civil *civil*
claro *of course*
claro/a *clear; light*
la clase *class, lesson* dar clases *to teach*
clásico/a *classical*
la clasificación *classification*
la claustrofobia *claustrophobia*
la clave *key*
la clienta, el cliente *client, customer*
el clima *climate*
la clínica *clinic*
el club *club*
la cobertura *covering*
cobrar *to collect (money)*
el coche *car*
coexistir *to co-exist*
cola: hacer cola *to queue up*
la colección *collection*
colectivo/a *collective*
el colegio *(high) school*
colgar (ue) *to hang (up)*
la colmena *beehive*
colocado/a *located*
la colonia *colony*
el color *colour*
combinar *to combine*
la comedia *comedy*
comentar *to comment on, discuss*
comenzar (ie) *to begin*
comer *to eat, to have lunch*
comercial *commercial*

la comida   *food; meal; lunch, dinner*
como   *like, as, such as*
¿cómo?   *how?, why?*
cómodo/a   *comfortable, agreeable*
el compadre   *friend*
compaginar   *to combine*
la compañera, el compañero   *colleague*
la compañía   *company*
comparar   *to compare*
compartir   *to share*
la competencia   *competition*
competir (i)   *to compete*
competitivo/a   *competitive*
la complacencia   *pleasing, liking*
complacer: ¿te complace ...?   *do you like ...?*
el complejo   *complex*
completamente   *completely*
completar   *to complete*
completo/a   *complete, full*
el comportamiento   *behaviour*
el compositor   *composer*
la(s) compra(s)   *shopping*
comprar   *to buy*
comprender   *to understand*
la comprensión   *understanding*
el compromiso   *promise*
la computación   *computing*
común   *common*
la comunicación   *communication*
la comunidad   *community; (LA) village*   la
   comunidad de vecinos   *residents' association*
   las comunidades autónomas   *autonomous
   communities (regional authorities)*
comunista   *communist*
con   *with*
concentrado/a   *concentrated*
conciencia: tomar conciencia de   *to become aware
   of*
la concienciación   *awareness*
concretamente   *precisely; specifically, to be exact*
concurrir   *to gather*
el concurso   *competition*
la condición   *condition*
el conductor   *driver*
confesar (ie)   *to confess*
la confianza   *confidence*
la configuración   *configuration*
confirmar   *to confirm*
conformarse con   *to be happy with*
confundir   *to confuse*

la congestión   *congestion*
congestionado/a   *congested*
conjuntamente   *jointly*
el conjunto   *group*   en conjunto   *all in all*
conocer (zc)   *to know, to get to know*
conocido/a   *known, well-known*
los conocimientos   *knowledge*
conseguir (i)   *to obtain; to make, bring about*
el consejo   *advice*
conservar   *to preserve*
conservarse   *to survive, still exist*
considerar   *to consider*
consistir en   *to consist*
constar de   *to consist of*
la constitución   *constitution*
la construcción   *construction, building*
construir   *to construct, build*
el consumo   *consumption*
el contacto   *contact*
la contaminación   *pollution*
contar (ue)   *to tell, explain*   contar con   *to count
   on, have*
contestar   *to answer*
el contexto   *context*
contigo   *with you*
la continuación   *continuation*
continuar   *to continue, go on*
contra, en contra de   *against*
contrario: al contrario   *on the contrary*
el contraste   *contrast*
contratar   *to contract*
el contratista   *contractor*
el contrato   *contract*
contribuir   *to contribute*
el control   *control, check*
controversial   *controversial*
la conversación   *conversation*
conversar   *to talk*
convertirse (ie)   *to become, be changed (into)*
el coñac   *brandy*
la copa   *cup; glass*   tomar una copa   *to have a drink*
la corona   *crown*
el coronel   *colonel*
correcto/a   *correct; all right*
corregir (i)   *to correct*
Correos   *Post Office*
correr   *to run*
corresponder   *to apply to, to rest with*
la corrida   *bullfight*
corriente   *common*

cortar   *to cut*
el corte   *court*
las Cortes   *Spanish parliament*
corto/a   *short*
la cosa   *thing; something*   cosa de   *something like, about*
coser   *to sew*
costar (ue)   *to cost*
el cristal   *glass*
la Cruz Roja   *Red Cross*
cuadrado/a   *square*
el cuadro   *picture*
cual: lo/la cual, los/las cuales   *which, whom*
¿cuál?, ¿cuáles?   *what?, which?*
cualquier/iera   *any*
cuando   *when*
¿cuándo?   *when?*
cuanto: en cuanto   *as*   en cuanto a   *as for, as regards*
¿cuánto/a?   *how much?*
¿cuántos/as?   *how many?*
cuarenta   *forty*
el cuarto   *quarter*   menos cuarto   *a quarter to*   y cuarto   *a quarter past*
el cuarto de baño   *bathroom*
cuarto/a   *fourth*
cuatro   *four*
cubierto/a   *overcast*   a cubierto   *undercover*
cubrir (*pp* cubierto)   *to cover*
la cucharada   *spoonful*
la cuenta   *bill, account*   darse cuenta   *to realise*   tener en cuenta   *to bear in mind*
el cuento   *short story*
el cuerpo   *body*
la cuestión   *question, matter*
el cuidado   *care*   ¡cuidado!   *watch out!*
cuidar   *to look after*
cuidarse   *to take care, to look after oneself*
cultivar   *to cultivate*
la cultura   *culture*
cultural   *cultural*
el culturismo   *body-building*
la cumbre   *height*
cumplir   *to fulfil*
la cuota   *quota*
curarse   *to heal up*
curioso/a   *odd, strange*
cursi   *vulgar, tacky*
el curso   *course*
cuyo/a   *whose*

CH

la chabola   *slum*
el chalet   (*detached*) *house*
la chamba (*Mex*)   *work*
el chándal   *tracksuit*
la chica   *girl*
el chico   *boy*
chico/a   *small, young*
chileno/a   *Chilean*
chino/a   *Chinese;* (*Arg*) *funny, sweet*
el chiscón   *cubby-hole*
chocar con   *to crash into*
el chocolate   *chocolate*
el chofer (*LA*)   *driver*
el chorizo   *spicy sausage*
chorrear   *to stream, gush*
el chubasco   *shower*

D

la dama   *lady*
daño: hacer(se) daño   *to hurt* (*oneself*)
dar*   *to give*
de   *of; from*
debajo de   *underneath, below*
deber   *to owe, to have to*
el deber   *duty*
el debut   *opening, beginning*
la década   *decade*
decidir   *to decide*
decir (i)* (*pp* dicho)   *to say, to tell*
   digamos   *let's say*   es decir   *in other words*
   querer decir   *to mean*
decisivo/a   *decisive*
declarar   *to declare*
dedicado/a   *devoted, dedicated*
dedicarse (a)   *to work* (*as*); *to take up*
el dedo   *finger; toe*
defenderse (ie)   *to defend oneself*
dejar   *to allow, to let; to leave*
del = de + el
delante (de)   *in front of, before*
la delegada   *delegate*
delgado/a   *slim, thin*
la delicia   *delight*
la delincuencia   *delinquency*
demás   *other, rest*
demasiado   *too*
demasiado/a   *too much*

demasiados/as *too many*
la democracia *democracy*
democrático/a *democratic*
denso/a *dense*
dentro (de) *in, inside*
depender (de) *to depend (on), to belong (to)*
el deporte *sport*
el/la deportista *sportsman, sportswoman*
deportivo/a *sporting*
la derecha *right*
el derecho *right; law*
el desafío *challenge*
desamparado/a *helpless, abandoned*
desaparecer (zc) *to disappear*
desarrollarse *to develop*
el desayuno *breakfast*
descansar *to rest*
el descendiente *descendant*
desconocido/a *unknown*
describir (*pp* descrito) *to describe*
el descubrimiento *discovery*
descubrir (*pp* descubierto) *to discover*
desde *from, since; upwards of*   desde luego *of course*
desear *to want*
desempeñar *to perform, carry out*
el deseo *wish*
desgraciadamente *unfortunately*
designado/a *designated*
después *after(wards)*   después de *after*
destacar *to stand out*
destinado/a *destined*
la desventaja *disadvantage*
el detalle *detail*
detectar *to detect*
deteriorarse *to deteriorate*
la determinación *determination*
determinado/a *particular*
detrás (de) *behind*
el día *day*   de día *in the daytime*   buenos días *good morning*
diario/a *daily*
el diccionario *dictionary*
la dictadura *dictatorship*
dicho: mejor dicho *rather*
dieciocho *eighteen*
el diente *tooth*
la dieta *diet*
diez *ten*
la diferencia *difference*

la diferenciación *differentiation*
diferenciarse *to be different*
diferente *different*
difícil *difficult*
digamos (*see* decir)
la dimensión *dimension, size*
dimitir *to resign*
la dinámica *dynamics, energy*
el dinero *money*
Dios *God*   gracias a Dios *thank God*
diplomático/a *diplomatic*
el diputado *member of Parliament*
directamente *directly, straight*
el directivo *executive*
directivo/a *executive*
directo/a *direct*
el director, la directora *director, manager(ess)*
el dirigente *leader, organiser*
dirigir *to direct*
dirigirse (a) *to go towards*
el disco *record*
la discoteca *discothèque*
la discusión *discussion*
la diseñadora *designer*
el diseño *design*
el disfraz *fancy dress*
disfrutar de *to enjoy*
el disgusto *annoyance, displeasure*
disímil (*LA*) *dissimilar*
el diskette *diskette, floppy disk*
disputarse *to fight over*
la distancia *distance*
distinguir *to distinguish, tell apart*
distintamente *differently*
distinto/a *different, various*
distribuido/a *distributed*
diverso/a *different, various*
divertido/a *enjoyable*
divertirse (ie) *to enjoy oneself*
divorciado/a *divorced*
el divorcio *divorce*
doblar *to turn*
doble *double*
doce *twelve*
el/la docente *teacher*
el doctor, la doctora *doctor*
el documento *document*
el dólar *dollar*
doler (ue) *to hurt*
el dolor *pain*   el dolor de cabeza *headache*

doméstico/a *domestic*
el domicilio *home*
la dominación *domination*
dominante *dominant*
domingo (*m*) *Sunday*
dominical (*of*) *Sunday*
donde *where*
¿dónde? *where?*
dormir (ue) *to sleep*
dos *two*
dramático/a *dramatic*
la droga *drug*
la duda *doubt*   sin duda *undoubtedly*
dudar *to doubt, hesitate*
el dueño *owner*
dulce *sweet*
los dulces *sweets*
duplicado/a *duplicated*
durante *during, for*
durar *to last*
duro/a *hard*

# E
e = y
económicamente *economically, financially*
económico/a *economic*
la edad *age*   ¿qué edad tiene …? *how old is …?*
la edificación *building (work)*
el edificio *building*
la editorial *publisher*
la educación *education*
educado/a *polite, civilised*
el educador, la educadora *teacher*
educar *to educate, bring up*
educativo/a *education(al)*
efectivamente *exactly*
el ejecutivo *executive*
el ejemplo *example*   por ejemplo *for example*
ejercer *to practise, perform*
el ejercicio *exercise*
el *the*   el que *the one*
él *he*
la elección *election*
electoral *electoral, voting*
elegante *elegant*
elegir (i) *to choose*
el elemento *element*
elevar *to raise*
la elite *elite*

ella *she; her*
ellas *they; them*
ello *it*
ellos *they; them*
la embajada *embassy*
embarazada *pregnant*
el embarazo *pregnancy*
embargo: sin embargo *however, nevertheless*
el emigrante *emigrant*
emitir *to produce*
emocionante *exciting*
empeorar *to get worse*
el emperador *emperor*
empezar (ie) *to begin*
el empleo *job*
la empresa *company, firm*
empujar *to drive, push*
en *in, into; on; at*
encantar *to delight*   me encanta … *I love …*
encargarse de *to see to, to take care of*
encender (ie) *to switch on*
encima de *above*
encontrar (ue) *to find*
encontrarse (ue) *to be, to be found, to be situated; to feel*
el encuentro *meeting, encounter*
enérgico/a *energetic*
enero (*m*) *January*
el énfasis *emphasis, stress*
la enfermera *nurse*
enfocar *to focus*
enfrentarse con *to face*
enfrente (de) *opposite*
engañar(se) *to deceive (oneself)*
englobar *to include, cover*
enojado/a *angry, annoyed*
enorme *huge*
enriquecer (zc) *to enrich*
ensayar *to rehearse*
la enseñanza *teaching*   la enseñanza media *secondary education*
enseñar *to show; to teach*
entender (ie) *to understand; to realise*
enterarse *to discover, find out*
entero/a *whole*
entonces *then; next*
la entrada *entrance; ticket*
entrar *to enter, go in, come in*
entre *between*
entregar *to hand over, give*

entretener (ie) *to entertain*
la entrevista *interview*
entrevistar *to interview*
entusiasmarse por *to be keen on, rave about*
el entusiasmo *enthusiasm*
entusiasta *enthusiastic*
el/la entusiasta *enthusiast*
enunciar *to enunciate*
enviar *to send*
envidia: tener envidia a *to envy*
la época *period, time*
el equipaje *luggage*
el equipo *team*
equivalente *equivalent*
equivocarse *to be wrong*
la escalera *staircase*
el escalón *stair, step*
el escaparate *shop window, showcase*
la escasez *scarcity*
escaso/a de *poor in, short of*
la escena *scene*
la escenografía *scenery, set design*
la esclusa *lock*
Escocia (f) *Scotland*
escoger *to choose*
escogido/a *chosen*
escolar *(of) school, education*
escribir (pp escrito) *to write*
escrito/a *written*
el escritor, la escritora *writer*
escuchar *to listen (to)*
el escudo *coat of arms, shield*
la escuela *school*
la escultura *sculpture, carving*
ese/a *that*
ése/a *that (one)*
esforzarse (ue) en *to make an effort to*
el esfuerzo *effort*
el esguince *sprain*
eso *that*   por eso *that's why*
el espacio *space, room*
los espaguetis *spaghetti*
España (f) *Spain*
español/ola *Spanish*
especial *special*
la especialidad *speciality*
especializado/a *specialised*
especialmente *specially*
específico/a *specific*
el espéctaculo *show, spectacle*

la espera *wait, waiting*
esperar *to hope (for); to wait (for)*
el espíritu *spirit*
el esquema *diagram, sketch*
establecerse (zc) *to set oneself up, to establish oneself*
la estación *station*
la estadística *figure, statistic*
el estado *state*
Estados Unidos (mpl) *United States*
estallar *to break out*
la estancia *stay*
estar* *to be*
estatal *state*
estático/a *static*
este (LA) *um, er, well*
este/a *this*
éste/a *this (one)*
la estela *stela, carved stone*
estimarse *to be estimated*
esto *this*
el estómago *stomach*
estos/as *these*
éstos/as *these (ones)*
el estrato *(social) stratum, level*
estrechar *to tighten*
estrecho/a *narrow*
la estrella *star*
el estrés *stress*
estricto/a *strict, severe*
el/la estudiante *student*
estudiar *to study*
el estudio *studio*
los estudios *studies, research*
estupendo/a *great, marvellous*
la etapa *stage*
etcétera *etcetera*
Europa (f) *Europe*
europeo/a *European*
Euskadi *Euskadi, Basque Country*
el euskera *Basque language*
evitar *to avoid*
la evolución *evolution*
exactamente *exactly, precisely*
el examen *examination*
la excavación *excavation*
excluir *to exclude*
exclusivamente *exclusively*
la excursión *excursion*
exigente *demanding, exacting*

el exiliado   *exile*
el exilio   *exile*
existir   *to exist*
el éxito   *success*
exótico/a   *exotic*
la expansión   *expansion*
expatriado/a   *taken out of the country*
la experiencia   *experience*
experimental   *experimental*
experimentar   *to undergo; to experiment*
la explicación   *explanation*
explicar   *to explain*
explorar   *to explore*
exponer* (*like* poner)   *to exhibit*
la exposición   *exhibition*
expresar   *to express*
la expresión   *expression*
extenderse   *to extend* (*oneself*)
extenso/a   *extensive*
extranjero: el extranjero   *abroad*
extranjero/a   *foreign*
extraño/a   *strange; outside*
extraordinario/a   *extraordinary*
extraordinariamente   *extraordinarily*
extremadamente   *extremely*
extremeño/a   *of/from Extremadura*
el extremo   *extreme*
extremo/a   *extreme*

F

la fábrica   *factory*
fabuloso/a   *great, wonderful*
fácil   *easy*
la facilidad   *facility*
fácilmente   *easily*
la faena   *chore*
falso/a   *false, counterfeit*
la falta   *lack*   hace falta   *it is necessary*
faltar   *to be lacking*
la familia   *family*
famoso/a   *famous*
fanático/a   *fanatic*
fantástico/a   *fantastic*
la farmacia   *chemist*
la farolita   *small* (*street*) *light*
la fase   *phase, stage*
fastidiarse   *to hurt* (*oneself*)
favor: por favor   *please*
febrero (*m*)   *February*

la fecha   *date*
felino/a   *feline, catlike*
feliz   *happy*
femenino/a   *feminine*
feminista   *feminist*
el fenómeno   *phenomenon*
feo/a   *ugly*
la feria   *fair*
el festejo   *celebration*
la fiebre   *fever*   tener fiebre   *to have a temperature*
fiel   *faithful*
la fiesta   *fiesta, festival*
figurar   *to figure, appear*
la filial   *subsidiary*
Filipinas (*fpl*)   *Philippines*
el filo   *edge, blade*
el fin   *end; aim, purpose*   el fin de semana   *weekend*   en fin   *in short, there you are*
el final   *end, ending*
la final   *final*
finalmente   *finally*
financiar   *to finance*
financiero/a   *financial*
el fino   *dry sherry*
fino/a   *refined*
firmar   *to sign*
físicamente   *physically*
físico/a   *physical*
la fisura   *fracture*
fláccido/a   *flaccid, flabby*
flaco/a   *thin*
el flamenco   *flamenco*
la flecha   *arrow*
la flor   *flower*
florecer (zc)   *to flourish*
flotante   *floating*
el foco   *focus*
folklórico/a   *folkloric*
fomentar   *to promote, foster*
los fondos   *funds*
el footing   *jogging*
la forma   *form, shape; way*
la formación   *training*
la formalidad   *formality*
la fortuna   *fortune*
la fotografía   *photograph*
el fotógrafo   *photographer*
fracasado/a   *failed, unsuccessful*
fracturado/a   *cracked, fractured*
francamente   *frankly, really*

francés/esa *French*
Francia (*f*) *France*
franquista *of Franco*
la frase *phrase, sentence*
frecuentemente *often*
fregar (ie) *to wash (up)*
freír (i) *to fry*
frente: frente a *towards* al frente de *in charge of*
la fresa *strawberry*
el fresco *fresh air*
fresco/a *cool*
el frijol (*Mex*) *black bean*
frío: hace frío *it's cold* (*weather*)
frío/a *cold*
la fruta *fruit*
la fruticultura *fruit-growing*
la fuente *fountain; source*
fuera (de) *out, outside*
fuerte *strong; hard; loud(ly)*
el fumador *smoker*
fumar *to smoke*
funcionar *to work*
la funcionaria, el funcionario *civil servant*
fundamentalmente *fundamentally, basically*
fundar *to found*
el fútbol *football*
el futuro *future*

G

el gabinete *cabinet*
las gafas *glasses* las gafas de sol *sunglasses*
gallego/a *Galician*
la galleta *biscuit;* (*Chile*) *coarse bread*
el gamberro *hooligan*
la gana *desire, wish* tener ganas de +*inf* *to want to, feel like*
la ganadería *cattle*
el ganador *winner*
ganar *to win*
garantizar *to guarantee*
la garganta *throat*
la gaseosa *fizzy lemonade*
gastar *to spend*
el gasto *expense, spending*
el gato *cat*
genealógico: el árbol genealógico *family tree*
la generación *generation*

general *general* en general *in general* por lo general *as a rule*
el general *general*
generalizarse *to become widespread*
generalmente *generally*
el genio *genius; temper*
la gente *people;* (*Mex*) *person*
la geografía *geography*
la gesticulación *gesticulation*
el gesto *gesture, sign*
el ginecólogo *gynaecologist*
el girasol *sunflower*
gitano/a *gipsy*
el gobierno *government*
el golf *golf*
el golpe (de estado) *coup d'état*
golpear(se) *to hit (oneself)*
gordo/a *fat*
gracias *thanks*
el grado *degree*
el graduado, la graduada *graduate*
la gramática *grammar*
Gran Bretaña (*f*) *Great Britain*
grande (gran) *large, big; great*
gratificar *to reward*
la gravitación *weight*
Grecia (*f*) *Greece*
griego/a *Greek*
la gripe *flu*
gris *grey* gris oscuro *dark grey*
gritar *to call, cry (out)*
el grito *cry, sound* dar gritos *to shout*
el gruñido *grunt, growl*
el grupo *group*
guapo/a *good-looking, pretty, attractive*
guardar *to keep, save*
la guardería *nursery*
la Guardia Civil *Civil Guard*
la guardilla *attic*
la guerra *war*
el guitarrista *guitarist*
gustar *to please* me gusta ... *I like ...* ¿te gusta ...? *do you like ...?*
el gusto *taste; pleasure*

H

el haba (*f*) *broad bean*
haber* *to have*
había (*imperfect of* hay) *there was, there were*

la habitación *room*

el/la habitante *inhabitant*

el hábito *habit*

el habla (*f*) *speech*

hablar *to speak, talk*

el hablar *speech*

habrá (*future of hay*) *there will be*

hace … … *ago*

hacer* *to make, to do*

hacerse* *to become*

hacia *to, towards*

haló (*LA*) *hallo (on phone)*

el hambre (*f*) *hunger*

harto/a *fed up*

hasta *even; until; up to; to, as far as*   hasta que *until*

hay *there is, there are*   hay que *one has to/must, you have to/must*   sigue habiendo *there is still*

el hecho *fact*

hecho/a *made, prepared*

la hembra *female*

herido/a *injured*

el hermano *brother*   los hermanos *brothers, brothers and sisters*

hermoso/a *beautiful*

hervir (ie) *to boil*

la hierba *herb*

el hierro *iron*

la hija *daughter*

el hijo *son*

los hijos *children*

hincapié: hacer hincapié en *to emphasise*

el/la hincha *supporter*

hispánico/a *Hispanic, Spanish*

el/la hispanista *Hispanist*

hispanoparlante *Spanish-speaking*

histérico/a *hysterical*

la historia *history*

históricamente *historically*

histórico/a *historic(al)*

el hogar *home*

la hoja *leaf; page*

el hojalatero *tinsmith*

hola *hello*

Holanda (*f*) *Holland*

el hombre *man*   ¡hombre! *well!, yes!*

el hombro *shoulder*

hondo/a *deep, profound*

el honor *honour*

la hora *hour; time*   ¿a qué hora? *when, (at) what time?*

el horario *timetable*   a horario (*LA*) *on time*

horrible *horrible*

el hospital *hospital*

el hostal *small hotel, pension*

el hotel *hotel*

hoy *today*   hoy en día *nowadays*

hubo (*preterite of* hay) *there was, there were*

el hueso *bone*

el huésped *guest; host*

el huevo *egg*

humano/a *human*

húmedo/a *wet, damp*

el humo *smoke*

I

-ico/a *ending added to words, often meaning 'little'*

el icono *icon*

la idea *idea*

idéntico/a *identical*

la identidad *identity*

identificar *to identify*

ideológico/a *ideological*

el idioma *language*

igual *(the) same; equal*   al igual que *the same as, just as*

la igualdad *equality*

igualmente *equally*

ilusionado/a con *excited about, looking forward to*

-illo/a *ending added to words, often meaning 'little'*

la imagen *image*

imaginarse *to imagine*

imitar *to imitate*

impacientarse *to grow impatient*

la imparcialidad *impartiality*

el imperio *empire*

imponer* (*like* poner) *to impose*

la importancia *importance*   dar importancia a *to attach importance to*

importante *important*

importar *to matter*

imposible *impossible*

imprescindible *essential*

impresionante *impressive*

impresionar *to impress*

la impresora *printer*

la inauguración *inauguration*

incaico/a *Inca*
el incendio *fire*
la incertidumbre *uncertainty*
el incidente *incident*
incisivo/a *incisive*
incluir *to include*
inclusive *including; even*
incluso *including; even*
incorrectamente *incorrectly*
la indicación *suggestion*
indicar *to show*
indígena *native, indigenous*
el indio *Indian*
individualmente *individually*
el individuo *individual*
indudablemente *undoubtedly*
industrial *industrial*
industrializar *to industrialise*
la ineficacia *inefficiency*
ineficaz *ineffective, inefficient*
ineludible *unavoidable*
inevitable *inevitable*
inevitablemente *inevitably*
la infanta *princess*
la influencia *influence*
influenciar *to influence*
la información *information*
informar *to report*
la informática *information technology*
la infraestructura *infrastructure*
la ingeniera (*woman*) *engineer*
Inglaterra (*f*) *England*
inglés/esa *English*
el ingrediente *ingredient*
ingresar *to admit*
inicial *initial*
iniciar *to start; set in motion*
el inicio (*LA*) *beginning*
inigualable *unequalled, incomparable*
inmediatamente *immediately*
el inmigrante *immigrant*
innecesario/a *unnecessary*
inocente *innocent*
inopinadamente *unexpectedly*
el inquilino *tenant*
insistir en *to insist on*
insoportable *unbearable*
la inspiración *inspiration*
la institución *institution*
el instituto *institute; high school*

instrucción: el juez de instrucción *examining magistrate*
instruir *to instruct*
insuficiente *insufficient*
integrante *integral*
intelectual *intellectual*
la inteligencia *intelligence*
inteligente *intelligent*
la intensidad *intensity*
intentar *to try* (*out*)
el intento *attempt*
el interés *interest*
interesado/a *interested*
interesante *interesting*
interesar *to interest*
interior *interior*
internacional *international*
interpretado/a *interpreted*
la interrogación *question mark*
el interruptor *switch*
la intervención *intervention*
el inti *Peruvian unit of currency*
intolerable *intolerable*
la introducción *introduction*
introducir (zc) *to introduce*
invadir *to invade*
invencible *invincible*
invertir (ie) *to invest*
la investigación *research*
investigar *to do research*
el invierno *winter*
invitar *to invite*
ir* *to go*   ir a +*inf* *to be going to*
    vamos *let's go; well*   vamos a ver *let's see*
irse* *to go* (*away*)
la irregularidad *irregularity*
-ísimo/a *ending added to adjectives, meaning 'very'*
Italia (*f*) *Italy*
italiano/a *Italian*
-ito/a *ending added to words, often meaning 'little'*
la izquierda *left*
izquierdo/a *left*

J

el jaleo *racket, din*
el Japón *Japan*
el jardín *garden*
la jefa, el jefe *boss, head*
el jinete *horse-rider, jockey*

la jornada (*working*) *day*
joven *young*
la jubilación *retirement*
jubilado/a *retired*
jubilarse *to retire*
la judía *bean*
jueves (*m*) *Thursday*
el juez *judge*
el jugador *player*
jugar (ue) *to play*
el juicio *opinion*
julio (*m*) *July*
juntarse *to join; to meet*
junto (a) *together* (*with*)
el jurado *juror*
justamente *exactly*
la justicia *law*
justo *right, just*
justo/a *just*

K

el kilo *kilo*
el kilómetro *kilometre*

L

la *the; her, it; the one*
la labor *task, job*
el laboratorio *laboratory*
el lado *side* al lado de *next to* por un
lado *on one hand* por otro lado *on the other
hand*
el ladrón *thief*
el lago *lake*
la lana *wool*
el lápiz *pencil*
largo/a *long*
las *the; them* las que *the ones, those who*
lástima: es una lástima *it's a shame*
el latín *Latin*
Latinoamérica (*f*) *Latin America*
latinoamericano/a *Latin American*
lavar *to wash*
el lazo *tie; link*
le (*to*) *you;* (*to*) *him,* (*to*) *her,* (*to*) *it*
el lector *reader*
la lectura *reading*
la leche *milk*

legal *legal*
legítimo/a *legitimate*
lejano/a *far away, distant*
lejos *far* (*away*)
la lengua *language*
el lenguaje *language*
lentamente *slowly*
lento/a *slow*
les (*to*) *you;* (*to*) *them*
la letra *letter*
levantarse *to get up*
la ley *law*
la libertad *freedom, liberty*
librar *to free, release*
libre *free*
libremente *freely*
el libro *book*
el líder *leader*
limitado/a *limited*
el límite *limit*
el limón *lemon*
la limosna *alms, charity*
limosnear *to beg*
limpiar *to clean*
la limpieza *cleaning*
lindo/a *pretty*
lingüísticamente *linguistically*
lingüístico/a *linguistic*
la lista *list*
literario/a *literary*
la literatura *literature*
el lizo *warp thread, heddle*
lo *him; it* lo+*adj* *the ... thing*
local *local*
loco/a *mad, crazy*
lógicamente *logically*
la lolita (*Chilean slang*) *girl*
Londres *London*
los *the; them* los que *the ones, those who*
luchar *to fight; struggle*
luego *then, next* desde luego *of course*
hasta luego *bye, see you later*
el lugar *place* dar lugar a *to lead to* tener
lugar *to take place*
lunes (*m*) *Monday*
el lustrabotas (*LA*) *bootblack*
la luxación *dislocation*
la luz *light* dar a luz *to give birth*

LL

llamar *to call*
llamarse *to be called*
la llave *key*
la llegada *arrival*
llegar *to arrive, get to; to reach*   llegar a +inf *to manage to, to go as far as to*
llevar *to bring, to take; to bear, carry; to wear; to lead; to spend (time), to take (time); to keep (accounts)*
llevarse con *to get on with*
llorar *to cry*
llover (ue) *to rain*
la lluvia *rain*

M

el machito (macho) (*LA*) *mule*
macho *male, masculine*
la madre *mother*
madrileño/a *of/from Madrid*
el madroño *strawberry tree, arbutus*
la madrugada *early morning*
maduro/a *ripe*
maestra: obra maestra *masterpiece*
la maestra, el maestro (*primary*) *schoolteacher*
majo/a *nice*
mal *bad(ly); unwell*
malo/a (mal) *bad*
la mamá *mother, mummy*
mandar *to send; to order*
la manera *way, manner*
la manifestación *statement*
manifestarse *to be apparent, to show*
la mano *hand*   a mano *by hand*
manso/a *tame, gentle*
la manteca *lard*
mantener (ie) *to maintain, to keep up; to hold*
mantenerse (ie) *to keep (oneself)*
la manzana *apple*
mañana *tomorrow*
la mañana *morning*
maño/a, mañico/a *nickname for someone from Aragon*
el mapa *map*
la maqueta *model*
la máquina de escribir *typewriter*
maravilloso/a *marvellous*
marcar *to lay down*

marcha: en marcha *working, 'on'*
marchar *to go*
marchar(se) *to go away*
la marea *tide*
el marido *husband*
marrón *brown*
Marruecos (*m*) *Morocco*
martiniqueño/a *of/from Martinique*
marzo (*m*) *March*
más *more, else; most* más ... de, más ... que *more ... than*   más bien *rather*
masivo/a *massive*
matar *to kill*
la materia *subject*
el material *material*
la maternidad *maternity*
matricularse *to enrol, sign up*
el matrimonio *marriage; married couple*
la matriz *matrix*
máximo/a *maximum*
mayo (*m*) *May*
mayor *main, major; bigger, greater; biggest, greatest; oldest*
la mayoría *most, majority*
mayormente *mainly*
me (*to*) *me; myself*
la medalla *medal*
medallero *medal table, tally*
media: y media *half past*
mediano/a *middle*
la medicina *medicine*
el médico *doctor*
médico/a *medical*
medida: a medida de *as, in line with*   en la medida que *as far as*
el medio *middle, medium; half; means*   el medio ambiente *environment*
medio/a *half; medium*   la enseñanza media *secondary education*
medir (i) *to measure*
mejicano/a *Mexican*
Méjico (*m*) *Mexico*
mejor *better; best*   mejor dicho *rather*
a lo mejor *probably*
la mejora *improvement*
mejorar *to improve*
mejorarse *to get better*
el melocotón *peach*
melodramático/a *melodramatic*
la memoria *memory*

la mendicidad *begging*
el menor *youngest; minor, young boy*
  menos *less; least* menos … de, menos … que
    less … than   menos cuarto *a quarter to*
    a menos que *unless*
la mentalidad *mentality*
la mentira *lie, falsehood*
  menudo: a menudo *often*
el mercado *market*
la merienda *picnic*
el mes *month*
la mesa *table*
  meter *to put*
  meterse (por/en) *to go (into), to get (into)*
el metro *metre; underground (railway)*
la mezcla *mixture*
  mezclar *to mix*
  mi, mis *my*
  mí *me*
  mío/a *mine*
el micro (*Chile, Peru*) *bus*
  miedo: tener miedo *to be afraid*
el miembro *member*
  mientras (que) *while*   mientras tanto *in the
    meantime*
  miércoles (*m*) *Wednesday*
la migración *migration*
  militar *military*
la minera (*woman*) *miner*
  minero/a *mining*
  mínimo/a *minimum*
el ministerio *ministry*
el ministro *minister*
el minuto *minute*
  mirar *to look* (*at*)
  miserable *miserable*
  mismo/a *same; very; (one)self*
la mitad *half*
la moda *fashion*   de moda *fashionable*
la modernización *modernisation*
  moderno/a *modern*
la modificación *alteration*
el modismo *idiom*
el modo *way, manner*   de todos modos *in any
    case*
  mojarse *to get wet*
  molestar *to bother; to hurt*
el momento *moment, time*   de momento *at the
    moment*   en el momento *on the spot*
    hasta el momento *up to now*

la monarquía *monarchy*
la moneda *coin*
  monetario/a *financial, monetary*
el montaje *production*
la montaña *mountains*
  montar *to ride*
el monumento *monument*
  moreno/a *dark (haired)*
  morir (ue) (*pp* muerto) *to die*
los moros *Moors*
la moto *motor-bike*
  moverse (ue) *to move*
  movido/a *lively*
el movimiento *movement*
  muchísimo *very much*
  mucho *a lot*
  mucho/a *a lot of, much*
  muchos/as *lots of, many*
la muerte *dead*
  muerto/a *dead*
la mujer *woman; wife*
  multilingüe *multilingual*
  mundial *world*
el mundo *the world*   todo el mundo *everybody*
  municipal *municipal*
el municipio *municipality*
el muñeco *doll*
el muro *wall*
el músculo *muscle*
el museo *museum*
la música *music*
  musical *musical*
  musulmán/ana *Moslem*
  muy *very*

N

  nacer (zc) *to be born*
la nación *nation*
  nacional *national*
la nacionalidad *nationality*
  nada *nothing*
  nadie *nobody*
la naranja *orange*
la nariz *nose*
la natación *swimming*
la nave *ship*
la Navidad *Christmas*   las Navidades *Christmas
    time*
    navideño/a *(of) Christmas*

necesariamente *necessary*
necesario/a *necessary*
la necesidad *need*
necesitar *to need*
negar (ie) *to deny*
el negocio *business*
negro/a *black*
la nevera *refrigerator*
ni *nor; not even* ni … ni *neither … nor*
el nieto *grandson* los nietos *grandchildren*
ninguno/a (ningún) *no, none, not one, not any*
la niña *girl*
el niño *boy* los niños *children*
el nivel *level*
no *no; not* ¿no? *no?, isn't it?, isn't that so?*
la noche *night*
nombrar *to name, to appoint*
el nombre *name*
la norma *regulation; condition*
normal *normal*
la normalidad *normality*
normalmente *normally, usually*
el norte *north*
norteamericano/a *(North) American*
nos *us; ourselves*
nosotros/as *we; us*
notar *to see, to note, to notice* es de notar *it should be noted*
el notario *solicitor, notary*
la novela *novel*
el novelista *novelist*
noventa *ninety*
noviembre *November*
novo/a *(Catalan word) new*
la nube *cloud*
nuboso/a *cloudy*
nuestro/a *our*
nueve *nine*
nuevo/a *new* de nuevo *again*
la nuez *nut, walnut*
nulo/a *none*
el número *number*
nunca *never*

Ñ

ñato/a *(LA) snub-nosed*

O

o *or* o … o *either … or*
el objeto *object*
la obligación *duty*
obligar *to compel, oblige*
obligatoriamente *compulsory*
la obra *work, play* obra maestra *masterpiece*
observar *to see, observe*
la obsesión *obsession*
obstante: no obstante *nevertheless*
obtener (ie) *to obtain*
obviamente *obviously*
occidental *western*
el occidente *west*
el océano *ocean*
el ocio *leisure time*
la ocupación *profession*
ocupar *to occupy*
ocurrir *to happen*
ocho *eight*
la oferta *supply, provision*
oficial *official*
la oficina *office*
el/la oficinista *office worker*
el oficio *job, profession*
ofrecer (zc) *to offer*
el oído *ear*
oír* *to hear*
el ojo *eye*
la ola *wave*
las Olimpíadas *Olympics*
olímpico: los Juegos Olímpicos *Olympic Games*
olvidar *to forget*
once *eleven*
la opción *choice, option*
la ópera *opera*
la operación *transaction*
opinar (de) *to think (of)*
la opinión *opinion*
la oportunidad *opportunity*
la oposición *opposition*
las oposiciones *public examinations*
el opresor *oppressor*
optimista *optimistic*
óptimo/a *very good*
el orden *order*
el ordenador *computer*
el organismo *body*
la organización *organisation*

organizar   *to organise*
el órgano   *organ*
el orgullo   *pride*
orgulloso/a   *proud*
la orientación   *orientation; training*
el oriente   *east*
el origen   *origin*
el original   *original*
originalmente   *originally*
os   *you; yourselves*
oscuro/a   *dark*
el oso   *bear*
la OTAN   *NATO*
otro/a   *other, another*
otros/as   *other(s)*
la oveja   *sheep*

P

paceño/a   *from La Paz*
el/la paciente   *patient*
el pacto   *pact, agreement*
el padre   *father*   los padres   *parents*
pagado/a: mal pagado/a   *badly paid*
pagar   *to pay (for)*
el pago   *pay, wages*
el país   *country*
el País Vasco   *Basque Country*
el paisaje   *landscape*
la palabra   *word*
el palacio   *palace*
palma: tocar las palmas   *to clap one's hands*
el pan   *bread*
panorámico/a   *panoramic*
el pantalón   *trousers*
la pantalla   *screen*
la pañería   *draper's*
el papá   *father, daddy*
el papel   *rôle*
el paquete   *parcel*
par: un par de   *a couple of*
para   *for; in order to; to, towards*   para que   *in order that, so that*
parado/a   *unemployed*
el paraguas   *umbrella*
pararse   *to stop*
parcial: a tiempo parcial   *part-time*
parecer (zc)   *to look, to seem*
¿te parece?   *what do you think?*
parecerse a   *to resemble (each other)*

parecido/a   *similar*
la pareja   *pair; couple*
paréntesis: entre paréntesis   *by the way, incidentally*
el parlamento   *parliament*
el paro   *unemployment (benefit)*
el parque   *park*
la parte   *part*   la mayor parte   *most*   a parte de   *apart from*   en gran parte   *to a great extent*   por parte de   *on the part of*   por otra parte   *on the other hand*
la participación   *participation*
participar   *to take part; to share*
particular   *particular*   en particular   *in particular*
el partido   *party; game, match*
partir   *to leave*   a partir de   *starting from*
el parto   *birth*
pasado/a   *past; last*
pasar   *to pass; to give; to go on; to happen; to spend (time); to go through*   pasar a ser   *to become*   ¿qué te pasa?   *what's the matter with you?*   pasarlo bien   *to have a good time*
pasear(se)   *to walk, go for a walk*
el paseo   *walk*   dar un paseo   *to go for a walk*
el paso   *step; passage, entry*   a dos pasos   *very near*
el pasodoble   *pasodoble, type of dance*
la pasta   *pasta*
la pastilla   *cake*
la pata   *paw*
la patata   *potato*
paterno/a   *paternal*
el patrón   *patron*
el pedazo   *piece*
pedir (i)   *to ask for*
peliagudo/a   *tricky, difficult*
la película   *film*
el peligro   *danger*
peligroso/a   *dangerous*
el pelo   *hair*
la pena: dar pena   *to cause sorrow*   vale la pena   *it's worth(while)*
pensar (ie)   *to think; to plan, intend*   pensar en   *to think about*
la pensión   *boarding house; pension*
la peña   *club*
pequeño/a   *little, small*   de pequeño/a   *as a little boy/girl*   los pequeños   *children*   en pequeño   *in miniature*
percibir   *to perceive*
perder (ie)   *to lose; to miss*
la pérdida   *loss*

perdido/a *lost*
perdón *excuse me, sorry*
el perejil *parsley*
el perezoso *sloth*
perezoso/a *lazy*
perfectamente *perfectly; completely*
perfecto/a *perfect*
la periferia *outskirts*
el periódico *newspaper*
el periodismo *journalism*
el/la periodista *journalist*
permanecer (zc) *to remain*
permanente *permanent*
permanentemente *permanently*
permitir *to permit, allow*
pero *but*
la perra *female dog, bitch*
el perro *dog*   el perro de aguas *spaniel*
la persona *person*
el personaje *character*
personal *personal*
la personalidad *personality*
personalmente *personally*
la perspectiva *prospect*
perspicaz *shrewd, perceptive*
pertenecer (zc) *to belong*
pesado/a *heavy; tedious, annoying*
pesar *to weigh*   a pesar de *in spite of*
la pesca *fishing*
el peso *weight*
pico: y pico *and a bit*
el pie *foot*   de pie *standing*
la piedra *stone*
la pierna *leg*
pillar *to catch*
la pimienta *pepper*
el pintor *painter, artist*
la piscina *swimming-pool*
el piso *floor; flat*
el pizarrón *blackboard*
el plan *plan*
planchar *to iron*
la planificación *plan*
la planta *plant; floor, storey*
el planteamiento *set-up*
el plato *dish*
la playa *beach*
la plaza *square*
pleno/a *full*   en pleno/a ... *in the middle of ...,
right in ...*

el plomero (*LA*) *plumber*
plural: en plural *in the plural*
la población *population, people*
el pobre *poor*
la pobreza *poverty*
poco *not much, little, not very*   un poco (de) *a
bit (of); a while*
poco/a *little, small; not much*
pocos/as *few, not many*
poder (ue)* *to be able, can, may*   se puede *it's
possible*
el poder *power*
la poesía *poetry, poem*
el poeta *poet*
policíaco/a *police*
el político *politician*
político/a *political*
poner* (*pp* puesto) *to put; to put on, to show; to
set up; to give (name)*   pongamos *let's say*
ponerse* *to become*   ponerse a +*inf* *to start*
popular *popular, of the people*
la popularidad *popularity*
por *by; in, around; for; because of*
¿por qué? *why?*
el porcentaje *percentage*
porque *because*
el porqué *the reason (for)*
el portal *main entrance*
la portera *caretaker, concierge*
la portería *caretaker's room*
la posibilidad *possibility; means*
posible *possible*
posiblemente *possibly*
postal: caja postal (de ahorros) *post office savings
bank*
posteriormente *later on*
potencialmente *potentially*
potente *strong, powerful*
el potingue *concoction*
el pozo *well*
la práctica *practice, practical work; exercise*
prácticamente *practically*
practicar *to practise, to do*
práctico/a *practical*
la pradera *meadow, field*
precario/a *precarious*
el precio *price*
precioso/a *lovely*
la preferencia *preference*
preferir (ie) *to prefer*

la pregunta *question*
preguntar *to ask*
el premio *prize*
prender *to take root*
la prensa *press*
preocuparse (por) *to trouble to*
la preparación *preparation; training*
preparar *to prepare*
prepararse *to prepare oneself, get ready (for)*
prepotente *presumptuous*
prescolar *nursery*
la presencia *presence*
presentar *to introduce; to present*
presentarse *to crop up*
presidente *president; chairperson*   presidente del gobierno *leader of the government, prime minister*
la presión *pressure*
el prestador *provider*
prestar *to lend, hire out*
el presupuesto *budget*
pretender *to attempt to*
primario/a *primary*
la primavera *spring*
primero *first (of all)*
primero/a (primer) *first; primary*
primordial *basic*
principal *main*
principalmente *mainly*
el príncipe *prince*
el principio *principle*   al principio *at the beginning*
la prioridad *priority*
prisa: a toda prisa *at top speed*
privado/a *private*
probablemente *probably*
el problema *problem*
proceder de *to come from*
el procesamiento de textos *word-processing*
la procesión *procession*
el proceso *process*
procurar *to try*
producir (zc) *to produce*
productivo/a *productive*
la profesión *profession*
profesional *professional*
el profesor, la profesora *teacher*
profundamente *profoundly, completely*
la profundidad *depth*
profundo/a *complete, total*

el programa *programme; curriculum*
progresar *to progress*
el progreso *progress*
prohibir *to ban*
proliferar *to mushroom, proliferate*
prolongar *to prolong*
la promoción *promotion*
promocionar *to promote*
pronto *quickly; soon*   de pronto (*LA*) *perhaps*
la pronunciación *pronunciation*
pronunciar *to pronounce*
la propaganda *publicity, advertising*
propiciar *to cause, bring about*
la propietaria, el propietario *owner*
la propina *tip*
propio/a *one's own; very (same)*
la proporción *proportion*
próspero/a *prosperous*
protegerse *to protect oneself*
la protesta *protest*
provenir (ie) de *to originate, to come from*
la provincia *province*
provincial *provincial*
la provisión *provision*
provisto/a *provided for*
proyectar *to plan*
el proyecto *project, plan*
publicar *to publish*
la publicidad *publicity*
el público *public*
público/a *public*
el pueblo *village; people*
la puerta *door*
el puerto *(mountain) pass*
pues *then; well, well now, well then*
la puesta en escena *staging*
el puesto *post, job; stall*
el punto *point, part*   el punto de vista *point of view*
la pureza *genuineness*
el puro *cigar*

Q

que *who; that; which; for, because; than*
¿qué? *what?*
¡qué ...! *how ...!, what a ...!*   ¡qué va! *far from it!, no way!*
quedar *to remain, to turn out*   quedar en *to agree on*

quedarse   *to stay, remain; to grow, become*
quejarse   *to complain*
querer (ie)*   *to want (to); to love*   querer decir   *to mean*
querido/a   *dear*
quien   *who, whom, someone who*
quienes   *who, whom, those who*
¿quién?, ¿quiénes?   *who?, whom?*
quince   *fifteen*   quince días   *fortnight*
quitar   *to take away; to take out*
quitarse   *to get away from; to take off*
quizá(s)   *perhaps*

R

la radio   *radio*
la raíz   *root*   'de raíces'   *'roots'*
rancio/a   *old (wine)*
la ranura   *slot*
rápidamente   *quickly*
la rapidez   *speed*
rápido   *quickly*
rápido/a   *quick*
raro/a   *rare*
el rasgo   *feature*
raspado/a   *threadbare*
el rato   *(short) time*   ratos libres   *spare time*
la razón   *reason*   tener razón   *to be right*
la reacción   *reaction*
real   *royal; real*
la realidad   *reality*
realizar   *to carry out, perform*
realmente   *really, in fact*
el/la recepcionista   *receptionist*
la receta   *recipe*
recibir   *to receive*
el recibo   *receipt, bill*
reciclar   *to recycle*
recién (*LA*)   *recently*
reciente   *recent*
recientemente   *recently*
el recipiente   *bowl, receptacle*
recoger   *to pick up, collect; to get*
recomendar (ie)   *to recommend*
reconocer (zc)   *to recognise*
la reconstrucción   *rebuilding*
reconstruir   *to rebuild*
recordar (ue)   *to bear in mind, remember*
el recreo   *leisure*
la recriminación   *recrimination*

rectificar   *to correct*
el recuerdo   *memory*
la recuperación   *recovery*
recuperar   *to make up*
recuperarse   *to get better*
el recurso   *resource*
la red   *network*
la redacción   *editorial work, writing*
redondo/a   *round*
referirse (ie) a   *to refer to*
reflejar   *to reflect*
la reforma   *reform*
reformar   *to reform*
reforzar (ue)   *to strengthen*
el régimen   *régime; diet*
la región   *region*
regional   *regional*
regir (i)   *to be in force*
regresar   *to return*
la regulación   *regulation, rule*
regular   *normal, average*
la rehabilitación   *rehabilitation*
el rehén   *hostage*
la reina   *queen*
el reino   *kingdom*
la reinstauración   *restoration*
reinterpretar   *to reinterpret*
reír (i)*   *to laugh*
la relación   *dealing; relation*
relacionado/a (con)   *connected (with)*
relajadamente   *slowly, in a relaxed way*
relativamente   *relatively*
el relax   *relaxation*
el relojero   *watchmaker*
el remedio   *remedy, cure*
remontarse a   *to go back to*
el renacimiento   *revival*
renovar (ue)   *to renew*
reparar   *to repair*
repartir   *to deliver*
repasar   *to review, look back over*
repente: de repente   *suddenly*
repetir (i)   *to repeat*
el reporte   *report*
reposar   *to rest*
el reposo   *rest*
representar   *to represent*
la represión   *repression*
requerer (ie)   *to require*
la resaca   *hangover*

resentido/a *suffering, affected*
el resentimiento *resentment*
el resfriado *cold*
residencial *residential*
resistirse *to resist, refuse*
resolver (ue) (*pp* resuelto) *to resolve*
respectar *to concern*
respecto: (con) respecto a *with regard to, in relation to*
responder *to respond*
la responsabilidad *responsibility*
responsable *responsible*
la respuesta *reply, answer*
el restaurante *restaurant*
el resto *the rest*
el resultado *result*
resultar *to be, to prove (to be)*
el resurgimiento *resurgence*
retomar *to pick up again, restart*
retroceder *to go back*
la reunión *joining, bringing together*
la revisión *re-examination, review*
la revolución *revolution*
revolucionario/a *revolutionary*
el rey *king*
ridículo/a *ridiculous*
rígido/a *stiff*
la riqueza *wealth, affluence*
la rodilla *knee*
la rodillera *knee-pad*
rojo/a *red*
romano/a *Roman*
romántico/a *romantic*
romper (*pp* roto) *to break*
la ropa *clothing*
rubio/a *fair-haired, blond(e)*
el rubro (*LA*) *business*
rufianesco/a *rough, roguish*
el ruido *noise*
ruidoso/a *noisy*
la ruina *ruin*
rural *rural*
la rutina *routine*

S

sábado (*m*) Saturday
saber* *to know*   que yo sepa *as far as I know*
el sabor *taste, flavour*
sacar *to take out; to get; to put out, dislocate*
  sacar adelante *to run, make work*

la sal *salt*
la sala (*large*) *room; gallery*
la salida *exit, departure; opening*
salir* *to go out; to leave; to get out*
saltar *to come out*
saltarse *to miss out, skip*
salto: dar el salto (*to make*) *the move*
la salud *health*
saludar: Le saluda muy atentamente *Yours faithfully*
salvar *to save, salvage*
el sanatorio *sanatorium*
la sangre *blood*
la sanidad *health*
sanitario/a *medical*
el santo *saint*
santo/a *holy*
saquear *to loot, plunder*
la sardana *dance from Cataluña*
la sartén *frying-pan*
el sastre *tailor*
satisfecho/a *satisfied*
se *yourself; yourselves; himself; herself; itself; each
    other, one another*
sea: o sea *in other words, that is*
seco/a *dry*
la secretaria, el secretario *secretary*
el sector *sector*
el secuestro *kidnapping, seizure*
la sede *seat*
seguida: en seguida *straightaway*
seguido/a *in one go, continuous*
el seguidor *follower*
seguir (i) *to follow; to carry on, go on, continue*
según *according to*
segundo/a *second*
la seguridad *security*
el seguro *insurance*
seis *six*
la selección *selection*
seleccionar *to pick, choose*
el sello *stamp*
la semana *week*
sencillo/a *simple*
sensible *sensitive*
sentado/a *sitting, seated*
sentarse (ie) *to sit down*
el sentido *sense*
sentir (ie) *to feel; to hear*
sentirse (ie) *to feel*
la señal *sign*

señalar   *to point out*

el señor   *gentleman; Mr; sir*   Muy Señor mío   *Dear Sir*

la señora   *lady; Mrs*

la señorita   *young lady; Miss*

sepa (*see* saber)

separarse   *to leave*

ser*   *to be*

el sereno   *night watchman*

la serie   *range, series*

serio/a   *serious*

el servicio   *service*   prestar servicio   *to serve*

servir (i)   *to serve; to be of use*   no servir de nada   *to be useless*

sesenta   *sixty*

la sesión   *session, showing*

setenta   *seventy*

el seto   *hedge, fence*

severamente   *harshly*

severo/a   *strict, severe*

las sevillanas   *type of folk song and dance from Seville*

sexual   *sexual*

si   *if*

sí   *yes*

sí mismo/a   *itself; oneself*

siempre   *always*

la sierra   *mountains*

siete   *seven*

el siglo   *century*

significar   *to mean*

significativo/a   *significant*

siguiente   *following*

la sílaba   *syllable*

silencioso/a   *quiet*

simbolizar   *to symbolise*

el símbolo   *symbol*

simpático/a   *nice, friendly*

simplemente   *simply*

simultáneamente   *simultaneously*

sin   *without*

la sinceridad   *sincerity*

sincero/a   *sincere*

el sindicato   *trade union*

sino   *but (rather)*

sintético/a   *synthetic*

el síntoma   *symptom*

el sismo (*more usually* seísmo)   *earthquake*

el sistema   *system*

el sitio   *place*

la situación   *place, situation*

el slogan   *slogan*

sobre   *on, on top of; about*   sobre todo   *especially*

social   *social*

socialista   *socialist*

la sociedad   *society*

el socio   *co-owner, partner*

la sociología   *sociology*

el sociólogo   *sociologist*

el sol   *sun*

solamente   *only*

el soldado   *soldier*

el soldador   *welder*

soleado/a   *sunny*

la soledad   *solitude*

soler (ue) +*inf*   *to be in the habit of*   suelo salir   *I usually go out*

solicitar   *to ask for*

la solidaridad   *solidarity*

solidario/a   *sharing, showing solidarity*

solitario/a   *solitary*

sólo   *only, just*   no sólo ... sino también   *not only ... but also*

solo/a   *alone*

soltero/a   *single*

la solución   *solution*

solucionar   *to solve, to deal with*

el sombrero   *hat*

somocista   *of Somoza*

sonar (ue)   *to sound*   sonar a   *to sound like*

el sonido   *sound*

la sonrisa   *smile*

los soportales   *arcade, colonnade*

sorprender   *to surprise*

su, sus   *your; his, her, its*

subdesarrollado/a   *under-developed*

el subgerente   *assistant manager*

subir   *to go up; to ascend, come to*

la sublevación   *revolt, rising*

la subvención   *subsidy*

suceder   *to happen*

sucesivamente   *little by little*

Sudamérica (*f*)   *South America*

sudar   *to sweat*

el sudeste   *south east*

el sueldo   *salary*

el suelo   *ground*

el sueño   *dream*   tener sueño   *to be tired*

la suerte   *luck; piece of fortune*

suficiente   *enough*

sufrido/a *long-suffering*
el sufrimiento *suffering*
sufrir *to suffer*
Suiza (*f*) *Switzerland*
suma: en suma *in short*
superior *higher; advanced*
el supermercado *supermarket*
supermoderno/a *ultra-modern*
el suplemento *supplement*
suponer* (*like* poner) (*pp* supuesto) *to suppose; to represent*
supuesto: por supuesto *of course*
el sur *south*
surgir *to arise*
el sustento *support*
suyo/a *yours; his, hers, its; their, their own*

T

el tabaco *tobacco*
el tablao *place where flamenco shows are held*
tal *such, as*   tal como *as, such as*   ¿qué tal? *how are things?*   ¿qué tal ...? *how is/was ...?*
el talento *talent*
el taller *workroom; workshop*
el tamaño *size*
también *as well, also, too*
tampoco *neither, not ... either*
tan *so*
tanto *so much*   mientras tanto *in the meantime*
tanto/a *as much, so much*   por lo tanto *so, therefore*   tanto ... como *both ... and*
tantos/as *as many, so many*
la tapa *bar snack*
el tapiz *tapestry*
tardar *to take* (*time*)
tarde *late*
la tarde *afternoon, evening*   buenas tardes *good afternoon, good evening*
te (*to*) *you, yourself*
teatral *theatrical*
teatralizar *to dramatise*
el teatro *theatre*
el teclado *keyboard*
teclar *to key in*
el técnico *technician*
la tecnología *technology*
tejer *to weave*
la tela *cloth*

el telar *loom*   el telar de alto lizo *heddle loom*
el teléfono *telephone*
el telegrama *telegram*
la televisión *television*
el tema *subject, theme*
la temperatura *temperature*
templado/a *mild*
la temporada *season*
temporal *temporary*
temprano *early*
tener (ie)* *to have*   tenga *here you are*   tener que +*inf* *to have to*
el teniente coronel *lieutenant colonel*
el tenis *tennis*
el tenista *tennis player*
la tensión *tension; blood pressure*
teñir (i) *to dye*
la teoría *theory*
tepiteño/a *of Tepito* (*area of Mexico City*)
tercero/a (tercer) *third*
terminar *to finish*
la ternura *tenderness*
terrible *terrible*
terriblemente *terribly*
el territorio *territory*
el testigo presencial *eye witness*
textil *textile*
el texto *text*
ti *you*
el tiempo *time; weather; tense*   ¿cuánto tiempo? *how long?*   mucho tiempo *a long time*
la tienda *shop*
la tierra *earth*
la tintada *dye*
el tinte *dye*
tinto *red* (*wine*)
el tío *uncle*
típicamente *typically*
típico/a *typical*
el tipo *type, sort*
tirar *to push*
tirarse *to throw oneself*
el tiro *throw*
titulado/a *qualified*
el título *title, degree*
el tobillo *ankle*
tocar *to touch*   tocar las palmas *to clap one's hands*   tocar a *to be someone's turn*
el tocino *salt pork*
todavía *still, yet*

todo *everything*   sobre todo *above all,
especially*
todo/a *all, every; the whole*
todos/as *all, every*
tolerante *tolerant*
la toma *taking, acquiring*
tomar *to take; to have*
el tomate *tomato*
el tono *tone*
el toque *clapping*
torcer (ue) *to turn, swerve*
la tormenta *storm*
tormentoso/a *stormy*
el toro *bull*   los toros *bulls, bull-fighting*
la tortilla *omelette*
total *total*
totalmente *totally*
trabajado/a *weary, worn out*
trabajador/ora *(hard) working*
trabajar *to work*
el trabajo *work, job*
la tradición *tradition*
tradicional *traditional*
traducir (zc) *to translate*
el traductor, la traductora *translator*
traer* *to bring (home); to take*
la tragedia *tragedy*
el traje *suit*
la tranquilidad *quietness, peace and quiet*
tranquilo/a *quiet, peaceful*
la transformación *transformation*
la transgresión *mixing up*
transitar *to pass through*
el transporte *transport*
trasladar *to transfer*
el tratamiento *treatment*
tratar *to treat*   tratar de *to try to*   se trata
de *it's a matter of*
través: a través de *across; through*
treinta *thirty*
el tren *train*
tres *three*
triste *sad*
el triunfo *victory*
el trono *throne*
tú *you*
tumbo: dar un tumbo *to take a tumble*
el turismo *tourism*
el/la turista *tourist*
turístico/a *tourist*

turno: por turno *in turn*
tu, tus *your*
Turquía (f) *Turkey*
el tuteo *using* tú

U

u = o
últimamente *recently*
último/a *last; latest; top*   por último *finally*
últimos/as *last few*
un, una *a/an*
la una *one o'clock*
únicamente *solely, only*
único/a *only; single*
unido/a (con) *together with*
universal *universal*
la universidad *university*
universitario/a *university*
uno/a *one*
unos/as *some, a few*
urbanístico/a *town planning*
urbano/a *urban*
la urdimbre *warp*
usado/a *second-hand*
usar *to use*
el uso *use*
usted, ustedes *you*
el ustedo *using* usted
útil *useful*
utilizar *to use*

V

las vacaciones *holidays*   de vacaciones *on holiday*
vacío/a *empty*
vago/a *lazy, idle*
valenciano/a *from Valencia*
valer* (*like* salir) *to be worth*   vale la pena *it's
worth* (*while*)   hacer valer *to be valued,
respected*   vale *OK, fine*
valioso/a *great*
el valor *value*
valorar *to value*
vamos (*see* ir)
la variación *variation*
variar *to vary*
la variedad *variety*
varios/as *several*

el varón *boy, male*
varonil *manly*
el vaso *glass*
el vecino *neighbour*
la vegetación *vegetation*
el vehículo *vehicle*
veinte *twenty*
el vencedor *winner, victor*
vencer *to win*
el vencido *loser, defeated*
el vendedor *seller*   el vendedor ambulante *pedlar*
vender *to sell*
venezolano/a *of/from Venezuela*
venir (ie)* *to come*   venir bien *to suit, be convenient*
la venta *sale*
la ventaja *advantage*
la ventana *window*
la ventanilla *counter ('little window')*
ver* (*pp* visto) *to see; to watch*   tener que ver que con *to have to do with*   vamos a ver *let's see*   verse *to see one another, meet*
veranear *to spend the summer*
el verano *summer*
la verbena *open-air fair*
la verdad *truth*   es verdad *it's true*   ¿verdad? *right?*   ¿verdad o mentira? *true or false?*
verdaderamente *really*
verdadero/a *true, real*
verde *green*   verde claro *light green*
la versión *version*
vestido/a *dressed*
vestir (i) *to dress*
la vez *time*   una vez *once*   tal vez *perhaps*   a veces, alguna vez *sometimes*   de vez en cuando *sometimes, from time to time*   otra vez *again*
viajar *to travel*
el viaje *journey, trip*   la agencia de viajes *travel agency*
la vida *life*
viejo/a *old*
viernes (*m*) *Friday*

vilo: en vilo *in suspense*
la villa *town*
el vino *wine*
la violencia *violence*
violentamente *violently*
violento/a *violent*
visible *visible*
visitar *to visit*
la vista *view*   el punto de vista *point of view*
la vitalidad *vitality*
la vitamina *vitamin*
la viuda *widow*
la vivienda *house, housing*
vivir *to live*
vivo/a *living, alive*
el vocabulario *vocabulary*
la vocación *vocation*
el voleibol *volleyball*
volver (ue) (*pp* vuelto) *to return*   volver a +*inf* *to ... again*
vos (*LA*) *you*
vosotros/as *you*
la votación *voting*
el voto *vote*
la voz *voice*
el vuelo *flight*
la vuelta *return*   a la vuelta *overleaf, over the page*   dar una vuelta *to go for a walk*

Y

y *and*
ya *now; yes, of course*
yo *I*
el yoga *yoga*

Z

la zanahoria *carrot*
el zapato *shoe*
la zona *area, district, part of town*

DEMOCRACIES
IN DEVELOPMENT
Politics and Reform in Latin America

WITHDRAWN

J. Mark Payne, Daniel Zovatto G., and Mercedes Mateo Díaz

Andrés Allamand Zavala, Fernando Carrillo-Flórez, Koldo Echebarría,
Flavia Freidenberg, and Edmundo Jarquín

**Published by the
Inter-American Development Bank,
the International Institute for Democracy and Electoral Assistance, and
the David Rockefeller Center for Latin American Studies,
Harvard University**

Washington, D.C.
2007

10376074

Produced by the IDB Office of External Relations

1st edition, 2002
Expanded and updated edition, 2007

To order this book, contact:
IDB Bookstore
Tel: (202) 623-1753
Fax: (202) 623-1709
E-mail: idb-books@iadb.org
www.iadb.org/pub

The views and opinions expressed in this publication are those of the authors and do not necessarily reflect the official position of the Inter-American Development Bank.

**Cataloging-in-Publication data provided by the
Inter-American Development Bank
Felipe Herrera Library**

Democracies in development : politics and reform in Latin America / J. Mark Payne ... [et al.]

"Expanded and updated edition, 2007"

     p. cm.
     Includes bibliographical references.
     ISBN 1-59782-036-9
     LCCN 2007920347

1. Elections—Latin America. 2. Latin America—Politics and government—1980-. 3. Latin America—Economic conditions—1982–. I. Payne, J. Mark. II. Inter-American Development Bank. III. International Institute for Democracy and Electoral Assistance. IV. David Rockefeller Center for Latin American Studies.

324 D36--dc21
JF1001 D36 2007

Contents

Foreword

More than 200 years ago, Charles de Montesquieu and Adam Smith identified the relationship between the well-being of nations and a sound legal framework capable of ensuring certain fundamental rights. Since that time, institutions have remained a significant focus of discussion and debate in both academic and political forums. Throughout the past century, the vital role played by institutions has been examined by Ronald Coase and neo-institutionalist academics like Douglass North, acquiring renewed salience in the 1990s as research and thinking in the area converged to shed light on major world events.

Today, demanding markets and increasingly globalized economies compel countries to have the capacity to adapt quickly to change. The necessary adaptability is built on many qualities—chief among them confidence in a predictable legal system and public policies; a reliable and flexible regulatory framework that stimulates business growth and labor market expansion; efficient investment in human capital and infrastructure; and social policies that cultivate both a well-prepared labor force and effective mechanisms of social protection. All these components necessarily depend on a system of strong institutions that facilitate the design and implementation of reforms that are sound, gradual, and well-adapted to specific realities.

During the past 25 years, countries in Latin America and the Caribbean have experienced the progressive consolidation of democratic freedoms, and political actors and citizens have accepted the rules of the electoral game. Representatives of the region's governments have agreed to take part in competitive electoral processes in which they subject their political performance to periodic voting. The current period is the region's most protracted and geographically extensive electoral phase in history. In some cases, this has brought considerable political realignment, the opening of representative institutions to new political groups and, certainly, along with that, the advancement of novel ideas. The current challenge is now to ensure that democratic institutions endure and are consolidated and strengthened by such processes.

The present study focuses precisely on these institutions. It examines prevailing reform trends as well as the principal governance challenges confronting the region. It is our thesis that while the interactions, negotiations, and agreements among political actors are certainly significant, even more significant are the institutions within which such interactions take place.

Written in this spirit, this book is the result of a joint effort initiated by the Inter-American Development Bank and the International Institute for Democracy and Electoral Assistance in 2002 with the publication of the first edition of *Democracies in Development*. The great demand for both the English and Spanish editions prompted the preparation of this expanded and updated edition. We hope that this book, like the first edition, stimulates useful debate on the central institutional questions shaping the course of development in the region.

Luis Alberto Moreno   Vidar Helgesen
President   Secretary-General
Inter-American Development Bank   International IDEA

Acknowledgments

Assembling this book depended on contributions from many people. Edmundo Jarquín, former chief of the State, Governance, and Civil Society Division of the Sustainable Development Department at the Inter-American Development Bank (IDB), and Bengt Säve-Söderbergh, the former secretary-general of the International Institute for Democracy and Electoral Assistance (International IDEA), provided solid intellectual and institutional support to the project. Marco Ferroni, deputy manager of the IDB's Sustainable Development Department, ensured that this institutional commitment was carried through to the completion of this revised edition. Special thanks are also due Andrés Allamand Zavala, who conceived the idea of producing the first edition of this book and, through his enthusiasm and leadership, helped to move it forward in its early stages.

The theoretical and conceptual discussions in each chapter drew on insights and analysis in the published works of numerous scholars. Given their studies' particular importance to the conceptual frameworks and theoretical ideas presented in various chapters of the book, we owe special gratitude to the following scholars: Manuel Alcántara, John Carey, Fernando Cepeda, Rodolfo Cerdas, Larry Diamond, Scott Mainwaring, Dieter Nohlen, Pippa Norris, Guillermo O'Donnell, Marc F. Plattner, Juan Rial, Dani Rodrik, Andreas Schedler, Timothy R. Scully, Amartya Kumar Sen, and Matthew Soberg Shugart.

We also thank Manuel Alcántara, Humberto de la Calle, Fernando Cepeda, Ricardo Córdova, Flavia Freidenberg, Mark P. Jones, Fabrice Lehoucq, José Enrique Molina, Dieter Nohlen, Guillermo O'Donnell, Juan Rial, Daniel Sabsay, and Michael Shifter for the valuable comments they provided on various chapters of the first edition. This new edition also benefited from comments from participants in the seminars and conferences at which the first edition was presented and discussed, and from the helpful remarks of two anonymous reviewers.

We are also grateful for the contributions of numerous country experts who enthusiastically committed themselves to filling gaps and checking the information on institutional rules and structures for particular countries—information that provided the foundation for the cross-country comparisons presented in the chapters and the country tables presented in Appendix 1. Without their generous collaboration, this book would not have been possible. The following persons deserve our deepest gratitude: Delia Ferreira Rubio, Laura Velásquez, Delia Matilde Ferreira, Daniel Sabsay, and Hernán Gonçalvez (Argentina); Jorge Lazarte, René Mayorga, and Alfredo Bocángel (Bolivia); David Fleischer, Torquato Jardim, Fernando Neves, and Bruno W. Speck (Brazil); Rolando Franco, Pedro Ignacio Mujica B., and Juan Ignacio García (Chile); Gabriel de Vega, Augusto Hernández Becerra, and María Magdalena Forero (Colombia); Rubén Hernández, Gonzalo Brenes, and Fabrice Lehoucq (Costa Rica); Flavio Darío Espinal, José Ángel Aquino, Luis Arias, and Isis Duarte (Dominican Republic); Alexandra Vela, Medardo Oleas Simón Pachano, and Andrés Mejía Acosta (Ecuador); Francisco Bertrand and Félix Ulloa (El Salvador); Jorge Mario García La Guardia and Gabriel Medrano (Guatemala); Mario Aguilar and Adán Palacios (Honduras); José M. Serna de la Garza, Carlos Vargas, Arturo Núñez, and Fabrice Lehoucq (Mexico); Rosa Marina Zelaya (Nicaragua); Eduardo Valdés and Ermitas Pérez (Panama); Rafael Dendia, Jorge Silvero Salgueiro, and Line Bareiro (Paraguay); Fernando Tuesta, Ximena Zavala, Jorge Valladares, and Adelaida Bolívar (Peru); Liliana Cella, Juan Rial, and Rodolfo González (Uruguay); Mercedes de Freitas, José Enrique Molina, and Jacqueline Mosquera (Venezuela), and Ronny Rodríguez (Honduras, Guatemala, and El Salvador).

For the care devoted to editorial production, we thank the IDB's Office of External Relations, where the work on this volume was coordinated by Rafael Cruz and Elisabeth Schmitt. The manuscript was edited by Steven B. Kennedy and proofread by Naomi Chernick-Berman. Michael Harrup served as production editor, and Cathy Conkling-Shaker provided editorial assistance. The cover was designed by Cinthya Cuba, and the interior design and layout were handled by Sandra Reinecke of The Word Express, Inc.

We are also indebted to Ileana Aguilar at International IDEA and Juan Cruz Perusia, Ana Inés Basco, Mauricio Granillo, and Ingrid Carlson of the IDB, for their valuable research and editorial assistance for this new edition. Nor can we fail to mention Marcelo Varela at International IDEA and Stephanie Hogan, Claudio Galán, Sean Reagan, and Elisa Vannini of the IDB, for their contributions to the first edition.

Preface

The extension of democracy in Latin America and its steady consolidation in some countries have brought major benefits to citizens, including guarantees of political and civil freedoms and the protection of fundamental human rights. Nevertheless, in the first decade of the new millennium, important challenges remain in the social, economic, and political spheres. Despite the adoption of market-oriented economic policy reforms, following the guidelines of the so-called Washington Consensus, economic growth since 1990 has been disappointing and has so far failed to sustain high levels of employment and increased living standards for the majority of citizens.

As a consequence, only in some countries have high poverty rates fallen, and even there only slightly. A June 2005 report of the Economic Commission for Latin America and the Caribbean (ECLAC) indicates that since 1990 Latin America's rate of progress in reducing the share of the population living in conditions of extreme poverty has been insufficient to meet the target established in the Millennium Development Goals for 2015 (ECLAC, 2005).[1] Advances in reducing hunger and childhood malnutrition have been greater for the region as a whole, but limited for the countries in which these problems are especially acute. Of the total population in the region, 18.6 percent (or 96 million people) live in conditions of extreme poverty, while 42.9 percent (or 222 million people) live in poverty. In general, the countries with the longest and most ingrained democratic traditions (such as Chile, Costa Rica, and Uruguay) are the ones that have made the most progress in reducing

---

[1] The Millennium Development Goals arose from an agreement between the governments of the 189 countries that took part in the United Nations Millennium Summit (2000). Eight development objectives were established that were to be fulfilled by 2015. They are to: (1) cut hunger and extreme poverty in half; (2) achieve universal primary education; (3) promote gender equality; (4) reduce infant mortality; (5) reduce mortality of women at childbirth; (6) halt the spread of HIV/AIDS and malaria; (7) guarantee the sustainability of the environment; and (8) promote a world partnership for development, with goals for assistance, trade, and reduction of the debt burden.

poverty. Other countries, such as Brazil, Colombia, Ecuador, and Mexico have made some, but still deficient, progress. Another group of countries, including Bolivia, Guatemala, and Nicaragua, have the farthest to go to meet the target.

In light of the experience in this and other developing regions, as well as a new body of theoretical and empirical research, there is a growing consensus that modernizing the state and consolidating the broader institutional framework at the foundation of a market-centered economy are essential to accelerate the pace of social and economic progress. The increased attention to the need to strengthen democratic institutions as a goal in and of itself, as well as for the sake of broader development objectives, is evidenced in various multilateral initiatives and in several recent publications. For instance, at the Quebec Summit of the Americas (April 2001) the countries of the region declared that "democracy and economic and social development are interdependent and mutually reinforcing as fundamental conditions to combat poverty and inequality." The adoption of the Inter-American Democratic Charter in Lima (September 2001) affirmed respect for core democratic values as a condition for membership in hemispheric organizations.

Democracy in Latin America: Towards a Citizens' Democracy, published by the United Nations Development Programme (UNDP, 2004) aimed to rally the multilateral community and the countries of the region around the objective of preserving and strengthening democracy. It called attention to the particular challenges to democratic consolidation posed by the limited fulfillment of civil and social rights in many countries of the region.

More recently, the Inter-American Development Bank (2006) published *The Politics of Policies* as its 2006 annual research report. That volume examined how relatively steady features of public policies—such as their stability, adaptability, and orientation to the public welfare—are affected by characteristics of the democratic policy-making process, including the independence of the judiciary, the professionalism of the civil service, and the capacity of the legislature.

This updated and expanded second edition of *Democracies in Development* underlines the importance of politics, and more specifically of how institutional features of democratic systems affect their functioning as well as the prospects for their consolidation. As in the first edition, we review Latin America's experience with democratic reform over the past quarter-century in order to identify the prevailing trends and to glean some lessons, however tentative and contingent, about the types of reforms that may or may not hold promise for strengthening democracy. We do not offer prescriptions or recipes. Rather, our purpose is to highlight many of the key issues, provide a map of the reform options available, and contribute conceptual tools and information to the debate about democratic reform.

Because the book aims to contribute to the debate over political reform, its structure and language are designed to be accessible and appealing to practitioners, policy makers, representatives of civil society, the media, and the development assistance community. The goal is not to break new theoretical ground or to test hypotheses. Instead, the book's main contribution is to apply a common conceptual framework to describing and analyzing the different institutional arrangements across Latin America.

We cover 18 Latin American countries over the period that begins with the arrival of the region's "third wave" of democracy (Table 1). The specific period examined for each country begins either in 1978 or at the point of the first reasonably free and fair democratic

Table 1. Latin America's Transition to Democracy, 1978–2005

Country	Transition year (first year of study)	Years of democracy since first year of study	Elections during the period of the study	
			Presidential	Legislative
Argentina	1983	21	1983, 1989, 1995, 1999, 2003	1983, 1985, 1987, 1989, 1991, 1993, 1995, 1997, 1999, 2001, 2003
Bolivia	1982	22	1980, 1985, 1989, 1993, 1997, 2002, 2005	1980, 1985, 1989, 1993, 1997, 2002, 2005
Brazil	1985	19	1989, 1994, 1998, 2002	1986, 1990, 1994, 1998, 2002
Chile	1990	14	1989, 1993, 1999, 2005	1989, 1993, 1997, 2001, 2005
Colombia[1]	1978	26	1978, 1982, 1986, 1990, 1994, 1998, 2002	1978, 1982, 1986, 1990, 1991, 1994, 1998, 2002
Costa Rica[1]	1978	26	1978, 1982, 1986, 1990, 1994, 1998, 2002	1978, 1982, 1986, 1990, 1994, 1998, 2002
Dominican Republic	1978	26	1978, 1982, 1988, 1992, 1994, 2000, 2004	1978, 1982, 1986, 1990, 1994, 1998, 2002, 2006,
Ecuador	1979	25	1978, 1984, 1988, 1992, 1996, 1998, 2002	1979, 1984, 1986, 1988, 1990, 1992, 1994, 1996, 1998, 2002
El Salvador	1984	20	1984, 1989, 1994, 1999, 2004	1985, 1988, 1991, 1994, 1997, 2000, 2003
Guatemala	1985	19	1985, 1990, 1995, 1999, 2003	1985, 1990, 1994, 1995, 1999, 2003
Honduras	1982	22	1981, 1985, 1989, 1993, 1997, 2001, 2005	1981, 1985, 1989, 1993, 1997, 2001, 2005
Mexico[2]	1982	22	1982, 1988, 1994, 2000	1979, 1982, 1985, 1988, 1991, 1994, 1997, 2000, 2003
Nicaragua	1990	14	1990, 1996, 2001	1990, 1996, 2001
Panama	1989	15	1989, 1994, 1999, 2004	1994, 1999, 2004
Paraguay	1989	15	1989, 1993, 1998, 2003	1989, 1993, 1998, 2003
Peru	1980	24	1980, 1985, 1990, 1995, 2000, 2001	1980, 1985, 1990, 1995, 2000, 2001
Uruguay	1985	19	1984, 1989, 1994, 1999, 2004	1984, 1989, 1994, 1999, 2004
Venezuela[1]	1979	25	1978, 1983, 1988, 1993, 1998, 2000	1978, 1983, 1988, 1993, 1998, 2000, 2005

[1] Colombia, Costa Rica, and Venezuela elected their leaders through reasonably free and competitive electoral processes before 1978, the initial year of the overall study. For these countries, the first year of the study is that in which the first president elected during the period 1978–2005 took office.
[2] Since Mexico underwent a long-term process of political liberalization and democratization during the period, a particular transition year is not assigned. Rather, political institutional change in Mexico is examined beginning in 1982, the year when the first elected president of the 1978–2005 period took office.

elections following that year. The definition of this transition point in some countries is a matter of controversy. The reason for setting such a dividing line for each country is to allow for a common starting point and to ensure that the reforms considered were adopted in a basically democratic context. The first edition analyzed political reforms and electoral outcomes through December 31, 2000—the current edition goes to December 31, 2005. In some cases of special relevance, we refer to some more recent events, either in the main text or in footnotes.

The book is organized in three parts: the first concerns electoral rules and regime design; the second, the organization and role of political parties; and the third, the participatory role of citizens and their attitudes towards democratic institutions.

Chapter 1 offers a broad, general overview, informed by a historical perspective, of the purpose behind the book. By highlighting the mechanisms through which the quality of democratic politics has historically affected development, we underline the particular relevance of democratic political reform to Latin America's development prospects. In looking at the region's political systems from this long-term perspective, we develop a typology of previous democratic experience on the assumption that these differences are likely to be central in shaping the nature and extent of the challenges faced in the current democratic period. In a few countries it is possible to speak of "the recovery of democracy," implying a situation in which countries already had a long tradition of democracy and solid adherence to the rule of law prior to the period of authoritarian rule. Other countries, which throughout the 20th century experienced repeated authoritarian interruptions of democracy or semi-democratic regimes, belong to the group of nations within the democratizing wave that have "returned to the process of democratic construction." A third group of countries that have lacked experience in democratic government over most of the period are referred to as "beginning the process of democratic construction."

The succeeding chapters each focus on a different institutional dimension of presidential democracy. First, they delineate the types of possible arrangements and define the relevant concepts. Second, they discuss from a theoretical perspective the possible effects of different institutional choices on democratic governance. Third, they examine current arrangements in countries of the region and identify the main regional reform trends over the period of the study. The chapters conclude with a partial and preliminary assessment of the reasonableness of the reforms in relation to the theoretical ideas elaborated earlier in the chapter, as well as their apparent impact in practical terms.

Part I
Institutions and Democracy (I):
Election Rules and Regime Design

Part I consists of four chapters that cover the election systems used for electing the president and representatives to the legislature, the balance of constitutional and partisan power between the executive and legislative branches, and institutions intended to support the holding of public officials and governmental institutions accountable to the law and to citizens. Chapter 2 examines the different systems used for electing presidents, as well as variations in the timing of presidential and legislative elections, the length of the presidential mandate, and rules in relation to presidential reelection. Chapter 3 focuses on the different systems used for electing legislative representatives. Chapter 4 analyzes the constitutional rules defining the formal balance of power between the executive and legislature, as well as the extraconstitutional, partisan-based factors shaping the capabilities of the two branches. Finally, Chapter 5 examines the authority and institutional origins and designs of three of the main types of "horizontal accountability" agencies: supreme audit institutions, the office of the attorney general or public prosecutor, and the office of the human rights ombudsman.

Part II
Institutions and Democracy (II): Political Parties

Pursuing the same broad objectives as the chapters in Part I, the two chapters in Part II concentrate on the relationship between characteristics of political parties and political party systems on the one hand, and democratic stability and governance, on the other. Chapter 6 examines political parties from the perspective of how they shape political participation and representation, while Chapter 7 concentrates on parties' internal processes of decision making and the financing of electoral campaigns and political party activity. Thus, the former focuses on the structure and degree of institutionalization of the political party system. The latter examines two important issues related to the functioning of political parties: (1) the rules and practices for parties' selection of candidates for public office, particularly the presidency, and (2) the rules governing campaign finance and the everyday activities of political parties, as well as the mechanisms of enforcing those rules.

Part III
Citizen Participation and Democracy

Part III, which consists of three chapters, examines the linkages between institutions and citizens. Chapter 8 focuses on the variety of mechanisms established to facilitate greater direct participation by citizens in national decision making. Chapter 9 examines the degree of citizen support for democracy as a form of government and for the institutions that comprise it, examining the region as a whole as well as individual countries. Finally, Chapter 10 considers the level and evolution of electoral participation by country, comparing Latin America with other world regions. It examines the degree to which trends in participation in electoral processes reflect changes in citizens' confidence in democracy.

Conclusions

In the book's final section, we set forth a series of recommendations that may be useful in efforts to reform public sector institutions in the region. It must be emphasized that these recommendations are tentative and should be interpreted with caution. There are no universal recipes, and the possibilities for and effects of reform very much depend on their context.

We recognize that political institutions are not the only factors that affect the performance of democratic systems. A host of noninstitutional factors—including the level of social and economic development; the intensity of ethnic, religious, geographic, and socioeconomic divisions; the proclivity of citizens toward association and cooperation; the independence and plurality of the news media; and international political and economic pressures—shape the operation of all democratic systems.

In addition, the quality of political leadership is central. Regardless of the structure of incentives provided by formal institutions, individual politicians still have room to influence the performance of the political system. Daring, capable, and unselfish leadership, in fact, is necessary to undercut entrenched interests and bring about meaningful political and institutional reform. Because of variation in the pool of political leadership and the collective learning of political actors, the same formal institutional structure may produce crisis in one historical context and stability and effective governance in another.

Limited resources and space prevented us from directly considering several topics of growing importance, notably the impact of political decentralization on democratic governability, the changing political role of indigenous peoples in some of the region's political systems, the reform of judicial institutions and the civil service, and the role of civil society organizations.

This publication tends to corroborate what is already known: specific institutions function differently depending on the socioeconomic and broader institutional and cultural context in which they operate. One possible response to this observation is a pessimistic, deterministic one: reforms are doomed to fail when the context does not offer the minimum conditions or "critical mass" needed to produce substantial change. But we take a different position. Institutions that are more democratic and efficient should contribute to an increase in democratic behavior in the populations they serve. Greater institutional efficiency should reverberate in greater public confidence in leaders and representative institutions—in other words, in enhanced legitimacy of the system and its institutions. In this fashion, a virtuous circle is generated in which institutions that are more democratic will produce types of behavior that are more democratic, which in turn will further strengthen institutions.

Appendixes

The CD-ROM that accompanies this publication contains three appendixes. Appendix 1 features for each country a table that describes the prevailing rules and structures pertaining to the institutional dimensions examined in the book. This provides a reference for the reader who wants to view in one place all of the rules for a particular country. Appendix 2 provides tables for each country regarding the level of electoral participation for each national election from the beginning of the study period through 2005. Appendix 3 features tables for each country that show the number of votes and percentage of the vote obtained by the political parties for presidential and legislative elections, as well as the distribution of legislative seats by party.

Sources

The bulk of the information on institutions and reforms considered in Chapters 2 through 8 is derived from extensive consultations with experts from the countries of the region, as well as from primary and secondary research carried out by the authors. This research covered the various constitutions, statutes, electoral laws, political party laws, and other laws in force at different points during the period studied. The information on electoral participation, as well as the votes by party for presidential and legislative elections, was drawn from the electoral oversight body for each country, the International Institute for Democracy and Electoral Assistance (International IDEA, 1997 and 2002), the *Enciclopedia electoral* (Nohlen, 1993), and national statistical publications. The discussion of citizen attitudes toward democracy in Chapter 10 is based mainly on the regional public opinion survey, *Latinobarómetro*, and on a survey carried out in a more limited group of countries by the Consorcio Iberoamericano de Empresas de Investigación de Mercado y Asesoramiento (CIMA), coordinated by the Gallup Institute of Argentina. Cross-regional comparisons are facilitated by use of the Eurobarometer and the Central and Eastern Eurobarometer.

The effort to obtain, assimilate, and ensure the accuracy of a detailed and comprehensive set of data on institutions and electoral outcomes in the region was a difficult one. Though attention to institutional variables has grown in recent years, the lack of reliable information reflects, at least in part, past scholarly neglect of such factors. Other complexities were present as well. For example, the legal source for a given set of institutional arrangements, such as mechanisms of direct democracy or audit agencies, is not necessarily the national constitution, but may be specific laws. Given the detailed knowledge required to understand how particular institutions are structured, and how they have been reformed, local expertise is essential.

The unavailability or unreliability of particular types of information—such as electoral registration data or votes by party for a given election—may also reflect the relatively weak capacity, and in some cases, the still limited transparency of some national political institutions. As a consequence, even if one relies exclusively on a single official source, it is common to find conflicting or missing information. The problem, of course, is multiplied when one is forced to rely on various secondary sources. The specific wording of laws is also quite different from how they are enforced or applied in practice. Constitutions and political laws are inherently rife with ambiguity, and the entities established to interpret them vary considerably in their degree of political independence and capacity. Thus, while the rules governing a particular institutional area may be correctly described in the book, the practical implications of such rules may be misinterpreted, given the leeway possible in their actual application. We simplify this problem somewhat by concerning ourselves mainly with a formal and literal reading of the rules and laws. Nevertheless, we also attempt to take into account as far as possible the divergences between rules and their practical application.

—The authors

References

CIMA (Consorcio Iberoamericano de Empresas de Investigación de Mercado y Asesoramiento). 2001. Public opinion survey undertaken in collaboration with the Instituto Gallup de Argentina.

ECLAC (United Nations Economic Commission for Latin America). 2005. *The Millennium Development Goals: A Latin American and Caribbean Perspective*. Santiago, Chile: ECLAC.

IDB (Inter-American Development Bank). 2006. *The Politics of Policies: Economic and Social Progress Report in Latin America*. Washington, D.C.: Inter-American Development Bank and Cambridge, MA: Harvard University Press.

International IDEA. 1997. *Voter Turnout from 1945 to 1997: A Global Report on Political Participation*. Stockholm: International IDEA.

————. 2002. *Voter Turnout since 1945: A Global Report*. Stockholm: International IDEA.

Latinobarómetro. 1996–2004. *Latinobarómetro: Opinión Pública Latinoamericana*. Santiago, Chile: Corporación Latinobarómetro.

Nohlen, Dieter, ed. 1993. *Enciclopedia electoral Latinoamericana y del Caribe*. San José, Costa Rica: Inter-American Institute for Human Rights.

UNDP (United Nations Development Programme). 2004. *Democracy in Latin America: Towards a Citizens' Democracy*. New York: UNDP.

CHAPTER 1

The Role of the State and Politics in Latin American Development (1950–2005)

An analysis of the institutional design of Latin American political systems has, until recently, been largely absent from explanations of development failure in the region.[1] While not attempting to define their causes, several political factors have been blamed for the region's economic instability.[2] Of these, one of the most prominent is political instability—as reflected in the frequency of constitutional change, coups d'état, irregular transfers of governmental power, armed insurgencies, and massive social protests. It is argued that the environment created by the frequent changes in power relationships and rules of the political game have been unsuitable for long-term investment and sustained economic growth.

The failures of Latin American development in the 20th century are not just associated with the episodic and deficient nature of economic growth, but also its lack of social equity (Thorp, 1998). Many countries in Latin America grew considerably over the past century, achieving significant progress. But the region continues to suffer overwhelming inequality across social classes, and its relative position in the world economy declined in the second half of the 20th century. Despite the significant economic reforms carried out over the past two decades, few countries have managed to achieve high and sustained rates of economic growth.

---

[1] As elsewhere throughout this book, this chapter considers only the Spanish-speaking countries of Latin America, and Brazil. The Caribbean Basin countries that have parliamentary systems are not included, given their distinct institutional, historical, and political conditions.

[2] Whether or not there is sufficient empirical evidence to demonstrate a cause-effect relationship between democracy and development has been the subject of considerable debate in academic forums. A stronger consensus does exist, however, on the relevance of several other institutional conditions. For example, the existence of an independent, competent, merit-based bureaucracy and adequate levels of security and confidence in the legal system have been found to be associated with higher levels of development. These conditions have generally not existed in much of Latin America.

In relation to the equity, depth, and sustainability of economic growth, the role of politics is best viewed as structural and long term in nature. This chapter briefly reviews the relationship between politics and growth over two major periods: between the end of World War II and the economic crises of the 1980s, and the years since—the "post-1980s"—when countries adopted significant economic reforms in response to these crises.

Development in Latin America, 1950–1980: The Price of the Democratic Deficit

The economic depression of the 1930s ravaged the international export markets for the raw materials that had been the cornerstone of Latin America's national economies since colonial times. Abruptly cut off from their sources of foreign exchange, the governments of the region suddenly found themselves unable to import the capital goods and manufactured products upon which their development depended. In response to this challenge, attempts were made to locally produce what had previously been imported. The National Financial Board in Mexico and the Corporation to Promote Production in Chile were among the state agencies created in the 1930s that gave impetus to new industrialization policies, which responded to the crisis in the primary product export model. A shift away from this model began in Mexico and the larger South American economies in the 1930s, then spread to Central American countries in the late 1950s as they embarked on a process of subregional integration. As a result of these economic efforts, states also became more active in the processes of development and social protection.

The initial work of the United Nations Economic Commission on Latin America and the Caribbean (ECLAC), under the leadership of Argentine economist Raúl Prebisch, provided an intellectual rationale for these policies. A new strategy that aimed to generate "growth from within" entailed a variety of tariff, fiscal, exchange rate, and credit instruments that were financed and implemented by the state to favor the industrial sector. At the same time, new social classes created by the industrialization process voiced demands for urban development, public education, health services, and social security arrangements. These could only be answered by social policies and public services also funded by the state. In this way, the state became a central actor in development, with a large bureaucracy that absorbed a growing amount of resources. Ministries of planning—the institutional outcome of this state-led development model—were created in order to coordinate the rational allocation of public investment resources.

Three major ideological currents converged in this post–World War II development model: a distrust of markets, influenced by the experiences of the Great Depression and wartime supply disruptions; the economic theories of John Maynard Keynes; and the influence of socialism.

The resulting state-led development model changed formerly rural societies into more urbanized ones, with rapidly growing cities and industrial sectors. Annual growth in the region between 1950 and 1970 averaged 5 percent. Despite extraordinary population growth, almost every country managed to double per capita income. But the enormous historical inequities in Latin American societies did not diminish; urban growth improved the standard of living of only a portion of the population. Slow growth in exports; insatiable demand for imported capital goods; discrimination against export commodities; and the extensive public, economic, and social role of the state contributed to significant imbalances in public sector finances and in the balance of payments. The effects of the 1971 devaluation of the U.S. dollar and the oil-price shocks in the middle of that decade finally made it clear that the state-led, import-substitution model was no longer sustainable. With a high level of international financial liquidity, fed by recycled earnings from the export of higher-priced petroleum, Latin American countries borrowed heavily in an effort to conserve the status quo. They accumulated large external debts in the process, creating the conditions for the debt crisis of the 1980s and changing the development paradigm.

The crisis in the traditional development model can be attributed to three major imbalances: (1) a growing trade deficit aggravated by excessive protectionism, a narrow export base, and distorted incentives; (2) deterioration in fiscal balances, brought on by the growing responsibilities of the state and the endemic weakness of its resources; and (3) rampant inflation triggered by the monetization of fiscal deficits. There is little doubt that the state-led model placed excessive faith in the capacity and neutrality of the state's role in the development process. Based on the idea that development was largely a technical matter, it was implicitly assumed that the design and implementation of countries' development policies simply required the growth and strengthening of the state or some of its essential components. To some extent, these same assumptions guided the development orientation of the so-called Asian tigers in recent decades. But while the Asian economies sustained high rates of growth and transformed themselves into industrial economies, the Latin American economies failed to take off. Aside from broad differences in the economic and industrial policies followed by the two regions, there is another, political and institutional, explanation consistent with the focus of this book.

The state in Latin America has been historically characterized by structural weaknesses that have left it little ability to play its assigned role. In the most successful Asian countries, the state's autonomy in relation to particular interests, as well as its strength, has been nurtured by centuries of bureaucratic tradition (in China and Japan) or the legacy of colonial administrations (Malaysia, Singapore, and even South Korea under U.S. occupation). These histories have created an effective, relatively autonomous state apparatus capable of acting independently from narrow group interests.

The situation in most Latin American countries is significantly different. The structural weakness that characterizes states in the region is caused by two principal factors: (1) an inadequate tax base, caused by the historical absence of a redistributional pact subscribed to by the highest income groups, and (2) the capture of tax resources—and the public sector apparatus itself—by private interests with disproportionate political and economic power. Throughout the period 1950–1980, most countries experienced a kind of privatization of the state as its central resources were captured by special interest groups that included political parties; economic groups, trade unions, and associations; local and regional groups; and, in extreme cases, strongmen, dictators, and their associates (Chehabi and Linz, 1998).

Thus, the differences between the industrialization policies of Asian and Latin American countries lie both in the quality of their implementation and in their design. Latin American bureaucracies have been hampered by their political incapacity to override private interests and establish proactive market regulation mechanisms, such as controlling monopolistic tendencies and eliminating barriers to entry. The absence of such capacity also explains the clientelistic public employment and budgetary practices, in which these resources of the state are used primarily for the purposes of building and maintaining bases of political support rather than for promoting the broader public good. In the 1950–1980 period, states became highly centralized, bloated, and captured—features that proved detrimental to their ability to effectively implement sound development policies. Authoritarian interventions in response to political crises often entailed the relinquishing of government control to the armed forces, but this usually failed to strengthen or rationalize government structures, or to imbue them with relative autonomy. The military acted in the role of guarantor of stability and political order, but it was unable or unwilling in most cases to act as an impartial referee between different societal forces and interests, and often introduced interests that hijacked the state's orientation away from ensuring the public good.

If a conclusion can be drawn from the experience of this period, it is that effective development promotion depends as much on the neutrality and capacity of the state as on the technical rationale and specific design of its policies (IDB, 2006). State characteristics that foster development could not be achieved in the political environment that prevailed during the period. Few countries made progress toward constructing a secure, democratic rule of law,[3] essential for achieving a reasonable level of independence from special interests and bolstering confidence in the political and legal systems. Such confidence is particularly critical to savings and productive long-term investment, both domestic and international. Instead, the period's legacy is political instability and institutional weakness, caused by three main factors:

- The bitterness of the political-ideological conflicts in most countries between capitalism and socialism, and between economic liberalism and different forms of authoritarian populism. These conflicts continued in at least half of the countries in the hemisphere into the late 1970s, and in some cases expressed themselves in the form of armed insurgent movements. Such struggles offered little capacity to build a consensus behind common national objectives. Instead, society was often under the threat of a radical redistribution or wholesale change of power.
- The persistence of poverty and inequality, despite the significant progress associated with the economic growth of the period 1950–1980. Slow growth in productivity and a concentrated distribution of assets in the agrarian sector encouraged an exodus from rural areas. Despite heavy state subsidization, the level of industrial expansion was insufficient to productively absorb all the migrants to urban centers.
- The application of a national security doctrine that emphasized the maintenance of social and political order and limited the scope of dissent, reinforcing the historical authoritarian tendencies in many countries.

---

[3] The notable exceptions are Costa Rica, Chile, and Uruguay, which developed more institutionalized legal systems.

Most countries in the region have been characterized by a "democratic deficit" that has occasionally been manifested in the phenomena of authoritarianism, clientelism, populism, corruption, and the capture of institutions and public policies by special interests. These phenomena have resulted in state actions that discourage efficient working markets, instead promoting rent-seeking behavior and speculation. At the same time, they have contributed to "a policy-making process in which the policies do not reflect the processing and aggregation of the demands of the majority of citizens but rather lead to the exclusion of broad sectors of society from the benefits of growth" (IDB, 2003).

The region's chronic democratic deficit has contributed to the noninclusive nature of its development (Iglesias, 2004). Despite experiencing reasonable economic growth between 1950 and the mid-1970s, countries in the region generally failed to become more socially cohesive, with lower levels of inequality and a broader sharing of economic opportunities. The inadequate relationship between the state and its citizens is a key reason for persistent political instability, and the consequent disincentives for savings and investment that have limited the possibilities of sustained growth. Thus, key factors impeding sustainable and equitable development in Latin America have been the ineffectiveness of the state in (1) regulating and promoting market growth, (2) providing evenhanded representation of citizen interests in the state's market interventions, and (3) providing public services.

Political and Economic Transformations in 1980–2005 and the Persistent Democratic Deficit

Beginning in the late 1970s, a process of dramatic and far-reaching transformation—the movement from authoritarian to democratic regimes—was initiated in parallel with economic reforms that significantly changed the previously state-centered and protectionist development model. Despite economic reforms' profound impact on states, little attention was paid to ensuring that the political and institutional requisites for their successful and sustained implementation were present. Similar to the previous period, reform design was treated as a technical problem rather than one inherently related to the institutional and political features of the processes through which such reforms were to be adopted and implemented (IDB, 2006).

Since the late 1970s, Latin America has also undergone a series of political changes that have displaced the old models of noninclusive governance, whether espoused and practiced by military-led governments, revolutionary movements, or civilian authoritarian governments under the tutelage of traditional parties. This period witnessed a movement toward democracy that was broader, more deeply engrained, and longer lasting than any in the region's history. In addition, the foundations were set and expectations raised for further citizen mobilization and organization, which presented new risks. In the past, democratic rule was established only in some countries for brief periods, or under conditions that limited political power to a small portion of the population. After the late 1970s, the reality became quite different. At present, cross-national indexes of civil and political rights show levels in the Latin American region that compare favorably with other regions of the world and approach those of high-income countries (Figure 1.1).

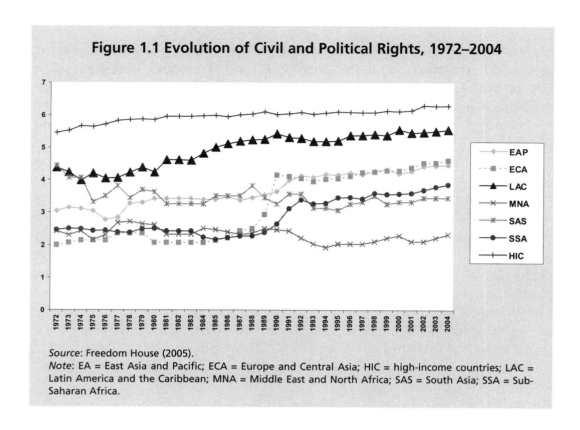

Figure 1.1 Evolution of Civil and Political Rights, 1972–2004

Source: Freedom House (2005).
Note: EA = East Asia and Pacific; ECA = Europe and Central Asia; HIC = high-income countries; LAC = Latin America and the Caribbean; MNA = Middle East and North Africa; SAS = South Asia; SSA = Sub-Saharan Africa.

Democratization has entailed a real redistribution of political power. First, political rights and freedoms have advanced enormously, allowing free and competitive elections to become an important factor in the political process. Competitive electoral processes have given the majority of citizens the ability to hold elected governments accountable—at least in the blunt sense of being able to vote them out of office. Power has been redistributed and democratized in geographic terms, thanks to its widespread decentralization in sub-national regions and municipalities. In many countries, ethnic minorities and women are represented at much higher levels than in previous decades and are more actively involved in the political process.

Free elections, though necessary, are an insufficient condition for democracy to function and respond effectively to the expectations of the majority. It is also essential to develop an intermediation process to translate the popular electoral mandate into policies and programs that are responsive to the will of citizens but do not overlook the need to objectively assess the nature of social problems and verify the viability and likely effectiveness of proposed policy changes. This process of aggregating individual preferences and expectations and resolving conflicting interests is affected by the structure of intermediate institutions such as political parties, legislative bodies, electoral rules, and civil society organizations. It is in these institutions that many of the region's democracies still face important limitations.

The weakness of such institutions, as well as of judicial and accountability agencies, is a key factor in the region's continued political instability. This weakness also contributes to

Democracies in Development

the precarious standing of several democratically elected leaders, the recurrent appeal of populism, the viability of clientelistic networks, and the growing influence of spontaneous social protest movements in some countries. Constructing stable institutions that can intermediate between citizen preferences and public policy, inspiring new confidence in legal and political institutions, is now the central challenge necessary for the consolidation and deepening of democracy in the region.

The prospects for such institutional stability are likely to be affected by the nature of the institutions and practices inherited from past experience. Thus, an analysis of countries' relative progress in advancing democracy can be facilitated by categorizing democratic transitions according to whether they represent a "recovery of democracy," the "resumption of processes of constructing democracy," or the "initiation of processes of constructing democracy." Prior to their authoritarian periods, only a few countries, such as Chile and Uruguay, experienced considerable advancement toward democratic rule and the development of effective representative institutions.[4] In the largest group of countries, where the democratic tradition was not deeply rooted, recent changes constitute the resumption of democratization efforts that had been halted by recurrent or prolonged authoritarian interventions.[5] In the other group—including Guatemala, Nicaragua, and El Salvador—the move toward democracy was, for practical purposes, initiated with the recent regime transitions.

The recent spread of democracy has taken place amid an adverse economic climate in which the majority of the population has perceived—and received—few concrete improvements in their living standards. The new democratic regimes have faced bouts of recession or sluggish growth, along with external economic shocks that have overpowered their ability to meet citizen expectations. As shown in Table 1.1, in a 25-year period marked by the debt crisis and economic reforms, most of the countries in the region have grown very little, and this growth has tended to be erratic. Poverty has not been significantly reduced in most cases, and in some cases, social inequalities have even increased. This situation is in stark contrast with the post–World War II history of democratization in many developed countries such as West Germany, Austria, Japan, and Spain, in which regime change coincided with cycles of robust growth and reduced poverty. In many of these developed countries, basic agreements in the areas of political power sharing, social welfare, and fiscal reform were reached at similar points in time and were therefore mutually reinforcing.

Aside from difficult initial conditions, the economic reform efforts overemphasized reducing the size and role of the state while overlooking the inherent interrelationship between the workings of the political system and the functioning of the public sector. An analysis of successful cases makes it clear that in order to build effective democracy and competitive markets—and fight against poverty and inequality—a capable, neutral, and fiscally endowed state is needed. In addition to concentrating state activities on those

---

[4] According to the criteria developed in Mainwaring, Brinks, and Pérez-Liñán (2001) for distinguishing democratic, semidemocratic, and nondemocratic regimes: over the twentieth century, Costa Rica experienced 98 years of democracy, Uruguay, 78, and Chile, 75.

[5] Among this group are the nations of Brazil (with 34 years of democratic government and 37 of semidemocratic government) and Argentina (with 19 and 48 years, respectively).

Table 1.1. Economic Growth, 1980–2004

	2004/1980 GDP per capita	Average annual growth in GDP per capita 1980–2004 (%)	1990/1980 GDP per capita	Average annual growth in GDP per capita 1980–1990 (%)	2004/1990 GDP per capita	Average annual growth in GDP per capita 1990–2004 (%)
Argentina	1.01	0.03	0.77	−2.52	1.30	2.04
Bolivia	1.01	0.05	0.86	−1.55	1.18	1.30
Brazil	1.13	0.53	0.95	−0.49	1.19	1.32
Chile	2.30	3.69	1.26	2.33	1.83	4.75
Colombia	1.33	1.24	1.21	1.94	1.10	0.71
Costa Rica	1.34	1.30	0.95	−0.51	1.42	2.71
Dominican Rep.	1.71	2.36	1.05	0.51	1.62	3.80
Ecuador	1.07	0.28	1.04	0.37	1.03	0.21
El Salvador	1.13	0.55	0.86	−1.53	1.32	2.17
Guatemala	0.97	−0.12	0.86	−1.46	1.13	0.93
Honduras	0.99	−0.06	0.94	−0.58	1.05	0.35
Mexico	1.16	0.64	0.98	−0.21	1.18	1.30
Nicaragua	0.68	−1.69	0.64	−4.35	1.05	0.40
Panama	1.31	1.18	0.87	−1.35	1.50	3.18
Paraguay	0.92	−0.37	0.97	−0.27	0.94	−0.45
Peru	0.98	−0.08	0.73	−3.11	1.35	2.32
Uruguay	1.14	0.57	0.93	−0.67	1.22	1.54
Venezuela	0.82	−0.87	0.86	−0.52	0.95	−0.38
Latin American average	1.17	0.51	0.93	−0.83	1.24	1.57
China	6.67	8.60	2.09	7.67	3.18	9.32
France	1.46	1.66	1.22	2.04	1.19	1.37
India	2.44	3.96	1.44	3.74	1.69	4.14
Indonesia	2.27	3.63	1.55	4.49	1.46	2.97
Malaysia	2.23	3.55	1.36	3.13	1.64	3.88
South Korea	3.88	6.07	2.02	7.28	1.92	5.15
Spain	1.75	2.46	1.28	2.53	1.36	2.42
Thailand	3.04	4.96	1.80	6.04	1.69	4.13
United Kingdom	1.65	2.20	1.27	2.43	1.30	2.03
United States	1.62	2.12	1.26	2.30	1.29	1.99

Source: Authors' calculations based on data from World Development Indicators online (World Bank, 2005).

Democracies in Development

functions that require its involvement, priority must be placed on making the state itself stronger and more effective.

In terms of the state's relationship to its citizens, the fundamental requirements for establishing an effective rule of law are still absent in many countries. Justice is neither impartial nor trusted, access is impeded or denied to large portions of the population, and the judicial system is incapable of providing legal protections such as safeguarding the exercise of rights and obligations and controlling illegal behavior enough to limit growing incidents of crime and threats to public safety. The limited redistributional capacity of the state is witnessed in the inadequate provision of basic social services, including those that would enable citizens to productively take part in both the economic and political system.

The relationship between the state and the market changed significantly with the economic reforms implemented in recent decades. Market sectors opened that had been previously dominated by inefficient state monopolies. However, the expansion of the market's role has often not been accompanied by the establishment of regulatory structures needed to foster competition and protect consumer interests. In addition, the process of market liberalization has in many cases been driven and shaped by organized interests with a particular stake in the outcome of the reform process rather than guided by broader societal interests. The absence of institutional mechanisms for consensus building has made it difficult to forge long-term national development strategies that would enable policies to be more sustainable and comprehensive. In many countries, fiscal reforms have also failed to advance as needed to sufficiently broaden the tax base and spread the tax burden more equitably. Together with other constraints, this has hobbled the government's capacity to invest in human capital and infrastructure, expand markets, and create the positive economic and social externalities essential for attracting greater private investment and creating an efficient market.

The nature of the relationship of the state to its citizens and the market is dependent on the capacity of the public administration to formulate and implement policies. In this regard, the development of a more effective state has been limited, given that public administration reforms over the past two decades have generally been aimed at paring back the state's size and budget in response to fiscal crises, rather than embodying deeper transformations of organizational and management structures and policies. It is important to note that most countries still lack a stable, competent, well-motivated, and merit-based civil service, which is the basis of an effective public sector.

Moving Ahead: The Centrality of Politics and Institutions

In their examination of the principal reasons for Latin America's progressive economic decline—relative to several other world regions—Beato and Vives (2005) identify one of the principal reasons as the absence of a basic social consensus to enable policy continuity across governments and over time. Countries have repeatedly bounced between mutually exclusive ideological paradigms, producing volatility in the rules of the game. Two starkly contrasting, but mistaken, perspectives have particularly impeded the reaching of a broader consensus on approaches to development. On the one hand, phenomena that are actually failures of the political system, such as the continuation of poverty and the concentration of the benefits of growth, have been attributed to market failures. Placing the blame on the market has hindered appropriate public interventions to distribute the benefits of growth and has fed an antimarket fundamentalism, manifested in recurrent episodes of populism. The other extreme has been to blame the state for interventions that resulted in market distortions when, in fact, it has often been the capture of the state by private interests that has resulted in ineffective state interactions with or participation in the markets. Thus, one extreme holds that there has been too much state intervention and the other, too much market, when an objective examination would show that in development terms, the region has needed better, stronger states *and* better, stronger markets.

The largely disappointing results of the first round of reforms make it clear that macroeconomic reforms alone are not sufficient to create dynamic market economies. The complex task of transforming economies in formerly communist states plainly demonstrates that market economies require solid institutional foundations. Broad-based, deep-rooted institutional reforms are essential in order to meet the key requirements of development: solid financial systems, competitive markets, legal predictability, property rights protection, effective investment in infrastructure, and steady advances in workforce skill and productivity. Rules governing competition and transactions in diverse markets need to be put in place at the same time that the effectiveness, professionalism, and neutrality of the regulatory agencies and courts required to enforce and adjudicate them need to be assured. Tax systems must be reformed to make them more encompassing, effective, and economically neutral. In addition, the state has to administer the use of available resources to guarantee the effective supply of infrastructure and equal access to quality education and health services.

However, because of their very nature, these institutional reforms—referred to as "second generation" reforms by some observers[6]—are considerably more complex and difficult to implement than the typical macroeconomic measures adopted in response to the public financial crises of the 1980s and early 1990s (Naím, 1995; Graham and Naím, 1998). Raising taxes, reducing state subsidies, eliminating price controls, lowering public sector wages, and reducing trade tariffs could be accomplished in some cases by executive decree and in others by legislative approval of a single bill. On the other hand, enhancing the management of public sector institutions, creating a more independent and effective judiciary, and establishing regulatory frameworks usually involves coordination and agreement among a wide array of public institutions and societal actors, as well as a series of legislative and bureaucratic actions over a long period.

Clearly, much is at stake for society in the creation of regulatory frameworks, the redesign of service delivery systems, and the restructuring of public sector institutions. Such changes inevitably entail taking on powerful interests, and privileging certain social groups

---

[6] The use of the term "second generation" has engendered some controversy. Some experts disagree with the implicit message that the effort to reform institutions should be subsequent to, or in any way secondary to, neoliberal, market-oriented economic reforms. Others oppose the neoliberal approach (e.g., "Washington consensus") and decline to adopt a terminology that associates support for institutional reforms with the backing of these economic policies.

or interests to the disadvantage of others. If the benefits of institutional change end up being overly concentrated on relatively narrow interests, then larger societal groups—such as consumers, workers, and entrepreneurs—will suffer. For instance, administrative reforms of the public sector—such as enhancing governmental transparency, controlling corruption, and establishing a professional civil service—require incumbent politicians to relinquish instruments of power and to open up their conduct and decisions to more intense public scrutiny.

Thus, it is clear that politics matters in the process of creating, implementing, and sustaining sound institutions and adopting public policies that work to the benefit of all citizens. More precisely, however, it is the *quality* of democracy that matters. Not only is the exercise of democratic freedoms and civil rights intrinsically valuable in expanding the range of possibilities and choices open to citizens, it is also instrumental in identifying and conceptualizing citizen needs and building the policies and institutions that will most effectively address them (Sen, 1999). Thus, contrary to a line of thinking prevalent in the past, the task of building a legitimate, representative, and effective democratic system is not something that can be put on hold until there is an adequate level of development. Rather, given its indispensability to strengthening institutions and implementing efficient and sustainable public policies, a well-functioning democracy seems to be a necessary condition for equitable and sustainable development.

Market institutions are necessarily embedded in a set of nonmarket political institutions (Rodrik, 2000). Efficient market institutions would appear to require democratic political institutions that can ensure that fair and efficient rules are created, and that these rules are evenhandedly and consistently enforced and adjudicated. Suitable and efficient market institutions must be well adapted to the particular social, economic, historical, and cultural conditions and needs of a given country. Given the impossibility of universal blueprints, the creation and maintenance of institutions depends upon broad and effective citizen participation through well-developed representative institutions. In light of this reasoning, democratic political institutions can be viewed as "meta-institutions" underlying the larger grouping of institutions that support a market economy. As stated in IDB (2000): "Politics exercises its greatest impact on development through its effect on institutions. The logic is clear: if politics matter for institutions, and institutions matter for development, politics must matter for development."

Thus, the effective practice of democracy would appear to be the basis of creating an effective public sector and establishing a legal framework propitious for social and economic development. The adoption of effective, fair, and sustainable public policies; the efficient and fair allocation of public resources; and the effective delivery of public services depend on the existence of representative institutions that take the preferences and interests of citizens into account. Public policies need to be adopted and implemented in a way that fully considers the views of diverse civil society organizations, without falling captive to any particular group or narrow set of interests. This requires that citizens and civil society organizations have opportunities to express their preferences and influence decision making, and that representative institutions have the capacity to effectively aggregate these preferences into consensual policies with broad bases of social support. Public decisions adopted in this manner are not only efficient—in their responsiveness to the preferences and needs of society—they are also more likely to benefit from legitimacy, social compliance, and sustainability over time.

Much attention has been paid to examining the economic reforms adopted by countries in the region over the past two decades. Such considerations have generated a lively and impassioned debate about the adequacy and appropriateness of the "neoliberal" thrust of much of the economic reforms. In contrast, few attempts have been made to study, in a systematic and broadly comparative manner, the political reforms of the period or to assess the extent to which they hold the possibility for reducing the governance problems plaguing the region's democracies. What are the major regional reform trends in respect to different political institutions? What are the likely effects of these changes on the functioning of democracy? What do past reforms suggest about the types of political reforms most needed in the near future? The chapters that follow provide at least partial and contingent answers to these questions.

References

Beato, Paulina, and Antonio Vives. 2005. ¿Porqué se está quedando atrás América Latina? Technical Reports Series of the Sustainable Development Department, Inter-American Development Bank, Washington, DC.

Chehabi, Houchang, and Juan J. Linz. 1998. *Sultanistic Regimes*. Baltimore: Johns Hopkins University Press.

Freedom House. 2005. *Freedom in the World: The Annual Survey of Political Rights and Civil Liberties*. Country ratings. [Retrieved November 2005 from http://www.freedomhouse.org]

Graham, Carol, and Moisés Naím. 1998. The Political Economy of Institutional Reform in Latin America. In Nancy Birdsall, Carol Graham, and Richard H. Sabot (eds.), *Beyond Tradeoffs: Market Reforms and Equitable Growth in Latin America*. Washington, DC: Brookings Institution Press.

IDB (Inter-American Development Bank). 2000. *Development Beyond Economics: Economic and Social Progress in Latin America, 2000 Report*. Washington, DC.

————. 2003. *Modernization of the State*. Strategy Document GN-2235-1. Washington, DC.

————. 2006. *The Politics of Policies: Economic and Social Progress in Latin America, 2006 Report*. Cambridge, MA: Harvard University Press.

Iglesias, Enrique V. 2004. Democracia y desarrollo: la política importa. In *La democracia en América Latina. Hacia una democracia de ciudadanas y ciudadanos. Contribuciones para el debate*. New York: United Nations Development Programme.

Mainwaring, Scott, Daniel Brinks, and Aníbal Pérez-Liñán. 2001. Classifying Political Regimes in Latin America, 1945–1999. *Studies in Comparative International Development* 36(1): 37–65.

Naím, Moisés. 1995. *Latin America's Journey to the Market: From Macroeconomic Shocks to Institutional Therapy*. San Francisco: ICS Press.

Rodrik, Dani. 2000. Institutions for High-Quality Growth: What They Are and How to Acquire Them. *Studies in Comparative International Development* 35 (3).

Sen, Amartya Kumar. 1999. *Development as Freedom*. New York: Knopf.

Thorp, Rosemary. 1998. *Progress, Poverty and Exclusion: An Economic History of Latin America in the 20th Century*. Washington, DC: Inter-American Development Bank.

World Bank. *World Development Indicators*. [Retrieved October 2005 from http://econ.world-bank.org]

Part I

Institutions and Democracy (I):
Election Rules and
Regime Design

CHAPTER 2

The Effects of Presidential Election Systems on Democratic Governability

A key feature of presidential democracies is the separate election of the head of government and legislature. With one partial exception, this basic criterion was fulfilled during the entire period of this study by all 18 of the Latin American countries reviewed.[1]

The separate selection process, basis of authority, and governing responsibilities of the executive and legislative branches of presidential governments imply a greater probability of conflict between them than is usually found in parliamentary regimes. Whether this inherent tension can be effectively managed depends, in part, on the methods used for electing the chief executive and legislators.

In the past 25 years, this conflict has not just been a matter for theoretical discussion. Efforts to overcome the impasse in dealings between the two branches have occasionally resulted in the usurpation of lawmaking powers by the executive branch through the making of extraconstitutional decrees. In more extreme cases, the executive has shut down congress or resorted to popular referenda in order to rewrite the constitution so as to bolster its power. In other cases, the standoff between the branches has been addressed by congressional actions to curb presidential powers or remove cabinet ministers—or to even impeach the president. Sometimes institutional governance problems have spilled out into the street, with massive social protests forcing presidents from office (Hochstetler, 2006; Pérez-Liñan, 2005).

In sum, if the methods for electing presidents and legislative representatives have an influence on power distribution in the legislature, and on parties' incentives to enter into

---

[1] In Bolivia, citizens vote to elect both the president and legislative representatives. However, the constitution stipulates that if no candidate obtains an absolute majority in the first round, then the congress makes the final selection by choosing between the two candidates with the most votes. Before a 1994 reform, the congress decided among the top three finishers from the first round. The 2005 election was the first election since the democratic transition of 1985 in which the second round was not necessary.

coalitions, these methods can play a vital role in affecting democratic governability. On the other hand, given the record described above, it is important to keep in mind that elections have not always been decisive in shaping the balance of power between the branches, and terms of office have not only been fixed by the electoral calendar (Chasquetti, 2001).

The electoral processes for the two branches are clearly not independent if the elections are held at the same time. Inevitably, the direct election of the head of government in a winner-take-all formula affects voter choices and party strategies in the legislative elections. Given that in a presidential race there can be only one winner, voters are constrained to choose among individual candidates who have a viable chance of winning. Smaller parties with little chance of winning by themselves have an incentive to band together and nominate a single candidate. Thus, when elections for the two branches are held on the same day, fewer parties are likely to receive significant shares of the vote in legislative elections. This is because many voters will hold to the "coattails" of their preferred presidential candidate by voting for legislative candidates or lists from the same party (Shugart and Carey, 1992).

Electoral systems influence the effectiveness of democratic governance in many ways. First, the legitimacy accorded an incumbent president is shaped by the president's apparent scope of victory, which is influenced by the election method used. Second, the interaction of the methods used for electing presidents and legislators affects the extent of party fragmentation and the percentage of the congressional seats controlled by the chief executive's party. Both of these factors affect the ability of presidents to obtain legislative support for their policy initiatives. Through its effect on the number of parties able to obtain representation in the legislature, the electoral system also influences the fairness of political representation.

This chapter will examine the influence of the system used for electing the president on the operation of democracy. The subsequent chapter will examine the influence of rules governing the election of legislators. Given the interactions between the two electoral processes, this chapter will also consider the matter of their timing and, in general, how the effects of presidential election systems may vary depending on the different methods chosen for electing legislative representatives.

Two related factors that will also be examined in this chapter are the length of the chief executive's term of office, and the matter of whether or not presidents can be reelected. Shorter terms of presidential office allow more frequent turnover and validation of popular support, and thus may alleviate the problem of the formal rigidity associated with presidential regimes (see Chapter 4). If a president loses all popular support and is rendered ineffective, there is less time to endure before someone else can be elected with a fresh mandate. However, short terms also limit the scope of the "honeymoon period" when the president is likely to be most effective in implementing major policy reforms.

Reelection presents both potential advantages and risks for democratic governability. First, accountability to citizens may be encouraged, since presidents' success in the next election is likely to depend on what they accomplish and how well they maintain the public trust in the current term. Second, reelection enhances electoral choice by allowing citizens the possibility to retain a popular and effective president in office. Finally, the possibility of reelection allows presidents to preserve congressional support longer into their term periods. Without the possibility of reelection, presidents have less to offer supporters and fewer tools with which to punish party defectors. The potential advantage cuts both ways, however, because this extra clout can also be used by presidents to dominate their parties and limit the degree of democracy within parties (Carey, 2003).

Considering the political history of many Latin American countries, bans on reelection have been deemed necessary in some countries to prevent elected presidents from using or abusing the power and resources of their position to perpetuate their terms in office. Without adequate horizontal and vertical checks on presidential authority, such constitutional limits may be necessary to prevent the emergence of "democratic dictatorships."

Presidential Election Systems

In general, presidents are elected by either plurality or majority (the latter is sometimes called a runoff, or *ballotage*). In plurality systems, the candidate with the most votes wins. In majority systems, a candidate must obtain one vote more than 50 percent of the total if a winner is to be declared in the first round. If no candidate reaches this threshold, then a second round is held between the top two finishers from the first round. Following the pioneering approach taken by Costa Rica in its 1949 constitution, several Latin American countries have adopted a threshold below a majority (40 percent in Costa Rica) for a candidate to be declared the winner in the first round (Lehoucq, 2004). In this chapter, such a system is referred to as a runoff with a reduced threshold.

Another matter is whether the president is elected directly or indirectly. Does the popular vote directly determine the winner of the presidential contest, or do voters elect representatives who, in turn, vote for the president? Prior to the adoption of the 1994 constitution, voters in Argentina elected delegates to an electoral college that was responsible for choosing the president.[2] In Bolivia, the congress is responsible for selecting the president if, as is common, no candidate obtains a majority in the first round. The first Brazilian president elected in the postauthoritarian period of the 1980s was chosen by a special assembly composed, in part, by the congress. Other than these instances, however, all the Latin American countries in this study have elected their presidents through direct popular vote.

Other key issues related to presidential elections are their timing—relative to legislative elections—and whether the votes for the two branches of government are linked together on the ballot. When the presidential elections occur on the same day as the congressional elections, they are considered concurrent, or simultaneous. Their degree of simultaneity is even greater when the elections are not only on the same day but the elector is limited to

---

[2] This system is similar to the one still used in the United States, where an electoral college composed of slates of delegates from each of the 50 states elects the president. The candidate winning a plurality of the vote is generally awarded all of the delegates from the state. The candidate who obtains the vote of the majority of electoral college delegates becomes president. It is extremely rare and in many cases illegal for delegates to vote against the candidate who won the plurality of the vote in their state. But as seen in the U.S. presidential election in 2000, the winner-take-all, state-by-state selection of delegates (especially given the overrepresentation of underpopulated states in the electoral college) makes it possible for a candidate to win a plurality of the vote at the national level but not be selected as president.

one vote that signifies his or her preference for both the presidential candidate and a legislative candidate or list from the same party. When the elector is able to vote for a presidential candidate of one party and a legislative candidate or list of another party (*voto cruzado* in Spanish), then the link between the elections is somewhat weaker.

The simultaneity of the two elections can be complete or partial. It is complete when the elections for president and the legislature are always held on the same day. It is partial when a portion of the legislative body is elected during the term of a sitting president. In Argentina, for example, half of the lower house and one-third of the senate are elected two years into the four-year presidential term.[3] The degree of simultaneity is even less when there are varying term lengths for both the presidency and legislature, meaning that elections are only rarely held at the same time. For example, until a 2005 reform reduced the presidential term from six to four years, presidential and congressional elections in Chile were set to coincide only once every 12 years. With the reform, the four-year election cycle of the legislature now coincides with that of the president.[4]

A number of different rules govern reelections. The most restrictive forbids a president from being reelected at any point after having served one term of office. Another, more lenient, rule allows reelection, but only after the passing of a period of at least one presidential term. The least restrictive allows at least one consecutive term of office, that is, a one-time reelection. Some systems that allow immediate reelection allow another additional term after the passing of at least one presidential term period out of office.

How Plurality, Majority, and Reduced-Threshold Systems Affect Governability

The manner in which presidents are elected has both direct and indirect effects on their legitimacy. A president's level of popular legitimacy is directly affected by the margin of the president's electoral victory. For example, a president who receives 60 percent of the votes in the first round, with a large advantage over all competitors, initiates his or her mandate with greater popular legitimacy and political backing than one who reaches power with a fairly small percentage of the vote, such as 30 percent. Election on the basis of a small percentage of the total vote can make it difficult for the elected president to govern effectively, and may lead to stalemate.

Whether the election is decided by plurality, majority, or some lower threshold does not directly affect the share of the votes received by the first-place candidate in the initial voting round. Rather, the results of the first round are related to the number of parties and candidates participating, as well as to circumstantial factors such as party strategies that influence the number of candidates competing and the popular appeal of individual candidates. The runoff system is designed to amplify the apparent mandate of the elected

---

[3] There is no law that requires presidential and legislative elections to be held simultaneously. In 2003, legislative elections were held a few months after the presidential election, at different times in different provinces. However, in 2005 all the provinces held legislative elections on the same day.

[4] Given the eight-year term of senators, only one-half of the upper house is elected every four years.

president by requiring a second round if no candidate receives a sufficient proportion of first-round votes. The second round guarantees that the president is ultimately elected with a majority of the vote, regardless of how small a share of the vote he or she received in the first round.

Thus, the runoff system would appear to directly increase the popular legitimacy of an elected president, at least when the leading candidate received one-third of the vote or less in the first round. However, a second-round majority vote is unlikely to provide a mandate equivalent to that bestowed on a president who won on the basis of a majority, or even somewhat less than a majority, in the first round. In the runoff, many people who vote for the winning candidate do so only because they see him or her as the lesser of two evils. The "manufactured" majority in the second round may alleviate, but usually does not solve, the problem of legitimacy for minority presidents. Nevertheless, considering only the direct effects, it seems that the majority runoff system bolsters the president's mandate to govern without any obvious costs. A majority runoff system, however, has indirect effects that may result in a president being elected with a weaker mandate, and with less legislative support, than would have been the case in a plurality system.

As mentioned above, if the elections are simultaneous, the presidential contest tends to narrow the field of parties competing for legislative seats. The extent of this effect depends on the system used for electing the president and the closeness of the link on the ballot between the elections for the two branches. In the plurality system, in which the candidate with the most votes in the first and only round wins, there is an incentive for parties (especially small- and medium-sized ones) to seek alliances or organize coalitions before the election, and for voters to focus their votes on those candidates and parties with a viable chance of winning. Given coattail effects, if the number of candidates and parties contending for the presidency is constrained, it is likely that the number of parties and party coalitions obtaining seats in the legislature will also be limited. In majority runoff systems, however, there are weaker incentives for parties to coalesce before the first-round election, since there are potentially two winners and the contest is unlikely to decide who will become president. Even relatively small parties have an incentive to put forth a presidential candidate, since this will improve their chances of winning legislative seats, and since a strong finish will enhance their bargaining position in relation to other candidates in the runoff. In addition, voters are more free to express their true preference in the first round, since they will have a second opportunity to choose among the two most viable candidates (Shugart and Carey, 1992; Shugart, 1995; Jones, 1996).

Thus, a majority runoff can be expected to encourage a larger number of parties to compete in the presidential race and obtain seats in the legislature than would a plurality system. This expectation has been confirmed in a number of cross-national studies (Jones, 1999; Shugart and Carey, 1992; Shugart and Taagepera, 1994). Over time, the movement from a plurality to a majority runoff system could, therefore, decrease democratic governability by reducing the share of the first-round vote typically received by the eventual victor, and that victor's partisan congressional support.

Of course, for the presidential election to limit the number of parties competing for seats in the legislative contest, the two elections must be held on the same day. Other things being equal, concurrent elections are likely to result in fewer parties being represented in congress than would result from elections separated in time. In addition, concurrent elections have the direct effect of providing a larger share of congressional seats to the president's party. But when presidents are elected by plurality, the constraints on the number of parties competing for, and obtaining, seats should be greater than in the case of majority runoff systems. The constraining effects of a single-round presidential race on the legislative contest should be even greater when the elector is restricted to a single vote for the two branches. In that case, the coattail effects are absolute, and the share of the vote for parties in the legislature exactly mirrors the share of votes received by the presidential candidates of those parties.

Runoff systems with a reduced threshold, such as 40 or 45 percent, act a little more like plurality systems in constraining the number of presidential candidates and the number of parties gaining legislative seats. Given the greater possibility that a candidate will be elected in the first round, parties still have some incentive to coalesce prior to the election, and voters have to be more strategic. But if no candidate obtains this lower threshold in the first round, the runoff provides the benefit of expanding the elected president's mandate.

Holding congressional election rules constant, Table 2.1 shows the expected effects of (1) the timing of the elections for the two branches and (2) the type of presidential election system. A plurality system combined with concurrent presidential and legislative elections is expected to lead to the greatest degree of party concentration. The most fragmented political administration would be expected to arise in the context of a majority runoff system with nonconcurrent elections.

The theoretical expectation that plurality or runoff-with-reduced-threshold systems are more inclined to promote effective democratic gov-

Table 2.1. Tendency toward Party System Concentration among Different Presidential Election Systems

	Concurrent	Not concurrent
Plurality	1	3
Runoff with reduced threshold	2	4
Majority runoff	4	6

Source: Authors' compilation.
Note: A score of one means the most concentrated outcome, six the least concentrated. Majority-runoff-with-concurrent-election systems are considered to have the same effects on party system concentration as runoff-with-reduced-threshold and nonconcurrent election systems, and so are given the same score.

ernance and stability may not always hold true in practice. For example, if party systems are ideologically polarized and fragmented, parties may be disinclined to coalesce prior to the first round. Thus, a presidential candidate representing an extreme segment of a polarized political spectrum may be elected with a small share of the vote, but attempt to govern as a majority president. The election by majority in the second round would impede the election of the candidate who is furthest from the political center. In addition, in a fragmented system in which the winner of the first round typically obtains 30 percent of the vote or less, a runoff may be necessary to provide the president-elect with some basic level of legitimacy.

Midterm Legislative Elections and Governability

Countries with midterm elections are set apart, since they combine concurrent elections for the executive and legislative branches with another, nonconcurrent, legislative election. If a plurality system is used, the concurrent presidential and legislative election should restrain the proliferation of parties. However, the nonconcurrent legislative election may provide opportunities for small parties to compete more effectively and gain representation.

The efficiency of governmental policy making may also be impeded for two additional reasons. First, the holding of an election that is not linked to the presidential outcome logically increases the probability that the president's party will lack a majority in the congress. In fact, the history of such elections suggests that opposition parties often gain ground as voters take the opportunity to protest the performance of the incumbent government. Second, the honeymoon period for elected governments is likely to be shortened, since in the period leading up to such elections the legislative blocs of the opposition parties, and even the governing party, are more likely to refrain from supporting politically controversial legislative initiatives. The positive side of midterm elections, however, is that they provide another opportunity for voters to hold the executive and the legislative representatives accountable for their performance.

Latin American Presidential Election Systems

Of the 18 countries in this study, five (Honduras, Mexico, Panama, Paraguay, and Venezuela) elect presidents using a plurality system. Nine countries employ a majority runoff system (Table 2.2). In one of these (Bolivia), the second round takes place in the congress. The other four countries (Argentina, Costa Rica, Nicaragua, and Ecuador) set a lower threshold for a candidate to be elected in the first round.

In Argentina, the winner of the first round becomes president if he or she has obtained either 45 percent of the valid votes, or 40 percent of the valid votes and at least a 10 percent advantage over the nearest competitor. In Costa Rica, the threshold is 40 percent, a level sufficiently low to have enabled first-round victories for every elected president from the adoption of the 1949 constitution until 2002, when a second round was necessary. As a result of a 1999 constitutional reform, Nicaragua now has a threshold of 40 percent, or 35 percent and at least a 5 percent advantage over the nearest competitor. In Ecuador, an absolute majority—or at least 45 percent of the vote and an advantage of 10 percent or more over the second-place finisher—is required. This threshold represents only a slight deviation from an absolute majority runoff system.

Six countries changed the formula used for electing presidents during the period of study. Colombia, the Dominican Republic, and Uruguay changed from a plurality to a majority runoff system, and Argentina and Nicaragua changed from a plurality system to a runoff with a reduced threshold. Nicaragua changed its system from a plurality to a runoff with a threshold of 45 percent in 1995, then reduced the threshold further in 1999. The only country that changed in the reverse direction was Ecuador, which went from a majority runoff system to a majority with a slightly reduced threshold. The second reform in Nicaragua, which

Table 2.2. Systems Used for Electing the President

Country	Majority runoff	Runoff with reduced threshold	Plurality	Year of change	Description of change
Argentina		X		1994	From plurality to runoff with a 45%, 40%, and 10% advantage over the nearest competitor; also, from indirect to direct
Bolivia	X[1]			1990	Instead of choosing among the top three finishers in the first round, the congress chooses between only the top two in the runoff
Brazil	X			1988	From indirect to direct
Chile	X				
Colombia	X			1991	From plurality to majority runoff
Costa Rica		X[2]			
Dominican Republic	X			1994	From plurality to majority runoff
Ecuador		X		1998	From majority runoff to runoff with a reduced threshold (50% +1 or 45% and a 10% advantage over the nearest competitor)
El Salvador	X				
Guatemala	X				
Honduras			X		
Mexico			X		
Nicaragua		X		1995	From plurality to runoff with a reduced threshold of 45%
				1999	The threshold was further lowered to 40%, or 35% with a 5% advantage over the nearest competitor
Panama			X		
Paraguay			X		
Peru	X[3]				
Uruguay	X			1997	From plurality to majority runoff
Venezuela			X		
Total	9	4	5		

Source: Authors' compilation.

[1] If no candidate obtains an absolute majority, the legislature selects a president among the candidates that finish first and second in the first-round election.

[2] The threshold is 40 percent of the votes.

[3] Absolute majority was adopted as the rule for election in the 1979 constitution, but a separate article provided that it would not apply to the 1980 election. Instead, only 33 percent of the vote was needed for that election. If this figure was not reached, the congress was to decide among the two top finishers. As it turned out, Fernando Belaúnde Terry received 45 percent of the vote and became president.

lowered the threshold for election in the first round, made the majority system resemble a plurality system.

Three additional reforms of a different nature were made to presidential election systems. Argentina and Brazil replaced their indirect systems with direct ones. Bolivia changed its second-round election—decided in congress—so that only the top two finishers, rather than the top three, are eligible for election. The overall trend of the period clearly shows a move away from the plurality system toward a runoff system.

Tables 2.3 and 2.4 examine the extent to which theoretical expectations of different systems' effects on presidential elections are consistent with electoral outcomes over the past two decades in Latin America. Table 2.3 shows that, in fact, plurality and runoff-with-

Table 2.3. Fragmentation of Party Systems According to Type of Presidential Election System

Type of election system, country, and year	Effective number of presidential candidates (first round)	Effective number of parties (lower house seats)
Plurality		
Argentina (1983, 1989 - 1985, 1987, 1991, 1993)	2.64	2.70
Colombia (1978, 1982, 1986, 1990 - 1991)	2.48	2.33
Dominican Republic (1978, 1982, 1986, 1990, 1994)	2.76	2.45
Honduras (1981, 1985, 1989, 1993, 1997, 2001)	2.14	2.15
Mexico (1982, 1988, 1994, 2000 - 1985, 1991, 1997, 2003)	2.50	2.37
Nicaragua (1990)	2.14	2.05
Panama (1989, 1994, 1999, 2004)	2.80	3.56
Paraguay (1989, 1993, 1998, 2003)	2.54	2.45
Uruguay (1984, 1989, 1994)	3.23	3.18
Venezuela (1978, 1983, 1988, 1993, 1998, 2000)	2.73	3.69
Average of country averages	*2.60*	*2.69*
Average for all elections	*2.60*	*2.70*
Reduced threshold		
Argentina[1] (1995, 1999, 2003 - 1997, 2001)	2.84	2.98
Costa Rica (1978, 1982, 1986, 1990, 1994, 1998, 2002)	2.31	2.51
Ecuador (1998, 2002)	5.46	6.71
Nicaragua (1996, 2001)	2.25	2.39
Peru (1980)	3.23	2.46
Average of country averages	*3.22*	*3.41*
Average for all elections	*2.89*	*3.13*

(continued)

Type of election system, country, and year	Effective number of presidential candidates (first round)	Effective number of parties (lower house seats)
Majority runoff		
Bolivia[2] (1980, 1985, 1989, 1993, 1997, 2002)	5.14	4.51
Brazil (**1989**, 1994, 1998, 2002 - 1990)	3.51	8.11
Chile[3] (1989, 1993, **1999** - 1997, 2001)	2.36	5.27
Colombia (1994, 1998, 2002)	2.69	4.24
Dominican Republic (**1996, 2000, 2004** - 1998, 2002)	2.89	2.52
Ecuador (1978, 1984, 1988, 1992, 1996 - 1986, 1990, 1994)	5.15	5.69
El Salvador (**1984, 1989**, 1994, **1999, 2004** - 1985, 1988, 1991, 1997, 2000, 2003)	2.68	3.17
Guatemala (1985, 1990, 1995, 1999, 2003 - 1994)	4.31	3.42
Peru (1985, 1990, 1995, 2000, 2001)	2.99	3.90
Uruguay (1999, 2004)	3.09	3.01
Average of country averages	*3.48*	*4.58*
Average for all elections	*3.74*	*4.57*

Source: Authors' compilation.

Note: The format for this table is based on Shugart and Carey (1992, Table 10.2), but different data are used. Most cases involve years in which simultaneous presidential and legislative elections were held; the listing of years when only legislative elections took place is preceded by a hyphen (e.g., Argentina); if only a presidential election was held, the years appear in boldface (e.g., El Salvador).

[1] The three candidates of the Justicialist (or Peronist) Party that ran on independent slates in the 2003 presidential elections were counted as a single slate. Had they been counted as running under separate party tickets, the average figure for the period would have reflected a value of 4.03 instead of 2.84.

[2] In Bolivia, the congress selects the president if no candidate obtains a majority in the first round.

[3] For Chile, computing the effective number of parties based on coalitions rather than individual parties would result in a much lower measure of fragmentation in the lower house (2.02).

reduced-threshold systems are associated with fewer significant candidates running for office and fewer parties being elected to seats in the legislature. Table 2.4 shows that in plurality and runoff-with-reduced-threshold systems, the winner of the first round averaged very close to 50 percent of the vote, while, in majority runoff systems, the winner typically received barely over 41 percent of the vote. In some countries, the winner averaged only about 30 percent of the vote.

The data in these tables, however, do not rigorously test hypotheses about effects of presidential election systems on party system fragmentation. The reason for this is that the influence can clearly go in both directions. Countries where many parties typically compete and present presidential candidates are precisely the ones that are most likely to adopt a

Table 2.4. Average Share of the Vote Obtained in the First Round by First- and Second-Place Candidates

Type of election system, country, and year	First place	Second place
Plurality		
Argentina (1983, 1989)	49.6	36.3
Colombia (1978, 1982, 1986, 1990)	50.9	37.0
Dominican Republic (1978, 1982, 1986, 1990, 1994)	42.8	36.9
Honduras (1981, 1985, 1989, 1993, 1997, 2001)	52.5	43.6
Mexico (1982, 1988, 1994, 2000)	54.7	24.2
Nicaragua (1990)	54.7	40.8
Panama (1989, 1994, 1999, 2004)	44.2	27.0
Paraguay (1989, 1993, 1998, 2003)	52.8	30.6
Uruguay (1984, 1989, 1994)	37.5	28.8
Venezuela (1978, 1983, 1988, 1993, 1998, 2000)	48.8	33.3
Average for all elections	*48.7*	*33.9*
Reduced threshold		
Argentina (1995, 1999, 2003)	40.9	29.9
Costa Rica (1978, 1982, 1986, 1990, 1994, 1998, 2002)	49.8	42.0
Ecuador (1998, 2002)	27.8	22.0
Nicaragua (1996, 2001)	53.6	40.1
Peru (1980)	46.5	28.2
Average for all elections	*45.4*	*35.7*
Majority runoff		
Bolivia[1] (1980, 1985, 1989, 1993, 1997, 2002)	29.6	22.7
Brazil (1989, 1994, 1998, 2002)	46.1	24.8
Chile[2] (1989, 1993, 1999)	53.7	33.9
Colombia (1994, 1998, 2002)	44.9	37.5
Dominican Republic (1996, 2000, 2004)	45.0	31.4
Ecuador (1978, 1984, 1988, 1992, 1996)	28.0	24.0
El Salvador (1984, 1989, 1994, 1999, 2004)	51.2	31.2
Guatemala (1985, 1990, 1995, 1999, 2003)	36.6	24.6
Peru (1985, 1990, 1995, 2000, 2001)	47.5	28.5
Uruguay (1999, 2004)	45.9	34.0
Average for all elections	*41.5*	*28.1*

Source: Authors' compilation.
Note: The format for this table is based on Shugart and Carey (1992, Table 10.2), but different data are used.
[1] In Bolivia, the congress selects the president if no candidate obtains a majority in the first round.
[2] The binominal election system for the legislature, along with the societal division among those for and against the Pinochet regime, encouraged the maintenance of party coalitions on the center-left and center-right, each of which presents a single candidate for the presidency.

majority runoff system. A more valid test would examine the change over time in the numerous instances when election systems either changed in one direction or another or stayed the same. Then, if the expected changes in the number of candidates competing and parties winning seats occur, one might have good grounds for upholding a particular hypothesis. Given the relatively short life of the region's democracies, along with the brief period that has passed since most of the reforms, it is not possible to conduct such a test with the limited sample of countries studied here. However, a significant effect of presidential election systems on the effective number of presidential candidates was found in a cross-national empirical study examining 33 countries over a 50-year period (Jones, 1999).

Simultaneity of Elections

In 12 of the 18 countries studied here, presidential and legislative elections are held simultaneously (Table 2.5). Of these, Brazil and Chile represent only a slight deviation, with a portion of the senate being elected on an alternating basis in a given presidential or legislative election. In these cases, elections for the two branches are nonetheless held on the same day. In Argentina and Mexico, the elections are partially simultaneous. In Argentina, elections for half of the lower house and one-third of the upper house are held simultaneously with the presidential election (but see Table 2.5, note 3), while the other half of the lower

		Table 2.5. Simultaneity of Presidential and Legislative Elections			
Country	Simulta-neous	Partially simulta-neous	Separate	Year of change	Description and direction of change
Argentina		X[1]		1994	Reduction of the presidential mandate from six to four years, and the senatorial mandate from nine to six years; this change maintained the system as partially simultaneous, but with one rather than two midterm elections
Bolivia	X				
Brazil	X[2]			1994	Reduction of the presidential mandate from five to four years transformed the system from separate to simultaneous
Chile	X			1993	Reduction of the presidential mandate from eight to six years transformed the system from partially simultaneous to separate
				2005	Reduction of the presidential mandate from six to four years transformed the system from separate to simultaneous

(continued)

Table 2.5. (continued)

Country	Simulta-neous	Partially simulta-neous	Separate	Year of change	Description and direction of change
Colombia			X[3]		
Costa Rica	X				
Dominican Republic			X	1994	In 1994, the decision to cut the disputed term of President Joaquín Balaguer from four to two years while maintaining the elected congress for four years trans-formed the system from simulta-neous to separate
Ecuador	X			1998	Elimination of the midterm elec-tions for provincial deputies trans-formed the system from partially simultaneous to simultaneous
El Salvador			X		
Guatemala	X				
Honduras	X				
Mexico		X[4]			
Nicaragua	X				
Panama	X				
Paraguay	X				
Peru	X				
Uruguay	X				
Venezuela			X[5]	1999	The 1999 constitution lengthened the president's term from five to six years, while legislators' terms remained at five years; thus, under the reform, the presidential and national assembly elections will only coincide once every 30 years
Total	12	2	4		

Source: Authors' compilation.

[1] Half of the lower house and one-third of the upper house are elected at the same time as the president. (But without a change to the electoral law, the system functioned as nonsimultaneous in 2003. See foot-note 3 in the text.)

[2] The system is considered simultaneous since the lower house and one- or two-thirds of the senate—on an alternating basis—are elected at the same time as the president, without any midterm elections.

[3] For the whole study period, congressional elections have been held two-and-a-half months prior to the presidential election, but in the same year.

[4] The system is considered partially simultaneous because, although the presidential elections always coin-cide with elections for the lower and upper house, the full lower house is renewed in the middle of the president's term.

[5] In 1998 a temporary reform moved the legislative elections to one month before the presidential elections. Under the current (1999) constitution, the system is considered separate, since it is only once every 30 years that a president is elected at the same time as the national assembly.

house and another third of the upper house are elected midway through the presidential term. In Mexico, the term of deputies in the lower house is three years so that one of the elections for the whole body is simultaneous with the presidential election, but a second election for the whole legislature is held at the midway point of the six-year presidential term. In the remaining four countries (Colombia, the Dominican Republic, El Salvador, and Venezuela), presidential and legislative elections rarely or never occur on the same day. Colombia is unusual among these five because the elections for the two branches occur in the same year in four-year cycles, but the legislative elections are held two-and-a-half months prior to the first round of the presidential elections.

The six countries where the timing of elections has been changed during the study period do not represent an obvious regional trend in the simultaneity of elections for the two branches. Chile, the Dominican Republic, and Venezuela shifted from systems with either fully or partially simultaneous elections (Chile) to ones with non-coterminous cycles. Then, in 2005, Chile moved back to simultaneous presidential and legislative elections while reducing the president's term from six to four years. Brazil also moved from nonconcurrent elections toward concurrent ones. With the elimination of the midterm election for legislators representing individual provinces, Ecuador transformed its system from partially simultaneous to simultaneous. In Argentina, there was a small move toward greater simultaneity. The reduction of the presidential term from six to four years and the reduction of senatorial terms from nine to six years maintained the partially simultaneous nature of the electoral system, but reduced the number of midterm elections from two to one.

Length of the Presidential Term

The length of presidential terms in the region vary between four and six years (Table 2.6). In nine countries (Argentina, Brazil, Chile, Colombia, Costa Rica, the Dominican Republic, Ecuador, Guatemala, and Honduras) the president has a four-year term; in seven (Bolivia, El Salvador, Nicaragua, Panama, Paraguay, Peru, and Uruguay), a five-year term; and in two (Mexico and Venezuela), a six-year term.

Seven countries changed the length of the presidential term during the period of the study. Five reduced the term of office, and two increased it. Several of the term reductions, however, are open to interpretation. Brazil and Argentina reduced the presidential term from five and six years, respectively, to four years, but at the same time they established the possibility of an immediate reelection. This permits a president to potentially remain in office for eight consecutive years. In the early 1990s, Chile reduced its presidential term from a single eight-year term to a somewhat more modest six years. Then, in 2005, it further reduced the term to four years. Guatemala reduced its presidential term from five to four years, and Nicaragua from six to five years. Bolivia increased the term of presidents from four to five years, and Venezuela from five to six years. With these changes, the average length of the presidential mandate in the region was reduced from 5.1 to 4.6 years.

Table 2.6. Presidential Term Length			
Country	Current term length	Previous term length	Year of change
Argentina	4	6	1994
Bolivia	5	4	1994
Brazil	4	5	1994
Chile	4	8 6	2003 2005
Colombia	4	4	
Costa Rica	4	4	
Dominican Republic	4	4	
Ecuador	4	4	
El Salvador	5	5	
Guatemala	4	5	1993
Honduras	4	4	
Mexico	6	6	
Nicaragua	5	6	1994
Panama	5	5	
Paraguay	5	5	
Peru	5	5	
Uruguay	5	5	
Venezuela	6	5	1999
Average	4.6	5.1	

Source: Authors' compilation.

Reelection of Presidents

Rules concerning the reelection of presidents vary considerably across the region (Table 2.7). While in five countries (Argentina, Brazil, Colombia, the Dominican Republic, and Venezuela) immediate reelection is permitted, in nine countries (Bolivia, Chile, Costa Rica, Ecuador, El Salvador, Nicaragua, Panama, Peru, and Uruguay) reelection is allowed only after the passing of at least one presidential term. The remaining four countries (Guatemala, Honduras, Mexico, and Paraguay) prohibit reelection at any time. In other words, reelection is favored in the region, with 14 of 18 countries allowing a president to be reelected at some point, either immediately or after one presidential term.

Ten countries changed the rules (or their interpretation of the rules) governing presidential reelection during the period studied. Argentina, Brazil, and Venezuela moved from a system that allowed reelection after the passing of at least one presidential period to one that allows immediate reelection. Ecuador and Costa Rica loosened the restrictions on reelection so that it is now allowed after one and two presidential terms, respectively. At the same time, two countries that had allowed consecutive presidential reelections at the be-

Country	Immediate	Not immediate	Prohibited	Year of change	Nature of change	Effect of change
Argentina	X			1994	Not immediate to immediate	Less restrictive
Bolivia		X				
Brazil	X			1997	Not immediate to immediate	Less restrictive
Chile		X				
Colombia	X			1991	Not immediate to prohibited	More restrictive
				2005	Prohibited to immediate	Less restrictive
Costa Rica		X[1]		2003	Prohibited to not immediate	Less restrictive
Dominican Republic	X			1994	Immediate to not immediate	More restrictive
				2002	Not immediate to immediate	Less restrictive
Ecuador		X		1996	Prohibited to not immediate	Less restrictive
El Salvador		X				
Guatemala			X			
Honduras			X			
Mexico			X			
Nicaragua		X		1995	Immediate to not immediate	More restrictive
Panama		X[2]		1994		
Paraguay			X	1992	Immediate to prohibited	More restrictive
Peru				1993	Not immediate to immediate	Less restrictive
		X		2000	Immediate to not immediate	More restrictive
Uruguay		X				
Venezuela	X[3]			1998	Not immediate to immediate	Less restrictive
Total	5	9	4			

Source: Authors' compilation.

[1] Nonimmediate reelection (reelection after two intervening presidential terms) was allowed until a 1969 referendum prohibited it (Carey, 1997). In 2003, however, the original rule was restored because the constitutional court decided that the process of reforming the rule was unconstitutional.

[2] Increased the required intervening period from one to two presidential terms (10 years).

[3] Under previous rules, the president could not be reelected until two presidential periods had passed.

ginning of the period no longer do. Paraguay now prohibits reelection at any point in time, and Nicaragua allows reelection after a single presidential term has elapsed.

The multiple reforms that took place in Peru, Colombia, and the Dominican Republic went in contrary directions. In Peru, consecutive reelection was put in place under the first Fujimori presidency in 1993, but was later disallowed in 2000. Colombia's 1991 constitution prohibited reelection, but then a 2005 reform permitted consecutive reelection for the first time. In the Dominican Republic, consecutive presidential terms were banned in 1994, but were once again allowed eight years later. Altogether, eight of the 13 modifications favored presidential reelection while five restricted it. In sum, reforms since the early 1980s generally loosened constraints on reelection, except for the reforms in Colombia in 1991 (overturned in 2005), the Dominican Republic in 1994 (overturned in 2002), Paraguay in 1992, Peru in 2000, and Nicaragua in 1995. All of the other reforms favored reelection (Peru, 1993; Argentina, 1994; Ecuador, 1996; Brazil, 1997; Venezuela, 1998; Dominican Republic, 2002; Costa Rica, 2003; and Colombia, 2005).

Conclusions

The governance capacity of presidential systems depends in part on the election of presidents who enjoy substantial popular legitimacy and can depend on a sizeable portion of the congress to work collaboratively with them to enact legislation. The system chosen for electing the president, along with the simultaneity of presidential and legislative elections, are two factors that can affect the likelihood that such conditions are met.

In the past two decades, many countries have reformed their presidential election systems, the relative timing of presidential and legislative elections, the length of the presidential term, and rules of reelection. The clearest trend has been a shift from a plurality system to a majority runoff or runoff-with-reduced-threshold system. Five countries moved in this direction, while only one (Ecuador) moved very slightly in the opposite direction. Abandoning the plurality formula was generally motivated either by a desire to amplify the mandate of the winner or by partisan power strategies (such as preventing a third minority party from obtaining the presidency).

Academic theory and the limited empirical evidence available would predict this change, under at least some circumstances, to work against democratic governability. This undesirable outcome would result from the tendency of a majority system to encourage the participation of more presidential candidates and increase the number of political parties gaining seats in congress. Thus, instead of broadening the mandate of the elected president, such a system may in fact undermine it.

The actual impact of majority runoff systems is difficult to judge in a rigorous manner. In most cases, too little time has passed since the implementation of reforms to assess their potential long-term impact on party system fragmentation. In the short term, it seems that one expected outcome, the immediate enhancement of the elected president's mandate, has not been fulfilled in most cases.

The failure of majority runoff systems to boost presidents' popular legitimacy may be because the first-round vote is perceived as a more valid reflection of true voter preferences.

It is difficult to turn a 25 percent vote into a mandate for government, even with a second-round majority vote. In fact, a particular legitimacy problem emerges when the candidate who is ultimately elected in the second round did not win the first round. Of the 23 instances in which runoff elections were held over the period of this study, in nine the winner of the first round failed to become president. Setting aside the two cases in Bolivia, in which the second-round decision was made by the congress, seven cases remain: President Jaime Roldós Aguilera, Ecuador, 1979; President León Febres Cordero, Ecuador, 1984; President Abdalá Bucaram Ortiz, Ecuador, 1996; President Alberto Fujimori, Peru, 1990; President Jorge Serrano Elías, Guatemala, 1993; President Andrés Pastrana, Colombia, 1998; and President Jorge Batlle Ibáñez, Uruguay, 1999. Most of these presidencies were characterized by highly conflictive relationships with the legislature and ineffective policy. Impeachment was threatened or attempted in four instances. Bucaram was ousted by the legislature for "mental incapacity." Fujimori and Serrano used "self-coups" to head off impeachment threats and difficult relations with the legislature. While Fujimori succeeded, Serrano's attempt ended in his resignation. Roldós's relations with congress were already strained when he was killed in an airplane accident two years into his five-year term, and Febres Cordero faced impeachment attempts.

Aside from the problem of conflict-ridden terms, the real capacity of presidents to govern may not be strengthened by runoffs, because the second round tends to encourage the formation of loose electoral coalitions among the two candidates and some minority parties, rather than more durable governing coalitions. Even though the president's institutional authority, reflected in votes or seats obtained, may not be increased by the second round, election by majority may give him an inflated sense of mandate and encourage attempts to circumvent or undermine democratic institutions.[5]

Regarding the timing of presidential and legislative elections, two countries moved toward separate elections while three shifted from separate to simultaneous elections, and another from partially simultaneous to simultaneous elections. Again, these changes are too recent for their effects to be ascertained. But it is interesting to note that two of the countries that moved toward making elections fully simultaneous (Brazil and Ecuador) are among those with the highest degree of party system fragmentation. Certainly the harmonization of the election cycles in Brazil has eased the problem of governing compared to what the situation could have been if presidents still had to face midterm congressional elections.

Midterm elections, whether in systems with or without coterminous cycles, clearly contribute to difficulties in governance. Presidents in all the nations with such elections (Argentina, Ecuador, and Mexico) have shown a tendency toward periodic, ineffective executive policy making over the course of their term because of the greater likelihood of a shift in the balance of partisan power, and because of the shift in congressional attention from the policy agenda to electoral strategizing and campaigning.

There is no clear trend in respect to rules on presidential reelection. Seven countries changed their systems in a direction favoring reelection (with two requiring at least one

---

[5] This problem can be cited particularly in the case of Bucaram.

intervening presidential term), while two banned consecutive reelection (one banned reelection altogether); Colombia, the Dominican Republic, and Peru adopted reforms in both directions. Reelection was introduced in Argentina, Brazil, and Peru, at least partly as a consequence of presidential popularity built on successes in taming hyperinflation and restoring economic growth. Even during the second terms of President Alberto Fujimori in Peru and President Carlos Menem in Argentina, reelection remained an issue, since each of these presidents or his supporters contended that the first term did not count under the new or reformed constitution. President Fujimori was controversially elected to a third term in 2000, while President Menem finally did not pursue a further extension of his mandate. In several other countries, including Guatemala, Ecuador, and Panama, attempts to lift the prohibition on immediate reelection were unsuccessful.

Again, it is difficult to assess the impact of the reforms in this area. The restrictions on reelection imposed in the Dominican Republic (1994), Nicaragua, and Paraguay appear to have been aimed at blocking the possibility that a strong leader might dominate politics over a long time period, as was the case with Joaquín Balaguer, Anastasio Somoza (or Daniel Ortega), and Alfredo Stroessner, respectively. In such circumstances, a ban on reelection marks a positive departure from a past style of politics, and may be necessary to ensure ongoing plurality in the division of national political power. As evident in the reversal of prohibitions on reelection in the Dominican Republic and Colombia, however, such rules are prone to being overturned.

Countries where constitutions were amended to permit reelection reveal the double-edged nature of the issue. Preventing the reelection of a popular president may stop, in midstream, a form of leadership that could make long-term contributions to the country's development. It may also create problems for the perceived legitimacy of the president's successor. However, reelection also reinforces the tendency—inherent in presidentialism—toward individualistic leadership, and undermines the development of a more pluralistic and institutionalized mode of exercising political authority. Although there have been a few successful presidencies that resulted from reelection, whether immediate or nonimmediate, the balance is not generally positive.

Beyond the substance of arguments in favor of or against presidential reelection, the fact remains that efforts to allow consecutive presidential terms have almost always been driven by presidents who have sought to remain in office by changing the rules under which they were elected. Such was the case with Menem in Argentina, Fernando Henrique Cardoso in Brazil, Hipólito Mejía in the Dominican Republic, Fujimori in Peru, and Hugo Chávez in Venezuela. Without analyzing specific cases in detail, it seems correct to say that the narrow motives behind the reforms make it less likely that they will be designed so as to contribute to the strengthening of democratic institutions in Latin America.

References

Carey, John M. 1997. Strong Candidates for a Limited Office: Presidentialism and Political Parties in Costa Rica. In Scott Mainwaring and Matthew Soberg Shugart (eds.), *Presidentialism and Democracy in Latin America*. New York: Cambridge University Press.

—————. 2003. Policy Issues. The Reelection Debate in Latin America. *Latin American Politics and Society* 45(1): 119–133.

Chasquetti, Daniel J. 2001. Democracia, multipartidismo y coaliciones en América Latina: evaluando la difícil combinación. In Jorge Lanzaro (ed.), *Tipos de presidencialismo y coaliciones políticas en América Latina*. Buenos Aires: Consejo Latinoamericano de Ciencias Sociales (CLACSO).

Hochstetler, Kathryn. 2006. Rethinking Presidentialism: Challenges and Presidential Falls in South America. *Comparative Politics* 38(4).

Jones, Mark P. 1996. *Electoral Laws and the Survival of Presidential Democracies*. Notre Dame: University of Notre Dame Press.

—————. 1999. Electoral Laws and the Effective Number of Candidates in Presidential Elections. *Journal of Politics* 61(1).

Lehoucq, Fabrice. 2004. Modifying Majoritarianism: The Origins of the 40 Percent Threshold. In Joseph M. Colomer (ed.), *The Handbook of Electoral System Choice*. New York and London: Palgrave.

Mainwaring, Scott, and Matthew Soberg Shugart (eds.). 1997. *Presidentialism and Democracy in Latin America*. New York: Cambridge University Press.

Pérez-Liñan, Aníbal. 2005. Democratization and Constitutional Crises in Presidential Regimes: Toward Congressional Supremacy? *Comparative Political Studies* 38(1).

Shugart, Matthew Soberg. 1995. The Electoral Cycle and Institutional Sources of Divided Presidential Government. *American Political Science Review* 89(2).

Shugart, Matthew Soberg, and John M. Carey. 1992. *Presidents and Assemblies: Constitutional Design and Electoral Dynamics*. Cambridge: Cambridge University Press.

Shugart, Matthew Soberg, and Rein Taagepera. 1994. Majority Versus Plurality Election of Presidents: A Proposal for a "Double Complement Rule." *Comparative Political Studies* 27(3).

CHAPTER 3

Legislative Electoral Systems and Democratic Governability

The design of systems for electing legislative representatives affects democratic governance by influencing, among other outcomes, the effectiveness of executive-legislative relations and the quality of political representation. This chapter examines several of the functions that electoral systems should ideally perform in a democratic system, and classifies electoral systems in Latin America in terms of how well they fulfill these theoretical functions. It also assesses the extent to which the regional electoral reforms made over the past two decades may alleviate governance problems.

An electoral system is defined here as a set of rules that determine how voters select the candidates and political parties of their preference, as well as how their votes shape the apportionment of seats (for congressional elections) and governmental offices (for presidential, gubernatorial, and mayoral elections) among contending political forces (Nohlen, 1998b).

The effect of electoral systems on democratic governance is mainly exerted through their indirect impact on the structure and functioning of the political party system. Such effects are far from being predictable, since, in exerting them, electoral systems interact with a host of other factors, including the depth and diversity of existing social, political, and economic cleavages; the nature of the political regime and political culture; and other more contingent factors (International IDEA, 1997). Electoral systems set in place an important array of incentives that shape the behavior of electors and other political actors, and influence both the structure of the party system and the orientation and conduct of elected officials. Even within the parameters of a given set of electoral rules, widely different behaviors and outcomes can result from differences in other aspects of the social and political setting.

Aside from structuring incentives, electoral systems exert a direct influence on a given allocation of power and authority. In other words, electoral rules have both mechanical and psychological effects (Duverger, 1954), and it may be helpful to distinguish between these.

Mechanical effects are the practical impacts of the seat-allocation method in determining what parties obtain representation and to what extent their share of the seats equates with their share of the votes. For example, first-past-the-post systems, where one legislator is elected by a simple plurality in each district, have the direct effect of underrepresenting minority parties. Even if such parties were to receive as much as 10 or 20 percent of the national vote, they would be unlikely to gain a single seat in the parliament if their support and that of other parties were distributed relatively evenly across the country.

Psychological effects are the reactions, over time, of the electorate and political actors to the constraints and opportunities presented by the electoral rules. As pointed out in the previous chapter, rational voters are unlikely to continue voting for a party or candidate with no realistic chance of winning. In the plurality system, where only the candidate with the most votes obtains a seat, electors may eschew their true preference for a minority party and instead vote for the best alternative among the larger parties. At the same time, rather than repeatedly being underrepresented in the legislature, minority parties may choose to join forces with larger parties in order to enhance their chances of winning seats. Over time, psychological effects are likely to reinforce the purely mechanical effects of the electoral system on the party system (Nohlen, 1998a).

Key Functions of Electoral Systems: Representativeness, Effectiveness, and Participation

Electoral systems can be differentiated by their intrinsic characteristics, which have expected consequences for the operation of democratic systems. Whether a given set of characteristics promotes or hinders democratic governability depends on the context. An electoral system may be workable and legitimate in one country, and not functional in another. Nevertheless, the general direction of change likely to be induced by a given reform in a particular country can be predicted with some degree of confidence. By understanding the incentives provided by different electoral systems, one can better hypothesize about the effects that given reforms will have on democratic operations in specific contexts.

One way to distinguish among electoral systems is to determine the extent to which they provide three functions: representativeness, effectiveness, and participation (Nohlen, 1998b, 1999).

An optimally representative electoral system is one in which political groups obtain legislative seats in nearly exact proportion to their share of the vote. In such a system, all votes count the same and no political groups competing for elected office are either over- or underrepresented (that is, receive a share of seats larger or smaller than their share of the vote). In assessing the degree of representation provided by an electoral system, a fairly restrictive definition of the term will be used here. For other purposes, the term has been reasonably applied to the matter of whether the full heterogeneity of the social fabric is adequately represented in the political process. However, whether minority or other previously excluded groups have a proportionate voice in the political system involves many factors (equity of political participation, level of voter turnout, capacity of groups to organize, etc.) that are not necessarily related to electoral rules. In our definition, we only consider whether those groups that form political parties or movements and enter electoral contests obtain representation in accordance with the proportion of the votes they receive.

An electoral system that fosters effectiveness is one that produces a sufficient concentration of power in the legislature to make it possible for diverse societal preferences to be aggregated and translated into acts of government. If a large number of parties obtain representation, then it is less likely that the governing party will enjoy reliable support in the legislature, and more difficult for legislators to reach the level of agreement needed to enact necessary reforms. In a presidential system, the problem of governing in the context of a fragmented legislature is a particularly difficult one. Since legislators' tenures do not depend on the success or failure of the government to adopt their legislative program (and since the presidency is a winner-take-all office that each party aims to occupy), there are weaker incentives for parties to form and maintain coalitions in presidential systems than in parliamentary ones.

Participation, or identifiability, is unique among the three functions. While representativeness and effectiveness involve the way that electors' aggregate preferences are translated into legislative seats, participation refers to how the voting system affects the strength of the connection between constituents and their representatives. For example, in a plurality system in which a single representative is elected in each district, the relationship is close and direct. Citizens can choose the individual candidate who they think will best represent them, and can reward or punish the incumbent based on his or her performance in office. This means that candidates and elected representatives are rewarded when they focus their attention on gaining and holding on to the support of constituents.

At the other end of the scale, in proportional representation systems with closed and blocked party lists, the connection between the elector and representative is looser and more distant. In such systems, party leaders or members in a convention put together an ordered list of candidates for each district. Citizens cast a vote for the party list of their choice (thereby affecting the share of seats won by that party), but have no role in deciding which individual candidates are elected. Candidates and incumbents do not have a strong incentive to cultivate relations with their constituents, and electors are discouraged from learning the identities of individual candidates or tracking the conduct of those who get elected (Carey and Shugart, 1995). Legislators enhance their reelection chances by winning the favor of party leaders and thus earning a high position on the party list. While individual electors can potentially hold the party accountable through their legislative votes, it is not realistically possible for them to hold legislators accountable on an individual basis.

Based on the above reasoning, it would seem at first glance that the best way to improve electoral systems in the region would be to simply maximize their provision of all three functions. However, it is not possible for electoral systems to satisfy these different demands simultaneously and in an absolute manner. Attempts to optimize performance in one function almost inevitably worsen performance in another (Nohlen, 1998b).

For example, enhancing the degree of representation afforded by a system (by making the translation of votes into seats more proportional) can lower effectiveness by increasing the number of parties that obtain representation in the legislature. In such a context, it is more likely that presidents will lack legislative support, and this may impede the development of expeditious responses to collective problems.

At the same time, reforms aimed at enhancing participation may reduce effectiveness by undermining party discipline and thereby inhibiting the executive-legislative cooperation needed to enact legislation. In addition, if efforts to enhance participation dilute the meaning of party labels and the programmatic focus of campaigns, then electors may lose the ability to hold representatives accountable for their decisions and positions on national policy issues. Instead of selling their constituents a package of policies and issue positions (or deeds in support of the public interest), legislative candidates will emphasize their personal qualities and the exchange of particularistic favors for electoral support (Carey and Shugart, 1995; Shugart and Wattenberg, 2001).

Theoretical Bases for Classifying Electoral Systems

Thinking in terms of the three functions and the trade-offs between them is useful in evaluating and distinguishing between the different electoral systems. The most basic and well-known classification of electoral systems differentiates between majority and proportional systems. Majority systems are those that award the seats in each district to the candidates with the most votes. As a consequence, such systems tend to systematically favor larger parties and make it difficult for small parties to gain representation. Classic examples of the majority system are found in the United States and Great Britain, where, in each district, one seat is awarded to the candidate with the most votes (or the "first past the post").

Proportional systems are those that award seats according to the percentage of the vote obtained by political parties. The logic behind these systems is to favor the election of a legislature that reflects the political heterogeneity of the electorate. Classic proportional systems, in their "pure" forms, can be found in Israel and the Netherlands, where there is effectively one electoral district (the whole nation), and the total vote determines the allocation of all legislative seats according to electoral district. In such systems, the share of the seats obtained almost exactly mirrors the share of the votes each party receives.

Within these two broad types of electoral systems, there are many variations. The prototypical majority systems are the first-past-the-post or plurality systems, where the candidate with the most votes wins, and the majority runoff systems, where an absolute majority of the votes is required. However, other forms are possible and are used in Latin America. Under the system called *majority with representation of the minority*, the party with the most votes obtains most of the seats in the district, but the party finishing second also receives one representative. Another variation of the majority system involves the awarding of multiple seats in each district in the order of the candidates who receive the most votes. In such systems, electors choose one or more candidates listed under different party labels, but the votes accrue and seats are awarded only on an individual basis.

While majority systems favor effectiveness and participation, they underrepresent smaller parties and work to the advantage of larger parties. Proportional systems, on the other hand, favor equitable representation but may result in a more cumbersome and inefficient decision-making process and weaker links between representatives and constituents.

Though this dichotomous classification is valuable for its simplicity, it is imprecise and does not distinguish electoral systems in terms of the degree to which they fulfill the expected functions, or their theoretical effects on democratic governance. In addition, this classification scheme is not very practical when it comes to distinguishing among the electoral systems found in Latin America. For electing members of the lower house, none of the 18 countries in the study uses a classic form of the majority system (either first past the post or majority runoff). Sixteen countries use a form of proportional representation for electing deputies to the legislature, but there are huge differences between these. Of these 16, Bolivia and Venezuela use a personalized proportional representation system.

Of the two nonproportional cases, Mexico uses a mixed, or segmented, system in which three-fifths of the seats are elected by plurality in single-member districts, and two-fifths are elected by proportional representation. Chile's system, labeled *binominal* in Spanish, is more difficult to classify within these two broad systems. Parties or coalitions present lists of candidates in two-member districts. Electors vote for one candidate, but the votes accrue to the party or party coalition. Each of the two parties with the most votes wins a seat unless the first party doubles the votes of the second. In this case, the first party obtains both seats. The effect is a particular form of the majority system that favors the largest parties, and particularly the second-largest party or coalition.

Sharper distinctions in the degree of representativeness associated with proportional representation systems can contribute to a more analytically useful classification scheme. Three characteristics of proportional representation systems exert the greatest influence on how closely the share of seats reflects the distribution of the vote: the size of the districts, the mathematical formula used to allocate seats, and the presence and size of legal thresholds required for parties to obtain representation.

District size, or more precisely the number of legislators elected in each district, is generally the most important variable. If we take the particular formula used for translating votes into seats as fixed, then, as the number of seats available for distribution increases, so will the degree to which the assignment of seats proportionally increases. This results in an increasingly greater possibility that parties receiving a small share of the vote can obtain representation.[1] There are systems that, despite being defined in a national constitution as proportional, have a significant number of districts that elect only one or two legislators. Obviously, when only one seat is being decided, the system operates as a majority one (the party with the most votes wins). When two seats are up for election, the system operates like the Chilean binominal system.

The decision about where to divide systems in terms of district magnitude is inevitably arbitrary. One expert considers districts of five seats or less to be small; between five and ten, medium; and over ten, large (Nohlen, 1998). These delineations seem reasonable when considering election outcomes at the district level. However, given the fact that most proportional representation systems are characterized by a fairly large number of districts with widely varying sizes (and some with a national district layered upon these territorial districts), categorizing systems in terms of district size is more complicated.

---

[1] The effect of district magnitude on the proportionality of the translation of votes into seats is conditioned by the number of parties and the distribution of the votes among them. Thus, a given average district magnitude might result in fairly proportional outcomes in a country with only a few significant parties, but produce a highly disproportional outcome in a country with a large number of significant parties.

One way of summarizing the size of electoral districts across a country is to consider the share of legislative seats that are elected in districts of a given size.[2] Systems in which more than half of the legislative body is elected in districts with five seats or less are considered to be proportional-representation-with-small-district systems. Proportional-representation-with-large-district systems are those in which more than half the seats in the legislature are elected from districts with 10 or more representatives. Systems that fall between these two extremes are considered proportional-representation-with-medium-sized-district systems.

Table 3.1 shows the classification of 14 of the 16 Latin American proportional representation systems, as well as data related to their district size. Though Bolivia and Venezuela are proportional representation systems, the personal nature of the voting in these nations warrants the creation of a different electoral system category. Using the criteria established in the previous paragraph, there are two large-district proportional representation systems, eight medium-sized systems, and four small ones—two of which (the Dominican Republic and Peru) moved into this category as a result of reforms passed since 2000.

Electoral Formulas

The degree to which proportional systems produce proportional outcomes is also affected by the mathematical formula used to transform votes into seats. Though there are many variations in the formulas used, in general most use either a divisor (highest average) system or a quota system.

The best-known divisor system—the D'Hondt system—is also the most common in Latin America. In this system, a series of divisors (1, 2, 3, etc.) is applied to the votes received by each party. Seats are assigned to parties in the order of the size of the quotients resulting from these divisions.

The most common quota system is the Hare (or simple quota) system, in which the total valid votes in the district are divided by the number of seats in contention. Parties then receive the number of seats corresponding to the number of times the district quotient goes into the valid votes received by the party. But since seats usually remain unallocated after this operation, a second process must be used to assign the remaining seats. The typical approach is to distribute the remaining seats to the parties with the largest remainder resulting from dividing the party's valid votes by the quotient.

The possibility of gaining a seat through remainders, which in some cases entails obtaining a vote percentage well below the single Hare quota, tends to encourage party system fragmentation and the proliferation of small parties contending for seats. These parties—or more accurately, electoral vehicles—have little hope of obtaining significant representation at the national level, aiming instead to elect a single individual or group of individuals to the congress. This phenomenon has been particularly evident in Colombia and Venezuela

---

[2] Another approach is to use the average magnitude, but this measure has some limitations. It requires that the frequency distribution of the size of the country's electoral districts approximate a normal distribution (or be fairly symmetric about the mean). But this is rarely the case.

Table 3.1. Classifying Proportional Representation Systems According to District Size, 2004

	District size classification	Average district magnitude	Share of districts with five seats or less (%)	Share of seats elected from districts with five seats or less (%)	Size of individual districts (the figure in parentheses is the number of districts of a given magnitude)
Argentina	Medium	5.4	84.0	49.2	35, 12, 10, 9, 5(2), 4(5), 3(8), 2(5)
Brazil	Large	19.0	0.0	0.0	70, 53, 46, 39, 31, 30, 25, 22, 18, 17(2), 16, 12, 10(2), 9, 8(11)
Colombia	Medium	4.9	72.7	45.9	18, 17, 13, 7(3), 6(3), 5(5), 4(4), 3(3), 2(12)
Costa Rica	Medium	8.1	42.9	24.6	21,10, 6(2), 5(2), 4
Dominican Republic[3]	Small	3.1	95.9	90.7	8, 6, 5(5), 4(8), 3(12), 2(21), 1
Ecuador	Small	4.8	85.7	60.0	18, 14, 8, 5(2), 4(7), 3(4), 2(5)
El Salvador[1]	Medium	5.6	80.0	50.0	20 (national), 16, 6, 5(2), 4(2), 3(8)
Guatemala[1]	Medium	6.6	69.6	36.0	22 (national), 12, 10, 8, 7, 6(2), 5, 4, 3(6), 2(5), 1(3)
Honduras	Medium	7.1	44.4	18.0	23, 20, 9(3), 8, 7(3), 6, 5, 4(2), 3(2), 2, 1(2)
Nicaragua[1]	Medium	5.0	72.2	36.7	20 (national), 19, 6(3), 4(1), 3(6), 2(5), 1
Panama	Small	1.8	97.5	91.5	6(1), 5(2), 4(3), 3, 2(7), 1(26)
Paraguay	Medium	4.4	76.5	42.5	17, 13, 6(2), 5, 4(2), 3(2), 2(4), 1(4)
Peru[2]	Small	4.8	88.0	58.3	37, 7, 6, 5(6), 4(3), 3(4), 2(7), 1(2)
Uruguay[4]	Large	99.0	0.0	0.0	44, 13, 4, 3(6), 2(10)

Source: Authors' compilation.

[1] El Salvador, Guatemala, and Nicaragua have a national district that coexists with numerous regional districts of varying size. In Guatemala and Nicaragua, electors vote twice—once for a party list in their departmental constituency, and once for a party list in the national district. In El Salvador, electors select a party, and that vote counts as their choice of a party list for the regional constituency and the national constituency. For the purpose of assessing districts' aggregate magnitudes in both these countries, the national constituency is treated as if it were another large regional constituency.

[2] For the 2001 election, Peru returned to a multimember district system of 25 districts. This system had been replaced by a single, national district system from 1993 to 2000. With a smaller congress in 2001 than in 1992, the system became a proportional-representation-in-small-district system, while prior to 1993 it was a proportional-representation-in-medium-sized-district system.

[3] The Dominican Republic had a system of medium-sized districts until 2002, when a reform was implemented that divided up eight of the larger districts and created a larger number of small districts.

[4] Uruguay is divided into 19 electoral districts of varying size, as can be seen from the last column. But even though electors vote for party lists in the districts, the formula for allocating seats is decided by percentages of the aggregate (national) vote, and the distribution of seats within districts is required to accommodate the distribution of national seats resulting from this calculation. In effect, the Uruguayan system functions in a manner similar to a single, national district system.

in recent years.[3] A way to impede this tendency would be to adopt the rule that only parties that obtain seats through Hare quotas are eligible to compete for seats on the basis of remainders. Or, as in Costa Rica, a second round of seat allocation can be carried out on the basis of a subquotient (in the case of Costa Rica, half of the Hare quotient) before considering the remainders.

Of the Hare and D'Hondt systems, the Hare-quota-and-largest-remainder system is the most impartial between large and small parties, and tends to yield closely proportional results. The D'Hondt formula tends to be less proportional, even relative to several other divisor systems, and systematically favors larger parties. In the hypothetical case shown in Table 3.2, the Hare formula results in at least one seat going to each party while the D'Hondt formula shuts out the smallest party and overrepresents the two largest parties.

Of the 14 proportional representation list systems in Latin America, six use some form of the Hare-and-greatest-remainder system, and eight apply a form of the D'Hondt system.

The usefulness of the classification of proportional representation systems can be examined by studying a measure of the disproportionality of the translation of votes into seats. Does a classification of systems in terms of district size, in fact, parallel the measure of proportionality of electoral outcomes? Does considering the type of electoral formula enhance the match between electoral system attributes and a measurement of their outcomes?

All of the different indexes of proportionality entail calculating, in some manner, the deviations between the vote and seat percentages obtained by each political party, and adding the results for each party competing for seats in the election. In the "least-squares" index used here,[4] the larger the value of the index, the greater the degree of disproportionality (or the lower the proportionality) of the relationship between vote shares and seat shares.[5]

Table 3.3 examines the extent to which the classification of small, medium, and large district proportional representation systems in Latin America align with the observed disproportionality of those systems.

Subdividing proportional representation systems according to the proportion of legislative seats elected in districts of a given size appears to make some sense. The large-district systems—Uruguay and Brazil—are characterized by a relatively small degree of deviation from proportionality, while the small-district systems in Peru and Panama are characterized by a relatively large deviation.[6] The index of disproportionality generally hovers in the middle of these two extremes for medium-sized districts. Nevertheless, the relationship

---

[3] In Colombia, the congress approved an electoral reform in 2003 that holds the potential to reduce this tendency toward party system fragmentation by limiting each party to presenting a single list in each district and by changing the seat allocation formula from the Hare-and-largest-remainder system to the D'Hondt system.

[4] In the least-squares index, the vote/seat share differences for each party are squared and then added; this total is divided by two; and then the square root of this value is taken. Low numbers indicate low disproportionality (or high proportionality), while high numbers indicate the opposite (Lijphart, 1994).

[5] Considering an index of disproportionality values for other countries in the world helps to gauge the meaning of the values for Latin American countries. Lijphart (1994) cites the following index values for the last electoral system in use in the period prior to 1990: Australia 10.24, Austria 1.43, Canada 11.33, France 11.84, Germany 0.67, Italy 1.12, Netherlands 1.32, Norway 4.84, Sweden 1.67, United Kingdom 2.94, and United States 5.41.

[6] The disproportionality index value shown in Table 3.3 for the Dominican Republic was calculated based on the 2002 elections which took place under the new, smaller-district system. Even though the disproportionality that arose in those elections was not extreme (5.7), it was higher than in previous elections.

Table 3.2. Application of D'Hondt and Hare Formulas in a Hypothetical Six-Member District with Four Parties

Seats allocated using D'Hondt divisors

Party	Votes (v)	Votes/1	Votes/2	Votes/3	Total seats	Seats (%)
A	41,000	41,000 (1)	20,500 (3)	13,667 (6)	3	50.00
B	29,000	29,000 (2)	14,500 (5)	9,667	2	33.33
C	17,000	17,000 (4)	8,500		1	16.67
D	13,000	13,000			0	0.00
Total	100,000				6	100.00

Note: The numbers in parentheses indicate the order in which the six seats are allocated to the parties.

Seats allocated using Hare-and-largest-remainder system

Hare quota = 100,000 [votes]/6 [seats] = 16,667 votes per seat

Party	Votes (v)	Hare quotas	Full quota seats	Remaining seats	Total seats	Seats (%)
A	41,000	41,000/16,667= 2.**45**	2	0	2	33.33
B	29,000	29,000/16,667= 1.**73**	1	1	2	33.33
C	17,000	17,000/16,667= 1.**02**	1	0	1	16.67
D	13,000	13,000/16,667= 0.**78**	0	1	1	16.67
Total	100,000		6.00	4	2	6	100.00

Note: The boldface decimal portion of numbers serves as the basis for the distribution of seats that remain following the quota-based distribution of seats.

between district size and the index is clearly imperfect, and there are several striking, outlying cases.

The nature of the electoral formula appears to account for at least part of the large variation in disproportionality among medium-sized districts. The systems in which the Hare formula is applied (e.g., Honduras, Nicaragua, and Costa Rica) are characterized by a lower degree of disproportionality, while those using the D'Hondt system (e.g., Argentina, Paraguay, and Guatemala) are characterized by a higher degree.

At the same time, however, it is clear that electoral system characteristics do not solely determine the proportionality of electoral outcomes. This is because other factors—such as the number of parties competing in the election,[7] the system used for electing the president,

---

[7] This is particularly evident from the index values cited in note 5 for the United States and the United Kingdom. Even though these countries use a single-member district system that heavily discriminates against minority par-

Table 3.3. Classification of Proportional Representation Systems versus Measurement of Disproportionality

	Classification by size of electoral districts	Average district magnitude	Formula used for the lower house	Least-squares index
Uruguay	Large	99.0	D'Hondt	1.52
Brazil	Large	19.0	Hare	0.90
Costa Rica[1]	Medium	8.1	Hare	5.18
Honduras	Medium	7.1	Hare	2.26
El Salvador	Medium	5.6	Hare	4.89
Argentina	Medium	5.4	D'Hondt	8.89
Nicaragua	Medium	5.0	Hare	4.48
Colombia[2]	Medium	4.9	D'Hondt	3.04
Guatemala[2]	Medium	6.6	D'Hondt	8.43
Paraguay	Medium	4.4	D'Hondt	8.47
Peru	Small	4.8	D'Hondt	8.87
Ecuador[2]	Small	4.8	D'Hondt	8.10
Dominican Republic	Small	3.1	D'Hondt	5.68
Panama	Small	1.8	Hare	11.56

Source: Authors' compilation.
Note: The least-squares index of disproportionality in this table is calculated on the basis of results from the most recent election.
[1] Costa Rica uses a Hare quotient, 50 percent subquotient, and greatest remainder system, which tends to exclude small parties to a greater extent than a pure Hare-and-largest-remainder system.
[2] As of the end of 2004, Colombia, Guatemala, and Ecuador had not yet held national elections under the rules defined by the recent electoral reforms. Thus, the disproportionality indexes have been calculated on the basis of electoral results shaped by the rules of the prior electoral system rather than the current system.

and the relative timing of presidential and legislative elections—can have significant effects on the actual functioning of the system. In general, the smaller the number of significant parties, the smaller the district magnitude that is required to produce a reasonably proportional outcome.

For example, it is likely that the wide deviation between Guatemala, and Honduras and Nicaragua, is due in great part to the differences in the degree to which their party systems are fragmented. According to a measure of the effective number of parties, Guatemala had about five or six significant parties competing for votes during the last 20 years, while Nicaragua[8] had about 2.5 and Honduras barely more than two. Thus, while the characteris-

---

ties, their indexes of disproportionality are fairly low. There is little inequity in the allocation of seats because in each case there are two parties that share most of the votes. It could be argued that the electoral system helped to create the two-party system over time, but this type of indirect effect is not captured by the index.
[8] This result for the effective number of parties in Nicaragua is based on counting the many parties in the 1990 center-right coalition as one single party.

tics of electoral systems affect party systems, there is an important component of inertia, which is a legacy of past political divisions and history. Consequently, at the same time that their development is shaped in part by electoral rules, party systems also mediate the influence of such rules in shaping political outcomes.

Legal Thresholds

Another factor that can affect the proportionality of seat allocation is whether there is a legally required threshold of vote percentage or other criteria that must be met before parties can obtain representation. The purpose of a threshold is to limit the fragmentation of the party system and enhance its effectiveness. However, few countries in Latin America have adopted a legal barrier to representation. The only one of the 14 party-list proportional representation systems with a vote threshold is Argentina, where, at the district level, a party must receive votes equivalent to 3 percent of all eligible voters. In addition, Bolivia (with a personalized proportional representation system) and Mexico (with a mixed system) have thresholds of 3 percent and 2 percent, respectively, applied at the national level. Finally, a January 2000 amendment to Nicaragua's election law requires each party to receive the equivalent of at least 4 percent of the entire country's registered votes to avoid disqualification. Other countries have practical thresholds that result from the combined effects of their mathematical formula, district magnitude, and the number of parties competing.[9]

Other Electoral Systems

Proportional Representation with Preference Vote

Another variation of proportional representation systems relates to the form in which voters manifest their preferences. In most of the proportional representation systems discussed in the preceding section, the elector is constrained to select among competing party lists. These types of lists are called *closed* (only those candidates on a given party list can be selected) and *blocked* (the elector votes only for the party and thus cannot alter the order of candidates on the list). In Brazil, the Dominican Republic, Panama, and Peru, however, the voter can specify a preference for a party list and for the individual candidates on the list. These lists are considered *unblocked*. In Peru, voters can select up to two candidates from a party list, while in Brazil and the Dominican Republic, they can select one.[10] In Panama, voters are given as many preference votes as there are seats to fill. Through a reform adopted

---

[9] In October 2005 a political party law reform in Peru established a threshold of 5 percent—or six deputies elected in more than one district—for parties to be awarded seats. For the 2006 election, the threshold was set at 4 percent or five deputies elected in at least two districts.

[10] Until its 1998 elections, the Dominican Republic used a system of blocked lists to select lower house legislators, but in 2002, a closed and unblocked ballot was introduced, whereby voters could mark their preference for a specific candidate within the list furnished by the party (Zovatto and Burdman, 2002).

in 2003, Colombia changed the electoral system in order to allow parties to decide whether or not voters can choose individual candidates.[11]

Another form of personal voting is found in Ecuador and Honduras, where voters can choose, from different party slates, as many candidates as there are legislative seats to be filled in the district. In this system, voters do not have the option of choosing a party list. This type of system is called proportional representation with open lists, or *panachage*. In both the closed- and open-list preference voting systems, seats are awarded to parties according to the percentage of votes each party receives in the district. These seats are then assigned to individual candidates within the parties according to the number of votes each receives. Given that the votes in these systems still accrue to the party list, and seats are awarded according to party vote shares, these systems all constitute different forms of proportional representation.

Mixed-Member Systems

Following the example of Germany, 29 countries around the world, including New Zealand, Italy, Israel, Japan, Hungary, and Russia, have adopted mixed-member electoral systems in which a portion of the legislative representatives are elected by majority rules in single-member districts, and another portion by proportional representation (Cox and Schoppa, 2002). In Latin America, such systems have been adopted in Mexico, Bolivia, and Venezuela. Within mixed-member systems one can distinguish between (1) mixed-member proportional systems, also called personalized proportional systems, in which the two tiers are connected so that the total number of legislative seats received by a party is proportional to the votes it receives in the list tier; and (2) mixed-member majority systems, in which seats in the two tiers are allocated independently, such that proportionality in the overall allocation of seats is not ensured (Shugart and Wattenberg, 2001). The former type of system, used in Bolivia and Venezuela, would be expected to produce a closer correspondence between vote and seat shares and to be more open to small parties (Thames and Edwards, 2006). In the mixed-member majority system used in Mexico, the election of three-fifths of representatives in single-member districts is separate from the election of the remaining two-fifths in large, multimember proportional districts. The principal of proportionality is built into part of the system, but not the system as a whole.[12]

---

[11] Prior to the reform, the parties could run on multiple lists in the same electoral district. The division of votes among many lists allowed most seats to be picked as remainders by the candidates at the head of each list. Thus, with candidates free to create their own lists within the same party, the system functioned as an open list type. The electoral reform confines parties to run on a single list, but voters can still select their candidates among those on the list.

[12] In reality, various and frequently changing rules have connected the two parts of the system in Mexico. For example, when the system was adopted in 1977, a party that had won more than 60 percent of single-member district seats was not eligible to receive any of the seats awarded through proportional representation. A subsequently adopted rule guaranteed an absolute majority in the lower house to any party obtaining 35 percent of the deputies elected through plurality, and 35 percent of the national vote. Currently, the deviation between the percentage of the total number of deputies a party is awarded and the national vote percentage is not allowed to exceed 8 percent.

Mixed-member systems have been seen to favor the development of more cohesive party systems (Shugart and Wattenberg, 2001). The existence of the single-member district tier of the system is expected to constrain the number of parties obtaining votes—even in the proportional tier of the system—for two reasons. First, voters will limit their vote in the single-member districts to candidates of parties with a viable chance of winning, and this will tend to also apply to their votes in the proportional tier of the system. Second, parties are expected to coalesce in order to improve their chances of winning seats in the single-member district tier of the system. But some empirical studies have questioned the extent of the winnowing effect this has on party numbers, given that small parties try to nonetheless maximize their votes in the proportional representation tier by maintaining a full slate of candidates in the single-member districts (Cox and Schoppa, 2002; Herron and Nishikawa, 2001). The extent to which mixed-member systems reduce party system fragmentation probably depends on whether or not the system is compensatory (mixed-member proportional rather than mixed-member majority), and the share of the seats that are decided by plurality rules versus proportional rules.

Mixed-member systems are also expected to allow constituents to hold legislators and their parties individually accountable on national policy matters (Shugart and Wattenberg, 2001). The election of a share of the legislators on an individual basis in single-member districts (or small multimember districts) is expected to strengthen the link between electors and their representatives. At the same time, the election of a significant share of the seats by party list favors the continued strength of national parties, and electoral accountability oriented around national policy concerns (Shugart, 2001). Also in relation to incentives, mixed-member proportional systems tend to foster more party-centered, and mixed-member majority systems more candidate-centered, forms of accountability (Bawn and Thies, 2003; Thames and Edwards, 2006).

Classification of Latin American Electoral Systems

The above discussion finds that the electoral systems used for the lower and upper houses in Latin America can be placed within one of eight different categories. Table 3.4 lists those categories and evaluates each in theoretical terms according to the three functions that electoral systems should ideally perform. The systems are listed roughly in order, from the most classically proportional systems to the most classically majoritarian systems.

Evaluations of system functions obviously depend on additional system features. A key issue already mentioned is whether the elector is limited to voting for a party list or is given the option of expressing a preference for an individual candidate or candidates on the list. Proportional representation systems with closed and blocked lists score low in participation, since the link between constituents and their individual representatives is weak. Systems with unblocked, or open, lists promote greater ties between voters and representatives—though the larger the number of representatives elected in a district, the more diffused this link becomes. First, with multiple seats at stake it is more difficult for the elector to be informed about all of the contending candidates and to track the performance of incumbents. Second, candidates are encouraged to develop close relations with only a

Table 3.4. Evaluating Electoral Systems by Function

Type of electoral system	Representativeness	Effectiveness	Participation
Proportional representation in large districts	+ +	– –	– –
Proportional representation in medium-sized districts	+	–	–
Proportional representation in small districts	±	+	–
Mixed-member proportional representation	+	–	+
Mixed-member majority	+	–	+
Binominal	–	+	+ +
Plurality with representation of the minority	–	+ +	+ +
Plurality	– –	+ +	+ +

Note: ++ = highly fulfilled; + = fulfilled; ± = partially fulfilled; –= not very well fulfilled; and – – = only minimally fulfilled.

portion of the constituency, since winning a seat entails capturing only a relatively small fraction of the total votes. Third, voters generally have only one vote each, and therefore can only hold one of the individuals representing them accountable.

The unblocking of party lists may also have a negative impact on effectiveness. With a preference vote, the main preoccupation of candidates is to distinguish themselves from other individuals on their party's list and to cultivate personal relations with a portion of their constituents. Thus, party leaders tend to lose the ability to discipline their legislative cohorts, and parties lose the ability to articulate and defend common programmatic objectives. Consequently, effectiveness is likely to be reduced (Shugart, 2001; Carey and Shugart, 1995).

In rating the general types of electoral systems, such particularities are ignored. When the specific Latin American electoral systems are evaluated, their individual traits will be considered more fully.

Proportional representation list systems score well in the degree of representation they afford, and poorly in their provision of effectiveness and participation. While systems with smaller districts tend to have lower representation scores, they score higher in effectiveness and—to a lesser extent—in participation. With smaller districts, fewer parties are likely to obtain representation. This makes majority governments more probable and facilitates interparty bargaining in the legislature. At the same time—and even with closed and blocked party lists—if only one, two, or three legislators are elected per district, then electors can vote, at least to some extent, according to their sentiments toward individual candidates.

Mixed-member proportional systems attempt to increase the degree of voter participation without reducing representativeness. The fact that a proportional formula is used to allocate all of the seats means that these systems can be relatively proportional, and thus representative. At the same time, the election of a large share of the legislature through single-member (or small) districts, and by personalized voting, tends to foster a stronger link between representatives and voters. As with other proportional representation systems, however, these systems run the risk of fostering a dispersed party system, which can make governing more difficult.

Mixed-member majority systems are similar to mixed-member proportional systems in that they promote stronger links between representatives and constituents while maintaining the electoral system's degree of proportionality. However, proportionality is an element—but not a universal principle—of segmented systems. Though segmented systems help guarantee the representation of minority parties, they do not guarantee that overall seat allocation will match the share of the votes that parties receive. Instead, it is likely that larger parties, which are able to win seats across the country in single-member districts, will receive a disproportionate share of seats. The majority, single-member district portion of the system is likely to have a greater impact on reducing votes for small parties even in the system's proportional representation tier (Cox and Schoppa, 2002). Thus, segmented systems are similar to personalized proportional representation systems in the degree of participation afforded, somewhat inferior in representativeness, and somewhat better in effectiveness.

Binominal systems clearly favor the two largest political forces at the expense of smaller parties. Their promotion of a two-party (or party block) system may be good for effectiveness, but is bad for representativeness. On the other hand, in two-member districts and—in the Chilean case—when citizens vote for individuals rather than party lists, the link between electors and representatives can be close.

Plurality-with-minority-representation and plurality systems are relatively similar in how they fulfill the main electoral system functions. The former may be somewhat better in terms of the representativeness afforded, because the system provides a guarantee that the first minority will be represented in each district. Nonetheless, both systems favor large parties at the expense of small parties, and both promote a concentration of seats in congress, thus facilitating effectiveness. In addition, both systems facilitate the building of relatively close links between representatives and constituents. Of course, these links are stronger in the single-member district plurality system, since only one candidate is elected and—in contrast to the plurality-with-minority-representation system—electors select individual candidates instead of party lists.

Tables 3.5 and 3.6 show the systems that are used in the lower and upper houses of Latin America, including information on district magnitude, electoral formula, and ballot form. With respect to the lower house, there are two systems of proportional representation in large districts, eight systems of proportional representation in medium-sized districts, four systems of proportional representation in small districts, two personalized proportional representation systems, one mixed system, and one binominal system. For the upper house, there are three systems of proportional representation in large districts, one plurality system, three plurality-with-minority-representation systems, one mixed system, and one binominal system.

In terms of the ballot structure, seven countries use closed and blocked party lists in the lower house: Argentina, Costa Rica, El Salvador, Guatemala, Nicaragua, Paraguay,

Table 3.5. Electoral Systems Used in the Lower House

	System	District magnitude	Average formula	Electoral ballot form
Argentina	Proportional representation in medium-sized districts	5.4	D'Hondt	Closed and blocked lists
Bolivia	Mixed-member proportional	14.4	D'Hondt	Candidate in single-member districts; closed and blocked lists
Brazil	Proportional representation in large districts	19.0	Hare and largest average[1]	Closed and unblocked lists
Chile	Binominal	2.0	First two finishers unless first doubles vote of second	One vote for candidate
Colombia[2]	Proportional representation in medium-sized districts	4.9	D'Hondt	Closed and unblocked lists, or blocked lists
Costa Rica[3]	Proportional representation in medium-sized districts	8.1	Hare quotient, 50% sub-quotient and greatest remainder	Closed and blocked lists
Dominican Republic	Proportional representation in medium-sized districts	3.1	D'Hondt	Closed and unblocked lists
Ecuador	Proportional representation in small districts	4.5	D'Hondt	Open lists with panachage
El Salvador	Proportional representation in medium-sized districts	5.6	Hare and largest remainder	Closed and blocked lists
Guatemala	Proportional representation in medium-sized districts	6.6	D'Hondt	Closed and blocked lists
Honduras	Proportional representation in medium-sized districts	7.1	Hare and largest remainder	Open lists with panachage
Mexico[4]	Mixed-member majority		Plurality; corrected electoral quotient	Candidate in single-member district; closed and blocked lists

(continued)

Table 3.5. *(continued)*

	System	District magnitude	Average formula	Electoral ballot form
Nicaragua[5]	Proportional representation in medium-sized districts	5.0	Hare and remainder quotient	Closed and blocked lists
Panama	Proportional representation in small districts	1.8	Single-member districts, plurality; multimember districts, Hare	Closed and unblocked lists
Paraguay	Proportional representation in medium-sized districts	4.4	D'Hondt	Closed and blocked lists
Peru	Proportional representation in large districts	4.8	D'Hondt	Closed and unblocked lists (two preference votes)
Uruguay[6]	Proportional representation in large districts		D'Hondt	Closed and blocked lists
Venezuela[7]	Mixed-member proportional	6.1	D'Hondt	Candidate in single-member district; closed and blocked lists

Source: Authors' compilation.

[1] "Hare and largest average" means that the valid votes are divided by the seats already obtained, plus one. This system tends to favor small parties more than does the largest remainder method.

[2] In Colombia, parties can decide if voters have the ability to select candidates from the list or are only able to select the party list.

[3] In Costa Rica, the Hare-and-largest-remainder-plus-subquotient formula means that parties that obtain at least half the electoral quotient are eligible to receive seats through remainders.

[4] Mexico's corrected quota system takes away the votes of those parties that do not reach the national threshold of 2 percent from the calculation of the electoral quotient. A second quotient is calculated in which the remaining effective votes (total votes minus those already used to allocate seats) are divided by the remaining seats. Following both procedures, the remaining seats are allocated to the parties with the greatest remainders, but only those already receiving seats are eligible.

[5] In Nicaragua, the Hare-and-remainder quotient formula means that the remainders for each party are summed across all of the districts and divided by the number of remaining seats to determine the quotient for the allocation of remaining seats. In the national district, the remaining seats are allocated under a quota calculated as the mean of four regional quotas.

[6] The Uruguayan election system is divided into 19 districts of varying size. However, even though the electors vote for party lists in the districts, the formula for allocating seats is applied to the aggregate (national) vote percentages, and the distribution of seats within districts is required to accommodate the national seat distribution resulting from this calculation. In effect, the Uruguayan system functions in a manner similar to a system of proportional representation in a single national district.

[7] In Venezuela, since the state vote totals are used to proportionally award the total seats contested in each state, the average district magnitude is calculated by dividing the size of the chamber by the number of state districts. But the system is really more proportional than this district magnitude would indicate, since additional seats (up to five) are available to parties that are underrepresented, as determined by their national vote totals relative to the national electoral quotient.

Table 3.6. Electoral Systems Used in the Upper House

Country	System	Average district magnitude	Electoral formula	Ballot form
Argentina	Plurality with minority representation	3	Plurality/ minority	Closed and blocked lists
Bolivia	Plurality with minority representation	3	Plurality/ minority	Closed and blocked lists
Brazil[1]	Plurality in single-member and two-member districts	1 and 2	Plurality	Open lists
Chile	Binominal	2	D'Hondt	One vote for a candidate
Colombia	Proportional representation in large (national) districts	100	D'Hondt	Closed and unblocked lists, or blocked lists
Dominican Republic	Plurality	1	Plurality	Vote for candidate
Mexico	Mixed-member majority: plurality with minority representation, and proportional representation in large (national) district	3 and 32	Plurality/ corrected Hare with greatest remainder	Closed and blocked lists
Paraguay	Proportional representation in large (national) districts	45	D'Hondt	Closed and blocked lists
Uruguay[2]	Proportional representation in large (national) districts	30	D'Hondt	Closed and blocked subparty lists

Source: Authors' compilation.
[1] When two-thirds of the senate is up for election and two senators are being elected per state, then electors have two votes for specific candidates who can be from different parties.
[2] In Uruguay, voters choose between closed and blocked subparty lists. The proportional representation formula is applied to the total votes of the party in order to determine the interparty allocation of seats. Then subparty list votes determine the allocation of seats within parties.

and Uruguay. In the mixed-member proportional systems (Bolivia and Venezuela) and the mixed-member majority case (Mexico), closed and blocked lists are used for the proportional representation component, but individual voting is found in the other component of the system. Among the proportional representation systems, preference votes are permitted

Democracies in Development

in a total of seven countries. In Brazil, Colombia,[13] the Dominican Republic, Panama, and Peru, the lists are closed and unblocked. In Ecuador and Honduras the lists are open and voters can vote multiple times for candidates from different parties. Personalized voting is also used in the binominal Chilean system.

Closed and blocked lists are used to elect senators in four countries (Argentina, Bolivia, Paraguay, and Uruguay). In Mexico, the proportional representation component uses closed and blocked lists, while the plurality component uses a personalized voting system. In the Dominican Republic and Brazil, voters can vote for individual candidates. In Colombia, parties may decide whether they want to allow voters to choose individual candidates or not.

Evaluation of Latin American Electoral System Functions

The next step is to evaluate the specific electoral systems used in Latin America in terms of the three functions previously discussed: representativeness, effectiveness, and participation. It is important to emphasize that the evaluations at this point are theoretical—and focused on the properties of the electoral systems—and are not based on the actual functioning of the political system in the specific countries. Table 3.7 evaluates the electoral system used for the lower house in each country in the study.

Given the prevalence of proportional representation and the use of multimember districts, Latin American electoral systems for the lower house tend to serve the function of representativeness to the detriment of effectiveness and participation. Even though the electoral systems in most countries use medium-sized districts, they generally provide opportunities for smaller parties to obtain representation. This would be expected to frequently result in governments that lack majorities in the legislature, and in a fairly high degree of party system fragmentation. Of the two wholly or partially majority systems, only Chile's is expected to concentrate legislative power and promote the election of majority governments. The segmented Mexican system may also tend to concentrate representation. The plurality portion of the system, the requirement that parties present candidates in at least 200 single-member districts in order to field lists in the regional proportional representation constituencies, and the 2 percent threshold may limit the ability of small parties to compete effectively. Despite their proportional design, the electoral systems of Panama and the Dominican Republic would also be expected to favor more concentrated representation given the small size of electoral districts. However, the separate election cycles for the presidency and legislative branch in the Dominican Republic tend to work against this tendency.

Rankings for participation are relatively low, but there has been a trend in the study period toward offering voters the opportunity to choose from individual candidates as well as different parties. The electoral systems in 11 of the 18 countries of the region allow voters a personalized vote in a mixed system (Mexico), under personalized proportional representation (Bolivia and Venezuela), in a binominal system (Chile), and through proportional repre-

---

[13] In the case of Colombia, parties are given the option of whether or not they want to allow voters to choose individual candidates.

Table 3.7. Theoretical Evaluations of Electoral System Functions in the Lower House

	Type of system	Represen-tativeness	Effective-ness	Participa-tion
Argentina	Proportional representation in medium-sized districts	+	–	–
Bolivia	Mixed-member proportional	+ +	–	±
Brazil	Proportional representation in large districts	+ +	– –	–
Chile	Binominal	–	+	+
Colombia	Proportional representation in medium-sized districts	+	–	±
Costa Rica	Proportional representation in medium-sized districts	+	–	–
Dominican Republic	Proportional representation in small districts	–	±	±
Ecuador	Proportional representation in small districts	±	–	–
El Salvador	Proportional representation in medium-sized districts	+	–	–
Guatemala	Proportional representation in medium-sized districts	±	±	–
Honduras	Proportional representation in medium-sized districts	+	–	–
Mexico	Mixed-member majority	+	–	±
Nicaragua	Proportional representation in medium-sized districts	+	–	–
Panama	Proportional representation in small districts	–	±	±
Paraguay	Proportional representation in medium-sized districts	+	–	–
Peru	Proportional representation in small districts	±	–	±
Uruguay	Proportional representation in large districts	+ +	–	–
Venezuela	Mixed-member proportional	+	–	±

Note: ++ = highly fulfilled; + = fulfilled; ± = partially fulfilled; – = not very well fulfilled; and – – = only minimally fulfilled.

sentation with open lists (Ecuador and Honduras) and proportional representation systems with preference voting (i.e., closed and unblocked lists in Brazil, Colombia, the Dominican Republic, Panama, and Peru). In the other countries, the system of proportional representation with closed and blocked lists prevails. This system encourages a party-centered type of representation, which inhibits electors from holding individual legislators accountable for their positions on issues or their conduct in office. Under this type of system, the accountability of political officials, if it can be achieved, depends on the existence of internal democratic mechanisms within parties that allow candidates and leadership to be selected through an open and competitive process. However, as is seen in Chapter 7, internal party democratization is in the beginning stages in most countries of the region.

In Bolivia, Mexico, and Venezuela, the selection of candidates for the plurality portion of the electoral system remains fairly centralized. Features designed to promote participation in the systems of Brazil, Ecuador, and Honduras would not be expected to fulfill this objective, given that personalized voting in such relatively large-district systems does not allow the development of a close link between constituents and their representatives. This was especially true in Peru between 1993 and 2000, when there was a single national district for electing the 120 members of the national assembly.

Different types of majority systems are the norm for the upper houses in the nine countries with bicameral systems (Table 3.8). Just three of these nine elect their senators through proportional representation, and all use a single national district. Included in this group are Colombia, Paraguay, and Uruguay. Among the majority systems, Argentina and Bolivia

Table 3.8. Theoretical Evaluations of Electoral System Functions in the Upper House

Country	System	Representativeness	Effectiveness	Participation
Argentina	Plurality with minority representation	−	+ +	+
Bolivia	Plurality with minority representation	−	+ +	+
Brazil	Plurality in single-member and two-member districts	−	+ +	+
Chile	Binominal	−	+ +	+
Colombia	Proportional representation in large (national) district	+ +	− −	− −
Dominican Republic	Plurality	−	+	+ +
Mexico	Mixed-member majority, plurality with minority representation, and proportional representation in large (national) district	+	±	+
Paraguay	Proportional representation in large (national) district	+ +	− −	− −
Uruguay	Proportional representation in large (national) district	+ +	− −	− −

Note: ++ = highly fulfilled; + = fulfilled; ± = partially fulfilled; − = not very well fulfilled; and − − = only minimally fulfilled.

elect their senators by plurality with minority representation; Brazil alternates between plurality in single-member districts and plurality in two-member districts; and the Dominican Republic uses plurality in single-member districts. The Chilean system is binominal. The Mexican system used to select the senate is segmented (like the system for its lower house), with three-quarters of senators elected by plurality with minority representation, and one-quarter by proportional representation in a national district.

Majoritarian systems generally receive low marks for representativeness but reasonably high marks for effectiveness and participation. Similar to projections for lower house systems, proportional representation in large, national district systems for upper house elections are expected to do well in representing the diverse political forces in society, and less well in producing effective governments and building personal links between representatives and constituents. As with its lower house system, Mexico's segmented upper house system is again a compromise between the principles of proportionality and majoritarianism. The Mexican system is scored with a "±" for representativeness, since the proportional representation part of the system should allow smaller parties to be represented, though not proportionately. It is scored "±" for effectiveness, since the election of three-quarters of the members through the plurality-with-minority-representation system should still tend to give large parties a substantial share of the seats. Finally, the system is rated a "+" for participation, since the plurality component allows constituents to get to know their senators reasonably well.

The next step is to examine whether the theoretical expectations of Latin America's electoral systems correspond, to any significant degree, with their actual functioning. Do electoral systems that appear to be designed to favor representativeness produce reasonably proportional results? Do electoral system designs that appear to favor a concentration of political forces and effectiveness actually do so? In this analysis, it will not be possible to compare theoretical expectations of participation rates with outcome measures. Though, in theory, it may be possible through public surveys or interviews of legislators to test the closeness of the relationship between constituents and their representatives, the data do not exist at the present time.

Figure 3.1 shows the degree of correspondence between the theoretical scores given for representativeness in each country and the measured degree of disproportionality taken from the most recent election results.[14]

Now that electoral formula, along with district magnitude, has been factored into the scoring of the proportional representation list systems, the least-squares index of disproportionality corresponds more closely to theoretical expectations of the systems. Where the systems have been scored "+" for representativeness, the index of disproportionality tends to be relatively small, as would be expected. The systems ranked low for representativeness (−) generally have higher indexes of disproportionality. The systems expected to moderately favor representativeness (±) generally have a moderate disproportionality measure as well.

Clearly, however, the theoretical properties of electoral systems do not accurately predict electoral outcomes. There remains a considerable range in proportionality in each of the

---

[14] The theoretical rankings of representativeness shown in the graph are based on the electoral systems in existence when these elections were held, and may no longer correspond to the current systems.

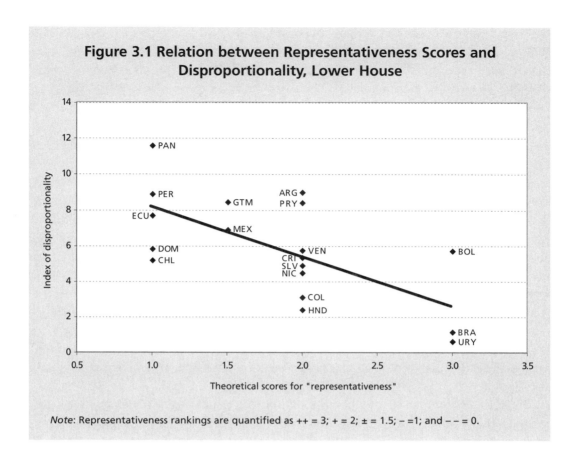

Figure 3.1 Relation between Representativeness Scores and Disproportionality, Lower House

Note: Representativeness rankings are quantified as ++ = 3; + = 2; ± = 1.5; – =1; and – – = 0.

possible theoretical scores for representativeness. Guatemala and Honduras are outliers. Guatemala has more disproportionate outcomes than would be expected, and Honduras, less. As already indicated, it is likely that differences in the nature of the party systems account for a large share of the differences in the proportionality of the results. While the Honduran party system has been dominated by two political groupings, in Guatemala several significant parties typically compete for the presidency and legislative seats.

The two-way, imperfect nature of the relationship between electoral system attributes and party system characteristics is even more evident when we compare the theoretical expectations for effectiveness with a measure of the effective number of political parties (Laakso and Taagepera, 1979).[15] The index of the effective number of parties measures the number of parties obtaining seats in the legislature, weighted by the proportion of seats they obtain.

---

[15] The index for the effective number of parties is computed by taking the inverse of the sum of the square of all parties' seat (or vote) shares. If there are three parties competing that receive close to an equal share of the vote, then the result for the index would be close to three. But if two of the three parties receive about 45 percent of the seats (or votes) each, and the third party receives only 10 percent, then the result would be about 2.4. The index attempts to capture the fact that despite also having three parties, the latter system functions closer to a two-party system, while the former functions more definitively like a three-party system.

We have already seen that a more fragmented party system contributes to higher disproportionality by making it more difficult for a given electoral system (based on formula, district magnitude, etc.) to fairly allocate seats among parties. More proportional systems are expected to allow more parties to be represented and to encourage more parties to compete for office. However, if this happens, a more proportional electoral system could paradoxically lead to an increase in the disproportionality of electoral outcomes (or a smaller decrease than expected) because of the greater number of parties contending for the seats available.

Similarly, an electoral system's properties do not exclusively determine the number of significant political parties competing for or holding political office. This is because the electoral system is clearly not the only factor affecting the nature of the party system. The structure of today's party systems is as much a product of long-term historical events and social and political divisions as it is of the current properties of any electoral system. In fact, one can view electoral systems themselves as products of this political history and of the evolution of the party system structure. Electoral systems do not emerge in a vacuum or from purely philosophical discussions. They are typically created by leading politicians in order to promote the interests of specific political parties or movements. In addition, as shown in the previous chapter, the presidential election system and the degree of concurrence between the presidential and legislative elections also influence the structure of the party system.

Thus, while highly proportional electoral systems create incentives for party system fragmentation, countries with such systems do not necessarily have a larger number of significant parties than countries with less proportional systems. Nevertheless, if a given country implements an electoral system reform that promotes greater proportionality, the expected trend is one of new party formation and more small parties obtaining representation in congress. A trend in the opposite direction may occur, but is not to be expected.

Table 3.9 and Figure 3.2 show that some countries match expectations fairly well. Brazil, which has an electoral system that favors representativeness and disfavors effectiveness, has a highly fragmented party system. With an electoral system that is not very proportional, a fairly large number of parties compete for seats in Guatemala, but few parties obtain significant representation.

There are, however, several countries with party systems that appear to diverge from expectations. Honduras, Costa Rica, and Uruguay, whose electoral systems would be expected to foster a relatively large number of effective parties, have had fairly concentrated party systems (as measured by the index of the effective number of parties). But there are signs that, at least in Costa Rica, this is changing, and given the factionalized nature of Uruguayan parties, it may not be correct to view this as a deviant case. While three major parties typically dominate, the parties themselves are composed of factions that compete internally for the party's seat share.

Among the countries that scored "–" for effectiveness, there is a range of party system outcomes, from a low of nearly two significant parties in Honduras and Paraguay to a high of more than five in Bolivia and Ecuador. Chile also has more political parties than would be expected in a binominal system; over the entire period, the average number of effective parties in its lower house was 5.3. However, when party alliances rather than individual

Table 3.9. Theoretical Expectations Compared with Outcome Measures, Lower House

Country	Represen-tativeness	Disproportion-ality index	Effective-ness	Effective number of parties (votes)	Effective number of parties (seats)
Argentina	+	8.89	–	3.80	2.82
Bolivia	+ +	5.69	–	5.14	4.51
Brazil	+ +	0.90	– –	7.70	7.06
Chile[1]	–	5.17	+	2.43	2.02
Colombia	+	3.04	–	3.34	3.05
Costa Rica[2]	+	5.18	–	3.02	2.51
Dominican Republic	–	5.68	+	2.96	2.47
Ecuador	±	8.10	–	7.21	5.90
El Salvador	+	4.89	–	3.42	3.17
Guatemala	±	8.43	–	5.36	3.42
Honduras	+	2.26	–	2.25	2.15
Mexico	±	6.87	–	2.84	2.37
Nicaragua	+	4.48	–	2.44	2.28
Panama	–	11.56	±	6.26	3.56
Paraguay	+	8.47	–	2.69	2.45
Peru	±	8.87	–	4.61	3.66
Uruguay	+ +	1.52	–	3.19	3.16
Venezuela	+	5.84	–	4.42	3.69

Source: Authors' compilation.
Note: ++ = highly fulfilled; + = fulfilled; ± = partially fulfilled; – = not very well fulfilled; and – – = only mini-mally fulfilled.
[1] The figures in parentheses are the values of the indexes if calculated on the basis of party alliances rather than individual parties.
[2] The least-squares index for the most recent election in Costa Rica was considerably higher than the 4.76 average score registered over the study period.

political parties are considered (values shown in Table 3.9), it is clear that Chile is not an atypical case. The electoral system appears to have had its intended effect of promoting government effectiveness by encouraging the formation and durability of two large alliances of the center-left and center-right.

Given the influence of other country-specific factors, the effect of electoral system properties on political outcomes may be obscured in cross-national comparisons such as those shown in Figure 3.2.[16] A preferable way to examine the impact of electoral systems would be

---

[16] As in Figure 3.1, the theoretical ranking of electoral effectiveness used in Figure 3.2 is based on the system used during the most recent election, and not necessarily on the current system.

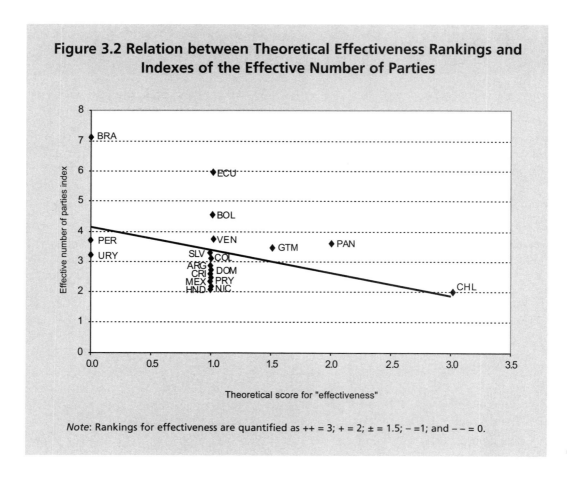

Figure 3.2 Relation between Theoretical Effectiveness Rankings and Indexes of the Effective Number of Parties

Note: Rankings for effectiveness are quantified as ++ = 3; + = 2; ± = 1.5; − =1; and − − = 0.

to analyze the effects of reforms in specific countries over time. In the case of an individual nation, the structural and historical factors that mediate between electoral system factors and political outcomes are more easily defined.

The next section of this chapter examines the electoral system reforms of the past few decades, and ventures to determine whether these reforms had the effects expected on political representation outcomes. Such analysis is complicated in many cases by the brief time period in which a reformed system has been in place, as well as by exogenous political events, such as the delegitimization of the political party system, which may have a greater impact on outcomes than changes to the electoral system.

Evolution of Latin American Electoral Systems[17]

In examining the electoral system reforms, it is clear that many reforms have been implemented during the period of this study, which begins in most countries after the transition

---

[17] Throughout this book, the period under review in each country starts when the transition to democracy took place (see Preface) or, if democratic rule existed prior to 1978, the year the first president who served a complete term took office after 1978. The study period goes to the end of 2005.

to democracy. To understand these reforms from the standpoint of democratic governance, they are examined in terms of their expected effects on the functions of representativeness, effectiveness, and participation. Many of the reforms are fairly subtle in nature, involving a slight adjustment of the electoral formula or small changes in the size of electoral districts. They would not be expected to have a significant impact on representation outcomes. Left out of this examination are many reforms that could be quite significant for the functioning of democracy, such as the creation of independent electoral commissions, or changes to the regulations of electoral campaign and political party financing. Also not considered in this review of national-level electoral reforms are far-reaching and significant reforms in the systems used for selecting subnational executive officials and representatives. The trend across the region has generally been one of adopting direct electoral popular elections for choosing such officials, and increasingly separating these processes from the influence of national electoral politics.

Changes in the following areas are noted:

- The type of electoral system, for example, from a proportional representation list system to a mixed-member proportional system
- The number of legislative seats and the magnitude of electoral districts
- The electoral formula, for example, from Hare to D'Hondt
- The existence of legal thresholds for parties to obtain representation
- The relative timing of presidential, legislative, and local elections
- The degree of connection on the ballot between presidential and legislative elections
- The type of voting choices available (strictly party list, candidate preference, multiple candidate preference, etc.)

Electoral Reforms Affecting the Lower House

Table 3.10 shows the reforms to systems for electing representatives to the lower house. Only three of the 18 countries studied did not change their legislative electoral system during the period of the study (Brazil, Chile, and Costa Rica). In five countries (Bolivia, the Dominican Republic, Ecuador, Peru, and Venezuela), changes were made in the type of electoral system. Each of these reforms involved changes from one type of proportional representation to another. In addition, significant changes in the voting choices presented to electors were made in several countries. It is worth noting that in Chile and Mexico, important electoral system reforms took place outside the period of the study. Chile moved to the binominal system and Mexico to the segmented system.

Of the countries that made changes in electoral system type, Bolivia and Venezuela adopted a mixed-member proportional system in place of a proportional representation list system in medium-sized constituencies. In Peru, there was a shift from a proportional representation list system in medium-sized districts to a "pure" proportional representation system in a national district (in both cases with preference votes). With the 2001 election, Peru returned again to a multimember district system consisting of 25 districts. The Dominican Republic changed from a system of proportional representation in medium-sized constituencies to a proportional representation list system in small constituencies.

Table 3.10. Lower House Electoral System Changes

Country	Year	Nature of change	Expected effect
Argentina	1994	Only one midterm election instead of two because of the shortening of the presidential term from six to four years[1]	Effectiveness +
Bolivia	1986	Seat allocation formula changed from D'Hondt to double quotient[2]	Representativeness – Effectiveness +
	1991	Seat allocation formula changed from double quotient to Saint-Lague divisor system	Representativeness + Effectiveness –
	1994	System changed from list proportional representation to personalized proportional representation (about half of deputies elected through plurality in single-member districts); plurality vote separated from vote for president, vice president, and senate; 3 percent threshold introduced at national level	Participation +
Brazil		No changes	
Chile[3]		No changes	
Colombia	1991	Reduction in the size of districts through the creation of new districts; reduction in congress size[4]	Representativeness – Effectiveness +
		Creation of special districts for indigenous groups	Representativeness +
	2003	Parties limited to presenting one list in each electoral district; in addition, parties given the option to allow voters to choose individual candidates instead of the party list	Representativeness – Effectiveness +
		Seat-allocation formula changed from Hare and greatest remainder to D'Hondt	Participation +
Costa Rica		No changes	
Dominican Republic	1985	Restoration of simultaneous vote for president legislators	Effectiveness + Participation –
	1990	Redivision of separate votes for president and legislators	Effectiveness – Participation +
	1994	Presidential and congressional elections separated into different four-year cycles, resulting in further separation of voting for president and congress	Effectiveness – Participation +
	1997	Size of lower house increased from 120 to 149 deputies; average district magnitude increased from four to five	Representativeness + Effectiveness –
	2002	Preferential voting introduced for election of representatives to the lower house; new electoral districts created through division of the eight largest districts	Participation + Representativeness –
Ecuador	1998	System changed from list proportional representation with small national district and regional multimember constituencies to	Representativeness – Effectiveness –

(continued)

Country	Year	Nature of change	Expected effect
		Table 3.10. (continued)	
		plurality in multimember districts; 20-member national constituency, maintained for 1998 election, eliminated for subsequent elections	
		All deputies elected at the same time as the president (previously provincial, district-based deputies had been elected every two years)	Effectiveness +
		Size of congress increased from 82 to 121 seats; for 1998 election, 20 national deputies instead of 12	
El Salvador	1988	Number of deputies increased from 60 to 84; creation of national constituency for election of 20 out of 84 deputies; electors still given one vote for congress	Representativeness +
Guatemala[5]	1990	Number of deputies increased from 100 to 116 (number of district deputies went from 75 to 87 and national deputies from 25 to 29)	Representativeness +
	1994	Number of deputies reduced and fixed at 80 with 64 district deputies and 16 national deputies	Representativeness – Effectiveness +
		Separate vote for national deputies (the vote for president previously entailed a vote for a party list for the national district)	Participation +
	1998	Number of deputies increased to 113, with 91 members elected in departmental constituencies and 22 in national constituency	Representativeness +
Honduras	1985	Number of deputies increased from 82 to 134; average district magnitude increased from 4.6 to 7.4	Representativeness + Effectiveness –
	1988	Decree established that congress be composed of a fixed number of 128 deputies; remainders allocated at national level on the basis of national quotient	
	1992	Separate vote for president and deputies to national congress; separate boxes on the same ballot for president, congress, and municipal councils	Participation +
	1993	Requirement for fully separate ballots for president, congress, and municipal councils (this system was first used in 1997)	Participation +
	2004	System changed from proportional representation with closed and blocked lists to proportional representation with open lists and panachage (electors can vote for as many candidates as there are seats to be filled and can select them from different party lists)	Participation + Effectiveness –

(continued)

Table 3.10. *(continued)*

Country	Year	Nature of change	Expected effect
Mexico[6]	1986	Number of proportional representation seats raised from 100 to 200; total size of chamber increased from 400 to 500; plurality winner assured majority in congress; change from two votes to one; the Institutional Revolutionary Party (PRI) given access to seats won through proportional representation	Representativeness +[7] Participation – Effectiveness +
	1989	Majority party limited to 70 percent of seats in lower house; electoral alliances prohibited; elector again given two votes, one for candidate in plurality and one for party list in proportional representation constituency	Participation +
	1990	Any party receiving 35 percent of plurality deputies and 35 percent of the national vote guaranteed an absolute majority in the lower house; limit of 60 percent of seats if party obtains more than 60 percent of popular vote	Representativeness - Effectiveness +
	1993	Thirty-five percent rule eliminated	Representativeness + Effectiveness –
	1996	Threshold for representation raised from 1.5 percent to 2 percent; no party to be awarded a percentage of total deputies over 8 percent of the national vote percentage it obtains (if this occurs solely in plurality seats, the rule does not apply)	Representativeness + Effectiveness +
	1996	Creation of five multiple member constituencies to replace national constituency	
Nicaragua	1988	One of three steps for assigning seats (based on the sum of district residuals and a new quotient) eliminated, but regional assignment of seats in order of more to less valid votes kept	Representativeness – Effectiveness +
	1992	Distribution formula for department level changed to favor very small parties	Representativeness + Effectiveness –
	1996	Electoral regions established in 1984 replaced by departmental districts of smaller populations and smaller numbers of deputies; creation of national constituency of 20 deputies	Representativeness + Effectiveness –
	2000	An electoral law established mandating that parties need to receive votes equivalent to 4 percent of all registered voters in order to retain their legal status	Representativeness – Effectiveness +
Panama	1993	A party restriction, introduced in 1988, eliminated (the restriction had prevented parties from obtaining seats through residuals that had not obtained a seat through quotas; remaining seats were allocated first to parties	Representativeness + Participation +

(continued)

Table 3.10. *(continued)*

Country	Year	Nature of change	Expected effect
		that had not obtained a seat but had minimally received a half quotient in the order of the votes received; if seats remained, they were allocated to the candidates receiving the most votes, counting each of the lists in which the candidate had postulated; the law eliminated the deduction of the half quotient as a means of assigning seats by residual); impediment—in place since 1930—against a party obtaining more than two-thirds of the seats in a district also eliminated; separate ballots put in place for each office	
Paraguay	1990	Separate ballots put in place for the election of senators and deputies	Participation +
	1990	Change from one national constituency to 18 multiple-member constituencies, corresponding to the country's 17 administrative departments and the capital	Representativeness – Participation +
Peru	1993	Change from a bicameral to a unicameral system; basis of representation changed from 25 multiple-member constituencies to one national constituency; size of lower house reduced from 180 to 120	Representativeness + Participation –
Peru	2000	Return to the use of 25 multiple-member constituencies to elect 120 representatives to the unicameral legislature	Representativeness –
Uruguay	1996	No change in legislative election system; replacement of simultaneous presidential election system with primaries (which had implications for a number of factions competing in the multiple simultaneous vote system in the legislative elections)	Effectiveness +
Venezuela	1990	Changed from proportional representation list in medium-sized districts to personalized proportional representation system; 35 percent of deputies elected by plurality (in single-member districts) and 65 percent by proportional representation; the vote for deputies separated from the vote for senators	Participation +
	1997	Several multiple-member constituencies created for plurality portions of the chamber in the cases of large municipalities that cannot be divided under the constitution; half of deputies elected by plurality and half by proportional representation	Participation +

(continued)

Country	Year	Nature of change	Expected effect
	1998	On a temporary basis, legislative elections moved to occur one month before presidential elections	Participation + Effectiveness –
	1999	Change to unicameral system; 60 percent of deputies elected by plurality and 40 percent by proportional representation; separation of presidential elections from congressional elections as a result of the lengthening of the presidential term from five to six years	Participation + Effectiveness –[8]
		Reduction in the number of legislators in the national assembly from 203 to 165	Representativeness – Effectiveness +

Table 3.10. *(continued)*

Source: Numerous sources were consulted in acquiring the information for this review of electoral reform in the region. Included among the important secondary sources are: Abente (1996); Archer (1995); Caballero Carrizosa (1998); Conaghan (1995); Fleischer (1998); Grullón (1999); IIHR (2000); Izaguirre (2000); Nohlen (1993); Urbina Mohs (2000).

[1] A new province was added (Tierra del Fuego in 1990), which increased the number of deputies in the lower house from 254 to 257.

[2] The double quotient requires that parties receive at least one quota (total valid votes/seats contested) before they can receive any seats through remainders.

[3] With the adoption of the 1980 constitution during the Pinochet regime (1973–1990), Chile replaced the proportional representation system with the binominal system. This change is not mentioned in the table since it occurred outside of the period of the study, i.e., before the transition to democracy in Chile.

[4] See Archer and Shugart (1997) for the broader impact of the change in terms of clientelistic practices. On the one hand, smaller districts make it harder to win with a narrow base of support. But expanding the number of districts may create some very underpopulated districts where particularistic appeals can flourish.

[5] The changes in the number of seats in the Guatemalan congress after 1994 result in part from a requirement that a fixed ratio between population and congressmen numbers be maintained.

[6] In Mexico, the segmented electoral system was adopted in 1977. This change is not mentioned in the table since it occurred outside of the study period.

[7] The increase in the size of the proportional representation part of the system would be expected to enhance the representation of minority parties. But the fact that the PRI was given access to the seats won through proportional representation could have enhanced the share of seats won by the majority party.

[8] The elimination of the senate tends to promote greater effectiveness, since one potential point of opposition to the government has been eliminated. But the separation of the presidential and legislative elections tends to undermine effectiveness by increasing the chances that a different party or coalition can control the legislature than that which controls the presidency. As pointed out in Chapter 2, it may also lead to an increase in the number of parties in the legislature. When presidential and congressional elections are held concurrently, legislative votes tend to be channeled toward the parties of the leading presidential candidates. This limits the number of parties that obtain representation and increases the chances that the president's party will obtain a large share of legislative seats.

Ecuador changed from a proportional representation system with closed and blocked lists to a plurality system in multimember electoral districts for the 1998 election. In the subsequent 2002 election, it changed back to proportional representation, but this time with open lists and *panachage*.

Although not representing a change in election system type as defined here, Honduras's 2004 change from a proportional representation system with closed and blocked lists to one with open lists also represents a significant reform. Though also not a formal change in electoral system, the recent electoral reform in Colombia was profound. By limiting each party to one list presented in each district and adopting a more restrictive formula for converting votes into seats, the reform should help restore significance to party labels and promote greater party system cohesion.

In addition to changing their electoral system, some countries changed the timing of presidential and legislative elections. As shown in Chapter 2 (see Table 2.5), Chile,[18] the Dominican Republic, and Venezuela shifted from systems with either fully or partially simultaneous elections to ones with nonconcurrent cycles. Brazil and Ecuador moved in the opposite direction, while Argentina moved slightly toward greater simultaneity.

Other important reforms were the separation of the election ballot for legislators from the ballots for other offices such as the presidency or upper house seats. Such reforms were adopted in the Dominican Republic, Guatemala, Honduras, Panama, Paraguay, and Uruguay.

The other types of changes noted in Table 3.10 relate mainly to the territorial distribution of legislative seats, the size of the chamber and the magnitude of electoral districts, and the type of formula used to assign seats.

Although one can observe a tendency toward strengthening representativeness and participation, the trend is not pronounced. There have been changes that favor representativeness in El Salvador, Guatemala, Honduras, Mexico, Nicaragua, and Panama. However, in a few of these cases, the changes were limited. The only countries that clearly moved in the opposite direction were the Dominican Republic and Paraguay, with a change from a proportional representation system using larger districts to one with smaller districts.

Since greater emphasis on representation usually entails a larger number of parties in the legislature and less chance of majority governments, the changes in these countries have generally coincided with less effectiveness. In the case of Guatemala, the changes reflected in Table 3.11 entail improvement in representativeness, but data from the last election (2003) also indicate that the number of parties in congress doubled (the effective number of parties rose from 2.35 to 4.56; see Table 3.12). In some cases, effectiveness decreased with the separation of legislative and presidential elections, either because of separate timing or because separate ballots were introduced—as was the case with representatives elected through a national list in Guatemala, the election of the president and legislators in Honduras, and representatives elected by plurality in Bolivia.

Though proportional representation with closed and blocked party lists remains the norm in the region, there has been a shift in favor of participation, giving voters greater choice over the individuals who will represent them. The moves to mixed-member proportional systems in Bolivia and Venezuela were the first changes in this direction. More recently, preference voting was adopted in Colombia (on an optional basis) and the Dominican Republic. Electoral lists were opened in Ecuador and Honduras in 1998 and 2004, respectively. The separation of legislative election ballots from those for the presidency and other offices, such as senate seats,[19] has also given voters greater discretion and

---

[18] With the reduction in the presidential term from six to four years in 2005, Chile returned to having simultaneous presidential and legislative elections.

[19] A significant trend has been the proliferation of elections for choosing representatives and leaders at the subnational level, and an increased separation of these elections from national ones, both in timing and ballot structure. A systematic treatment of this matter, however, is beyond the scope of this chapter.

weakened the hold of parties over voter decisions. Nevertheless, in many of the countries, party leaders or party organizations still exercise considerable control over determining the particular individuals who are elected and reelected to congress. This undermines the link between representatives and constituents.

Table 3.11 shows changes over time in the disproportionality of outcomes produced by the Latin American lower house electoral systems. Examining the regional average (see Table 3.11), it is clear that there has not been a dramatic shift in the function of representativeness over the period. On average, Latin American systems continue to generate relatively proportional outcomes, neither discriminating strongly against smaller parties nor unduly favoring large parties. Nor have there been many dramatic changes in individual countries. Peru experienced a substantial increase in proportionality after 1993, as a consequence of the change from medium-sized, multimember constituencies to a single national district. In 2001, the proportionality of outcomes decreased with the reinstatement of the original multimember district system.

How do Latin American election systems perform with respect to effectiveness? To answer this question completely, of course, one would need to determine the number of effective parties most compatible with a well-performing presidential democracy. But this depends on other factors such as the degree of ideological polarization between the parties, the disposition of political parties toward cooperation, and parties' internal cohesiveness. In several countries of the region the problem of governing in the context of multiparty systems has been addressed by forming party alliances and coalitions (what might be called "presidentialism through coalitions," to be examined further in Chapter 4). Nevertheless, the possibilities for effective government would still seem to be complicated in numerous cases by the high degree of party system fragmentation reinforced by the proportional representation system.

Figure 3.3 shows changes over time in the effective number of parties represented in the legislature. On average, a substantial increase occurred in the region between the 1980s and the 1990s. While in the first period, the number of parties ranged from 2.5 to 3.0, in the second they ranged from 3.5 to 4.0. The years 2000–2005 are also characterized by growth in the number of parties, though whether or not this trend will hold throughout the decade remains to be seen.

Table 3.12 shows the effective number of parties of individual countries underlying these regional trends. First, one can see that the increase in the number of parties between 1980 and 1990 is not explained by the inclusion of new countries with greater party fragmentation; in fact, the countries of most recent democratization (Brazil, Chile, and Nicaragua) had lower than average levels of fragmentation when they were incorporated into the sample.

Second, the regional trend was characterized by considerable increases in a relatively small number of countries. By far the most pronounced increases in party system fragmentation occurred in Brazil from 1986 to 1990, and in Venezuela from 1988 to 1993 and again in 1998. In neither case could the change be attributed to an electoral system reform, since in Brazil no significant reform occurred, and in Venezuela the reform should not have strongly affected the proportionality of the system. There was also a large increase in the number of effective parties represented in the legislature in Peru between 1985 and 1990, but the trend ended in 1995 despite a constitutional reform that emphasized greater proportionality. Less pronounced increases in the number of effective parties occurred in Bolivia, Ecuador, El

Table 3.11. Evolution of Latin American Electoral Systems: Representativeness

Index of disproportionality based on elections to the lower house

Country	1978–1981	1982–1985	1986–1989	1990–1993	1994–1997	1998–2001	2002–2004
Argentina	—	5.23	6.28	6.04	5.75	8.61	8.89
Bolivia	5.72	3.80	6.94	6.48	4.41	—	5.64
Brazil	—	—	3.46	3.20	3.08	2.65	0.90
Chile	—	—	7.02	5.59	8.20	5.17	—
Colombia	3.23	1.43	3.26	2.87 (1990) 3.11 (1991)	4.90	3.47	3.04
Costa Rica	5.47	3.18	3.25	4.59	5.50	6.57	5.18
Dominican Republic	3.46	5.57	5.64	4.95	4.83	5.04	5.68
Ecuador	11.06	11.82	17.04	4.60	5.18	8.10	—
El Salvador	—	10.45	4.87	3.88	4.70	4.58	4.89
Guatemala	—	11.41	—	11.03	12.42	11.72	8.43
Honduras	0.93	1.34	2.70	2.13	2.92	2.26	—
Mexico	1.42	6.91	3.53	2.52	7.08	6.37	6.87
Nicaragua	—	—	—	1.79	2.14	4.48	—
Panama	—	—	—	—	15.55	12.52	11.56
Paraguay	—	—	8.23	5.91	—	2.28	8.47
Peru	9.30	7.88	—	6.63	2.80	1.54 (2000) 8.87 (2001)	—
Uruguay	—	0.41	0.54	—	0.43	0.60	1.52
Venezuela	4.22	4.97	4.02	3.85	—	5.42 (1998) 6.25 (2000)	—
Average	4.98	5.72	5.37	4.81	5.16	5.53	6.39

Source: Authors' compilation.

Note: Indexes are presented for four-year periods (except the last period from 2002 to 2004). In general, elections are held every four years, so the number for a given country reflects the election held in that period. Among the exceptions are Peru, where elections were held in 2000 and 2001, and Argentina, where part of the lower house is elected every two years. In these cases, the numbers for the corresponding periods reflect the average of the index value for the two contests covered. The same procedure is used for Table 3.12. Dashes indicate absence of data, either because during the years indicated elections were not held, or because the country was not yet considered to have made its transition to a democratic system.

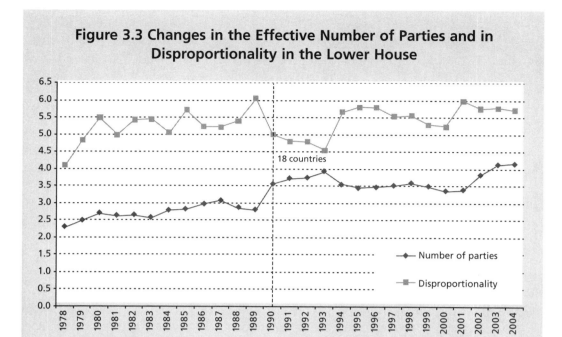

Figure 3.3 Changes in the Effective Number of Parties and in Disproportionality in the Lower House

18 countries

← Number of parties

■ Disproportionality

Note: Countries are included in the regional average beginning with their first year of inclusion in the study, as defined in the Preface. The regional average for any given year includes values from all of the countries for which the start year has already been passed, with the index values from a given election being held constant until the subsequent election.

Salvador, and Mexico. In each of these cases, an electoral system reform favored the function of representativeness at the expense of effectiveness. But it is doubtful, at least in the case of Ecuador and Mexico, that electoral reform was the main factor driving the increase in the number of effective parties.

Table 3.12 shows that on the basis of the data from the most recent elections, in four countries (Bolivia, Brazil, Colombia, and Ecuador) there are more than five parties with significant representation in the legislature. When there are three or more parties with significant representation, the president is unlikely to be elected with a majority in congress. On the basis of data from the most recent elections, nearly all of the countries studied are in this situation. The exceptions are Chile (when one considers its stable coalitions rather than its parties), the Dominican Republic, Honduras, Nicaragua, and Uruguay.

Electoral Reforms Affecting the Upper House

Among the 11 countries that had bicameral systems at the start of the study period, there have been relatively few changes affecting the representativeness of the electoral system for the upper house (Table 3.13). In Peru and Venezuela, there has been a shift to a unicameral system that in both cases could be seen to favor effectiveness since it eliminated an important potential source of opposition to the executive's initiatives and eased the problem of developing legislative compromises.

Democracies in Development

Table 3.12. Effective Number of Parties According to Number of Legislative Seats in the Lower House

Country	1978–1981	1982–1985	1986–1989	1990–1993	1994–1997	1998–2001	2002–2004
Argentina	—	2.32	2.77	3.01	2.68	2.86	3.82
Bolivia	4.13	4.31	3.92	4.29	5.36	—	5.06
Brazil	—	—	2.83	8.68	8.15	7.13	8.49
Chile	—	—	2.04	2.00	2.01	2.03	—
Colombia	2.06	1.98	2.45	2.17 (1990) 3.00 (1991)	2.72	3.21	6.80
Costa Rica	2.38	2.27	2.21	2.21	2.29	2.56	3.68
Dominican Republic	1.99	2.25	2.53	3.05	2.43	2.32	2.72
Ecuador	3.94	6.15	5.87	6.58	5.28	5.73	7.69
El Salvador	—	2.56	2.41	3.01	3.60	3.47	3.54
Guatemala	—	2.98	—	4.44	3.10	2.35	4.56
Honduras	2.17	2.12	2.00	2.03	2.18	2.41	—
Mexico	1.77	1.79	3.04	2.21	2.58	2.55	3.02
Nicaragua	—	—	—	2.05	2.79	1.99	—
Panama	—	—	3.72	—	4.33	3.26	2.92
Paraguay	—	—	1.89	2.45	—	2.27	3.18
Peru	2.46	2.31	—	5.83	2.91	4.00 (2000) 6.63 (2001)	—
Uruguay	—	2.92	3.33	—	3.30	3.07	2.41
Venezuela	2.65	2.42	2.83	4.74	—	6.05 (1998) 3.44 (2000)	—
Average	2.62	2.80	2.84	3.87	3.51	3.04	4.62

Source: Authors' compilation.
Note: Dashes indicate absence of data, either because during the years indicated elections were not held, or because the country was not yet considered to have made its transition to a democratic system.

The adoption of a national district in Colombia, a proportional representation component in Mexico, and a system of plurality with minority representation in Argentina would be expected to enhance representativeness to some degree. The separation of the vote for senators from the vote for other offices in the Dominican Republic and Paraguay favors participation, since voters have more freedom to select the particular candidates or parties they prefer. But this change—especially in the Dominican Republic, where not only the

Table 3.13. Changes in Upper House Electoral Systems

Country	Year	Nature of change	Expected effect
Argentina	1994	Change in direct election of senators (previously they were elected by provincial assemblies); senators' terms reduced from nine to six years; number of senators elected per district increased from two to three, with one seat for representation of the first minority[1]	Participation + Representativeness +
Bolivia		No changes	
Brazil		No changes	
Chile		No changes	
Colombia	1991	Regional multimember districts replaced by a single national district of 100 members Creation of special districts for indigenous persons and persons of African descent	Representativeness + Participation – Representativeness +
Dominican Republic	1985	Return to simultaneous vote for president and congressmen	Representativeness – Effectiveness + Participation –
	1990	Return to system of two votes, one for the president and one for congressmen	Representativeness + Effectiveness – – Participation +
	1994	Presidential and legislative elections separated into different four-year cycles	Representativeness + Effectiveness – – Participation +
	1994	Vote for senatorial candidates separated from vote for lower house party lists	Representativeness + Effectiveness – –
Mexico	1993	Number of each state's senators increased from two to four, with three seats going to the party receiving the most votes and one seat to the first minority	
	1996	Number of senators in each state reduced from four to three, and a 32-member national constituency created; the senate electoral system segmented like the lower house system, with three-quarters of the members elected by plurality with minority representation, and one-quarter by proportional representation in a national constituency	Representativeness + Participation – Effectiveness –
Paraguay	1990	Separate ballots put in place for the election of senators and deputies	Participation +
Peru	1993	Change from bicameral to unicameral system (the senate was previously elected in a large national district)	Effectiveness + Representativeness –
Uruguay	1996	No changes	
Venezuela	1990	Vote for deputies separated from vote for senate; electors given three votes for congress; for the lower house, electors may choose a candidate in the plurality districts and a party list in the proportional representation part of the system; they also choose a party list for senate	Participation +
	1999	Change to unicameral system	Effectiveness +

Note: ++ = highly fulfilled; + = fulfilled; ± = partially fulfilled; – = not very well fulfilled; and – – = only minimally fulfilled.
[1] The senate chamber increased from 46 to 48 due to the addition of Tierra del Fuego as a province in 1990.

ballot structure but the timing relative to the presidential election was changed—could undermine effectiveness, since it increases the chance that the senate may be controlled by the political opposition. The move to direct election of senators in Argentina also clearly favors the function of participation.

Conclusions

The most common system used for electing representatives to the lower house (or the national assembly in the case of unicameral systems) is proportional representation with closed and blocked party lists. Medium-sized districts, averaging about five to six representatives per constituency, are also the norm. Five of the nine bicameral systems use a form of plurality system for electing senators, while one uses a mixed system (Mexico) and three use a pure proportional system. Thus, with respect to the lower house, the function of representativeness is favored by most Latin American electoral systems, but not to an extreme degree. Small parties have a chance to obtain representation, although usually not in full proportion to their electoral strength. Given the predominance of proportional electoral systems in lower houses, effectiveness is relatively deemphasized. In such systems, there is little assurance that presidents will obtain majorities in congress, and a fairly large number of parties can typically obtain significant representation. In the context of presidential systems, where the head of government and legislators have separate bases of legitimacy and fixed tenures, it could be difficult to establish a consensual basis for governing when political power is so fragmented.

The bicameral nature of nine of the political systems would be expected to complicate effectiveness even further, since the executive must try to amass majorities in two chambers simultaneously. This problem may be mitigated to some extent in the case of plurality systems, or when upper house elections are held simultaneously with that for the president. But effectiveness may be particularly compromised when the upper house is elected through a pure proportional representation system.

Regarding the function of participation, the predominance of closed and blocked party lists in the electoral systems for both the lower and upper houses tends to impede the development of close links between constituents and their representatives. In many cases, constituents typically do not know who their representatives are, let alone monitor legislators' votes in congress or levels of job competence. In many of the cases, all—or a significant share—of the votes made in congress are not recorded (Carey, 2004). For their part, representatives have little incentive to appeal to their constituents on the basis of policy positions or constituents' particular needs. This tendency is also reinforced by the relatively low proportion of legislators who seek or obtain reelection in many of the countries in the region (Cox and Morgenstern, 2001). Thus, incentives generally lead legislators to focus their attention on pleasing national or regional party leaders in order to obtain privileged positions in the party list for the next election, or to be favored as candidates for other elected or appointed political offices. Partly as a consequence of electoral-system-based incentives, the legislature in most countries has failed to develop an assertive and independent role in policy making or in overseeing the executive branch (as discussed further in Chapter 4).

Theoretically, proportional representation systems with closed and blocked lists would be expected to foster the development of "strong" parties, if only in one sense of the word. Legislators in such systems typically tend to follow the orders of their particular leaders, and thus parties can operate with some cohesion. But these systems do not necessarily help build parties that earn the loyalty and respect of citizens, or that represent clear sets of principles and programmatic orientations. Individual legislators' lack of accountability has likely contributed to the growing sense of disconnection between citizens and political parties, as well as the eroding legitimacy of politicians in general.

During the period of this study, most countries have reformed the rules governing the election of legislators in some way; several have adopted multiple, and sometimes contradictory, reforms. Only in five countries, however, did the reforms represent a change in the type of electoral system (as defined in this chapter). In all five cases, the changes were from one form of proportional representation to another. Though there are few reforms that would be expected to profoundly affect the proportionality of electoral outcomes, in general these reforms have tended to favor representativeness at the expense of effectiveness.

Thus, while the region had fairly fragmented party systems in the beginning of the study period, electoral system reforms seem to have only strengthened this tendency. The reforms, therefore, have not followed the conventional wisdom, found in academic writings, that a more concentrated party system is necessary to make presidential democracy work more effectively.

There have also been different types of reforms aimed at enhancing the discretion of voters in choosing their representatives. The most comprehensive reform was the adoption of personalized proportional representation systems in Bolivia and Venezuela. It is difficult to assess the impact of these changes in terms of democratic governability. In Venezuela, it is clear that the reform neither caused nor prevented the breakdown of the traditional party system or the onset of the broader crisis of the legitimacy of the nation's democratic system. This reform was probably implemented at a time when the discrediting of traditional leaders and institutions had already reached a critical point. Others have criticized the reform as not going far enough to curtail the power of central party leaders in selecting legislative candidates (Crisp, 1997; Kulisheck, 1997; Shugart, 2001).

Brazil, Colombia, the Dominican Republic, Ecuador, Honduras, and Peru have different forms of preference votes in their legislative election systems that might be expected to promote a stronger link between voters and representatives. However, given the demands of information and time, it is difficult for citizens in multimember district systems to make an informed choice among the large number of contending candidates and parties. In addition, the uncohesive and often unprogrammatic nature of parties—characteristics that are likely to be reinforced under such a system—undermine the ability of electors to use their votes to signal preferences to politicians about important policy issues, and to hold legislators accountable on that basis.

Another type of reform, adopted in several countries, that has enhanced citizen discretion in choosing leaders is the separation of ballots for legislative offices from those for the presidency and subnational political offices. When this has been done without separating the timing of presidential and legislative elections, it has usually enhanced participation without significantly undermining effectiveness.

Clearly, determining the appropriate electoral system design for a given country is fraught with difficulties. There are significant trade-offs entailed in adopting reforms aimed at enhancing performance in a given function—be it representativeness, effectiveness, or participation. Adopting the combined system is one way to increase ties between citizens and legislators without sacrificing too much in the functions of representativeness or effectiveness. This goal could also be advanced by the adoption of reforms that lie outside the scope of the narrow electoral system traits considered in this chapter. For example, adopting primaries for selecting candidates and using democratic procedures to choose party leaders could also help to strengthen the credibility of parties and enhance the ties between voters and legislators. This issue is the focus of Chapter 7.

In sum, while many electoral system reforms have been adopted in Latin America during the period of this study, relatively few have involved a dramatic change in system design. The electoral reforms implemented do not appear to have significantly alleviated the problems of governability, or to have raised the credibility of representative institutions in the region. In some cases, the frequent changes in the rules may, in fact, have contributed to increased uncertainty and volatility. Twenty-six years after the onset of the wave of democratic transitions in the region, the 18 countries in this study have, for the most part, retained their proportional electoral systems.

References

Abente Brun, Diego. 1996. Paraguay: Transition from Caudillo Rule. In Jorge I. Domínguez and Abraham Lowenthal (eds.), *Constructing Democratic Governance: South America in the 1990s*. Baltimore. MD: Johns Hopkins University Press.

Archer, Ronald P. 1995. Party Strength and Weakness in Colombia's Besieged Democracy. In Scott Mainwaring and Timothy R. Scully (eds.), *Building Democratic Institutions: Party Systems in Latin America*. Stanford, CA: Stanford University Press.

Archer, Ronald P., and Matthew Soberg Shugart. 1997. The Unrealized Potential of Presidential Dominance in Colombia. In Scott Mainwaring and Mathew Soberg Shugart (eds.), *Presidentialism and Democracy in Latin America*. New York: Cambridge University Press.

Bawn, Kathleen, and Michael Thies. 2003. A Comparative Theory of Electoral Incentives: Representing the Unorganized under PR, Plurality, and Mixed-Member Electoral Systems. *Journal of Theoretical Politics* 15: 5–32.

Caballero Carrizosa, Esteban. 1998. Elecciones y Democracia en el Paraguay, 1989–1996. In Juan Rial and Daniel Zovatto G. (eds.), *Elecciones y democracia en América Latina 1992–1996: urnas y desencanto político*. San José, Costa Rica: Interamerican Institute of Human Rights.

Carey, John M. 2004. Visible Votes: Recorded Voting and Legislative Accountability in Latin America. Working paper, Dartmouth College, Hanover, NH.

Carey, John M., and Matthew Soberg Shugart. 1995. Incentives to Cultivate a Personal Vote: A Rank Ordering of Electoral Formulas. *Electoral Studies* 14.

Conaghan, Catherine M. 1995. Politicians against Parties: Discord and Disconnection in Ecuador's Party System. In Scott Mainwaring and Timothy R. Scully (eds.), *Building Democratic Institutions: Party Systems in Latin America*. Stanford, CA: Stanford University Press.

Cox, Gary, and Scott Morgenstern. 2001. Latin America's Reactive Assemblies and Proactive Presidents. *Comparative Politics* 33(2): 171–190.

Cox, Karen E., and Leonard J. Schoppa. 2002. Interaction Effects in Mixed-Member Electoral Systems: Theory and Evidence from Germany, Japan, and Italy. *Comparative Political Studies* 35(9).

Crisp, Brain F. 1997. Presidential Behavior in a System with Strong Parties: Venezuela, 1958–1995. In Scott Mainwaring and Matthew Soberg Shugart (eds.), *Presidentialism and Democracy in Latin America*. New York: Cambridge University Press.

Duverger, Maurice. 1954. *Political Parties: Their Organization and Activity in the Modern State*. New York: Wiley.

Fleischer, David. 1998. Elecciones y sistema electoral en Brasil 1990–1997. In Juan Rial and Daniel Zovatto G. (eds.), *Elecciones y democracia en América Latina 1992–1996*. San José, Costa Rica: Interamerican Institute of Human Rights.

Grullón, Sandino. 1999. *Historia de las elecciones en la Dominican Republic desde 1913 a 1998*. Santo Domingo, Dominican Republic: Oficina Nacional de Derecho de Autor.

Herron, Erika S., and Misa Nishikawa. 2001. Contamination Effects and the Number of Parties in Mixed Superposition Electoral Systems. *Electoral Studies* 20.

IIHR (Interamerican Institute of Human Rights). 2000. *Sistemas de elecciones parlamentarias y su relación con la gobernabilidad democrática en América Central y Dominican Republic*. San José, Costa Rica: Instituto Interamericano de Derechos Humanos.

International IDEA. 1997. *The International IDEA Handbook of Electoral System Design*. Stockholm: International IDEA.

Izaguirre, Ramón. 2000. Análisis del caso de Honduras. In Instituto Interamericano de Derechos Humanos, *Sistema de elecciones parlamentarias y su relación con la gobernabilidad democrática en América Central y Dominican Republic*. San José, Costa Rica: Instituto Interamericano de Derechos Humanos, Unidad para la Promoción de la Democracia/OEA.

Kulisheck, Michael R. 1997. Electoral Laws and Politicians: The Behavioral Effects of Electoral Reform in Venezuela. Presentation at the meeting of the American Political Science Association, Washington, DC, August 28–31.

Laakso, Markku, and Rein Taagepera. 1979. The Effective Number of Parties: A Measure with Application to Western Europe. *Comparative Political Studies* 12(1).

Lijphart, Arend. 1994. Presidential and Majoritarian Democracy: Theoretical Observations. In Juan J. Linz and Arturo Valenzuela (eds.), *The Failure of Presidential Democracy*. Baltimore: Johns Hopkins University Press.

Nohlen, Dieter (ed.). 1993. *Enciclopedia Electoral Latinoamericana y del Caribe*. San José, Costa Rica: Instituto Interamericano de Derechos Humanos.

————. 1998a. *Sistemas electorales y partidos políticos.* México: Fondo de Cultura Económica.

————. 1998b. Sistemas electorales parlamentarios y presidenciales. In Dieter Nohlen, Sonia Picado, and Daniel Zovatto (eds.), *Tratado de derecho electoral de América Latina.* México: Fondo de Cultura Económica.

————. 1999. El distrito electoral. Paper presented at the International Seminar on Election Legislation and Organization, Lima, February 9–11.

Shugart, Matthew Soberg. 2001. Electoral Efficiency and the Move to Mixed-Member Systems. *Electoral Studies* 20(2).

Shugart, Matthew Soberg, and Martin P. Wattenberg (eds.). 2001. *Mixed-Member Electoral Systems: The Best of Both Worlds?* New York: Oxford University Press.

Thames, Frank C., and Martin S. Edwards. 2006. Differentiating Mixed-Member Electoral Systems: Mixed-Member Majoritarian and Mixed-Member Proportional Systems and Government Expenditures. *Comparative Political Studies* 39(7).

Urbina Mohs, Sandra. 2000. El sistema de elección de diputados en Costa Rica. In Instituto Interamericano de Derechos Humanos, *Sistema de elecciones parlamentarias y su relación con la gobernabilidad democrática en América Central y Dominican Republic.* San José, Costa Rica: Instituto Interamericano de Derechos Humanos.

Zovatto, Daniel, and Julio Burdman. 2002. Análisis de los procesos electorales 2002. Working paper, Observatorio Electoral. [http://www.observatorioelectoral.org]

CHAPTER 4

Balancing Executive and Legislative Prerogatives: The Role of Constitutional and Party-Based Factors

At the onset of the third wave of democratization in Latin America, a debate over the fundamental structure of political regimes hung over the political landscape. Many academic studies asserted that among the reasons for the previous collapse of Latin American democracies in the 1960s and 1970s were the inherent deficiencies of presidentialism,[1] the form of democracy of all 18 Latin American countries in this study. This conclusion was shared by a significant group of scholars and political elites in the region, who argued that a second transition to a parliamentary system of government was necessary if both new and restored Latin American democracies were to survive.

Pessimism about the viability of presidentialism is rooted in three broad concerns (Shugart and Mainwaring, 1997). The first is that the separate election of the president and legislature, and a consequent "dual legitimacy," often results in political stalemate. Especially in the case of relatively fragmented party systems, it is common for the president's party to lack a majority in the legislature. This outcome is even more likely if the legislature is bicameral, given that lower and upper houses often elect members through different rules, out of different geographical constituencies, and at different times. In the context of presidentialism, governing can be quite difficult when the president's party lacks a majority, because opposition parties have relatively weak incentives to cooperate (Jones, 1995). Opposition parties are not disposed to help the executive because, while they are unlikely to receive much of the credit for policy successes, they are likely to absorb a good share of the blame for policy

---

[1] See Linz (1978, 1990), Valenzuela (1978, 1994), Di Palma (1990), Lijphart (1990), Suárez (1982), and Mainwaring (1990, 1993).

failures. In addition, refusal to support the executive branch does not jeopardize legislators' tenure in office in a presidential system as it might in a parliamentary one. As a consequence, presidents may find it difficult to rally support from members of even their own party.

The second concern about presidentialism is that the executive and legislators' fixed terms of office can contribute to instability; the system may be politically paralyzed for an intolerable period or stuck with an incompetent or unpopular president. The very stability of the constitutional order could be threatened by various factors, including attempts to extend the term of a successful and admired president, or oust a lame-duck and ineffective president. In contrast, parliamentary systems are considered to be more flexible; unpopular governments can be removed by votes of no confidence, while popular and effective ones can be reaffirmed and strengthened through the calling of new elections.

Finally, critics lambaste the winner-take-all nature of presidential elections. Though presidents are rarely elected with the support of more than a slim majority of the electorate (and often considerably less), they gain sole possession of the nation's single most prestigious and powerful political office for a defined period of time. Nevertheless, their direct popular election from a national constituency is likely to give them an inflated sense of legitimacy and dissuade them from engaging in the painstaking and troublesome task of negotiating and building coalitions with the opposition (Linz, 1994). In contrast, the norm in European parliamentary systems is a coalition government founded on the support of two or more parties, which together represent an often large majority of the electorate.

More balanced political observers, however, point out that presidential regimes also have several advantages, and parliamentary systems are not without flaws (Shugart and Carey, 1992; Nohlen and Fernández, 1991; Mainwaring and Shugart, 1997). First, presidential regimes provide voters with more electoral choices, allowing them to choose a head of government and representatives who can more closely reflect their specific preferences.

Second, presidential systems provide citizens with a more direct mechanism by which to hold the government accountable and indicate their preferences in government policy (Samuels and Shugart, 2003). While in multiparty parliamentary contexts, citizens often cannot know the implications of their vote for the partisan composition of government, in presidential systems they can reward or punish the incumbent president and governing party with their votes and directly signal a preference for a particular governing agenda.

Third, presidential regimes give legislators more freedom to debate alternative policy options, since opposition to the government does not endanger the survival of the government or risk the calling of new elections. Open debate in the legislature can promote a broader consensus behind laws, avoid the enactment of poorly considered legislation, permit constituent-centered political representation, and enhance oversight of the executive branch. However, the potential cost of the checks and balances revered by the founding fathers of the United States is the political stalemate derided by critics of presidentialism.

The fourth argument in favor of presidential systems is that the fixed terms of presidents may provide more stability than can sometimes be achieved in parliamentary systems. The possibility of recomposing the government or calling new elections in parliamentary systems is a potentially beneficial escape valve that allows a way—short of a coup—out of a crisis or stalemate. However, in the context of weak, fragmented, or polarized party systems it may be difficult to sustain a viable coalition government. The consequence could be a high level of cabinet instability, which impairs government performance and possibly desta-bilizes the political system.

Finally, presidentialism may not necessarily encourage winner-take-all attitudes more than parliamentary systems. The balance of power in presidential systems should impede the possibility that the winner of the presidential election will assume all power. In parlia-mentary systems with single-party majorities, it is more likely for the winner of the election to assume a dominant status with few restraints on the exercise of public authority.

Even in theory, it is difficult to sustain the idea that parliamentary systems are un-equivocally superior. In practice, parliamentary systems have failed to gain enough support, both among the elite and general populations of Latin American countries, to be chosen as a system of government. Despite the sympathy of certain elite elements for parliamentary government, only in a couple of countries have proposals to change democratic regime design been seriously considered by politicians and the broader public. In each of these cases, the move to a parliamentary system was rejected. Given that a massive shift of politi-cal regimes in the region is highly unlikely, attention has focused on the impact that more specific types of institutional arrangements may have on presidential system performance (Mainwaring, 1997; Mainwaring and Shugart, 1997; Shugart and Carey, 1992; Nohlen and Fernández, 1991; Chasquetti, 2001; Lanzaro, 2001).

The efficiency and stability of presidential democracies is largely dependent on the manner in which the inherent tension between the executive and the legislative branches is resolved. This tension is muted in parliamentary systems, in which the government is elected by the legislature and must maintain its confidence. If the governing cabinet loses the support of the legislature, either the partisan composition of the cabinet is reshuffled or the parliament is dissolved and new elections held. Given the separate election of the executive and legislative branches—usually through different electoral procedures, out of different constituencies, and sometimes at different times—and their consequently sepa-rate bases of legitimacy, conflict between the two branches is more obvious and pervasive in presidential systems than in parliamentary ones.

The actual experience of presidential systems in the region has been somewhat mixed. The record disagrees with the most pessimistic prognostications of presidentialism's crit-ics, but does not contradict the expectation of frequent and significant interbranch conflict. Despite the frequency of minority governments and fragmented party systems, constitu-tional crises have not resulted—with only a few exceptions—in the breakdown of democratic systems. However, on several occasions, conflict between the branches of government has contributed to the premature interruption of elected mandates as a result of impeachment, forced resignation, or the suspension of congress. While in previous decades such changes of government were often led by the military and entailed the dissolution of congress, in the period after 1978, congress and societal groups became the lead actors in the impeach-ment or forced resignation of presidents (Pérez-Liñán, 2003). Some scholars have noted that the formal rigidity of presidential regimes has been circumvented to some extent by the introduction of this quasi-parliamentary practice of congress- or populace-led removal of presidents (Carey, 2002; Hochstetler, 2006). From 1978 through the end of 2005 there were 15 cases in which either presidents were forced to leave office before the end of their terms, or congress was suspended and replaced by a constituent assembly (Negretto, 2006).

A growing body of research questions the correlation between the absence of a partisan majority for the president and the likelihood of governing crises (Cheibub, 2002; Negretto, 2006; Chasquetti, 2001). Presidents who lack an outright partisan majority in congress still possess mechanisms and powers with which to foster interbranch cooperation. These include constitutional powers, such as agenda setting and decree and veto making. Bargaining mechanisms include policy trades, cabinet posts, and pork spending that can be used to build informal legislative coalitions or more formal cabinet coalitions (Negretto, 2006). The risks of instability in the cases of a presidential party minority in congress are likely to depend on an array of factors, including the extent of the president's powers, whether or not a governing cabinet majority can be formed, and the policy position of the president's party relative to that of the median legislative party (Colomer and Negretto, 2005).

Two caricatures of executive-legislative relations in Latin America are common in the literature. In one, the executive is perceived as the dominant actor, with the legislature serving as little more than a rubber stamp on the president's policy agenda. If the legislature balks at a presidential proposal, then the president uses decrees and other powers to railroad the proposal through. The legislature is also weak in its monitoring and control of executive activities, opening the way for corruption and public fund mismanagement.

The second caricature is of an executive lacking in partisan support whose plans are constantly thwarted by an obstructionist congress. The president alleviates or overcomes this situation only by abusing his or her decree and emergency powers or by dispensing favors to the constituencies of wavering legislators, providing concessions on legislation, or giving outright bribes. Sometimes the partisan stalemate results in a constitutional crisis in which either the president is prematurely removed or the congress is dissolved.

Even if these caricatures are believed to have some validity, they are at least partially contradictory. Is the primary difficulty in the operation of presidentialism in Latin America one of legislative gridlock, or of executive domination and legislative submission? Or perhaps both of these imbalances can be observed in various historical and regional contexts?

These stereotypes have one common feature: the relative lack of legislative capacity for positive, collective action in the lawmaking and oversight processes. In both caricatures, the legislature is portrayed as an agent that mainly reacts to the initiatives and agendas of the executive, rather than one that also directs and steers the legislative or oversight processes. If factual, the relative weakness of legislatures in pursuing policy goals or carrying out oversight responsibilities through collective action could be due to a number of different factors. These include the fragmented character of both party and broader representation systems (multiple parties or regionalized representation), the nature of electoral system incentives (see Chapter 3), the institutional weakness of political parties (see Chapter 6), the alignment of partisan political forces, the large constitutional powers of presidents, the weak institutional capacity of legislatures, and cultural traditions. Given the incentives flowing from these and other sources, legislators may find it more rewarding to orient themselves toward delivering goods to their constituents or courting the favor of party leaders than pursuing broader national policy goals.[2]

---

[2] See Shugart (2001) and Carey and Shugart (1995) for a discussion of the role of the electoral system in influencing legislators to focus on national policy matters.

To the extent that congress refrains from positive engagement in national policy matters, it might be responsible for the particular difficulties encountered in the event of a legislature controlled by opposition parties. This may also account for congress's failure to implement effective oversight of the executive branch. If congress is accustomed to merely reacting to the president's initiatives, then a congress dominated by parties other than the president's is more likely to result in gridlock. If congress traditionally has a more proactive role, then policy stalemates in such circumstances might be alleviated by shifting the responsibility for pushing a legislative agenda to the legislature itself.

The caricatures mentioned are obviously too simplistic to capture the full reality of the dynamic between executives and legislators in Latin America. There is a tremendous diversity in the political makeup and social and cultural contexts of the 18 countries considered in this study. Certainly there is also a great range in the assertiveness of Latin American congresses in amending or blocking executive proposals, initiating legislation, and overseeing the execution of government programs (Cox and Morgenstern, 2001; Morgenstern and Nacif, 2002).

Generalizations about Latin American legislatures have typically been based on casual observation rather than in-depth studies of specific countries. Legislative actions to modify or support executive proposals are usually not done in plain view. This is especially the case in those systems where roll calls and votes are normally not published and debates not recorded—matters likely to undermine the representative function of the congress and the disposition of legislators to concern themselves with their record on policy issues (Carey, 2006). But even when proceedings and votes are fully on the public record, the true role of congress is obscured by the fact that much of the deal making done between the executive and legislators (particularly those in the governing party or coalition) typically takes place behind closed doors. In some cases the real influence of legislators may be greater than what is seen on the surface.

Types of Presidential Powers

This chapter does not aim to substantiate any particular assessment of the state of executive-legislative relations in Latin America or any other region. Instead, it concentrates on comparing the countries of the region in relation to two factors that are expected to exert a direct influence on the effectiveness of these relations: (1) the nature of the president's constitutional powers; and (2) the degree of his or her partisan powers, or partisan support in congress.[3]

Both influence the extent to which a president is able to mold policy. The first is built into the formal design of the presidential system, as embodied in the constitution, and changes only as a consequence of explicit reforms of constitutional norms or related laws. The president's constitutional powers can be divided into two sets—direct powers in the

---

[3] These powers are delineated and assessed for Latin American countries in Shugart and Carey (1992). The power categories and scoring criteria for the powers set forth by these authors are the starting point for those followed in this chapter, but the measurements are taken from UNDP (2004).

lawmaking process (legislative powers), and powers to form the cabinet and appoint other governmental officials (nonlegislative powers).

Among the president's legislative powers is the power to veto bills approved by the congress, enact legislation by decree, take exclusive initiative in some policy matters, convoke referenda or plebiscites, and shape the budget. Nonlegislative powers involve powers of the president to exclusively determine the makeup of the cabinet. This is determined both by the exclusivity of the president's powers to appoint and dismiss cabinet members and the powers of the congress to censure and remove cabinet ministers.

In contrast, partisan powers are derived from many different factors, some institutional (such as electoral laws and party system structure) and some circumstantial (such as election outcomes and the quality of presidential leadership), that vary over time. The party backing that the president can count on in congress depends on both the share of seats controlled by the president's party or party coalition and the extent to which parties are disciplined—that is, the extent to which legislators tend to vote in a bloc as instructed by party leadership.

Neither the president's constitutional nor partisan powers are individually sufficient to account for the degree to which the president is able to put his or her own stamp on policy, or the overall dynamic of executive-legislative relations. A president who is endowed with strong constitutional powers may nonetheless be weak in the face of a highly fragmented party system and an unreliable base of support in the legislature. Similarly, a president with fairly weak constitutional powers may appear to dominate the policy-making process if his or her party controls a majority of the seats in congress and is highly disciplined (Samuels, 2000).

Even these two broad types of power may be insufficient to understand the real nature of executive-legislative relations. Formal constitutional rules may not, in fact, be followed, and in many instances are ambiguous. Informal and cultural norms also exert considerable influence. Thus, the cross-national examination presented in this chapter is unavoidably incomplete. Nonetheless, given the importance of a president's constitutional and partisan powers in the operation of presidential systems, examining these is a valuable starting point for promoting better understanding and educating would-be reformers.

Presidential Powers and Democratic Governability

The concept of democratic governability entails the capacity to make and implement decisions that respond adequately to a country's pressing social and economic problems. The term implies that these decisions also be democratically legitimate and sustainable; that is, that they be adopted on the basis of an open, participatory process. In addition, the government should carry out its duties efficiently and in a manner that upholds the broader public interest.

One aspect of democratic governability is policy efficiency, meaning the capacity to adopt policy changes directed at improving social and economic conditions. However, this is not sufficient in itself, since the essential requirements of democratic government are that decisions respond to public preferences and interests, both of individuals and organized groups. In addition, the government must execute laws and implement policies efficiently, fairly, and honestly.

Gauging what balance of a president's constitutional and partisan powers is optimal for democratic governability is a complex matter. If the goal were merely policy-making efficiency, then it would be desirable for a presidency to be endowed with a large amount of both types of power. But when presidents dominate congress, there is a greater risk that decisions will be adopted that do not reflect the interests and demands of the majority of citizens (and thus are not legitimate and sustainable). There is also a greater probability that laws and policies will not be executed fairly and efficiently, and that public funds will be mismanaged or directed toward private ends.

Thus, for the optimal functioning of presidential democracy, it seems better that legislatures share lawmaking power with the executive and develop the capacity to regularly oversee the implementation of government programs and regulations. In order for the congress to play such a role, it is necessary for individual legislators to have enough freedom from the party hierarchy to be accountable and responsive to their constituencies and able to engage in real policy debates. At the same time, the incentives of the institutional environment (including electoral system, party system, and constitutional rules) should encourage legislators to concern themselves with national policy matters rather than just the delivery of particularistic goods and services to constituents (Carey and Shugart, 1995; Shugart, 2001; Moreno, Crisp and Shugart, 2003). Aside from the challenges facing individual legislators, party systems represented in the legislature cannot be so fragmented that congress as a whole is unable to take collective action.[4] In order to avoid gridlock, however, the president must have sufficient formal power and partisan support in congress to play a proactive role in moving the policy-making process forward.

Moving beyond the simple dichotomy of strong and weak presidents, there are other issues to consider. How much of each type of power should a president have if the democratic government is to perform well and be consolidated? The next section describes each type of presidential power in more detail. By assigning numerical scores along each power dimension, the powers of presidents in the region are compared.

A later section also examines national differences in the degree of partisan congressional support that presidents typically enjoy. Given the importance of other contextual factors, however, the full effects of constitutional and partisan powers on both executive-legislative relations and democratic governability cannot be determined without more careful study of individual cases.

Legislative Powers of Presidents

This section describes the types of legislative powers held by Latin American presidents, and the criteria used to evaluate them.

---

[4] For a more extensive discussion of these trade-offs, see Shugart (2001), Carey and Shugart (1995), and Shugart and Wattenberg (2001).

Package Veto

The package veto is the power of the president to block the enactment of a law to which he or she objects even after it has been approved by congress. This and the partial veto power described next are the only formal means a president has to directly influence legislative policy making. In most presidential systems, it is the congress that is responsible for enacting all of the laws of the country. Even a president's package veto power is usually not absolute, since the congress is given the power to persist in the passage of legislation.

Presidential veto power is weak when the congress can override it with the votes of only a simple or absolute majority. When only a simple majority is required, the veto may delay the implementation of legislation, but the president is relatively limited in his ability to curb the actions of a congress determined to adopt policy changes. The veto power is stronger when it must be overcome by an absolute majority (50 percent plus one of the total membership of the legislative body), given that a significant number of legislators are typically absent or abstain from voting. A president's veto power is stronger still when the votes of a qualified majority, such as two-thirds of all congress members, are required to override it. In this case, the president would be very powerful, since it would be extremely difficult for the legislature to take any action with which the chief executive disagrees.

The veto power allows presidents to protect the status quo against legislative efforts to change it. However, this power is not as useful when it is the president who wants to bring about policy changes (Shugart and Mainwaring, 1997).

The strongest presidential veto powers in the region are found in Ecuador, where the congress cannot override the veto and the vetoed legislation cannot be brought up again until the following year. Veto powers are also relatively strong in the Dominican Republic, El Salvador, Guatemala, and Panama, where two-thirds of the full congressional membership is needed for the override. Slightly weaker but still strong veto powers are found in Argentina, Bolivia, Chile, and Mexico, where the votes of two-thirds of the legislators present at the time are required to override the president. In Uruguay, a slightly lower threshold of three-fifths of present members is required. In the remaining eight cases (Brazil, Colombia, Costa Rica, Nicaragua, Paraguay, Peru, Uruguay, and Venezuela), the veto power is weaker because the vote of only an absolute majority of the membership or present members is required to override the presidential veto.

Partial Veto

The partial, or item, veto is the power of the president to veto particular, objectionable provisions of an approved bill. When this power is fully in place, the effect of the president's action is the promulgation of the unobjectionable portion of the bill, unless the congress insists on its original version with the majority vote required in the constitution.

Many Latin American constitutions specify that a president may object to a legislative bill, whether in whole or part. But a partial veto power, in our definition, does not exist unless the implication of the partial objection put forward by the president is that the remainder of the bill is automatically promulgated, absent a congressional vote insisting on the enactment of the bill as it was initially approved by congress (Shugart and Carey, 1992).

Though the power of partial promulgation is not explicitly provided in many constitutions, numerous presidents have asserted this right, and—in some instances—courts have accepted its validity. A president is considered to have partial veto power when the effect of partial promulgation is either explicitly stated in the constitution or has occurred without legal contest or been previously sanctioned by the courts. Like the package veto, the partial veto is a power that presidents can use to block undesired changes in the status quo. However, it engages the president more closely in the lawmaking process, since it allows the president to interject his or her views into the details of legislation, influencing its final form, rather than merely submitting a broad yes or no opinion.

The capability to object to portions of bills already approved by congress is present in all of the countries studied except Bolivia, Costa Rica, El Salvador, Guatemala, Honduras, and Mexico. In most countries, the threshold required for overriding the partial veto is the same as that for the package veto.

Decree-Making and Agenda-Setting Powers

A few constitutions in Latin America provide presidents with the power to directly make laws by issuing decrees, thus circumventing the congress altogether. By using this power, the president participates directly in the process of lawmaking to alter the status quo. However, it is rare for presidents to be provided a decree-making power without limits. In some cases the president is restricted to particular policy areas over which the power can be applied; in others, the power only becomes effective in particularly traumatic circumstances in the life of the nation.

It is important to not confuse the power to issue decrees of a regulatory or administrative nature with the power to legislate by decree. Most presidents do enjoy the former power, as does the U.S. president, who commonly issues executive orders. Nevertheless, the scope of this regulatory power varies substantially. In some cases, the president is even given ample latitude to interpret the intentions of the legislature in its execution of the law (Carey and Shugart, 1998; Mainwaring and Shugart, 1997; Shugart and Carey, 1992).

In addition, some constitutions explicitly permit the congress to delegate the power to legislate by decree to the president. In other cases, constitutions do not address the issue, but decree powers have been delegated in practice and unsuccessfully challenged in court. Regardless, the delegation of decree power cannot be considered on par with a constitutionally embedded power to legislate by decree. Delegated powers are temporarily issued by a congressional majority and can be carefully circumscribed. The same majority can also rescind these powers. Therefore, delegated powers cannot be used to enact a package of legislation contrary to the wishes of the majority in congress (Carey and Shugart, 1998). Acting on its own, however, a legislative majority may not be able to enact the individual measures that can be implemented through the delegated decree power.

In several countries, the president is granted the power to legislate by decree only on particular matters, and in the event of exceptional circumstances such as a state of emergency. Given the ambiguity inherent in interpreting what constitutes an emergency situation, such a provision potentially opens the door to a fairly extensive form of decree power. The extent of this power depends in part on whether there is an independent body, such as a constitutional court, with the responsibility to determine whether the use of the decree-making power is valid or not. Aside from the explicit right to legislate by decree, constitutions in some countries permit the president to declare a bill urgent, thus requiring congress to act on it within a specified time period. If congress does not act within the required time period, the bill automatically becomes law. While congress has an opportunity to reject the president's proposal before it becomes law, this constitutes an important presidential power, since practical and procedural barriers as well as problems of coordination may give the president the upper hand over congress. If the president issues a series of such urgent measures, it would be even more difficult for congress to coordinate against particular bills. Thus, this power gives the president great capacity to shape the legislative agenda.

Some form of explicit capability to legislate by decree or otherwise control the legislative agenda is present in Argentina, Brazil, Chile, Colombia, Ecuador, Guatemala, Honduras, Peru, and Uruguay. In Brazil, the constitution provides the president with the power to issue "provisional measures" in times of "relevance and urgency." In the provision of the 1988 constitution, such measures expired after 30 days unless passed as law. However, this provision was interpreted as allowing presidents to reissue the provisional measures indefinitely. A 2001 reform lengthened the time period before these measures had to be converted into law to 60 days, but also specified that they could only be renewed one time. In Colombia, aside from extensive power to administer the law, the president can acquire substantial lawmaking power by declaring a state of "internal commotion" or economic emergency. The former can be declared for a period of 90 days, and can be renewed once by the president acting alone, and then again with senate consent. The constitutional court may revoke decrees issued under a state of internal commotion if they violate constitutional guarantees, and the congress may revoke or amend them at any time. Under states of economic emergency, the president can issue decrees that remain in force even when the special circumstance expires. In practice, presidents have been able to declare such states of emergency with little justification (Archer and Shugart, 1997).

The power of decree is more restricted in Argentina, Guatemala, and Honduras, where it is only supposed to be used in exceptional or emergency circumstances. Decree authority in Argentina, Guatemala, Honduras, and Chile is also restricted in its application to only specified areas of policy, a limitation that is particularly constraining in Chile. Before the 1995 constitutional reform, the president in Nicaragua could adopt laws related to spending and taxation by decree, but now such powers are restricted, in principle, to administrative matters.[5] This reform also removed the ability of congress to delegate decree powers to the president.

There is no decree power in Ecuador and Uruguay, but the executive may declare items of legislation urgent, in which case the congress must act within a certain time period or the legislation becomes law. The adoption of the 1998 constitution in Ecuador changed the time period in which congress must explicitly reject the urgent bill from 15 to 30 days. There are no restrictions on the number of bills that the executive can term urgent. In Uruguay, the

---

[5] In practice, decrees have been occasionally objected to by legislators or leaders of opposition parties on the basis that they went beyond administrative matters related to taxation. Several have been overturned by the legislature on such grounds.

legislature has 45 days to take action on the bill, which does not have to be explicitly voted down to be prevented from becoming law. In addition, only one piece of legislation can be designated as urgent at one time. Along with the power to issue provisional measures, the president in Brazil can declare matters urgent with the same effect as in Uruguay.

The constitutions of Chile, Colombia, Mexico, Panama, Peru, and Venezuela explicitly authorize the legislative delegation of decree-making powers to the president.

In Bolivia, Costa Rica, the Dominican Republic, El Salvador, Guatemala, Nicaragua, and Paraguay, presidents do not have any form of legislative decree authority, though constitutions may permit decrees to be issued for administrative purposes. In Panama, Mexico, and Venezuela, presidents only possess decree powers if the congress delegates them.

Exclusive Initiative

Several constitutions give the president the exclusive right to introduce legislation in specific policy areas. It is particularly common in the region for the president to have the exclusive right to introduce budgetary laws, international treaty agreements, and trade tariff legislation. Because executive power in these areas is common, it is not considered exclusive initiative. The power of exclusive initiative is deemed present when presidents have an exclusive ability to introduce legislation in other areas of policy, such as public employment, defense appropriations, and auxiliary public spending.

Like the veto, exclusive initiative enables the president to prevent congress from changing the status quo in the particular policy areas to which it applies. A president who wants to keep an opposition congress from making changes in a given area can just refrain from introducing legislation. But this power is not very effective if the president wants to change the existing policy situation, since the congress theoretically can modify any proposal as it wishes. In some cases, however, the congress is restricted in its ability to modify the budget, a matter taken up in the next section.

Exclusive initiative powers are fairly extensive in Brazil, Chile, and Colombia. They extend beyond budgetary law and trade matters in Bolivia, Ecuador, Panama, Peru, and Uruguay.

Budgetary Law: The Power to Define

Given the importance of budgetary law in the working of government and the nature of executive-legislative relations, presidential powers in this area are considered separately.

In contrast with the U.S. Congress, many Latin American legislatures are restricted in the nature and scope of the changes they can make to the budget laws proposed by the executive.[6] In several systems—including Brazil, Chile, Colombia, Ecuador, El Salvador, and, since 1993, Peru—the congress is not authorized to increase either allocated amounts in the president's submitted budget, or the overall level of spending.

---

[6] Formally, in the United States, the congress is exclusively responsible for initiating and enacting the budget bill, as it is for all other pieces of legislation. The budget, in particular, must originate in the House of Representatives. In practice, representatives from the president's party submit the executive budget proposal, which serves as at least a foundation for initial discussion. Any other legislator is also free to propose an alternative budget.

A nation's congress is somewhat freer to modify the budget when it is explicitly allowed to switch spending between different items, even if prevented from raising the overall level of spending. This is the case in Nicaragua, Panama, Uruguay, and Venezuela. A somewhat greater capacity is given when congress can increase spending as long as it also provides for new revenue sources to cover the expenses. This is the case in Costa Rica and the Dominican Republic, although in the latter such modifications require the vote of two-thirds of each chamber of congress.

The president has the weakest power over the budget when the congress can modify it without restrictions. Argentina, Bolivia, Guatemala, Honduras, Mexico, and Paraguay give congress free rein to amend the national budget. In Mexico, however, the congress cannot create new expenditures after the budget is enacted.

Another factor that affects the president's budgetary leverage is what happens if congress does not approve a budget by the required deadline or before the start of the fiscal year. In some cases, the executive's proposal is automatically implemented. This is the case in Bolivia, Chile, Colombia, Ecuador, Panama, and Peru. Under this arrangement, the president can win if his or her legislative supporters merely succeed in postponing debate or preventing another budget from obtaining a majority. In Argentina, the Dominican Republic, El Salvador, Guatemala, Paraguay, Uruguay, and Venezuela, the budget of the previous year remains in effect for the next fiscal year until a new budget can be approved. In the other nations studied, there is no provision for such an event. The implication is that a new bill must be approved for the work of government to continue; otherwise, stopgap measures must be adopted.

Convoking a Referendum or Plebiscite

The power to convoke a referendum or plebiscite enables the president to put forward general matters of policy or particular laws to be voted on by citizens, in some cases after such provisions have been rejected by congress. Plebiscites are part of a larger group of direct, democratic instruments that will be considered in Chapter 8. If given fairly unrestricted application, the power to convoke a referendum or plebiscite can be an important tool, used by presidents to apply pressure on legislators to go along with their policy proposals, and to reaffirm their popular mandate and legitimacy (Shugart and Carey, 1992). This power is most extensive in Peru, since the congress there does not share it. If congress also has the power to call a plebiscite or referendum, as in Ecuador, Guatemala, Nicaragua, and Venezuela, then presidential power is weaker. The symmetric power of the congress gives it the potential to avoid a presidential veto or to pressure the president to refrain from applying veto power. If the president can convoke only a nonbinding plebiscite or referendum, as in Argentina, it becomes a less significant tool for pushing the president's legislative agenda.

Nonlegislative Presidential Powers

This section describes the nonlegislative powers of Latin American presidents and the criteria used to score them.

The central feature of presidential systems is the separate origin and tenure of the executive branch relative to the legislative. In contrast to parliamentary systems, the president is separately elected by the people, and appoints and dismisses cabinet members. These officials usually cannot be members of the legislature while they are serving the executive, and they are appointed and dismissed by the president rather than by the legislature. In the presidential system's pure form, it is the prerogative of the president to appoint cabinet members whom he or she can trust, and to dismiss them at his own discretion. Exclusive power over the formation of the cabinet, and the tenure of its members, is valuable for securing the president's government against shifting political forces in the congress, and for building political coalitions.

But the separation of the two branches is not complete in all cases. While all of the Latin American nations studied grant the powers of cabinet appointment and dismissal to presidents, there are some cases in which congress is also authorized to censure and remove cabinet ministers.

Cabinet Formation

The president has exclusive power over cabinet appointments in all countries of the region. Unlike in the United States, Latin American presidents do not have to obtain the advice and consent of their legislative bodies to make cabinet appointments. Even in the United States, cabinet appointments are almost always approved, though they may be considerably delayed. In the few instances when appointments have been rejected, it has usually been on the basis of purported personal character flaws or a lack of competence rather than the political views of the nominee, given the broad acceptance of the president's prerogative in forming his or her cabinet.[7]

Cabinet Dismissal

In all Latin American countries, as well as in the United States, presidents are free to dismiss their cabinet members at will, without providing a justification to the congress or obtaining its assent. Therefore, presidents can ensure that the making and execution of cabinet policy in all areas conforms to their wishes. Any time there is a deviation from the president's policy preferences, a perception of policy failure, or even a problem related to personal character, the president can remove the cabinet member in question.

Censure of Cabinet Members

An area in which there are substantial differences between countries is in the ability of the legislature to take action against cabinet members on its own initiative. The censure and

---

[7] One possible explanation for the U.S. Senate's deference to the president on cabinet appointments is that this body understands the relative weakness of its position in the appointment process. Even if the senate majority risks its political capital in rejecting a nominee, the president has the prerogative to nominate another cabinet secretary who may be equally objectionable on political grounds. And if the senate initially succeeds in gaining the appointment and confirmation of a cabinet secretary who runs the department in a manner that is closer to the preferences of the senate majority, the president can still dismiss that cabinet member (Shugart and Carey, 1992).

subsequent removal of cabinet members is the strongest form of such powers. When this is allowed, and regularly exercised, the separation of powers crucial to the presidential model is severely undermined. When cabinet members become accountable to the congress and dependent on legislators' continued support to remain in office, the presidential regime takes on distinctly parliamentary characteristics. These characteristics are especially pronounced when accompanied by presidential power to dissolve the congress. The latter power, however, is present only in Peru, Uruguay, and Venezuela, and can only be exercised after a successful motion of censure against one or more governmental officials (cabinet ministers in Peru and Uruguay, and the vice president in Venezuela).

The power of censure raises the potential for political stalemate and instability, given the contradiction between the popularly elected president's right to appoint his or her cabinet and the opposition legislature's right of censure (Shugart and Carey, 1992). The legislature may censure a cabinet member because of his or her approach to policy, but then the president can turn around and appoint a replacement with the same views. However, the censure power obviously weakens the president, since it provides a tool that the legislature can use to undermine and harass the executive.

In many cases the censure power is restricted, either because it does not necessarily produce the removal of the government official in question, or because it must be supported by a large congressional majority, such as two-thirds or three-fifths. Some form of censure power is present in Argentina, Colombia, Ecuador, Guatemala, Panama, Peru, Uruguay, and Venezuela.

Under Argentina's 1994 constitution, congress has the power to censure and remove the chief of the cabinet, but not any of the other cabinet members. The motion of censure and the vote to remove cabinet members requires the support of two-thirds of the membership of both houses of congress. Thus far, this power has not been exercised.

Under Colombia's 1991 constitution, each chamber can propose to censure ministers for matters related to their performance. The motion of censure must be proposed by at least one-tenth of the members of a particular chamber, and approved by an absolute majority of the members of each chamber. The consequence of the approval of the motion of censure is the removal of the cabinet member in question. Thus far, a censure motion has not been approved, given the difficulty of obtaining an absolute majority in both houses of a fairly fragmented congress.

In Ecuador, the 1998 constitution took away the ability of the legislature to oust cabinet members. During the 1980s and early 1990s, this weapon had been used frequently, with the effect of seriously undermining the authority of the president and fostering a climate of political uncertainty and instability. Under the current constitution, cabinet members can be "politically judged" at the request of one-fourth of the members of the congress, but this does not imply their removal from office.

In Guatemala, the 1985 constitution established that, following a citation of a cabinet member, a no-confidence vote can be solicited by at least four deputies. The vote must be approved by an absolute majority of the members of congress. The president can accept the dismissal of the cabinet member, or can desist on the basis that the act for which the official was censured is defensible in accordance with national interests and government policies. In the latter case, the congress may reaffirm the censure and remove the cabinet member with the vote of two-thirds of congress. The congress can cite and censure as many as four cabinet members at the same time.

Panama's constitution states that the legislative assembly can censure cabinet members if, in its judgment, they are responsible for crimes or have committed grave mistakes that have caused serious harm to the nation. The vote of censure must be proposed by at least one-half of all legislators and approved by two-thirds. Though the constitution does not spell out the effect of the censure, it has been interpreted as only a moral sanction, not to result in the removal of the cabinet member concerned.

In Peru, the 1993 constitution maintained the previous constitution's provision that the congress can hold either the entire cabinet or its individual members accountable through a censure vote or the rejection of a confidence measure. The censure needs to be presented by no less than 25 percent of congress members, and its approval requires the vote of an absolute majority. If censured, the entire cabinet or the member in question must resign, but the president is empowered to dissolve the congress if it has censured or declared its lack of confidence in two cabinet members or more. The president cannot dissolve the congress in the last year of his or her term, or during a state of emergency.

In Uruguay, the 1966 constitution establishes that either chamber of the congress can judge the performance of a cabinet member by proposing a motion of censure with the support of the majority of those present. The censure can be directed at an individual, several members, or the cabinet as a whole. The censure must be approved by an absolute majority of the members of the full congress. The approval of a motion of censure calls for the resignation of one cabinet member, group of members, or the entire cabinet. When the censure is approved by less than two-thirds of the members of the general assembly (the combined assembly of both houses of congress), the president can refuse to dismiss the cabinet members in question. In this event, the general assembly has to vote again. If less than 60 percent of the legislators uphold the censure, the president can dissolve the congress. The president can dissolve the congress only once during his or her term, and not during the last year of an assembly's term. In the current democratic period, no cabinet member has been censured and the matter of dissolution has not come up.

The 1999 Venezuelan constitution provides for the removal of a cabinet member through a motion of censure supported by three-fifths of the deputies present in the national assembly. With a vote of two-thirds of the national assembly membership, the vice president can also be removed from office. If the legislature approves motions of censure three times against a vice president in one presidential term, then the president can dissolve the national assembly, but not in the last year of the president's term.

Comparing the Constitutional Powers of Presidents in Latin America

Legislative Powers

The constitutional power of presidents varies significantly across the region. Considering the sum of all formal legislative powers (Table 4.1), the presidents in Chile, Ecuador, Brazil,

Table 4.1. Legislative Powers of Latin American Presidents
In descending order of total legislative powers

| | **Proactive powers** | | | | **Reactive powers** | | | | |
	Decree	Budget	Proactive power (subtotal)	Veto	Partial veto	Exclusive initiative	Reactive power (subtotal)	Power to convoke plebiscite	Total legislative powers
Chile	0.33	0.73	0.50	0.85	0.85	0.67	0.77	1.00	0.68
Ecuador	0.33	0.73	0.50	1.00	0.69	0.33	0.62	1.00	0.62
Brazil	1.00	0.91	0.96	0.15	0.15	0.67	0.38	0.00	0.60
Colombia	0.67	0.64	0.66	0.31	0.31	0.67	0.46	1.00	0.57
Peru	0.67	0.73	0.70	0.15	0.15	0.33	0.23	1.00	0.49
Argentina	0.33	0.45	0.38	0.85	0.85	0.00	0.48	0.50	0.47
Panama	0.17	0.55	0.33	0.77	0.77	0.33	0.58	0.00	0.45
Uruguay	0.17	0.64	0.37	0.54	0.54	0.33	0.45	0.00	0.39
El Salvador	0.00	0.82	0.35	0.77	0.00	0.00	0.22	1.00	0.35
Guatemala	0.33	0.18	0.27	0.77	0.00	0.00	0.22	1.00	0.31
Venezuela	0.33	0.64	0.46	0.08	0.08	0.00	0.04	1.00	0.31
Dominican Republic	0.00	0.64	0.27	0.92	0.15	0.00	0.31	0.00	0.30
Honduras	0.33	0.36	0.34	0.77	0.00	0.00	0.22	0.00	0.28
Mexico	0.17	0.36	0.25	0.92	0.00	0.00	0.26	0.00	0.26
Costa Rica	0.00	0.64	0.27	0.77	0.00	0.00	0.22	0.00	0.25
Bolivia	0.00	0.27	0.12	0.85	0.00	0.33	0.38	0.00	0.24
Paraguay	0.00	0.64	0.27	0.23	0.23	0.00	0.13	0.00	0.20
Nicaragua	0.00	0.73	0.31	0.15	0.15	0.00	0.09	0.00	0.19

Source: United Nations Development Programme (UNDP, 2004).
Note: This table is based on UNDP (2004) Table 43 and the scoring system is described in the UNDP table notes. The values shown are the normalized scores of indexes with different scales. The proactive and reactive power subtotals are calculated by the authors based on the weights used by UNDP (2004) in the calculation of total legislative powers. The proactive power subtotal is computed according to the formula: [(decree powers subindex * 4) + (budget powers subindex * 3)] / 7. The reactive power subtotal is computed according to the formula: [(average of package and partial veto subindexes * 4) + (exclusive initiative subindex * 3)] / 7. The total legislative power index is calculated by adding all of the subindex values for the proactive powers and the reactive powers (using the same weights as above) and also the plebiscite subindex (weighted by 1), and then dividing by 15 (the sum of all of the weights).

Colombia, Peru, Argentina, and Panama are the most powerful. In formal terms, the weakest presidents overall appear to be those of Mexico, Bolivia, Costa Rica, Paraguay, and Nicaragua. However, it is misleading to simply add up the scores, since individual forms of power do not all have the same impact on the nature and extent of presidential influence.

The powers that are likely to be most important to a president's ability to imprint policy are the veto and decree powers. The reactive veto power shapes the president's effectiveness in blocking policy changes that the congress hopes to enact (Shugart and Mainwaring, 1997). In the United States, the package veto is the only constitutional power a president can use to shape the direction of policy. Thus, on most occasions, the U.S. president has the power to prevent undesired changes in the status quo, but does not have the power to positively influence the adoption of the legislation he or she prefers. Through surrogates, the president may introduce a legislative bill, but congress decides when and if it will be debated in committee or on the floor, and has full freedom to modify the bill, reject it, or introduce an alternative. Therefore, the president depends on more informal, indirect approaches to influencing policy, as well as advantages such as powers of persuasion based on popular legitimacy, leadership of a major political party, appointment powers, and the information and resources that come with being the head of the executive branch of the government.

In terms of reactive powers, the U.S. president is relatively strong, since the support of two-thirds of the present members of each house of Congress is needed to override the package veto. Most Latin American presidents are endowed with reactive powers that exceed even those of the U.S. president. In some cases, these powers are greater because the package veto power itself is greater. For example, in the Dominican Republic, El Salvador, Guatemala, and Panama, a larger share of congress is needed to override the president (two-thirds of the total membership of each house of congress—rather than just the present membership), while in Ecuador a package veto means the matter cannot be taken up until the following year. In other cases, reactive powers are larger because the president can also partially veto legislation or has exclusive ability to initiate legislation in certain policy areas. Explicit or de facto partial veto powers are strong in Argentina, Chile, Ecuador, and Panama. Considering the power of exclusive initiative as well as overall veto power, the countries in which presidents' reactive powers are greatest are Chile, Ecuador, Panama, and Argentina. The weakest reactive powers are found in Venezuela, Nicaragua, and Paraguay.

In contrast with the U.S. president, some Latin American presidents are also endowed with powers that are proactive in the sense that they can influence the adoption of policies that represent a change in the status quo. The most important forms of proactive powers are: (1) decree powers and (2) the power to control the legislative agenda. By issuing decrees or declaring matters of legislation to be urgent, the president can directly engage in the lawmaking process and potentially bypass the congress altogether. Another proactive power is the ability to set budget spending and revenue levels, or to set spending priorities without the possibility of congressional interference. The partial veto itself may also be considered a form of proactive power, since it can be used to influence the smaller details of enacted legislation. Considering decree and budgetary powers, the proactive powers of presidents are greatest in Brazil, Colombia, and Peru. Proactive powers are weakest in Bolivia, Mexico, Costa Rica, Paraguay, Guatemala, and the Dominican Republic.

Table 4.2. Presidential Power in Latin American Political Systems

	Strong proactive	Moderate proactive	Weak proactive
Strong reactive		Chile	
Moderate reactive	Brazil Colombia	Argentina Ecuador Panama Uruguay	Bolivia
Weak reactive	Peru	El Salvador Honduras Venezuela	Costa Rica Guatemala Nicaragua Mexico Paraguay Dominican Republic

Source: Authors, based on data from UNDP (2004).

In terms of the proactive and reactive powers of presidents, Latin American political systems can be grouped in the categories shown in Table 4.2. Strong presidents are in the upper left-hand section of the table. Presidents in Brazil, Colombia, and Peru have strong proactive powers but moderate veto powers. In contrast, presidents in Chile, Panama, and Ecuador have strong veto powers but moderate decree and budgetary powers.

The weakest presidents, in constitutional terms, are found in Costa Rica, Mexico, and Paraguay, both in proactive and reactive types of power. Venezuelan and Uruguayan presidents have fairly weak veto powers but have stronger powers to define the budget; in Venezuela, presidential decree powers are delegated by the congress. Mexico and Paraguay are similar to the United States in that presidents have relatively strong package veto powers but little power to autonomously turn proposals into policy.

Presidents in Argentina, Bolivia, El Salvador, Guatemala, and Nicaragua have intermediate levels of power, and are endowed with either some decree authority—or the possibility that congress may delegate such authority—or special authority over the budget. Presidents in Argentina, El Salvador, and Guatemala also have stronger veto powers than the chief executive in the United States, but not as much as those categorized in the "strong reactive power" category.

Nonlegislative Powers

As mentioned, there is no significant variation in the powers to appoint and dismiss cabinet members across the region. In contrast with the United States, presidents have full discretion in filling their cabinet; but similarly to the United States, they do not have to consult congress in their decisions to dismiss cabinet members. Thus, in terms of appointment and dismissal powers, the Latin American cases conform to the archetypal form of presidentialism in which the origin and survival of members of the two branches are fully

Table 4.3. Nonlegislative Powers of Latin American Presidents

In descending order of total nonlegislative powers

Country	Power of censure	Executive authority to dissolve legislature	Total nonlegislative powers
Bolivia	1.00	0.00	0.50
Brazil	1.00	0.00	0.50
Chile	1.00	0.00	0.50
Costa Rica	1.00	0.00	0.50
Ecuador	1.00	0.00	0.50
El Salvador	1.00	0.00	0.50
Honduras	1.00	0.00	0.50
Mexico	1.00	0.00	0.50
Nicaragua	1.00	0.00	0.50
Panama	1.00	0.00	0.50
Paraguay	1.00	0.00	0.50
Dominican Republic	1.00	0.00	0.50
Argentina	0.75	0.00	0.38
Uruguay	0.50	0.25	0.38
Guatemala	0.50	0.00	0.25
Venezuela	0.25	0.13	0.19
Peru	0.00	0.25	0.13
Colombia	0.00	0.00	0.00
Average	**0.78**	**0.04**	**0.41**

Source: UNDP (2004).
Note: These scores are taken from Tables 41 and 42 of UNDP (2004). The values for the power of censure and the executive authority to dissolve the legislature have been normalized from 0 to 1. The scoring systems are described in the notes to these two tables.

separated.[8] All of these nations receive a top score for the areas of cabinet formation and dismissal.

Several Latin American countries, however, deviate from the archetypal presidential model in giving congress the power to censure and subsequently remove cabinet members (Table 4.3). This provision could have a potentially important effect on the dynamic of executive-legislative relations, while also setting up the possibility of a tit-for-tat conflict. Though the congress may be able to remove a cabinet member, the president's exclusive powers of appointment mean that he or she can immediately name a person who might be

---

[8] Another matter is the scope of a president's appointment powers. Until fairly recently, the appointment powers of Latin American presidents were vast, since they included the right to name governors, department heads, and mayors in some countries—as well as the presidents of numerous public agencies, such as state enterprises and national banks. With the political decentralization and privatization that has occurred in most countries of the region, the scope of appointment powers has been reduced over the past two decades.

equally objectionable to the legislative body. Given the difficulty of obtaining the majorities required for censure, and the president's countervailing power to dissolve congress in some countries, this power has not been a major factor in most cases.[9] Thus, the semiparliamentary features that have been incorporated into several constitutions have not been used in practice to a significant extent. The nature of executive-legislative relations would appear to be much more affected by the influence of the legislative powers described in the previous section.

Impeachment of the President

Another institutional dimension relevant to executive-legislative relations is the mechanism for the impeachment of the president. In keeping with the structure of a presidential regime, it is the intention of most constitutions in the region that impeachment provisions be invoked only if the president is alleged to be guilty of serious common crimes, abuses of authority, or violations of the constitution or the law. However, as Pérez-Liñán (2000) writes, legislators and public officials are not easily able "to detach themselves from the broader social and political context in which a presidential crisis takes place. Congress may protect the chief executive by blocking further exposure of a scandal. Or, on the other hand, it may press charges against the president when there is not real proof or public sentiment in favor of impeachment."

Some constitutions deviate from a pure form of presidentialism by permitting legislatures to remove the president not just in the case of the commission of serious crimes, but for poor performance of duties. Thus, impeachment is a mechanism that can be used to circumvent the inflexibility of presidential regimes, allowing the removal of corrupt or unpopular presidents before their terms expire. If overly politicized, however, impeachment can be a source of political instability and may aggravate partisan conflict.

The potential vulnerability of presidents to impeachment varies greatly across the region. As in other matters, constitutions are not definitive, since they can be interpreted and applied in ways that might not have been intended by their authors.

In Latin America, there are three main models for impeaching the president. They entail different procedures for implementation, depending on the bicameral or unicameral nature of the congress (Table 4.4) (Pérez Liñán, 2000).

- *Congressional model.* Unicameral: the legislative assembly acts as both the accuser and jury. Bicameral: the lower house acts as the accuser, and the upper house as the jury.
- *Dual model.* Depending on the nature of the offense, the senate or the supreme court acts as the jury, upon accusation by the lower house.
- *Judicial model.* Unicameral: the legislative assembly acts as the accuser and the supreme court as the jury. Bicameral: one or both branches of congress make the accusation and the supreme court acts as the jury.

---

[9] The case of Ecuador is one important exception since the censure and removal of cabinet members was common in many of the administrations of the period and added to the difficulties of governing in a fragmented political system.

Table 4.4. Impeachment Models

	Unicameral	Bicameral
Congressional model	Ecuador Guatemala[1] Honduras[1] Nicaragua[2] Panama Peru	Argentina Chile Dominican Republic Mexico Paraguay Uruguay
Dual model		Brazil[3] Colombia[4]
Judicial model	Costa Rica El Salvador Venezuela[5]	Bolivia

Source: Author's compilation based on Pérez Liñán (2000).

[1] The unicameral legislature has the power to accuse the president of wrongdoing; however, the constitution does not explain the full procedures for impeachment of the head of state.

[2] The national assembly can declare the head of state to be permanently incapacitated by a vote of two-thirds of its members.

[3] Trial is held in the supreme court in the case of common criminal offenses and in the senate in the case of the criminal abuse of power.

[4] The lower house issues the indictment and the senate suspends the president from office. In the case of common criminal offenses, the trial takes place in the supreme court, but in the case of disqualification due to performance, the senate acts as jury.

[5] The Venezuelan process has features somewhat unique among judicial models: the supreme court first decides if there are grounds for presidential impeachment. Then, the national assembly must authorize such a trial through a simple majority vote. If so authorized, the supreme court holds the trial and makes a ruling, which could result in the removal of the head of state.

In almost all of the cases with a bicameral congressional model of impeachment, following the accusation of the lower house, the senate must provide a two-thirds majority vote to convict and remove the president. The only exception is the Dominican Republic, where a three-fourths majority is required for conviction. The unicameral cases are more varied. In Guatemala, Honduras, Peru, and Panama, no extraordinary majority is stipulated in the constitution, while in Nicaragua and Ecuador a two-thirds majority is required. The constitutions in Guatemala and Honduras, however, are unclear about the impeachment process once charges are brought by a simple majority in the national assembly.

Brazil and Colombia are intermediate cases; the institutional venue for the trial depends on the nature of the crime. In both countries, common crimes are tried in the supreme court, while abuse of power and failure to perform duties are tried in the senate.

Of the four countries where the judicial model is used, only Costa Rica requires an extraordinary majority (two-thirds) to authorize the trial in the court system. In Venezuela, the supreme court must first determine if the case has merit before the national assembly can authorize a trial by a simple majority vote. In Bolivia, a simple majority is sufficient to authorize a trial, but a two-thirds majority is necessary for the supreme court to convict the president. In El Salvador, only a simple majority is needed to authorize the trial, which takes place in the court of appeals.

Guatemala, Honduras, Panama, and Peru appear to be the countries where presidents are most vulnerable to impeachment. However, it should be noted that in Guatemala and Honduras the process is left somewhat undefined by the constitution. Given the three-fourths majority required both for accusation in the lower house and for conviction in the upper house, the Dominican Republic would appear to be the nation in which the president is most secure.

Several constitutions also have a provision for presidential removal in the event that the president becomes physically or mentally incapacitated. The removal of President Abdalá Bucaram in Ecuador in 1997 for alleged "mental incapacity" has elevated such clauses to relevance in the discussion of impeachment. In Ecuador, only a simple majority was required to remove a president for this reason, while a two-thirds majority would have been required for impeachment. This type of provision also exists in Chile, El Salvador, Guatemala, and Colombia. In Chile, a prior ruling is required by the constitutional tribunal, while in El Salvador and Guatemala a panel of doctors must confirm the applicability of the provision before the congress can remove the president on this basis. In Colombia, the provision is limited to physical incapacity, and the text implies that the president has already voluntarily taken a leave of absence.

In addition to Bucaram, there have been three other cases where impeachment or imminent threat of impeachment led to presidential removal or resignation: President Collor de Melo in Brazil (1992), President Carlos Andrés Pérez in Venezuela (1993), and President Raúl Cubas Grau in Paraguay (1999). There were unsuccessful impeachment attempts in Ecuador in 1987 (against President Febres Cordero), in Colombia in 1996–97 (against President Ernesto Samper), and in Paraguay in 1998 (against President Cubas Grau). Threats of impeachment also anticipated the self-coups of President Alberto Fujimori in Peru and President Jorge Serrano Elías in Guatemala. President Fujimori succeeded in keeping himself in office, while President Serrano resigned from his position.

Partisan Powers of Latin American Presidents

In addition to presidents' constitutional powers, the nature of the party system plays an important role in shaping the operation of presidential systems. Both the number of significant parties and their cohesiveness and discipline affect the chances for a workable accommodation between the executive and legislative branches.

When the party system is highly fragmented, it is unlikely that the party of the president will control more than a small share of legislative seats. Given the incentives built into the presidential system, it is difficult in such a scenario for the president to put together and sustain a reliable governing coalition. But this does not necessarily mean that it is desirable that the president and a hierarchically organized majority party control the government.

In fragmented systems, governments are likely to be ineffective, which eventually may weaken the legitimacy of democratic institutions and increase their risk of instability. Yet in cases of majority party control, presidential systems' inherent restraints on the potential for the abuse of authority are substantially reduced; the government may be less representative and more prone to mismanagement and corruption. A middle ground, in which the president's party does not fully dominate or is not rigidly disciplined, is more likely to permit sufficient congressional backing—and at the same time restrain the executive from the temptation to act unilaterally and abuse the public trust.

As shown in Chapter 6 (Table 6.10), the degree of party system fragmentation varies widely across the region. Given the fairly concentrated legislative seat distribution in Honduras, Paraguay, Mexico, Costa Rica, and the Dominican Republic, majority or near-majority governments have been a common occurrence during the period of this study; however, the situation in many of these countries has changed in recent years. Except for the Dominican Republic, these are cases in which the president's formal powers are relatively weak.

In contrast, single-party majoritarian governments are improbable in Ecuador, Brazil, Bolivia, and Peru, where five to seven significant parties compete for public offices. Possibly as compensation for their weak partisan powers, presidents in Ecuador, Brazil, Peru—and, to a lesser extent, Bolivia—have been bolstered by significant legislative powers. Chile is also characterized by a fragmented party system, but the binominal election system established under the 1980 constitution has created strong incentives for consolidating the party system into two competing party blocs. As a consequence, all the elected presidents in the post-Pinochet period have been backed by a reliable majority in the fully elected lower house.

The regional average for the period—a little more than three significant parties—suggests that single-party majorities are fairly rare in most Latin American presidential systems. The improbability of single-party majorities is compounded by the bicameral character of nine of the 18 countries in the study. The problem of electing and sustaining majorities in two chambers of congress simultaneously was probably one of the principal motivations for the switch to a unicameral legislature in Peru (1993) and Venezuela (1999).

In cases where party unity and discipline is fairly weak, even a majority of the legislative seats does not guarantee reliable support for the president. Fragmented party systems in combination with undisciplined parties tend to make it especially difficult for presidents to assemble majorities behind a policy agenda.

Coalitions in presidential systems are usually not as formalized, durable, or binding (for legislative voting) as they are in parliamentary systems. Parties may agree to join forces before an election in order to enhance the chances of a particular presidential candidate, but support is not ensured after the president's inauguration.

Postelection governing coalitions may entail the participation of members of allied parties in the cabinet or other public agencies, but this does not necessarily ensure the support of individual legislators from these parties, or imply a binding commitment to the party. Allied parties and politicians can switch to the opposition without risking new elections or the downfall of the government. Nonetheless, coalitions do present a potential means to at least partially overcome the gridlock that might arise from a president's weak base of partisan support in congress.

Coalitions, in a variety of forms and with varying practical consequences for the management of executive-legislative relations, became increasingly common in Latin America in the 1990s (Lanzaro, 2001; Chasquetti, 2001). To some extent, this fact contradicts the expectations of critics of presidentialism, who did not foresee coalitions as a viable possibility for avoiding dual legitimacy and the tendency toward stalemate endemic in the separation of powers. When ideological and policy differences between parties are not very salient, a comparison between benefits and costs may make it more favorable to join a coalition than anticipated by critics of presidentialism. Refusing to join a coalition may result in marginalization for the party and its leaders, while participation gives the party more prominence and provides leaders with positions of power and prestige. When parties are elite-driven rather than mass-based, then the interests of party elites to obtain access to power may offset the potential costs in compromised principles or long-term electoral strategy.

Table 4.5 summarizes the frequency with which presidents are elected by single-party majorities or assembled coalitions that, at least on paper, provide legislative majorities. The unit of analysis is the period during which the balance of power resulting from the previous election remained the same. When the president and legislators are elected at the same time, the period is simply the president and the legislators' terms of office, unless the president is replaced by someone else (usually the vice president) due to death or some other cause of irregular succession. When presidential and legislative elections are not concurrent, a new period commences when either a new president or new congress is elected. During the time frame of this study, there have been a total of 131 such periods in the 18 countries examined. In 52 of these periods (39.7 percent), some form of interparty coalition supported the president for a significant block of time.[10] The case was counted as a coalition government only if a formal agreement was reached between the president and the coalition partners, or when cabinet or other governmental posts were shared with another party (rather than with independents from parties). Ad hoc party coalitions formed to support particular legislative initiatives were not considered a coalition government. Clearly, coalitions have been a necessary and important characteristic of executive-legislative relations in Latin America over the period of the study. Given the large number of countries examined and the length of the period, however, it is difficult to fully evaluate the efficacy of coalitions in fostering reliable legislative support for presidential policy initiatives.

In 29 percent of all of the presidential-legislative periods, the president's own party held a majority of the seats in the lower house (or the national assembly in the case of unicameral systems). The proportion for the upper house was 40.3 percent. But only in 25.2 percent of the cases did the president's party hold a majority of the seats in the whole congress.

However, when one also counts the seats of coalition partners (in the event that a coalition existed), then the government held a majority in the lower house in 49.1 percent of the cases, and in the upper house in 57.1 percent.[11] When the seats of coalition partners were also counted, the government held an overall majority in 43.8 percent of the 131 cases.

Single-party majority governments (considering the whole congress) were most common in Honduras, Mexico, Colombia, Costa Rica, and Guatemala. This partisan alignment with the president contributed to fairly strong presidents in all those countries, except Colombia. Given the highly factionalized and undisciplined nature of the two main par-

---

[10] In three other cases, the coalitions did not last more than one year during the presidential term, and were thus not counted.

[11] These are percentages of the 131 cases that were considered. If a coalition was identified, then the share of the seats controlled by all of the parties in the coalition was summed to determine if the government held a majority. If there was no identifiable coalition, only the seats controlled by the president's party were considered.

Table 4.5. Frequency of Majority Governments in Latin America

Country	Presidential/ legislative periods	Periods when official party held majority in lower house (%)	Periods when official party held majority in upper house (%)	Periods when official party held majority in both houses (%)	Periods of majority rule in lower house (including coalitions) (%)	Periods of majority rule in upper house (including coalitions) (%)	Periods of majority rule in both houses (including coalitions) (%)
Argentina	11	36.4	63.6	18.2	36.4	63.6	18.2
Bolivia	7	0.0	28.6	0.0	71.4	71.4	71.4
Brazil	8	12.5	12.5	12.5	50.0	50.0	50.0
Chile	5	0.0	0.0	0.0	100.0	20.0	20.0
Colombia	8	50.0	62.5	50.0	62.5	75.0	62.5
Costa Rica	7	42.9	—	42.9	42.9	—	42.9
Dominican Republic	10	30.0	60.0	20.0	40.0	70.0	30.0
Ecuador	13	0.0	—	0.0	7.7	—	7.7
El Salvador	10	20.0	—	20.0	30.0	—	30.0
Guatemala[1]	7	60.0	—	60.0	80.0	—	80.0
Honduras	6	66.7	—	66.7	83.3	—	83.3
Mexico	9	66.7	77.8	66.7	66.7	77.8	66.7
Nicaragua	3	33.3	—	33.3	66.7	—	66.7
Panama	4	25.0	—	25.0	75.0	—	75.0
Paraguay	5	20.0	20.0	20.0	40.0	40.0	40.0
Peru	6	50.0	0.0	20.0	66.7	33.3	50.0
Uruguay	5	20.0	20.0	20.0	60.0	60.0	60.0
Venezuela	7	14.3	16.7	14.3	28.6	16.7	28.6
Total periods	**131**	**29.0**	**40.3**	**25.2**	**49.6**	**57.1**	**43.8**

Source: Authors' compilation.
Note: — = data not available.
[1] Information is available for only five of Guatemala's presidential-legislative periods; accordingly, percentages correspond to only five of the seven periods.

ties in Colombia, partisan majorities did not necessarily imply reliable legislative support. Single-party majoritarian governments did not arise in Bolivia, Chile, Ecuador, Nicaragua, Panama, Peru, or Uruguay.

Even when considering the potential support of legislators from parties allied with the government, an overall majority did not occur in Chile and was found to be rare in Argentina, Ecuador, and Venezuela. Though obtaining a majority in the lower house, the Concertación coalition in Chile was repeatedly denied a majority in the senate because of the presence of unelected, conservative senators.[12]

---

[12] This problem was compounded by the fact that many of the institutional reforms that the Chilean government wanted to enact required extraordinary majorities. The Concertación obtained a majority in both houses for the first time after the December 2005 legislative elections.

Coalitions contributed significantly to the legislative backing of presidents in Bolivia, Brazil, Chile, Nicaragua, Uruguay, and—to a somewhat lesser extent—Paraguay. In these cases, interparty agreements and power sharing frequently allowed minority presidents to gain the support of parties that together controlled a majority or near-majority of the legislative seats. Particularly in Brazil, but also to some extent in the other cases, a theoretical majority status did not mean that the president could always count on the support of individual legislators from parties in the coalition. The interparty coalitions, when they existed, were strongest in Bolivia and Uruguay, and greatly contributed to governmental action. But even in Brazil and Nicaragua, where the coalitions were weaker and had less of an influence on the positions taken by individual legislators, government effectiveness was clearly facilitated by the support of coalition partners.

Tables 4.6 and 4.7 show the shares of seats held by the president's party and governmental coalition, respectively, for each country over each of the presidential-congressional periods. The unraveling of traditional party systems is evident in Colombia, Peru, and Venezuela, where the parties of presidents at one time typically controlled a substantial share of the seats, but more recently have been less assured of such support. Increasingly open and competitive elections have also resulted in greater party system fragmentation in Mexico and Paraguay, and the end of governments dominated by a single party and a powerful president. In Uruguay, the ascendancy of the Broad Front and New Space parties resulted in a three- or four-way division of the party system, making it less likely for a single party to gain a majority on its own.

As a consequence of the tendency toward increasingly dispersed party systems, as well as the weakening of parties in some countries, coalitions are likely to become even more necessary in the future. Figure 4.1 shows that the steady decline in the percentage of single-party majority governments has been matched by an increase in coalition-backed governments. The result of these parallel trends is a relatively modest decline in the percentage of governments with a majority in congress, even when the presidential party's coalition partners are considered.

Throughout the whole period, the viability of governments in Bolivia, Brazil, Chile, and Ecuador has depended on coalitions. Given the increased fragmentation of party systems, however, coalitions also appear to have become more necessary in Argentina, Costa Rica, Colombia, El Salvador, Mexico, Panama, Paraguay, Peru, and Uruguay. The reduced partisan powers of presidents in Paraguay and Mexico are especially relevant given that, in these cases, presidents have few constitutional resources with which to move their agendas forward. The breakdown of the traditional party system in Venezuela also presents the chance of a more fractured division of power should the unifying influence of President Hugo Chávez fade.

Comparing Constitutional and Party Powers of Presidents

In countries with fragmented party systems, presidents generally have been granted fairly deep constitutional powers, especially proactive powers such as decree and budget making (Shugart and Carey, 1992). All countries with low partisan powers have granted presidents at least moderately proactive powers (Figure 4.2). Given their need to deliver goods (the benefits of a growing economy, jobs, budgetary resources, etc.) to their constituents, leg-

Table 4.6. Percentage of Seats Held by Governing Party

Country		By period 1	2	3	4	5	6	7	8	9	10	11	12	13	Average
Argentina	LH	50.8	50.8	44.5	48.0	45.5	49.0	53.1	46.3	48.3	45.5	50.2			48.4
	UH	39.1	39.1	39.1	58.7	62.5	62.5	54.2	54.2	27.8	55.6	59.7			50.2
Bolivia	LH	**36.2**	33.1	25.4	40.0	25.4	28.0	0.0							26.9
	UH	**37.0**	59.3	29.6	63.0	40.7	40.7	0.0							38.6
Brazil	LH	**41.8**	53.4	2.6	8.0	8.0	12.1	19.3	17.7						20.4
	UH	**29.2**	62.5	0.0	6.2	6.2	12.4	16.7	16.1						18.6
Chile	LH	31.7	30.8	31.7	31.7	16.7									28.5
	UH	27.7	29.8	29.8	29.8	7.9									25.0
Colombia	LH	55.8	41.2	49.3	59.8	53.7	54.7	17.4	36.1						46.0
	UH	55.4	43.0	50.9	57.9	54.9	54.9	26.5	29.4						46.6
Costa Rica		**47.4**	57.9	50.9	50.9	49.1	47.4	33.3							48.1
Ecuador		**42.0**		12.7	16.9	43.7	19.7	15.6	3.9	23.2	0.0	26.5	21.5	9.0	19.5
Dominican Republic	LH	52.8	51.7	46.7	35.0	41.7	10.8	32.9	55.7	48.7	27.3				40.3
	UH	40.7	63.0	70.0	53.3	50.0	3.3	13.3	80.0	90.6	6.3				47.1
El Salvador		55.0	36.7	51.7	46.4	46.4	33.3	33.3	34.5	32.1	32.1				40.2
Guatemala		51.0	15.5			53.8	55.8	29.8							41.2
Honduras		53.7	34.3	55.5	55.5	52.3	47.7								49.8
Mexico	LH	74.0	74.8	72.5	52.0	64.0	60.0	47.8	44.2	30.2					57.7
	UH	100.0	98.4	98.4	93.8	95.3	66.7	60.2	35.9	35.9					76.1
Nicaragua		55.4	**45.2**	56.6	52.6										52.4
Panama		**82.1**	43.1	25.4											50.8
Paraguay	LH	66.7	25.0	22.5	22.5	46.3									36.6
	UH	66.7	22.2	20.0	22.2	35.6									33.3
Peru	LH	54.4	59.4	22.5	17.8	55.8	37.5								41.3
	UH	43.3	49.2	22.6											38.4
Uruguay	LH	41.4	39.4	32.3	33.3	53.5									40.0
	UH	43.3	38.9	35.5	33.3	53.3									40.8
Venezuela	LH	42.2	56.5	48.3	48.3	12.8	17.2	48.5							39.1
	UH	47.7	63.6	47.8	47.8	12.0	14.8								39.0

Source: Authors' compilation.

Note: LH = lower house; UH = upper house. Values appearing in boldface indicate seats held by a governing coalition and appear in the absence of data for the governing party. The president of Bolivia in period 7 was Carlos Mesa, who took office after the resignation of Sánchez de Lozada. Mesa had no party affiliation. Álvaro Uribe came into office in Colombia via an independent political movement (Primero Colombia) in period 8. The pro-Uribe portion of the elected legislators associated with the Liberal Party is included in these percentages. Since period 4, the Peruvian congress has been unicameral, as has the Venezuelan congress since period 7.

Table 4.7. Percentage of Seats Held by Governing Coalition

Country		1	2	3	4	5	6	7	8	9	10	11	12	13	Average
Argentina	LH	50.8	50.8	44.5	48.0	45.5	49.0	53.1	46.3	**48.3**	45.5	50.2			48.4
	UH	39.1	39.1	39.1	58.7	62.5	62.5	54.2	54.2	**27.8**	55.6	59.7			50.2
Bolivia	LH	36.2	64.6	54.6	60.8	73.8	51.5	0.0							48.8
	UH	37.0	96.3	59.3	66.7	81.5	59.3	0.0							57.1
Brazil	LH	41.8	77.6	2.6	24.5	52.6	58.9	64.3	28.3						43.8
	UH	29.2	83.3	0.0	37.0	66.7	70.4	77.8	22.0						48.3
Chile	LH	**57.5**	**58.3**	**58.3**	**58.3**	**51.7**									56.8
	UH	**46.8**	**44.7**	**42.6**	**42.6**	**52.6**									45.8
Colombia	LH	**97.5**	41.2	49.3	59.8	53.7	54.7	**69.6**	**65.1**						60.8
	UH	**99.1**	43.0	50.9	57.9	54.9	54.9	**78.4**	**61.8**						62.6
Costa Rica	LH	**47.4**	57.9	50.9	50.9	49.1	47.4	33.3							48.1
Dominican Republic	LH	52.8	51.7	46.7	35.0	41.7	**52.5**	**44.3**	55.7	**48.7**	27.3				45.6
	UH	40.7	63.0	70.0	53.3	50.0	**53.3**	**20.0**	80.0	**90.6**	6.3				52.7
Ecuador		**42.0**	22.5	22.5	22.5	**50.7**	22.5	23.4	**11.7**	**25.6**	0.0	26.5	47.9	9.0	25.4
El Salvador		55.0	36.7	51.7	46.4	52.4	33.3	33.3	34.5	32.1	32.1				40.8
Guatemala		51.0	**74.1**			53.8	55.8	**29.8**							52.9
Honduras		53.7	**81.3**	55.5	55.5	52.3	47.7								57.7
Mexico	LH	74.0	7.8	72.5	52.0	64.0	60.0	47.8	44.2	30.2					57.7
	UH	100.0	98.4	98.4	93.8	95.3	66.7	60.2	39.9	35.9					76.5
Nicaragua		**55.4**	**45.2**	56.6											52.4
Panama		**82.1**	**50.0**	**33.8**	**53.8**										54.9
Paraguay	LH	66.7	**66.3**	22.5	22.5	46.3									44.8
	UH	66.7	**60.0**	20.0	22.2	35.6									40.9
Peru	LH	**60.0**	59.4	22.5	55.0	55.8	37.5								48.4
	UH	**53.3**	49.2	22.6											41.7
Uruguay	LH	41.4	39.4	**63.6**	**55.6**	53.5									50.7
	UH	43.3	38.9	**67.7**	**56.7**	53.3									51.9
Venezuela	LH	42.2	56.5	48.3	48.3	**24.6**	**29.1**	61.2							44.3
	UH	47.7	63.6	47.8	47.8	**22.0**	**24.1**								42.2

Source: Authors' compilation.

Note: UH = upper house; LH = lower house. Boldface numbers indicate president-congress periods when governments were supported by interparty coalitions.

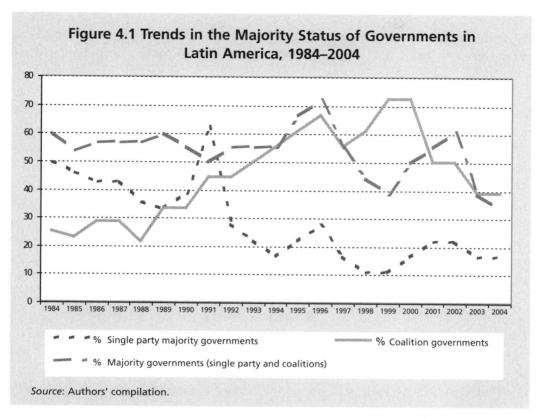

Figure 4.1 Trends in the Majority Status of Governments in Latin America, 1984–2004

- - - % Single party majority governments   ——— % Coalition governments

- - - % Majority governments (single party and coalitions)

Source: Authors' compilation.

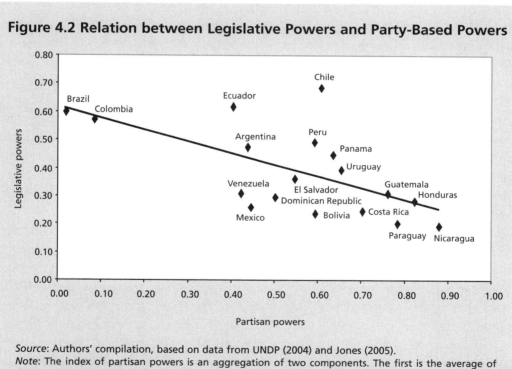

Figure 4.2 Relation between Legislative Powers and Party-Based Powers

Source: Authors' compilation, based on data from UNDP (2004) and Jones (2005).
Note: The index of partisan powers is an aggregation of two components. The first is the average of the indexes for decentralization and nationalization of party systems found in Jones (2005). The second is an index based on the percentage of seats held by the party of the president in the two most recent elections.

islators may be willing to grant presidents considerable power when they know that they are unable to get things done themselves (Archer and Shugart, 1997). Presidents in several countries—such as Bolivia, El Salvador, and Uruguay—are relatively weak in both partisan and constitutional powers.

In contrast, countries that have traditionally had relatively concentrated party systems tend to be those in which the president's legislative powers are weaker, such as Honduras and Guatemala.

Compensating for a fragmented party system with a president endowed with proactive legislative powers, however, may not be the best scenario for building a strong system of checks and balances and a legitimate system of representation. To meet this objective, there is no substitute for a congress that has a capacity for collective action and that develops the professional capabilities to participate jointly in the policy-making process and in the oversight of the executive branch. Though constitutional powers may be useful in extreme moments of crisis, it is valuable for the institutionalization of the checks-and-balances system that presidents develop policies through consensus with parties in the legislature, no matter how difficult this may sometimes be.

Conclusions

The governability of presidential democracies is closely connected to how the inherent tensions and competing responsibilities between the executive and legislative branches are sorted out. On the one hand, governments need to be able to act. They need to respond efficiently and effectively to pressing social and economic problems and to adopt policies that will promote the well-being of society over the long term. Presidents, in particular, are elected with a broad mandate to manage these national problems. Thus, presidents need to have sufficient constitutional powers and partisan support for effective government.

On the other hand, intrinsic to the idea of democracy is the need for government to be responsive to the views and interests of citizens. Elected officials should be held accountable for how they exercise public authority and use public funds. Thus, effective execution of the representative and oversight responsibilities of the legislative branch is also essential to democratic governability. While these functions are clearly at odds with an imperial presidency, they are important for the implementation of effective governmental responses to social problems.

For the congress to develop its representation and oversight capacities, presidents must not be endowed with such a high degree of proactive legislative powers that they can develop policies—including budgetary ones—in relative isolation, at times bypassing the congress altogether (Eaton, 2000; Negretto, 2004). In addition, opposition forces must have a voice in congress. Progovernment legislators need sufficient independence from the party hierarchy, and the proper electoral incentives, to play a role in shaping and overseeing policy choices.

Developing legislative policy-making and oversight capacities is also likely to be impaired if there is an overly fragmented division of seats among political parties. A legislature strongly divided along partisan lines—especially if that partisanship is exacerbated by regional and ethnic divisions—may block positive policy actions proposed by the executive.

At the same time, the legislature may be unable to act collectively to develop alternative approaches or to effectively monitor the executive.

Thus, the evidence discussed in this chapter suggests that democratic governability is complicated in several countries by an excessively fragmented party system. This may be rooted, at least in part—as we saw in Chapter 3—in characteristics of the electoral system. Moreover, the extent of party system fragmentation has been growing over the last two decades. This could complicate effective policy making and increase the incentive of presidents to take advantage of their proactive lawmaking powers and reduce the role of legislatures.

This is precisely the dangerous scenario that critics of presidentialism warn can limit its effectiveness and stability. Despite the growing tendency toward multiple parties, however, no country has changed the fundamental structure of its political regime from presidentialism to parliamentarism or semipresidentialism. However, a few countries have incorporated several semiparliamentary or semipresidential features that had previously existed in other countries of the region. These have included providing congress with the power to censure and remove cabinet members; providing the president with the power, in highly specified circumstances, to dissolve the legislature; and, in one case, establishing the position of a cabinet chief held partly accountable to the legislature. But these features, whether adopted prior to or during the region's recent democratization period, have not significantly affected how the systems function in practice except in a couple of cases. Another incipient, though still fairly weak, trend has been to attempt to control or limit presidential decree powers and strengthen the capacity of the legislature by modernizing information systems and increasing staff support for legislators and legislative committees.

A clear reaction to the fragmentation of party systems has been the growing tendency of elected presidents to forge coalitions with other parties in order to govern more effectively. As a consequence of the increased dispersion of party systems, and in some cases the weakening of parties, coalitions are likely to become even more necessary in the future. Figure 4.1 shows that the steady decline in the percentage of single-party majority governments has been matched with an increasing number of coalition-backed governments. The result of these parallel trends is a relatively modest decline in the percentage of governments with a majority in congress when the coalition partners of the president's party are considered.

Clearly, government effectiveness has been facilitated by resorting to this somewhat parliamentary form of presidential governance. Maintaining coalitions has been facilitated in two particular cases (Bolivia and Chile) by features of the electoral system that provide fairly powerful incentives for parties to form alliances. But determining the general viability of coalitions for alleviating governability problems in multiparty presidential systems is a matter that demands more detailed study.

The endowment of presidents with inordinate legislative powers has also, in several cases, impaired the development of the legislature's capacity to engage itself effectively in policy making and executive oversight. Of course, the development of such capacity has also been occasionally limited by electoral system features such as the lack of democratic procedures within political parties and the excessive degree of control exerted by leaders in the selection of candidates. The high turnover rate of legislators—whether because of mandated term limits, party nominating procedures, or the lack of prestige and rewards of a legislative career—has also in some cases deterred the strengthening of the legislative branch. If legislators have little desire or ability to build a career in the legislature and remain in office, they also have little incentive to be responsive to their constituents or to invest in developing the knowledge and capacities necessary to perform a more proactive policy-making and oversight role.

To a great extent, the circumstances in which Latin American democracies operated during the 1980s and early 1990s have also influenced their approach to policy making. Economic crises and growing problems of public safety provided the incentive and a justification for centralized policy-making structures and a relatively minimal role for congress.

References

Archer, Ronald P., and Matthew Soberg Shugart. 1997. The Unrealized Potential of Presidential Dominance in Colombia. In Scott Mainwaring and Matthew Soberg Shugart (eds.), *Presidentialism and Democracy in Latin America*. New York: Cambridge University Press.

Carey, John M. 2002. Legislatures and Political Accountability. *Revista: Harvard Review of Latin America* 2(1).

———. 2006. *Legislative Voting and Accountability*. Unpublished manuscript. [http://www.dartmouth.edu/~jcarey/publications.htm#lv]

Carey, John M., and Matthew Soberg Shugart (eds.). 1995. Incentives to Cultivate Personal Vote: A Rank Ordering of Electoral Formulas. *Electoral Studies* 14(4).

———. 1998. *Executive Decree Authority*. Cambridge: Cambridge University Press.

Chasquetti, Daniel. 2001. Democracia, multipartidismo y coaliciones en América Latina: evaluando la difícil combinación. In Jorge Lanzaro (ed.), *Tipos de presidencialismo y coaliciones políticas en América Latina*. Buenos Aires: Consejo Latinoamericano de Ciencias Sociales.

Cheibub, José Antonio. 2002. Minority Governments, Deadlock Situations, and the Survival of Presidential Democracies. *Comparative Political Studies* 35: 284–312.

Colomer, Josep, and Gabriel L. Negretto. 2005. Can Presidentialism Work Like Parliamentarism? *Government and Opposition* 40(1): 60–89.

Cox, Gary, and Scott Morgenstern. 2001. Latin America's Reactive Assemblies and Proactive Presidents. *Comparative Politics* 33(2).

Di Palma, Giuseppe. 1990. *To Craft Democracies : An Essay on Democratic Transitions*. Berkeley and Los Angeles: University of California Press.

Eaton, Kent. 2000. Parliamentarism versus Presidentialism in the Policy Arena. *Comparative Politics* 32(3): 355–373.

Hochstetler, Kathryn. 2006. Rethinking Presidentialism: Challenges and Presidential Falls in South America. *Comparative Politics* 38(4).

Jones, Mark P. 1995. *Electoral Laws and the Survival of Presidential Democracies*. Notre Dame, IN: University of Notre Dame Press.

—————. 2005. The Role of Parties and Party Systems in the Policymaking Process. Paper prepared for the Inter-American Development Bank Workshop on State Reform, Public Policies and Policymaking Processes, February 28–March 2, Washington, DC.

Lanzaro, Jorge. 2001. Tipos de presidencialismo y modos de gobierno en América Latina. In Jorge Lanzaro (ed.), *Tipos de presidencialismo y coaliciones políticas en América Latina*. Buenos Aires: Consejo Latinoamericano de Ciencias Sociales.

Lijphart, Arend. 1990. Presidencialismo y democracia de mayoría. In Oscar Godoy Arcaya (ed.), *Hacia una democracia moderna: la opción parlamentaria*. Santiago: Ediciones Universidad Católica de Chile.

Linz, Juan J. 1978. Crisis, Breakdown and Reequilibration. In Juan J. Linz and Alfred Stephan (eds.), *The Breakdown of Democratic Regimes*, Vol. 1. Baltimore: Johns Hopkins University Press.

—————. 1990. The Perils of Presidentialism. *Journal of Democracy* 1(4).

—————. 1994. Presidential or Parliamentary Democracy: Does It Make a Difference? In Juan J. Linz and Arturo Valenzuela (eds.), *The Failure of Presidential Democracy: The Case of Latin America*, Vol. 2. Baltimore: Johns Hopkins University Press.

Mainwaring, Scott. 1990. Presidentialism in Latin America. *Latin American Research Review* 1(25).

—————. 1993. Presidentialism, Multipartism and Democracy: The Difficult Combination. *Comparative Political Studies* 26(2).

—————. 1997. Multipartism, Robust Federalism, and Presidentialism in Brazil. In Scott Mainwaring and Matthew Shugart (eds.), *Presidentialism and Democracy in Latin America*. New York: Cambridge University Press.

Mainwaring, Scott, and Matthew Soberg Shugart. 1997. Presidentialism and the Party System. In Scott Mainwaring and Matthew Shugart (eds.), *Presidentialism and Democracy in Latin America*. New York: Cambridge University Press.

Moreno, Erika, Brian F. Crisp, and Matthew Soberg Shugart. 2003. The Accountability Deficit in Latin America. In Scott Mainwaring and Christopher Welna (eds.), *Democratic Accountability in Latin America*. New York: Oxford University Press.

Morgenstern, Scott, and Benito Nacif (eds.). 2002. *Legislatures and Democracy in Latin America*. New York: Cambridge University Press.

Negretto, Gabriel L. 2004. Government Capacities and Policy Making by Decree in Latin America: The Cases of Brazil and Argentina. *Comparative Political Studies* 37(5): 531–562.

————. 2006. Minority Presidents and Democratic Performance in Latin America. *Latin American Politics and Society* 48(3).

Nohlen, Dieter, and Mario Fernández (eds.). 1991. *Presidencialismo versus parlamentarismo, América Latina*. Caracas: Editorial Nueva Sociedad.

Pérez-Liñán, Aníbal. 2000. The Institutional Determinants of Impeachment. Paper presented at the 23rd International Congress of Latin American Studies Association, Miami, March 16–18.

————. 2003. Democratization and Constitutional Crises in Presidential Regimes: Toward Congressional Supremacy? *Comparative Political Studies* 38(1): 51–74.

Samuels, David J. 2000. Fiscal Horizontal Accountability? Toward a Theory of Budgetary "Checks and Balances" in Presidential Systems. Paper presented at the conference, "Institutions, Accountability and Democratic Governance in Latin America," Kellogg Institute, Notre Dame University, Notre Dame, IN, May 8–9.

Samuels, David J., and Matthew Soberg Shugart. 2003. Presidentialism, Elections and Representation. *Journal of Theoretical Politics* 15(1).

Shugart, Matthew Soberg. 2001. Electoral Efficiency and the Move to Mixed-Member Systems. *Electoral Studies* 20(2): 173–193.

Shugart, Matthew Soberg, and John M. Carey. 1992. *Presidents and Assemblies: Constitutional Design and Electoral Dynamics*. Cambridge: Cambridge University Press.

Shugart, Matthew Soberg, and Scott Mainwaring. 1997. Presidentialism and Democracy in Latin America: Rethinking the Terms of the Debate. In Scott Mainwaring and Matthew Soberg Shugart (eds.), *Presidentialism and Democracy in Latin America*. New York: Cambridge University Press.

Shugart, Matthew Soberg, and Martin P. Wattenberg (eds.). 2001. *Mixed-Member Electoral Systems: The Best of Both Worlds?* New York: Oxford University Press.

Suárez, Waldino. 1982. El poder ejecutivo en América Latina: Su capacidad operativa bajo regímenes presidencialistas de gobierno. *Revista de Estudios Políticos* [Madrid: Instituto de Estudios Políticos] 29.

UNDP (United Nations Development Programme). 2004. *Democracy in Latin America: Toward a Democracy of Citizens. Statistical Compendium*. New York: UNDP.

Valenzuela, Arturo. 1978. *The Breakdown of Democratic Regimes: Chile*. Baltimore: Johns Hopkins University Press.

————. 1994. Party Politics and the Crisis of Presidentialism in Chile: A Proposal for a Parliamentary Form of Government. In Juan J. Linz and Arturo Valenzuela (eds.), *The Failure of Presidential Democracy: The Case of Latin America*, Vol. 2. Baltimore: Johns Hopkins University Press.

CHAPTER 5

Institutions of Democratic Accountability in Latin America: Legal Design versus Actual Performance

While the question of how to hold democratic public officials accountable has long been debated, the issue has been subject to renewed scrutiny in studies of Latin America's third-wave democracies.[1] Recent democratic transitions in the region have included efforts to constitutionalize agencies responsible for controlling the exercise of public authority—an objective that runs against once-prevalent approaches to governance in the region, and also differs from the classic conception of three separate and counterbalancing branches of power. The idea has been to make these agencies independent of traditional branches of government. Until recently, governmental institutions—particularly those connected with the executive branch—have been rarely controlled, either by their own monitoring systems or by other government branches.

The traditional concept of democratic accountability includes the supervision and control of public authority both by citizens (through elections) and other branches of government. Though important, elections have long been recognized as insufficient in the provision of full accountability.[2] Where representative institutions are inadequately developed and legislator accountability mechanisms poorly configured, there is a particular need for additional layers of protection against the abuse of public authority (O'Donnell, 1994). In hopes of increasing governmental accountability, over the past two decades countries in

---

[1] See O'Donnell (1994, 1999, 2000); Schedler, Diamond, and Plattner (1999); Centro Latinoamericano de Administración para el Desarrollo (CLAD) (2000); Fox (2005); Smulovitz and Peruzotti (2003); and Moreno, Crisp, and Shugart (2003).

[2] The limits and possibilities of elections and representative institutions in ensuring accountability are examined in Przeworski, Stokes, and Manin (1999); Lupia and McCubbins (1998); and Moreno, Crisp, and Shugart (2003).

the region have adopted constitutional and institutional reforms affecting both traditional instruments and innovative institutions.

Other reforms also have the potential to enhance accountability, even if this was not their principal aim. Many countries have introduced mechanisms for direct citizen participation, thus providing opportunities for the populace to provide decision-making input and, in limited cases, to revoke the mandate of public officials (see Chapter 8).

In addition, far-reaching judicial reforms in the region have helped redefine the role of the judicial system. Though the process is ongoing and the changes required profound, rules and codes—as well as the administration and management of the system itself—have been reformed in many countries. Such reforms have been necessary to respond to the need for more secure and legally predictable property rights, greater citizen access to and trust in the judicial system, and the improved efficiency and quality of judicial decisions. Legal system reform has been seen as an essential part of the broader processes of democratic consolidation and economic reform (Hammergren, 1998).

An important objective of many of the judicial reforms that have been carried out in the region has been to establish a more independent judiciary that can better exercise legal accountability and ensure adherence to constitutional precepts and universal protection of civil rights. An independent and effective judiciary is necessary to protect against public authority infringement of the constitution and other laws, provide for evenhanded interpretation and enforcement of laws, and administer criminal justice in an unbiased fashion. As is evident in still-lagging perceptions of judicial independence, this is an area where ongoing and long-term efforts are needed (Figure 5.1) (Domingo, 1999).

A reconceptualization of the state as a creation and servant of its citizens has notably contributed to the recognition that it is important to hold public officials accountable and ensure transparency in the management of public funds. Redefining the public domain as an area of citizen responsibility and ownership has paralleled the elevation of the "participative" concept of democracy in democratic theory. According to this perspective, public accountability and transparency are irreplaceable elements of good governance and policy (Avritzer, 2000; Cohen, 2000; Bohman, 2000).

Over the past decade, the terms *accountability* and *governability* have been prominent in academic analyses of the new Latin American democracies. These studies have focused attention on the potential tension that exists between the need for oversight of political power and the need for effective government. On the one hand, for government to adequately respond to pressing social problems and citizen demands, power must be sufficiently concentrated to enable the making of sound and timely decisions. On the other, it is dangerous to confer great power upon particular individuals or institutions, since doing so increases the risk that such authority will be abused. The logical conclusion is that the use of power should be effectively monitored and controlled, but in a way that is not detrimental to the efficacy of the decision-making process.

In addition to reforming their judicial systems, many Latin American countries have developed and strengthened institutions overseeing the exercise of public authority. To reduce governmental corruption, it is particularly important to introduce and strengthen merit systems in public administration, as well as internal mechanisms for the monitoring and control of official actions in public agencies. Such reforms have been beneficial where

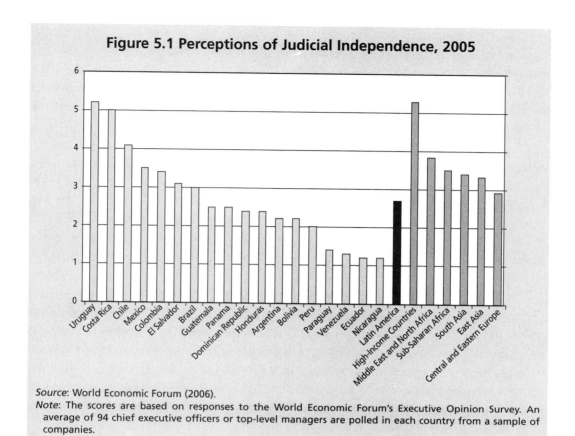

Figure 5.1 Perceptions of Judicial Independence, 2005

Source: World Economic Forum (2006).
Note: The scores are based on responses to the World Economic Forum's Executive Opinion Survey. An average of 94 chief executive officers or top-level managers are polled in each country from a sample of companies.

they have been successfully implemented, but much work remains to be done. How they are implemented is important; by themselves, these accountability-building mechanisms are insufficient.

The concept of accountability can also be expressed in the word *answerability*. Ensuring that government officials are answerable for their actions entails the use of three different mechanisms: (1) officials must be obligated to inform citizens and public agencies about their decisions, with the understanding that their conduct is monitored externally; (2) those who wield power must explain or justify their decisions and actions if so demanded by citizens, other public officials, or institutions; and (3) evident abuses of power or the public trust must be subject to negative sanctions (Schedler, 1999). Though public documentation of authority abuses is indispensable, it is, on its own, insufficient for the achievement of accountability. Effective deterrence requires the implementation of predictable, negative consequences for those who violate the public trust (Fox, 2005). The three aspects of accountability—transparency and monitoring, justification, and enforcement—are all needed to manage the diverse forms that the abuse of authority might take.

Ensuring accountability in practice requires attention to a wide range of capabilities and structures in an array of organizations and legal and procedural areas. Not only must public officials and agencies be compelled to fully and accurately disclose their decisions and budgetary accounts, but a diverse body of independent, motivated, and capable people must monitor the information provided, detect improprieties, determine legal responsibility, and impose sanctions when appropriate. At the same time, a participatory citizenry, a vibrant and well-organized civil society, and a pluralistic and independent media are essential to monitor government activities, expose abuses of power and violations of civil rights, raise public expectations of state performance, and bring political pressure to bear so that overseeing institutions can take the appropriate remedial actions.

There are several types of accountability enforcement mechanisms in the Latin American legal tradition, depending on the nature of the transgression. In some cases, several enforcement mechanisms operate at the same time (Groisman and Lerner, 2000). The first type of enforcement mechanism inherent in a democratic system is political sanction, through which a public official can be removed by defeat in a competitive election or—in the context of some constitutions or particular circumstances—through the revocation of the official's mandate either through the vote of citizens (recall) or congress (censure or political judgment). Such a sanction may not necessarily result from a violation of the law. At times, it may be merely due to beliefs that the official performed unsatisfactorily or was insufficiently responsive to his or her constituents. The second type of enforcement, administrative sanction, comes into play when the rules, procedures, or ethical norms of an organization are breached. The third, civil sanction, consists of the obligation to repair damages caused by an action that constitutes a violation of the law. Finally, criminal sanction is applied when a crime or misdemeanor is committed. A fiscal sanction implies, in addition to criminal liability, the need to remedy monetary or proprietary harm to the state or particular groups of citizens.

Accountability, when promoted through actions and institutions within the state, can be referred to as "horizontal accountability." Accountability promoted through the actions of individual citizens, civil society organizations, or other nonstate actors is considered "vertical accountability." The effectiveness of accountability depends on the positive interaction between both horizontal and vertical dimensions (Figure 5.2). Proper mechanisms for electoral accountability and strong civil society organizations are needed to generate constant pressure to uncover and punish abuses of authority, and to develop and sustain accountability agencies with sufficient authority, capability, and political independence. However, without the existence of independent and properly authorized state agencies, vertical accountability mechanisms will not result in the sanctioning of officials who abuse their powers, and instead will likely fuel citizen frustration, cynicism, and apathy (O'Donnell, 1999; Fox, 2005; Moreno, Crisp, and Shugart, 2003). Horizontal agencies such as independent and effective electoral management bodies and courts are also necessary to allow vertical electoral mechanisms to function credibly, fairly, and without corruption.

Recently, there has been particular emphasis placed on the establishment of horizontal accountability agencies to fight corruption and promote transparency in Latin America. Anticorruption initiatives have focused on creating national entities solely devoted to fighting corrupt practices. As in the case of other semiautonomous accountability agencies, to be effective these entities must enjoy broad public respect, maintain credibility, operate transparently, and remain open to the scrutiny of the press and civil society (Pope and Vogl, 2000). Nonetheless, they must also be afforded considerable political autonomy to avoid being undermined, ignored, or manipulated by the political elite.

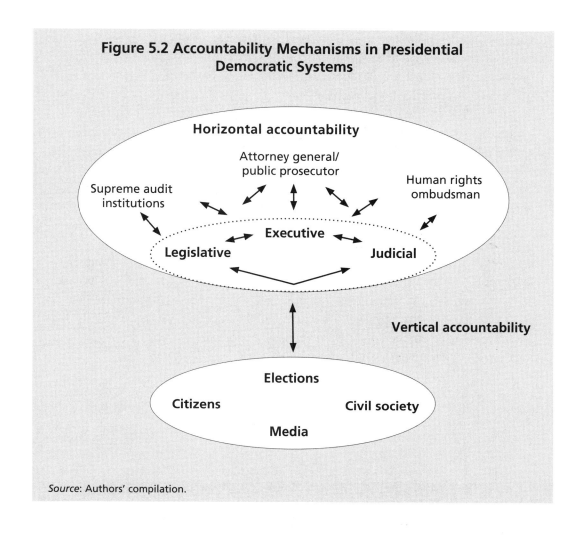

Figure 5.2 Accountability Mechanisms in Presidential Democratic Systems

Horizontal accountability

Attorney general/ public prosecutor

Supreme audit institutions

Human rights ombudsman

Executive

Legislative

Judicial

Vertical accountability

Elections

Citizens

Civil society

Media

Source: Authors' compilation.

O'Donnell (1999) has defined horizontal accountability as "the existence of state agencies that are legally enabled and empowered, and factually willing and able, to take actions that span from routine oversight to criminal sanctions or impeachment in relation to actions or omissions by other agents or agencies of the state that may be qualified as unlawful." This definition not only takes into account endogenous factors, such as the legal authority and institutional design of the agencies responsible for enforcing such controls, but also exogenous factors that enable these agencies to act according to their legal authorization.

Horizontal accountability is practiced by two types of institutions (O'Donnell, 2003):

- *Balance institutions*. These traditional institutions exercise horizontal balance accountability, or control, through a balance between separate branches of authority with somewhat distinct, though overlapping, responsibilities and powers. The separate origin and distinct missions of these institutions gives their members an incentive to prevent infringements on the jurisdiction and authority of others and to check large-scale abuses of constitutional power. Such a check involves reactive and relatively sporadic control, since, in theory, it is only wielded when a branch of government senses that its authority has been infringed upon by other institutions, or when constitutional rights or important laws have been violated.

- *Mandated agencies.* These are public institutions (many of them recently created or institutionalized) that practice horizontal mandated accountability. Most were not established as much to regulate the overall balance between the main branches of government as to curb more specific, though still fairly undefined, risks of infringement. Agencies with similar names and purposes across countries differ greatly in their institutional origins, the nature of their relationship with the three traditional branches of authority, the procedures through which their top officials are appointed, the range of their authority, and the source of their financing (Table 5.1). As a consequence, the nature and degree of their political autonomy and their capacity to monitor, investigate, and punish abuses of power or violations of citizen rights also vary. Since their precise function is to exercise control, they are proactive in their job of monitoring transgressions of authority or corruption. The result of the efforts to complement traditional accountability institutions are complex and sometimes overlapping agencies that include auditor generals, courts of accounts, attorney general's offices, public prosecutor offices, public defender, and human rights ombudsman. These agencies perform their assigned tasks with varying degrees of effectiveness and political independence.

The actual results of mandated agencies' efforts in fostering democratic accountability are quite difficult to determine, given the diverse institutions involved and the wide variation across nations in the nature of their responsibilities and powers and the extent to

Table 5.1. English and Spanish Terms for Horizontal Accountability Agencies

Supreme audit institutions

Comptroller General's Office	Contraloría General
General Accounting Office	Tribunal de Cuentas
Auditor General's Office	Auditoría General
Court of Accounts	Corte de Cuentas
Inspectors General	Fiscalización Superior

Prosecutorial/investigative agencies

Public Prosecutor	Procuraduría General
Prosecutor General	Ministerio Público
Special Prosecutor	Fiscalía General
Attorney General's Office	

Agencies for the defense of citizens' rights

Human Rights Ombudsman	Procuraduría para la Defensa de los Derechos Humanos
Public Defender	Defensoría del Pueblo
Civil Rights Commission	Comisión Nacional de Derechos Humanos

Source: Authors' compilation.

which they exercise these in practice. Within the limitations imposed by the relative novelty of mandated institutions, and the deficiency of available information, this chapter examines their institutional design. Specifically, it seeks to evaluate the actual performance of three of the most important mandated agencies: supreme audit institutions, offices of the public prosecutor or attorney general, and ombudsman's offices.

Supreme Audit Institutions

Institutions created to oversee the execution of the budget were established around the region in the early part of the 20th century. Most were designed to be dependent on the legislature, though in functional terms, they are semiautonomous. The most significant modernization and institutionalization of supreme audit institutions has resulted from the efforts over the past 20 years to make them in practice truly independent of the traditional branches of government. The trend has been a gradual shift away from purely formal legal control of budgetary execution toward evaluations based on the measured criteria of efficiency, effectiveness, and economy.

The jurisdictions of supreme audit institutions differ across countries. There are three models relevant to Latin America (Groisman and Lerner, 2000). The first is the French model of the court of accounts (*Cour des Comptes*), which has a collegiate directorate and, though part of the national public administration, has substantial independence.

The second is based on the Italian (*Corte dei Conti*) and Spanish (*Tribunal de Cuentas*) models. This model also has a collegiate directorate, is independent from the executive and legislative branches, and has the power to enforce the laws governing the administration of the budget, and to sanction abuses of authority. This model was adopted by Guatemala, Brazil, and El Salvador. It was also used in Argentina until 1993, when the *Auditoria General*, which lacks judicial powers, replaced the *Tribunal de Cuentas*.

The third is the Anglo-American model of the unipersonal comptroller or accounting office. This office originates in and reports to the legislative branch and possesses no judicial powers, although it does monitor execution of the budget to confirm compliance with budgetary law. The Anglo-American model has been adopted by most of the countries in the region. However, in Nicaragua, the comptroller's office was replaced by a court of accounts because the executive believed that the former institution had too much power.

The court of accounts aims to ensure formal and legal conformity of budget execution with budgetary law, and focuses on this over efficiency criteria (Groisman and Lerner, 2000). Courts of accounts with judicial enforcement powers may establish administrative legal responsibility for the misuse of public funds or violations of the law. This procedure is followed in Brazil, Chile, El Salvador, Guatemala, and Panama. Some institutions that do not have judicial powers, however, may urge other public institutions to prepare the legal case and procedures to be followed in order to determine responsibility. This is the procedure established in Uruguay, Paraguay, Costa Rica, and Nicaragua.

Regardless of whether institutions have judicial functions, some have prior or ex ante powers of control. The purpose of this control is to verify the legality or appropriateness of administrative actions before their implementation, and to authorize or suspend them ac-

Table 5.2. Central Audit Institutions

Country/ name of institution	Control, ex ante	Institution tied to the executive branch	Institution tied to the legislature	Degree of independence[1]	Issuable in- dictments: *juicio de cuentas* and violations of law[2]
Argentina Auditoría General de la Nación			X	Financial and operational independence	
Bolivia Contraloría General de la República		X			
Brazil Tribunal de Cuentas de la Unión			X	Financial and operational independence	X (*juicio de cuentas*)
Chile Contraloría General de la República				Institutional independence	X (Both)
Colombia Contraloría General de la República				Institutional independence	X (*juicio de cuentas*)
Costa Rica Contraloría General de la República	X		X	Financial and operational independence	
Dominican Republic Contraloría General Cámara de Cuentas	X	X			
Ecuador Contraloría General del Estado				Administrative, budgetary, and financial autonomy	
El Salvador Corte de Cuentas de la República	X		Reports to congress	Institutional independence	X (*juicio de cuentas*)
Guatemala Contraloría de Cuentas de la República			X	Operational independence	X (*juicio de cuentas*)
Honduras Contraloría General de la República			X	Operational and administrative independence	
Mexico Entidad de Fiscalización Superior de la Federación			X	Technical and administrative autonomy	

(continued)

Democracies in Development

Table 5.2. *(continued)*

Country/ name of institution	Control, ex ante	Institution tied to the executive branch	Institution tied to the legislature	Degree of independence[1]	Issuable indictments: *juicio de cuentas* and violations of law[2]
Nicaragua Consejo Superior de la Contraloría General de la República			X	Operational and administrative autonomy	
Panama Contraloría General de la República	X			Institutional independence	X (*juicio de cuentas*)
Paraguay Contraloría General de la República Tribunal de Cuentas			X		
Peru Contraloría General de la República	X			Institutional independence	
Uruguay Tribunal de Cuentas de la República	X		X	Operational autonomy	
Venezuela Contraloría General de la República			Citizen power; operational, administrative, and organizational autonomy		

Source: Authors' compilation.

[1] The column reflects specifically what the constitution or law establishing the institution says in respect to the independence of the body.

[2] Generally, a *juicio de cuentas* implies the finding of legal responsibility by the audit institution and the initiation and execution of the judicial process. A violation of the law requires the involvement of another judicial body.

cordingly. This is the procedure followed in the Dominican Republic, El Salvador, Panama, Peru, and Uruguay, although several of these countries are considering moving to a results-based approach (Table 5.2).

Although supreme audit institutions (mainly *Contralorías*) that follow the Anglo-American model have no judicial functions, they do have instruments of control that can be very effective in certain cases. The recommendations and findings made in their reports are not binding, but these agencies generally use follow-up mechanisms that serve as deterrents. In such cases, the controls seek to correct rather than to penalize. This approach has been used in Argentina (since 1993), Bolivia, Colombia, Ecuador, and Venezuela.

Among Latin America's supreme audit institutions, most are connected to the legislative branch, while several are independent or tied to the executive. In Argentina, Brazil, Costa Rica, Guatemala, Honduras, Mexico,[3] Nicaragua, Paraguay, and Uruguay, audit institutions are dependent on the legislature. In Chile, Colombia, Ecuador, Panama, and Peru, they are independent; in Bolivia and the Dominican Republic,[4] they are tied to the executive branch. The court of accounts in El Salvador is not associated with the legislative branch, but does submit an annual report to the legislature. A noteworthy case is Venezuela, where the comptroller's office is connected with *Poder Ciudadano*, or "citizen power," defined in the constitution as a separate branch of government. In theory, this affords it extensive independence from the three traditional branches of government. For all of these institutions, however, the real litmus test of independence is the extent to which they are autonomous in budgetary and functional terms. This varies from country to country, and does not exist simply as a result of a constitutional stipulation.

There is a greater variety among the directorships of supreme audit institutions (Table 5.3). Four countries appoint directors for five-year terms (Honduras, Panama, Paraguay, and Uruguay); three for four years (Colombia, Ecuador, and Guatemala); two for eight years (Argentina and Costa Rica); two for seven years (Peru and Venezuela); one for 10 years (Bolivia); one for six years (Nicaragua); one for three years (El Salvador); one for one year (Brazil, although members of the directorate stay indefinitely until the age of 70); and one that is appointed and removed at the pleasure of the president (the Dominican Republic). In Mexico, the director of the supreme audit institution is appointed for eight years, while the director of the Secretariat of Comptrollership and Administrative Development is appointed for an indefinite period by the president.

Directors are generally designated by the legislative branch in Argentina, Colombia, Costa Rica, El Salvador, Guatemala, Honduras, Mexico (the federal audit authority), Nicaragua, Panama, Paraguay, Peru, Uruguay, and Venezuela. In Brazil, the president of the court of accounts (*Tribunal de Cuentas*) is appointed by the members of the tribunal. Two-thirds of tribunal members are appointed by the congress and the remainder by the president, subject to senate confirmation. In the other countries, the executive appoints the directors. In Chile, however, the president designates the controller general subject to approval of a majority in the senate.

Institutional design varies even more in the process for removing comptrollers from office. In 11 countries, the comptroller can be removed by the same power through which he or she is appointed. In Brazil, Colombia, and Panama, the judiciary issues the order. In Colombia, Ecuador, Nicaragua, Paraguay, and Venezuela, candidates for comptroller are presented on a short list of three candidates to be selected by another branch of government. Only the secretary of comptrollership and administrative development in Mexico, and the comptroller in the Dominican Republic, are freely appointed and removed by the president.

---

[3] Mexico has two audit agencies: the Supreme Auditing Office of the Federation, and the Secretariat of the Comptrollership and Administrative Development. The first agency reports to the legislative branch, the second to the executive.

[4] The Dominican Republic also has the *Camara de Cuentas*, associated with the legislature. However, this institution has few resources and little power.

Table 5.3. Supreme Audit Institution Directors

Country/title of director	Appointment of director/directorate	Term of office (years)	Removal of director/ directorate
Argentina Presidente de la Auditoría	Legislature	8 (renewable)	
Bolivia Contralor General de la República	Executive (proposed by the senate)	10	Legislature through a trial by the supreme court
Brazil Ministro-presidente del Tribunal de Cuentas de la Unión	*President*: By collegial tribunal de cuentas *Ministers*: one-third by the president, with senate confirmation; two-thirds by the congress	1 Until age 70	Supreme federal tribunal
Chile Contralor General de la República	Appointed by the president, subject to consent of majority in senate	Indefinite term until 75 years of age	Chamber of deputies carries out accusation and the senate removes
Colombia Contralor General de la República	Legislature (from list presented by the constitutional court, the supreme court, and the council of state)	4	Supreme court, after previous accusation of public prosecutor
Costa Rica Contralor General de la República	Legislature	8 (renewable)	Legislature
Dominican Republic Contralor General de la República	Executive	Indefinite	
Ecuador Contralor General del Estado	President (from list presented by congress)	4	Legislature (after impeachment)
El Salvador Presidente de la Corte de Cuentas de la República	Legislature	3 (renewable)	Legislature
Guatemala Contralor General de Cuentas	Legislature	4 (single term)	Legislature
Honduras Contralor General de la República	Legislature	5	Legislature

(continued)

Country/title of director	Appointment of director/directorate	Term of office (years)	Removal of director/directorate
Mexico Titular de la Entidad de Fiscalización Superior de la Federación	Legislature	8	Legislature, or through impeachment
Secretario de Contraloría y Desarrollo Administrativo	Executive	Indefinite	Executive, freely; also through impeachment
Nicaragua Presidente del Consejo Superior de la Contraloría General	The superior council of the comptrollership chooses its president and vice president from its five members	5	Legislature
Miembros del Consejo Superior de la Contraloría General de la República	Legislature (from a list proposed by the president and representatives to the legislative assembly)		
Panama Contralor General de la República	Legislature	5 (renewable)	Supreme court
Paraguay Contralor General de la República	Legislature	5	Executive, after consent of senate
Peru Contralor General de la República	Legislature (proposed by the president)	7	Legislature
Uruguay Presidente del Tribunal de Cuentas	Legislature	5	Legislature, after final decision of courts of justice or competent court
Venezuela Contralor General de la República	Legislature (from a list presented by a group of citizens)	7 (renewable)	Legislature, after determination by the supreme court of justice

Source: Authors' compilation.

Performance of Supreme Audit Institutions

In the process of formulating, enacting, and executing the budget, the separation of powers of the executive and legislative branches is the chief source of public accountability. As pointed out in Chapter 4, the budgetary powers divided between the two branches include the power to propose budgetary law (a power that is formally conferred upon presidents throughout the region), the power of the legislative branch to modify the budget proposed by the president, and the power of the president to veto the budget or to modify it after it has been approved by the legislature. Aside from these constitutionally embedded powers, the balance of partisan forces in the congress can also significantly influence the roles of the two governmental branches in the budgetary process.

In Latin American presidential systems, the executive tends to dominate this process throughout its various stages. This does not necessarily mean that the executive infringes upon the powers of the legislative branch, but rather that his or her formal authority is broad in this area. This excessive power over the budget has been seen as an impediment to horizontal and vertical accountability, leading some critics to allege that Latin American presidents are budgetary dictators. Thus, the process of establishing compliance with budgetary law not only depends on the existence of independent audit institutions with considerable capability and authority. It also depends on an adequate balance of power in budgetary matters between the legislative and executive branches, which tends to be absent in Latin America.

Several recommendations for the ideal design of supreme audit institutions appear in the specialized literature. These recommendations point to the need for highly professional members, functional and administrative autonomy, and—to the extent possible—budgetary autonomy. Autonomy and independence may be advantageous and necessary, but sometimes they are not exclusively dependent upon institutional design. For example, while financial autonomy may be called for in the constitution, the actual means for putting its requirements into practice—such as guaranteeing a fixed share of the budget—requires additional steps. During previous authoritarian periods, courts of accounts in many countries were formally independent. However, despite wielding broad powers and judicial authority, their actions were limited to reporting excesses, and perpetrators were seldom prosecuted. When their work caused trouble for the ruling government, the president would typically remove court members from office illegally and replace them with presidential allies. This was possible because of the strong control wielded by the president over the legislative branch and judicial system. Even under the current democratic systems, formal independence does not always guarantee it in practice. For example, in Nicaragua, reports submitted by the comptroller's office led to an intense clash, the immediate consequence of which was the adoption of the current collegial directorate system.

Factors beyond institutional design also influence the effectiveness of agencies responsible for horizontal accountability. These agencies need timely access to reliable information, and require the ongoing support and participation of civil society and external actors (O'Donnell, 1999).

Thus, a mutually reinforcing and positive interaction between the elements of horizontal and vertical accountability is essential. In fact, a great deal of the success achieved by

Latin American supreme audit institutions has resulted from citizen cooperation in reporting to and working with the control authorities to expose public authorities' legal violations. The organization of the political system also influences the development of effective accountability in public financing. Divided government, for example, can contribute to the creation of such a capacity. However, divided government also increases the potential for conflict between the legislative and executive branches, and subsequent governmental ineffectiveness, which under certain circumstances can endanger the stability of the democratic regime. Thus, the short- and long-term development of effective oversight capability may conflict with the political requirements for effective decision making (Kenney, 2003).

This dilemma must be resolved according to the values prioritized by society at a given time. There is a tendency to blame new oversight mechanisms for impeding efficient decision making. The reality, however, is quite different: when they have not been undermined by the executive branch, new control institutions have been key to controlling abuses in the exercise of power.

Comptroller general offices have been the most common form of supreme audit institution adopted in Latin America in the 20th century, due partly to the influence of the Kemmerer Missions.[5] However, they have been often limited in their performance because of the different, overlapping legal functions of the diverse public institutions involved in law enforcement and justice administration.

Attorney General's/Prosecutor General's Office

The role of initiating the process of determining legal and criminal responsibility has been constitutionally assigned to different entities, including the *Ministerio Público*, *Procuraduría General*, and more recently, the *Fiscalía General*. Given the diverse institutional natures and functions of these distinct entities across the region, it is not possible to develop a consistent classification for describing them. Nor is it easy to link the functions of the common Anglo-American versions of these entities (such as the offices of the public prosecutor, solicitor general, and attorney general) with their Spanish-language equivalents in Latin American political systems. At the risk of conceptual imprecision, "attorney general" is used to refer to the Latin American *Ministerio Público*, although their functions often differ.

The duties of the attorney general vary from country to country. They include issuing indictments and carrying out accusatory and criminal proceedings, directing and promoting procedural and criminal procedural investigations, defending the legal authority and the interests of the state, and defending the civil and human rights of citizens. The most important actions against corruption taken over the past decade have been headed by the offices of the attorney general or prosecutor general. The independence and competence of these agencies is critical to democratic governability in the region.

---

[5] The Kemmerer Missions, led by a U.S. banking official named Edwin W. Kemmerer, were carried out across many countries in Latin America during the 1920s with the purpose of strengthening financial institutions and procedures. These missions generally recommended the creation of comptroller general's offices.

In some countries, more than one institution performs the most important function of the attorney general. In Colombia, the attorney general's office oversees and brings legal proceedings against top-level public officials, protects civil rights, and defends the legal authority of the state. But the accusatory function is carried out by the general prosecutor's office, which is under the judiciary system rather than the attorney general's office. In Ecuador, within a single ministry—the *Ministerio Público*—the functions of criminal prosecution and representation of the state's interests in legal matters are divided between two agencies—the attorney general's office (*Procuraduría General*) and the prosecutor general's office (*Fiscalía General*).

During the 1990s, most countries in the region began to introduce major reforms in their criminal justice systems. These included Colombia (1991); Argentina (1992); Guatemala (1994); Costa Rica (1998); El Salvador (1998); Paraguay (1999); Venezuela (1999); and Bolivia, Chile, Ecuador, and Honduras (2000). These reforms have been described as a change from inquisitorial, or quasi-inquisitorial, systems to more accusatorial, or adversarial, systems. This change has entailed the introduction of oral arguments and public trials instead of written proceedings, and the creation of a sharp distinction between the roles of investigation and prosecution on the one hand, and adjudication on the other. In addition, reforms have involved the introduction of some degree of prosecutorial discretion and alternative dispute resolution mechanisms in order to streamline criminal processes.

One of the important matters in the debate over the institutional design of attorney general's offices is their institutional position. There is an ongoing discussion regarding the advantages and disadvantages of linking the attorney general's office with the executive branch or the judiciary, or establishing it as an independent entity (in Spanish, an *extrapoder*) outside the other branches of government (Duce, 1999). Table 5.4 shows that in six countries (Brazil, Costa Rica, the Dominican Republic, Mexico, Panama, and Paraguay) the attorney general's office is under the judiciary, while only in Uruguay is it under the executive branch. Even though officially under the judicial branch, the attorney general in Mexico is appointed by the president, with the performance of his or her duties under the jurisdiction of the executive branch.[6] Thus, the formal connection to a given branch of government such as the judiciary is not always an indicator of the attorney general's true functional relationship to the government.

Attorney general's offices in other countries of the region are independent from the traditional branches of government. Colombia is atypical, with an autonomous attorney general's office; however, its prosecutor general's office, which carries out accusatory duties, is formally part of the judiciary but functionally autonomous. In Venezuela, the attorney general's office is under the citizen branch, or "citizen power" (*Poder Ciudadano*). Starting with the 1988 constitutional reform, Brazil's attorney general was made truly independent from the other branches of government. The office was given broader jurisdiction and new powers to control abuses of power and to defend social and collective rights by means of public actions. Thus, the regional trend is toward independence from the executive branch, whether through operational autonomy—the creation of an additional branch outside any other of the government (*extrapoder*)—or the establishment of links under the judiciary.

---

[6] The administration of President Vicente Fox proposed a reform in 2004 that would create a general prosecuting attorney's office that is independent of the executive branch. This had not yet been enacted by the end of 2005.

Country	Name of entity	Tied to the judiciary[1]	Independent, outside branch	Tied to other institutions
Table 5.4. Attorney General's Offices (*Ministerio Público*)				
Argentina	Ministerio Público Fiscal y Ministerio Público de la Defensa		X	
Bolivia	Fiscalía General de la República		X	
Brazil	Ministerio Público de la Unión o de los Estados	X	Operational and administrative autonomy	
Chile	Ministerio Público		X	
Colombia	Procuraduría General de la Nación		X	
Costa Rica	Fiscalía General de la República	X	Full operational independence	
Dominican Republic	Ministerio Público	X		
Ecuador	Ministerio Público		X	
El Salvador	Procuraduría General de la República		X	
Guatemala	Fiscalía General and Procuraduría General de la Nación		X	
Honduras	Ministerio Público		X	
Mexico	Ministerio Público Federal	X		
Nicaragua	Ministerio Público		X	
Panama	Ministerio Público	X		
Paraguay	Ministerio Público	X	Operational and administrative independence	
Peru	Ministerio Público		X	
Uruguay	Ministerio Público		Technical independence	X Executive
Venezuela	Ministerio Público			X Citizen power

Source: Authors' compilation.

[1] In Mexico and the Dominican Republic, the attorney general is appointed by the president but, according to the constitution, is tied to the judicial branch.

Despite the importance of the debate over the institutional position of the attorney general's office, in many cases the discussion has been overly theoretical, with limited attention to the problems these institutions confront in practice.

A second matter of debate involves the function of attorney general's offices in the new criminal procedure model. In this model, the prosecuting function of the attorney general's office is responsible for preliminary investigation and accusation, whereas previously these had been the responsibility of other criminal investigation entities. The new model has been instituted in most Latin American countries, though the previous system was retained in specific cases, such as under the reform of the Argentine federal system in 1992. The attorney general's office's specific role in the new context of the accusatory system of criminal procedure varies from one country to another, but it is generally a central actor in the new criminal prosecution process.

In most countries in the region, the executive and judicial branches have a clear role in appointing and removing the attorney general. Appointment of the attorney general is made by the executive in nine countries, although in several of these the consent of a chamber of the legislature (usually the senate) is needed, or the executive selects from a list of candidates prepared by either the legislature or part of the judiciary (Table 5.5). In Chile, the supreme court recommends candidates and the president appoints someone from this list with the assent of two-thirds of the senate. The supreme court also has the power to remove the incumbent from office. In Brazil, the president appoints the attorney general from among career civil service officials after the candidate has been designated by an absolute majority of the senate. Only in Colombia (since 1991) are all three branches of government involved in appointing and dismissing the attorney general. The senate appoints from a short list of candidates presented by the president, the supreme court, and the council of state.

Table 5.5. Appointment and Period of Service of the Attorney General

Country	Period of service (years)	Reappoint-ment	Institution that appoints head of agency	Institution that removes head of agency
Argentina	Not defined in the constitution	Not defined in the constitution	Executive (with consent of two-thirds of senate)	Not defined in the constitution
Bolivia	10	Yes (after one term period)	National congress	Chamber of deputies
Brazil	2	Yes (one time)	President (with approval of majority of senate)	President (with approval of majority of senate)
Chile	10	Yes (but not consecutive)	President (proposed by the supreme court with consent of senate)	Supreme court (after motion by the president of the chamber of deputies)
Colombia	4	Yes	Senate (from list of candidates proposed by the president, the supreme court, and the Consejo de Estado)	Supreme court (after indictment by the Fiscal General de la Nación)
Costa Rica	4	Yes	Supreme court	Supreme court
Dominican Republic	Not limited	Yes	President	President (total discretion)

(continued)

Table 5.5. *(continued)*

Country	Period of service (years)	Reappoint-ment	Institution that appoints head of agency	Institution that removes head of agency
Ecuador	6	No	National congress (from a list of candidates presented by the Consejo Nacional de la Judicatura)	National congress
El Salvador	3	Yes	Legislative assembly	Legislative assembly
Guatemala	5	Yes	President	President
Honduras	5	Yes (one time)	National congress	National congress
Mexico	Not limited	Yes	President (ratified by the senate or, specifi-cally, the permanent commission of the congress)	President (discretional) or by court trial or impeachment
Nicaragua	5	Yes	National assembly (from list of candidates presented by the president and deputies)	President
Panama	10	Yes	Cabinet and the president (with the approval of the legislative assembly)	Supreme court
Paraguay	5	Yes	Executive (with the approval of the senate from a list of candidates proposed by the Consejo de la Magistratura)	Senate (after articles of impeachment issued by the chamber of deputies)
Peru	3	Yes (for two more years)	Junta de Fiscales Supremos	Congress
Uruguay	Not limited		Executive (with the consent of the senate or its permanent commission)	Executive (with consent of senate or its perma-nent commission)
Venezuela	7	Yes	National assembly (from a list of candidates presented by the citizen branch; if agreement is not reached in 30 days, the list is submitted to a popular vote)	National assembly (after opinion from the supreme court)

Source: Authors' compilation.

Democracies in Development

The term of office of the attorney general varies widely. The term is indefinite in Mexico and the Dominican Republic; ten years in Bolivia, Chile, and Panama; seven years in Venezuela; six years in Ecuador; five years in Guatemala, Honduras, Nicaragua, and Paraguay; four years in Colombia and Costa Rica; three years in El Salvador and Peru; and two years in Brazil.

Reelection is explicitly permitted in most countries, although in a restricted manner in several. In Brazil, the incumbent attorney general may be reelected only once. In Bolivia and Chile, the attorney general may be reelected only after the lapse of the 10-year term of his or her successor. In Honduras, the incumbent can be reelected for only one additional term, while in Peru the term can be extended two years through reelection. Where the term of office is indefinite (Mexico and the Dominican Republic), continuation depends on reappointment by the president. In other countries, such as Colombia, El Salvador, Guatemala, Nicaragua, Panama, Paraguay, and Venezuela, the attorney general can be reelected indefinitely.

Performance of the Attorney General's Office

Undue emphasis on issues such as the optimal institutional design or procedural model for attorney general's offices has led analysts to overlook other problems not directly related to these issues. Problems associated with implementing reforms or the relationship between the attorney general's office and other state entities, for example, have been ignored.

As indicated earlier, the office's autonomy does not depend solely on institutional design. What is important is whether the organization has sufficient operational autonomy to function properly—more so than whether it operates from an institutional position formally independent from the branches of government. The issue of operational autonomy is also the chief problem faced by many judicial systems in the region.

The risk involved in linking the attorney general's office with the executive branch is the potential for the office to become politicized. One of the most serious problems currently facing the attorney general's office in several Latin American countries is "the intervention of the executive branch in determining its policies" (Duce, 1999). This not only leads to the possible politicization of criminal prosecution, but also to impunity in cases of political or administrative corruption, or even in cases of human rights violations.

The chief risk involved in judicial intervention in the public prosecutor's office is the potential for what might be called "judicialization." In many countries, judges have had to assume the responsibility for leading investigations. The judiciary has had to perform the functions of the attorney general by directing criminal prosecutions. In such cases, the role of the courts as an independent and fair adjudicator of the legal process is likely to be compromised.

These problems of politicization and judicialization have led to the conclusion that the formal institutional design of the attorney general's office as an independent agency is insufficient to make it function in a truly autonomous fashion. Thus, the issue of its independence from the traditional branches of power should be reexamined in a way that takes into account the more practical aspects of autonomy.

On the other hand, there has been little discussion of the negative consequences that might result from an attorney general's office being afforded too much autonomy. The experience of the office in Brazil shows that undue autonomy can be detrimental to effective internal control. The autonomy conferred by the 1988 constitution on the new Brazilian attorney general's office, together with its low level of institutionalization, "gives its members a great deal of freedom, leaving the identity of the institution open and reliant upon the individual characteristics of its members" (Sadek and Cavalcanti, 2000). Institutional credibility is a factor in legitimizing public decisions, especially in cases when officials have not been elected by popular vote. The attorney general's office in Brazil has been described by the media in terms ranging from a "true defender of human rights" to an "irresponsible exhibitionist." Settling the issue of who controls the controller is a requirement for the establishment of a true rule of law.

A second problem facing attorney general's offices throughout the region is the lack of coordination between this agency and other organizations connected to the criminal justice system, particularly the executive and judicial branches and police forces. Because of this lack of coordination, a certain level of institutional isolation constrains the efficiency of the attorney general's office. Problems related to criminal investigation are largely due to the lack of coordination between judges, prosecuting attorneys, and the police.

A third problem has been that, in most cases, the organizational capacity of attorney general's offices has not been sufficient to cope with an overload of work. Managing this workload is critical to both efficiency and legitimacy. The legal instruments available to attorney general's offices have been insufficient for developing an effective policy to streamline the daily work process. Such inefficiency carries with it the potential negative consequence of a loss of legitimacy, giving rise to a private system of justice fraught with abuses and inequities. Such a loss of legitimacy may also undermine vertical accountability mechanisms necessary to strengthen the potential ability of the attorney general's office to enforce horizontal accountability. This is especially true in cases where the citizenry has placed great faith in the capability of these new institutions to alleviate many of the problems they perceive in the operation of democracy in their countries.

A fourth, potential, problem is in the implementation of reforms, the success of which depends not only on well-conceived institutional designs but also on the way in which proposed changes are implemented. In some countries, inadequate implementation has been one of the chief problems of the reform process. Reforms need to be carried out in such a way that the interests of the other traditional actors in the judicial system are taken into account.

A final factor to consider is the need for these agencies and their staff to be professionalized. There is an obvious shortage of professionals in charge of managing the offices of attorney generals across the region. Poor or inefficient career or civil service systems have weakened or failed to develop the pool of human resources that serves as the hiring base for management.

The Ombudsman's Office

An ombudsman is generally an independent investigator authorized to receive complaints from citizens, make the state answerable for its abuses of authority or failures to protect citizen rights, and provide compensation to victims for damages caused by ineffective or unfair governmental actions or human rights violations.

The concept of the ombudsman's office has its roots in 19th-century Scandinavia, where the institution of a parliamentary commissioner was created to monitor public administration and provide citizens with an instrument to defend their rights. By the second half of the 20th century, the concept of the ombudsman had spread to other European countries and, through the influence of Great Britain, to the British commonwealth. France and Spain exported the concept to some African and Latin American countries. Finally, with the fall of the Berlin Wall, this concept has recently reached countries in Central and Eastern Europe.

Over the past two decades, ombudsman's offices have been established throughout Latin America in the context of the transition from authoritarianism to democracy. Guatemala was first to adopt the institution in 1985, followed—after 1990—by Mexico, El Salvador, Colombia, Costa Rica, Paraguay, Honduras, Peru, Argentina, Bolivia, Nicaragua, Panama, and Ecuador. Several states in Brazil and Venezuela have one, and the establishment of an ombudsman's office is currently on the political agenda in Chile and Uruguay. In December 2003 the Chilean government introduced a bill to create an ombudsman's office (*Defensoría de los Ciudadanos*). This agency is still not functioning, but the Comisión de Defensoría Ciudadana de Chile is performing some of its main functions.

While the first ombudsman models in Scandinavia and Europe were limited to cases of poor administration or governmental negligence, the influence of the 1978 Spanish constitution has extended the jurisdiction of such offices in modern Latin America to the oversight of accountability for human rights violations. More recently, ombudsman cases have also included environmental protection, freedom of the press, and the supervision of elections.

As in Spain, ombudsman's offices in much of Latin America have formed part of efforts to overcome legacies of human rights violations associated with past authoritarian regimes. Within the context of democratic transition, ombudsman's offices were granted a high level of legitimacy.

Moreover, the institutional design and mechanisms of these offices have developed according to the specific needs and demands of citizens of each country. In Colombia, the ombudsman's office has become involved in peace efforts; in El Salvador and Guatemala, in monitoring human rights in the context of the peace accords; in Bolivia, in narcotics eradication programs; in Costa Rica, in some sensitive privatization processes involving state-owned businesses; and in Peru, in the monitoring of electoral processes. With high levels of inequality and inequity, it is natural that the orientation of ombudsman's office services is geared toward the promotion, defense, and protection of economic and social rights.

The basic characteristics of this institution are the nonbinding nature of its decisions or recommendations, its powers of investigation into the actions of public officials, its full autonomy from the government and the courts, and its obligation to report to the congress.

Ombudsman's offices are generally associated with the legislative branch, although most are operationally, administratively, and, in some cases, financially autonomous (Table 5.6). Thus, in most countries ombudsman's offices report to congress, though they may be otherwise autonomous or linked with other institutions. In Honduras and Nicaragua, the ombudsman's office is an autonomous, independent entity with its own legal status, but it submits a report annually to the national assembly. In Colombia, the office is under the attorney general's office, while in Venezuela, it answers to the citizen branch (*Poder Ciudadano*), although it still reports to the legislature.

Even though their decisions or recommendations are nonbinding, rulings of these agencies can include effective instruments of accountability. In Argentina, the ombudsman's office can perform an active role in the legal process. In Bolivia, it can file for the reversal of judgments on grounds of their unconstitutionality, file direct appeals to reverse verdicts, or apply for a writ of habeas corpus without having to make a ruling. In Colombia, it can lodge protective legal actions, while in Guatemala it can denounce administrative behavior injurious to the interests of individuals, and condemn presidential acts. These actions, if they also receive the support of other players or control agencies, can contribute to the process of enforcing accountability.

Ombudsman's offices also carry out other functions that help create a bridge between society and the government. They may have the authority to undertake and initiate lawsuits, receive and act on complaints from citizens, assist victims of certain offenses, or instruct citizens on how to defend their rights.

In almost all of the Latin American countries, the legislative branch has the authority to appoint the ombudsman (Table 5.7). Such appointments generally require a qualified majority, usually two-thirds of the votes cast by members of the institution. Panama is distinct in that the president appoints the ombudsman, albeit based on a list of candidates proposed by the legislature.

In some countries, selection of the ombudsman involves mechanisms for including participants from civil society. Such is the case in Ecuador, where the congress elects the ombudsman after conferring with legally recognized human rights organizations, and in Nicaragua, where legislative deputies propose a list of candidates after consulting with major civil society organizations.

Most ombudsmen in Latin America are permitted reelection, except in the case of Venezuela. In some countries, the legislature is authorized to remove the ombudsman from office, while in others, such as Bolivia, Colombia, the Dominican Republic, and Panama, the supreme court wields this authority.

Ombudsman's Functions

As already pointed out in the cases of supreme audit institutions and attorney general's offices, formal autonomy may be constructive and necessary, but it does not depend solely on institutional design. According to most constitutional and legal provisions in the region, the ombudsman's office is typically part of the legislative branch, but functionally and

Table 5.6. Ombudsman's Offices

Country	Year established	Under the legislature?	Type of formal independence	Link to other institutions
Argentina Defensoría del Pueblo	1993	X	Operational and financial independence	
Bolivia Defensor del Pueblo	1994	X	Institutional independence	
Colombia Defensor del Pueblo	1991			X (public ministry)
Costa Rica Defensoría de los Habitantes de la República	1992	X	Operational and discretionary independence	
Dominican Republic Defensor del Pueblo	2001			
Ecuador Defensoría del Pueblo	1998	X	Operational and financial independence	
El Salvador Procuraduría para la Defensa de los Derechos Humanos	1993	X	Institutional independence	
Guatemala Comisión de Derechos Humanos	1985	X	Operational independence	
Honduras Comisionado Nacional de los Derechos Humanos	1992	X	Operational and financial independence	
Mexico Comisión Nacional de Derechos Humanos	1990	X	Operational and financial independence	
Nicaragua Procuraduría para la Defensa de los Derechos Humanos	1995	X	Institutional independence	
Panama Defensoría del Pueblo	1997		Institutional independence	
Paraguay Defensoría del Pueblo	1992	X	Functional independence	
Peru Defensoría del Pueblo	1993	X	Operational independence	
Venezuela Defensoría del Pueblo	1999		Institutional independence	X Poder Ciudadano (citizen branch)

Source: Authors' compilation.

Table 5.7. Ombudsman Appointments and Terms of Office

Country	Terms of office (years)	Reappoint- ment	Appointing institution	Institution that re- moves office holder
Argentina	Five	Yes (one time)	Congress	Congress
Bolivia	Five	Yes (one time)	Congress	Supreme court
Colombia	Four	Yes	Lower house (from short list proposed by the president)	Supreme court (follow- ing indictment by prosecutor general)
Costa Rica	Four	Yes (one time)	Legislative assembly	Legislative assembly
Dominican Republic	Six	Yes (one time)	Senate	Supreme court
Ecuador	Five	Yes (one time)	Congress (upon recommendation by recognized human rights organizations)	Congress
El Salvador	Three	Yes	Legislative assembly	Legislative assembly
Guatemala	Five	No	Congress (based on short list presented by the human rights commission)	Congress
Honduras	Six	Yes	Congress	Not defined
Mexico	Five	Yes (one time)	Senate	Senate (by impeach- ment) or lower house (by declaration sustain- ing a criminal matter)
Nicaragua	Five	Yes	National assembly (based on list of candidates, in consultation with corresponding civil society organizations)	National assembly (after hearing with head of public ministry)
Panama	Five	Yes (one time)	President of the republic (candidates chosen by the human rights commission of the legislative assembly)	Supreme court
Paraguay	Five	Yes	Chamber of deputies	Senate (after indict- ment of chamber of deputies)
Peru	Five	Yes (one time)	Congress	Congress
Venezuela	Seven	No	National assembly (from a short list submitted by the applicant assessment committee of the citizen branch); if agreement is not reached in 30 days, the short list is submitted to popular vote	National assembly (after opinion from the supreme court)

Source: Authors' compilation.

administratively autonomous. It generally reports to the legislative branch, and thus indirectly to citizens.

In such a design, the autonomy of the ombudsman's office depends on the division of political forces in power. In divided governments, political incentives may be such that the actions of the ombudsman's office elicit the support and follow-up of the legislature, thus increasing the ombudsman's effectiveness. However, this close connection with the legislature may increase the probability of executive-legislative conflict, with a potentially negative effect on democratic governance.

If the president commands a majority in the legislature, any initiative of the ombudsman aimed at sanctioning executive irregularities may be blocked. This was the case in Peru, where President Fujimori's control over the legislature blocked action on the ombudsman's initiatives to punish abuses committed by the armed forces and intelligence organizations. Nevertheless, wide dissemination of information about human rights abuses and corruption charges, and resulting public pressure, likely contributed, at least indirectly, to the fall of the government.

Establishing an appointment process that requires a qualified majority of legislators, and providing for input from civil society organizations, may be constructive from the standpoint of democratic governance, but does not always ensure that an ombudsman will take office in a timely manner or will be independent from partisan politics and competent. For example, even though Paraguay's 1992 constitution created the *Defensoría del Pueblo*, the first ombudsman was not appointed until November 2001. Similarly, in El Salvador, because of the polarization between the governing *Alianza Republicana Nacionalista* (ARENA) party and the opposition *Frente Farabundo Martí para la Liberación Nacional* (FMLN), the national assembly became deadlocked over the selection of an ombudsman on multiple occasions. In addition, the partisan-based appointment process resulted in the naming of persons who lacked political independence, ample experience, and commitment to carrying out the mission of the institution to defend human rights (Dodson and Jackson, 2004).

Agencies of horizontal accountability cannot function in an isolated fashion. In order to be effective, the work of ombudman's offices needs to be linked with other public institutions related to justice and civil society associations (O'Donnell, 2003). In Peru, for example, the 1993 constitutional reform established the office of the ombudsman, formally endowing it with the authority to wield control. However, at the same time, the nucleus of power centered on the presidency, the armed forces, and the intelligence agency was reinforced. Consequently, though the constitution authorized and legally empowered the ombudsman's office to wield control within its jurisdiction, the concentration of power reinforced by a self-coup (*autogolpe*) did not allow this agency to, in practice, take actions to protect citizens from civil rights violations.

This factor is even more important if the agencies responsible for enforcing accountability are not authorized to make binding decisions. If no support is available from other state agencies, particularly from the courts, accusations made by institutions such as ombudsman's offices may have the effect of building the hostility of public opinion without actually sanctioning the culprits—in some cases—threatening the governance of democratic regimes.

The level of legitimacy of a control official or agency can be very important to the practice of horizontal accountability. The Peruvian ombudsman's office, for example, achieved a high level of legitimacy, largely due to the leadership wielded by its director. Such leadership is another factor that can work in favor of accountability even when other state agencies are not willing to cooperate with the control efforts of ombudsman's offices. Strong leadership, however, requires a complementary relationship between horizontal accountability, enforced through the ombudsman's office, and vertical accountability stemming from public opinion. Since the decisions handed down by ombudsman's offices are nonbinding, they must persuade and mobilize society to demand respect for citizen rights. Thus, positive interaction between the ombudsman's office and civil society organizations is essential.

Conclusions

It is evident that political systems in Latin America have made progress toward establishing semiautonomous institutions to control the exercise of public authority. More than ever, the strength of democracy depends on their performance. The need to protect and guarantee fundamental citizen rights and equality under the law underlies the trend toward creating and strengthening such institutions.

Over the past two decades, constitutional and legal reforms have led to the creation of ombudsman and attorney general's offices in many countries. During this period, reforms have also sought to root these institutions more firmly in the democratic system and to develop their independence and capabilities. Such efforts toward institutionalization have also been directed at supreme audit institutions. Most of these were created in the first half of the 20th century, but have not generally functioned as independent agencies.

It has been suggested that in the creation of Latin American horizontal accountability agencies, it should be considered how these agencies would react in given situations, such as if the head of the executive branch were to be accused of serious abuses of authority. In fact, such an eventuality has already been faced by many presidential regimes in the region. Public prosecutors, attorney generals, comptrollers, and ombudsmen have exercised legal authority in many cases over the past decade in the hemisphere, with mixed results. Such experiences have corroborated the need to endow these entities with sufficient constitutional and legal authority to deal with cases of dereliction of duties of office and abuses of power. The cases involving the comptroller's office in Nicaragua, the attorney general's offices in Colombia and Venezuela, the public prosecutor's office in Brazil, and the ombudsman's office in Peru have served as strong tests of the role and authority of these agencies in relation to the executive branch. Recent actions, such as those undertaken by the prosecutor general of Costa Rica in response to acts of corruption by former presidents, confirm the importance of these control mechanisms.

In order for democracy and horizontal accountability agencies to gain legitimacy, the public must see that investigations eventually lead to effective trials, judgments, and sanctions that are consistent with ethical and legal standards. In each case, the agency must possess and be capable of exercising the political autonomy required to earn the respect of the citizenry.

One factor essential for the effectiveness of horizontal accountability agencies is that they not work separately, but rather in the context of a "network of relatively autonomous powers" (O'Donnell, 2003) supported by an active civil society and a favorable climate of public opinion. In cases of control agencies working in relative institutional isolation, positive feedback between vertical and horizontal accountability is even more important, since the backing of public opinion may encourage and mobilize other state institutions to support initiatives to hold public officials accountable.

Overlapping and redundant forms of control have been proposed as a way to enhance the ethics of public decision making, but this can lead to stalemate and less effective public policy. Thus, there needs to be clearer specification of the responsibilities and authorities of the different horizontal accountability agencies in order for them to efficiently carry out their monitoring and controlling tasks, while also permitting the government to perform effectively.

Another problem facing accountability agencies in the region is the lack of institutional coordination between these organizations and others that participate in or form part of the criminal justice system. The result is a certain institutional isolation that endangers the efficiency and effectiveness of these agencies. The growth of impunity, for instance, is at least partly attributable to the lack of coordination between judges, prosecuting attorneys, ombudsmen, comptrollers, attorney generals, and the police.

Essential to establishing an autonomous accountability agency is guaranteeing that it will act responsibly. Several different mechanisms may be established to ensure public participation in policy formulation and supervision in order to further transparency, though this may not be advisable when carrying out criminal and disciplinary proceedings, where secrecy is essential to the success of investigations. Citizen participation mobilizes the support of other public and private institutions and constitutes a proper response to the classic question: "Who controls the controller?" Without significant public participation, the legitimacy and effectiveness of these institutions may well be undermined by public opinion, and accountability agencies may face challenges to their power on many fronts.

Similarly, an evenhanded analysis must start with an acknowledgment of the wide gap between Latin American institutions' formal legal authority and their real world performance, independence, and authority. While it is true that these horizontal accountability agencies can help surmount the deficit of democracy in the region, their institutional and cultural context may contribute to their failure. When operating in unfavorable national and cultural contexts, institutions that are sophisticated from the standpoint of institutional design will have a limited impact if not accompanied by systematic civic education and public campaigns against governmental corruption and mismanagement. It must not be forgotten that the importance of accountability institutions lies as much in their contribution to overall democratic development and civic education as in the particular legal outcomes they might achieve.

References

Avritzer, Leonardo. 2000. Teoría democrática, esfera pública y deliberación. *Revista Metapolítica* 14(4).

Bohman, James. 2000. La democracia deliberativa y sus críticos. *Revista Metapolítica* 14(4).

CLAD (Centro Latinoamericano de Administración para el Desarrollo). 2000. *La respon-sabilización en la nueva gestión pública latinoamericana*. Buenos Aires: Inter-American Development Bank and Editorial Eudeba.

Cohen, Joshua. 2000. Procedimiento y sustancia en la democracia deliberativa. *Revista Metapolítica* 14(4).

Dodson, Michael, and Donald Jackson. 2004. Horizontal Accountability in Transitional Democracies: The Human Rights Ombudsman in El Salvador and Guatemala. *Latin American Politics and Society*. 46(4): 1–27.

Domingo, Pilar. 1999. Judicial Independence and Judicial Reform in Latin America. In Andreas Schedler, Larry Diamond, and Marc Plattner (eds.), *The Self-Restraining State: Power and Accountability in New Democracies*. Boulder, CO: Rienner.

Duce, Mauricio. 1999. Problemas en torno a la reconfiguración del Public Prosecutor en América Latina. Translation of Chapter 3 of *Criminal Justice System in Latin America*. Master's thesis, International Legal Studies Program, Stanford University Law School, May.

Fox, Jonathan. 2005. Civil Society and Political Accountability: Propositions for Discussion. *Perfiles Latinoamericanos*, no. 27, December.

Groisman, Enrique, and Emilia Lerner. 2000. Responzabilización por los controles clásicos. In CLAD (Centro Latinoamericano de Administración para el Desarrollo), *La responsabilización en la nueva gestión pública latinoamericana*. Buenos Aires: Inter-American Development Bank and Editorial Eudeba.

Hammergren, Linn. 1998. *Institutional Strengthening and Justice Reform*. Center for Democracy and Governance. Washington, DC: U.S. Agency for International Development.

Kenney, Charles D. 2003. Horizontal Accountability: Concepts and Conflicts. In Scott Mainwaring and Christopher Welna (eds.), *Democratic Accountability in Latin America*. New York: Oxford University Press.

Lupia, Arthur, and Mathew D. McCubbins. 1998. *The Democratic Dilemma: Can Citizens Learn What They Need to Know?* Cambridge: Cambridge University Press.

Moreno, Erika, Brian F. Crisp, and Matthew Soberg Shugart. 2003. The Accountability Deficit in Latin America. In Scott Mainwaring and Christopher Welna (eds.), *Democratic Accountability in Latin America*. New York: Oxford University Press.

O'Donnell, Guillermo. 1994. Delegative Democracy. *Journal of Democracy* 5(1).

———. 1999. Horizontal Accountability in New Democracies. In Andreas Schedler, Larry Diamond and Marc Plattner (eds.), *The Self-Restraining State: Power and Accountability in New Democracies*. Boulder, CO: Rienner.

———. 2003. Horizontal Accountability: The Legal Institutionalization of Mistrust. In Scott Mainwaring and Christopher Welna (eds.), *Democratic Accountability in Latin America*. New York: Oxford University Press.

Pope, Jeremy, and Frank Vogl. 2000. Making Anticorruption Agencies More Effective. *Finance and Development* 37(2).

Przeworski, Adam, Susan C. Stokes, and Bernard Manin (eds.). 1999. *Democracy, Accountability and Representation*. Cambridge: Cambridge University Press.

Sadek, Maria Tereza, and Rosângela Batista Cavalcanti. 2000. The New Brazilian Public Prosecution: An Agent of Accountability. In Scott Mainwaring and Christopher Welna (eds.), *Democratic Accountability in Latin America*. New York: Oxford University Press.

Schedler, Andreas. 1999. Conceptualizing Accountability. In Andreas Schedler, Larry Diamond, and Marc Plattner (eds.), *The Self-Restraining State: Power and Accountability in New Democracies*. Boulder, CO: Rienner.

Schedler, Andreas, Larry Diamond, and Marc Plattner (eds.). 1999. *The Self-Restraining State: Power and Accountability in New Democracies*. Boulder, CO: Rienner.

Smulovitz, Catalina, and Enrique Peruzotti. 2003. Societal and Horizontal Controls: Two Cases about a Fruitful Relationship. In Scott Mainwaring and Christopher Welna (eds.), *Democratic Accountability in Latin America*. New York: Oxford University Press.

World Economic Forum. 2005. *The Global Competitiveness Report, 2005–2006*. New York: Oxford University Press.

Part II

Institutions and Democracy (II):
Political Parties

CHAPTER 6

Party Systems and Democratic Governability

In the modern era, democracies revolve around a political party system in which at least two viable parties compete freely for shares of power. Political parties are indispensable to the working of democracy. They recruit and select candidates for political office; organize the electoral process; and structure public political support around identifiable sets of policy programs, socioeconomic interests, and values. Parties also aggregate citizen interests and preferences in the policy-making process, form governments, and finally, reach legislative policy agreements (Sartori, 1976; Lipset and Rokkan, 1967; La Palombara and Weiner, 1996).

Political party systems have at least three characteristics that affect how well a democratic government functions: (1) their level of institutionalization; (2) their degree of fragmentation; and (3) their degree of polarization. Following Mainwaring and Scully (1995) party systems can be considered to be institutionalized when: patterns of interparty competition are relatively stable; parties have fairly stable and deep bases of societal support; parties and elections are viewed as legitimate and as the sole instruments for determining who governs; and party organizations are characterized by reasonably stable rules and structures.

The degree of party system fragmentation relates to the number of parties that regularly obtain a significant share of legislative votes and seats. The degree of polarization is a measure of how drastically parties differ in political ideology and their social bases of political support.

When party systems are institutionalized, parties are important actors in channeling and aggregating political demands.[1] With identifiable political programs and entrenched societal support, reasonably cohesive parties facilitate the representation of citizens' preferences and interests and enhance the possibility that citizens can hold elected officials

---

[1] See Mainwaring and Scully (1995) for a more extensive analysis of the importance of party system institutionalization for the governance of democratic systems. This discussion of the link between party systems and democratic governability draws significantly on their framework of analysis.

accountable. Given the great costs in determining the policy positions and conduct of individual candidates and incumbents, programmatic parties enable citizens to vote according to broad political philosophies, sets of values, and policy directions. At least to some degree, citizens' judgments of candidates can be based on the programs and performance of the party with which these candidates are affiliated, rather than merely their individual personalities and patrimonial links with voters. Likewise, in more institutionalized party systems, politicians are at least somewhat dependent on parties for their positions and career advancement. Thus, citizens are better able to signal their preferences; politicians, meanwhile, are more constrained to adhere to the rules of the democratic game, to adopt decisions that conform with the programmatic objectives of their party, and to refrain from making populist and demagogic appeals to the masses.

Institutionalized party systems also tend to promote greater political stability and governmental effectiveness. When parties are institutionalized, societal actors come to accept that electoral and legislative channels influence policy making most propitiously. (Mainwaring and Scully, 1995). Citizens and civil society organizations articulate their demands through legitimate and established institutions, lowering the risk that conflicts will intensify and overwhelm the political system.[2] Citizens and social groups trust political parties and political leaders to act in their interest, and are therefore more prepared to grant some degree of decision-making authority in times of crisis, when difficult and controversial decisions must be made. Compromise is an accepted inevitability. No societal group or interest can obtain all of its demands. Yet working through political parties and the legislature, few demands will be totally ignored.

Similarly, in an institutionalized party system, politics become more predictable. Election results do not dramatically change from one election to the next, with some parties vanishing and many others being born (Mainwaring and Scully, 1995). The rules of conduct and interaction are better known and accepted, and political actors know reasonably well how to best pursue their interests. In contrast, political actors in less institutionalized settings are more worried about the future and more prone to follow narrow, short-term interests, even when this entails potential long-term costs for themselves or for the government as a whole. Such uncertainties about the future can also cause some political actors to take actions that undermine the democratic system.

Finally, institutionalized party systems favor governability because they enhance the likelihood that the executive will obtain support in the legislature (Mainwaring and Shugart, 1997). When parties are weak and undisciplined, it is less likely that the president will be able to count on stable partisan support in the legislature. In such systems, presidents are more likely to be elected without the backing of an established party. Therefore, their victories will not necessarily translate into numerical strength for their party in the congress. Even when the governing party obtains a significant share of seats, the lack of party discipline could make the support of copartisans in the legislature more tenuous. When the

---

[2] As Arriagada (2001) points out, a strengthened civil society in the context of a weakening political party system can be a source of political instability. Thus, the strengthening of civil society is valuable for improving democratic performance, but only if intermediary representative institutions, such as political parties, can adequately perform their roles.

president is popular, legislators may find it in their interest to "join the bandwagon" and lend their support. But given the weak significance of party labels and low levels of party cohesion, legislators have little incentive to remain loyal to the president when his or her popularity fades.

In a presidential system, there are inherent difficulties in sustaining a government supported by a coalition of diverse parties (see Chapter 4). Given the independent bases of legitimacy and tenure of the executive and legislative branches, the government's coalition partners have less incentive to adhere to the coalition than they do in parliamentary systems. These impediments to coalition building in presidential systems are likely to be even more magnified when parties are weakly institutionalized. In such contexts, parties are generally unable to act as a unit under a defined leadership, their members bound to a given course of action. Often, the support of individual legislators must be acquired through the promise of budgetary resources, legislative concessions, and outright bribes. Given the limited degree of cohesion within parties, coalitions are more likely to be transitory.

The more traditional factors used to distinguish party systems—the number of relevant parties and the degree of ideological polarization—can also affect the governability of democratic systems.[3] The number of parties affects the likelihood that the president's party will control a majority of the seats in the legislature, and the possibilities for building majority legislative support behind the executive's legislative program. The more fragmented the party system, the more likely it is that coalitions will be required, and the more difficult it will be to sustain them. A fragmented party system does not ensure executive and legislative gridlock, but gridlock is more likely in this type of system than in one with fewer parties. Governmental paralysis is a negative outcome by itself, but it also provides a justification for actions aimed at subverting or circumventing democratic institutions, and thus may contribute to the destabilization of the democratic system.

Highly polarized party systems, which remain more likely in multiparty contexts, tend to create greater difficulties for democratic governance than those systems characterized by low or moderate polarization. In highly polarized party systems, interparty coalitions and piecemeal agreements that smooth the workings of the legislature are more difficult to forge and sustain. In governments led by parties near the center of the political spectrum, a high degree of polarization may impair governmental stability and performance. This probable dynamic exacerbates the polarization of the system, and then endangers the stability of the regime (Sartori, 1976; Sani and Sartori, 1983).

However, representation and accountability are facilitated when parties are distinguishable in programmatic or ideological terms. In order for elections to be effective in allowing citizens to signal their policy preferences and hold parties accountable, party labels need to mean something in terms of policy positions (Coppedge, 1998; Jones, 2005).

The above reasoning implies that systems with relatively few significant parties and low or moderate levels of polarization are more conducive to stable and effective governance in democratic systems. This does not mean that electoral laws that artificially concentrate the party system or discourage mobilization along ideological lines are necessarily advan-

---

[3] Sartori (1976) developed the conventional classification of party systems centered on the number of parties and their degree of ideological polarization.

tageous for democracy. Aside from decision-making efficiency, the long-term health of a democracy depends on the legitimacy of its democratic institutions, and how representative such institutions are of the citizenry.

It is also important to note that a given type of party system does not determine success or failure in democratic governance. Certainly emerging democracies, with their (almost by definition) weakly institutionalized party systems, are not all doomed to failure. Party systems can evolve based on the conscious and unconscious behavior of the political elite and the influence of the broader social and economic context. In Latin America, fairly well institutionalized party systems have unraveled in recent decades, while a few once weakly institutionalized systems have developed steadily. In some countries, the same structural features that appeared to contribute to democratic breakdowns in the 1960s and 1970s now appear compatible with reasonably effective and stable democratic governance. Thus, institutionalized party systems with moderate degrees of ideological polarization and a limited number of relevant parties facilitate democratic governability. But these characteristics neither guarantee success nor stand as prerequisites.

With the advent of television and other forms of mass communication and the narrowing of traditional ideological rifts, the present-day context of party system development is very different than that of the northern and western European countries when their democracies took root. Across the globe, citizens' attachments to parties are becoming more loose, and the party systems that develop in new or restored democracies will probably not have the stability and depth of connection to society that they once had in more established democracies. In addition, the greater incentives toward the personalization of electoral competition, and the greater focus on vote-seeking rather than policy-oriented behaviors associated with presidential systems, are likely to affect the nature of party organizations in Latin America (Samuels, 2002).

Assessing the Institutionalization of Party Systems in Latin America

The party systems that Latin American countries carried over into the past two decades were formed at different points in their respective histories. In some cases, the major parties entering the period were formed as far back as the 19th century, along the classic liberal and conservative rift that influenced party evolution in Western Europe. In other cases, the major parties entering the 1980s arose as recently as the latter half of the 20th century. In addition to the differing ages of Latin American party systems, there are also considerable differences in national experiences with democracy. In countries such as Colombia, Costa Rica, and Venezuela, there had been decades of uninterrupted political competition prior to the 1980s. In a second group of countries, including Argentina, Chile, and Uruguay, the party system that took shape after the transition from authoritarianism was largely a continuation of that which had existed in prior periods of electoral competition. In other countries—including Brazil, Mexico, Paraguay, and most of the Central American countries—the transition entailed construction of new parties to compete against the party or military faction that headed the prior, more restrictive regime.

The level of party system institutionalization is, for the most part, a product of each country's political history. Party system institutionalization facilitates the governance of democratic systems. However, in countries where democratization entails the construction of interparty competition that scarcely existed before, a certain degree of deinstitutional-ization must occur before a democratic party system can be institutionalized. This dein-stitutionalization entails the entrance of new parties, the shifting of voter allegiances, and potentially, the weakening of existing parties. Such systems may be handicapped relative to those that can simply resurrect a dormant party system. Yet the construction of party politics is a necessary and sometimes lengthy process on the way toward the consolidation of democratic systems.

This section compares Latin American countries' different dimensions of party system institutionalization. An overall index of party system institutionalization aggregates these individual dimensions.[4] The dimensions to be examined are those that, as defined earlier, characterize an institutionalized party system: (1) patterns of interparty competition are relatively stable; (2) parties have fairly stable and deep roots in society; (3) parties and elections are viewed as legitimate and as the sole instruments for determining who governs; and (4) party organizations have reasonably stable rules and structures.

Stability of Patterns of Interparty Competition

The stability or regularity of patterns of interparty competition can be measured through an index of electoral volatility.[5] The index measures the net change in the seat (and vote) shares of all parties from one election to the next. For example, assume that, in a prior election, Party A received 60 percent of the seats and Party B received 40 percent, while in the current election Party A receives 40 percent and Party B receives 60 percent. In this case, the volatility between the two elections is 20 percent. Party A loses 20 percent of the seats and Party B gains 20 percent, with a net change of 20 percent. Volatility can result either from shifts in the votes (and seats) from a given group of parties to another, or from the appearance or disappearance of parties.

Table 6.1 shows the mean volatility calculated according to lower chamber seats and vote percentages in presidential elections for the 18 countries covered in this study. The countries are listed in order of lowest to highest volatility, based on average volatility according to both types of measures.

The table shows that there is a huge range in the mean volatility among the countries of the region. Volatility has been minimal in Honduras, Nicaragua, Chile, and Uruguay, but extremely significant among the countries in the lower third of the table. Among lower chamber seats, there has been practically no change in the partisan breakdown from one election to the next in Chile, and little change in Honduras. However, in Peru and Guatemala, more

---

[4] This analysis follows the structure laid out by Mainwaring and Scully (1995) but updates their measures and adds others. The additional measures are derived from data from the *Latinobarómetro* survey, which were not available to these authors.

[5] Pedersen's index of electoral volatility (1983) is used here. This index is derived by adding the net change in the percentage of the seats (or votes) gained or lost by each party from one election to the next, then dividing by two.

Table 6.1. Electoral Volatility in Latin America

Country	Lower chamber seats			Presidential vote			Mean volatility $\frac{(A) + (B)}{2}$
	Time span	No. of electoral periods	Mean volatility (A)	Time span	No. of electoral periods	Mean volatility (B)	
Honduras	1981–2001	4	7.67	1981–2001	4	6.23	6.95
Nicaragua	1990–2001	2	15.05	1990–2001	2	10.50	12.77
Chile	1989–2001	3	3.47	1989–1999	2	22.17	12.82
Uruguay	1984–2004	4	14.65	1984–2004	4	14.59	14.62
Costa Rica	1978–2002	6	16.96	1978–2002	6	12.95	14.95
Mexico	1979–2003	9	14.23	1982–2000	4	18.43	16.33
El Salvador	1985–2003	6	18.09	1984–2004	4	19.48	18.79
Dominican Republic	1978–2002	6	19.09	1978–2004	7	23.08	21.09
Paraguay	1989–2003	3	19.86	1989–2003	3	28.70	24.28
Argentina	1983–2003	10	18.35	1983–2003	4	31.70	25.02
Colombia	1978–2002	7	17.51	1978–2002	6	33.64	25.58
Panama	1994–2004	3	19.36	1994–2004	3	34.78	27.07
Brazil	1986–2002	5	28.67	1989–2002	3	36.35	32.51
Venezuela	1978–2000	5	28.98	1978–2000	5	37.04	33.01
Bolivia	1980–2002	5	29.09	1980–2002	5	38.68	33.88
Ecuador	1979–2002	9	32.55	1978–2002	6	46.26	39.41
Guatemala	1985–2003	5	46.95	1985–2003	4	48.95	47.95
Peru	1980–2001	5	51.83	1980–2001	5	52.21	52.02
Total		96	22.35		76	28.65	25.50

Note: The structure of this table is based on Table 1.1 in Mainwaring and Scully (1995), but the measures cover the period of this study, updated through 2004.

Democracies in Development

than 45 percent of the seats have shifted on average among parties. Average volatility percentages of 25 to 40 percent were registered in Ecuador, Brazil, Venezuela, and Bolivia.

The volatility of the vote in presidential elections yields roughly the same ordering of countries as that for legislative seats. Chile provides one example of deviation between the two measures; here, the increase in voting for the center-right candidate in 1999 contributed to a greater figure for volatility in presidential elections than for lower chamber seats. Ecuador, Colombia, and Argentina also have greater volatility rankings when one considers voting in presidential elections.

In comparison with Western European democracies, at least half of the Latin American countries experienced very high electoral volatility. A study of all of the elections in 13 Western European countries from 1885 to 1985 revealed that the highest single instance of volatility—that of Germany from 1919 to 1920—was 32.1 percent.[6] The highest mean volatility over the whole period—registered in France—was 15.2 percent. In several Latin American countries, the average volatility exceeds the greatest recorded value in this 100-year period of Western European democracy. And in terms of the period averages, more than two-thirds of Latin American countries experienced more electoral volatility than the most volatile European democracy.

Over the period, average electoral volatility measurements conceal considerable change in the party systems of some countries. Prior to the 1990s, patterns of electoral competition in Venezuela were among the most stable in the region. But the collapse in the legitimacy of its major political parties resulted in surging electoral volatility and the emergence of an extraordinarily large number of new parties and movements. In Colombia, changes in the electoral system and growing fragmentation in the two main parties have also resulted in a significant, albeit less dramatic, increase in volatility. In recent elections, a similar trend has affected Argentina, Bolivia, and Costa Rica. Peru's party system collapsed in the early 1990s, but then partially recovered after the fall of the Fujimori government in 2000 (Kenney, 2003). In contrast, Brazil's party system evolved during the period from extreme volatility to reasonable stability. In part, this pattern of evolution reflects the fact that the democratic transition was marked by the emergence of new political forces that filled the gaps left by the two-party system imposed during much of the period of military rule. With little inheritance from the previous democratic period, the transition in Brazil entailed the creation of a new party system. But the consecutive electoral victories of President Fernando Henrique Cardoso and the growing strength of President Lula da Silva's Worker's Party (Partido dos Trabalhadores, PT) increased the stability of political competition from 1994 to 2004.

Stability and Depth of Party Roots in Society

The second dimension of party system institutionalization is the depth of the links between parties, citizens, and organized groups. It would be expected that stronger ties between parties and society would contribute to more stable patterns of voting. That is, when a large share of voters feel close to a political party, it is less likely that there will be dramatic shifts

---

[6] Bartolini and Mair (1990), as cited in Mainwaring and Scully (1995).

in the partisan distribution of the vote from one election to the next. Nevertheless, the two dimensions do not necessarily go hand in hand, and they measure different aspects of the concept of party system institutionalization (Mainwaring and Scully, 1995).

The most direct way to measure how deeply parties penetrate society would be through comparable cross-national election surveys, which would make it possible to examine the stability of voters' party preferences, the depth of their attachment to parties, and the consistency of voting among given socioeconomic groups. But such comprehensive and comparable election surveys do not exist for the range of countries considered here. In lieu of such information, two alternative measures are developed, based on citizen responses to the *Latinobarómetro* survey and long-term shifts in electoral outcomes.

A party's endurance over long periods of electoral competition provides one indication of how stable its links are to voters. If parties keep fading out of existence and new parties keep emerging, then it is doubtful that parties have obtained the strong allegiance of citizens, or have sunk their roots in society. Table 6.2 compares the share of legislative seats controlled by the significant parties at the beginning of the study period to the share these same parties controlled following the most recent election. Parties are considered "significant" if they gained 10 percent or more of the seats in the lower house in the first election of the study period. The last column shows the percent decline over the period in the share of the seats controlled by these parties.

The table shows a tremendous variation across the region in the fate of the parties that were politically dominant at the beginning of the period. In Venezuela and Peru, the major parties experienced significant losses, while in Guatemala and Ecuador they practically disappeared. By the 2000 election, the stature of the two previously well-established parties in Venezuela—Comité de Organización Político Electoral (COPEI) and Acción Democrática (AD)—had severely eroded. In Peru, a similar dynamic took place, even though in the 2001 elections the Partido Aprista Peruano (PAP) recovered part of its historic electoral support behind its presidential candidate, former president Alan García, and the Partido Popular Cristiano (PPC) experienced a partial resurgence in the form of electoral support for Lourdes Flores Nano's Unidad Nacional (UN) coalition (Kenney, 2003).[7]

In contrast, the level of electoral support for the major parties in Nicaragua, Uruguay, Chile, Honduras, and Panama remained quite stable. The major parties also held on to their status reasonably well in Paraguay, Mexico, the Dominican Republic, and Costa Rica. The loss of seats among the traditional parties in these countries ranged roughly between 25 and 30 percent, though, with increased electoral competition in Mexico, this figure was likely to increase over time. In Costa Rica, two new parties, Acción Ciudadana and Movimiento Libertario, burst upon the political scene and managed to capture about 35 percent of the legislative seats in 2002 at the expense of the two traditional major parties—Partido de Liberación Nacional (PLN) and the Partido Unidad Social Cristiana (PUSC).[8]

To some extent, the varying lengths of the countries' recent democratic periods may distort the comparison. However, only in Chile, Nicaragua, Panama, and Paraguay has the

---

[7] The PPC was a member of this electoral alliance and Flores Nano was associated with the PPC (Kenney, 2003).

[8] The fact that these two parties maintained this share in the 2006 elections suggests that this represents a durable change in the party system in Costa Rica.

Table 6.2. Share of Legislative Seats Controlled by Significant Parties at the Beginning and End of Study Period

Country	Significant parties at moment of transition (10% or more of seats)[1]	Percent of seats at beginning of study period	First election year	Percent of seats after most recent election	Most recent election year	Percent decline
Nicaragua	Nationalist Opposition Union (UNO) (APC, MDN, PALI, PAN, PC, PDCN, PLC, PLI, PNC, PSD, PSN) FSLN	98.9	1990	98.9	2001	0.0
Uruguay	PC, PN, FA/EP	98.0	1984	96.9	2004	1.1
Chile	PDC, PPD, RN, UDI	78.3	1989	76.7	2001	2.1
Honduras	PLH, PNH	95.5	1981	90.6	2001	5.1
Panama	PRD, MOLIRENA, PDC, PPA	91.0	1989	79.5	2004	12.7
Paraguay	ANR, PLRA	95.8	1989	72.5	2003	24.4
Mexico	PRI, PAN	100.0	1979	74.6	2003	25.4
Dominican Republic	PRD, PR/PRSC	100.0	1978	72.7	2002	27.3
Costa Rica[2]	PLN, Coalición Unidad/PUSC	91.2	1978	63.2	2002	30.8
Argentina	UCR, PJ	94.5	1983	63.1	2003	33.3
Bolivia	ADN, MIR, MNR, MNRI	80.8	1982	49.3	2002	39.0
El Salvador	ARENA, PDC, PCN	96.7	1985	57.1	2003	40.9
Colombia	PCC, PLC	97.5	1978	46.3	2002	52.5
Brazil	PMDB, PFL	77.6	1986	30.8	2002	60.3
Peru	AP, PAP	86.7	1980	24.2	2001	72.1
Venezuela	AD, COPEI	86.4	1978	22.4	2000	74.1
Ecuador	CFP, ID, PCE	78.3	1979	14.0	2002	82.1
Guatemala	DCG, UCN, MLN, PDCN, PR	92.0	1985	0.6	2003	99.3

Source: Authors' compilation.

[1] For a key to the abbreviations used in this column, see Appendix 7.1.

[2] The Partido Unidad Social Cristiana (PUSC) was formed in 1983 as a regrouping of the Coalición de la Unidad, the conservative alliance that presented candidates in 1978 and 1982. The Partido Republicano Calderonista (PRC), Renovación Democrática (PRD), Partido Demócrata Cristiano (PDC), and Partido Unión Popular (PUP) were the parties that merged to form the PUSC. Given the continuity in bases of support and elites, the PUSC is considered as a successor to the Coalición de la Unidad and not as a new party.

period since the democratic transition been significantly shorter than in the other countries. Given that the major parties in Chile actually gained seats, the passage of more time would probably not make a substantive difference in the measure of party system stability. But the interpretation of the situations in Nicaragua, Panama, and Paraguay might be expected to change once they experience a comparable number of elections.[9]

A second way to gauge the depth of public allegiance to parties is through public opinion surveys. The 1996, 1997, and 2003 rounds of the *Latinobarómetro* survey asked respondents whether they consider themselves to be close to any particular political party, and if so, how close. Table 6.3 shows countries' party identification scores computed as a weighted average of the proportion of respondents making the four possible responses ("very close" is weighted as 1.0; "somewhat close," 0.67; "merely a sympathizer," 0.33; and "not close," 0.00). The percentage change from 1996/1997 to 2003 in the party identification score is shown in the last column.

The figures in Table 6.3 show fairly low levels of identification with political parties in the region. In only Paraguay and Uruguay did more than 25 percent of those surveyed identify with political parties in 2003. In Paraguay, the comparatively high degree of identification of citizens with political parties may reflect the intense traditional rivalry between the Asociación Nacional Republicana (ANR) (or Colorado Party) and the Partido Liberal Radical Auténtico (PLRA) (or Blancos Party), but it could also have been reinforced by the political patronage practiced by the *Colorados* during the authoritarian period. The low level of party identification in Chile is surprising; voting patterns are very stable, and historically, political parties have maintained a strong presence in Chilean society. Apart from the general trend of political detachment that appears to be affecting the region as a whole, it is possible that the electoral system-imposed competition between two encompassing coalitions of the center-left and center-right has weakened citizen attachment to individual parties.

According to survey results from the 1996 Eurobarometer,[10] the level of identification with political parties in Western Europe is somewhat higher than in Latin America. In 1996, around 29 percent of European respondents identified with political parties; in Latin America, the figure for roughly the same time period (an average of 1996 and 1997) was around 24 percent. In Europe, the level of identification recorded in the Netherlands (35 percent of the surveyed population) and Austria (37 percent) was notably higher than in the other countries. In Latin America, the highest levels were found in Paraguay, where the level of affinity to parties was roughly the same as the European average, followed by Uruguay and Panama.

Between 1989 and 1996, the average level of identification with parties in Europe fell slightly from 31 percent to 29 percent, reflecting a percent reduction as a share of the

---

[9] Divisions in the Partido Liberal Constitucionalista (PLC) and the Frente Sandinista de Liberación Nacional (FSLN) that emerged as a consequence of efforts to displace the dominant status of the two parties' leaders (Arnoldo Alemán and Daniel Ortega, respectively) have altered the political landscape in the run-up to the 2006 election.

[10] Given the fact that the Eurobarometer question used the same scale of responses (one to four), the weighted index of party identification is formed in the same way as in *Latinobarómetro*. The Eurobarometer includes the following 15 Western European countries: France, Belgium, Netherlands, Germany, Italy, Luxemburg, Denmark, Ireland, the United Kingdom, Sweden, Spain, Portugal, Finland, Switzerland, and Austria.

Table 6.3. Extent that Citizens Feel "Close" to a Political Party

In descending order of countries' scores for 2003

Country	Party identification score		
	Average 1996/97	2003	Percent change 1996/97–2003
Paraguay	0.36	0.31	−14.7
Uruguay	0.38	0.26	−30.5
Panama	0.22	0.22	1.4
Honduras	0.34	0.22	−35.6
Nicaragua	0.36	0.21	−43.4
Bolivia	0.20	0.20	0.4
El Salvador	0.28	0.20	−28.2
Ecuador	0.23	0.19	−17.1
Peru	0.14	0.18	23.3
Venezuela	0.18	0.18	−00.8
Mexico	0.23	0.17	−27.6
Brazil	0.14	0.16	13.9
Costa Rica	0.18	0.16	−12.8
Colombia	0.24	0.15	−36.0
Guatemala	0.21	0.15	−32.0
Chile	0.18	0.14	−26.2
Argentina	0.17	0.11	−35.6
Average	0.24	0.19	−21.2

Source: Latinobarómetro (1996, 1997, and 2003).

previous total of 6 percent. In contrast, from 1996/97 to 2003, the level of party identification observed in Latin America dropped more significantly, from around 24 percent to 19 percent. Identification with political parties declined in 13 out of 17 countries, and by more than 30 percent in six countries (Argentina, Guatemala, Colombia, Nicaragua, Honduras, and Uruguay).

The third indicator used to gauge the depth of party support among citizens is the percentage of Latinobarómetro survey respondents that are able to name a party that they would vote for if elections were held within the next week.[11] As is evident in Figure 6.1, Mexico and Uruguay, followed by Honduras and Paraguay, have the highest percentage of respondents that are able to identify a specific political party for which they would vote. It

---

[11] The question is: "If elections were held next Sunday, which party would you vote for?" Taking the average over a nine-year period helps control for the fact that proximity to elections is likely to increase the percentage of respondents who know the party for which they would vote.

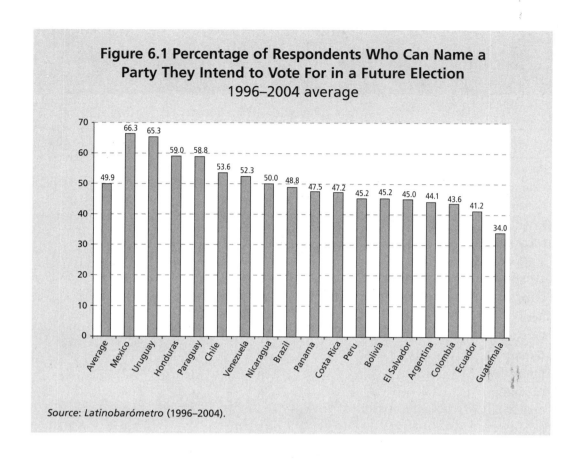

Figure 6.1 Percentage of Respondents Who Can Name a Party They Intend to Vote For in a Future Election
1996–2004 average

Source: Latinobarómetro (1996–2004).

is not surprising that—except Mexico—all of these countries are also among those with the most stable electoral support, as shown in Table 6.2. At the other extreme, the low level of party identification in Colombia, Ecuador, and Guatemala reflect the diminishing importance of traditional parties in recent years, and the relatively high level of party system fragmentation.

Parties and Elections Accorded Legitimacy and Parties Perceived as Central to Determining Who Governs

The third dimension of party system institutionalization refers to the extent to which citizens and organized interests accord the electoral process and political parties legitimacy, and perceive parties and elections as the main route to government. Based on questions in the *Latinobarómetro* surveys, three measures are used to compare countries: (1) respondents' degree of confidence in political parties; (2) respondents' perceptions of the integrity of electoral processes; and (3) respondents' perceptions of the importance of political parties to the progress of the country.

Table 6.4 shows the percentage of respondents in each year of the survey that expressed "a lot" or "some" confidence in political parties. The countries are arranged in descending order of the average value of this percentage across the eight surveys, from 1996–2004.

Democracies in Development

Table 6.4. Percentage of Survey Respondents with Confidence in Political Parties, 1996–2004

Country	1996–1997	1998–2000	2001–2002	2003–2004	1996–2004
Uruguay	38.1	34.7	33.0	23.9	32.4
El Salvador	35.0	12.0	17.4	17.6	23.4
Panama	22.1	22.9	21.3	22.5	22.2
Mexico	24.4	33.7	16.6	12.7	21.9
Chile	31.1	22.1	17.3	16.6	21.8
Honduras	31.1	9.0	18.8	16.8	21.6
Costa Rica	20.5	26.3	21.9	15.5	21.1
Venezuela	16.1	19.3	24.6	17.8	19.4
Paraguay	31.9	21.0	11.2	13.3	19.3
Nicaragua	32.1	4.9	17.5	9.4	18.2
Brazil	17.1	16.0	16.2	19.1	17.1
Peru	19.5	17.7	18.1	9.4	16.2
Guatemala	22.8	18.4	8.8	9.8	14.9
Colombia	16.1	16.1	11.2	14.9	14.6
Argentina	22.6	16.3	8.4	10.3	14.4
Bolivia	18.4	15.9	10.1	6.5	12.7
Ecuador	16.9	11.0	7.9	5.4	10.3
Average	24.5	18.7	16.5	14.2	18.9

Source: Latinobarómetro (1996–2004).

Based on this measure, parties appear to be accorded some legitimacy in Uruguay. But in the rest of the countries, between 75 percent and 90 percent of respondents have little or no confidence in political parties. Similar to the case of party identification, citizen confidence in political parties has declined. While about 25 percent of respondents had a lot or some confidence in political parties in 1996–1997, by 2003 and 2004 this figure had fallen to 14 percent. Trust in parties fell in all countries except Brazil, Venezuela, and Panama; in these countries, trust levels remained relatively stable.

In addition to public confidence in political parties, this dimension also refers to the legitimacy of electoral processes. Table 6.5 shows the percentage of respondents that view elections as being conducted fairly. Again, the countries are arranged in descending order of the average percentage of respondents (1996–2000) that view elections as clean. The table shows that there is a very wide variation in the legitimacy accorded electoral processes. While 70 percent of respondents in Uruguay, Chile, and Costa Rica perceive elections to be fair, only around 25 percent of respondents feel this way in Colombia, Ecuador, Mexico, and Paraguay. Regardless of whether such perceptions reflect real deficiencies, they certainly impair the ability of representative institutions to assume their full roles in the democratic

Table 6.5. Percentage of Survey Respondents Who Perceive Elections as Clean

Country	1996	1997	1998	1999/2000	Average, 1996–2000
Uruguay	83.39	80.77	77.71	78.63	80.13
Chile	74.22	73.41	71.04	80.47	74.78
Costa Rica	79.41	62.27	74.87	73.83	72.60
Panama	62.99	49.34	50.22	76.68	59.81
Nicaragua	74.32	52.11	—	43.89	56.77
Argentina	52.53	56.48	52.59	63.94	56.38
Honduras	42.80	56.54	—	51.91	50.42
Guatemala	38.42	38.51	48.09	70.34	48.84
El Salvador	42.50	40.54	—	39.91	40.99
Peru	53.76	28.56	23.92	41.23	36.87
Brazil	29.25	16.49	32.45	44.84	30.76
Venezuela	8.22	11.88	27.84	67.01	28.74
Bolivia	28.57	28.89	28.67	25.90	28.01
Paraguay	34.57	14.15	36.30	26.61	27.91
Mexico	14.32	41.35	29.30	23.81	27.20
Ecuador	37.59	18.86	23.70	19.80	24.99
Colombia	15.32	13.10	22.60	28.41	19.85
Average	45.42	40.19	42.81	50.42	44.80

Source: *Latinobarómetro* (1996–2000).
Note: This question was not asked in the *Latinobarómetro* surveys from 2001 to 2004.

process, and in some circumstances, may deprive governments and political parties of the legitimacy necessary to govern effectively.

The third measure related to this dimension assesses the extent to which political parties are viewed as central to the democratic political process. It is based on a question from the 1997 and 2003 *Latinobarómetro*, which asked respondents to pick institutions—both from a list of governmental and nongovernmental ones—that they thought were "indispensable to the progress of the country." Table 6.6 shows the percentage of respondents that selected political parties.

Again, there is an extremely wide range across the region. More than half of respondents in Uruguay, Mexico, and Honduras believed political parties to be indispensable; relatively few shared this view in Ecuador, Guatemala, Bolivia, and Colombia. The high percentage of respondents mentioning political parties in Mexico in 1997 was likely due to the historically close relationship between the Partido Revolucionario Institucional (PRI) and the state, and this party's deep penetration into societal organizations. The sharp decline in 2003 may reflect the weakening presence of the PRI in government, with the defeat of the

Table 6.6. Percentage of Survey Respondents Who Consider Political Parties Indispensable to the Progress of the Country, 1997 and 2003

Country	Average, 1997–2003	1997	2003	Percentage change from 1997 to 2003
Uruguay	61.7	64.5	58.9	–8.7
Mexico	59.6	77.4	41.8	–46.0
Honduras	54.5	61.2	47.8	–21.9
Costa Rica	43.7	53.1	34.4	–35.3
Nicaragua	40.1	41.1	39.1	–4.9
Venezuela	39.9	42.2	37.7	–10.7
El Salvador	37.6	42.5	32.6	–23.2
Chile	36.1	40.2	32.0	–20.3
Brazil	35.0	27.2	42.9	58.0
Peru	35.0	30.0	40.1	33.7
Argentina	32.6	34.8	30.4	–12.7
Panama	32.4	37.2	27.6	–25.9
Paraguay	32.0	19.8	44.2	122.7
Colombia	31.9	39.1	24.7	–36.9
Bolivia	30.3	30.4	30.2	–0.8
Guatemala	28.1	30.5	25.7	–15.6
Ecuador	22.6	27.3	17.8	–34.9
Average	38.4	41.1	35.7	–13.0

Source: Latinobarómetro (1997 and 2003).

PRI in the 2000 presidential election, and its decreasing influence in the social and political life of the country.

According to this measure as well, the public image of parties in the region declined between the mid-1990s and 2003. The only cases in which the perceived importance of parties increased were Brazil, Peru, and Paraguay.

Strength of Party Organizations

The fourth dimension of party system institutionalization refers to the strength of party organizations. To what extent are political elites and legislators loyal to their parties? To what extent is the party label associated with a set of ideals, programmatic objectives, and a diverse portfolio of leaders, rather than a single personality? To what extent do party organizations have a presence at the local and national levels, during elections, and between elections? How much money is available for parties to spend on their activities, apart from what is exclusively devoted to particular electoral campaigns?

On a theoretical level, the responses to these questions are extremely important in gauging the relative strength of party organizations, which is essential in estimating the relative institutionalization of party systems. In order to accurately gauge the strength of party organizations, it would be necessary to have comparative information on a variety of indicators, such as the number of party members and activists, the breadth of the geographic distribution of these members, the parties' annual operating budgets, and the extent to which parties are perceived to represent distinct programmatic orientations. However, this information, particularly concerning the activities of organizations and party structures, remains unavailable on a comparative basis.

Given the deficiencies in measuring party organization strength, this dimension is not included in the index of party system institutionalization. But an attempt to measure the strength of party organizations was made by Jones (2005). Jones compiled an index comprised of two dimensions: (1) party continuity, measured on the basis of responses to a question in a survey of legislators conducted by the Latin American Elites Project (PELA, 2005), which probes legislators' perceptions of the extent to which their party exists as a permanent organization rather than merely being an election-time vehicle for electing candidates to office; and (2) party age, which is an average of the percentage of currently existing parties that were present 10 and 25 years ago (Table 6.7).

Based on these criteria, the countries that appear to reflect the greatest party strength are the Dominican Republic, Nicaragua, Uruguay, and Argentina. At the other extreme, the countries with the weakest party organizations are Guatemala, Ecuador, Paraguay, and Brazil.

Index of Party System Institutionalization

The measures developed for the first three dimensions of party system institutionalization are aggregated into a single index in Table 6.9. The values of the component variables and subindexes that went into the calculation of the aggregate index are summarized in Table 6.8. For the reasons mentioned above, the measure of party organization strength is left out of the index. The absence of this dimension is obviously a significant limitation of the index.

In the calculation of the index score for each country, the raw value for each measure within the three dimensions was first rescaled from 1 to 3. The rescaling was carried out considering only the party systems of Latin America. Thus, the rescaling is based on a range of variation that is not as wide as it would be if a larger world sample were considered. The average of the rescaled values of the measures within each dimension was then calculated (criterion 1 had only one measure; criterion 2, two measures; criterion 3, three measures). The index of party system institutionalization was computed as a simple average of the scores for each dimension, thus giving all dimensions equal weight.

According to the measures considered, the most institutionalized party systems are those in Uruguay, Honduras, Mexico, Chile, and El Salvador. In contrast, Ecuador, Peru, Guatemala, Brazil, Colombia, and Bolivia have weakly institutionalized systems. Depending on where the dividing lines are drawn, one can say that the party systems of Costa Rica,

Table 6.7. Strength of Party Organizations, 2005

Country	Index of strength of party organization (average of A and B)	A Party continuity[1]	B Party age (average of C and D)	C % of current parties that existed 10 years ago	D % of current parties that existed 25 years ago
Dominican Republic	98.0	96	100	100	100
Nicaragua	98.0	96	100	100	100
Uruguay	96.5	93	100	100	100
Argentina	94.0	88	100	100	100
Mexico	85.3	87	83.5	100	67
Panama	82.8	82	83.5	100	67
El Salvador	78.3	90	66.5	100	33
Chile	76.8	91	62.5	100	25
Peru	75.0	83	67	67	67
Honduras	74.0	48	100	100	100
Colombia	73.0	46	100	100	100
Venezuela	72.5	78	67	67	67
Bolivia	72.3	82	62.5	75	50
Costa Rica	67.0	84	50	67	33
Brazil	66.0	82	50	100	0
Paraguay	64.5	79	50	50	50
Ecuador	61.5	73	50	75	25
Guatemala	57.5	90	25	50	0

Source: Jones (2005) using data from PELA (2005) for the measure of party continuity.
Note: In the cases of Panama and Brazil, the party organization measure is based only on party age, not party continuity, since these countries were not included in the legislator survey. For these cases, the value in the party continuity column is the regional average.
[1] Percentage of legislators polled who declared that their party was a "permanent organization."

Panama, Paraguay, and Venezuela are moderately institutionalized, while those of Argentina and Nicaragua are characterized by relatively weak institutionalization.

Considering the measures of the three criteria, the countries are ranked in a roughly similar fashion, but some variation is expected, given that the measures relate to different aspects of the broader concept of institutionalization. For example, given the recent opening and broadening of political competition in Mexico and Paraguay, measures showing low electoral volatility and high party system stability over the period of the study are compatible with the finding that citizens remain skeptical about the integrity of the electoral process. Some deviations between the measures, however, are a little more puzzling. For example, the level of identification with parties is lower than might be expected in Chile,

Table 6.8. Summary of Measures Used in the Computation of the Party System Institutionalization Index

Country	Criterion 1: electoral volatility	Criterion 2: party system stability (0 = highest; 100 = lowest)	Criterion 2: party identification (1996/97 and 2003)	Criterion 3: confidence in parties (1996–2004)	Criterion 3: legitimacy of electoral processes (1996–2000)	Criterion 3: parties indispensable to country's progress (1997 and 2003)
Argentina	25.0	33.3	13.8	14.4	56.4	32.6
Bolivia	33.9	39.0	20.2	12.7	28.0	30.3
Brazil	32.5	60.3	15.0	17.1	30.8	35.0
Chile	12.8	2.1	15.7	21.8	74.8	36.1
Colombia	25.6	52.5	16.8	14.6	19.9	31.9
Costa Rica	15.0	30.8	19.5	21.1	72.6	43.7
Ecuador	39.4	82.1	20.8	10.3	25.0	22.6
El Salvador	18.8	40.9	23.6	23.4	41.0	37.6
Guatemala	48.0	99.3	18.0	14.9	48.8	28.1
Honduras	7.0	5.1	28.1	21.6	50.4	54.5
Mexico	16.3	25.4	19.8	21.9	27.2	59.6
Nicaragua	12.8	0.0	28.3	18.2	56.8	40.1
Panama	27.1	12.7	21.9	22.2	59.8	32.4
Paraguay	24.3	24.4	33.5	19.3	27.9	32.0
Peru	52.0	72.1	16.1	16.2	36.9	35.0
Uruguay	14.6	1.1	32.1	32.4	80.1	61.7
Venezuela	33.0	74.1	17.6	19.4	28.7	39.9
Total	**25.8**	**38.5**	**21.2**	**18.9**	**45.0**	**38.4**

Source: Authors' compilation of both original data and data from *Latinobarómetro* (1996–2004).

Table 6.9. Party System Institutionalization in Latin America

Country	Criterion 1: electoral volatility	Criterion 2: party system stability	Criterion 2: party identification (1996/97 and 2003)	Criterion 3: confidence in parties (1996–2004)	Criterion 3: legitimacy of electoral processes (1996–2000)	Criterion 3: parties indispensable to country's progress (1997 and 2003)	Institutionalization index
Uruguay	2.2	3.0	3.0	3.0	3.0	3.0	2.72
Honduras	2.8	2.9	2.7	2.3	2.2	2.8	2.67
Mexico	2.4	2.3	2.2	2.3	1.7	2.9	2.32
Chile	2.7	3.0	1.0	2.0	2.8	1.7	2.30
El Salvador	2.3	2.2	2.4	2.4	2.0	2.2	2.27
Costa Rica	2.6	2.4	1.4	2.0	2.7	2.1	2.26
Panama	2.0	2.7	2.3	2.3	2.5	2.0	2.25
Paraguay	2.1	2.4	3.0	2.2	1.7	2.0	2.25
Venezuela	2.2	1.0	2.6	3.0	2.3	3.0	2.24
Nicaragua	2.6	3.0	2.7	2.1	2.4	2.3	2.06
Argentina	2.2	2.3	1.0	1.4	2.2	1.5	1.85
Bolivia	1.8	2.2	1.6	1.2	1.3	1.4	1.66
Colombia	2.2	1.9	1.1	1.4	1.0	1.5	1.66
Brazil	1.9	1.8	1.0	1.6	1.4	1.6	1.60
Guatemala	1.2	1.0	2.0	1.9	2.2	1.9	1.56
Peru	1.0	1.1	2.0	2.0	1.9	2.1	1.50
Ecuador	1.6	1.3	1.5	1.0	1.0	1.0	1.33
Total	**2.1**	**2.1**	**2.0**	**2.0**	**2.0**	**2.1**	**2.03**

Source: Authors' compilation based on Table 6.8.

considering that electoral support for parties has been relatively stable. In addition, the percentage of Chilean respondents that view parties as critical to their country's progress is not as high as might be expected. As mentioned above, the two-way competition among party coalitions may be a factor in weakening the salience of parties in Chilean politics, or perhaps parties are weakening for other reasons.

Assessing Party System Fragmentation and Polarization

Apart from their level of institutionalization, party systems' fragmentation and polarization are also factors that affect the governance and stability of democratic systems.[12] The number of parties affects the likelihood that the party of the president will obtain a majority of seats in the legislature, and provide sustained legislative support for the executive's policy proposals. A large number of parties also tends to be associated with a higher level of polarization.

Clearly, the effects of a multiparty system, which is most often polarized, in part depend on the level of the institutionalization of the parties involved. For example, when parties are weak, one would expect executive and legislative relations to be more problematic, and the possibilities for forming durable governmental coalitions more limited. On the other hand, it could be argued that more inflexible, highly cohesive parties with loyal societal followings might actually aggravate governance problems if there is already a high level of ideological polarization.

Party System Fragmentation

The fragmentation of party systems is measured using the index of the effective number of parties introduced in Chapter 3.[13] Table 6.10 shows the average of that index for the full study period, as well as the value for the most recent election for each country. Focusing on the figures for the most recent election, it is clear that Latin American party systems range from a few that are close to being two-party systems, to four countries in which between five and seven parties typically obtain significant shares of the legislative seats.

Considering the outcomes of the most recent election, Honduras and Nicaragua have the most concentrated party systems. The party system in Honduras is the only one that remains close to a purely two-party system, with the Partido Liberal de Honduras (PLH) and the Partido Nacional de Honduras (PNH) gaining most of the legislative seats, although they lost some seats to smaller parties in the 1997, 2001, and 2005 elections. Until 1996, a considerable number of parties sought seats in the Nicaraguan congress, although most of them were part of the center-right coalition, called the Unión Nacional Opositora during the 1990 elections, and of Alianza Liberal in the 1996 and 2001 elections. A political reform in 2000 introduced a party extinction clause that set stringent new requirements for the establishment of new parties, and designated the Supreme Electoral Council—controlled

---

[12] These two factors are the basis for the conventional classification of party systems developed by Sartori (1976).
[13] See note 15 in Chapter 3 for an explanation.

Table 6.10. Effective Number of Parties

Based on lower chamber seats

Country	Time span	Number of elections	Effective number of parties	
			Period average	Most recent election
Nicaragua[1]	1990–2001	3	2.28	1.99
Honduras	1981–2001	6	2.15	2.41
Uruguay	1984–2004	5	3.02	2.49
Dominican Republic	1978–2002	7	2.47	2.72
Panama	1994–2004	4	3.56	2.92
Mexico	1979–2003	9	2.37	3.02
Paraguay	1989–2003	4	2.45	3.18
Venezuela	1978–2000	6	3.69	3.44
El Salvador	1985–2003	7	3.17	3.54
Costa Rica	1978–2002	7	2.51	3.68
Argentina[2]	1983–2003	11	2.82	3.82
Peru	1980–2001	6	3.66	4.50
Guatemala	1985–2003	6	3.42	4.56
Bolivia	1980–2002	6	4.51	5.06
Chile[3]	1989–2001	4	5.27	5.94
Colombia	1978–2002	8	3.05	6.80
Ecuador	1979–2002	10	5.90	7.69
Brazil	1986–2002	5	7.06	8.49
Average			3.52	4.24

Source: Authors' compilation using the method of Laakso and Taagepera (1979).
[1] The Union National Opositora (UNO) and the Alianza Liberal in 1996 are each treated as a single party.
[2] The Alianza is treated as one party in 1997 and 1999.
[3] In Chile, the center-left and center-right party coalitions have been unusually durable, in large part because of incentives stemming from a binominal electoral system. Thus, a measure of the effective number of parties that would better reflect the system's actual functioning might be one computed on the basis of party coalitions. If this is done, the average index value for the period would be 2.02 and the value for the most recent election, 2.03.

almost entirely by the Partido Liberal Constitucionalista (PLC) and the Frente Sandinista de Liberación (FSLN)—as arbiter of the new elections law. The result was that 89 of the 90 seats up for election were obtained by the two major parties in the 2001 elections. Nonetheless, the divisions that emerged within the PLC during the government of President Enrique Bolaños (2001–2006) began to give the party system a somewhat more fragmented character in practice.

The Dominican Republic, Uruguay, and Panama also have relatively concentrated party systems, with about 2.5 effective parties each. The Dominican Republic went from a two-party system to the equivalent of a three-party system (2.7 effective parties), with the Partido Revolucionario Social Cristiano (PRSC), the Partido Revolucionario Democrático (PRD) and the Partido de Liberación Democrático (PLD) competing for legislative seats. Outside of these five countries, party systems in the region typically have three or more parties. The last several elections in Paraguay, Costa Rica, and Mexico marked transitions from one or two dominant parties to situations in which three or more political parties came to occupy significant blocs of seats. In Paraguay, the two-party hold of the Colorados and Blancos was loosened by the upsurge of Encuentro Nacional (EN) in 1993 and 1998. The 2003 elections confirmed the trend toward lower party concentration in congress, as the appearance of new political groupings cut into the seats formerly held by the two traditionally dominant parties.

In the 1998 elections in Costa Rica, the PLN and PUSC won significant blocs of seats, and a number of small groupings each obtained a few seats. In the 2002 elections, with the success of Partido Acción Ciudadana (PAC) and Movimiento Libertario (ML), the structure of the party system was transformed from one with two major parties and several small parties represented, to one with four significant parties with the same set of small parties.

The 1997 congressional elections in Mexico spelled the end of the longstanding domination of the Partido Revolucionario Institucional (PRI), which lost its legislative majority for the first time since 1929. Thereafter, the PRI was forced to seek support from representatives of the Partido de Acción Nacional (PAN) or the Partido Revolucionario Democrático (PRD), which each won about one quarter of legislative seats. The trend toward a multiparty system continued in the 2000 elections, when the PRI not only lost the presidency but also obtained fewer legislative seats than the PAN-led alliance. Although the PRI regained a plurality of the seats in the 2003 legislative elections, the three-party system appeared to be well entrenched.

The most fragmented party systems in recent years have been those of Brazil, Ecuador, Chile, Colombia, and Bolivia, with more than five significant parties each. However, given the binominal nature of Chile's electoral system, and the manner in which it pressures parties into forming two broad coalitions, the Chilean political system may be thought to operate as if it were a two-party system. If one considers coalitions rather than parties, the Chilean effective-number-of-parties index is only slightly greater than two.

In Colombia, two parties—the Partido Liberal and the Partido Conservador—traditionally dominated the system, though they were highly factionalized. In the past decade, their strength has declined, leading to a proliferation of parties and small electoral movements. In the 2002 elections, some 37 parties (for the most part, electoral lists aimed at electing a single individual to office) managed to win at least one seat.[14] Thus, the effective number of electoral parties grew from just above three to seven (counting each list as a party).

---

[14] In Colombia, the electoral formula (Hare and greatest remainder) and public financing for campaigns encourage individuals to create separate electoral lists (movements) in order to increase their chance of obtaining seats through remainders. Given the proliferation of electoral lists, most of the seats are awarded through remainders rather than by simple quota. By limiting parties to presenting a single list in each district and by changing to the D'Hondt formula for allocating seats, the 2003 electoral reform aimed to contain this fragmentation in the party system.

In sum, the typical system in Latin America is now a multiparty system with between three and four effective parties. The average number of parties across Latin American countries has grown significantly since the beginning of the study period. Most of the two-party systems found at the beginning of the study period have given way to two-and-a-half or three-party systems. This change reflects a greater democratic competition in countries such as Brazil, Mexico, and Paraguay. The party system became more concentrated in just a few countries (Uruguay and Panama, in particular), while increased fragmentation could be observed in Argentina, Bolivia, Colombia, Costa Rica, Ecuador, and Peru.

Party System Polarization

Though clearly important to the functioning of democratic systems, the polarization of party systems in the region is more difficult to measure than fragmentation.

High polarization levels indicate that parties at each end of the spectrum represent very different approaches to policy. Polarization can be problematic for democratic governance, especially when differences between parties are so significant that compromise solutions are not possible. But differences between parties in programmatic terms also can be beneficial for the quality of representation and the efficiency of electoral accountability mechanisms.

Polarization at the level of the electorate is assessed using data from *Latinobarómetro*, and an approach combining the elite and electorate level developed by Jones (2005), using data from *Latinobarómetro* and the legislative surveys of the Latin American Elites Project (PELA).

Without considering any systematic data, it seems clear that in most countries the degree of polarization along the traditional left and right ideological divide declined considerably among both the general public and the elite between the 1960s and the 1990s. The fall of communism in Eastern Europe and the decline of the extreme left have closed this gap across much of the world. However, there remain bases for impassioned political differences along this traditional rift, as well as in respect to general political values, religion, ethnicity, and cultural issues. Recently, ideological differences appear to be deepening in some countries, with leftist or populist candidates gaining influence or winning the presidency. Over the past decade, the potential for political conflict has surfaced in the continued guerrilla warfare in Colombia, and in outbreaks of mass demonstrations and violent social protests in several other countries. If not readily apparent, the potential for upheaval simmers below the surface when economic opportunities are limited, the middle class is relatively small, and severe social and economic inequality remains widespread.

The decrease in ideological polarization clearly contributed to the durability of the current wave of democracy. Countries where prior experiences with democracy had been disrupted by sharp political divisions—and at times, open subversion from the left and the right—benefited in the 1980s and 1990s from societal and elite attitudes that were more favorable to the functioning of democracy.

The first approach to assessing polarization is one that focuses simply on ideological polarization among citizens. In each year of the *Latinobarómetro* survey, respondents were asked to place themselves on an ideological scale from 0 to 10, with 0 marking the furthest left and 10 the furthest right. The degree of polarization in public attitudes is assessed by calculating the standard deviation (or the spread) in the distribution of the responses to this question. Assuming a normal distribution,[15] if the mean response in a given country is 5, a standard deviation of 2 implies that about 68 percent of the responses are between 3 and 7. On the other hand, if the standard deviation is 3, a wider range, from 2 to 8, is required in order to include the same percentage of responses. Thus, in the second case, respondents' ideological placements reflect a much greater degree of polarization.

Table 6.11 shows the average, for four survey years, of the standard deviations of self-placement on the ideological scale. According to this measure, polarization of general public opinion is greatest in Nicaragua, Venezuela, Honduras, and El Salvador. In addition to having the greatest ideological distance between citizens, these countries are among those in which these differences have increased the most in recent years. One finds the least polarization among citizens in Argentina, Peru, Bolivia, and Chile.

Jones (2005) developed a more sophisticated index that attempts to more specifically gauge the extent to which ideological divisions in the electorate are reflected in divisions in the party system. This index measures the extent of the relationship between citizens' left and right placements and their party preferences, and legislators' assessments of their own party's left and right placement, as well as that of other parties. The measure of mass opinion is based on two questions from the *Latinobarómetro* for the years 2002 to 2004: (1) "If elections were held next Sunday, which party would you vote for?" and (2) the ideological scale question considered above. Legislator opinion is calculated on the basis of two questions from a survey of legislators conducted by PELA (2004). Respondents were asked: (1) "On an ideological scale from 1 to 10, from left to right, how would you rate all the parties?" and (2) "On a ideological scale from 1 to 10, from left to right, where would you place your own party?"

Data from these questions were used to calculate one measure of ideological polarization for parties in the electorate and two measures of ideological polarization for parties in congress, which were then averaged to yield a general gauge of ideological polarization in the 18 Latin American countries studied, as shown in Table 6.11.

According to this measure, El Salvador stands out as having the most ideologically structured party system in the region, followed by Nicaragua, Uruguay, Chile, and Brazil. At the other end of the spectrum, Paraguay, Colombia, Costa Rica, Honduras, and Panama have relatively low ideological polarization among the electorate and in congress.[16]

Given the difficulty of capturing the concept of polarization, and given that the various measures classify the countries differently, only a very tentative classification of countries

---

[15] A normal distribution means that the distribution pattern of the responses is roughly symmetric on both sides of the mean and is shaped like a bell curve—meaning that the bulk of the responses is clustered fairly close to the mean, and gradually recedes as one moves further from the mean.

[16] Recent studies by Rosas (2005) and Luna and Zechmeister (2005) represent more rigorous and comprehensive approaches to using mass and elite survey data to analyze the programmatic character of parties. Rosas finds, for instance, that legislatures in Chile, Mexico, and Uruguay are organized in fairly ideological terms, while those in Brazil, the Dominican Republic, Ecuador, Peru, and Venezuela are not. Argentina, Colombia, and Costa Rica are found to be intermediate cases.

Table 6.11. Polarization in the Electorate and among Party Elites, 1996–2004

Country	Spread of left-right placements (average, 1996–2004)	Overall polarization
El Salvador	2.99	10.00
Nicaragua	3.30	5.66
Uruguay	2.63	4.92
Chile	2.53	4.61
Brazil	2.98	2.84
Peru	2.34	2.06
Mexico	2.61	1.74
Ecuador	2.90	1.56
Guatemala	2.94	1.52
Venezuela	3.19	1.32
Bolivia	2.43	1.08
Argentina	2.19	1.00
Panama	2.84	0.86
Honduras	3.02	0.75
Costa Rica	2.68	0.70
Colombia	2.79	0.60
Paraguay	2.55	0.52
Average	2.76	2.46

Source: Authors' compilation, based on *Latinobarómetro* data (1996–2004) and Jones (2005).
Note: The measure of overall polarization is based on Jones (2005).

is possible.[17] This tentative classification, based on the two different approaches considered above, ranks the 18 countries studied as follows:

- Between high and moderate: El Salvador, Nicaragua, Uruguay, and Brazil
- Moderate: Guatemala, Panama, Ecuador, Mexico, Bolivia, Peru, Chile, and Venezuela
- Low: the Dominican Republic, Costa Rica, Argentina, Colombia, Paraguay, and Honduras

Conclusions

In keeping with the considerable differences in political histories across Latin America, and in particular, the extent of previous national experiences with democracy, the nature of party

---

[17] For instance, according to the public opinion survey, Chile is characterized by a low level of polarization, but this changes to a fairly high level of polarization when one considers the opinions of legislators about their own party's ideological placement relative to that of other parties.

systems and how they have evolved varies greatly across the region. This chapter has found that party systems in a small group of countries are reasonably well institutionalized, while in other systems few parties are able to maintain citizen support, party organizations remain weak, and representatives show little loyalty to the party through which they were elected.

In a few countries, including Peru, Ecuador, Venezuela, and Colombia, party systems have clearly weakened. Colombia and Venezuela had relatively institutionalized party systems at the beginning of the study period, but by the end, their party systems were much more fragmented, with more diffuse bases of social support. Party systems in Peru and Ecuador did not reach such a relatively high level of institutionalization, and the parties that did compose the system at the beginning of the period were seriously weakened or replaced by the end of it. In contrast, the party systems in Chile, Uruguay, Honduras, and El Salvador either maintained or built on their relatively high level of institutionalization. With the emergence of more vigorous and fair electoral competition, the party system in Mexico can also be viewed as progressing toward institutionalization in democratic terms.

During the period of the study, the party systems in the region became more fragmented, with several two-party systems gradually becoming two-and-a-half or multiparty systems. The group of countries with three-and-a-half or more parties has expanded to include seven countries.

Several countries have party systems in which two or, at most, three parties have dominated the political arena. In these countries—Honduras, Paraguay, Mexico, Costa Rica, Guatemala, Argentina, Chile (considering its coalitions), and Colombia—it has been fairly common for presidents to be elected with their party winning a majority or near-majority in congress, or for presidents to build governing coalitions—though not always in a durable and effective manner. However, in the remaining countries, and particularly those with four or more effective parties (Ecuador, Brazil, Bolivia, and Peru), minority governments have been more common, and governing through normal representative channels has in many instances been extremely difficult. Brazil has at least temporarily and partially managed some of these difficulties through reasonably successful interparty coalitions backing the governments of Presidents Fernando Henrique Cardoso and Luiz Inácio Lula de Silva. But implementing reforms remains laborious at times and potentially costly in the efficiency of resource allocation. At the same time, in Bolivia the second-round election of presidents by the legislature facilitated the formation of government coalitions during the 1980s and 1990s, in circumstances in which this might otherwise have been difficult.

In Peru, President Alberto Fujimori overcame the difficulties of governing a fragmented congress by remaking the constitutional framework (with the backing of the military), which greatly amplified his power. The impact of the more fragmented party system in Venezuela initially worked to the benefit of a populist president, who also has succeeded in obtaining the acquiescence of other institutions that might serve to check his power. But in a different political context, such a high level of party system fragmentation could complicate the achievement of stable and effective democratic governance.

Classifying Latin American party systems according to their degree of ideological polarization is more difficult. While differences between countries clearly exist, they are not as readily measurable or discernable as other party system features. Other forms of polarization, such as those reflecting support or opposition to given political personalities, or different sets of moral values, may not be captured by traditional measures of ideological polarization. Based on the measures examined, polarization may be a factor compromising governance capacity and political stability in El Salvador, Nicaragua, and Venezuela—countries in which polarization is fairly high and seems to have increased in the last few years. Since most systems appear to be less polarized than they were in the 1960s and 1970s, the impact that different degrees of polarization have on the performance of democratic systems is less clear. Amid high levels of poverty, underdevelopment, and extreme inequality, latent bases for political conflict may be as important as the visible level of polarization among political elites. Such conditions are favorable for the emergence of populist leaders who can suddenly and profoundly alter the structure of political competition, as has recently been observed in Venezuela, Bolivia, and other countries in the region.

References

Arriagada Herrera, Genaro. 2001. Crisis de los sistema de partidos en América Latina. *Democratización del estado: el desafío pendiente*. Lima: Asociación Civil Transparencia.

Bartolini, Stefano, and Peter Mair. 1990. *Identity, Competition, and Electoral Availability: The Stabilization of European Electorates, 1885–1985*. Cambridge: Cambridge University Press.

Coppedge, Michael. 1998. The Dynamic Diversity of Latin American Party Systems. *Party Politics* 4(4): 549–570.

Eurobarometer. 1991. *European Elections, 1989. Pre-Election Survey, March–April* 1989. Ann Arbor, MI: Inter-University Consortium for Political and Social Research.

Jones, Mark. 2005. The Role of Parties and Party Systems in the Policymaking Process. Paper presented at the seminar "State Reform, Public Policies and Policymaking Processes," organized by the Inter-American Development Bank, February 28–March 2, Washington, DC.

Kenney, Charles D. 2003. The Death and Rebirth of a Party System, Peru, 1978–2001. *Comparative Political Studies* 36(10).

Laakso, Markku, and Rein Taagepera. 1979. The Effective Number of Parties: A Measure with Application to Western Europe. *Comparative Political Studies* 12(1).

La Palombara, Joseph, and Myron Weiner (eds.). 1996. *Political Parties and Political Development*. Princeton: Princeton University Press.

Latinobarómetro. 1996–2004. *Latinobarómetro: Opinión Pública Latinoamericana*. Santiago, Chile.

Lipset, Seymour Martin, and Stein Rokkan. 1967. *Party Systems and Voter Alignments*. New York: Free Press.

Luna, Juan P., and Elizabeth J. Zechmeister. 2005. Political Representation in Latin America: A Study of Elite-Mass Congruence in Nine Countries. *Comparative Political Studies* 38(4).

Mainwaring, Scott, and Timothy R. Scully (eds.). 1995. *Building Democratic Institutions: Party Systems in Latin America*. Stanford, CA: Stanford University Press.

Mainwaring, Scott, and Matthew Soberg Shugart (eds.). 1997. *Presidentialism and Democracy in Latin America*. New York: Cambridge University Press.

Pedersen, Mogens N. 1983. Changing Patterns of Electoral Volatility in European Party Systems, 1948–1977: Explorations in Explanations. In Hans Daalder and Peter Mair (eds.), *Western European Party Systems: Continuity and Change*. Beverly Hills, CA: Sage.

PELA (Proyecto de Elites Latinoamericanas). 1996–2005. Manuel Alcántara, Director. Salamanca, Spain: Universidad de Salamanca.

Rosas, Guillermo. 2005. The Ideological Organization of Latin American Legislative Parties: An Empirical Analysis of Elite Policy Preferences. *Comparative Political Studies* 38(7).

Samuels, David. 2002. Presidentialized Parties: The Separation of Powers and Party Organization and Behavior. *Comparative Political Studies* 35(4).

Sani, Giacomo, and Giovanni Sartori. 1983. Polarization, Fragmentation and Competition in Western Democracies. In Hans Daalder and Peter Mair (eds.), *Western European Party Systems: Continuity and Change*. Beverly Hills, CA: Sage.

Sartori, Giovanni. 1976. *Parties and Party Systems: A Framework for Analysis*. New York: Cambridge University Press.

CHAPTER 7

Intraparty Democratic Processes and the Financing of Political Parties

The examination of political party systems in the previous chapter shows that on the whole those systems are weakly institutionalized, moderately to highly fragmented, and moderately polarized. That analysis leaves out two critical dimensions of party politics: the internal processes by which party officials are selected and candidates nominated, and the rules for financing political parties and electoral campaigns. Those topics are the subject of this chapter.

Citizens' perceptions that politicians and parties are out of touch with their concerns, are corrupt, and tend to serve the interests of their financial patrons have contributed to disenchantment with democratic politics. Control of parties by long-standing *caudillos* and local bosses, and parties' limited connection to rank and file members, undermine public respect for political parties. At the same time, the growing importance of money in electoral campaigns calls into question basic democratic principles of political equality and accountability and increases the prevalence of corruption and illicit activities. These perceived limitations of the democratic systems that took hold in the 1970s and 1980s have given rise to growing demands for reforms to democratize the selection of party leaders and candidates for public office and to regulate the financing of politics so as to curb the influence of money.

The Internal Democratization of Political Parties

The development and operation of political parties are affected by the relationships that evolve within parties, particularly the interaction between the party chairperson, the leader of the party in the legislature, and the president. Perpetual conflict among party factions and individual politicians appears to be at odds with the kind of leadership necessary for effective policy making in the broader public interest. As important as this topic is, particularly with respect to the operation of presidential systems, it is not directly addressed in this chapter. Instead, our main focus is on the processes by which party leaders are selected and candidates are nominated for elected offices.

How these matters are addressed is influenced by the dual nature of political parties. While the strict internal organization of political parties—that is, their administration and the configuration of their leadership—could be conceived as a private matter, the nomination of candidates for political office is by nature public. It is in this latter area where demands for transparency and participation have been strongest.

These demands have resulted in the emergence of two prevalent mechanisms for selecting candidates for public office: party conventions and primaries. A third mechanism—the selection of candidates by the top party leadership—has become less common, particularly with regard to the nomination of candidates for the presidency, but also in the nomination of candidates for other elected offices.

The first and more traditional mechanism—conventions—involves an assembly of representatives that has the power to elect party officials and nominate candidates for public office. Although this mechanism has begun to be displaced by primaries, it continues to be important in the nomination processes of many parties in the region. The second, more recent mechanism is primaries, which have been adopted as a means to further open the process of selecting candidates. Primaries entail the selection of candidates for public office through free, fair, competitive, and direct elections by secret vote either by party members (closed primaries) or by all citizens who wish to participate (open primaries).

The move toward greater intraparty democracy has broad benefits. First, such reforms deepen democracy by extending it to the internal workings of the political parties. Politicians can hardly speak out with authority in the name of democracy if their leaders and candidates emerge from nondemocratic practices. Second, competition at the heart of political parties can enhance mobility among party elites and diversify the leadership structure. Third, primaries raise the competence and legitimacy of candidates both within the party and among the broader public, as well as the degree to which they represent the different interests within the party and society as a whole.[1] Fourth, broader segments of society, or at least a broader range of activists, are encouraged to participate and take on leadership responsibilities in political parties, and thereby become more engaged in the democratic process and in strengthening one of its key institutions. Finally, internal party democracy is expected to lend added legitimacy to democratic processes and trust in political parties by helping to offset negative practices such as political nepotism, patronage networks (*clientelismo*), and control of the party from the top by bosses (*caciquismo*)—thereby also enhancing responsiveness to citizens.[2]

Nonetheless, internal democratization may not bring immediate benefits to specific political parties and may present some trade-offs with respect to political representation. Primaries may disrupt the internal harmony or the unified external image and ideological

---

[1] A recent empirical study of the use of primaries in Latin America supports the conclusion that the use of these mechanisms has resulted in more viable candidates (Carey and Polga-Hecimovich, 2006).

[2] Citizen confidence in political parties has tended to be higher in countries that have legislated primaries (Alcántara Sáez, 2002).

coherence of parties. Weakening the programmatic character of parties could make elections less effective as mechanisms for holding officials accountable for their policies (as discussed in Chapters 3 and 6). In addition, adverse results for incumbent leaders, such as victories by outsider candidates, could initially cause instability and uncertainty, and thereby weaken individual political parties, if only in the short term. Some scholars have argued that because primaries tend to be dominated by more extreme party activists, weaker candidates, less representative of the broader society, could gain control of their party's banner (Buquet and Chasquetti, 2004; Colomer, 2002). Profound reforms of constitutions and laws governing political parties and elections were adopted during the final two decades of the 20th century, a reflection of the transition in many countries from authoritarianism to democracy. These reforms initially sidestepped the issue of the internal democratization of political parties and the more difficult subject of party financing. However, intraparty democratization was addressed more directly in a wave of reforms that began in the second half of the 1990s.

Since then, the trend in the 18 countries of the region has been toward higher levels of transparency, openness, and participation in the selection of political party leaders and in the nomination of presidential candidates. In a growing number of countries, where party standard-bearers were once selected mainly by top party leaders or closed party caucuses, various types of primary processes are now used.

Electing Party Officials and Nominating Candidates

The internal democratization of political parties is shaped by different factors, including the rules of the political system. In particular, national laws influence intraparty processes for selecting party leaders and nominating candidates for public office (Bendel, 1998). Those laws vary in type and scope (Tables 7.1 and 7.2).

Reflecting the complex distinction between what is considered private and public, few Latin American constitutions stipulate how political party leaders should be elected, but many regulate the way parties nominate their candidates for public office. Notable examples are Uruguay and Venezuela. The internal functioning of parties generally is considered a private matter—up to the point of selecting candidates for public office. The trend toward the democratization of candidate selection has brought with it a greater control of parties under public law, as has occurred in Bolivia and Colombia.

In Argentina, Colombia, Costa Rica, Honduras, Panama, Paraguay, Peru, Dominican Republic, Uruguay, and Venezuela the election of party officials is regulated by law. By contrast, in Bolivia, Brazil, Chile, Ecuador, El Salvador, Guatemala, Mexico, and Nicaragua, neither the constitution nor electoral laws deal in any way with the selection of party officials, allowing political parties to organize themselves according to their own rules (Table 7.1).

The picture is somewhat different for the selection of candidates. In some countries, such as Costa Rica, Uruguay, and Venezuela, the nomination process is regulated by the constitution, whereas in other countries it is governed by legislation, as in Argentina, Bolivia, Colombia, Costa Rica, the Dominican Republic, Honduras, Panama, Paraguay, Peru, and Uruguay (Table 7.2).

Table 7.1. Constitution, Electoral Law, or Bylaw? Regulation of the Process of Selecting Party Leaders

Country	Is selection process regulated by national law?	Do electoral laws clearly establish the mechanism for selecting party leaders?	Does law defer to party bylaws?
Argentina	Yes	Yes[1]	
Bolivia	No	No	✓
Brazil	No	No	
Chile	No	No	
Colombia	Yes, electoral law	Yes, internal caucuses[2]	✓
Costa Rica	Yes	Ambiguous; selection must be consistent with "principles of internal democracy"	✓
Dominican Republic	Yes, electoral law	Yes. Compulsory for all parties, simultaneously held, organized, controlled, and judged by Electoral Court, with voluntary vote open to all registered voters	✓
Ecuador	No	No	✓
El Salvador	No	No	✓
Guatemala	No	No	✓
Honduras	Yes, electoral law	Yes, internal elections, direct, secret vote of members at all party levels	✓
Mexico	No	No	✓
Nicaragua	No	No	✓
Panama	Yes, electoral law	No	✓
Paraguay	Yes	Yes, elections by free, direct, secret, equal vote of members	✓
Peru	Yes	Ambiguous; selection must be governed by rules of internal democracy[3]	✓
Uruguay	Yes, constitution	Yes	✓
Venezuela	Yes, constitution	No	✓

Source: Freidenberg (2005).

[1] According to Law 23,298 of 2002, as amended, elections of party leaders and nomination of candidates for public office, except the presidency and the vice presidency, are governed by the constitution, by party bylaws, and to the extent applicable, by electoral law.

[2] Basic statute on political parties and movements and *Ley de Consultas Internas* (article 1).

[3] Article 25 of Law 28,094 provides that intraparty elections are to be conducted according to party bylaws and that they must be consistent with the law of the land; article 19 indicates that intraparty elections are to be governed by the rules of internal democracy set forth in the law and in party bylaws.

Table 7.2. Regulation of the Nominating Process

Country	Is the nominating process regulated by the constitution?	Is the nominating process regulated by national law (electoral law, law on political parties, or other laws)?
Argentina	No	Yes, Organic Law on Parties 25,611, with amendments of Law 23,298
Bolivia	No	Yes[1]
Brazil	No	No
Chile	No	No[2]
Colombia	No	Yes,[3] Basic Statute on Parties and Movements and Special Law on Internal Popular Consultations. Law 130 of 1994
Costa Rica	Yes	Yes, Electoral Code (article 74)
Dominican Republic	No	Yes, Electoral Law
Ecuador	No	No
El Salvador	No	No
Guatemala	No	No
Honduras	No	Yes, Electoral and Political Organization Law (articles 18–19)
Mexico	No	No
Nicaragua	No	No
Panama	No	Yes, Law 22 of 1997
Paraguay	No	Yes, Electoral Code of 1996 (article 33)
Peru	No	Yes
Uruguay	Yes	Yes, Law 17063 of 1998 (articles 1, 3, 5–8)
Venezuela	Yes	No

Source: Freidenberg (2005); Zovatto (2006).

[1] The political party law establishes the electoral character of internal party mechanisms. Each party defines the mechanism it will use to choose candidates.

[2] The law on political parties requires that the party leadership (Consejo General) submit its presidential candidate for ratification by party members. The candidate is proclaimed official only once accepted by the party members.

[3] Electoral legislation does not require parties to hold primary elections, but it does regulate them if parties choose to hold them.

Political parties use various mechanisms for nominating presidential candidates (Table 7.3). These can be classified according to the scope of participation and the method used. The classification based on scope hinges on whether candidates are elected by party members alone or in primaries open to citizens who are not party members. Classification by method requires determining whether the party uses primaries, conventions, nomination by party leaders (followed in some cases by internal elections), or primaries subject to ratification by national party conventions (Freidenberg, 2003).

Table 7.3. How Latin America's Political Parties Nominate Presidential Candidates, 1978 (or Transition Year) to 2004

Country	Open primaries	Closed primaries	Conventions	Party leadership	Party leaders propose candidates; internal primaries are then held	Primaries subject to ratification by national party conventions
Argentina	IU (1989), FREPASO (1994), FREPASO-UCR (1999), UCR (2002)	PJ (1988)[1]	PJ (1982, 1994, 1999, 2002),[1] UCR (1982, 1989, 1994)			
Bolivia	MNR (1999), MIR (1999)[1]		UCS,[2] MNR,[2] MIR,[2] ADN,[2] MAS (2002)	UCS		
Brazil		PT (2002)	PDT, PMDB, PSDB, PFL			
Chile	Concertación (1993, 1999, 2001)	PS	PPD (1993, 1999, 2001)		PDC, RN, UDI (the three parties in 1993, 1999, 2001)	
Colombia	PLC (1990, 1994)[1]	PCC (1998)	PCC (1990, 1994, 2002), PLC (1998, 2002)[1]			
Costa Rica	PLN (1985, 1989, 1993, 1997, 2001), PUSC (1989, 1993, 2002)[1,4]					
Dominican Republic	PRSC (1996, 2002)	PRD (since 1982)	PRSC[2] PRD (2002), PLD (1999)	PRSC (1999)	PLD (2002)[3]	
Ecuador	ID (1987), DP (2002)		ID (1984,1991, 1998, 2002), DP, PSC (1978,1984, 1991, 2002)	PRE, MUPP-NP (1996, 1998, 2002)		

(continued)

Table 7.3. (continued)

Country	Open primaries	Closed primaries	Conventions	Party leadership	Party leaders propose candidates; internal primaries are then held	Primaries subject to ratification by national party conventions
El Salvador		FMLN (1994, 1999, 2003)	ARENA (1994, 1999, 2003)			
Guatemala		PAN (2003)	FRG (2002), PAN			
Honduras		PLH, PNH (both parties 1985, 1993, 1997, 2000)				
Mexico	PRI (1999)	PRD, PAN (2000), PRI (since 2001)[5]	PAN, PRD (2000)	PRI (until 1999)		
Nicaragua			PLC (1996, 2001)	PLC		FSLN (1996, 2001)
Panama		PA (1998), PRD (1998, 2004), PDC (1998)	PA (1993, 2003), PRD (1993)[2]			
Paraguay		ANR-PC (1990, 1994, 1999), PLRA (1990, 1994, 1999), PEN (1990, 1994, 1999)				
Peru		APRA/PAP (1985, 2000)	APRA/PAP, AP			

(continued)

Table 7.3. (continued)

Country	Open primaries	Closed primaries	Conventions	Party leadership	Party leaders propose candidates; internal primaries are then held	Primaries subject to ratification by national party conventions
Uruguay	EP-FA (1999, 2003), PC (1999, 2003), PN (1999, 2003)[4]		EP-FA,[2] PC,[2] PN[2]			
Venezuela	COPEI (1993)	AD (1968, 1978, 1983, 1993, 1998)	AD, COPEI (1987), MAS (1988, 1998)	MVR, PPT, PV		

Source: Freidenberg (2005).
Note: The full names of the parties are listed in Appendix 7.1.
[1] More than one actor participates in the process.
[2] The mechanism was used until electoral reforms were implemented and electoral norms modified.
[3] The national party conventions qualify the candidates, who then compete among themselves.
[4] According to party rules, the leadership has the right to ratify the results of the primaries (or conventions) in which party members choose the presidential nominee. In practical terms, the primaries are open, since electors declare their affiliation to a party at the polling place.
[5] No election has yet been held under the new party rule.

The Latin American Experience with Primary Elections

Since the trend in the region favors primaries, we will focus on this mechanism for selecting candidates. The countries of the region can be divided into three groups according to their current position with respect to primaries: (1) countries in which primary elections are mandated and regulated by law; (2) countries in which primaries have been held but are not regulated by law; and (3) countries in which primaries have been held only very rarely and are not regulated by law (Table 7.4).

Primaries can be further distinguished based on the following criteria (Figure 7.1 and Table 7.5):

- Are they open (all citizens may participate) or closed (only party members may participate)?
- Are they held separately (each party holds its elections on different days) or simultaneously (all on the same day)?
- Are they overseen by an electoral management body?
- Is public funding provided?

Countries in Which Primary Elections Are Legally Recognized

The constitutions or national legislation of 11 Latin American countries contain provisions regarding the use of primaries (see Table 7.4). In all of these countries except Colombia, the law requires that parties hold primary elections and regulates those elections. In Colombia the law does not require parties to conduct primaries but does regulate those that parties choose to hold. Costa Rica was the first to adopt such provisions, followed by Honduras in 1985–89; Colombia in 1994; Paraguay in 1996; Panama in 1997; and Uruguay, Bolivia, and Venezuela in 1999. Recently, Argentina (2002), Peru (2003), and the Dominican Republic (2004) have also passed laws governing the selection of candidates.

For years in *Costa Rica*, electoral legislation has mandated a system of party primaries (known as "national conventions") as a free, universal, direct, secret polling mechanism for nominating presidential candidates. In some electoral districts, popular elections are also held for other representative offices. Political parties decide whether these will be open or closed and when to schedule them. Formally, the results of the primaries are subject to ratification by the party leadership, but it is doubtful that the results would in fact be overturned. The two main political parties—the Partido de Liberación Nacional (PLN) and the Partido Unidad Social Cristiana (PUSC)—hold open primaries on different days. No public funding is provided specifically for this activity. The national voter registry is used, and the country's electoral management body gets involved only if conflicts arise.

In *Uruguay*, the 1996 constitutional reform established an open primary procedure for political parties seeking to field presidential candidates. The parties hold their primaries simultaneously on the last Sunday in April (the general election is in October). The 1998 Internal Elections Law for Political Parties provides that the Electoral Court is responsible for hearing cases dealing with primary elections. Enforcement of the law began in April 1999. The same law requires that the party primaries are to be held simultaneously.

Table 7.4. Primary Elections in Latin America

Country	Regulated by the constitution or political/ electoral legislation	Observed in practice
Costa Rica	Yes	Yes
Honduras	Yes	Yes
Panama	Yes	Yes
Paraguay	Yes	Yes
Uruguay	Yes	Yes
Venezuela	Yes	Yes
Argentina	Yes	Yes (sometimes)
Bolivia	Yes	Yes (sometimes)
Dominican Republic	Yes	Yes (sometimes)
Peru	Yes	Yes (sometimes)
Colombia	Yes (not mandatory)	Yes (sometimes)
Chile	No	Yes (sometimes)
El Salvador	No	Yes (sometimes)
Mexico	No	Yes (sometimes)
Nicaragua	No	Yes (sometimes)
Ecuador	No	Yes (twice)
Brazil	No	Yes (once)
Guatemala	No	Yes (once)

Source: Alcántara (2002), with updates by the authors.
Note: The shaded countries are those in which primaries are regulated by law. The nonshaded countries are those where primaries are not required but have been held sometimes at least by some parties.

Figure 7.1 Classifying Primary Elections

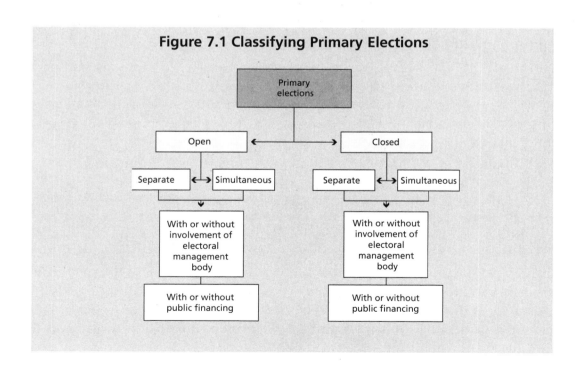

Democracies in Development

Table 7.5. National Regulation of Nominating Procedures

	Are intraparty elections regulated by the constitution or national law?		What electoral mechanisms are regulated?		Characteristics of intraparty elections		
	Constitution	Law	Primary	Other	Are elections supervised by an electoral agency?	Are primaries simultaneous or separate?	Is public financing provided?
Argentina	No	Yes	Yes, open	n.a.	Yes, judges appointed by Justicia Electoral (upon request of political parties)	Simultaneous for each party	No
Bolivia	No	Yes	Yes	n.a.	No[1]	Separate	No
Brazil	No	No	No	n.a.	n.a.	n.a.	No
Chile	No	Yes	No	Yes, ratification by plebiscite	n.a.	n.a.	No
Colombia	No	Optional	Yes, open	n.a.	Yes, CNE	Separate	Yes
Costa Rica	Yes	Yes	Yes, closed/ open	n.a.	Only to settle disputes	Separate	No
Dominican Republic	No	Yes	Yes, open	n.a.	n.a.	n.a.	No
Ecuador	No	No	No	n.a.	n.a.	n.a.	No
El Salvador	No	No	No	n.a.	n.a.	n.a.	No
Guatemala	No	Yes	No	Yes, convention	n.a.	n.a.	No
Honduras	No	Yes	Yes, open	n.a.	Yes, TSE	Simultaneous	No
Mexico	No	No	No	n.a.	n.a.	n.a.	No

(continued)

Table 7.5. (continued)

	Are intraparty elections regulated by the constitution or national law?		What electoral mechanisms are regulated?		Characteristics of intraparty elections		
	Constitution	Law	Primary	Other	Are elections supervised by an electoral agency?	Are primaries simultaneous or separate?	Is public financing provided?
Nicaragua	No	No	No	n.a.	n.a.	n.a.	No
Panama	No	Yes	Yes, closed	n.a.	No (only to settle potential conflicts)	Simultaneous	Yes
Paraguay	No	Yes	Yes, closed	n.a.	No	Separate	No
Peru	No	Yes	Yes, closed/open	Yes, convention	Yes, ONPE	Separate	No
Uruguay	Yes	Yes	Yes, open	n.a.	Yes, CE	Simultaneous	No
Venezuela	Yes	Yes	Yes, closed	n.a.	Yes, CNE	Separate	No

Sources: Freidenberg (2006); Zovatto (2006).
Note: n.a. = not applicable.
[1] An oversight agency was given regulatory authority in 1991 but it was withdrawn in 2001.

Democracies in Development

Because no party membership registries exist, the primary election for all political parties begins and ends on the same day; voting for a political party is tantamount to affiliating with it. Although voting is not mandatory, primary elections are backed by all the guarantees and requirements characteristic of any national electoral process. Any candidate obtaining one vote more than 50 percent of the total vote is automatically nominated as the party's presidential candidate for the general election. If no candidate wins a majority, the candidate is elected by political party convention, with no restrictions on the field of potential candidates.

Since the return to democracy in 1989, political parties in *Paraguay* have regularly held internal closed elections to constitute national and departmental assemblies that then elect the party's leadership bodies. A reform adopted in April 1996 requires that candidates for any elected office must be elected by party members through a free, fair, direct and secret closed primary.

Each political party organizes elections to be held on a date of its choosing and has its own rules and supervisory mechanisms. No specific public funding is available, and there is little oversight by national electoral authorities. To vote in the primary one must be registered with the respective party.

In *Panama*, closed primary elections were adopted through reforms to the electoral code enacted in 1997. Those reforms require that parties with candidates on the presidential ballot must hold primary elections, but they do not apply to allied parties endorsing the presidential candidate of another party. In 1998, the first primary elections were held to elect presidential and vice presidential candidates within the Partido Arnulfista (PA), the Partido Revolucionario Democrático (PRD), and the Partido Democrático Cristiano (PDC), currently known as the Partido Popular (PP). Other parties allied with one of these three parties, rather than putting forth their own candidates.

In 2001 the nation considered a proposal for a system of primaries for all elected positions, in addition to president and vice president. However, the proposal failed to receive sufficient support, and it was agreed that the system then in effect would be maintained. Even so, the government eliminated from the broader set of electoral reforms the proposal to require the selection of presidential candidates through primaries, in favor of having primaries be optional and for all elected offices. This represented a step back from the 1997 reform, because parties that had conducted primaries in 1999, no longer did so in 2004. Elsewhere the new law provides that voters must register with a political party before casting a primary ballot. Approval was also given for the allocation of public funds to cover expenses related to the holding of primary elections.

The national elections tribunal has no jurisdiction or power over the internal procedures of political groups; it only sends delegates to act as mediators to resolve potential conflicts or to collaborate in organizing conventions or primaries, all at the request of the parties. Because the tribunal maintains the electoral registry, however, the parties depend on it to some extent (for example, to determine quorums).

Bolivia introduced primary elections in 1999. The law on political parties stipulates that any party, when formed, must be officially recognized and adopt rules and procedures ensuring fully democratic primaries by means of free, direct, and secret voting under the supervision of the national and departmental electoral courts. The law reinforces the institutionalization of the primary process by prohibiting waivers of compliance with party rules, in essence forbidding extraordinary procedures or exemptions from the rules for individuals or groups of party members. In short, the legislation ensured that party leaders at all levels, including candidates for all elected posts in the country, would be elected. But this innovative reform was circumscribed by a series of decisions of the National Electoral Court in 2001, which argued that it was not advisable for the parties to hold primaries. In addition, the decisions withdrew the National Electoral Court from the supervision of intraparty electoral processes. The parties then placed the final decision on nominating procedures in the hands of national party conventions. Those decisions reflected the party leaders' lack of confidence in the capacity of their bases to conduct primary elections, and the view that primaries had negative consequences for the parties by increasing internal conflicts and weakening party cohesion.

Electoral legislation in *Honduras* requires that political parties hold primary elections through a direct vote among their members if there are at least two different groups competing to nominate candidates. Political parties with only one internal bloc may choose another process to ratify a single slate of candidates. In practice primaries have been held on various occasions since 1989 to manage the internal fragmentation of the two principal parties.

In *Venezuela*, the 1999 constitution requires political parties to hold primary elections. Nevertheless, in the 2000 elections not one political party held them, allegedly owing to the absence of regulations to implement the constitutional requirement.[3]

In *Argentina*, the discussion of the mechanism of nominating candidates took place in distinct stages. The senate passed a bill in 2001 establishing simultaneous, open primaries. A year later, the president issued a decree (subsequently approved by the congress) that made simultaneous primaries mandatory. Primaries were to be open to all citizens, whether affiliated with a party or not, and without the involvement of the electoral agency, unless requested by the parties. These provisions were set aside for the 2003 elections because President Duhalde feared that former president Carlos Menem would win an open primary in the Partido Justicialista (PJ, the Peronist party). In February 2005, President Néstor Kirchner of the PJ "resurrected" the law to require primaries in every district prior to the legislative elections.

Even before Kirchner's move, some parties had held primaries on their own initiative. Indeed, in 1988, the PJ held closed primaries in which Carlos Menem and Antonio Cafiero competed to become the party's presidential candidate. The Frente País Solidario (FREPASO) held an open primary in 1995, in which José Octavio Bordón and Carlos Álvarez competed. The country's first open primary was held in 1989 by the Izquierda Unida, when Luis Zamora and Néstor Vicente campaigned to lead the ticket. In both cases, the processes were conducted within political coalitions and not within the individual parties. In 1999, primaries were used to select the candidate of the Alianza, a coalition that brought together the Unión Cívica Radical (UCR) and FREPASO.

Peru enacted a political party law in October 2003 on the basis of a broad national agreement involving several major parties. This new regulatory structure forced the parties

---

[3] In 2006 opposition groups had planned to hold a primary before deciding to unite behind Manuel Rosales.

to adapt to new rules of the game, including the need to hold separate primaries, open or closed, with the help of the national office of electoral processes. These internal elections were to be held between 210 and 180 days before the general election. Prior to 2003, several parties had held primaries without being required by law to do so.

Since 1982, in the *Dominican Republic*, some parties have sporadically held primaries notable for the scant levels of citizen participation. Often these have been conducted by the political elite to dampen the threat of internal divisions. For the 2000 elections, the Partido Revolucionario Dominicano (PRD) held a closed primary, while the Partido de la Liberación Dominicana (PLD) and the Partido Reformista Social Cristiano (PRSC) held conventions among their membership. The influence of party strongman Joaquín Balaguer was evident in the internal conventions of the PRSC. In August 2004, the congress passed a reform that introduced simultaneous internal party elections through a universal, direct, secret vote open to all voters.

Colombia's election laws do not require political parties to hold primary elections, but on two occasions (1990 and 1994) the Partido Liberal (PL) has held primaries to select its presidential candidate. (The party has since used a convention system). When primaries *are* held they must follow the provisions of a special law on intraparty consultations, *and* they must be simultaneous. In addition, the law provides for public financing and for supervision by the national electoral council. The Partido Conservador (PC) has conducted just one (closed) primary, in 1998.

Countries in Which Primaries Are Held but Not Regulated

In a second group of countries, political parties hold primary elections at least sporadically (that is, some parties hold them some of the time) without regulation or sanction by the government.

Internal elections are sometimes held within the framework of electoral coalitions. In *Chile*, the binominal electoral system[4] and the political division between supporters and opponents of former president Augusto Pinochet has kept most of the center-left coalition known as *Concertación* united since the group successfully organized to vote against the dictator in the 1988 plebiscite. The need to hold together the heterogeneous coalition led to the adoption of primaries as the means to select presidential candidates in 1993 and 1999.

Mexico's Partido Revolucionario Institucional (PRI) held a primary election in 1999 to choose its presidential candidate, an historic departure from the unpopular practice of allowing the outgoing president to handpick his replacement, a method that was in clear contradiction with democratic principles. The primary aimed to boost the legitimacy of a political party whose credibility has been damaged. Holding the most open elections possible to pick the candidate for president was regarded as the best way to make up for the PRI's past errors and to project the party into the future. However, according to some observers and

---

[4] In the binominal system, legislators are elected from two-member districts, with the two seats being awarded to the two party lists that won the most votes, unless the victorious party won at least twice as many votes as the second, in which case the winning party takes both seats.

certain groups within the party, this election was not a thoroughly open process, although it did represent clear progress from past practices.

In the 2000 elections the Partido Acción Nacional (PAN) used a closed primary, whereas the Partido de la Revolución Democrática (PRD) used a party convention to choose their candidates.[5]

Primary elections (known as *consultas populares*) were also held in Nicaragua by the Frente Sandinista de Liberación Nacional (FSLN) in 1996 and 2001. These elections for selecting the FSLN's candidates were open to all citizens. However, the winners of the primary elections had to be ratified by the FSLN council before the general elections. In one case the council made its own choice for vice president after rejecting the selection of the voters in the primary election. For the November 2000 municipal elections, the Sandinistas returned to the practice of selecting their candidates through primaries that were restricted to party members.

Finally there is the case of El Salvador, where primaries are not regulated by law but are regulated in the bylaws of some parties and have been held occasionally. In other cases, party conventions have been used. The bylaws of the Frente Farabundo Martí para la Liberación Nacional (FMLN) require the use of closed primaries, whereas those of the Alianza Republicana Nacional (ARENA) stipulate the use of party conventions.

Countries That Do Not Have a Significant Tradition of Primaries

In Brazil, Ecuador, and Guatemala primary elections are not regulated by law and are not a common method for choosing presidential candidates, although they have been used by particular parties in some cases. Brazil's Partido dos Trabalhadores (PT) held primary elections in 2002. In Ecuador, Izquierda Democrática (ID) and Democracia Popular (DP) held primaries in 1987 in 2002, respectively. The Partido de Acción Nacional (PAN) in Guatemala held a primary in 2003. In none of the three cases, however, is the primary tradition engrained to a degree that would lead one to predict greater intraparty democracy in the near future. Factors that might have discouraged the adoption of primaries in Brazil and Ecuador include the elitist nature of the political parties and the fear that politics might become more highly regionalized. In Guatemala, the weakness of the political party system and the high level of personalization of political parties have so far prevented the issue from receiving consideration.

Summary of Primary Election Experiences

This review of the region's experience with primary elections illustrates that primaries may be enshrined in national legislation, or each political party may be left free to decide for itself whether and how to organize internal elections. Even without the benefit of legislation, the second approach may result in primaries becoming general practice.

---

[5] The PAN and the PRI also used closed primaries to nominate candidates for the 2006 presidential elections. In the case of the PRD, one of the two potential candidates dropped out, so a primary was not needed.

To be sure, strategic considerations, both internal and external, guide political parties' choice of how and when to hold primaries when they are free to make such choices. The desire to improve the quality of democracy is at best a secondary consideration. To date, the most favorable circumstances for the introduction of primaries are those in which the formation of party alliances or the management of internal party conflict makes them useful. For example, primaries may be perceived as the best solution for settling potential disputes among the leadership of the parties in the coalition or a way to gather popular support for the coalition before the general presidential election. Such was the case in Chile in 1993 and 1999, and in Argentina in 1999, in the selection of presidential candidates for the Concertación and Alianza coalitions, respectively.

In Chile, Argentina, Mexico, Nicaragua, and Colombia, the opening up to new democratic methods in the nomination of presidential candidates was largely dictated by internal circumstances specific to each political party. Except in the case of Colombia, national election agencies did not involve themselves in the organization, administration, oversight, or funding of the primaries.

By contrast, Costa Rica, Uruguay, Paraguay, Bolivia, Panama, Honduras, Venezuela—joined recently by Argentina and Peru—have adopted a different approach, one in which primaries have been institutionalized and placed under the supervision of electoral management bodies that regulate primaries in different ways.

Regulation of the Financing of Elections and Political Parties

The relationship between money and politics is crucial to the health and quality of democracy. Contrary to democratic ideals, monetary assets—not just individual votes and political activity—are in practice important tools for exerting influence on elected officials.

The importance of this issue is matched by its complexity. Regulating the use of money in politics gives rise to a conflict between the principle of freedom of expression and those of impartiality and fairness in electoral competition. Whether attention is centered on principles or on the protection of status and privileges, however, the issue invariably prompts heated debate, not to mention efforts to circumvent whatever rules are created. Even highly developed democracies have yet to resolve the dilemma posed by campaign finance. Nor have they avoided scandals, as illustrated over the years by cases in the United States, Japan, France, Spain, England Germany, and elsewhere (Nassmacher, 1992).

Although the issues of campaign finance are not new, their salience has risen with the cost of electoral campaigns based increasingly on costly television marketing, consultants, opinion polls, and focus groups.

In Latin America, the issue of campaign financing is closely related to the current disenchantment with politics (see Chapter 10). Continuous scandals involving corruption, bribery, influence peddling, and even narco-trafficking reinforce the aversion many citizens feel toward politics and politicians, who are perceived as corrupt, lacking transparency, oriented primarily towards promoting their own interests, and frequently reneging on their campaign promises. Political parties and candidates attempt to exploit popular disgust by accusing one another of obtaining funds from questionable sources or handling them improperly.

To address these problems, the idea of using public resources to help political parties carry out campaigns, and in certain cases their day-to-day operations, has been introduced over the past few decades. Other laws have been devised to regulate activities involving private contributions and to exert greater public control over party finances. But despite these attempts to clean up the playing field, parties' political independence remains in jeopardy because of the need to obtain ever-larger sums of money. At the same time, very little information is available on the amount and sources of campaign spending. In addition, little is known about the effects of public financing measures on the strength of parties and the control of corruption (Posada-Carbó and Carlos Malamud, 2005).

Despite recognition that a balanced and equitable system of party funding is an indispensable requirement for truly competitive and fair elections (Njaim, 2000; González-Varas, 1995), the issue of campaign finance was largely neglected during the initial stage of the region's recent political transition. Once elections began to gain credibility, however, issues related to the quality and enhancement of democracy—among them campaign finance—gained a place on the political agenda. Over the past two decades, several countries have introduced laws related to the financing of political parties and electoral campaigns (Table 7.6).

In recent years campaign finance has become a serious point of contention in several countries of the region because of its critical role in: (1) guaranteeing fairness in electoral contests; (2) ensuring a modicum of transparency and accountability with regard to the origin and use of public and private funds; (3) preventing influence peddling and opportunities for political corruption; and (4) preventing the influx of money from organized crime, particularly drug money, into the political arena.

Critical Issues in Campaign Finance

The consolidation of democracy in Latin America has helped political parties reassume their role as main actors on the political scene, affording them constitutional legitimacy as autonomous entities with full legal status. At the same time, political and campaign spending have grown exponentially, largely because of the escalating costs of electoral campaigns, which require increasingly large expenditures on television advertising, marketing, consultants, opinion surveys, and the use of focus groups.

The need to run ever-more expensive campaigns and keep political party mechanisms in permanent operation has gone hand in hand with a decline in the collection of party membership dues. Faced with the need to raise large sums, it is tempting to divert one's attention from the source of the money, thus opening the door to illegal funding.

The debate over political financing in Latin America centers on four topics. The first has to do with whether to regulate party financing, and if so, to what extent. There is no consistent pattern in this area among the countries of the region. Some, such as Mexico, have a detailed regulatory framework, while others, such as Uruguay and El Salvador, have very few regulations. The issue is complex, and there are limits to what can be done. Although there is a need to establish clear rules of the game to achieve greater public control over the

Table 7.6. The Advent of Public Financing in Latin America

Country	Year
Uruguay	1928
Costa Rica	1949
Argentina	1957 (indirect) and 1961 (direct)
Peru	1966 (indirect) and 2003 (direct)
Venezuela	Established in 1973, eliminated in 1999
Nicaragua	1974
Mexico	1977
Ecuador	1978
Honduras	1981
El Salvador	1983
Colombia	1985
Guatemala	1985
Chile	1988 (indirect) and 2003 (direct)
Paraguay	1990
Brazil	1995
Bolivia	1997
Dominican Republic	1997
Panama	1997

financial operations of political parties, there also is a risk of overregulation that could lead to more elaborate schemes to obscure party finances and evade the law.

The second key issue is the mode of financing—private, public, or mixed. With mixed systems, there is the further question of the proper balance between public and private funds. Various political and social actors have questioned whether it is appropriate for the state to invest large amounts of public funds in political parties, especially in the context of the fiscal crises afflicting many Latin American governments. Public opinion against public financial support has gained strength with the widespread credibility crisis confronting political parties and politicians.

The third issue revolves around mechanisms to lower the demand for money in electoral activity and ensure a sounder use of public funding. Proponents of curbs on escalating campaign costs contend that the infusion of money on such a large scale undermines the fairness of electoral competition, raises the risk of illegal forms of funding, and increases the prevalence of corruption and influence peddling (Zovatto, 1998, 2003a, 2003b).

Finally, there is the matter of establishing or strengthening controls and sanctions to improve transparency, accountability, and compliance with political finance legislation.

Key Features of Campaign Finance Systems in Latin America

Our analysis of campaign finance legislation in Latin America focuses on 10 specific areas of potential regulation: funding systems, the activities eligible for public funding, legal barriers, allocation criteria, prohibitions against contributions from certain sources, limits on private contributions, disbursement scheduling, access of parties to the media, enforcement, and sanctions. Each variable is discussed below.

- *Funding systems.* All Latin American countries except Venezuela use a mixed funding system in which political parties receive public funds and raise private money to finance their electoral campaigns and meet operating expenses. All but Venezuela have some form of public financing, either direct (in cash or secured credits) or indirect (services, tax benefits, media access, training) (Figure 7.2).
- *Activities eligible for public funding.* Ten of the Latin American countries studied here provide direct public funding for campaigns *and* operational expenses, whereas six countries fund only electoral campaigns (Table 7.7). In the past few years, a proportion of public funds have been allocated to support research and training activities by political parties in Argentina, Bolivia, Brazil, Colombia, Mexico, Panama, and Peru.
- *Legal barriers.* Twelve of the countries that provide direct public funding impose an eligibility requirement, such as obtaining a minimum percentage of votes or a minimum level of parliamentary representation (Table 7.8).

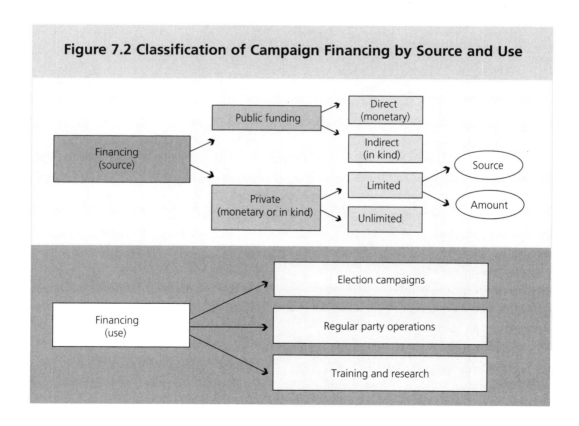

Figure 7.2 Classification of Campaign Financing by Source and Use

Table 7.7. Activities Eligible for Public Funding

Country	Campaigns and operations	Campaigns only	Operations only	Training and research
Argentina	Yes	No	No	Yes
Bolivia	No	Yes	No	Yes
Brazil	Yes	No	No	Yes
Chile	No	Yes	No	No
Colombia	Yes	No	No	Yes
Costa Rica	Yes[1]	No	No	No
Dominican Republic	Yes	No	No	No
Ecuador	Yes	No	No	No
El Salvador	No	Yes	No	No
Guatemala	Yes[2]	No	No	No[2]
Honduras	No	Yes	No	No
Mexico	Yes	No	No	Yes
Nicaragua	No	Yes	No	No
Panama	Yes	No	No	Yes
Paraguay	Yes	No	No	No
Peru	No	No	Yes	Yes
Uruguay	No	Yes	No	No
Venezuela	No	No	No	No

[1] Although the legislation does not specifically authorize it, public funds can be used to cover organization and election expenses.
[2] The legislation does not earmark spending for specific objectives, so expenditures are discretionary.

- *Allocation criteria.* Public funds are allocated to political parties (1) as a proportion of votes received in nine countries, (2) in equal shares plus additional amounts in proportion to votes received in seven countries, and (3) in amounts proportional to votes received and to the share of legislative seats in one country (Table 7.8). Currently, only a few countries (Argentina, Chile, Colombia, Honduras, Mexico, and Panama) provide public financing for political groups taking part for the first time in elections, and with different conditions.

- *Prohibitions against contributions from certain sources.* Most countries impose restrictions on the origins of private contributions. The most common restrictions prohibit donations by foreign governments, institutions, or individuals (thirteen countries), government contractors (nine countries), and anonymous sources (nine countries). Bans on donations by particular social organizations—such as unions, associations, special interest groups, religious groups—are less common (Table 7.9).

- *Ceilings on private contributions.* Argentina, Bolivia, Brazil, Colombia, Costa Rica, Chile, Ecuador, Guatemala, Mexico, Paraguay, and Peru have set upper limits on private contributions from individuals and, to a lesser degree, from firms and organizations.

Table 7.8. Direct Public Financing in Latin America: Access Conditions and Allocation Criteria

Country	Conditions for access to financing and legal barriers	Allocation criteria
Argentina	Officially recognized parties that have listed their national candidates receive equal shares of that part of the financing pool that is set aside for equal distribution among all eligible parties (30%). The balance of the financing pool (70%) is distributed, in proportion to votes obtained, to parties that participated in the most recent legislative election. No threshold is required.	Combined (equal shares + in proportion to votes won)
Bolivia	Parties must obtain a minimum of 3% of all valid votes cast nationwide in the preceding general elections (or municipal elections).	In proportion to votes won
Brazil	For basic accreditation parties must be registered with the election oversight body. To qualify for funding parties must have won 5% of all valid votes cast nationally and a minimum of 2% of votes cast in at least one-third of the states.	Combined (equal shares + in proportion to votes won)
Chile	Financing is made available to all parties and candidates registered with the election oversight body (Servicio Electoral).	In proportion to votes won
Colombia	Candidates must be registered by a party or movement that won at least 4% of the votes in the previous election for the senate or the lower house. The party or movement must be endorsed by a number of citizen signatures equivalent to 3% of the total number of votes cast in the previous presidential elections.	In proportion to votes won
Costa Rica	National parties must obtain at least 4% of the valid votes cast nationally. Parties registered at the provincial level must obtain at least 4% of the votes cast in their respective provinces or succeed in electing at least one deputy.	In proportion to votes won

(continued)

Country	Conditions for access to financing and legal barriers	Allocation criteria
Dominican Republic	Parties must be legally established and maintain this status by obtaining a minimum of 2% of the valid votes in the previous presidential election or representation in the national assembly or city council (Sala Capitular).	In proportion to votes won
Ecuador	Parties must obtain a minimum of 4% of the votes cast in national legislative elections.	Combined (equal shares + in proportion to votes won)
El Salvador	Parties must be legally incorporated and register with election authorities. No threshold.	In proportion to votes won
Guatemala	Parties must obtain at least 4% of all valid votes cast in the first round of the presidential elections.	In proportion to votes won
Honduras	Parties must have obtained a minimum of 10,000 votes in the previous presidential, legislative, or municipal elections.	In proportion to votes won
Mexico	Parties must obtain 2% of all valid votes cast in elections for either the lower house, senate, or presidency. New parties must be legally registered.	Combined (equal shares + in proportion to votes won)
Nicaragua	Parties must obtain a minimum of 4% of all valid votes cast.	In proportion to votes won
Panama	Parties must obtain 4% of the valid votes cast in either presidential, legislative, or local elections. Independent candidates need to have received the number of votes required of parties.	Combined (equal shares + in proportion to votes won)
Paraguay	Parties must be legally registered, organized, and in operation. They must present accounts to the election oversight body. No threshold.	Combined (by votes obtained and legislative representation)
Peru	Parties must be represented in congress.	Combined (equal shares + in proportion to votes won)
Uruguay	No conditions.	In proportion to votes won
Venezuela	No public financing for political campaigns or party operations.	n.a.

Table 7.8. *(continued)*

Table 7.9. Prohibitions against Political Contributions

Country	Foreign entities	Social or political organizations	Corporations and NGOs	Government contractors	Anonymous
Argentina	Yes	Yes	Yes	Yes	Yes
Bolivia	Yes[1]	Yes	No	Yes	Yes
Brazil	Yes	Yes	No	No	Yes
Chile	Yes	Yes	Yes	Yes	No[4]
Colombia	No	No	Yes	No	No[2]
Costa Rica	Yes[3]	No	No	No	No[2]
Dominican Republic	Yes	No	No	No	No
Ecuador	Yes	No	No	Yes	Yes
El Salvador	No	No	No	No	No
Guatemala	Yes[3]	No	No	No	Yes
Honduras	Yes	No	Yes	Yes	Yes
Mexico	Yes	Yes	Yes	Yes	Yes
Nicaragua	No[5]	No	No	Yes	Yes
Panama	No	No	No	No	No[2]
Paraguay	Yes	Yes	Yes	Yes	No[2]
Peru	Yes	No	No	No	No[6]
Uruguay	No	No	No	No	No
Venezuela	Yes	No	No	Yes	Yes

[1] Donations from foreign, legally registered entities are allowed but only for technical assistance and training.
[2] There is no explicit ban; however, regulations require parties and political movements to justify the source of funds received, which in practice entails a prohibition.
[3] Contributions are prohibited, except for donations designated for training and technical assistance.
[4] There are limits on anonymous contributions, set in development units.
[5] Not prohibited, but it is expected that foreign donations will be for training and technical assistance.
[6] Not explicitly regulated. Nevertheless, support from unidentified donors directed toward campaign activities must not exceed 30 annual "UIT" tax units (= 106,000 sucres at 2006 rates).

- *Disbursement scheduling.* The most common pattern of disbursement of public financing (found in ten countries) is that some of the subsidy is provided before and some after the elections. In four countries the entire reimbursement is provided after the elections; only in Argentina is it provided in full before elections (Table 7.10).
- *Access to the media.* Politics is communicated, more than ever before, through the mass media, notably television. Political parties' access to the electronic media in Latin America can be viewed as a continuum (Griner and Zovatto, 2004). Brazil and Chile provide parties free broadcast time during campaigns and, between elections, free time for publicizing their policy positions. In Brazil, commercial campaign advertising is prohibited; instead, the parties receive daily airspace during the campaign. Chile prohibits

Table 7.10. Timing of Disbursements of Direct Public Funds

Country	Before elections	After elections	Before and after elections	Provisions for new political parties	Other (ongoing financing)
Argentina	Yes	No	No	Yes	Yes
Bolivia	No	No	Yes	No	No[1]
Brazil	No	No	No	No	Yes
Chile	No	No	Yes	Yes	No
Colombia	No	No	Yes	Yes	Yes
Costa Rica	No	Yes	No	No	No
Dominican Republic	No	No	Yes	No	Yes
Ecuador	No	Yes	No	No	Yes
El Salvador	No	No	Yes	No	No
Guatemala	No	No	Yes[2]	No	Yes
Honduras	No	No	Yes	Yes	No
Mexico	No	No	Yes	Yes	Yes
Nicaragua	No	Yes	No	No	No
Panama	No	No	Yes	Yes	Yes
Paraguay	No	Yes	No	No	Yes
Peru	No	No	No	No	Yes
Uruguay	No	No	Yes	No	No
Venezuela	No	No	No	No	No

[1] In nonelection years parties receive funding for citizen education and program dissemination.
[2] In Guatemala, the calculation and payment of public financing is done after the elections in four annual installments; in practice, the last installment is paid during the subsequent electoral campaign.

paid commercials on broadcast television, where free airtime is made available, but airtime can be purchased from radio stations, cable television, and the print media.

Elsewhere in the region one finds combinations of free airtime in public and private media and options to purchase additional advertising. Thirteen of the region's countries provide airtime to parties in the electronic media, particularly public television, in most cases only during campaigns. Only Brazil, Colombia, Mexico, Panama, and Peru provide continuous access to the media. Party access to the print media is broad in most countries, although in some cases, such as Costa Rica, Bolivia, Ecuador, and Nicaragua, there are restrictions. In all countries state media time slots have become irrelevant because of their small audiences; in some places state media no longer exist. Paid advertising makes up a very large, and rising, share of campaign spending.

Despite state-supported access to the media, most countries could do more to ensure the equity of political competition and control campaign spending, a topic explored later in the chapter.

Table 7.11. Agencies Responsible for Enforcing Campaign Finance Regulations

Country	Supervisory agencies
Argentina	Federal judges with electoral jurisdiction
Bolivia	Election oversight body
Brazil	Election oversight body
Chile	Election oversight body
Colombia	Election oversight body
Costa Rica	Election oversight body / Comptroller General's Office
Dominican Republic	Election oversight body / Comptroller General's Office
Ecuador	Election oversight body
El Salvador	Court of Accounts[1]
Guatemala	Election oversight body
Honduras	Election oversight body
Mexico	Election oversight body
Nicaragua	Comptroller General's Office / election oversight body[2]
Panama	Election oversight body / Comptroller General's Office [3]
Paraguay	Election oversight body
Peru	Election oversight body
Uruguay	None
Venezuela	Election oversight body

[1] In practice, the court does not exercise its authority.
[2] Contributes to the control efforts of the Office of the Special Prosecutor for Elections, under the national Office of the Prosecutor General. Opened six months prior to elections, the office closes again once its work is over.
[3] The role of the Comptroller General's Office concerns public funding.

- *Application of the law and control agencies.* In all cases except Uruguay electoral legislation specifies an entity responsible for the monitoring or oversight of political party and election campaign funding (Table 7.11). In most cases, the organization responsible for overseeing political party funding is the electoral management body.
- *Systems of sanction.* Finally, most countries provide for a system of sanctions for violations of laws and regulations governing electoral and party finances. The most common are fines (fifteen countries), followed by administrative or other sanctions (nine countries), which lead either to revocation of party registration or the suspension of public financing for parties that have broken the law. In seven countries, candidates are subject to criminal sanctions; in six of these, donors, too, may face criminal sanctions.

Trends in Campaign Finance Reform

The mixed funding system is used in all countries with the exception of Venezuela, where no public funding is provided. There is no clear trend in the region favoring either public or private funding at the expense of the other, although the focus of the 1996 Mexican reform stressing public funding has been emulated in proposals for electoral reform in Argentina, Brazil, and Colombia. Venezuela, however, has gone against this trend by *eliminating* public funding, while Chile and Peru reformed their systems so as to incorporate direct public financing.

Two emerging trends in campaign spending are (1) to limit spending on political advertising and (2) to increase public outlays to strengthen, modernize, and train political parties and politicians. Along these lines, electoral reforms in the region—some already adopted, others proposed—have opened up a third window for public funding designed to fortify the democratic political culture, and contribute to research and training for political parties.

Limiting Private Contributions

Scandals involving corruption and the connections of political parties and their candidates with money made through illicit activities, particularly drug trafficking, have led to limitations on or prohibitions against private contributions from certain sources or in amounts above a certain level. Another reason for these measures is to avoid great disparities in the financial resources of political parties and candidates and to limit the influence of very wealthy donors.

Two main trends prevail in funding prohibitions. The first is increased efforts to prevent donations from abroad (from foreign governments, institutions, or individuals), even if earmarked for instruction, training, or education. Experience suggests that allowing such contributions opens a dangerous loophole, hindering control over their actual use. The second trend entails efforts to forbid contributions made anonymously, except for those obtained through collections taken up in public.

Ensuring Equitable Media Access

Making access to the media, particularly television, more equitable is a topic of growing importance, as noted earlier, because of the key role of media in electoral campaigns. Most recent legislation provides for free access to the media, chiefly those run by the state. This television or radio airtime is known as "antenna rights" or "antenna time." Despite this trend, most countries in the region still have a long way to go to counteract the inequitable environment in which political forces compete. The sources of the imbalance can be traced to the following factors:

- Most countries combine free media access with the option to purchase additional airtime in the private media, which by and large is not closely regulated and is hard to control.
- Owners and administrators of the media frequently associate with powerful economic and political groups. Commonly, even among the collectively owned media, those who hold a controlling interest favor certain political groups, sometimes offering them better or longer time slots.

- The small size of the audiences of state-funded television and radio stations oblige even small parties to purchase airtime from private media concerns.
- Swift changes in communications technology (e.g., satellite and cable television) are giving rise to gaps in regulations designed to promote more equal media access among political parties.
- Even though regulations establish free time slots in many countries, very few provide support for the production of advertising, an undertaking that normally requires large sums of money.
- The news may present biased treatment of certain parties or candidates.
- Incumbent governments may use their easy access to state media to convey their achievements and the outcomes of their policies, giving unfair advantages in electoral campaigns.
- Lack of legislation governing advertising rates makes it difficult to ensure that political parties are not charged different rates for access.

Another incipient trend in the region is toward greater involvement of election oversight bodies in the monitoring and enforcement of provisions dealing with equitable media access for political parties. At present, most of these bodies have insufficient capacity or resources to effectively handle the issue of political advertising and the media. Perhaps the greatest progress has been made in Mexico, where the powers of the broadcasting commission (*Comisión de Radiodifusión*) of the federal electoral institute were considerably broadened by the 1996 electoral reforms. One of the commission's chief responsibilities is to monitor, but not enforce, the fairness of campaign broadcasting time slots and equal treatment in newscasts, and to widely publish reports of its findings.

Improving Accountability and Transparency in the Use of Financial Resources

A few countries of the region require political parties to account for their use of public and private resources. This trend is just getting started, however, and in most cases, the required accounting is limited to the publication by parties of their financial statements in bulletins, official gazettes and registers, which few citizens read. Publication in official dailies has little impact on enforcement or control efforts, because it does not bring information on party revenues and expenses to the vast majority of the population. New mechanisms are needed to ensure that parties and candidates produce transparent information on their financial activities, the manner in which their resources are administered, and the source and destination of the funds used to finance their activities.

Strengthening Enforcement Mechanisms and Law Enforcement Entities

Although oversight bodies in most countries have the legal authority to supervise and control the financial actions of political parties, their ability to carry out their responsibilities is severely limited. There is a trend toward reinforcing their authority and their economic, technical, and human capacities to audit the reports submitted by political parties, as well as their powers to investigate the origin, management, and actual use of resources.

Moreover, in some countries other types of control agencies have been involved, such as the comptroller (as in El Salvador), or a combination of both election oversight bodies and comptroller's offices, as in Costa Rica, Nicaragua, the Dominican Republic, and Panama.

The chief measures adopted in recent years to strengthen control mechanisms have been (1) to make the supervision of political parties an ongoing rather than a temporary activity; (2) to regulate the duty of political parties to submit reports on their revenues and expenditures; (3) to establish the obligation to conduct bona fide audits to verify and supervise financial resources, with all the technical rigor that this requires; (4) to require standardized procedures and the regular submission of reports; (5) to make audits a constant practice as a means of preventive intervention; (6) to call for the widespread dissemination of the results of audits as well as of reports submitted by political parties (preferably before elections); (7) to improve the quality and clarity of donor records; (8) to establish ethics control councils within political parties; (9) to require that resources pass through the financial system rather than through cash transactions; and (10) to establish the position of sole financial executive as the single authority over the management of party funds.

Toughening Sanctions Systems

Despite extensive legislative changes, sanctions systems in most countries remain insufficient and ineffective (Griner and Zovatto, 2004). Among the main reasons for the low level of application of sanctions, the most noteworthy are: (1) the institutional and technical weaknesses of the agencies responsible for enforcement; (2) lack of independence from the government and from political parties of some election oversight bodies and judicial institutions; and (3) corruption and bribery of officials in these institutions. Because of these limitations, sanctions often have no practical effect on the amounts and origins of contributions or on the administration of financial resources by the parties.

To address these weaknesses, reforms have been adopted in several countries aimed at toughening the sanctions and, at the same time, strengthening enforcement mechanisms and institutions. For example, aside from fines (the traditional and still most common sanction), in some countries, illegal contributions have been classified as a criminal offense, and new penalties have been introduced, such as disqualifying candidates for a specified time (as in Honduras, Nicaragua, and Ecuador, among others). Other sanctions include disqualification of election results and removal from office, as in Colombia and Ecuador. Nine countries have enacted criminal sanctions against candidates or donors; of these, four specifically require detention (Costa Rica, Mexico, Paraguay, and Venezuela). At the other extreme, two countries fail to provide any sanction at all for violations of the law (El Salvador and Guatemala).[6]

In short, if campaign finance regulations are to have some teeth, it seems clear that those who violate campaign finance laws must face not just fines but the possibility of a prison sentence. Most appropriate is a mixed strategy that offers both adequate incentives to parties and candidates for voluntary compliance, and a strict system of penalties for violations.

---

[6] Guatemala's 2004 reform contemplates the introduction of administrative and criminal sanctions, but without a clear definition of their application within the legal framework.

Box 7.1. The Ten Commandments of Campaign Finance

1. The revenues and expenses of political parties and their campaigns shall be transparent and available to the public.
2. A reasonable amount of public financing shall be made available to parties. This financing shall be devoted to promoting greater equity in political contests, lessening the economic dependence of political parties on economic groups, and strengthening the political party system and political culture.
3. To prevent privileged groups from wielding undue influence over elected governments, it is essential to lower the demand for campaign money by controlling the factors that have driven up campaign spending.
4. No foreign contributions shall be allowed.
5. No anonymous contributions shall be allowed.
6. No contributions shall be made from sources linked to organized crime or other illicit activities.
7. Equitable access to the public as well as private media shall be guaranteed, particularly with regard to television.
8. Regulations shall avoid violations of the freedom of expression.
9. Competent, efficient authorities shall enforce these regulations.
10. Violators shall be punished.

Source: de la Calle (2001).

If the requirements to observe political finance rules are minimal, the laws become insignificant; but if they are too strictly enforced, the system could become subject to excess rigidity. So regulatory enforcement must be calculated and properly balanced to avoid either the *overregulation* or *criminalization* of politics. "Given the institutional weaknesses prevalent in the region, the drive to penalize can lead to a debasement of the law, and in this regard reform efforts in this field should always be undertaken prudently" (de la Calle, 2003).

Key guidelines for reform in this difficult area of political finance are spelled out in Box 7.1.

Conclusions

After years at the bottom of the region's reform agenda, the internal democratization of political parties and the reform of systems for financing political parties and electoral campaigns emerged to command significant attention. Despite substantial progress on both fronts, however, much remains to be done to strengthen the credibility of political parties and the fairness of electoral competition in the region.

The internal democratization of political parties has proceeded gradually and unevenly. Although slow, the reforms appear to be headed in the right direction and hold the potential to strengthen the quality of democratic political representation. The issue attained prominence in some cases in response to growing social demands for broader participation in political parties and more transparency in their activities. In other cases, democratization has emerged as a strategy by political parties to build coalitions or rejuvenate their bases of electoral support. Before this process got underway, most countries had very closed political parties, usually organized around exclusive forms of leadership, such as *caudillos*, or traditional leaders.

After a series of reforms across the region in recent years, internal elections for the nomination of presidential candidates are now regulated by law in 11 of the 18 countries examined here (Argentina, Bolivia, Colombia, Costa Rica, the Dominican Republic, Honduras, Panama, Paraguay, Peru, Uruguay, and Venezuela). In four countries (Chile, El Salvador, Mexico, and Nicaragua), primaries are not regulated, but political parties have occasionally used them in different forms on some occasions. In Brazil, Ecuador, and Guatemala, primaries are neither regulated nor widely used.

Progress in democratizing has been slower in respect to the election of party officials than in respect to the nomination of candidates for elected public office. This situation appears to be rooted in the resistance of traditional leadership structures to change, and in the ongoing tendency to treat political parties in some circumstances as purely private entities.

Comparative analysis suggests a growing consensus in Latin America on the benefits of using primary elections for selecting presidential candidates. Even from the narrow vantage point of party electoral strategies, primaries appear valuable in strengthening public backing for candidates in the general election. More importantly for democracy as a whole, primaries enhance the legitimacy of those elected to the presidency, broaden the circle of potential party leaders, and provide voters with a greater range of choices, hopefully leading to the selection of more competent and responsive leaders.

However, practical experience shows that primaries can also produce negative effects. A clear example has been the loss of parties' organizational autonomy in open primaries. In some cases (e.g., Argentina in 1995) supporters of one party have voted en masse in another's primary in order to produce an outcome they deemed favorable to their party. In other cases, governments have interfered in the internal operations of opposing parties for their own benefit (as occurred in the Dominican Republic). In some situations, party primaries have reinforced the power of existing party elites and the maintenance of the status quo (in Bolivia, the Dominican Republic, Ecuador, Honduras, Paraguay, and Uruguay). In others, they have undermined citizen confidence in the party, due to allegations of fraud (e.g., the FMLN in El Salvador in 2003) or corruption and fraudulent financial management of party primaries, all of which can exact high costs for parties (as in Bolivia).

When the candidates chosen by grassroots constituencies are not the national leaders of the party, conflicts have sometimes arisen between the bureaucratic and electoral faces of the party, especially when the leaders are not accustomed to sharing power and see themselves playing second fiddle to the party's candidate. If the primary elections result in greater party fragmentation, the candidate elected president may have difficulty dealing with party leaders and legislative representatives (as occurred in Paraguay). When primaries lead to party fragmentation the electoral process can become more personalistic and open to outsiders who use the party purely as a vehicle to get elected (Freidenberg, 2005).

Primary election processes have also led party leaders to confuse the preferences and demands of party loyalists with those of the broader electorate. Because successful candidates may place the values of the general electorate (at least those values that polling results attribute to the general electorate) above the values of party loyalists, conflicts may arise between popular candidates and those more respectful of party ideology. In order to capture the maximum number of votes, catch-all strategies have been employed, which generate a reluctance in candidates to take well-defined ideological stands.

The relationship between internal democracy and success at the polls is problematic. Primaries have been no guarantee of ultimate electoral success. Party primaries tend to enjoy lower rates of participation than general elections; they are less competitive; and according to one account, more likely to result in the selection of unsuccessful presidential candidates (Colomer, 2002: 119). Disciplined, highly centralized, highly cohesive parties tend to prevail in general elections. If parties' main purpose is to win elections, the belief that primaries do not help them do this discourages their use.

This is a central challenge, given citizens' marked indifference to and profound mistrust of political parties across much of the region (see Chapter 10). The current high level of popular disenchantment with politics may be alleviated to the extent that people see politicians and the party itself as necessary for the country to function. The solution may lie in part in professionalizing parties and strengthening the institutions that oversee their activities. If they are to function better, parties must be more open to society at large, which means responding to the demands of citizens as well as stimulating the participation of a broader segment of the electorate. But at the same time parties must protect their organizations against external interference. The internal democratization of political parties is one means of promoting the objective of enhancing the representativeness of parties, but it is not a panacea.

Electoral reforms during the past two decades have brought important advances in the financing of politics in the region. Nevertheless, progress has not been even across countries, and there remains much to do. Financing issues are dynamic and constantly changing, so it is likely that a series of legal reforms tailored to the specific needs and context of each country is required. It is not surprising that in Germany, where the issue has been addressed repeatedly over the past 40 years, political financing laws have been dubbed an area of "interminable legislation."

A comparative survey of the region reveals that, with the passage of legislation in 2003 for direct public financing in Peru and Chile, a regional trend toward indirect and direct state financing was consolidated—to the point that now only Venezuela lacks any form of such funding. A mixed system of public and private financing prevails in the region, with a tendency toward public financing and an inclination to strengthen the legal limits on private contributions. These formal features contrast, however, with the widespread perception that in most Latin American countries private contributions, whose true totals are unknown, greatly exceed the amounts of public funds going to electoral campaigns. That assumption is bolstered by frequent scandals involving corruption, illegal financing, and drug money.

Several factors—among them inadequate regulation, inefficient enforcement, ineffective systems of sanctions, and political practices prone to abuse—have come together to make public funding a supplement to private funding rather than a replacement for it. Its impact has been limited, though that impact varies from country to country.

A movement to rein in campaign spending by capping contributions and shortening the campaign period has had mixed results across the region. At the same time, public resources devoted to the financing of politics have been redirected in some cases toward strengthening political parties through support for research and training activities.

While some issues have been dealt with adequately, others—notably more equitable media access—are weakly or scarcely regulated. Fairer access to television, in particular, is one of the greatest deficiencies in the political finance systems of most countries of the region.

Transparency levels continue to be low, notwithstanding reforms aimed at strengthening accountability and improving public disclosure of financial statements. In this area, the media and civil society are playing a growing and positive role.

Despite some progress, most recent reforms have failed to strengthen relevant enforcement agencies or the system of sanctions applied to violations. This vacuum constitutes the Achilles' heel of the financing systems of many countries in the region.

In short, the region has made uneven progress toward the following six objectives:

- Reducing the influence of money by diminishing its impact and controlling the factors that contribute to the rapid rise of campaign spending.
- Promoting fairer conditions for electoral competition.
- Making wiser use of public money by investing in activities that are more productive for democracy and that strengthen political parties.
- Promoting greater transparency and improved accountability in relation to both the source and use of public and private funds.
- Strengthening national bodies charged with electoral control and oversight, and the independence, efficacy, and professional performance of enforcement agencies.
- Increasing the severity of existing sanctions.

The issues examined in this chapter lead us to two main conclusions. First, financing for political parties and electoral campaigns is a complex, controversial, and unresolved issue, for which there are no panaceas or magic formulas. Improvements will require a sequence of steps and a variety of approaches rather than broad and ambitious reform initiatives. This is a subject that at bottom is a political rather than a technical matter, but one essential to the quality and healthy functioning of democracy.

Secondly, the establishment of an equitable, transparent and well-enforced system of financing must correspond to the general and specific objectives being pursued, as well as the particular needs and circumstances of each country. Moreover, it must be comprehensive and well coordinated, a product of an effective legal framework, efficient enforcement institutions, and a vigilant civil society and mass media. However, in most Latin American countries today, legal compliance is poor, transparency is low, enforcement and oversight institutions are weak, and systems of sanctions are ineffective. Thus, legislative and regulatory reforms will not be sufficient. As de la Calle (2001, 2003) has argued, the cultural context needs to be addressed and efforts to educate the general public are required.

The current period demands a new convergence between action and ethics, and between ethics and politics. Strengthening the health and quality of the region's democracy is a strategic objective that requires democratization within political parties. This is where political financing plays a decisive role.

References

Alcántara Sáez, Manuel. 2002. Experimentos de democracia interna. Las primarias de partidos en América Latina. Working Paper 293, Helen Kellogg Institute for International Studies, University of Notre Dame, South Bend, IN.

Bendel, Petra. 1998. "Los partidos políticos: condiciones de inscripción y reconocimiento legal, democracia interna, etc." In Dieter Nohlen, Sonia Picado and Daniel Zovatto (eds.), *Tratado de derecho electoral comparado de América Latina*. Mexico: Fondo de Cultura Económica.

Buquet, Daniel, and Daniel Chasquetti. 2004. Presidential Candidate Selection in Uruguay. Paper presented at the symposium "Pathways to Power: Political Recruitment and Democracy in Latin America," Wake Forest University, Winston-Salem, NC.

Carey, John M., and John Polga-Hecimovich. 2006. Primary Elections and Candidate Strength in Latin America. *Journal of Politics* 68(3).

Colomer, Joseph. 2002. Las elecciones primarias presidenciales en América Latina y sus consecuencias políticas. In Marcelo Cavarozzi and Juan Abal Medina, Jr. (eds.), *El asedio a la política. Los partidos latinoamericanos en la era neoliberal*. Rosario, Argentina: Editions Homo Sapiens.

de la Calle, Humberto. 2001. La perspectiva desde los partidos políticos. El caso de Latinoamérica. Report presented to the First Special Session of the Congress on Money and Politics, Mexico, December.

————. 2003. Presentation at the Third Meeting of the Inter-American Forum on Political Parties, Cartagena de Indias, Colombia, November.

Freidenberg, Flavia. 2003. *Selección de candidatos y democracia interna en los partidos de América Latina*. Lima: Asociación Civil Transparencia and Internacional IDEA.

————. 2005. Democracia interna en los partidos políticos. In Dieter Nohlen, Sonia Picado, and Daniel Zovatto (eds.), *Tratado de derecho electoral comparado de América Latina*. 2nd edition. Mexico: Fondo de Cultura Económica.

————. 2006. La democratización de los partidos políticos: entre la ilusión y el desencanto. In Fernando Sánchez and José Thompson (eds.), *Fortalecimiento de los partidos políticos en América Latina: Institucionalización, democratización y transparencia*. Cuadernos de CAPEL 50. San José, Costa Rica: IIDH/CAPEL.

González-Varas, Santiago. 1995. *La financiación de los partidos políticos*. Madrid: Dyckinson.

Griner, Steven, and Daniel Zovatto (eds.). 2004. *De las normas a las buenas prácticas. El desafío del financiamiento político en América Latina*. San José, Costa Rica: OAS/IDEA.

Nassmacher, Karl-Heinz. 1992. Comparing Party and Campaign Finance in Western Democracies. In Arthur B. Gunlicks (ed.), *Campaign and Party Finance in North America and Western Europe*. Boulder, CO: Westview.

Njaim, Humberto. 2000. La financiación de la política. In *Diccionario electoral*. San José, Costa Rica: IIDH/CAPEL.

Posada-Carbó, Eduardo, and Carlos Malamud (eds.). 2005. *The Financing of Politics: Latin American and European Perspectives*. London: Institute for the Study of the Americas.

Zovatto, Daniel. 1998. La financiación política en Iberoamérica: una visión preliminar comparada. In Daniel Zovatto and Pilar del Castillo (eds.), *La financiación de la política en Iberoamérica*. San José, Costa Rica: IIDH/CAPEL.

―――. 2003a. *Estudios sobre financiamiento de partidos políticos en Centroamérica y Panamá*. Cuadernos de CAPEL 48. San José: IIDH/CAPEL.

―――. 2003b. Estudio comparado de las características jurídicas y prácticas del financiamiento de los partidos políticos y las campañas electorales en América Latina. In Manuel Alcántara and Elena Martínez-Barahona (eds.), *Política, dinero e institucionalización partidista en América Latina*. Mexico: Universidad Iberoamericana, Instituto Federal Electoral, Facultad Latinoamericana de Ciencias Sociales.

―――. 2006. *Regulación jurídica de los partidos políticos en América Latina*. Mexico City: International IDEA and Universidad Nacional Autónoma de México.

Appendix 7.1. Political Parties in Latin America

Country and party abbreviation	Full name of party	English translation
Argentina		
FREPASO	Frente País Solidario	Country Solidarity Front
PJ	Partido Justicialista	Justicialista (Peronist) Party
UCR	Unión Cívica Radical	Radical Civic Union
IU	Izquierda Unida	United Left
Bolivia		
ADN	Alianza Democrática Nacionalista	Nationalist Democratic Alliance
MIR	Movimiento de Izquierda Revolucionaria	Revolutionary Left Movement
MNR	Movimiento Nacionalista Revolucionario	Nationalist Revolution Movement
UCS	Unión Cívica Solidaridad	Civic Solidarity Union
Brazil		
PDT	Partido Democrático Trabalhista	Democratic Workers Party
PMDB	Partido Movimento Democrático Brasileiro	Brazilian Democratic Movement
PSDB	Partido de Social Democracia Brasileira	Brazilian Social Democratic Party
PT	Partido dos Trabalhadores	Workers Party
PFL	Partido de Frente Liberal	Liberal Front
Chile		
PDC	Partido de la Democracia Cristiana	Christian Democratic Party
PPD	Partido por la Democracia	Party for Democracy
PS	Partido Socialista	Socialist Party
RN	Renovación Nacional	National Renewal
UDI	Unión Demócrata Independiente	Independent Democrat Union
Colombia		
PC	Partido Conservador	Conservative Party
PL	Partido Liberal	Liberal Party
Costa Rica		
PLN	Partido de Liberación Nacional	National Liberation Party
PUSC	Partido Unidad Social Cristiana	Social Christian Unity Party
Dominican Republic		
PLD	Partido de la Liberación Dominicana	Dominican Liberation Party
PRD	Partido Revolucionario Dominicano	Dominican Revolutionary Party
PRSC	Partido Reformista Social Cristiano	Social Christian Reform Party
Ecuador		
DP	Democracia Popular	Popular Democracy
ID	Izquierda Democrática	Democratic Left

(continued)

Appendix 7.1. Political Parties in Latin America

Country and party abbreviation	Full name of party	English translation
PRE	Partido Roldosista Ecuatoriano	Ecuadorian Roldosista Movement
PSC	Partido Social Cristiano	Social Christian Union
El Salvador		
ARENA	Alianza Republicana Nacional	Nationalist Republican Alliance
FMLN	Frente Farabundo Martí para la Liberación Nacional	Farabundo Martí Front for National Liberation
Guatemala		
FRG	Frente Republicano Guatemalteco	Guatemalan Republican Front
PAN	Partido de Avanzada Nacional	National Advancement Party
Honduras		
PL	Partido Liberal de Honduras	Liberal Party of Honduras
PN	Partido Nacional de Honduras	National Party of Honduras
Mexico		
PAN	Partido Acción Nacional	National Action Party
PRI	Partido Revolucionario Institucional	Institutional Revolutionary Party
PRD	Partido de la Revolución Democrática	Democratic Revolution Party
Nicaragua		
FSLN	Frente Sandinista de Liberación Nacional	Sandinista Front for National Liberation
PLC	Partido Liberal Constitucionalista	Liberal Constitutionalist Party
Paraguay		
ANR	Asociación Nacional Republicana	National Republican Association
PEN	Partido Encuentro Nacional	National Meeting Party
PLRA	Partido Liberal Radical Auténtico	Authentic Radical Liberal Party
Panama		
PA	Partido Arnulfista	Arnulfista Party
PDC	Partido Democrático Cristiano (or Partido Popular)	Christian Democratic Party (or People's Party)
PRD	Partido Revolucionario Democrático	Democratic Revolutionary Party
Peru		
PAP	Partido Aprista Peruano	Peruvian Aprista Party
Uruguay		
FA	Frente Amplio	Broad Front
PC	Partido Colorado	Colorado Party
PN	Partido Nacional	National Party
Venezuela		
AD	Acción Democrática	Democratic Action
COPEI	Comité de Org. Político Electoral	Political Electoral Organizing Committee (Christian Democrat)

(continued)

Appendix 7.1. Political Parties in Latin America		
Country and party abbreviation	**Full name of party**	**English translation**
MAS	Movimiento al Socialismo	Movement toward Socialism
MVR	Movimiento V República	Fifth Republic Movement
PPT	Patria Para Todos	Fatherland for All
PV	Proyecto Venezuela	Project Venezuela

Note: This table presents the names of some of the principal political parties referred to in Tables 6.2 and 7.3.

Part III

Citizen Participation and Democracy

CHAPTER 8

Direct Democracy Institutions

Since 1978 a growing number of Latin America's representative democracies have adopted mechanisms for direct citizen participation in decision making. Often referred to as institutions of direct democracy, these mechanisms are a means of political participation through direct and universal suffrage.[1] Their aim is to involve citizens directly in the decision-making process rather than having elected representatives make all of their decisions for them.

As an ideal, direct democracy certainly has appeal, but do such mechanisms function well in practice? History shows that in early Greece—specifically Athens—and in some medieval urban communes, experiments in direct democracy were short-lived and incomplete, and that any concrete achievements in terms of "pure" democracy were rather limited. However, experiences in Liechtenstein, Italy, the United States (at the subnational level), and especially Switzerland demonstrate the potential of direct democracy as a mechanism for giving expression to the popular will (Thibaut, 1998; Bogdanor, 1994). Popular consultations have become increasingly common across Europe, with such mechanisms having been introduced recently in several German states and used for ratification of the European integration process in Denmark, France, Ireland, Norway, and Sweden (Dalton, Bürklin, and Drummond, 2001). Examinations of experiences in Europe and the United States, however, do not necessarily provide insights into how similar institutions operate in Latin America.

Given the region's generally low levels of public trust in legislative bodies and political parties (see Chapter 10), some segments of the electorate view direct democracy mechanisms as valid options for improving the quality and depth of political representation, boosting participation, and strengthening the legitimacy of democratic institutions (Barczak, 2001). As a result, a debate has opened in the region with respect to the potential

---

[1] Given this book's focus on political institutions at the national level, in this chapter analysis of direct democracy mechanisms will also be limited to that level.

benefits and risks of these institutions. Critics suggest that direct democracy mechanisms may undermine institutions of representative democracy, and that they may be used by an authoritarian-minded president to circumvent and thereby weaken the legislature and political parties.[2] Defenders of such mechanisms contend, however, that institutions of direct democracy can enhance the legitimacy of the political process and lead to greater social integration. In addition, they point out that there is not necessarily a contradiction between direct democracy and representative democracy. There is no reason, they argue, why institutions of direct democracy cannot complement, rather than supplant or weaken, representative democracy.

Types of Institutions

Several types of direct democracy institutions are in use in Latin America, and there are several ways to describe them. National constitutions often refer to similar institutions using different terminology. Some of the most common terms include popular legislative initiative (*iniciativa popular legislativa*); referendum, plebiscite, or the more direct translation, "popular consultation" (*consulta popular*); recall (*revocatoria de mandato*); and open town meeting (*cabildo abierto*). As a result of the variations in usage, it is not possible to arrive at a common terminology for the purpose of cross-country comparison that is faithful to the diverse set of concepts currently in use throughout the region.

This chapter classifies mechanisms of direct democracy into three types: *popular consultations* (by far the most commonly used term), *popular legislative initiatives*, and *recall votes*. Given that these mechanisms are interconnected (for instance, a legislative initiative can lead to a popular consultation), the classification is somewhat loose and is intended merely to enhance the clarity of the description of the various mechanisms in the region.

Popular Consultations

Popular consultations encompass both plebiscites and referendums. Although some experts distinguish between the two (the first being a direct vote of the people on important political matters and the second a direct popular vote on the approval of laws or constitutional texts), we will use the term popular consultation to refer to both. In general, popular consultations refer to votes by citizens to decide or express opinions on constitutional matters or legislative issues of national importance.

The second mechanism, popular legislative initiative, expresses the citizens' right to introduce bills to make partial or complete reforms to laws or the constitution. The third mechanism, the recall vote, gives citizens the power to vote to remove an elected official from office.

A more comprehensive classification of the various mechanisms of direct democracy takes into consideration their area of application and origin (Figure 8.1). Such a classifica-

---

[2] See Thibaut (1998), Barczak (2001), and Dalton, Bürklin, and Drummond (2001) for discussions of different perspectives on the potential advantages and disadvantages of direct democracy.

Figure 8.1. Classification of Direct Democracy Mechanisms

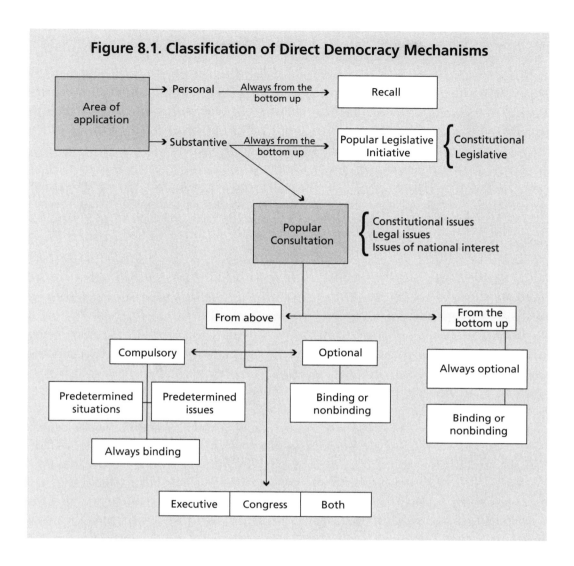

tion differentiates between mechanisms targeted at individual elected officials and those with a substantive, lawmaking purpose, as well as distinguishing among mechanisms that are triggered from the bottom up, from the top down, or as a result of a specific institutional requirement (Thibaut, 1998).

Popular consultation may be either compulsory or optional. Compulsory mechanisms can be subdivided into two categories: (1) consultations called for in relation to predetermined issues specifically set out in the constitution, and (2) consultations established for predetermined situations, which are set in motion only when a predefined circumstance arises, such as a dispute between the executive branch and congress that cannot be resolved within the framework of the representative system (Thibaut, 1998).

Compulsory popular consultations on predetermined issues are provided for in El Salvador, Panama, and Guatemala. These mechanisms require that certain decisions affecting national sovereignty be put to popular vote. In El Salvador, consultations are convoked to make decisions regarding the political unification of Central American countries; in

Panama, for deciding the future of the Panama Canal; and in Guatemala, for establishing laws related to the border dispute with Belize.

The Chilean and Peruvian constitutions mandate compulsory popular consultations in predetermined situations. Peru requires that constitutional reforms backed by an absolute majority in congress, but lacking the two-thirds majority required for enactment, be put to popular vote. Constitutional reforms are put to popular vote in Chile only if the executive branch and the legislature cannot reach an agreement.

Optional popular consultation mechanisms may be divided into two additional categories, according to whether (1) the call for a popular vote is imposed from the top down (that is, where the branches of government have the exclusive right to implement the mechanism), or (2) the initiative for the consultation comes from the bottom up, that is, from the citizenry itself. Popular consultations coming from the top down may originate from either the executive or legislative branch, or from the two acting together. Popular consultations driven from the bottom up result from citizens' initiatives that must pass some type of threshold for the process to advance, such as obtaining the signatures of a minimum percentage or number of registered voters or citizens.

Optional popular consultations have been legislated in at least 16 countries in the region. In Argentina, Bolivia, Brazil, Colombia, Nicaragua, Panama, and Paraguay, the initiative lies chiefly or exclusively with the legislature. In Guatemala, both citizens (or registered voters) and the legislature have the power to initiate a consultation. In Chile, Costa Rica, Honduras, Peru, Uruguay, and Venezuela the process may be initiated by the executive branch, the legislative branch, or by the citizenry. In El Salvador, only the executive branch has the authority to propose a referendum to call a constitutional convention. In Ecuador, both the executive branch and the citizenry have the authority to initiate a consultation.

The results of popular consultations may be binding or nonbinding, and if they are binding, they may or may not require a quorum. In Latin America, the results of popular consultations carried out to ratify constitutional reforms are in all cases binding. In only a few countries is a minimum level of participation necessary for the approval of binding consultations. These countries include Colombia, which requires that at least 25 percent of registered voters participate; Uruguay, which requires at least 35 percent of registered voters; Honduras, which requires a minimum of 51 percent of registered voters; and Costa Rica, which requires a minimum of 40 percent of registered voters.

In Colombia, Ecuador, Uruguay, and Venezuela, the results of popular consultations called to ratify laws are binding. In Nicaragua, results are binding for popular consultations proposed by at least 60 percent of the members of congress. In Argentina, congress determines whether the results of a given popular consultation will be binding. However, the results of popular consultations initiated by the president are always nonbinding, as are the results of those initiated by congress in cases where legislation has not been passed calling for the vote. In Colombia, the results of popular consultations are binding when the process is initiated by the president and approved by congress. In Costa Rica, the results are binding when a minimum of 30 percent of registered voters participate. Results are also binding in Bolivia under the 2004 referendum law, which stipulates that the outcomes of popular consultations must be put into effect immediately.

In many countries the list of issues that may be submitted to popular consultation is restricted, while in others there are no stated limits. For example, in Bolivia, Colombia, Costa Rica, Peru, Paraguay, Uruguay, and Venezuela, certain issues are excluded by law. In other cases, such as Ecuador, Honduras, Guatemala, and Colombia, the issues that qualify are specified. In contrast, in countries such as Argentina, Brazil, and Nicaragua, there are no restrictions on the types of issues that may be submitted for consideration. Finally, only in Colombia and Uruguay may popular consultations be used to abrogate as well as ratify laws. Nevertheless, in both of these countries certain types of legislation (such as tax policy) may not be put to popular consultation.

Popular Legislative Initiatives

Popular legislative initiatives are mandated in the constitutions of 13 of the region's countries. Except in Uruguay, however, their use has been limited. This mechanism is usually *ad parlamentum*, meaning that proposals presented through citizen-driven initiatives are sent for deliberation to the legislature, which then reaches a decision without consulting with the electorate. However, a few countries provide for legislative initiatives that result in a popular vote to decide the matter, without consideration by the legislature. For example, in Uruguay constitutional reforms or other legal initiatives originating from at least 10 percent of the electorate must be put to a popular consultation. In Colombia, when a bill introduced by popular initiative has been rejected by congress, it must be put to a vote in a "referendum of approval" if 10 percent of the registered voters so request.

Recalls

Recall votes are limited in most cases to the subnational level, but in Colombia, Ecuador, Panama, and Venezuela they can be held at the national level. In Venezuela, this option has been established for the offices of all popularly elected national officials, including the president. In fact, Venezuela is the only country in which the mechanism has been applied, when a vote was held in August 2004 on whether the mandate of President Hugo Chávez should be revoked. The measure did not succeed. Nevertheless, at the subnational level, recall votes have been introduced and applied in numerous countries, including Argentina, Ecuador, Peru, Bolivia, and Colombia.

Table 8.1 classifies countries into three groups, according to whether the various direct democracy mechanisms have been incorporated into the constitution and whether they have been used in practice. In the first group of 11 countries (dark shading), at least one of the mechanisms exists and at least one has been applied. The five countries in the second group (light shading) have some type of direct democracy mechanism in the constitution, but it has not yet been applied. Finally, in the third group of two countries (no shading), no provision is made at the national level for these types of mechanisms.

In the early 1990s, direct democracy mechanisms proliferated throughout Latin America. This trend reflected a popular desire to broaden public participation to remedy serious problems of representation and combat pervasive corruption in the political system. As a consequence of constitutional reforms in the 1980s and particularly the 1990s, 16 of the

Table 8.1. Direct Democracy Mechanisms at the National Level in Latin America

Country	Popular legislative initiative		Plebiscite/ referendum		Recall	
	Exists	Used	Exists	Used	Exists	Used
Argentina	Yes	No	Yes	Yes	No	No
Bolivia	Yes	No	Yes	Yes	No	No
Brazil	Yes	No	Yes	Yes	No	No
Chile	No	No	Yes	Yes	No	No
Colombia	Yes	Yes	Yes	Yes	Yes	No
Ecuador	Yes	No	Yes	Yes	No	No
Guatemala	Yes	No	Yes	Yes	No	No
Panama	No	No	Yes	Yes	Yes	No
Peru	Yes	No	Yes	Yes	No	No
Uruguay	Yes	Yes	Yes	Yes	No	No
Venezuela	Yes	No	Yes	Yes	Yes	Yes
Costa Rica	Yes	No	Yes	No	No	No
El Salvador	No	No	Yes	No	No	No
Honduras	No	No	Yes	No	No	No
Nicaragua	Yes	No	Yes	No	No	No
Paraguay	Yes	No	Yes	No	No	No
Mexico	No	No	No	No	No	No
Dominican Republic	No	No	No	No	No	No

Source: Author's compilation.
Note: The darker shading indicates countries in which direct democracy mechanisms both are in place and have been used. The lighter shading indicates those in which such mechanisms are in place but have not yet been used. Absence of shading indicates those in which such mechanisms are not in place.

18 countries in our study now provide for direct democracy in their national constitutions. (The exceptions are Mexico and the Dominican Republic.) Nevertheless, only Uruguay and, to a lesser extent, Ecuador have made frequent use of these mechanisms. Despite the wide variety of direct democracy mechanisms provided for in its 1991 constitution, Colombia has formally used only one of them (and only once) at the national level.[3] In 5 of the 16 countries where such mechanisms are in the constitution—Costa Rica, El Salvador, Honduras, Nicaragua, and Paraguay—they have never been used.

Every new constitution adopted in Latin America during the 1980s and 1990s included direct democracy mechanisms. The reasons behind their introduction varied throughout

---

[3] The 1990 popular consultation that led to the drafting of the 1991 constitution did not follow formal constitutional procedures.

the region, but two conditions were important in several of the cases. The first was the rise in influence of "outsider" political interests, including neopopulist presidents or previously excluded parties that came to dominate constituent assemblies. The second was strong popular pressure to democratize political institutions dominated by traditional political interests (Barczak, 2001). The fact that direct democracy mechanisms sprang from very specific conditions may account for the infrequency of their subsequent use and their relatively small effect on democratic representation and legitimacy.

Use of Direct Democracy Institutions

Between 1978 and 2005, 35 popular consultations were held in 11 countries (Table 8.2). Significantly, five were held in authoritarian regimes: in Panama in 1983, Uruguay in 1980, and Chile in 1980, 1988, and 1989. In Panama, the plebiscite approved in 1983 was aimed at reforming the constitution to strengthen the authoritarian regime of General Manuel Antonio Noriega. The results of the 1980 plebiscite in Uruguay were unfavorable to the military and thus opened the way to four years of negotiations culminating in the reinstatement of democracy. In contrast, the authoritarian regime of General Augusto Pinochet prevailed in Chile in 1980 and imposed a new constitution. However, the results of the 1988 consultation, which the 1980 constitution had envisioned as a means of endorsing Pinochet's continued rule, proved unfavorable. The purpose of the 1989 popular consultation was to modify the constitution in such a way as to promote the withdrawal of Pinochet from power and facilitate the democratic transition.

The remaining 30 cases involved a great variety of issues and outcomes. The popular consultations held in Argentina in 1984, Colombia in 1990 and 1997, and Ecuador in 1986 and 1997 (the *consultas-encuestas*, or consultation surveys) were not binding. The 1997 vote in Ecuador led to the creation of a constituent assembly, which subsequently incorporated into its proposed constitutional reform a good portion of what had been approved in the popular consultation.

The other cases of popular consultation were binding. Of these, eighteen were held to approve or reject constitutional reforms: seven in Uruguay, with four rejected and three approved; two in Chile, both approved; one in Brazil, which was rejected; three in Panama, with one approved and two rejected; two in Guatemala, with one approved and one rejected; and one each in Ecuador, Peru, and Venezuela, all approved. Three of the popular consultations, all in Uruguay, were aimed at overturning legislation. The popular consultation in Colombia in 1990 served simultaneously to create and legitimize the constituent assembly. The same procedure was followed in Venezuela in April 1999. In December 2000, President Chávez's government called another referendum to test support for holding labor union elections within a 180-day period. However, convoking a referendum on this issue conflicted with International Labour Organization regulations. Citizens subsequently responded to a request by labor unions to boycott the vote, and the initiative was rejected, with a turnout of only 20 percent.

The referendum held in Colombia in 2003 submitted to the voters a series of 15 government reform proposals covering a wide range of issues, including reducing the number of congressional seats; narrowing the grounds for dismissal from office; prohibiting the use

Table 8.2. Applications of Direct Democracy Mechanisms from 1978 to 2005

Country	Date	Mechanism	Issue	Outcome	Effect
Argentina	Nov. 1984	Popular consultation	The Beagle Channel decision.	Approved	Legitimizing, non-binding. Support for the administration of President Raúl Alfonsín, author of the proposal.
Bolivia	Jul. 2004	Referendum	Consultation on national energy policy.	Approved	The result allowed a change in the rules for entering into contracts with international oil companies. Binding.
Brazil	April 1993	Plebiscite	Monarchy vs. republic.	Rejected	Endorsement of the prevailing republican form of government. Binding.
Brazil	April 1993	Plebiscite	Parliamentarism vs. presidentialism.	Rejected	Endorsement of the prevailing presidential system.
Chile	Sep. 1980	Plebiscite	New constitution establishing the new regime.	Approved	New constitution and electoral system.
Chile	Oct. 1988	Plebiscite	In accordance with the 1980 constitution, a vote on whether to extend Pinochet's rule.	Rejected	A rejection of the military government's proposal, put to direct popular vote as anticipated in 1980. This subsequently allowed the acceleration of the democratization process.
Chile	Jun. 1989	Plebiscite	Constitutional reform.	Approved	Confirmation of negotiations on the democratic transition.
Colombia	Mar. 1990	Informal popular consultation	Possibility of reforming the constitution by extra-congressional means. Direct popular vote advanced by "7th ballot" students.	Affirmative	Because of this consultation, a constituent assembly was convened and its members were elected in December 1990.

(continued)

Table 8.2. *(continued)*

Country	Date	Mechanism	Issue	Outcome	Effect
Colombia	Oct. 1997	Popular consultation	Support for pacification.	Approved	Irrelevant. An attempt by the president to legitimize the peace process.
Colombia	Oct. 2003	Referendum	Consultation on 15 proposals submitted by President Uribe to popular vote, including reducing the number of congressional seats and imposing new restrictions on candidates for public office.	All but one rejected	Failure of the majority of President Uribe's proposals to be approved.
Ecuador	Jan. 1978	Plebiscite	Constitution.	Approved	Endorsement of the transition to democracy.
Ecuador	Jun. 1986	Popular consultation	Whether to allow candidacies independent of the political parties.	Approved	Irrelevant, nonbinding.
Ecuador	Aug. 1994	Survey consultation with seven questions[1]	To strengthen the legitimacy of the president.	Approved except for a question on the congressional budget	Nonbinding. Display of support for President Sixto Durán, who initiated the process. Items not implemented.
Ecuador	Nov. 1995	Survey consultation	Authority of the president to dissolve congress one time during his or her term of office; also, changing the term of provincial legislators from two to four years.	All points rejected	Nonbinding. Became a plebiscite to oppose the administration of President Sixto Durán, who initiated the process.

(continued)

Table 8.2. *(continued)*

Country	Date	Mechanism	Issue	Outcome	Effect
Ecuador	May 1997	Survey consultation with 11 questions	Support for removal from office of President Abdalá Bucarám and his replacement by Fabián Alarcón.	Approved	Endorsed the removal of the president and the confirmation of his replacement. Because of the consultation, a constitutional convention was convened, which approved a new constitution containing some of the measures put to popular consultation.
Guatemala	Jan. 1994	Referendum	Constitutional reform.	Approved	Approval of constitutional reforms necessitated by the institutional adjustments made in the wake of the unsuccessful self-coup of President Jorge Serrano.
Guatemala	May 1999	Referendum	Constitutional reforms made to implement peace accords.	Rejected	Became primarily a demonstration of hostility toward the government instead of focusing on the constitutional issue under consideration.
Panama	April 1983	Referendum	Constitutional reform.	Approved	Strengthened the authoritarian regime of President Noriega.
Panama	Nov. 1992	Referendum	58-point constitutional reform.	Rejected	Attempted endorsement of reforms introduced by the democratic regime.
Panama	Aug. 1998	Plebiscite	Constitutional reform, immediate presidential reelection, and other points.	Rejected	President Pérez Balladares' reelection was not allowed.

(continued)

Table 8.2. (continued)

Country	Date	Mechanism	Issue	Outcome	Effect
Peru	Oct. 1993	Plebiscite	New constitution.	Approved	Legitimization of the new regime of President Alberto Fujimori.
Uruguay	Nov. 1980	Plebiscite	New constitution proposed by the military government.	Rejected	Rejection exerted pressure on the military to begin political liberalization.
Uruguay	April 1989	Referendum	General amnesty law covering the military and police.	Approved	Lent popular backing to a very controversial decision.
Uruguay	Nov. 1989	Plebiscite	Constitutional reform.	Approved	Public endorsement of agreements previously reached by party leaders.
Uruguay	Dec. 1992	Referendum	Proposal to over-turn law partially privatizing the state-owned telephone company.	Approved	Expressed the continued statist sentiments of the majority of the electorate.
Uruguay	Aug. 1994	Plebiscite	Constitutional reform establishing separate ballots for municipal and national elections.	Rejected	
Uruguay	Nov. 1994	Plebiscite	Constitutional reform to establish regulations to protect retired persons and those receiving pensions.	Approved	Modified constitution to add protections for these citizens.
Uruguay	Nov. 1994	Plebiscite	Constitutional re-form allocating 27 percent of the bud-get for education.	Rejected	
Uruguay	Dec. 1996	Plebiscite	Constitutional reform to modify the electoral system.	Approved	Resulted in important changes in the electoral system, eliminating the double simultaneous vote and replacing it with primary and general elections.

(continued)

Table 8.2. *(continued)*

Country	Date	Mechanism	Issue	Outcome	Effect
Uruguay	Oct. 1999	Plebiscite	Two constitutional reforms: one prohibiting members of state enterprises from running for office, and another allocating a fixed percentage of the budget for the judiciary.	Rejected	
Uruguay	Dec. 2003	Referendum	Attempt to repeal law authorizing national fuel agency (ANCAP) to join with private firms; sought to eliminate the monopoly on fuel imports by 2006.	Approved	ANCAP barred from forming joint ventures for the purposes spelled out in the law. Binding.
Venezuela	April 1999	Referendum	Authorization of executive resolution to create a constituent assembly and elect its members.	Approved	Referendum made up part of President Chávez's efforts to reform the political system.
Venezuela	Dec. 1999	Plebiscite	Constitutional reform.	Approved	Endorsement of reform enacted by the constituent assembly.
Venezuela	Dec. 2000	Referendum	Replacement of union leadership.	Approved	Created a coalition of forces favorable to the government. Binding.
Venezuela	Aug. 2004	Referendum	Recall vote on presidency of Hugo Chávez.	Rejected	Popular endorsement of President Chávez's continued rule.

Source: Author's compilation
[1] The term "consultation survey" (*consulta-encuesta*) was used in Ecuador because the format of the ballot for the direct popular vote was similar to that of questionnaires used in public opinion polls.

of public resources by elected officials to support political campaigns or provide personal rewards; introducing elections to fill leadership posts in public enterprises; and granting new resources for education, among other measures. Although those who voted were overwhelmingly in favor of all of the proposals, in only one case was the necessary quorum (25 percent) reached.

The consultation held in Bolivia in 2004 resulted in the approval of the government's proposed energy policy. Finally, the 2004 referendum in Venezuela to recall President Hugo Chávez was rejected, signaling voters' support for his continued rule. The *autogolpes* (self-coups) of President Fujimori in Peru, which succeeded, and President Serrano Elías in Guatemala, which failed, led to popular consultations in both countries in 1993 and 1994, respectively. The processes resulted in the formation of constituent assemblies in both countries, the establishment of a new constitution in Peru, and constitutional reform in Guatemala. A profound political crisis in Venezuela in the 1990s eroded the party system that had been in existence since the 1961 *Punto Fijo* pact and led to popular consultations in 1999. The first created a constituent assembly, and the second ratified the constitution proposed by the assembly. The only popular consultation carried out in the context of a peace process was in Guatemala in 1999; it was broadly rejected by voters. Popular consultations were not used in the peace processes in either Nicaragua or El Salvador.

Most of the popular consultations held during the 1978–2005 period were top-down initiatives. The executive branch convoked the popular consultations in Argentina in 1984, Bolivia in 2004, Colombia in 1997 and 2003, and Venezuela in 2000, as well as the four consultations in Ecuador, comprising a total of nine cases. Where popular consultations were used to approve constitutional reforms, in six of sixteen cases the executive branch initiated the process, although all were officially endorsed by legislative bodies or constitutional conventions. The six cases include Guatemala (1994), Panama (1998), Peru (1993), Venezuela (1999), and under military regimes, Chile (1980) and Uruguay (1980).

In summary, the executive branch initiated 15 of the 35 popular consultations that were held. Another 11 stemmed from agreements among politicians that resulted in constitutional reform proposals being either approved or rejected, or involved constitutional provisions agreed on beforehand, such as the aforementioned 1993 popular consultation in Brazil and the one in Chile in 1988. Altogether, 26 of the 35 popular consultations held arose from initiatives coming from the top down.

The last nine cases involved bottom-up initiatives. Seven took place in Uruguay: two that approved constitutional reforms (1989 and 1994), two that rejected constitutional reforms (1994 and 1999), and three referenda that successfully repealed laws. The eighth case, as indicated above, was that of Colombia in 1990, which was extra-constitutional and led to the drafting and adoption of the 1991 constitution. The ninth case, the recall vote against Venezuelan President Hugo Chávez, was presented for popular vote in August 2004 after opposition sectors collected the required number of signatures to call the referendum.

Assessment of Direct Democracy Institutions

Frequency of Use

Over the past two decades, countries have made only modest use of mechanisms for direct citizen participation at the national level. In fact, direct democracy institutions have been applied in only 11 of the 16 countries where they figure in the constitution. In Chile, the mechanisms have been used only under the previous authoritarian regime (as they were under nondemocratic regimes in 1980 in Uruguay and in 1983 in Panama). Overall, during the period under study, direct democracy institutions were used most often in Uruguay, followed by Ecuador. They have been used several times recently in Venezuela.

Although these mechanisms have been used fairly infrequently, there has been an increase in their use over time. Nine popular consultations took place during the 1980s (five under authoritarian regimes), while 20 took place during the 1990s, and five since 2000.

No general rule explains why some countries have used these mechanisms more than others. The prevailing circumstances in the two countries in which they have been used most often could hardly be more different. In Uruguay, these mechanisms had been in existence long before the restoration of democracy, and the party system was relatively institutionalized.[4] In contrast, in Ecuador the weak and fragmented party system sometimes prompted presidents to use popular consultations as defensive measures, in vain attempts to fend off harassment by the legislature and bolster declining public support. Direct democracy mechanisms have been rarely used in the region's three largest countries. Argentina and Brazil have used them only once each, and no provisions for them exist in the Mexican constitution.

Origins of Use

We have noted that 26 of the 35 popular consultations during the period of the study came from the top down and only nine originated from the bottom up—with seven of those in just one country, Uruguay. This experience is consistent with the fact that, while some countries do provide for citizen initiation of popular consultations, it is more common for the initiation of referendums to be limited by law to the executive branch or congress.

The top-down approach to direct democracy has been pursued across the region with mixed results for those in power. In Panama, former president Pérez Balladares failed in his attempt to modify the constitution to permit his reelection. In Ecuador, President Sixto Durán got a favorable response in the first popular consultation undertaken during his administration, but he lost the second one, weakening his administration. The Uruguayan government suffered a defeat in 1994 when it attempted to impose a constitutional reform to separate municipal and national voting lists, a reform that had already been approved by two-thirds of congress. (The reform was subsequently approved in 1996.) President Fujimori in Peru and President Chávez in Venezuela successfully employed direct democracy mechanisms to help consolidate their political programs. In Colombia, President Álvaro Uribe, buoyed by significant public support, attempted to win popular backing for a series of policy changes. The result? All but one of the proposals failed because of insufficient voter turnout. Finally, in Bolivia the referendum on national energy policy called by President Carlos Mesa succeeded in involving citizens directly in political decision making. The referendum was approved, lending support to Mesa's political style based on sustaining a direct relationship with citizens.

---

[4] The possibility of using referendums to repeal laws was an innovation that occurred after the democratic transition.

The constitutions of several countries allow citizens to initiate constitutional reforms, thus giving them a significant decision-making role. Each country requires a certain percentage of registered voters to sign a petition to advance the process. To date this mechanism has been used only in Uruguay. Reform initiatives launched there by civil society organizations in 1989, 1994, and 1999 aimed at increasing the budget or benefits of workers in the retirement system, education sector, and the judiciary, respectively. The initiatives in 1989 and 1994 were approved; the one in 1999 failed.

Popular initiatives have led to referendums to overturn laws in Uruguay. A coalition of left and center-left parties and an ad hoc civil society movement sponsored the ultimately unsuccessful 1989 referendum aimed at revoking the amnesty law, which had been designed to protect members of the armed forces from prosecution for human rights violations committed during the military regime (1973–85). The 1992 referendum in Uruguay, which successfully overturned a law that would have partially privatized the state-owned telephone company, was spearheaded by a similar coalition of forces working in tandem with labor unions representing telephone workers. The 2003 referendum to repeal this law was promoted by the workers' union of the state fuel company, with the support of parties on the left. The participation of Uruguayan civil society organizations was limited, since in both cases ad hoc social movements sought alliances with political parties. In Colombia, the "7th Ballot" student movement (*movimiento estudiantil de la 7ª papeleta*) exerted pressure leading to the 1991 constitutional reform. In Venezuela, the August 2004 referendum to recall President Chávez was promoted by civil society groups and opposition forces, which jointly organized the effort to gather the required number of signatures.

Several countries allow citizens to propose legislative initiatives, provided a certain percentage of the population backs the petition. The constitutions of some countries, including Brazil and Venezuela, also stipulate that if the legislature rejects a bill introduced by popular initiative, a certain percentage of the citizens may request that it be put to a referendum. The constitutions of Paraguay, Peru, and Uruguay also provide for this mechanism, but as is the case with some of the other countries mentioned above, the laws needed to implement the mechanism have yet to be enacted.

The use of these mechanisms at the national level generally has not increased the influence of civil society in public decision making. Greater citizen control over the government and other representative institutions has resulted in very few cases. The only clear examples are the popular consultations held in Uruguay for the purpose of repealing laws. But even in this case, three attempts after 1992 to abolish laws through referenda failed because the required number of signatures on the petition (25 percent of registered voters) was not obtained. The only other examples are the approval of an anti-kidnapping law in Colombia; the consultation in Peru in 1998 on the possible reelection of President Fujimori; and the recall vote in Venezuela in 2004 on Chávez's presidency. In the case of Peru, the government blocked the consultation, despite the popular support behind it, by amending a law to make congressional approval a prerequisite for holding the referendum. In the end, this approval was not obtained. In Venezuela, opposition groups successfully led the effort to collect the required number of signatures to hold the recall referendum, but the initiative ultimately was rejected.

In short, civil society's use of direct democracy has centered on efforts to control and restrain rather than to create and innovate. In part this distinction reflects the fact that, despite constitutional provisions for implementing these mechanisms, initiatives are not easy to carry out. They require the convergence of political will around a relevant, motivating issue and the development of a social movement to carry the process forward.

Direct Democracy and the Behavior of the Electorate

During the past 27 years, citizens' behavior with respect to direct democracy has varied, with no overall trend having emerged in the region. It is clear that Latin Americans frequently fail to vote in a manner that focuses on the particular issue put before them; rather, they use the vote as an opportunity to vent their frustration at the poor performance of the government in power. Therefore, popular consultations in some cases have served as a means of expressing overall disenchantment with politics and politicians.

One example is the unequivocal rejection by Uruguayan citizens of the 1994 "mini" constitutional reform, which had the backing of all major political parties. Apparently, the outcome had little to do with the specific content of the issues presented to the public. Another example is the popular consultation in Guatemala in 1999. The reforms designed to ratify the peace accords that ended the 36-year-long civil war did not induce a significant level of participation. Additionally, a high percentage of those who did participate voted "no" primarily as a means of expressing dissatisfaction with the government in power at the time.

Citizens also have not demonstrated a clear tendency for either preserving the status quo or bringing about significant change. While the rejection of legislative reforms in Brazil's 1993 referendum preserved the status quo, the "7th Ballot" student movement initiative in Colombia promoted substantial political change. Likewise, even though the recall referendum in Venezuela sought a major change in government leadership through the president's removal, the outcome supported his continued rule.

As a result of this generalized unpredictability, elected officials may be becoming more cautious about using direct democracy mechanisms, resorting to their use only when they feel fairly confident that the outcome will be favorable, or applying them only when obliged to do so, as in the case of constitutional reforms.

Low levels of electoral participation in popular consultations reflect considerable apathy on the part of voters. The Guatemalan and Colombian examples are particularly noteworthy for their low levels of participation, although high abstention rates are also typical of regular elections in these countries. Some popular consultations have been approved or rejected with the participation of fewer than 50 percent of registered voters. Nonetheless, the results were accepted even by groups whose positions on the matter at hand were not favored.

Consequences for the Political System

There is no clear evidence that the use of direct democracy at the national level has either significantly improved or damaged the performance of political systems around the world.

With few exceptions, the democracies of Europe and North America either do not provide for national popular consultations, or rarely invoke them. Experience at the national level in Latin America indicates that these mechanisms, at least as used to date, have not had the desired effects on representation or participation.

Similarly, direct democracy mechanisms have not had a substantial impact on political stability. Just as with any other feature of the electoral system, their functioning must be examined relative to the broader institutional framework. In general, these mechanisms have not been used to resolve disputes between the legislature and the executive branch. Rare examples of their use in this way include the cases in which Ecuadorian presidents Sixto Durán and Fabían Alarcón unsuccessfully resorted to popular consultations to enhance the popular legitimacy and legislative backing of their weakened administrations.

In particular countries at certain moments, the use of these mechanisms may have been counterproductive for political stability. An example is Ecuador, where the nonbinding character of popular consultations and their lack of implementation has actually exacerbated the country's problems of democratic governability.

The complexity of economic and financial issues at the national level makes it difficult to try to address them through institutions of direct democracy, because they require a high level of citizen participation. As a result, constitutions in most Latin American countries have expressly excluded such matters from popular consultations.

However, in Uruguay and Ecuador these mechanisms have been used by civil society organizations tied to center-left parties seeking to impose limits on economic reforms. The paradigmatic case is the 1992 referendum to repeal the law enacted by the Uruguayan government to partially privatize the state-owned telephone company. However, a similar attempt several years later to overturn a law regulating the distribution of electricity and gas failed, as did a challenge to the private retirement and pension system. Then in 2003 a referendum repealed a law that allowed Uruguay's national fuel agency to form joint ventures to refine and distribute petroleum products. In Ecuador, attempts by civil society groups to call a popular consultation to challenge President Gustavo Noboa's dollarization policy and economic plan failed after the election oversight body reported that the required number of signatures had not been obtained.

Finally, it is again worth noting the attempt of Colombian President Álvaro Uribe in 2003 to enact multiple reform proposals via referendum. By not turning out to vote in sufficient numbers, citizens in effect blocked most of the reforms. In contrast, the approval by Bolivian voters of President Mesa's July 2004 proposal led to the repeal of a hydrocarbons law originally promulgated by Gonzalo Sánchez de Lozada and resulted in the recovery of government ownership of all fossil fuels within the country's borders.

Conclusions

In most Latin American countries both the use and impact of direct democracy mechanisms at the national level have been limited. These mechanisms have been used for a variety of reasons, ranging from demagogic manipulation to the defense of conservative or traditionalist interests and the implementation of reforms sought by voters. Their results have been mixed and, at times, unanticipated. For instance, in two extreme cases where prevailing authoritarian regimes resorted to these mechanisms to keep themselves in power—Chile in 1988 and Uruguay in 1980—their use backfired tremendously.

An assessment of the impact of direct democracy mechanisms in the region should take into account how recently they have been adopted. With the exception of Uruguay, direct democracy mechanisms are a relatively new feature of Latin American democracy. Hence, more time is needed to evaluate their effects and their scope of application.

Based on the review of this relatively limited regional experience, it would seem that a proper legal framework is essential for these mechanisms to function well. For example, the law must explicitly address the various options available for activating such mechanisms. Experience has shown that between 1978 and 2004, direct democracy mechanisms were primarily initiated from the top down. Additionally, legal norms should clearly specify the situations and issues that may be dealt with through various direct democracy mechanisms.

In general, democracy will be strengthened to the extent that the use of direct democracy mechanisms is rooted in and contributes to strengthening citizenship. This is possible only when efforts to reinforce democracy include civic education to support the development of values associated with the exercise of political participation beyond its electoral form. As the situation now stands, very low levels of interpersonal trust and confidence in political institutions in Latin America (see Chapter 10) make it difficult to mobilize and coordinate civil society and improve and broaden political participation.

In societies such as those of Latin America, where poverty and inequality are persistently high, the wise use of direct democracy mechanisms may help offset the worrisome trend toward delegitimization of the political system. Because direct democracy institutions provide an additional means for political expression, they can be a valuable way for people to signal their frustrations to those in positions of power. At the same time, it is important to avoid the danger of these mechanisms being used for demagogic purposes; hence clear limits should be established regarding the types of issues that they may be used to address.

It is also important that direct democracy mechanisms be viewed as instruments for strengthening democracy that complement rather than supplant the institutions of representative democracy. While the exercise of direct democracy can strengthen political legitimacy and open channels of participation that bring together citizens and their representatives, the primary institutions for articulating and aggregating citizen preferences remain political parties and congress. These institutions themselves need to be strengthened in order to improve the quality and legitimacy of democratic representation.

Finally, the fact that direct democracy mechanisms have rarely been used and have had little impact at the national level—not only in Latin America but in democracies around the world—suggests that they may be more suitable and beneficial at the subnational level. This notion finds some support in cases where such mechanisms have been employed at the subnational level in Europe and North America, as well as in some Latin American countries.

It is important to recognize that whatever their impact, direct democracy mechanisms are likely to remain part of the democratic system. Our main concern, therefore, should be to determine how and when to use them—and for what purposes.

References

Aguilar de Luque, Luis. 1986. Participación política y reforma. Aspectos teóricos y constitucionales. *Revista de Derecho Público* [Madrid], no. 102.

Barczak, Monica. 2001. Representation by Consultation? The Rise of Direct Democracy in Latin America. *Latin American Politics and Society* 43(3).

Bogdanor, Vernon. 1994. Western Europe. In David Butler and Austin Ranney (eds.), *Referendums around the World: The Growing Use of Direct Democracy*. Washington, DC: American Enterprise Institute Press.

Cronin, Thomas E. 1998. *Direct Democracy: The Politics of Initiative, Referendum and Recall*. Cambridge, MA: Harvard University Press.

Dalton, Russell J., Wilhelm Bürklin, and Andrew Drummond. 2001. Public Opinion and Direct Democracy. *Journal of Democracy* 12(4).

Thibaut, Bernhard. 1998. Instituciones de democracia directa. In Dieter Nohlen, Sonia Picado, and Daniel Zovatto (eds.), *Tratado de derecho electoral comparado de América Latina*. Mexico: Fondo de Cultura Económica.

CHAPTER 9

Trends in Electoral Participation

Power can be taken, but not given.
The process of the taking is empowerment in itself.
—Gloria Steinem

Contrasted with taking part in elections—a rather formal and sporadic form of citizen participation—democratic political participation is a broad concept connoting ongoing involvement in the political system. It embraces not only voting but involvement in political campaigns or party meetings, membership in community organizations, joining protests, and communicating with legislative representatives. Of the various forms of citizen participation, voting is the only one in which more than 50 percent of the citizenry of democratic countries normally take part. The others imply a level of commitment and engagement in public affairs that rarely attracts more than a quarter of the adult population (CAPEL, 1989). Thus electoral participation is central to the functioning of democratic systems: people otherwise scarcely involved in a nation's political life nonetheless express their preferences among competing candidates on election day.

Because cross-national, quantitative data are available for electoral participation, but are more uneven and sparse for the broader notion of political participation, this chapter focuses specifically on the former. Evidence does suggest, however, that the two types of participation are connected: people who vote are more likely than those who do not to be interested in politics and to participate more regularly in other forms of political activity (Putnam, 2000). Political participation should be measured along at least two dimensions: first, the *level* of participation, meaning the relative number of citizens who vote or otherwise participate to some degree in the political system; and second, the *intensity* of participation, specifically the extent to which citizens engage in more demanding forms of participation, and the level of information citizens have about politics (IDB, 2000).[1]

---

[1] The level of information about politics to which citizens have access through the mass media, a factor not measured directly in this chapter, influences the quality and intensity of political participation.

References to voting and its value for democracy often operate under implicit assumptions about how the electoral process works. For example, it is often assumed that wherever elections occur, democratic freedoms are fully protected and the voting process itself is transparent and fair. Such assumptions have not always been warranted in Latin America. But over the past 20 years, considerable progress has been made throughout the region in improving the integrity and fairness of elections. Electoral management bodies now exist in every country of the region, and in many countries these institutions have taken on a more permanent character and assumed a growing array of functions. As a consequence, only in a relatively few cases over the past decade have election procedures or vote counts been perceived as fraudulent by objective observers.

Despite this important accomplishment, developing more permanent professional and managerial capacity in electoral bodies could further enhance the electoral process. Greater capacity would allow election authorities to maintain accurate and complete voter registration lists and effectively enforce regulations pertaining to electoral and party financing and access to the media. In some countries the political independence and public credibility of the electoral management agency remain in doubt, thus endangering popular acceptance of election results and leaving the system vulnerable to fraud.

Electoral fairness also requires relatively equal access to campaign resources for candidates, a politically independent media, and transparency in the origins and use of campaign finance (see Chapter 7). Efforts in all these areas have been undertaken throughout the region, but just as in some of the world's oldest democracies, serious problems remain. As a consequence, citizens in some countries remain skeptical about the integrity and fairness of the electoral process.

Importance of Electoral Participation

The extent to which citizens exercise their right (or duty) to vote clearly determines how well elections are performing the functions expected of them in a modern democracy, including (1) legitimizing governmental authority; (2) forming governments; (3) recruiting political leaders; (4) fostering public discussion and debate about issues; and (5) facilitating the development and exercise of citizenship (Heywood, 1997). While all of these functions are important, this chapter focuses on two that are central to the notion of democracy: signaling preferences about public policy and holding public officials accountable for their performance.

Democratic representation entails a form of bargain between citizens and elected officials. Citizens confer authority (by voting) in exchange for promises by elected officials to pursue a given package of policy goals, serve the public good, and respect the law and the constitution. Given the informality of this transaction, the infrequency of elections, and gaps in citizens' information, the process never produces fully responsive or even always honest politicians. But the effectiveness of democracy can be traced in part to the quality of this two-way exchange (Lupia and McCubbins, 1998; Przeworski, Stokes, and Manin, 1999).

The likelihood that elections will produce effective and accountable political representation hinges on a range of institutional factors, including the nature of the electoral system

(Chapters 2 and 3), the capacity of the legislature (Chapter 4), the independence and effectiveness of agencies of horizontal accountability (Chapter 5), and characteristics of the political party system (Chapters 6 and 7). Nevertheless, it can be argued that a well-informed and highly participatory citizenry is the foundation of any "good" government.

The fewer citizens who participate, individually and as members of civil society organizations, the more probable it is that the public's needs and demands will be ignored—and the more likely that public officials will give in to the temptation to pursue private interests at the expense of the public good. Low levels of electoral participation can have a range of adverse effects on the functioning of the democratic system.

One such effect stems from the fact that, when turnout is low, it is also often skewed. This means that certain groups participate less actively in the electoral process, both as voters and candidates. Such groups frequently include the poorest and least educated sectors of the population, as well as women, youth, the elderly, ethnic minorities, and people in rural, less-populous regions. Low participation affects election results and therefore the composition and representativeness of the political system (Hajnal and Trounstine, 2005; Bernhagen and Marsh, 2004). To the extent that some groups fail to participate, elected officials have less incentive to address their needs; thus the interests of underparticipating groups may be ignored in the making and implementation of public policies. This can lead to a vicious cycle in which underparticipating groups are ignored in the decision-making process, further alienating them from the political system and reinforcing bias in public policies.

Another adverse impact of low levels of participation is that the actions of public officials are subjected to less public scrutiny, increasing the possibility that unresponsive or corrupt behavior will go unnoticed and unpunished at the polls (IDB, 2000). Societies with low levels of political participation and information are less able to foresee and signal to public officials the policies that may lead to superior performance, and are less determined to press for the effective implementation of such policies. However, as shown in previous chapters, participation cannot be considered independently of other factors and mechanisms of institutional oversight. Higher participation alone will not ensure greater oversight of political leaders.

A low or declining level of electoral participation may not only hinder efficient democratic representation, it may also reflect a lack of confidence in democratic institutions, something that can delay the consolidation of a democratic regime and even threaten its stability. Low electoral participation is of particular concern in societies where the transition to democracy is recent and a broad foundation of democratic values and practices is lacking. If large numbers of people do not vote, it is difficult to build a democratic culture and strengthen the legitimacy and functional capacity of democratic institutions, such as the legislature and the judiciary. It is also difficult to promote transparent, responsible management of public finances and to ensure that public employees and officials embrace the public interest and refrain from improper conduct. In sum, low levels of political participation can set off a deteriorating cycle in which disappointment in the performance of politicians breeds further distrust and political alienation, in turn further reducing participation and incentives for better performance. Disenchantment with democratic actors and institutions can open the doors of power to leaders and movements that govern without regard for the constitution.

Factors Affecting Electoral Participation

An extensive literature examines why some citizens and not others participate actively in civic affairs, and why levels of participation vary across countries.[2] Various attempts have been made to understand, on the one hand, the characteristics of politically active citizens in a particular country (the micro level of electoral participation), and on the other, the types of political systems that produce incentives for citizens to participate in spite of the associated costs (the macro level). While we will not provide an exhaustive analysis of this matter here, we offer some insights into the major factors that influence levels of electoral participation. Although certain factors have been shown to influence turnout, much of the variance remains unexplained in the existing literature. The reality is that even in established democracies, citizen participation in decision-making processes is limited, as evidenced in part by the progressive decline of participation over the past decades—even in customary practices like elections and referenda.

Macro Factors Affecting Levels of Electoral Participation

The fairly stable *macro* (country-level) factors that help explain comparative levels of electoral participation—but not sudden shifts in voter turnout—can be divided into two major groups. As shown in Table 9.1, these include (1) factors related to the socioeconomic and cultural context, and (2) factors specifically related to institutions and political processes.[3] This chapter focuses primarily on political factors, referring only briefly to socioeconomic factors.

Socioeconomic factors include the level of educational attainment, the level of economic development, and the degree of ethnolinguistic and religious homogeneity. Factors related to political culture, measured by levels of interpersonal trust and civic cooperation, do not fit neatly into either of the two broad categories. Clearly, citizens are more likely to vote in large numbers in societies in which individuals are more trusting of one another and therefore more inclined to join civic organizations. Moreover, more years of education and higher incomes would be expected to enhance citizens' political awareness as well as their capacity to participate in politics. However, given the minimal demands of voting, income and education may have a greater effect on the intensity of political participation than on the level of electoral participation per se.

The political and institutional dimension includes structural elements, such as the intensity of linkages between political parties and major lines of cleavage in society (social class, religion, ethnicity); the nature of the electoral system; the comprehensiveness of voter registration lists; the legal status of voting (compulsory or voluntary); and the nature of the voter registration process. Included among the contextual political factors is whether

---

[2] See Almond and Verba (1965); Nie and Verba (1975); Verba, Nie, and Kim (1971); Powell (1980, 1986); LeDuc, Niemi, and Norris (1996); International IDEA (1997, 2002); Jackman (1987); and Fornos, Power, and Garand (2004).

[3] For further discussion of the various factors, see Powell (1980); Jackman (1987); Jackman and Miller (1995); and Fornos, Power, and Garand (2004).

Table 9.1. Socioeconomic and Political Factors Affecting Electoral Participation at the Macro Level

	Socioeconomic factors	Political factors
Structural factors	Educational attainment Economic development Ethnolinguistic and religious homogeneity	Political culture Linkages between political parties and major groups Electoral system • proportionality • size and type of voting district/precinct • compulsory voting • voter registration Efficiency, integrity, and transparency of political processes
Contextual factors	Economic crisis Passage of unpopular socioeconomic reforms Social mobilization	Electoral process Foundational elections Election timing Electoral campaign

Source: Authors' compilation.

or not the elections are "foundational," that is, whether they mark a return to democracy after a prolonged period of undemocratic rule. Turnout may be unusually high in elections inaugurating a democratic transition, because regime change often is accompanied by considerable citizen mobilization and enthusiasm for the exercise of recently acquired democratic freedoms. However, after this relatively brief period has passed, and the populace experiences the realities of governing in complex circumstances, turnout usually begins to decline. Other contextual factors discussed briefly below include the character of the election campaign and the environment in which voting takes place.

When parties represent important lines of cleavage in society—such as religion or social class—electoral outcomes take on a more readily identifiable significance, and politicians can more easily mobilize their less-informed or less-interested supporters. Also, greater ethnolinguistic diversity likely reduces electoral participation, because the sense of national community is weaker, and ethnolinguistic or cultural barriers may impede political activity and voting by members of minority groups.

Other factors may increase or reduce turnout. National electoral districts may provide an incentive for political parties to deploy their resources throughout the entire national territory, which may increase voter turnout (Powell, 1986). Some authors suggest that "disproportional" electoral systems reduce incentives for the constituencies of political groups with low chances of winning to take part in the electoral process (Jackman and Miller, 1995). Finally, if voters perceive that their votes matter to outcomes, participation tends to be higher. According to Jackman (1987), this perception is more prevalent in countries with a unicameral legislature.

Factors such as whether voter registration is automatic, compulsory, or voluntary can also influence voter turnout. If the government is responsible for maintaining current lists of registered voters or periodically canvassing citizens to create or update lists, then the registration process itself should not present a significant obstacle to voting. Mandatory registration may encourage more citizens to register and therefore to vote. However, if citizens are required to undertake procedural steps to register, many may avoid the process and thus not vote.

More citizens may be expected to participate in elections when voting is mandatory rather than voluntary. In fact, studies done in relatively well established democracies suggest, not surprisingly, that compulsory voting laws result in somewhat higher levels of turnout (Powell, 1980; Jackman, 1987). However, the degree to which legal requirements make a difference depends on the severity of the penalty and the likelihood of being caught and punished. If the penalty is minimal or rarely enforced, then the law likely will have little effect. Such conditions may be more likely to obtain in democracies such as those in Latin America, where the rule of law is less well established than in Europe, for example. In most countries of Latin America, registration and voting are compulsory, although the requirement is hotly debated. Advocates of penalties for nonvoting view voting as a public duty and believe that such legislation can increase electoral participation above what it would be otherwise. Critics of legal mandates believe that voting is a right, and that including votes of citizens who participate only for fear of being penalized may spoil the election process.

In Argentina, Brazil, Costa Rica, Ecuador, and Peru, voter registration is automatic, while in 11 other countries it is compulsory; it is voluntary only in Colombia and Chile (Table 9.2). Voting is obligatory in 15 of the 18 countries in this study. In Chile, voting is mandatory only for those registered to vote; in Colombia and Nicaragua voting is not mandatory. Colombia is the only country where both registration and voting are entirely voluntary.

However, only five countries—Bolivia, Chile, Ecuador, Peru, and Uruguay—can be considered to have a comprehensive system of compulsory voting, with voting required by law, sanctions contemplated for those who abstain, and effective mechanisms for applying the penalties. As a result, each of these countries can be considered to have a comprehensive system of compulsory voting, with the caveat that in Chile obligatory voting rules apply only to those who are registered. All other countries in the region have mixed systems in which either no penalties exist, or the penalties are not enforced in practice.

Micro Factors Affecting Levels of Electoral Participation

Given that in some countries voter turnout varies considerably from one election to the next, elements other than the macro (country-level) factors must affect electoral participation.

Why do some individuals choose to vote and others do not? As discussed in Chapter 1, citizens generally need incentives to make the effort to vote. Civic duty and political attitudes may not be enough; instead, incentives should take the form of benefits that voters hope to gain. The various micro (individual-level) factors that contribute to short- and long-term fluctuations in turnout can be divided, like the set of macro factors, into two major

Table 9.2. Types of Registration and Voting Rules in Latin America

Country	Type of Registration			Compulsory voting?	Penalties for abstention?	Penalties enforced?
	Automatic	Compulsory	Voluntary			
Chile[1]			X	Yes	Yes	Yes
Ecuador[2]	X			Yes	Yes	Yes
Peru[3]	X			Yes	Yes	Yes
Uruguay		X		Yes	Yes	Yes
Bolivia		X		Yes	Yes	Yes
Argentina[4]	X			Yes	Yes	No
Brazil[5]	X			Yes	Yes	No
Honduras		X		Yes	Yes	No
Mexico		X		Yes	Yes	No
Paraguay		X		Yes	Yes	No
Costa Rica	X			Yes	No	n.a.
Dominican Republic		X		Yes	No	n.a.
El Salvador		X		Yes	No	n.a.
Guatemala		X		Yes	No	n.a.
Panama		X		Yes	No	n.a.
Venezuela		X		No	n.a.	n.a.
Colombia			X	No	n.a.	n.a.
Nicaragua		X		No	n.a.	n.a.

Source: Authors' compilation.
Note: n.a. = not applicable.
[1] Voting is mandatory only for citizens who are registered to vote.
[2] Voting is mandatory for those up to the age of 65 who are literate.
[3] Voting is mandatory for those up to the age of 70 who are literate.
[4] Voting is mandatory up to the age of 70.
[5] Voting is mandatory for those 18–70 who are literate, and optional for those 16–17 years old, over 70, or illiterate.

Table 9.3. Classification of Micro Factors Affecting Levels of Electoral Participation

	Sociodemographic factors	Political factors
Structural factors	- Educational attainment - Socioeconomic status (income, occupation) - Age - Membership in a minority and/or underrepresented group	- Political/civic attitudes a) interest in politics, political knowledge b) objective and subjective competence c) sense of efficacy, alienation - Relationship between citizenry and institutions, in terms of proximity, access, and quality - Legitimacy and integrity of political institutions, actors, and processes
Contextual factors	- Perception of individual and national economic situations - Satisfaction with general quality of life	- Electoral campaign a) field of candidates and their relative popularity b) salience of election issues

Source: Authors' compilation.

groups. One group comprises elements related to sociodemographic context, whereas the other is made up of factors more closely related to the political process (Table 9.3).

The level of educational attainment is one of the strongest sociodemographic factors that affects the decision of citizens to exercise their right (or duty) to vote. (The relationship between socioeconomic status and access to education is quite strong, particularly in countries where differences in access to services are extremely large.) Similarly, both age and membership in a minority group or another traditionally excluded group, such as indigenous persons and women, may also be significant factors in explaining why citizens decide to vote or not.

Political factors include citizens' level of interest in politics and their degree of political knowledge. These factors form a significant part of electoral participation and influence not only whether citizens decide to vote, but also *how* they vote. Closely related to these factors are what Gabriel Almond and Sidney Verba term "objective competence" and "subjective competence." In *The Civic Culture* (1965), Almond and Verba define a citizen as an individual capable of engaging in some way with the political system. They emphasize the importance of political competence, characterized as a person's knowledge of political matters (objective competence) and their belief in their own ability to understand political issues and actively engage in the political system (subjective competence). The first dimension is clearly very much related to both level of interest in politics and degree of political knowledge, while the second has to do with people's sense of efficacy within, or alienation from, the political system. This is significant because citizens who are well informed are more likely to be politically active. Citizens who believe they can understand and affect the workings of the system will seek out information and consequently be far more likely to be politically involved.

Among the purely political factors that influence electoral participation, several elements stand out: first, the relationship between political institutions and the citizenry in terms of proximity, access, and the quality of services provided; second, the legitimacy and integrity of political institutions and democratic practices, including whether citizens perceive the electoral process to be clean and fair, and the level of popular trust in politicians; and finally, as a contextual factor, the characteristics of the election contest. This last factor includes two components: the attractiveness of the field of candidates and their relative popularity, and the importance voters accord to the issues at stake in the campaign.

Participation, therefore, may fluctuate from one election to the next in response to contextual factors narrowly related to a particular campaign cycle, or in response to larger structural factors, such as the legitimacy and credibility of institutions and political processes. Thus, long-term patterns of electoral participation can to some degree reflect public perceptions of how well the democratic system is performing.

Voter Turnout in Latin America

How does the level of electoral participation in Latin America compare with that of other regions of the world? On average 61 percent of the eligible population in the 18 Latin American countries in this study turned out to vote in national elections during the period 1990–2004. That level of turnout is significantly less than that in Oceania, Central and Eastern Europe, and Western Europe, where participation generally exceeds 70 percent (Figure 9.1). In the countries of East Asia and the former Soviet Union, the average is also slightly higher than in Latin America. But in four other regions—Sub-Saharan Africa, the United States and Canada, the Middle East, and North Africa—turnout was lower than in Latin America.[4]

Average voter turnout for the region, however, masks a large degree of variation between countries. Table 9.4 shows electoral participation in presidential and legislative elections from 1978 to 2004 as a percentage of registered voters and as a percentage of the voting age population in each of the 18 Latin American countries included in the study. The average turnout in presidential elections measured as a share of registered voters ranges from a low of 44.5 percent to 56.8 percent in Colombia, El Salvador, and Guatemala to a high of about 90 percent in Chile and Uruguay. Electoral participation in legislative elections is somewhat lower than in presidential contests in most countries.

---

[4] The relative positions of the regions with respect to electoral participation do not change substantially if one restricts the sample of countries to those whose political systems are reasonably democratic, as measured by the Freedom House indicators of political liberties and civil rights.

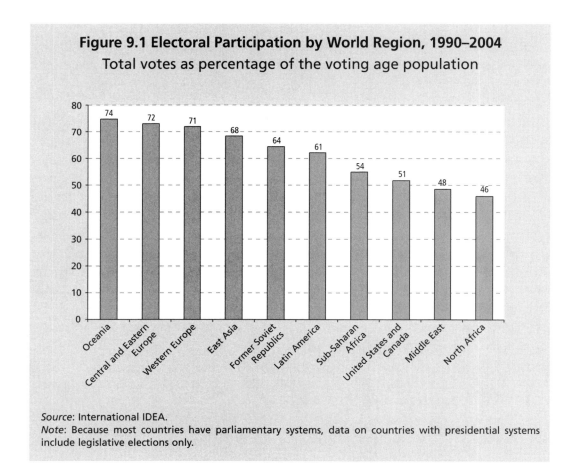

Figure 9.1 Electoral Participation by World Region, 1990–2004
Total votes as percentage of the voting age population

Source: International IDEA.
Note: Because most countries have parliamentary systems, data on countries with presidential systems include legislative elections only.

Examining the more meaningful measure of votes as a share of the voting-age population shows that in some countries the number of citizens who are not registered to vote is quite significant. In Chile and Guatemala, where registration is optional, turnout is about 10 and 12 percentage points less, respectively, when measured as a share of the voting age population. Turnout is also lower as a share of the voting-age population in Bolivia, Paraguay, and to a somewhat lesser extent, the Dominican Republic and Venezuela—all countries where a significant number of citizens are not registered to vote despite compulsory registration laws.

While participation trends by country are examined in more detail below, Table 9.4 provides a useful first approximation. Results show that in only three countries—Paraguay, El Salvador,[5] and Colombia—did turnout significantly increase from the earliest to the most recent election for which data are available. In another five countries—Uruguay, Panama,

[5] For El Salvador the absence of data on the number of registered voters for the founding 1984 election prevents the calculation of turnout as a share of registered voters for this election. But a continuous series could be calculated for turnout calculated in terms of voting-age population, and this is the basis for the inclusion of El Salvador in this group.

Table 9.4. Electoral Participation in Latin America, 1978–2004

| Country | Presidential elections | | | | Legislative elections | | |
| | Turnout (% of registered voters) | | | Turnout (% of voting-age population) | Electoral participation (% of registered voters) | | |
	First election	Most recent election	Average of all elections	Average of all elections	First election	Most recent election	Average of all elections
Uruguay	87.9	91.8	89.8	94.6	87.9	91.3	89.8
Chile	94.7	89.9	92.0	82.3	94.7	87.1	90.1
Argentina	86.0	78.2	82.5	80.2	85.9	71.5	81.1
Brazil	88.1	79.5	82.8	77.0	95.0	68.9	82.1
Nicaragua	86.2	—	81.3	75.4	86.3	—	81.7
Panama	76.8	76.9	75.9	72.2	—	76.3	74.6
Honduras	76.5	66.3	73.3	72.2	76.5	66.3	73.3
Costa Rica	81.3	68.9	78.1	72.1	81.2	68.9	77.6
Peru	79.1	82.3	80.8	69.5	71.1	80.4	74.6
Venezuela	87.6	56.5	72.8	63.4	87.6	56.6	71.0
Ecuador	81.4	65.0	71.6	62.8	80.3	—	70.6
Dom. Rep.[1]	72.9	72.8	73.3	62.8	—	51.6	62.0
Mexico	74.8	64.0	66.5	61.8	85.1	41.4	62.0
Paraguay	54.0	64.3	67.1	53.3	52.0	64.1	66.1
Bolivia	74.3	72.1	74.3	52.9	74.3	72.1	74.2
El Salvador[2]	—	67.3	52.6	46.9	—	—	49.8
Guatemala	69.3	57.9	56.8	44.1	69.2	61.3	51.0
Colombia	40.3	46.5	44.5	37.7	33.2	43.0	41.3
Average	**77.1**	**70.6**	**73.1**	**65.6**	**77.4**	**66.7**	**70.7**

Source: Authors' compilation based on data from electoral agencies.

Note: — = Data not available.

[1] Figures for several years reflect valid votes cast, not total votes (see Appendix 2).

[2] For the 2004 presidential elections, figures reflect valid votes cast instead of total votes; turnout in 2003 legislative elections not included.

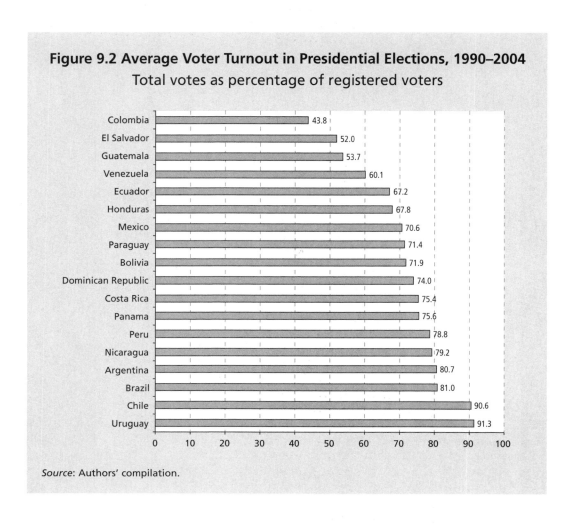

Figure 9.2 Average Voter Turnout in Presidential Elections, 1990–2004
Total votes as percentage of registered voters

Colombia	43.8
El Salvador	52.0
Guatemala	53.7
Venezuela	60.1
Ecuador	67.2
Honduras	67.8
Mexico	70.6
Paraguay	71.4
Bolivia	71.9
Dominican Republic	74.0
Costa Rica	75.4
Panama	75.6
Peru	78.8
Nicaragua	79.2
Argentina	80.7
Brazil	81.0
Chile	90.6
Uruguay	91.3

Source: Authors' compilation.

Peru, the Dominican Republic, and Bolivia—turnout remained relatively even over time. In the remaining 10 countries, there was considerable decline in participation levels.

When just the elections from 1990 to 2004 are considered (Figure 9.2), most countries are clustered in the range between 67 percent and 80 percent of registered voters participating in elections. However, in four countries—Colombia, El Salvador, Guatemala, and Venezuela—turnout was 60 percent or less, with Colombia at the bottom end at 44 percent. However, there are grounds for optimism with regard to El Salvador, where turnout for presidential elections increased from 39 percent in 2000 to 69 percent in 2004. At the other end of the scale, voter turnout as a share of registered voters for the same period in Uruguay, Chile, Brazil, Argentina, and Nicaragua was 80 percent or more.

Consequently, it appears that registration and voting laws alone cannot account for the varying levels of electoral participation in Latin America. Although voting is compulsory in all countries except Colombia, Guatemala, and Nicaragua, the range in voter turnout is still very large. Despite the existence of mandatory voting laws, between 9 percent and 48 percent of registered voters still abstain from voting. And though not compelled to do so by law, the percentage of citizens who turn out to vote in Nicaragua is among the highest in the region.

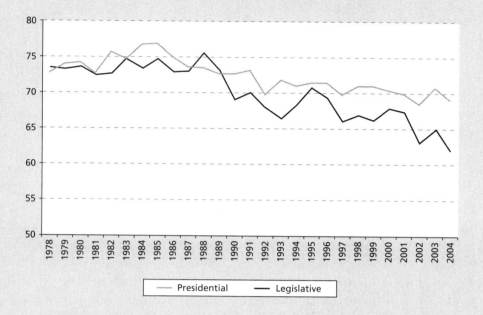

Figure 9.3 Evolution of Electoral Turnout in Latin America, 1978–2004
Percent of registered voters

Source: Authors' compilation.
Note: The computation of the regional average for a given year includes turnout figures for countries considered at that time to be democratic. The elections included are the same as those in the tables in Appendix 2.

Trends in Electoral Participation

How has the level of electoral turnout in Latin America evolved from 1978 to 2004? Is there a clear and persistent upward or downward trend in electoral participation? Figure 9.3 plots the average turnout for 18 Latin American countries in presidential and legislative elections from 1978 to 2004. Given that elections occur only every four or five years in most countries, the turnout value for one election is included in the computation of the regional average for a period of four years, including the year before the election actually took place; the year of the election; and the two years following the election. In this way the figure computed for the average regional turnout is not distorted by the differences in the particular set of countries included in each year's average.

The average turnout in presidential elections fell from 77 percent in 1985 to 69 percent in 2004. Turnout in legislative elections declined by a sharper 13 percent—from 75 to 62 percent. This downward trend may not reflect a general decline in turnout in most countries of the region, but rather the gradual inclusion after 1985 of four newly democratic countries characterized by lower levels of turnout than the 14 countries included previously. However, a careful analysis shows that the downward trend does indeed reflect a decline in turnout in the countries of the region. The average turnout in the four countries added to the sample after 1985 is, if anything, greater than in the 14 countries previously included. Thus, the average decline in turnout could actually be slightly higher than 7 percent.

However, this aggregate trend, although significant, is not yet cause for serious alarm. Supporting this benign assessment is the fact that average turnout as a share of registered voters for presidential elections has remained steady since 1991, hovering around 70 percent. Nevertheless, it is important that the trend should not accelerate, and that the gap in turnout between presidential and legislative elections should not widen in the future.

The aggregate trend lines in Figure 9.3 conceal widely divergent patterns in different countries across the region: Data for individual countries do not show a neat conformity to the aggregate regional trend of gradual decline. Some countries show unambiguous declines or increases in turnout, while others show relative stability and unpredictable upward and downward movements (Table 9.4 and Appendix 2).

Turnout has clearly fallen during the period in Venezuela, Ecuador, and Honduras. In Venezuela, turnout as a share of registered voters declined from approximately 87 percent in 1978 to 56 percent in 2000; in Ecuador, the shift was from 81 percent in 1979 to 65 percent in 2002; and in Honduras, from 76 percent in 1981 to 66 percent in 2001.

Apart from these three countries, where the turnout trend is unambiguously downward, there are a few countries where there is a visible, but more moderate, reduction in voter turnout. Turnout in Costa Rica was stable at around 80 percent until the 1994 elections, but then dropped in the subsequent three elections (1998, 2002, and 2006) when it fell to a level of about 65 percent. In Argentina, since the elections of 1983 there has been a fairly moderate but steady decline in turnout, from 86 percent in 1983 to 78 percent in 2003. In the case of Chile, turnout fell slightly from an extraordinarily high initial level of more than 94 percent in 1990 to about 90 percent in 1999 and 87 percent in 2005. But measured as a percentage of the voting-age population, turnout fell much more dramatically in Chile—from 89 percent to 63 percent.

Several cases show an inconclusive trend in voter turnout. For example, in Nicaragua turnout fell by 10 percent between 1990 and 1996. However, this reflected an increase in the number of registered voters, not a decline in the absolute number of voters; furthermore, data for 2001 are quite consistent with data for previous years. In Guatemala, Brazil, and El Salvador downward trends have reversed in the most recent elections.[6] In Guatemala and Brazil, increased levels of turnout have persisted for two consecutive elections. In El Salvador, where turnout had fallen steadily since 1984, turnout for the 2004 elections reached a historic high of about 67 percent.

Only in two countries was there an upward trend in turnout during the period of study, but in neither case was it very pronounced or definitive. In Paraguay, turnout as a

---

[6] The complexities of the ballot in Brazilian legislative elections resulted in an extremely large proportion of blank or invalid votes cast (close to 30 percent) until the 1998 election. As a result of improvements in the voting system, 15 percent more ballots in legislative elections were validly cast for a party or candidate in the 1998 elections than previously. This increase offset the decrease in votes cast as a share of registered voters.

share of registered voters rose dramatically from 54 percent in 1989 to 69 percent and 81 percent in 1993 and 1998, respectively. But given that the number of voters who actually went to the polls decreased between 1989 and 1993, the apparent increase between the first two elections in the democratic period was due to the inflated voter registry used in the 1989 election. As a consequence, turnout as a share of registered voters was underestimated for the 1989 election (Riquelme and Riquelme, 1997). Nevertheless, there were real increases in absolute and relative turnout between the 1993 and 1998 elections, since turnout as a share of the voting-age population approached 60 percent after having hovered in the 50 percent range. However, there was a deterioration in the 2003 elections to turnout levels below those of 1993 (47 percent, in terms of voting-age population). In Uruguay, there was a clear though not very significant upward trend from 87 percent in 1984 to 91 percent in 1999. Although this trend is not very significant, it is remarkable nonetheless that Uruguay has maintained such a high level of electoral participation over the last 20 years.

In the five remaining countries in the study, no clear trend can be discerned. In Mexico and Colombia, turnout has moved up and down erratically with no apparent trend in either direction. In the Dominican Republic, turnout declined from 1978 to 1990, but rose in the three presidential elections after 1990, surpassing the 1978 level, only to fall again in 2004.[7] In Panama, turnout has been relatively constant over four elections. In Peru, a downward trend that started with the second post-transition election of 1985 was reversed in 2000 and 2001, as turnout rose from about 74 percent in 1995 to about 82 percent (as a share of registered voters) in 2000 and 2001. Taking all the countries into account—even those where the trend is not very significant or long-term—we find that turnout has declined in eight countries and risen at least modestly in two countries. In the remaining eight countries, there has been little long-term change, or the trend is ambiguous.

Effects of Macro Factors

It is useful to examine some of the macro factors (shown in Table 9.1) that may have influenced the patterns of voter turnout discussed in the previous section.

To what extent could the overall downward trend in voter turnout be due to a post-transition voting effect? As previously mentioned, unusually high turnout is expected during the first or "foundational" elections in a democratizing country. Given that most of the countries included in the study experienced transitions from authoritarian to democratic regimes during the 1978–2004 period, the overall drop in turnout could be a function of a decline in electoral participation in each country after an unusually high initial level. The data, however, do not convincingly support this scenario. Fourteen countries in the region experienced definitive transitions to democracy in which foundational elections can be identified. In eight of those—Argentina, Brazil, Chile, Ecuador, El Salvador, Guatemala, Nicaragua, and Panama—turnout in the transition-year election was indeed higher than

---

[7] The dramatic fall in participation in the 1998 legislative elections can be attributed to the fact that, beginning in that year, elections for president were not held concurrently.

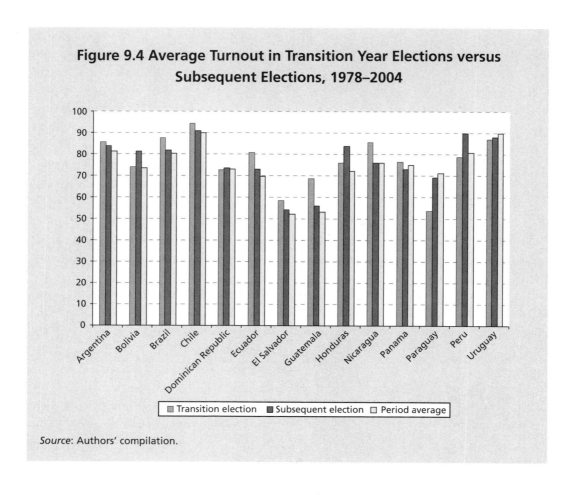

Figure 9.4 Average Turnout in Transition Year Elections versus Subsequent Elections, 1978–2004

Legend: ▨ Transition election ■ Subsequent election □ Period average

Source: Authors' compilation.

that in the following election, as well as higher than the average turnout in all other post-transition elections (Figure 9.4). Data for the remaining six countries, however, are less conclusive. When turnout is measured as a share of the voting age population, in only five countries is turnout in a foundational election higher than in the following election, or higher than the average turnout in all other post-transitional elections. In short, although foundational elections can produce a temporary increase in voter turnout owing to initial popular enthusiasm, they do not appear to be a determining factor in the overall downward trend in the region.

Laws related to registration and voting are also among the various politico-institutional factors that can affect turnout. Based on the classification of countries shown in Table 9.2, we computed the average number of registered voters and average turnout by type of registration system (voluntary, compulsory, or automatic) and type of voting system (voluntary or compulsory, and with or without enforced sanctions). Table 9.5 reveals a clear, significant correlation between mandatory voting and turnout as a share of registered voters. Accordingly, countries like Bolivia, Chile, Ecuador, Peru, and Uruguay, where voting is mandatory and penalties for abstention are enforced, tend to have higher voter turnouts than do countries with voluntary voting systems, such as Venezuela, Colombia, Guatemala, and Nicaragua.

Table 9.5. Correlation of Types of Registration and Voting Systems with Levels of Registration and Turnout

		Average number of registered voters, 1990–2004 (% of voting age population)	Average turnout, 1990–2004 (% of registered voters)
Type of registration system	Voluntary	82.5	n.a.
	Compulsory	88.0	n.a.
	Automatic	94.4	n.a.
Type of voting system	Voluntary	n.a.	58.0
	Compulsory, no penalties	n.a.	65.3
	Compulsory, penalties not enforced	n.a.	72.0
	Compulsory, penalties enforced	n.a.	81.5
Correlation between average number of registered voters over period and registration system		0.417	
Correlation between type of voting system and average turnout		0.608**	

Source: Authors' calculations.
Note: Averages include legislative and presidential elections from 1990 until 2004. n.a. = not applicable.
** Correlation is significant at the 0.01 level.

Although the correlation between the type of voter registration system and the proportion of the voting-age population that is registered is not significant, regional averages for each type of registration system suggest that levels of voter registration tend to be greater under automatic systems than in systems with voluntary registration, the difference being in excess of 10 percentage points.

What these data confirm is that the combination of automatic voter registration and mandatory voting with enforced penalties is the institutional arrangement that favors the highest level of voter participation.

The perceived efficiency, integrity, and transparency of political processes and institutions affect levels of electoral participation, as indicated in Table 9.1. In the following figures we examine the impact of these factors with reference to an index of political freedom and measures of corruption and government effectiveness.

Countries in which democratic freedoms are more highly respected tend to have somewhat higher rates of turnout (Figure 9.5). This correlation appears to be higher when just the Latin American countries are considered. Even when other factors such as income levels, literacy rates, and the degree of ethnolinguistic fragmentation are considered, the influence of the scope and depth of democratic freedoms remain weak, but significant. Thus, the ex-

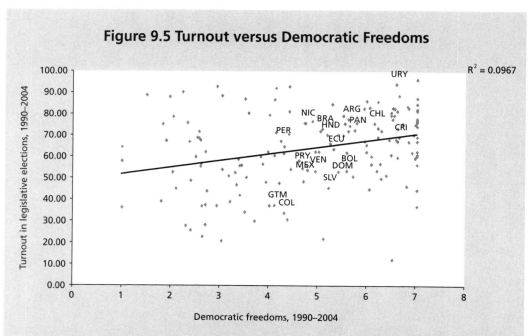

Figure 9.5 Turnout versus Democratic Freedoms

Source: Authors' compilation based on data from International IDEA (2006) and Freedom House (2005).
Note: The figure plots for each country the average percentage of the voting age population that voted in legislative elections from 1990 to 2004 against an index of democratic freedoms calculated as the average of the Freedom House ratings for political rights and civil liberties (inverted so that larger scores equate to more freedom).

tent of political freedom and competition, and perhaps the depth of respect for democratic principles, appear to play a role in motivating or sustaining electoral participation.

Moreover, the level of electoral participation appears to affect the quality of governance. Higher levels of electoral turnout are associated, at least to some degree, with the absence of corruption and better governmental performance (Figure 9.6). This relation is stronger when one takes into account the extent of political information (or inquisitive capacity) of citizens (Adserà, Boix, and Payne, 2003).

Effects of Micro Factors

The previous section focused on the influence of macro (country-level) factors on cross-national variation in levels of electoral participation. This section centers on the factors that affect whether *individuals* decide to participate or not in the electoral process. Most of the data on these micro factors come from *Latinobarómetro* (1996–2004), the only source that covers a large number of countries (18) using a consistent methodology and similar sets of questions. This analysis draws on the results of a 2004 survey, the most recent at the time this work was carried out.

Educational attainment is one of the micro factors presented in Table 9.3 that influences the level of electoral participation. This indicator, which partially captures the concept of socioeconomic status, is a key factor in understanding participation. As previously men-

Democracies in Development

Figure 9.6 Turnout versus Government Performance

a. Turnout and the absence of corruption

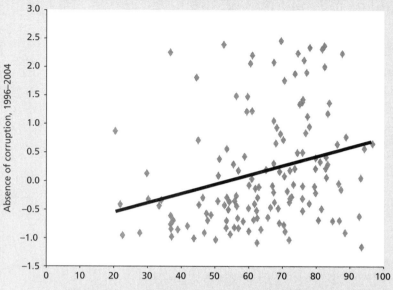

Electoral turnout in legislative elections (% voting age population), 1990–2004

b. Turnout and government effectiveness

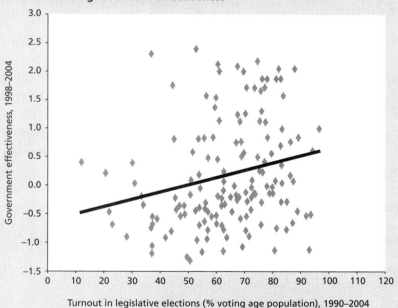

Turnout in legislative elections (% voting age population), 1990–2004

Sources: Authors' compilation based on data from Kaufmann, Kraay, and Mastruzzi (2005) (absence of corruption and government effectiveness) and from International IDEA (2006) (electoral participation).
Note: Countries with an average score of 2.5 or less in the average Freedom House rating of political rights and civil liberties (i.e., countries rated as "not free") are left out of the analysis. It is assumed that in such countries, electoral participation has little value in holding officials accountable, given that voting is not free and voluntary. In some of these cases, higher turnout levels may reflect the coercive capacity of the government.

tioned, it is very closely linked conceptually both to political attitudes, such as degree of interest in politics and level of political knowledge, and to civic attitudes, such as objective and subjective competence. Gender is another micro factor that would be expected to affect electoral participation. To the extent that this factor affects who decides to vote, it may also affect the degree to which women are effectively represented in the political process. The relevance of ethnicity is not examined since comparable data were not available.

To explore the factors affecting individual choices to participate (or not) in elections, we considered responses from the following question from *Latinobarómetro*: "If elections were held this Sunday, for which party would you vote?" Those who responded by answering either "I don't vote," "For none," or "I'm not registered" were classified as individuals planning not to participate in elections, while all other respondents were identified as intending to vote. Included in the second group were not only individuals who mentioned a particular party, but also those who indicated they were "undecided" about which party they preferred and those who replied that they would cast blank or invalid votes, given that all those responses still indicate an intention to go to the polls. Survey respondents who failed to answer the question were not included in the analysis.[8]

Before continuing our exploration of the effects of variables related to citizen attitudes toward politics and the performance of democratic institutions, we pause to ask if those who are fundamentally opposed to democracy as a system of government are also those least likely to vote (or, more precisely, to express an intention to vote). One would expect that individuals who believe in the democratic system would be more likely to want to take part in one of its fundamental processes. However, our results indicate that an individual's preference for a democratic or authoritarian form of government is not strongly related to his or her tendency to either vote or abstain (Table 9.6). Contrary to what may be expected, the probability that individuals who prefer democracy will go to the polls is barely four percentage points higher than the probability that those who, under some circumstances would prefer authoritarian rule. In contrast, results show that those who express indifference about the type of regime they prefer are 10 percentage points less likely to vote than those who express a preference for democracy. These results indicate that alienation from the system or apathy about politics (expressed by the "indifferent" response) have a more significant impact on an individual's disposition to vote.

In the analysis that follows, in addition to educational attainment and gender, we include two variables that measure what has been termed "election efficacy," that is, the extent to which citizens believe that elections offer a genuine opportunity for choosing parties and candidates and that a change in the government's composition can have a real impact on policies. Two additional variables are trust in government and trust in political parties, both of which are used as measures of satisfaction with democracy institutions. Two final variables gauge individuals' subjective knowledge of political and social issues and their

---

[8] It is to be expected that declared intentions to vote in a survey would exceed the actual percentage voting in a typical election, because intention is obviously different from action and respondents may not want to admit to an interviewer that they will not vote, especially when voting is obligatory. Whereas 70 percent of respondents across the region declared an intention to vote, only 61 percent of the voting-age population typically turns out.

Table 9.6. Intention to Vote and Support for Democracy

	Voters' intentions (percent)	
	Abstain	Vote
Democracy is preferable to any other form of government	26.0	74.0
In some circumstances, authoritarian government may be preferable	29.4	70.6
People like me don't care if the system of government is democratic or of any other type of rule	35.7	64.3
Total	**28.8**	**71.2**

Source: Authors' compilation using data from *Latinobarómetro* 2004.
Note: $N = 19{,}605$; $\chi^2 = 129.54$, 2 degrees of freedom; $p = .000$.

level of interest in politics. Variables associated with contextual factors are not included because data on election campaigns in each country are lacking.

The Pearson correlations among the above-mentioned variables are given in Table 9.7. The coefficients can have a value between 0 and 1, or 0 and −1, with plus or minus signs (+, −) showing whether the correlation between two variables is positive or negative, and the value itself showing the magnitude or strength of the correlation. Thus, the larger the coefficient, the stronger the association between the variables. Coefficients marked by asterisks indicate whether and to what extent the correlation found from the sampled population is statistically significant, that is, generalizable to the whole population. A single asterisk indicates that the probability is 95 percent, while two asterisks indicate a probability of 99 percent. The correlation coefficients lacking an asterisk are not statistically significant.

Highly educated men are the group most likely to participate in elections. However, the low coefficients and lack of statistical significance of the relationships in many countries suggest that the variation in intention to vote between genders and across levels of educational attainment is not large. Education does seem to play an important role in predicting a subject's level of interest in politics. Respondents with higher levels of educational attainment are significantly more likely to be interested in politics than those who are less educated. Likewise, levels of interest in politics are very closely related to whether individuals decide to vote. The correlation between these two variables for the regional sample is 0.254, and remains significant at the level of individual countries.[9] It can be argued that an interest in politics is a bridge between political participation and education, in the sense that

---

[9] Argentina −0.147; Bolivia −0.124; Brazil −0.207; Colombia −0.245; Costa Rica −0.330; Chile −0.300; Ecuador −0.139; El Salvador −0.289; Guatemala −0.280; Honduras −0.342; Mexico −0.137; Nicaragua −0.306; Panama −0.283; Paraguay −0.232; Peru −0.083; Uruguay −0.154; Venezuela −0.274; Dominican Republic −0.274. (All correlations are significant at the 0.01 level.)

Table 9.7. Factors Affecting Citizens' Choice to Participate in Elections

		Sociodemographic factors		Belief in efficacy of elections		Trust in institutions		Performance of democratic system	Information	
	Country	Gender	Education	Elections offer real option to choose parties and candidates	Importance of voting	Trust in government	Trust in political parties	Satisfaction with democracy	Knowledge of political and social issues	Attention given politics in TV news broadcasts
Intention to vote in future elections	Argentina	−0.002	0.008	−0.139**	−0.089**	−0.199**	−0.152**	−0.114**	−0.060*	−0.125**
	Bolivia	−0.019	−0.115**	−0.096**	0.002	−0.081**	−0.164**	−0.116**	0.023	−0.014
	Brazil	−0.029	0.000	−0.129**	−0.019	−0.158**	−0.190**	−0.110**	−0.065*	−0.099**
	Chile	−0.053	0.011	−0.153**	−0.082**	−0.220**	−0.224**	−0.137**	−0.197**	−0.248**
	Colombia	0.014	−0.049	−0.117**	−0.063*	−0.200**	−0.237**	−0.151**	−0.004	−0.107**
	Costa Rica	0.028	0.006	−0.115**	−0.148**	−0.276**	−0.278**	−0.146**	−0.025	−0.158**
	Dominican Republic	−0.003	−0.049	−0.069*	−0.108**	−0.097**	−0.190**	−0.011	−0.056	−0.127**
	Ecuador	−0.070*	0.004	−0.015	−0.073*	−0.145**	−0.141**	0.002	−0.037	−0.057
	El Salvador	−0.073*	0.144**	−0.118**	−0.170*	−0.128**	−0.210**	−0.047	−0.215**	−0.200**
	Guatemala	−0.114**	0.066*	−0.137**	−0.093**	−0.217**	−0.245**	−0.112**	−0.103**	−0.202**
	Honduras	−0.090**	−0.064*	−0.087**	−0.083*	−0.218**	−0.364**	−0.104**	−0.019	−0.228**
	Mexico	0.012	−0.015	0.005	−0.084**	−0.041	−0.024	−0.101**	−0.036	−0.045
	Nicaragua	−0.109**	−0.044	−0.077*	−0.064	−0.150**	−0.300**	−0.081*	−0.066	−0.191**
	Panama	0.027	−0.021	−0.083*	−0.123**	−0.134**	−0.267**	−0.039	−0.018	−0.202**
	Paraguay	−0.035	−0.027	−0.082*	−0.051	−0.191**	−0.248**	−0.130**	−0.057	−0.119**
	Peru	−0.053	−0.031	−0.072*	0.019	−0.067*	−0.215**	−0.108**	−0.018	−0.025
	Uruguay	0.020	0.007	−0.082**	−0.027	−0.051	−0.094**	−0.020	0.010	−0.046
	Venezuela	−0.064*	0.006	−0.083**	−0.082**	−0.218**	−0.167**	−0.171**	−0.130**	−0.171**
	Total Latin America	−0.031**	0.015*	−0.100**	−0.088**	−0.161**	−0.233**	−0.114**	−0.075**	−0.146**

(continued)

Table 9.7. (continued)

| | Country | Sociodemographic factors | | Belief in efficacy of elections | | Trust in institutions | | Performance of democratic system | Information | |
		Gender	Education	Elections offer real option to choose parties and candidates	Importance of voting	Trust in government	Trust in political parties	Satisfaction with democracy	Knowledge of political and social issues	Attention given politics in TV news broadcasts
Interest in politics	Argentina	0.027	−0.284**	0.058*	0.190**	0.168**	0.237**	0.055	0.381**	0.503**
	Bolivia	0.133**	−0.312**	0.067*	0.146**	0.192**	0.203**	0.052	0.267**	0.300**
	Brazil	0.088**	−0.311**	0.042	0.137**	0.174**	0.241**	0.095**	0.409**	0.453**
	Chile	0.145**	−0.337**	0.124**	0.225**	0.363**	0.321**	0.306**	0.391**	0.502**
	Colombia	0.091**	−0.290**	0.094**	0.152**	0.190**	0.213**	0.143**	0.331**	0.467**
	Costa Rica	−0.011	−0.164**	0.088**	0.179**	0.210**	0.252**	0.101**	0.227**	0.364**
	Dominican Republic	0.043	−0.120**	−0.005	0.188*	0.153**	0.333**	0.006	0.261**	0.394**
	Ecuador	0.089**	−0.179**	−0.007	0.080**	0.153**	0.163**	0.103**	0.251**	0.269**
	El Salvador	0.137**	−0.300**	0.103**	0.186**	0.148**	0.341**	−0.011	0.419**	0.466**
	Guatemala	0.119**	−0.237**	0.054	0.181**	0.193**	0.252**	0.078*	0.351**	0.420**
	Honduras	0.064*	−0.102**	0.084**	0.129**	0.239**	0.397**	0.124**	0.237**	0.377**
	Mexico	0.081**	−0.079**	0.001	0.220**	0.060*	0.072*	0.039	0.075**	0.108**
	Nicaragua	0.122**	−0.187**	0.040	0.165**	0.171**	0.286**	0.068*	0.299**	0.376**
	Panama	0.046	−0.182**	0.072*	0.118**	0.131**	0.278**	0.016	0.256**	0.409**
	Paraguay	0.096*	−0.262**	0.050	0.182**	0.172**	0.268**	0.194**	0.306**	0.427**
	Peru	0.155**	−0.295**	0.050	0.181**	0.101**	0.176**	0.059*	0.348**	0.370**
	Uruguay	0.140**	−0.305**	0.103**	0.197**	0.047	0.300**	−0.046	0.374**	0.436**
	Venezuela	0.072**	−0.069*	0.093**	0.118**	0.237**	0.315**	0.209**	0.279**	0.362**
	Total Latin America	0.087**	−0.226**	0.074**	0.174**	0.165**	0.279**	0.093**	0.316**	0.405**

Source: Authors' compilation using data from *Latinobarómetro* 2004.
Note: N = 19,605.
* = significant at the 0.05 level. ** = significant at the 0.01 level.

education fosters interest in politics, which in turn stimulates the search for information on political and social affairs and increases the likelihood that citizens will be politically active and participate by voting.

Taking the pooled averages for the entire sample of countries, the variables that are most closely associated with electoral participation at the individual level are, in descending order: trust in political institutions (particularly in political parties), the amount of information received through the mass media, the degree of satisfaction with democracy, and the importance attributed to elections as mechanisms for choosing among different political parties and candidates.

When the data are aggregated at the national level, comparisons can be made among countries, and a more accurate picture emerges of how countries are situated along both dimensions (Figures 9.7–9.10).

Among the most striking results is that voters who are dissatisfied with how the system is working and do not consider elections as opportunities to bring about change find less reason to vote. And countries whose citizens consider elections to be effective in achieving change are those with the highest levels of electoral participation. People abstain from voting not because they consider their vote to have no chance of changing the election results—a belief that would be rational, given the low mathematical probability of one vote influencing the outcome—but rather because they believe that, regardless of who wins,

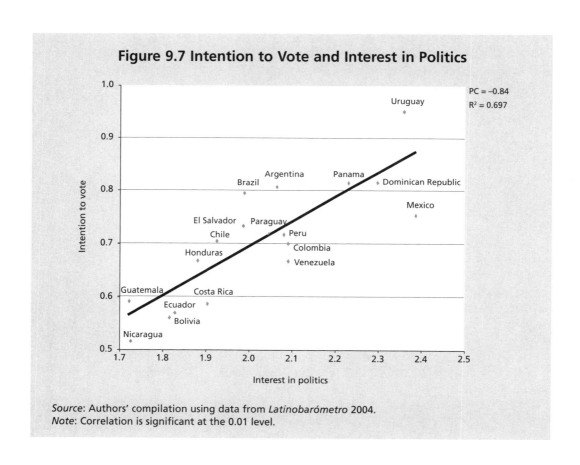

Figure 9.7 Intention to Vote and Interest in Politics

$PC = -0.84$
$R^2 = 0.697$

Source: Authors' compilation using data from *Latinobarómetro* 2004.
Note: Correlation is significant at the 0.01 level.

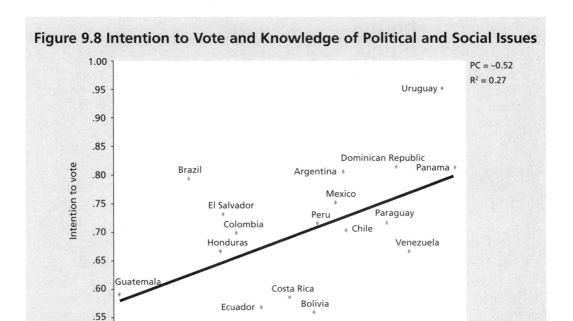

Figure 9.8 Intention to Vote and Knowledge of Political and Social Issues

PC = −0.52
R² = 0.27

Source: Authors' compilation using data from *Latinobarómetro* 2004.
Note: Correlation is significant at the 0.05 level.

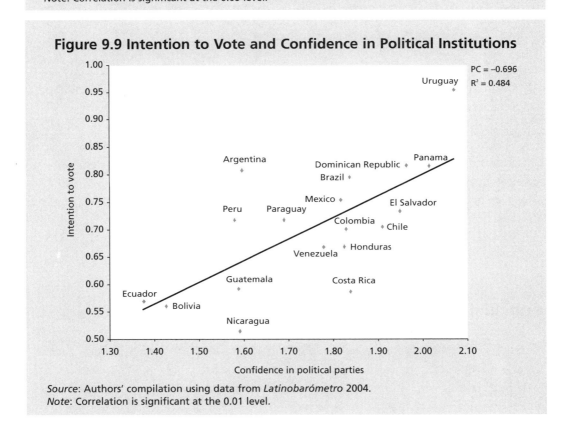

Figure 9.9 Intention to Vote and Confidence in Political Institutions

PC = −0.696
R² = 0.484

Source: Authors' compilation using data from *Latinobarómetro* 2004.
Note: Correlation is significant at the 0.01 level.

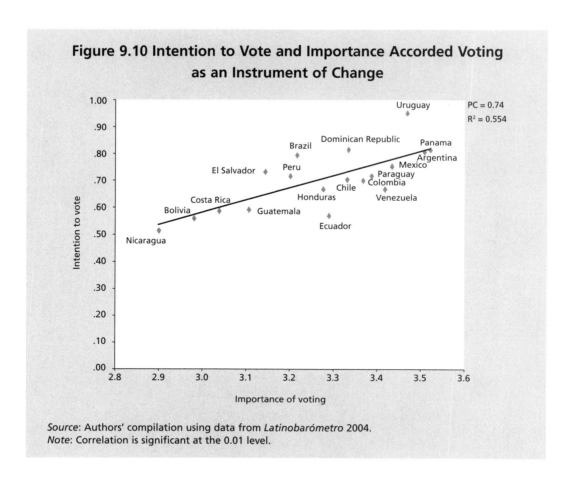

Figure 9.10 Intention to Vote and Importance Accorded Voting as an Instrument of Change

Source: Authors' compilation using data from *Latinobarómetro* 2004.
Note: Correlation is significant at the 0.01 level.

significant changes will not occur. In other words, they consider that the existing field of candidates and parties does not offer opportunity for real change.

Related to this, a final political factor presented in Table 9.3 that influences levels of electoral participation is the belief in the integrity and fairness of the electoral process. Data from the 18 Latin American countries in the study indicate that this factor is clearly associated with levels of electoral participation (Figure 9.11). Despite efforts in the region to reduce or eliminate electoral fraud, citizens in various countries are not persuaded that electoral processes are sufficiently clean or fair. This factor's relationship to electoral participation suggests that measures to strengthen public confidence in elections could increase voter turnout.

Conclusions

Electoral participation varies considerably from one country to another in Latin America. Based on recent election results, in only two countries does more than 80 percent of the voting-age population participate in elections. In five countries, between 70 percent and 80 percent participate; in another five, between 60 percent and 70 percent participate. In the

Democracies in Development

Figure 9.11 Intention to Vote and the Integrity of the Electoral Process

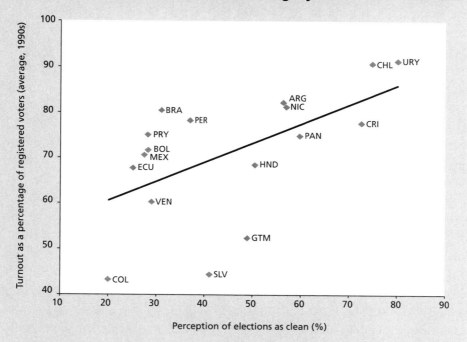

Source: Authors' compilation using data from *Latinobarometro* 1999–2000 and electoral turnout data from Appendix 2 for 1990s.
Note: The percentage of respondents who perceive elections as "clean" is the average of responses obtained in each country in the *Latinobarómetro* public opinion surveys for 1999–2000.

remaining six countries fewer than 60 percent of voters participate, and in a couple of these the figure is as low as 40 percent.

The level of electoral participation has declined modestly across the region since the mid-1980s, although it appears to have stabilized in more recent presidential elections. On the whole, turnout appears to have declined consistently in eight countries. Of these, the decline was especially sharp in three countries. Only in two countries has the trend been at least modestly positive. In the rest, there has either been little change or an ambiguous pattern of change.

Thus, in the region as a whole, the trends in turnout point neither to a clear crisis of representation nor to a growing legitimization of democracy. On average, about 61 percent of eligible citizens vote in major national elections. In absolute terms, the regular abstention of almost 40 percent of Latin Americans of voting age from a process so fundamental to the workings of democracy would appear to suggest a substantial deficiency in the region's democratic systems. However, given that a lower proportion of citizens vote in some stable and apparently successful democracies, such as the United States (50 percent) or Switzerland (45 percent), this fact by itself may not be cause for serious concern. Relative to other regions, Latin American turnout is roughly in the middle of the pack: below Western and Central Europe but above the poorer and less democratic regions of Sub-Saharan Africa, the Middle East, and North Africa. If participation levels of the more established democracies are taken as a standard, then one could argue that the Latin American systems could benefit from higher levels of voting.

But these conclusions suggest that the reasons why people abstain from voting are just as important as turnout levels. While the relative quantity of electoral participation is important, essentially for what these numbers can reveal about legitimacy and inclusion across sectors, understanding the underlying reasons for abstention is fundamental. Individuals' rationales for not voting can vary extensively from one case to the next and so have different implications for democracy. There is a significant difference between having a large number of citizens stay away from the polls because they are alienated from the system or protesting it, and having them stay away because they are more or less satisfied ("things are not going as well as I'd like, but not so bad that I'll make the effort to vote"). In the first case, individuals fail to vote because they believe they simply cannot affect the workings of the system and that regardless of their actions, real change will not occur. The second case reflects relative satisfaction with and trust in the system: since no imminent hazards seem to threaten one's current quality of life, there is less need for action.

Finally, among the various reasons that explain why citizens vote or abstain, the public perception that voting has a tangible purpose is of particular importance. Countries whose citizens perceive that the electoral process functions well, that viable options exist, and that change can bring concrete improvements in living conditions are also the countries with higher relative numbers of politically active citizens, at least in terms of participation in elections. The logic is quite clear: there are no benefits without costs, but it is unreasonable to expect citizens to assume costs with no benefits in sight.

Democracies in Development

References

Adserà, Alícia, Carles Boix, and Mark Payne. 2003. Are You Being Served? Political Accountability and Quality of Government. *Journal of Law, Economics and Organization* 19(2): 445–490.

Almond, Gabriel, and Sidney Verba. 1965. *The Civic Culture.* Boston: Little, Brown.

Bernhagen, Patrick, and Michael Marsh. 2004. Turnout Matters: Sometimes. Paper presented at the European Consortium for Political Research Joint Sessions, Uppsala, Sweden, April 13–18.

CAPEL (Center for Electoral Promotion and Assistance). 1989. *Diccionario electoral.* San José, Costa Rica: IIHR/CAPEL.

Fornos, Carolina A., Timothy J. Power, and James C. Garand. 2004. Explaining Voter Turnout in Latin America, 1980 to 2000. *Comparative Political Studies* 37(8): 909–940.

Freedom House. 2005. *Freedom in the World: The Annual Survey of Political Rights and Civil Liberties.* Washington, DC: Freedom House. [Retrieved from http://www.freedomhouse.org]

Hajnal, Zoltan, and Jessica Trounstine. 2005. Where Turnout Matters: The Consequences of Uneven Turnout in City Politics. *Journal of Politics* 67(2): 515–535.

Heywood, Andrew. 1997. *Politics.* London: Macmillan.

IDB (Inter-American Development Bank). 2000. *Development beyond Economics: Report on Economic and Social Progress in Latin America.* Washington, DC: Inter-American Development Bank.

International IDEA. 1997. *Voter Turnout from 1945 to 1997: A Global Report on Political Participation.* Stockholm: International IDEA.

———. 2002. *Voter Turnout since 1945: A Global Report.* Stockholm: International IDEA.

———. 2006. Voter Turnout Database. Stockholm: International IDEA. [Retrieved September 2006 from http://www.idea.int/vt]

Jackman, Robert W. 1987. Political Institutions and Voter Turnout in the Industrial Democracies. *American Political Science Review* 81(June).

Jackman, Robert W., and Ross A. Miller. 1995. Voter Turnout in the Industrial Democracies during the 1980s. *Comparative Political Studies* 27: 467–492.

Kaufmann, Daniel, Aart Kraay, and Massimo Mastruzzi. 2005. Governance Matters 5: Governance Indicators for 1996–2004. Policy Research Paper 3630. World Bank, Washington, DC.

Latinobarómetro. 1996–2004. *Latinobarómetro: Opinión pública latinoamericana, 1996–2004.* Santiago, Chile: Corporación Latinobarómetro.

LeDuc, Lawrence, Richard G. Niemi, and Pippa Norris (eds.). 1996. *Comparing Democracies: Elections and Voting in Global Perspective.* London: Sage.

Lupia, Arthur, and Mathew D. McCubbins. 1998. *The Democratic Dilemma: Can Citizens Learn What They Need to Know?* Cambridge: Cambridge University Press.

Nie, Norman, and Sidney Verba. 1975. Political Participation. In Fred I. Greenstein and Nelson W. Polsby (eds.), *Handbook of Political Science.* Reading, MA: Addison Wesley.

Powell, G. Bingham, Jr. 1980. Voting Turnout in Thirty Democracies: Partisan, Legal and Socio-Economic Influences. In Richard Rose (ed.), *Electoral Participation: A Comparative Analysis.* London: Sage.

———. 1986. American Voter Turnout in Comparative Perspective. *American Political Science Review* 80.

Przeworski, Adam, Susan C. Stokes, and Bernard Manin (eds.). 1999. *Democracy, Accountability and Representation.* New York: Cambridge University Press.

Putnam, Robert D. 2000. *Bowling Alone: The Collapse and Revival of American Community.* New York: Simon & Schuster.

Riquelme, Marcial A., and Jorge G. Riquelme. 1997. Political Parties. In Peter Lambert and Andrew Nickson (eds.), *The Transition to Democracy in Paraguay.* New York: St. Martin's.

Verba, Sidney, Norman H. Nie, and Jae-On Kim. 1971. *The Modes of Democratic Participation: A Cross-National Comparison.* Beverly Hills, CA: Sage.

CHAPTER 10

Gauging Public Support
for Democracy

Democracy is like oxygen.
People neither talk nor worry about it,
but if you take it away from them,
they will react and begin to stir.
—Fernando Henrique Cardoso

With tremendous challenges posed by economic volatility, high levels of poverty and inequality, and high rates of crime and violence, democracy remains under stress in many countries in Latin America. Because the consolidation of democracy rests, at least partly, on public support that accumulates over time, it is understandable that in many countries the advent of democratic regimes has not yet been accompanied by full institutionalization of democratic practices and rules.

The legitimacy of the democratic system depends in part on public acceptance of the set of values on which the political system rests. This first dimension of support for democracy is what David Easton identifies as "diffuse support" (1975). Diffuse support implies that citizens share a set of deep-seated political values that permeate the society's collective imagination. However, ideas and values are not the sole determinants of public attitudes toward democracy. The way values are translated into concrete political practice is also essential in determining the level of public support for democracy, a form of support that Easton terms "specific support." In other words, prospects for expanding the legitimacy of democratic systems hinge significantly on the performance of the system's institutions and political actors, and on the results of the policies adopted through its decision-making processes (Norris, 1999; Dalton, 1999; Klingemann, 1999).

In this chapter we examine attitudes toward democracy in the countries of Latin America between 1996 and 2004. The primary emphasis is on comparing levels of support for democracy as a system of government and for its institutions across countries of the region. But to broaden the perspective, the findings for Latin America are also compared with those of other world regions. Given the absence of cross-national comparative data, it is not possible to systematically study the evolution of public attitudes toward democracy over the entire period of the study. However, we use data from the *Latinobarómetro* surveys to analyze recent trends in the region and to underpin our assessment of changes over time in particular countries. One reason to assess public attitudes toward democracy and its institutions is to examine progress toward legitimizing and consolidating democratic regimes. Two decades after the onset of Latin America's "third wave" of democratization, how solid are the region's democracies? To what extent can they be expected to withstand current and future pressures and threats?

Clearly, the actions and decisions of politicians affect levels of public satisfaction with and trust in not only politicians, but also the political system and, therefore, in democracy. Levels of public satisfaction and trust, in turn, affect the performance of politicians and democratic institutions, and therefore the political system itself. A certain minimum level of public trust is necessary to enable the government to make the tough decisions that have to be made when managing an economy and implementing public policies, especially during a crisis. In addition, where public trust in politicians and the democratic system is low, one may expect that fewer citizens will participate in politics (as the previous chapter showed). Low levels of citizen involvement and interest are likely to undermine the accountability of elected officials to the citizenry and may create biases in representation, spurring further disenchantment. Similarly, if citizens do not trust political parties, those parties will be less able to perform their key functions of articulating and aggregating citizens' preferences. A weakening of political parties will tend to promote an increasingly personalistic and particularistic form of representation in which the broader public interest is lost in a cacophony of narrow and regionally concentrated demands.

According to a classification set forth in Norris (1999), a refinement of the typology of Easton (1975) referred to above, support for democracy may be assessed at several different levels, ranging from a fairly diffuse basis of evaluation to a more specific one. The first level we consider here refers to support for the *political community*, meaning that citizens are bound together by a sense of pride in their nation and are able to cooperate politically in pursuit of common objectives.[1] The second level refers to support for core *regime principles*. Survey questions addressing this matter gauge the extent to which citizens agree with such democratic values as freedom, participation, tolerance, and compromise, and whether they agree that democracy is the best form of government.

The third level of evaluation concerns *regime performance*, meaning support for how democratic or authoritarian regimes function in practice. In cross-national surveys, this is usually measured by citizens' responses to a question asking them to rate their degree of "satisfaction with the functioning of democracy" (or "satisfaction with the way democracy works"). This measurement is more ambiguous than that for the previous dimension, however, since alternative interpretations are possible. Some respondents may still center their attention on democracy as a value, while others will primarily consider the performance of the incumbent government or a series of previous governments.

The fourth level of evaluation relates to support for *regime institutions* such as the government, executive, legislature, judiciary, public administration, political parties, police, and

---

[1] See also Linz and Stepan (1996).

military. Survey items focusing on institutions gauge confidence in the institution broadly considered, rather than in particular individuals associated with it. This level of evaluation allows for a deeper and more differentiated consideration of regime performance, separating somewhat the matter of incumbent government performance from that of the more permanent institutional elements of the regime.

Finally, the fifth level of evaluation is that of support for *political authorities*, meaning trust in both the political class as a whole and in individual political leaders. This is usually measured by citizens' responses to a question asking them to rate their degree of trust in politicians.

The regional trends evaluated below are based mainly on our analysis of results from the eight surveys done by *Latinobarómetro* from 1996 to 2004.[2] We used those surveys to make comparisons across countries and to analyze trends over time in attitudes toward democracy. In addition, comparisons are made with European countries and the United States using data from the Eurobarometer and the World Values Survey.[3]

Reasons for Discontent with Democracy

Citizens' discontent with democracy's performance can spring from a range of sources, some of which may particularly affect new democracies. In the late 1970s, democratic transitions in Ecuador, the Dominican Republic, and Peru launched a regionwide trend that culminated with democratic transitions in Panama, Paraguay, Chile, and Nicaragua around 1990. Despite the fact that the transition process was accompanied by great uncertainty and left areas of social conflict unresolved in some cases, citizens generally embraced the advent of democracy and felt a renewed sense of optimism and confidence in their country's political future.

Citizens and political parties reactivated quickly, and democratic institutions resumed or initiated the performance of their basic functions, filling the void left by departing military officers or nondemocratic civilian incumbents. In the countries that had had little previous experience with democratic governance, the transition process was inevitably more difficult, since it entailed not only the creation of democratic institutions and procedures but also the formation of a new institutional culture that had to be internalized by participants. Where democratic institutions had already functioned but had ceased to operate during military rule, establishing the basic rule of law and democratic practices was typically more rapid and less complicated.

The predominant public attitude during the first years of democracy was to give the recently restored or created institutions some time to assume their responsibilities and fulfill their roles. But the democratic honeymoon in most cases did not last very long. Citizens' demands grew, social conflicts reactivated, and in most cases public disappointment in the performance of democratic governance escalated.

---

[2] In 1999 and 2000 just one survey was completed. Thus, surveys are available for the years 1996, 1997, 1998, 1999/2000, 2001, 2002, 2003, and 2004.

[3] Eurobarometer 48 (1997) to Eurobarometer 61 (2004); Inglehart (2000), which presents the World Values Surveys for 1990–93 and 1995–97.

Some of this growing disenchantment can be attributed to the always-negative correlation between idealized expectations of democracy and actual performance under difficult political and economic circumstances. The democracies that emerged in the late 1970s endured unfavorable economic conditions that were due in part to debt burdens inherited from preceding authoritarian regimes. Countries faced the collapse of the existing economic development model, limited access to international financial resources, and shocks in the international financial system. In addition, these difficulties occurred during a period of large-scale change in the international terms of trade and the imposition of difficult deprivations stemming from structural adjustments, which in many cases constrained and undermined state capacity to provide services to citizens.

Tensions over the principles that legitimize a political system typically intensify during periods of rapid change or instability. When an institution loses legitimacy, the basis for its authority and its very existence come into question. At the same time, incipient political regimes generate expectations and demands. From the perspective of rational utility, taking on the cost of regime change can be justified only if the benefits one expects in return are significantly greater than the benefits already existing in the current regime. In relatively new regimes, legitimacy is earned in large part through the outputs generated by the system. New institutions cannot depend on the strength of tradition; they must earn public acceptance through concrete action.

Thus, two types of mechanisms are fundamental for increasing the legitimacy of democratic systems: one type is oriented toward results and the delivery of goods and services; the other is oriented toward inputs, or the processes by which decisions are made. Sartori (1997) and Scharpf (1999) use the term *output-oriented* to refer to the first dimension, in which the focus is "government for the people" (that is, on what goods and services the government provides) rather than on "government by the people" (that is, the processes through which power is allocated and decisions made).

The second type of mechanism for generating legitimacy is oriented toward processes, or the "factors of production" of democracy (Sartori, 1997: 521). From this perspective, the legitimacy of a political system comes from citizens' acknowledgement and acceptance of the rules of decision making and power sharing that govern the system independent of the results generated through these rules.

Naturally, the two mechanisms are complementary rather than mutually exclusive. It is reasonable to assume that levels of satisfaction with democracy and, therefore, of the legitimacy of the democratic system are directly proportional to the degree of satisfaction with democratic institutions along both dimensions. However, it is also logical that in a newly established democracy, in which institutions have not had the chance to acquire legitimacy over a period of time, assessments of the regime will tend to be based to a greater degree on regime outputs. As a result, it is important in comparing attitudes toward democracy across the countries in the region to take into consideration the extent of their democratic experiences.

As noted above, the socioeconomic context of many countries during the 1978–2004 period contributed to the erosion of the initial reserve of public trust in democratic institutions. The cutoff of foreign lending, public financial crises, and skyrocketing inflation signaled that the previous statist and protectionist models of development were no longer viable. Faced with large macroeconomic imbalances and financing constraints, democratic governments were forced to adopt austerity policies and, in some cases, reduce the scope of the state and its role in the economy. While their aim was to promote long-term growth, these polices exacerbated immediate economic difficulties, especially for the poor, and heightened social tensions. Regardless of the real causes of these economic problems, democratic governments and institutions absorbed the blame for the painful remedies adopted to surmount the economic crisis. And Latin America's fledgling democracies were not alone in dealing with such problems. Severe economic distress and the need for structural adjustment and economic transformation also prompted public disillusionment with many of the emerging democracies in Central and Eastern Europe, Africa, and, after 1997, Asia.

Among the process- or input-oriented mechanisms affecting legitimacy, the poor performance of politicians and political institutions appears to have contributed to growing frustration in many countries. Citizens reacted negatively to the inability of governments to make sound and effective decisions either on their own or in the face of recalcitrant legislative opposition. They also objected to the poor and deteriorating quality of public services and to the dishonest and corrupt conduct of politicians, as well as their remoteness from constituents. Though such problems may not have been worse than under previous regimes, they were certainly more exposed and intensely reported by the media in the new democratic setting.

Public management in most cases lacked suitable institutions to ensure the neutrality, efficiency, and transparency of public policies. The absence of fair, consistent, consensus-based rules of power sharing meant that public policies were more likely to benefit the few—and respond to particularistic interests—and less likely to ensure a certain degree of universality in public policy outputs.

Growing public dissatisfaction was also a result of ongoing deficiencies in the fulfillment of democratic values. As shown in Chapter 1 (Figure 1.1), the average scores of the region's countries in Freedom House's 2004 indexes of political rights and civil liberties placed it in the category "partly free" rather than "free." Nine of the 18 Latin American countries in the study were rated as "free," while the other half were considered "partly free," the latter due to deficiencies in guaranteeing civil rights or in the scope afforded free expression and political organization.[4]

Trends in political support for democracy across the world—including the more established democracies—suggest that other, more global, phenomena may also have contributed to growing citizen disenchantment with democratic institutions. Studies by Norris (1999) and Dalton (1999) show a mixed trend in established democracies with respect to the different dimensions of support for democracy. Support for the ideal of democracy remains quite strong; but the level of satisfaction with the performance of democratic regimes varies across time and place without exhibiting any clear trend. Available survey data from the 1950s onward show a significant, though not severe, decline in trust in political authorities, as well as in political institutions such as parties and legislatures.

---

[4] The countries rated as free were Argentina, Bolivia, Chile, Costa Rica, the Dominican Republic, El Salvador, Mexico, Panama, and Uruguay. Those rated as partially free were Brazil, Colombia, Ecuador, Guatemala, Honduras, Nicaragua, Paraguay, Peru, and Venezuela.

Several factors may underlie disenchantment with politicians and institutions in established as well as emerging democracies, among them the change in the modalities of political representation that resulted from the weakening of ideological divisions associated with the end of the Cold War, the ascendance of television and other forms of mass communication, and the globalization of politics. As a consequence of these factors, traditional social class and ideological bases for citizens' political identity and for the cohesion of political parties have been undermined. Thus, citizens and parties have to some degree lost their bearings, while at the same time new issues have emerged—such as the environment, human rights, and crime—that traditional structures of representation are struggling to incorporate (Inglehart, 1990 and 1997). Meanwhile, the growing importance of television news and advertising has enhanced the personalization of the links between public officials and citizens, undermining the salience and importance of political parties as intermediary institutions. The decline in citizen identification with particular political parties and the loss of confidence in representative institutions in established democracies may stem from this blurring of the historic lines of social division, and from changes in the forms of electoral competition and representation.

Like mass communication, the erosion of the power of national governments (or nation-states) transcends the regions of the globe. That loss has come from above, with the globalization of politics and economic policy, and from below, with decentralization. Abetted by the ever-expanding reach of international economic forces, the creation of transnational governmental and trading institutions such as the European Union, the World Trade Organization, Mercosur, and the North American Free Trade Agreement is shifting economic power away from nations and toward external actors and forces. In many countries decentralization has weakened the authority and responsibilities of national governments. While this "outsourcing" of what used to be national governmental responsibilities in the end may be beneficial for citizens, public perceptions of the efficacy of national governments and institutions may, at least in the short term, be negatively affected.

Diffuse Support for the Political Community

In recent years scholars have renewed their interest in the importance of trust and social capital for the effective functioning of representative governments and for social and economic development (Putnam, 1993; Fukuyama, 1995; Boix and Posner, 1998). One hypothesis is that a decline in social capital, in the form of social networks and levels of interpersonal trust, may infect the relationship between citizens and government and lead to a loss of trust in political institutions.

To the extent that social trust captures the disposition of citizens to cooperate on behalf of common objectives, it can be taken as one measure of support for the *political community*. Interpersonal trust measures the capacity of citizens to create and maintain relationships of trust with one another. It is therefore intimately related to a sense of belonging to a community of peers. Levels of interpersonal trust have some effect on political participation and attitudes, such as the level of public trust in political institutions, as shown below.

Table 10.1. Interpersonal Trust in Latin America

Percentage of respondents who agreed with the proposition

	1996	1998	1999/2000	2002	2004	1996–2004
One can trust in the majority of people	20	21	16	18	15	18
One can never be sufficiently careful in relations with others	77	76	82	78	81	79
No response	3	3	2	4	3	3

Source: *Latinobarómetro* 1996–2004.

One of the most salient features of Latin America's political culture is the low level of interpersonal trust. Responses to the *Latinobarómetro* surveys for the past five years (Table 10.1) show that from an already low level of about 20 percent, the share of respondents who say that they trust most people fell to a still lower level of 15 percent in 2004. Only in Uruguay do more than 30 percent of respondents say they can trust other people most of the time. In 14 of the countries surveyed, the level of interpersonal trust is below 20 percent. In Brazil, it has been around or below 5 percent since 1997.

Data from the World Values Survey (1990–93) reveal considerably higher levels of interpersonal trust in most countries of Western Europe, as well as in the United States, Canada, and Japan. On average, about 47 percent of respondents in Western European countries say that they can trust others, while 51 percent, 53 percent, and 42 percent say so in the United States, Canada, and Japan, respectively.

The efficient operation of markets, governmental institutions and other forms of social relations requires an environment in which mutually beneficial transactions can be regularly carried out between individuals and groups, without undue reliance on outside enforcement. Greater trust among individuals should foster greater cooperation in the pursuit of social ends and encourage participation in civic associations and community affairs, as well as greater cooperation within organizations (including legislatures and government agencies), thus enabling them to be more effective in the pursuit of the public good.

Responses to the *Latinobarómetro* surveys provide some support for the notion that there is a link between interpersonal trust and the proclivity to participate in politics. Respondents who said that they trust others are 27 percent more likely than those who distrust others to say that they participate in their communities, and 23 percent more likely to say that they talk about politics with friends.

The relationship between trust and the effectiveness of political institutions is bidirectional. Given the great reach of the government and the lower density and intensity of social relations in modern communities, political institutions may be expected to play an important role in shaping the more diffuse and fragile trust that can develop. For trust to develop in the modern age, rules of conduct must be enforced consistently and impartially.[5] Without

---

[5] See Newton (1999) for a discussion of the impact of modernization and social change on the development and maintenance of social trust.

the consistent and structured social interactions that might have existed naturally in the past, the development of social trust would appear to be more closely dependent on reliable institutions that gain the trust of citizens. Thus, while high levels of interpersonal trust ease the problems of governing (as well as the costs of exchange in economic markets), steady work in building trust in governmental institutions may help foster trust in society.

Interpersonal trust is fairly weakly associated with trust in political institutions; Table 10.2 presents correlations of the two variables. A detailed analysis by country indicates that while the correlations between these variables are statistically significant in Chile, Guatemala, Paraguay, Uruguay, and Venezuela they are not significant in the rest of the countries.

The low level of interpersonal trust in Latin America coexists with the broadly critical view that citizens have of other citizens. For example, only 28 percent of Latin Americans believe that the citizens of their own country are very or fairly honest (2001); only 34 percent believe that other citizens are aware of their duties and obligations (2003); and 77

Table 10.2. Correlations between Interpersonal Trust and Trust in Institutions

	Congress	Political parties	Judiciary	Presidency	Democratic institutions
Argentina	0.049	0.057	0.009	0.009	0.063*
Bolivia	0.000	0.039	0.049	0.095**	0.042
Brazil	0.012	0.051	0.016	0.029	0.061*
Chile	0.082**	0.097**	0.077**	0.076*	0.106**
Colombia	0.025	0.072*	0.048	0.060*	0.088**
Costa Rica	0.009	0.022	0.006	−0.008	0.008
Dominican Republic	0.033	0.037	−0.008	0.007	0.080*
Ecuador	0.028	0.020	−0.028	0.082**	0.036
El Salvador	0.004	0.043	−0.017	−0.029	−0.003
Guatemala	0.080*	0.079*	0.098**	0.062	0.086**
Honduras	0.036	0.094**	0.042	0.036	0.034
Mexico	0.001	−0.001	0.022	−0.001	0.028
Nicaragua	−0.010	0.034	0.030	0.042	0.024
Panama	0.056	0.048	0.048	0.017	0.040
Paraguay	0.118**	0.091*	0.100*	0.026	0.067
Peru	0.003	0.022	0.000	0.073*	0.028
Uruguay	0.148**	0.164**	0.145**	0.088**	0.063*
Venezuela	0.172**	0.191**	0.140**	0.111**	0.142**
Latin America	**0.046****	**0.075****	**0.037****	**0.030****	**0.048****

Source: Latinobarómetro 2004.
Note: For an explanation of how to interpret the indicators, see Chapter 9.
* Correlation is significant at the 0.05 level; ** correlation is significant at the 0.01 level.

percent think that their fellow citizens either never or seldom comply with the law (2003) (*Latinobarómetro*, 2001, 2003). These values and attitudes contribute to the weak associative inclinations of Latin American societies and the particularly low levels of participation in neighborhood councils, parent-teacher organizations, and other civil society organizations. This feature of the political culture encourages the development of a social and political order in which people typically relate individually to the political sphere instead of doing so through social networks and associations that have the capacity to exert greater influence on public decision making and governmental conduct.

Support for Democratic Ideals

Latinobarómetro surveys prior to 2001 reflected a fairly high level of support for democracy, understood as a set of ideals and a form of government. On average, 61 percent of those surveyed from 1996 to 1999/2000 endorsed the view that "democracy is preferable to all other forms of government" (Figure 10.1). Only about 18 percent thought an authoritarian form of government might sometimes be preferable, and about 16 percent were indifferent between authoritarian and democratic regimes.

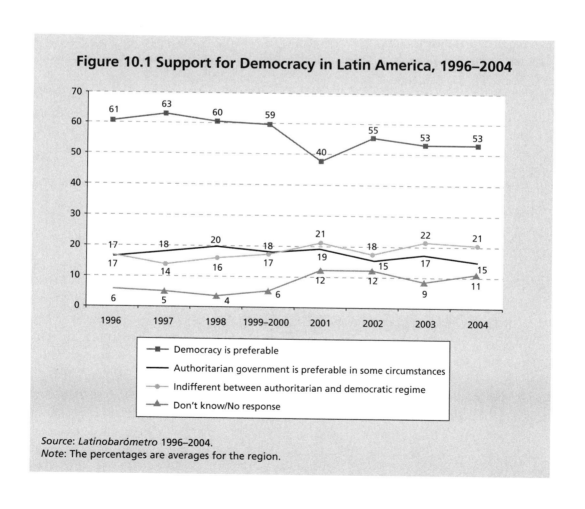

Figure 10.1 Support for Democracy in Latin America, 1996–2004

Source: *Latinobarómetro* 1996–2004.
Note: The percentages are averages for the region.

However, the 2001 survey revealed a dramatic drop in the share of respondents who unequivocally embraced democracy as their preferred system of government. Less than half (48 percent) of the respondents in that survey expressed a clear preference for democracy. While the average levels of support for democracy in subsequent surveys were not as low as those of 2001, the level in the years following 2001 remained appreciably lower (eight to nine percentage points less) than in the second half of the 1990s.

Despite the decline in support for democracy, the percentage of respondents who, at least in some circumstances, would favor authoritarianism barely changed. The highest share registered in the entire period was about 19 percent, in 2001. Evidently, the decline in support for democracy was replaced by apathy and indifference, entailing an increase in the percentage of respondents who either expressed indifference about the potential types of government, answered "don't know," or did not respond.

It is worth noting that the extent of the decline in support for democracy in the region reflected in the 2001 survey was influenced by a dramatic fall in a handful of countries. Although democracy was supported by an average of 62 percent of respondents in El Salvador from 1996 to 2000, that support fell to 27.3 percent in the 2001 survey. Sharp declines were also observed in Panama (69.9 percent to 34.3 percent), Colombia (58.4 percent to 36.3 percent), and Nicaragua (63.6 percent to 42.7 percent). In Argentina, Brazil, Ecuador, Guatemala, and Paraguay the share of those affirming a preference for democracy also fell by at least 10 percentage points.

Since then, however, support for democracy has partially recovered in these countries, although it still has not reached the levels existing prior to 2001. Table 10.3 shows averages by country for the two earliest years (1996 and 1997) and the two most recent years (2003 and 2004) of the *Latinobarómetro* surveys covered here. The share of respondents unequivocally backing democracy fell in varying degrees in all countries except Ecuador and Mexico. Colombia, Nicaragua, Bolivia, Panama, and Guatemala recorded declines of more than 15 percentage points. Brazil and Peru recorded slightly smaller declines, though the portion of respondents expressing support for democracy still fell below 40 percent.

These results indicate a fairly consistent reduction in public support for democracy in the Latin American region. Although the changes have not been extremely significant, the survey results suggest that the pro-democracy consensus that appears to have existed in the late 1990s weakened over the past few years.

The 2003 and 2004 surveys show that the highest percentage of respondents who in some circumstances would favor authoritarianism is found in Paraguay (42 percent, versus 39 percent supportive of democracy). This is followed by Ecuador, at 32 percent, and Bolivia, at 21 percent. The lowest percentages are found in Costa Rica (7 percent), Uruguay (8 percent), and Nicaragua (10 percent). In general, however, the reduction in unambiguous support for democracy has resulted from an increase in indifference (and nonresponses) rather than increases in support for authoritarianism.

It is probable that persistent dissatisfaction with social and economic conditions and government performance has begun to erode public trust in the more abstract conception of democracy as a set of ideals and form of government. This topic merits steady examination in the coming years, given its importance for the future of democratic governance in the region.

Table 10.3. Support for Democracy as a System of Government in Latin America, 1996–97 and 2003–04

Percent

	Democracy preferable		Authoritarianism sometimes preferable		Indifferent between authoritarian and democratic regime		Don't know/ No response	
	Avg. 1996–97	Avg. 2003–04	Avg. 1996–97	Avg. 2003–04	Avg. 1996–97	Avg. 2003–04	Avg. 1996–97	Avg. 2003–04
Argentina	73	66	15	19	10	12	3	3
Bolivia	65	47	17	21	14	21	5	11
Brazil	50	38	22	18	21	31	8	13
Chile	58	54	18	14	22	29	3	3
Colombia	64	46	17	13	17	26	2	15
Costa Rica	81	72	8	7	7	14	4	7
Dominican Rep.[1]	—	65	—	11	—	12	—	12
Ecuador	46	46	20	32	26	19	8	3
El Salvador	61	48	13	10	19	22	8	20
Guatemala	49	34	24	11	18	24	10	31
Honduras	53	50	16	12	22	27	9	11
Mexico	52	53	27	14	16	30	4	3
Nicaragua	63	45	16	10	15	27	5	18
Panama	73	57	10	13	13	20	4	9
Paraguay	52	39	34	42	12	17	3	2
Peru	61	48	15	20	14	23	10	9
Uruguay	83	78	8	8	6	10	3	4
Venezuela	63	71	18	13	14	13	4	4
Latin America	**62**	**53**	**17**	**16**	**16**	**21**	**5**	**10**

Source: *Latinobarómetro* 1996, 1997, 2003 and 2004.
Note: Boldface indicates countries that experienced a decline in support for democracy of 15 or more percentage points. — = Data not available.
[1] Data available only for 2004.

The level of support for democracy in Europe provides a basis for comparison with that observed in Latin America. Data from the 1990 Eurobarometer, which included 12 Western European countries, showed that about 96 percent of respondents viewed democracy as preferable to all other forms of government. Fewer than 2 percent thought that authoritarianism at times might be preferable.

In summary, data from the most recent *Latinobarómetro* surveys indicate that the fairly robust support for democracy present at the beginning of the study period has shown some signs of slippage. While there is little support for authoritarian alternatives, people evince fairly high levels of indifference or apathy with respect to the basic form of their government. As the contrast between the survey results for Latin America and Europe clearly shows, the reservoir of support for democracy in many Latin American countries is not deep enough to give us confidence that democracy will consistently withstand future stresses and threats.

Satisfaction with Democracy

Public perceptions of democracy as an ideal and as a form of government are distinct from the issue of whether citizens are satisfied with how the democratic system is working in practice. Satisfaction with democratic performance varies more extensively over time and is more sensitive to changes in economic conditions. For instance, support for the ideal of democracy barely wavered in Western European countries during the 1970s, but given spiraling inflation and growing unemployment, satisfaction with democratic performance declined considerably in many countries.

Although the two factors are not directly related, several scholars have concluded that sustained, effective democratic performance and, particularly, success in addressing social and economic problems contribute to broad and fundamental support for the legitimacy of democracy (Lipset, 1993; Diamond, Linz, and Lipset, 1989; McAllister, 1999). Thus, satisfaction over the long term with governmental performance may be a precondition for consolidating support for democratic regimes, because it allows for a reservoir of fundamental support to be built. The regime, in turn, can draw on that support in times of crisis. Clearly, however, the legitimacy of democratic regimes is also derived from many other factors, including the political culture, perceptions of feasible alternative regimes, the performance of the regime in providing valued political goods, such as order, human rights, and political freedom.

Social and economic outcomes are likely to exert a strong effect on popular perceptions of the performance of democratic regimes in Latin America, where income levels are relatively low, poverty is widespread (40 percent of the population lives below the poverty line), and trust in politicians and political institutions is low (Lagos, 2001). Thus, the findings of the 2004 *Latinobarómetro* do not augur well for further legitimization of democracy: in 14 of the 18 countries in the study, more than half of respondents believed that the economic situation in their country was heading in the wrong direction; only 8 percent felt that the economic situation in their country was good, and a growing portion—from 13 percent in 1996 to 23 percent in 2004—said that they could not provide for their basic needs with their present incomes. Similarly, it is troublesome that 65 percent of respondents thought that little or no progress was being achieved in the fight against crime.

Given the relatively poor assessments of the performance of democratic regimes, it is not surprising that from 1996 to 2000, an average of just 35 percent of respondents (across the 17 countries for all four years of the survey)[6] reported that they were satisfied with the

---

[6] Until 2004, when the Dominican Republic was added, the *Latinobarómetro* survey included 17 countries. The exception was 1998 when El Salvador, Honduras and Nicaragua were also excluded.

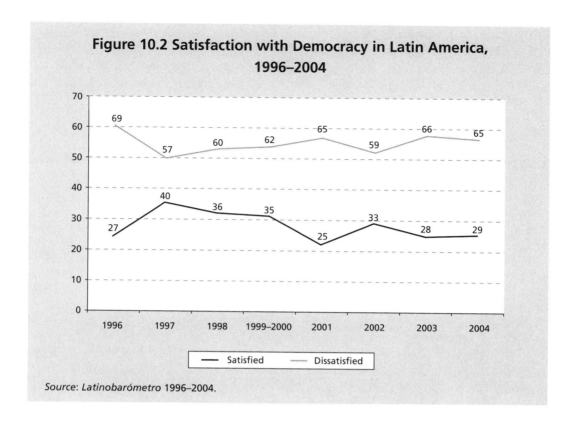

Figure 10.2 Satisfaction with Democracy in Latin America, 1996–2004

Satisfied: 27, 40, 36, 35, 25, 33, 28, 29
Dissatisfied: 69, 57, 60, 62, 65, 59, 66, 65

1996, 1997, 1998, 1999–2000, 2001, 2002, 2003, 2004

—— Satisfied   —— Dissatisfied

Source: Latinobarómetro 1996–2004.

functioning of democracy. Worse, however, the 2001 survey revealed an even lower proportion of respondents satisfied with democracy (only one out of every four citizens). In the 2002 to 2004 surveys, levels of satisfaction were lower than those of the late 1990s (Figure 10.2). It is at least some consolation that this decline in satisfaction did not translate into a dramatic increase in the expressed level of dissatisfaction.[7] As in the case of support for democratic principles, much of the observed reduction in satisfaction with democracy was converted into responses of indifference or no responses rather than into outright dissatisfaction.

The most recent data available show that Latin Americans are just slightly more satisfied with democracy than Central and Eastern Europeans (2004), where democracy is a still more recent development (Figure 10.3).[8] The average level of dissatisfaction with democracy for Central and Eastern Europe was 69 percent, 4 points higher than in Latin America.

As might be expected, in the more established democracies and advanced economies of Western Europe, the level of satisfaction with democracy is considerably higher. Even though the average level of satisfaction with democracy in these countries fell in 2004 rela-

---

[7] The percentage of those characterized as "satisfied" includes both those who responded that they were "very satisfied" and those who responded that they were "fairly satisfied." Those characterized as "dissatisfied" include respondents who said that they were "not very satisfied" and those who were "not satisfied at all."

[8] The countries examined in the Central and Eastern European group were Bulgaria, Cyprus, Czech Republic, Estonia, Hungary, Latvia, Lithuania, Malta, Poland, Romania, Slovakia, Slovenia, and Turkey (Central and Eastern Eurobarometer, 2004).

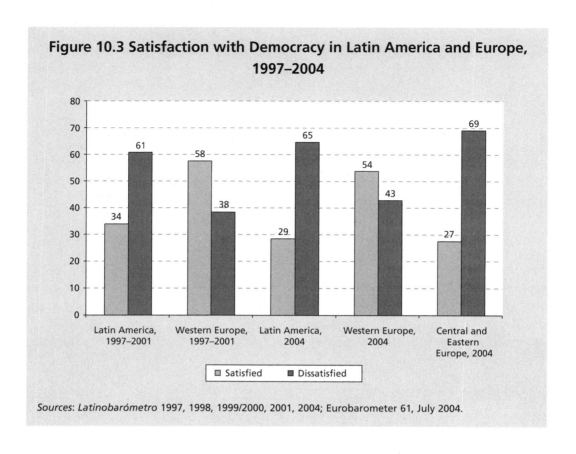

Figure 10.3 Satisfaction with Democracy in Latin America and Europe, 1997–2004

Sources: *Latinobarómetro* 1997, 1998, 1999/2000, 2001, 2004; Eurobarometer 61, July 2004.

tive to the 1997–2001 period, it is significantly higher than the level in Latin America. An average of 54 percent of respondents sampled in Western Europe in 2004 said they were satisfied with democracy, while just 43 percent were dissatisfied. None of the 15 Western European countries surveyed had levels of satisfaction with democracy below the average levels observed in Latin America for the 1997 to 2001 period or for 2004.

The individual country responses validate the view that perceptions of the efficacy of democracy do not necessarily go hand in hand with beliefs in its legitimacy. Many countries in which an ample majority supports democracy as a form of government are nonetheless characterized by a low level of satisfaction with the performance of the regime. On average, about 30 percent of the people who responded to the 2004 *Latinobarómetro* survey can be labeled "dissatisfied democrats." They prefer democracy as a system of government but are displeased with how their governments and institutions are performing. By contrast, just 20 percent of respondents are "satisfied democrats," believing both in the ideal of democracy and that their democratic systems are performing reasonably well. The crucial question is how well beliefs in the legitimacy of democracy can hold up in the face of persistent dissatisfaction with the performance of the regime.

Given the impact of economic performance and of the government's success at satisfying basic needs on perceptions of the effectiveness of democratic regimes, it is understandable that the measure of satisfaction with democratic performance varies more widely than does the measure of level of support for democracy as a system. Figures 10.2 and 10.3 show

Democracies in Development

that the average level of satisfaction with democracy in the region as a whole decreased slightly. Table 10.4 breaks down the results by country and year, thus providing a more detailed view of regional trends. Averages across the region show a wide variation, with Costa Rica (57 percent) and Uruguay (56 percent) clearly standing out from the rest of the countries of the region. They are the only countries in which more than half of the respondents expressed satisfaction with democracy. Next, with considerably lower averages than the first two, is a group of countries led by Venezuela, where levels of satisfaction average between 30 percent and 40 percent. Mexico and six South American countries make up the lower end of the scale, with levels of satisfaction at or below 25 percent.

Trends in the degree of satisfaction with democracy have also varied considerably at the level of individual countries during the nine-year period of the *Latinobarómetro* survey. Changes in economic performance or perceived government efficiency in addressing social problems, heightened expectations associated with the inauguration of newly elected governments, political crises or scandals, or a combination of these may account for the wide fluctuations in observed satisfaction with democracy.

Table 10.4. Satisfaction with Democracy

Share of respondents "very satisfied" or "fairly satisfied" with democracy

	1996	1997	1998	1999/ 2000	2001	2002	2003	2004	1996– 2004
Costa Rica	51	68	54	61	51	75	47	47	57
Uruguay	51	65	68	69	56	53	43	45	56
Venezuela	30	36	35	55	41	40	38	42	40
Honduras	19	49	—	44	35	62	37	30	39
Dominican Rep.	—	—	—	—	—	—	—	36	36
Panama	28	39	34	47	21	44	24	35	34
Argentina	34	42	49	46	20	8	34	34	33
El Salvador	26	48	—	27	21	38	33	37	33
Nicaragua	24	51	—	16	24	59	31	21	32
Chile	27	37	32	34	23	28	33	41	32
Guatemala	17	40	57	36	17	35	21	20	30
Bolivia	25	33	34	22	16	24	25	17	25
Mexico	12	45	21	37	26	18	18	18	24
Ecuador	33	31	34	23	14	16	23	14	23
Brazil	20	23	25	19	21	21	28	28	23
Colombia	16	40	24	27	8	11	22	30	22
Peru	28	21	18	24	16	18	11	7	18
Paraguay	21	16	24	13	11	7	9	13	14
Latin America	**27**	**40**	**36**	**35**	**25**	**33**	**28**	**29**	**32**

Source: Latinobarómetro 1996–2004.
Note: — = Data not available.

For example, in Nicaragua just over half (51 percent) of respondents expressed satisfaction with democracy after both the 1996 and 2001 elections, but sharp declines were observed in subsequent survey years. In Colombia, levels of satisfaction were very low in 2001 and 2002 (8 percent and 11 percent respectively), but then rose to 22 percent in 2003 and 30 percent in 2004. In Argentina, only 8 percent of respondents expressed satisfaction with democracy in the 2002 survey, which was administered when the country was experiencing the effects of the drastic peso devaluation. Levels of satisfaction rose fourfold in the following two years with the election of the new government and the restoration of economic growth.

Thus, while support for the principles of democracy has been fairly strong, and was especially so in the first four years of the *Latinobarómetro* survey, there has been far less satisfaction with its actual operation and performance. Clearly, broad sectors of the population feel that democratic systems, which they support in principle, are not meeting their expectations.

The rest of this section examines more rigorously the relationship between the performance of democratic governments and citizen satisfaction with democracy. It is reasonable to expect that subjective perceptions of government performance rather than macroeconomic outcomes have more direct influence on how citizens evaluate democratic performance. This may be especially true in Latin America, where, because of stark inequality in access to resources and in the distribution of wealth, increases in economic growth do not necessarily improve the conditions of the most underprivileged social groups.

It is worth returning for a moment to the distinction made above between legitimacy as gauged by popular satisfaction with and support for the outputs of the system, and legitimacy derived from people's belief in political processes and institutions. The political system is the instrument through which the state undertakes its public management function. Whereas elections provide citizens with occasional, periodic links to politics and politicians, the actual outputs of public services make up the daily connection between citizens and the state. Presented in Table 10.6 are the correlations between respondents' stated level of satisfaction with democracy and their assessments of (1) whether their country is headed in the right or wrong direction; (2) their personal economic situation; (3) their satisfaction with health and education services; (4) the autonomy, impartiality, and universality of interest representation as reflected in government policies; and (5) the progress achieved in reducing corruption in state institutions.

As might be expected, the results in Table 10.5 show that respondents tend to be more satisfied with democracy when they perceive the country to be making progress and the government to be effective. At the regional level the correlations between satisfaction with democracy and all variables are statistically significant. In most cases, they remain fairly significant when one considers just individual country samples. Respondents who believe that their country is headed in the right direction and that their country is governed for the common good are most likely to be satisfied with democracy, but the other variables are almost as powerful in predicting respondents' level of satisfaction with democracy.

As a further exploration of the impact of performance on citizens' assessments of democracy, we examine the influence of general indicators of economic performance and

Table 10.5. Correlations between Satisfaction with Democracy and Satisfaction with Public Services and Government Performance, 2004

	Outputs				Processes	
	Belief that country is headed in the right (wrong) direction[1]	Satisfaction with current personal economic situation[2]	Satisfaction with health services[3]	Satisfaction with education services[3]	Belief that country is (not) governed for the common good[4]	Belief that progress has (not) been made in reducing corruption in state institutions[5]
Argentina	0.374**	0.159**	0.106**	0.137**	−0.285**	0.181**
Bolivia	0.207**	0.140**	0.076*	0.122**	−0.044	0.130**
Brazil	0.354**	0.198**	0.244**	0.225**	−0.261**	0.059
Chile	0.430**	0.247**	0.154**	0.159**	−0.284**	0.306**
Colombia	0.319**	0.192**	0.142**	0.106**	−0.179**	0.220**
Costa Rica	0.320**	0.158**	0.124**	0.121**	−0.260**	0.145**
Dominican Rep.	0.174**	0.060	0.083*	0.026	−0.167**	0.098**
Ecuador	0.148**	0.131**	0.109**	0.144**	−0.117**	0.187**
El Salvador	0.393**	0.279**	0.279**	0.239**	−0.325**	0.252**
Guatemala	0.251**	0.137**	0.138**	0.124**	−0.128**	0.099**
Honduras	0.262**	0.091**	0.103**	0.131**	−0.198**	0.170**
Mexico	0.102**	0.169**	0.071*	0.048	0.069*	0.195**
Nicaragua	0.266**	0.138**	0.215**	0.191**	−0.197**	0.168**
Panama	0.185**	0.101**	0.085**	0.089**	−0.103**	0.085*
Paraguay	0.271**	0.174**	0.125**	0.149**	−0.176**	0.085*
Peru	0.174**	0.145**	0.055	0.105**	−0.174**	0.262**
Uruguay	0.234**	0.159**	0.213**	0.143**	−0.156**	0.114**
Venezuela	0.524**	0.276**	0.165**	0.175**	−0.447**	0.365**
Total	**0.319****	**0.179****	**0.182****	**0.184****	**−0.214****	**0.188****

Source: *Latinobarómetro* 2004.
Note: *N* = 19,605.
[1] On a scale from 1 to 2, where 1 = right direction; 2 = wrong direction
[2] On a scale from 1 to 5, where 1 = very good; 5 = very bad
[3] On a scale from 1 to 4, where 1 = very satisfied; 4 = not satisfied
[4] On a scale from 1 to 2, where 1 = powerful interests; 2 = common good
[5] On a scale from 1 to 4, where 1 = a lot; 4 = none
* Correlation is significant at the 0.05 level; ** correlation is significant at the 0.01 level.

experts' perceptions of levels of corruption (Table 10.6). To proxy national economic performance, we use 2003 GDP growth and inflation rates; for the degree of corruption we use Transparency International's Corruption Perceptions Index for 2004. As in Table 10.5, we use 2004 *Latinobarómetro* data to calculate the average level of satisfaction with democracy and a measure of whether or not citizens think the country is going in the right direction.

Table 10.6. Correlations between the Economic and Sociopolitical Situation and Satisfaction with Democracy and the General Direction of the Country

		Satisfaction with democracy	Country headed in the right or wrong direction
Perception indicators	Satisfaction with current personal economic situation	0.332	0.709**
	Country governed for the benefit of a few private interests or for the common good	−0.461	−0.493*
	Progress made in reducing corruption	0.211	0.423
	Satisfaction with health services	0.699**	−0.011
	Satisfaction with education services	0.771**	0.058
Economic and sociopolitical indicators	Corruption Perception Index	−0.459	−0.268
	GDP growth (annual percentage)	0.113	−0.065
	Inflation, consumer prices (annual percentage)	−0.324	−0.216

Source: Macroeconomic data are from World Bank (2004); indicators based on public perceptions are from *Latinobarómetro* 2004; the corruption index is from Transparency International.
Note: N = 18.
* Correlation is significant at the 0.05 level; ** correlation is significant at the 0.01 level.

Again, as might be expected, the subjective perceptions of individuals appear to account better for their level of satisfaction with democracy than do objective indicators. Even though the relationship between the corruption index and satisfaction with democracy is relatively strong and the direction is consistent with expectations (−0.459), it is not statistically significant. Respondents' evaluations of their personal economic situation and perception of corruption in the political system seem to be less significant in determining their degree of satisfaction with democracy than the perceived quality of public health and education services. Nevertheless, public opinion about whether the country is generally heading in the right or wrong direction correlates with both respondents' perceptions of their personal economic situation and the degree to which governmental policies are perceived to reflect common interests.

At the macro level—that is, at the level of country averages—public perceptions of the quality of health and education services are the variables that are most closely tied to the degree of satisfaction with democratic performance. Figures 10.4 and 10.5 show countries' positions in terms of respondents' satisfaction with democracy and with education and health

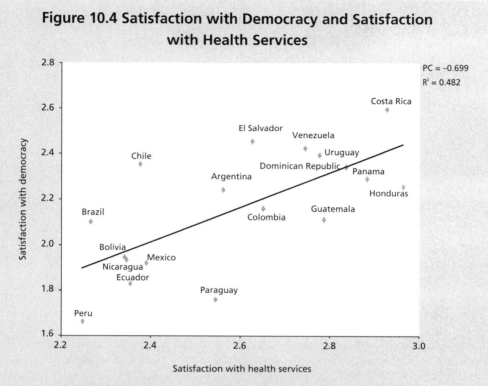

Figure 10.4 Satisfaction with Democracy and Satisfaction with Health Services

Source: Authors' compilation based on data from *Latinobarómetro* 2004.
Note: Correlation is significant at the 0.01 level. Both measures are calculated as a weighted average of the four possible responses where 1 = "not at all satisfied," 2 = "not very satisfied," 3 = "somewhat satisfied," and 4 = "very satisfied."

services. Figure 10.6 shows that satisfaction with democracy is also associated with the level of public spending on health care, expressed as a percentage of gross domestic product (GDP). It was not possible to examine the relationship between satisfaction with democracy and levels of public spending on education, because comparable data were lacking.

Figures 10.4 and 10.5 reveal very similar distributions of countries along the two axes. The placement of Peru, Ecuador, Nicaragua, and Bolivia indicates that in these countries a low level of satisfaction with available health and education services is linked to a low level of satisfaction with democracy. By contrast, in Costa Rica levels of satisfaction with public services and democracy are both relatively high. Chile and Paraguay are at least partial outliers. In Chile, satisfaction with education and health services is relatively low but satisfaction with democracy is comparatively high. The opposite holds true for Paraguay, with one of the lowest levels of satisfaction with democracy and moderate levels of satisfaction with these key public services.

Clearly, regardless of the particular content of policies and the levels of public spending, public opinion toward democracy is influenced most directly by citizens' perceptions of how effectively public services are delivered in practice. Expenditure levels alone reveal very little about how fairly and efficiently resources are allocated and how well they are put

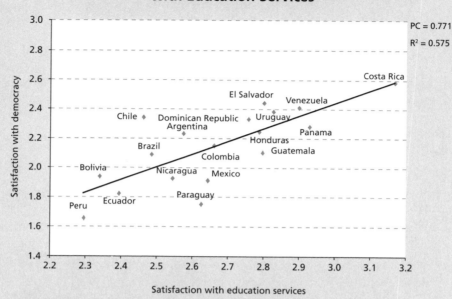

Figure 10.5 Satisfaction with Democracy vs. Satisfaction with Education Services

Source: Authors' compilation based on data from *Latinobarómetro* 2004.
Note: Correlation is significant at the 0.01 level. Both measures are calculated as a weighted average of the four possible responses where 1 = "not at all satisfied," 2 = "not very satisfied," 3 = "somewhat satisfied," and 4 = "very satisfied."

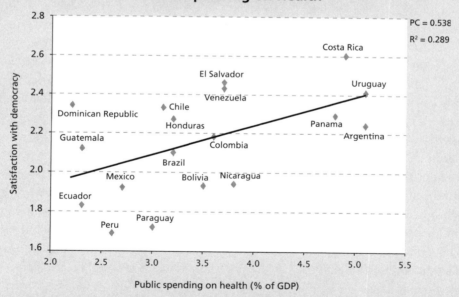

Figure 10.6 Satisfaction with Democracy and Level of Public Spending on Health

Sources: Public spending on health services from World Bank (2004); satisfaction with democracy from *Latinobarómetro* 2004.
Note: Correlation is significant at the 0.05 level. Satisfaction with democracy is calculated as a weighted average of the four possible responses where 1 = "not at all satisfied," 2 = "not very satisfied," 3 = "somewhat satisfied," and 4 = "very satisfied."

Democracies in Development

to use. This qualitative dimension can be captured to a certain extent by subjective indicators, such as that in Figure 10.5. Even though the level of public spending is somewhat related to citizen satisfaction with democratic performance—since expenditure levels are an important element of the relationship between the state and citizens—levels of satisfaction with the functioning of public services appear to be even more strongly associated with the degree of satisfaction with democracy.

Confidence in Democratic Institutions

In a representative system not all citizens participate in the decision-making process, but they must consent to the rules governing the distribution of power so that they are prepared to abide by the resulting decisions. Citizens' acceptance of the fairness of the rules of the game is the source of the state's authority to impose law and order and make binding decisions. Democracy is an uncertain game in which actors must accept that sometimes they will win, and sometimes they will lose. To accept losing today, one has to believe that the political process is fair—that is, that those that won really obtained a majority and were not unduly privileged by their connections to persons in power—and that one has a possibility of winning the next election. In short, the legitimacy of a democratic system depends heavily on the legitimacy of the processes and institutions that comprise it.

Examining the credibility of political institutions allows a more direct assessment of support for democracy than we have been able to carry out thus far, one less prone to the fluctuations associated with appraisals centered on outcomes, which are inevitably affected by intervening and short-term factors outside the control of the political system. That said, citizens' perceptions of outcomes (e.g., economic performance) are also likely to color their appraisals of institutions as well.

One institution that enjoys considerable prestige in Latin America is the Catholic Church (Figure 10.7). In the 1996–2004 *Latinobarómetro* surveys, around 73 percent of respondents consistently said that they had "much" or "some" confidence in the church. Given that this institution's private role likely plays a central role in people's perceptions, while its public role is not always so visible, such a high rating is not that surprising.[9] Political parties and other representative government institutions, by contrast, play more clearly public roles—they reflect and give expression to conflicting interests in society, ranging from those that are fairly narrow and personal to those that are more universal.

Citizens also place a fairly high level of confidence in television (44 percent), although that figure is considerably lower than the level of confidence in the Catholic Church. The prestige and visibility of television relative to that of other democratic institutions reflects the modern mode of politics, in which image is at least as important as substance. To be successful, politicians must work on developing an appealing persona on television, a task to which they often invest considerable financial resources. Television personalities, in turn,

---

[9] While the church is a public institution, it was also established largely to guide norms of conduct in the private sphere.

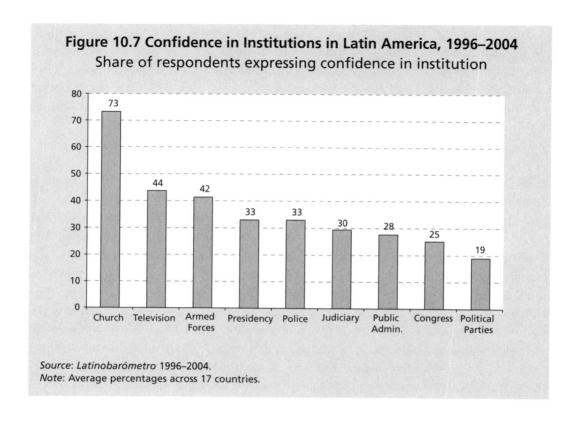

Figure 10.7 Confidence in Institutions in Latin America, 1996–2004
Share of respondents expressing confidence in institution

Source: *Latinobarómetro* 1996–2004.
Note: Average percentages across 17 countries.

often play an important role in focusing and moving the political debate and agenda, shaping images of politicians and filtering the news reported to the public.

The institution enjoying the third-highest level of public confidence is the armed forces, which on average over the eight survey years had a 42 percent confidence rating. However, the level of trust varies substantially across countries. In Bolivia, Guatemala, Nicaragua, and Argentina, confidence in the armed forces is scarcely greater than confidence in the major representative institutions, whereas in Ecuador, Brazil, and Venezuela confidence in the armed forces is more than double that expressed in the fundamental democratic institutions. Across the region, the generally positive image of the armed forces does not translate into a high level of support for military authoritarianism, as seen in Table 10.3. Similarly, variations in popular confidence in democratic institutions are not associated with citizens' disposition to support a military government (Figure 10.8). Although a significant percentage of respondents in Paraguay and, to a lesser extent, in Honduras and Peru, said they would support a military government "if the situation got very bad" (*Latinobarómetro* 2004), a plurality of respondents in all other countries selected the option that "under no circumstances" would they support a military government.

The presidency ranks next in terms of the level of public confidence, with an average level of 33 percent. Across time and countries, however, it is also the institution that exhibits the highest degree of variability. Rather than judging the institution with any kind of permanence, respondents in this instance naturally evaluate the executive on the basis of their feelings toward the incumbent and the current government. As is well known, the

Democracies in Development

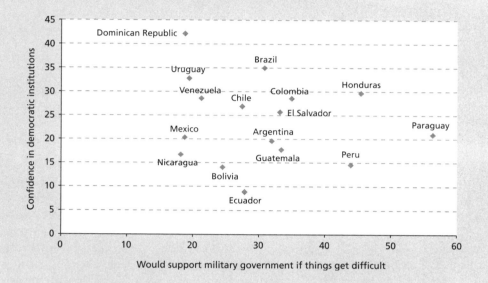

Figure 10.8 Confidence in Democratic Institutions and Support for Military Government in a Difficult Situation, 2004

Source: Latinobarómetro 2004.
Note: The democratic institutions considered here are the congress, judiciary, and political parties.

popularity of presidents changes according to perceptions of governmental performance and the integrity and competence of the president and cabinet. Because presidents have the advantage of being able to represent the nation as a whole and appear decisive, it is not surprising that, on average, the presidency would enjoy greater respect than the more diffuse representative institutions.

Just below the presidency in terms of public trust are the police and the judiciary, which on average enjoy the confidence of 33 percent and 30 percent of citizens sampled, respectively. Considering data from individual countries, it is clear that these institutions are rated in comparable fashion.

The institutions in which citizens place the least confidence are the public administration (civil service) and two of the principal institutions of representative democracy: the legislature and political parties. Only 19 percent of respondents place "much" or "some" confidence in political parties, making them less esteemed than even congress or the public administration, whose confidence ratings are 28 percent and 25 percent, respectively.

This ranking of citizen confidence in institutions is consistent with that revealed in a regional survey conducted by the Consorcio Iberoamericano de Empresas de Investigación de Mercado y Asesoramiento (CIMA) and the Gallup Institute of Argentina in 2001. That survey, which included 13 of the 18 countries covered in this study, reported that 71 percent of respondents had confidence in the Catholic Church, 51 percent in the armed forces, 26 percent in the judicial system, 19 percent in the congress, and 14 percent in political parties.

The average level of confidence in democratic political institutions in Latin America is considerably below that of Western Europe, even considering the decline in confidence in the latter region over the past two decades. Relative to Latin America, legislatures in Western Europe enjoy a confidence level among respondents that is 15 percentage points higher. The gap for the judicial system is 19 points; for public administration, 15 percent points; and the executive, 4 points. However, according to the same data, political parties enjoy somewhat greater prestige in Latin America than in Western Europe (19 percent instead of 17 percent) (Table 10.7).

Hidden behind Latin America's regional averages is considerable variation in levels of confidence in the principal democratic institutions (Table 10.7). The eight-year averages

Table 10.7. Confidence in Democratic Political Institutions, 1996–2004

Average percentages of respondents who expressed "a lot of" or "some" confidence

Country	Congress	Parties	Judiciary	Public administration	Presidency	Democratic institutions (average)
Uruguay	38	32	47	42	37	39
Chile	36	22	33	43	54	37
Costa Rica	30	21	44	26	36	31
Honduras	31	22	33	24	37	29
Brazil	25	17	40	29	35	29
Venezuela	28	19	33	25	40	29
El Salvador	28	23	31	27	34	29
Panama	23	22	30	32	32	28
Mexico	27	22	24	27	31	26
Paraguay	25	19	27	27	29	25
Nicaragua	23	18	26	30	26	25
Colombia	20	15	31	20	33	24
Argentina	20	14	20	21	36	22
Guatemala	20	15	24	27	24	22
Peru	22	16	18	26	27	22
Bolivia	20	13	22	21	25	20
Ecuador	13	10	19	25	22	18
Latin America	25	19	30	28	33	28
Western Europe	40	17	49	43	37	37

Sources: For Latin American countries, Latinobarómetro (1996 to 2004); for Western Europe, Eurobarometer 51 (1999), 55 (2001), 57 (2002), 59(2003), and 61(2004).
Note: For Latin American countries, average percentages are for the period 1996–2004, except for public administration, for which data are available only from the 1996 and 2001 surveys. In addition, the figures for the Dominican Republic are based only on 2004 data, while the averages for El Salvador, Guatemala, and Honduras do not include data from 1998. For Western Europe, averages are for 1999 and 2001–04, except for the judiciary, for which no data are available for 1999, and for public administration, for which no data are available for 2003 and 2004.

for confidence in the legislature range from a high of around 39 percent and 37 percent in Uruguay and Chile, respectively, to a low of 17 percent in Ecuador, and 20 percent to 22 percent in Bolivia, Peru, Guatemala, and Argentina. Very low levels of confidence in political parties extend across a broader group of countries, including Ecuador (10 percent), Bolivia (13 percent), Argentina (14 percent), and Colombia and Guatemala (15 percent). Only in Uruguay (32 percent) do political parties hold the respect of what might be viewed as a significant share of the citizenry. The widest range in confidence across countries is observed in the case of the judiciary. This institution enjoys a substantial degree of trust in Uruguay (47 percent) and Costa Rica (44 percent), but it is not trusted very highly in Peru (18 percent), Ecuador (19 percent), Argentina (20 percent), or Bolivia (22 percent). Faith in public administration is highest in Chile (43 percent) and Uruguay (42 percent), and lowest in Colombia (20 percent), Argentina (21 percent), and Bolivia (21 percent).

The lack of esteem for congress and political parties is further illustrated by responses to a question included in the 2001 *Latinobarómetro* survey about a hypothetical closure of congress and abolishment of political parties. Overall, 35 percent of respondents in the region said that they would approve of such a move, while 54 percent said that they would disapprove. However, in Colombia, Ecuador, Mexico, and Paraguay the share who said that they would approve (51 percent, 71 percent, 46 percent, and 56 percent, respectively) exceeded the share who said that they would disapprove.

In summary, dissatisfaction with democracy does not appear to be simply a reflection of bad economic times or unhappiness with the more visible and concrete outputs of democratic governance. Rather, given the lack of confidence expressed in particular institutions, dissatisfaction with democracy seems to be rooted in a more basic disenchantment with the operation of the fundamental processes, actors, and organizations of the democratic system. Though a certain level of cynicism is common in all democratic systems, the perception that politicians and political parties are primarily concerned with gaining and keeping power and enriching themselves, rather than pursuing the public interest, appears to be pervasive in Latin America. Of course, it is difficult to disentangle these sentiments, since it is certainly the case that citizens' views of democratic institutions are colored by governmental performance in delivering public goods and managing the economy.

Conclusions

The past years have witnessed a growing debate centered on the implications of empirical evidence related to support for democracy, both in established and emerging democracies. Pippa Norris and other scholars (1999) have argued that the identification of what appear to be contradictory trends may be explained by a failure to adequately distinguish among different dimensions of support for the political system. These scholars propose a more rigorous and refined distinction among different forms of support, based on the work of David Easton (1975). The evidence presented in this chapter confirms the findings of this body of work: despite relatively low levels of confidence in democratic institutions and widespread dissatisfaction with their functioning, there is generalized support for democratic ideals and principles.

Our examination of public attitudes has indicated that most Latin Americans appear to support democracy as a form of government, at least relative to perceived alternatives. Citizens may express more confidence in the military as an institution than in congress or political parties, but most do not support the assumption of power by the armed forces. Democracy is supported in part because citizens believe that they should have the right to select their leaders and influence the making of public policy. It is also supported because citizens believe that, while less than perfect, democracy is better than all feasible alternative regimes.

Whether based on principle or on more pragmatic considerations, support for democracy as a form of government remains fairly strong in most Latin American countries. However, that support also shows signs of deterioration. This is cause for concern, since a continued decline in legitimacy across the region impedes the consolidation, and even threatens the survival, of democratic regimes. Support for democracy has shown particular vulnerability in a few countries (Brazil, Bolivia, Colombia, Ecuador, Guatemala, and Paraguay). At the same time, it appears to be strengthening in Mexico and holding relatively steady in most other countries.

Despite general support for the idea of democracy and the rejection of authoritarian alternatives, most citizens are disenchanted with the performance of their democratic systems. Governments and the larger processes of democracy have not met their expectations with respect to delivering goods and services and solving social problems. Nor do citizens appear to place much confidence in the processes through which public functions are carried out. The disenchantment is relatively generalized, and its political consequences have varied across countries. Polls in some countries suggest a kind of nostalgia for strong leadership, which has helped bring to power by electoral means leaders (at the national and subnational levels) who had previously attempted to access power through coups d'état, who had been generals in the military, or who had previously participated in more restrictive, if not oppressive, regimes. In other countries, disenchantment has propelled to power political outsiders with weak or no ties to established political parties, or who had distanced themselves from their party associations. In all such cases, political discourse acquired a clear antiparty orientation, reinforcing a more personalistic form of representation.

The end result is that in some countries, the political party system has been seriously weakened, and the credibility of congress, other democratic institutions, and politicians has eroded. This has led, in some cases, to the practical disappearance of long-standing and important political parties and has made it more difficult for traditional representative institutions to carry out their critical functions. In the wake of these changes democratic competition has tended to become more uncertain and fraught with tension, representation more personalistic, and accountability between politicians and constituents looser. In some cases, the loss of credibility of elected officials, political parties, and the legislature has clearly weakened the capacity of government to effectively respond to economic and social problems, given the fragility of public trust in the integrity and reasonableness of whatever actions that are initiated. The weakened reputation of political parties and legislatures also tends to move such systems more firmly into the category of "delegative" democracies, in which the executive predominates in decision making, with only weak oversight from other institutions (O'Donnell, 1994).

The relatively low level of confidence in and satisfaction with democratic institutions and politicians impedes progress toward the consolidation of democracy. Broadening the group of citizens who strongly support democracy for reasons of principle rather than just for instrumental or conditional reasons ("democracy is better than visible alternatives") depends on improving perceptions of the *performance* of democracy. When democracy is supported only instrumentally, it is more vulnerable to sabotage by leaders who offer efficient solutions to the country's problems in exchange for reduced checks on their power.

Possibly associated with the lack of confidence in institutions in Latin America is a relatively low level of trust among individuals in society. This lack of interpersonal trust may impede the willingness of citizens to participate in their communities and in the political system and is likely associated with widespread problems of crime and corruption—and the difficulties in fighting them.

There is still much to understand about the processes through which citizens opt to submit to rules that limit their capacity to act and that empower authorities to make decisions and exercise the use of force. No matter how attractive democratic ideals appear to be, citizens' expectations—which range from hopes for expanded freedoms and rights to participation to a broader sharing in the benefits of economic growth and state services—need to be reflected to some extent in concrete results. As mentioned above, in emerging democracies it seems logical that citizens tend initially to judge the political system according to results (*government for the people*) rather than by a somewhat abstract appreciation for the processes that generate those results (*government by the people*). However, as various authors have emphasized, to ensure the permanency, stability, and consolidation of a democratic regime, citizens must perceive that the processes and mechanisms used to reach decisions are legitimate, and they must feel that they belong to a community in which risks are both spread and shared, and where there is a collective sense that all are "in the same boat" on equal terms (Rokan, 1999; Thomassen and Schmitt, 2004).

References

Boix, Carles, and David Posner. 1998. The Origins and Political Consequences of Social Capital. *British Journal of Political Science* 28.

CIMA (Consorcio Iberoamericano de Empresas de Investigación de Mercado y Asesoramiento). 2001. Public opinion survey, in collaboration with the Instituto Gallup de Argentina.

Dalton, Russell J. 1999. Political Support in Advanced Industrial Democracies. In Pippa Norris (ed.), *Critical Citizens: Global Support for Democratic Governance*. New York: Oxford University Press.

Diamond, Larry, Juan Linz, and Seymour M. Lipset, eds. 1989. *Democracy in Developing Countries*. London: Amantine.

Easton, David. 1975. A Reassessment of the Concept of Political Support. *British Journal of Political Science* 5.

Eurobarometer 48. 1997. *Public Opinion in the European Community*. Brussels: INRA.

Eurobarometer 51. 1999. *Public Opinion in the European Community*. Brussels: INRA.

Eurobarometer 53. 2000. *Racism, Information Society, General Services and Food Labeling*. Brussels: INRA.

Eurobarometer 55. 2001. *Public Opinion in the European Community*. Brussels: INRA.

Eurobarometer 57. 2002. *Public Opinion in the European Community*. Brussels: INRA.

Eurobarometer 59. 2003. *Public Opinion in the European Community*. Brussels: INRA.

Eurobarometer 61. 2004. *Public Opinion in the European Community*. Brussels: INRA.

Freedom House. 2000. *Freedom in the World: The Annual Survey of Political Rights and Civil Liberties, 1999–2000*. New York: Freedom House.

Fukuyama, Francis. 1995. *Trust: The Social Virtues and the Creation of Prosperity*. New York: Free Press.

Inglehart, Ronald F. 1990. *Culture Shift in Advanced Industrial Society*. Princeton: Princeton University Press.

————. 1997. *Modernization and Postmodernization: Cultural, Economic and Political Change in 43 Societies*. Princeton: Princeton University Press.

————. 2000. *World Values Survey (1990–93 and 1995–97)*. Ann Arbor, MI: Inter-University Consortium for Political and Social Research.

IUCPSR (Inter-University Consortium for Political and Social Research). 2004. Central and Eastern Eurobarometer. Ann Arbor, MI: IUCPSR.

Klingemann, Hans D. 1999. Mapping Political Support in the 1990s: A Global Analysis. In Pippa Norris (ed.), *Critical Citizens: Global Support for Democratic Governance*. New York: Oxford University Press.

Lagos, Marta. 2001. How People View Democracy: Between Stability and Crisis in Latin America. *Journal of Democracy* 12(1).

Latinobarómetro. 1996–2004. *Latinobarómetro: Opinión pública latinoamericana, 1996–2004*. Santiago, Chile: Corporación Latinobarómetro.

Linz, Juan J., and Alfred C. Stepan. 1996. *Problems of Democratic Transition and Consolidation: Southern Europe, South America and Post-communist Europe*. Baltimore: Johns Hopkins University Press.

Lipset, Seymour Martin. 1993. The Centrality of Political Culture. In Larry Diamond and Marc F. Plattner (eds.), *The Global Resurgence of Democracy*. Baltimore: Johns Hopkins University Press.

McAllister, Ian. 1999. The Economic Performance of Governments. In Pippa Norris (ed.), *Critical Citizens: Global Support for Democratic Governance*. New York: Oxford University Press.

Newton, Kenneth. 1999. Social and Political Trust in Established Democracies. In Pippa Norris (ed.), *Critical Citizens: Global Support for Democratic Governance*. New York: Oxford University Press.

Norris, Pippa, ed. 1999. *Critical Citizens: Global Support for Democratic Governance*. New York: Oxford University Press.

O'Donnell, Guillermo. 1994. Delegative Democracy. *Journal of Democracy* 5(1).

Putnam, Robert D. 1993. *Making Democracy Work*. Princeton: Princeton University Press.

Rokkan, Stein. 1999. *State Formation, Nation Building, and Mass Politics in Europe: The Theory of Stein Rokkan*. Edited by Peter Flora, with Stein Kuhnle and Derek Urwin. Oxford: Oxford University Press.

Sartori, Giovanni. 1997 [1987]. *Teoría de la democracia. Los problemas clásicos*. Vol. 2. Madrid: Alianza Editorial.

Scharpf, Fritz W. 1999. *Governing in Europe: Effective and Democratic?* Oxford: Oxford University Press.

Thomassen, Jacques, and Hermann Schmitt. 2004. Democracy and Legitimacy in the European Union. *Tidsskrift for Samfunnsforskning* 45(1): 377–410.

Transparency International. 2005. [Retrieved from http://www.transparency.org/policy_research/surveys_indices/cpi]

UNDP (United Nations Development Programme). 2004. *Human Development Report: Cultural Liberty in Today's Diverse World*. New York: UNDP.

World Bank. 2004. World Development Indicators 2004. CD-ROM. Washington, DC: World Bank.

Trends in Democratic Reform in Latin America

This book addresses issues essential to the study and understanding of political reform in Latin America. Building on the first edition, it identifies the main reform trends in the region and discusses their effects on the functioning of democracy. It also provides at least partial and contingent answers to the question of what types of political reforms may be considered in the future to enhance democratic governability in the region.

Over the past two decades, the analysis and practice of development have increasingly acknowledged the importance of institutions and of a legitimate, stable, and effective political system. Modernizing the state and consolidating the broader institutional framework at the foundation of a market-centered economy are essential to accelerate the pace of social and economic progress. At the same time, a well-functioning democracy appears to be indispensable to strengthening the broader set of development-supporting institutions (civil service, courts, regulatory frameworks, and so on) and to implementing efficient and effective public policies. In Latin America, countries have progressed to varying degrees in the task of building legitimate, representative, and effective democratic political institutions.

The political and institutional reforms adopted across the region have pursued different and sometimes conflicting purposes. If reforms are to be adopted into law, they must be compatible with the interests of leading political and social groups. Thus, reform processes are inevitably driven, or at least constrained, by the narrow motives of power and privilege. In some instances such motives are more transparent than in others, though proponents of reforms inevitably portray reforms as means to enhance democratic governance in one way or another. But reforms of political institutions at times are also prompted—especially during a political crisis or dramatic shifts in the stature of political groups—by demands from citizens and civil society organizations for more effective and representative democratic governance. At least for brief periods of time, such demands can change politicians' calculus of the costs and benefits of reform. This in turn makes it possible to pass reforms with the prospect of producing more general benefits for the democratic system and its citizens.

Several factors complicate an analysis of the effects of political reforms and the task of developing reform recommendations. First, there is limited agreement on the ultimate objectives of reform and on how those objectives should be prioritized. Considering them separately, most analysts and citizens would agree on the merits of several objectives, including: political stability, political freedom, decision-making efficiency, inclusive political participation, law and order, responsive and equitable representation, political legitimacy, transparency, and accountability. But it is more difficult to obtain agreement on the main deficiencies of democratic functioning in a given country and how the above objectives should be ranked. Second, given the inherent trade-offs—such as between more inclusive representation and decision-making efficiency—one must calibrate the reform so that correcting one perceived deficiency does not harm other aspects of the democratic system. Third, designing reforms and predicting their effects are impeded by inadequate theory related to the interactions among different institutional factors as well as contextual ones, such as socioeconomic structure, political culture, and history (IDB, 2006).

The importance of narrow political interests and customary practices (or political culture), the trade-offs among competing reform objectives, and the uncertainty surrounding the effects of reform help explain not only the frequent and sometimes contradictory nature of reform efforts, but also the limited number of reforms that succeed in producing broad benefits for the democratic system and the frequent slippages and backslides in reform implementation. In addition, these factors complicate the task of evaluating the effects of political reforms in the region and setting forth recommendations.

The recommendations laid out in this chapter are presented primarily in the form of trade-offs. Our aim is to emphasize the advantages and disadvantages associated with selecting a certain model of political reform over another. We do not pretend to offer prescriptions or recipes regarding the types of reforms that are desirable in the region as a whole or in particular countries. Institutional reform options, like the institutions themselves, are extremely complex and ideally must emerge from discussion and debate among the social and political actors of the country in which they will be applied. Only in this way will the reforms be suited to the context and therefore seen as legitimate.

Election Rules and Regime Design

The broader issues of constitutional design (and their implications for the operation of presidential regimes) cannot be understood without taking into account the nature of the electoral system and other rules that affect the incentives of political actors. Among these are the nature of the electoral system, the degree of fragmentation of the party system, and the cohesiveness of parties themselves.

Presidential Election Systems

In order to reform presidential election systems, one should consider the effects of different sets of rules and their interactions with one another, including the election rule itself (is election by plurality, majority, or reduced threshold?), the concurrence of presidential and legislative elections, and the possibility of presidential reelection and the length of the presidential term.

Plurality and Majority Runoff Systems

The region is clearly moving from plurality to majority runoff (or *ballotage*) systems, or runoffs with a reduced threshold. The expectation of reform proponents is that a shift away from a plurality system to a majority runoff system will strengthen the mandate of the elected president by ensuring the winner a higher proportion of votes. But in practice the goal of strengthening mandates has in many cases not been fulfilled. In fact, experience indicates that majority runoff systems can have some undesirable effects, including: (1) not reflecting true voter preferences as well as plurality systems; (2) tending to encourage party system fragmentation in the long run; (3) potentially weakening the legitimacy of the president, such as when the candidate who wins the second round is not the largest vote-earner in the first round; and (4) tending to encourage the formation of loose electoral coalitions between each of the two candidates and some minority parties, rather than more durable governing coalitions. Consequently, over time the movement from a plurality to a majority runoff system could end up worsening the problem of democratic governability. This suggests that a compromise of sorts—such as, a majority runoff system with a reduced threshold—may be an appropriate intermediate solution. Several countries have moved in this direction.

Concurrence of Presidential and Legislative Elections

No clear trend can be observed with respect to the concurrent or nonconcurrent nature of presidential and legislative elections. Mid-term legislative elections can be beneficial for democracy in the sense that they allow voters the chance to hold legislators and the government accountable on a more regular basis and remove some of the "rigidities" associated with the fixed terms of presidential systems. But nonconcurrent legislative elections can be problematic for democratic governability given the likelihood that such elections will lower the chance for majority government, promote party system fragmentation, and shorten political time horizons. Given coattail effects, when presidential and legislative elections are concurrent, there is a tendency for the distribution of votes in the congressional elections to reflect that in the presidential election. Thus, especially when a plurality system is used to elect the president, votes in congress will tend to be more concentrated and will tend to give the president's party a share of votes in the legislative elections similar to the share the president won. In the case of nonconcurrent presidential and legislative elections, or mid-term legislative elections, this connection does not exist, and it is much more likely for the congressional results to be more dispersed and for the president's party to end up in a weaker position in the congress. Two additional benefits of concurrent elections are: (1) cost-effectiveness: holding simultaneous elections eliminates the duplication of costs; and (2) turnout: electoral participation may be greater because citizens are more motivated to vote in the legislative election when it occurs alongside the presidential election.

Reelection and Length of Presidential Term

Some systems strictly prohibit presidential reelection; others permit immediate reelection; and still others allow for reelection only after the passage of at least one presidential term (nonconsecutive reelection). Though all three models are found in the region, there has been a general movement toward less restrictive standards. The primary rationale for prohibiting presidential reelection is to avoid the concentration of presidential power over successive terms. Despite the fact the terms are won through democratic means, the lack of alternation of power reduces political pluralism. As a result, restrictions on reelection aim in part to promote the renewal and circulation of elites. In addition to exposing the political system to the risk of electoral dictatorship, reelection may reinforce the tendency inherent in presidentialism toward personalistic and hegemonic leadership.

Yet there are arguments in favor of reelection. Blocking reelection may: (1) stop a capable, popular leader from making long-term contributions to the country, while also weakening the legitimacy of his successor; (2) lower the time horizons of governments; (3) impede the ability of citizens to hold the incumbent and government accountable for performance; (4) reduce the president's political capital or power to negotiate and, therefore, limit the executive's ability to generate support for policies among legislators from his own party and from outside (the lame-duck effect); and (5) reduce incentives for forging social and political accords that help provide continuity and a stable framework for policy implementation.

If presidential reelection is not to present the risks of power concentration, it may be necessary to put in place reasonable checks and balances, such as independent and effective legislative and judicial branches and institutional provisions that ensure a level playing field for political competition between the incumbent and opposition groups. In addition, it may be advisable when such requisites are achieved to combine the possibility of reelection with modest term lengths (such as four years, as opposed to six).

Restrictions on presidential reelection have generally served as checks against the reemergence of authoritarian practices in countries in which rule by strongmen has been historically common. Nevertheless, the suitability of reforms of reelection rules, as of the broader presidential election system, must always be judged relative to each country's distinct cultural, historical, and political context.

Legislative Electoral Systems

Debates on the structure of legislative electoral systems typically center on three issues: (1) majoritarian versus proportional representation and the degree of proportionality of electoral systems; (2) closed and blocked party lists versus preferential voting; and (3) unicameral versus bicameral legislatures. The basic trade-offs in most cases can be conceived as those between efficiency and representativeness and between party-centered and candidate-centered representation.

Majoritarian versus Proportional Electoral Systems

Over the past quarter century the region generally has maintained proportional representation, except in the case of the upper house, where more than half of the countries now use plurality systems. In two countries (three, counting the 1977 Mexican reform) a shift has been made to a combined (or mixed, in the case of Mexico) electoral system in which characteristics of both types are present in the same system.

Because proportional systems favor the election of a legislature that reflects the political heterogeneity of the electorate, proportional representation is generally believed to encourage participation and provide greater legitimacy of representation than majoritarian systems, which favor larger parties and make it difficult for small parties to gain representation. Nevertheless, the high degree of party system fragmentation that may result from systems that are excessively proportional, and the consequent complications for executive-legislative relations, support the case for a majoritarian system of representation, at least in theory.

The details of the design of a system of either type may have a considerable impact on the system's effects. For example, to function well a majoritarian system must be designed in such a way that the drawing of districts and the rules governing access to the ballot do not impede genuine political competition. Similarly, a system of proportional representation should be designed so that it does not encourage excessive party system fragmentation or discriminate too heavily against smaller parties. Achieving the appropriate balance entails focusing on the particularities of the design of the system, such as the size of electoral districts, the formula used for translating votes into seats, and whether or not to put in place vote thresholds for obtaining legislative seats. Other electoral rules, such as requisites for forming and maintaining political parties and the rules for distributing public financing (where such financing exists), will also affect the tendency toward party system fragmentation under a proportional system. Empirical evidence appears to indicate that in relatively homogeneous societies the choice between the two types of systems does not have a significant impact on the stability of democracy. In highly fragmented societies, however, proportional arrangements, particularly in presidential systems, tend to offer more benefits for democratic stability than do majoritarian arrangements (Adserà and Boix, 2004).

Closed and Blocked Party Lists versus Preferential Voting

Democratic governability is also affected by whether electors in a proportional system are limited to voting for a party list or are given the option of expressing a preference for an individual candidate or candidates on the list. In open-list systems, voters may choose both the party and the particular individual or individuals they would like to have represent them, while in systems with closed and blocked lists, voters must accept the order and preferences imposed by parties. Closed systems with preference voting allow voters to vote for a party list or to choose individual candidates within the list.

In single-member-district plurality systems, candidate-centered voting is privileged, even more so than in preference voting under proportional representation systems. Given the relatively low information costs entailed in distinguishing among a limited number of candidates and tracking the performance of a single incumbent, such systems tend to favor accountability. The downsides are those discussed above with respect to equity and legitimacy of representation. Other disadvantages are the possibility that the excessive candidate focus may weaken the importance of party distinctions and the power of electors to hold representatives accountable on broad matters of governmental performance and national policy. Thus, accountability for personal behavior and constituent service may be efficient, while accountability on issues of importance to the nation as a whole and to broader groups of citizens may be weaker.

The introduction of preference voting in a system of proportional representation with closed lists increases the extent to which electors are able to hold incumbents individually accountable and to ensure that parties do not become unduly controlled by the party leadership. But the larger the number of seats being elected per district, the higher the information costs for voters in choosing the right candidates and tracking performance. In addition, the more representatives elected per district, the more narrow is the likely constituency of each representative and the greater the incentives for the representative to prioritize the satisfaction of particularistic over more general interests. As a result, the actual probability of voters being able to hold elected officials accountable on issues of broad importance is fairly low, at least in large-district systems. Preferential voting also tends to reduce party cohesiveness, because success as a candidate comes to rest more on personal popularity and on the delivery of targeted benefits than on loyalty to the party. In fact, such a system tends to encourage intraparty competition.

On the other hand, closed and blocked lists tend to support a party-centered form of accountability that theoretically should favor accountability centered on parties' performance in government and broad issues of policy and service delivery. But for this form of accountability to work effectively, parties need to be programmatically distinguishable and internally democratic to ensure that they remain accountable to their membership and that their leadership is subject to circulation and renewal. In such a system the information demands on voters are lower (and, therefore, the effectiveness of representation is possibly greater) than in systems with preference voting.

Thus, the choice of electoral system involves a complex set of trade-offs. Avoiding extremes in restricting or opening access of minor political parties to electoral competition and representation is one guiding parameter. Similarly, on the other dimension, a balance must be struck between candidate-centered and party-centered competition and representation, such that in systems biased toward the former politics does not become overly localized and personalized, and in those biased toward the latter it does not become excessively centralized in party leaders and unresponsive to citizens and local interests (Shugart, 2001). Otherwise, as with other institutional dimensions covered in this book, it is vital to base reform on broad consensus, while reconciling the system with the history, sociopolitical structure, and culture of the country.

Unicameral and Bicameral Legislatures

The effects of a bicameral legislature on democratic governability largely depend on the system used to elect representatives to each chamber, and on the territorial structure and the overall size of the country. In theory, a unicameral system functions more efficiently, because it eliminates an important potential source of opposition to the executive's initiatives (the upper house) and eases the problem of developing legislative compromises. But in some cases the upper house is designed (through different terms of office, electoral rules, and territorial bases of representation) to be a somewhat more sober and experienced body that can provide a wider and longer perspective on policy as well as a check on the quality and appropriateness of legislation. In addition, in federal or decentralized systems the upper house can provide a means of enhancing territorial representation essential to the stability and legitimacy of the political order. Thus the main trade-offs in choosing a bicameral system would appear to involve efficiency, legislative quality, and representation: potential gains in terms of oversight, quality, and representation may come at the cost of losses in efficiency—the ability to gain approval for necessary reforms. But context is essential in determining whether a particular institutional design is appropriate or not.

Balancing Executive and Legislative Prerogatives

The governability of presidential democracies is closely connected to how the inherent tensions and competing responsibilities between the executive and legislative branches are sorted out. In effect, executive-legislative relations depend on the art of combining a capacity for action with a capacity for legislative oversight and effective citizen representation. The legislature needs to be sufficiently independent from the executive to exercise oversight, but at the same time, it should not have the capacity or incentive to systematically obstruct executive actions required to address national problems efficiently and effectively. Rather, the legislature should play a constructive role, helping to improve the quality or policy acceptability of executive proposals through the formulation of concrete and viable alternatives, while ensuring that the executive does not overstep its authority or misuse public resources. The capacity to check the executive and to propose alternatives without obstructing needed action depends on many factors, including electoral-system incentives, the degree of party system fragmentation and institutionalization, and the constitutional powers and technical capacities of the congress vis-à-vis the executive.

Strengthening the Legislature

A strengthened legislature can play a significant role in improving democratic governability. Endowing presidents with substantial formal powers is one factor that can impede the development of proactive policy-making and oversight capacity in congress. To achieve a balance in executive-legislative relations that permits effective policy making, it may be necessary (1) to limit the power of the president to issue decrees and control the legislative agenda; (2) to ensure that legislators have incentives to build a legislative career and some degree of independence from national party leaders; and (3) to strengthen the operational capacity of the legislature by providing it with advisory agencies staffed by independent experts. High turnover rates for legislators are not conducive to the development of a long-term perspective in policy making or to the development of the knowledge and capacities necessary for the legislature to play an active role in policy making and to exercise effective oversight over the executive.

Presidentialism and Parliamentarianism

After being a topic of debate in some countries in the first decade of democracy, the parliamentary or presidential structure of the political regime does not appear to be an area in which reform is likely in the near future. While presidential regimes (like all systems of government) are not without flaws, they also have several advantages. Among the traditionally recognized merits of presidential regimes are the fact that they: (1) favor accountability by providing citizens with a more direct mechanism to hold the government accountable and to indicate their preferences in government policy; (2) provide potentially more stability than parliamentary systems, in which it may be difficult under some circumstances to sustain viable coalition governments; and (3), in theory, give legislators more freedom to debate alternative policy options, since opposition to the government does not endanger the survival of the government or risk the calling of new elections.

Nevertheless, in countries with fractious societies and fragmented party systems, presidentialism, with its majoritarian electoral arrangement, can be problematic for obtaining and sustaining majority governments with sufficiently broad legitimacy. The presidency's winner-take-all nature and broad national constituency generates a tendency for presidents to assert their authority to govern by developing their personal relations with citizens, even when they may not have obtained majority support in the elections. At the same time, given the fact that legislators' terms are fixed and not dependent on the government maintaining legislative support, there are fewer incentives than in parliamentary systems for parties to form and maintain governing coalitions.

But it is one thing to compare regimes in their abstract, ideal forms, and another to consider how they function in specific contexts. Clearly, how either type of regime functions will depend on factors such as the particular allocation of constitutional powers to the two branches, the characteristics of the electoral and party system, the capacities of the legislature, and the nation's political culture and history. The focus of reform in Latin America today is on making presidential systems function better rather than on changing the broad structure of the regime. This means working to achieve a reasonable balance among the above dimensions so that it is possible for the two branches to cooperate and for the legislature to participate constructively in the making of legislation and in overseeing the executive.

Institutions of Democratic Accountability

One of the major achievements of the process of democratic consolidation in Latin America has been the establishment of horizontal accountability agencies, such as audit institutions, public prosecutor's offices, and human rights ombudsmen. Several semi-autonomous agencies overseeing the exercise of public authority have been developed in Latin American democracies, in part due to the ineffectiveness of more traditional sources of accountability, such as elections and representative institutions. Reforms have aimed to improve the functioning of these institutions in relation to others and to develop their independence, capabilities, and legitimacy. In order for them to gain legitimacy, the public must see that investigations eventually lead to clear findings of fact, prosecution where appropriate, and sanctions. In each case, the agency must possess the authority and capability to exercise its functions autonomously in order to earn the respect of citizens and successfully carry out its constitutional mission.

In addition, the effectiveness of horizontal accountability agencies depends on their ability to work in collaboration with other democratic institutions and support from an active civil society and favorable climate of public opinion. Responsibilities and authorities need to be clearly specified so that agencies can carry out their responsibilities and collaborate effectively with other institutions, especially when their control functions overlap with those of other agencies. But the broader institutional and cultural context in a country is also important to their success. The importance of accountability institutions lies at least partly in their contribution to overall democratic development and civic education, not merely in the legal outcomes they achieve.

Political Parties

Three aspects of political party systems are fundamental to democratic governability: their degree of fragmentation, level of institutionalization, and intensity of polarization. Again, as mentioned above, political parties cannot be considered in isolation from the electoral systems in which they operate.

Party Systems

Fragmentation

With fragmentation, there is a trade-off between representativeness and efficiency. On the one hand, fragmentation can be seen as a measure of the pluralism of the political forces represented in congress and the extent to which the distinct social groups and ideological currents in society are represented. On the other hand, fragmentation in extreme cases may become counterproductive because it damages executive-legislative relations. Political divisions in the legislature can make reaching agreements difficult and so impede decision making. Internal party divisions can add to these problems by making it more difficult for parties to make and enforce interparty agreements and weakening the lines of accountability between citizens and representatives.

Institutionalization

Ideally, parties should have fairly durable bases of social support and represent positions that are clearly identifiable to voters, so parties are decisive actors in determining who will govern and how. Institutionalized parties, which forge ties with their constituencies on the basis of coherent political programs (as opposed to the discretional distribution of benefits that are the hallmarks of clientelism) make a significant contribution to democratic representation and accountability. Institutionalized parties promote predictability in public policy and help build acceptance and respect for rules of behavior and interaction among political actors.

Parties that endure because of restrictions on the entry of new participants into the system and limits to free electoral competition are not democratically institutionalized parties. A well-functioning democracy depends on a high degree of competition among parties.

Polarization

Some degree of polarization can be seen as a functional necessity of political parties. For elections to function properly, voters need to be able to signal their broad policy preferences through their electoral choices, which requires parties with clear programmatic differences. In addition, if parties do not appear to stand for different approaches to governing, and if it is unclear how the election could make a difference, then the incentives for citizens to participate are weakened. On the other hand, when polarization is extreme, the possibility of dialogue and negotiation between political forces is greatly reduced. In this context, it is difficult to form stable governments, and actors may not be able to reach consensus or make the interim agreements necessary to pursue a coherent, sustainable set of public policies.

Intraparty Democratic Processes and Financing of Political Parties

Intraparty Democratization

The 1980s and 1990s saw profound reforms of constitutions and laws governing political parties and elections in most Latin American countries. Nevertheless, in their first stage, these reforms failed to focus on the internal democratization of political parties, beyond granting them constitutional recognition. However, party democratization was addressed more directly in the phase of reforms that began in the second half of the 1990s, with special attention devoted to the processes for nominating presidential candidates.

In a growing number of countries, the presidential candidate is no longer chosen by the highest-ranking party leaders or in internal party conventions, but through various types of primary processes that tend to strengthen the legitimacy of the individual who is ultimately elected president. The expectation is that these reforms will afford parties a higher degree of accountability to their members and the broader society; a greater capacity to represent diverse interests present in the party and society; the possibility of settling conflicts among competing currents of leadership; and an increased level of legitimacy for the organization in the eyes of the public.

Comparative analysis suggests a growing consensus in Latin America regarding the advantages of holding primary elections to select presidential candidates. In fact, even from the narrow vantage point of campaign strategy, primaries appear to be (1) a valuable resource to strengthen public backing for candidates in the general elections; (2) a source of greater legitimacy for the candidate elected to the presidency; (3) a way to broaden the circle of potential party leaders; and (4) a way to offer voters a broader range of options, which should lead to the selection of more competent and responsive leaders.

The adverse effects of opening parties up to democratic processes are mainly evident in how the democratization process has affected internal cohesion and accord. In some cases internal democratization has created conflicts among party factions, increased party fragmentation, and even contributed to the splitting up of parties.

Despite the progress made in the internal democratization of political parties, given the varied and divergent national experiences and the short time that has passed since their initiation, no definitive conclusions can be drawn about either the effects, positive or negative, of intraparty democratization on political representation and democratic governance.

Political Financing

Two main conclusions stand out with respect to the regulation of political financing in the region: first, financing for political parties and election campaigns is a complex, controversial, and unresolved issue for which there are no panaceas or magic formulas. Improvements will require a sequence of mostly modest measures and approaches, rather than broad and highly ambitious reform initiatives. Second, important advances have occurred in the past 20 years, though progress has not been even across the region. Having been virtually absent from the political agenda in Latin America, the issue has been receiving increasing attention not only at the national level, where an intense process of reforms is taking place, but also in discussions at conferences attended by experts on the subject, among heads of state throughout the hemisphere, and within political parties themselves.

In Latin America, a system of mixed public and private financing predominates, with a trend toward public financing and stricter limits on private contributions. Owing to several factors, however, including inadequate regulation, weak oversight and control, ineffective enforcement, and political practices that encourage contempt for the rules, public financing has in many cases functioned less as a partial substitute for private funding than as an extra funding source. Accordingly, despite some positive effect, the impact of public financing has been modest and uneven.

Increasingly common are attempts to control election activities that trigger spending, to impose spending ceilings, and to cut back on the length of campaigns. Results in different countries have been mixed. These developments have occurred in conjunction with a redirection in the use of public funds toward (what is budgeted as) electoral investment, with resources allocated to strengthen political parties through support for research and training activities.

All in all, transparency in campaign finance remains low, notwithstanding a growing number of reforms aimed at strengthening accountability and better disclosure, and a growing positive role played by the mass media and civil society in this area. The large majority of recent reforms have failed to provide for the need to strengthen oversight mechanisms, enforcement agencies, and the framework for penalties against violations. In this area new legislation alone will be insufficient. What is required to produce an effective system is to combine a broader regulatory framework with effective control and enforcement agencies geared toward raising vigilance among the public and mass media.

In short, a good financing system must safeguard open and free political competition that is fair and equitable, while contributing, through greater transparency, to stronger public confidence in parties, politics, and democracy. That goal will require a mixed system (public and private), with full disclosure, and a strong regulatory agency supported by an effective system of enforcement with penalties. Public financing provided to parties should be commensurate with efforts to develop parties' own resources, and should involve a system for matching funds or reimbursements. Private financing must include a share raised from grassroots contributions, but because of its limited size, that share will not be the sole source of funding. The imperative of disclosure entails publication of regular financial statements, auditing, and public access to accounting records and advertising contracts. Enforcement requires a politically independent authority with financial budgetary independence, which must be adequately empowered by legislation to exercise authority to oversee, verify, investigate, and when appropriate, hand up indictments. All of these arrangements will require strong, genuine political will in favor of authentic reforms.

Citizen Participation and Democracy

Institutions of Direct Democracy

A preliminary overview makes clear that, despite the general inclusion of arrangements for direct democracy in their constitutions, in most Latin American national political systems the role of popular referendums and similar initiatives continues to be small.

In general, the record in most cases in Latin America gives little indication that the arrangements for direct democracy have had the desired impact on the expansion of representativeness or participation. Nor is it evident that these arrangements have helped to reduce discontent with politics and parties; rather, in many cases they have served as channels, separate from regular elections, to express public disenchantment. The record of referendums, "popular consultations," and other such schemes has been one of little substantial impact, for good or for bad, on political stability. As with any component of the electoral structure, these mechanisms are part of a larger framework, and their function in practice has to be considered as such.

The effect of direct democracy mechanisms on political reforms can either favor conservative outcomes or create support for change. Particularly complex policy reforms, such as economic and financial matters, are unlikely to lend themselves to resolution through citizen participation in direct democracy. For that reason, legislation in most countries expressly precludes these issues from the purview of popular consultations.

Consultations, referendums, and initiatives can introduce distortions in the absence of efficient representative democratic institutions based on a stable multi-party system. If they are used by the executive as a means to bypass the legislature they can contribute to the weakening of representative institutions both by making them seem less relevant and by allowing the adoption of reforms aimed at strengthening the executive's hand.

The mechanisms of direct democracy are likely to be more useful at the subnational level, where the scale of government is smaller and decision making takes place in closer proximity to constituents. If properly employed, direct democracy can strengthen the legitimacy of the system by providing citizens with a direct opportunity to voice their opinions on policy. Otherwise, these mechanisms, far from serving as instruments available to citizens for direct participation in policy making, become a means of social protest, separate from elections, that may serve to discredit representative institutions to the detriment of democratic governance.

Electoral Participation

Recent trends in electoral participation may not be cause for serious concern, but there is significant room for improvement, with about 60 percent of the voting-age population turning out to vote. Although this figure may be taken to indicate that Latin American democracies are in relatively good health—given that the level of participation in Latin America is not dramatically different from that found in some advanced democracies—levels of voter turnout alone are not a clear indicator of confidence in the democratic system. Instead, individuals' *reasons for abstention* (are they alienated from the system or satisfied with how things are going, and thus apathetic?) are a more accurate gauge of the health of democracy in a given system.

Chapter 9 examined the characteristics of politically active individuals by country (the "micro level"), and explored which systems produce the greatest incentives for citizens to make the effort to vote (the "macro level"). The political-institutional factors considered at the macro level included, among others, the type of voter registration system, whether voting is compulsory or voluntary, the electoral formula used to award seats, the legal and constitutional framework, and the party system. In terms of institutional design, results indicate that higher turnout levels are associated with (1) automatic voter registration and compulsory voting with enforceable penalties; (2) systems that hold concurrent presidential and legislative elections; and (3) systems in which levels of political freedoms and civil liberties are relatively high.

Transitional elections tended to have higher levels of turnout than subsequent democratic elections, but not by a large amount. The perception of transparency and effectiveness in the electoral process are also important motivators of participation. Countries whose citizens perceive that the electoral process functions well, that viable options exist, and that change can bring concrete improvements in living conditions have higher relative numbers of politically active citizens. Therefore, it is the responsibility of political parties and of candidates to make the electoral process attractive to voters. Substantive, programmatic politics is fundamental in this regard. Parties need to demonstrate that the issues included in their platforms *matter* and that their political proposals are sufficiently viable for voters to turn out at the polls. Also worth noting is the correlation between electoral participation and perceptions of the legitimacy and integrity of political institutions, actors, and processes, including political parties and the executive and legislative branches of government.

Public Support for Democracy

A majority of Latin Americans prefer democracy to any other type of regime. Although the proportion (53 percent) is relatively modest, democracy still appears to be supported by the majority and to have reached a certain equilibrium that limits the chances for authoritarian reversals—at least ones involving sharp departures from democratic practices. Curiously, even during periods of poor economic performance, support for democracy has not plummeted—a considerable accomplishment.

Citizens' prevailing preference for democracy contrasts with the low level of satisfaction with democratic *performance* and to the lack of confidence in the institutions of democratic representation. Citizens do not want to forgo democracy; but they do appear to blame politicians and elites for the system's failure to promote adequate social and economic development and to effectively deliver public services. Widespread discontent and lack of confidence has affected the degree of electoral volatility, which, in turn, has contributed to political uncertainty—and in some cases, instability. Fed by campaign promises made by those aspiring to govern, democracy has produced high expectations, leading citizens to look for results that are greater than what the political system can realistically offer, especially considering the adverse economic context in which democratic processes were initiated or restored in most of the region.

Democratic governance requires effective institutions that have the capacity to produce results. Trust in public policies and public institutions are gained based on the quality of the outcomes of those policies. Therefore, while the risk of an authoritarian reversal appears minor, given the generally small share of citizens who express any preference for authoritarian rule, there are still dangers that threaten democracy if it fails to transform formal rights into concrete results. Democracy enables the broad exercise of freedoms of speech and association, whose effects can include not only electoral losses for incumbents who perform poorly, but also the resignation of presidents in the face of popular unrest, as has occurred various times over the past 20 years. If the fruits of democratic government continue to be limited, the balance may again tip toward a change in regime, particularly among the roughly 40 percent of the public who express apathy or indifference about the type of government under which they live or who may even envisage supporting an authoritarian regime in difficult circumstances.

References

Adserà, Alicia, and Carles Boix. 2004. Constitutional Engineering and the Stability of Democracies. Paper presented at the Annual Conference of the ISNIE (International Society for New Institutional Economics), Tucson, AZ, September 30–October 3.

IDB (Inter-American Development Bank). 2006. *The Politics of Policies: Economic and Social Progress in Latin America*. Washington, DC: Inter-American Development Bank and Cambridge, MA: Harvard University Press.

Shugart, Matthew Soberg. 2001. Electoral Efficiency and the Move to Mixed-Member Systems. *Electoral Studies* 20(2).

About the Authors

Andrés Allamand Zavala

Andrés Allamand Zavala holds a law degree from the University of Chile. He has written and contributed to several books, including *Chile y México: dos transiciones frente a frente* (Editorial Grijalbo, 2000) and *La travesía del desierto* (Editorial Alfaguara, 1999). He served as a deputy in the Chilean congress from 1994 to 1998 and was elected to the senate in 2005. He worked as a consultant at the Inter-American Development Bank in Washington, D.C., from 1999 to 2001 and then was Dean of the School of Government at the University Adolfo Ibáñez and a principal partner in the law firm Allamand & Schaulsohn.

Fernando Carrillo-Flórez

Fernando Carrillo-Flórez is the Principal Advisor in the Special Office in Europe of the Inter-American Development Bank. He is also Professor of Political Institutions at the Institute of Political Studies of Paris—Sciences Po. He served as Minister of Justice in Colombia and was elected a member of the constituent assembly in 1991. He is trained as a lawyer and social economist and obtained a master's in law, finance and public administration from Harvard University.

Koldo Echebarría

Koldo Echebarría holds a doctorate in law from the University of Deusto in Spain. He is currently the Country Representative of the Inter-American Development Bank in Chile. Previously he served as Principal Specialist in the IDB's State, Governance and Civil Society Division. Before coming to the IDB he served as director of the Public Management Institute of ESADE (Barcelona) and taught courses in several European and Latin American universities on reform of the state and public management.

Flavia Freidenberg

Flavia Freidenberg holds a doctorate in political science and a master's degree in Latin American studies from the University of Salamanca. She is Assistant Professor in Political Science and Administration and Professor of Latin American Political Systems in the Latin American Studies Program of the Interuniversity Institute of Iberoamérica (Instituto Interuniversitario de Iberoamérica) at the University of Salamanca. She has published several books about politics in Ecuador and about the organization and functioning of political parties in Latin America.

Edmundo Jarquín

Edmundo Jarquín is a lawyer and economist from Nicaragua. He served as cabinet minister, Nicaragua's ambassador to Spain, and legislator in the 1980s and 1990s. He was Chief of the State, Governance and Civil Society Division of the Sustainable Development Department at the Inter-American Development Bank and then Chief of the Cabinet of the Iberian American Secretary General before returning to Nicaragua in 2006. He was the presidential candidate for the Sandinista Renovation Movement in the November 2006 elections.

Mercedes Mateo Díaz

Mercedes Mateo Díaz is a Modernization of the State Specialist in the State, Governance and Civil Society Division of the Sustainable Development Department of the Inter-American Development Bank. Previously she was an honorary research fellow of the Belgian National Research Fund. From 2002 to 2004, she was a Marie Curie Fellow of the Robert Schumann Center at the European University. She holds a doctorate in political science and international relations from the University of Lovaina.

J. Mark Payne

J. Mark Payne is a Modernization of the State Specialist in the State, Governance and Civil Society Division of the Sustainable Development Department of the Inter-American Development Bank. He holds a doctorate in political science from Ohio State University. He contributed as a coauthor to the Inter-American Development Bank's 2006 Report on Economic and Social Progress entitled *The Politics of Policies*. He has written several journal articles, book chapters and working papers related to democratic institutions, judicial reform and public administration.

Daniel Zovatto G.

Daniel Zovatto G. holds a doctorate in international law from the Complutense University in Spain and a master's degree in public management from the Kennedy School of Government at Harvard University. He is the regional director of the Latin American Program of International IDEA and is a member of the International Advisory Council of *Latinobarómetro*. He has written numerous articles and several books on human rights, democracy, and elections in Latin America.

Index

Production, 2; direct democracy institutions, 224, 227, 233, 238; early democratic development in, 7; electoral participation, 246; Freedom House 2004 indexes, 275n4; legislative electoral system in, 41, 51, 55, 58, 60–61, 63, 69–70, 72; legislature's powers, 102; ombudsman office, 137; party system fragmentation and polarization, 170, 172–174; party system institutionalization, 152–153, 155–156, 158, 161, 164–165, 168, 174; presidential electoral system in, 28, 31; presidential powers, 88, 90–92, 95, 97–98, 103, 105–106, 111; primary elections, 193, 209; public support for democracy, 273, 278, 289, 295; supreme audit institutions, 123, 126; voter turnout, 249–250, 252, 254–256

churches, 291, 292*fig*

The Civic Culture (Almond and Verba), 248

civil and political rights, *6fig*

civil sanctions, 120

civil service, 9, 136, 293

civil society, 143, 150

clientelismo, 180, 310

coalitions, 103–104, 106, 111

coattail effects, 21–22, 303

collegiate directorates, 123

Collor de Melo, Fernando, 102

Colombia: attorney general's office, 131, 133, 135, 142; campaign finance regulation, 198–199, 203, 205; candidate selection, 181, 195; direct democracy institutions, 224–227, 233, 235–237; electoral participation, 246; Freedom House 2004 indexes, 275n4; guerrilla warfare, 171; legislative electoral system in, 42, 44n3, 48, 55–57, 68, 72–73, 76; legislature's powers, 94, 101–102; ombudsman office, 137–138; party system fragmentation and polarization, 170–174; party system institutionalization, 152, 155, 159–162,

164, 174; presidential electoral system in, 23, 30–31, 33, 35; presidential powers, 88, 90–92, 97–98, 104–106; primary elections, 187, 193, 209; public support for democracy, 280, 286, 295–296; supreme audit institutions, 125–126; voter turnout, 249–250, 252, 255–256

Comisión de Radiodifusión, 206

compromise, 150

comptrollers, 123, 126, 130, 142, 207

Consorcio Iberoamericano de Empresas de Investigación de Mercado y Asesoramiento (CIMA), 293

consulta popular. See plebiscites

Contralorías, 125

conventions, 180

corruption, 119, 225, 275, 288

Corruption Perceptions Index, 287

Corte dei Conti, 123

Costa Rica: attorney general's office, 131, 135, 142; campaign finance regulation, 199, 203, 207; candidate selection, 181, 195; direct democracy institutions, 224–226; early democratic development in, *7n4*; electoral participation, 246; Freedom House 2004 indexes, 275n4; legislative electoral system in, 44–45, 51, 60, 63; legislature's powers, 101; ombudsman office, 137; party system fragmentation and polarization, 170–174; party system institutionalization, 152, 155–156, 161, 164; presidential electoral system in, 19, 23, 31, 33; presidential powers, 88–89, 92, 97–98, 103–104, 106; primary elections, 187, 209; public support for democracy, 285, 289, 295; supreme audit institutions, 123, 126; voter turnout, 254

Cour de Comptes, 123

crime, 282

criminal investigations, 136

criminal procedure model, 132–133

168, 172–174; party system institutionalization, 153, 156, 159, 162, 164, 168, 174; presidential electoral system in, 23, 30–31; presidential powers, 89–90, 92, 103–104, 110; primary elections, 187, 192, 209; public support for democracy, 292; supreme audit institutions, 126; voter turnout, 254

horizontal accountability, 120–123, 142, 307–308

human rights violations, 137

Hungary, 48

identifiability, 39

impeachment, 83, 100–102

import-substitution model of development, 2–3

inflation, 3

institutional reform, 10–11

institutional weaknesses, 6–7

internal democratization of political parties: advantages of, 180, 208–209; candidate selection methods, 180; factionalism, 179–180; nomination of presidential candidates, 184*fig*, 185*fig*, 186*fig*; party official selection, 181, 182*fig*; primary elections, 187; regulation of nominating process, 183*fig*; trends in, 310–311. *See also* campaign finance; public funding of campaigns

International Labour Organization (ILO), 227

interpersonal trust, 276–279, 297

Ireland, 221

Israel, 40, 48

Italy, 48, 221

item veto, 88–89

Japan: campaign finance, 195; electoral system in, 48; interpersonal trust levels, 277; poverty reduction in, 7

judicial system: attorney general's office and, 135; perceptions of independence of, 119*fig*; public trust for, 293; reforms of, 118

judicialization, 135

Kemmerer, Edwin W., 130*n5*

Kemmerer Missions, 130

Kirchner, Néstor, 192

Latin American Elites Project (PELA), 171

Latinobarómetro surveys, 158–163, 166, 171–173, 258, 260, 272–273, 277–295

least-squares index, 44, 58

legal thresholds for seat allocation, 47

legislative election systems: average magnitude approach, 42*n2*; binominal system, 41, 51, 103, 193*n4*; democratic governability and, 37–38; district size in, 41–47; effective number of, 62*fig*, 73*fig*; electoral formulas for, 42–47; first-past-the-post systems, 38, 40; and fragmentation of party systems, 46, 70, 76; key functions of, 38–40; in the lower house, 52*tab*, 53*tab*, 59*tab*, 61*tab*, 63–72; majority systems, 40, 58; mechanical effects, 38; midterm, 23, 34; plurality, 39; psychological effects, 38; simultaneous with presidential elections, 19–21, 28–30, 303–304; theoretical bases for classification of, 40–42; theoretical effectiveness and effective number of parties, 62*fig*; theoretical expectations and outcome measures, 61*tab*; trends in, 304–305; unicameral legislatures, 72, 103, 307; in the upper house, 54*tab*, 57*tab*, 72–75. *See also* proportional representation

legislatures: censure of cabinet members by, 93–95, 99–100; high turnover in, 111–112, 308; impeachment by, 83, 100–102; lack of capacity for action in, 84; opposition party control of, 85; public mistrust of, 293; trends in strengthening, 307–308. *See also* executive-legislative relations

North American Free Trade Agreement (NAFTA), 276
Norway, 221

objective competence, 248
ombudsman office: appointments and terms of office, 140*tab*; autonomy of, 142; as democratic achievement, 309; functions of, 138–142; Latin American models for, 137–138; offices by country, 139*tab*
open town meetings, 222
Ortega, Daniel, 35
overregulation, 208
oversight, 118

package veto, 88, 97
panachage, 48, 68
Panama: attorney general's office, 131, 135; campaign finance regulation, 198–199, 203, 207; candidate selection, 181, 195; direct democracy institutions, 223–224, 227, 233–234; Freedom House 2004 indexes, 275*n4*; legislative electoral system in, 44, 47, 55–56, 69; legislature's powers, 94–95, 101–102; ombudsman office, 137–138; party system fragmentation and polarization, 170–173; party system institutionalization, 156, 158, 161, 165; presidential electoral system in, 23, 35; presidential powers, 88, 91–92, 97–98, 105–106; primary elections, 187, 191, 209; public support for democracy, 273, 280; supreme audit institutions, 123, 125–126; voter turnout, 250, 255
Panama Canal, 224
Paraguay: attorney general's office, 131, 135; campaign finance regulation, 199; candidate selection, 181, 195; direct democracy institutions, 224–226, 235; Freedom House 2004 indexes, 275*n4*; legislative electoral system in, 45, 51, 55, 57, 60, 69, 73; legislature's

powers, 102; ombudsman office, 137, 141; party system fragmentation and polarization, 170–174; party system institutionalization, 152, 156, 158–159, 161, 163–165; presidential electoral system in, 23, 30, 33, 35; presidential powers, 88, 91–92, 97–98, 103, 106; primary elections, 187, 191, 209; public support for democracy, 273, 278, 280, 289, 292, 295, 296; supreme audit institutions, 123, 126; voter turnout, 250, 254–255
parliamentary systems, 39, 81–83, 308
partial veto, 88–89
participation of citizens, 38–40, 55
party lists, 39
party systems: democratic governance and, 149–152, 168–171; electoral volatility in Latin America, 154*tab*; evolution of, 152; fragmentation in, 25*tab*, 26, 28, 46, 70, 76, 103, 106, 110–111, 149, 151, 168–171, 309–310; index of institutionalization, 164–168; institutionalization of, 149–151, 167*tab*; perceived legitimacy of parties and elections, 160–163; polarization in, 149, 151, 171–173, 310; societal identification with political parties, 155–160; stability of interparty competition patterns, 153–155; strength of party organizations, 163–164
Pastrana, Andrés, 34
Pérez, Carlos Andrés, 102
personalized proportional representation, 41, 51, 55, 57, 76
Peru: attorney general's office, 135; campaign finance regulation, 198–199, 203, 205, 210; candidate selection, 181, 195; direct democracy institutions, 224–225, 233; electoral participation, 246; Freedom House 2004 indexes, 275*n4*; legislative electoral system in, 42, 44, 47, 55–57, 63, 70, 72, 76;

television, 291–292

terms of office, 18, 30, 31*tab*, 82, 304

third-wave of democratization, 81, 117, 272

Transparency International, 287

trends in democratic reform: bicameral vs. unicameral legislatures, 307; in campaign finance, 204–205, 211–212; concurrent presidential and legislative elections, 303–304; electoral participation, 253–255, 313–314; executive vs. legislative prerogatives, 307; institutions for democratic accountability, 308–309; institutions of direct democracy, 238, 312–313; intraparty democratization, 310–311; legislative election systems, 304–305; majoritarian vs. proportional electoral systems, 305; party system fragmentation, 309–310; party system polarization, 310; political financing, 204–205, 211–212, 311–312; presidential election systems, 303; presidential terms and reelection, 304; presidential vs. parliamentary systems, 308; primary elections, 305–306; problems in analysis of, 302; in public funding of campaigns, 210, 311; public support for democracy, 314; runoff systems, 303; strengthening the legislature, 307–308

Tribunal de Cuentas, 123

trust: in institutions, 278*tab*, 282, 291–295; interpersonal, 276–279, 297; in judicial systems, 293; levels in Europe, 277, 294; levels in Japan, 277; levels in the U.S., 277; in political parties and voter turnout, 260, 264; social, 276, 278

unicameral legislatures, 72, 103, 307

United Kingdom, 45*n7*, 137, 195

United Nations Economic Commission on Latin America and the Caribbean (ECLAC), 2

United States: budget legislation, 91*n6*; cabinet appointments, 93*n7*, 98; campaign finance, 195; direct democracy, 221; electoral college, 19; electoral disproportionality, 45*n7*; interpersonal trust levels, 277; presidential veto authority, 97–98; voter turnout, 249

upper legislative houses, 54*tab*, 57*tab*, 72–75

urbanization, 2

Uribe Vélez, Álvaro, 237

Uruguay: attorney general's office, 131; campaign finance regulation, 196; candidate selection, 181, 195; direct democracy institutions, 224–226, 227, 233–238; early democratic development in, 7; electoral participation, 246; Freedom House 2004 indexes, 275*n4*; legislative electoral system in, 44, 54–55, 57, 60, 69, 72; legislature's powers, 94–95; ombudsman office, 137; party system fragmentation and polarization, 170–173; party system institutionalization, 152–153, 156, 158–159, 161–162, 164, 174; presidential electoral system in, 23, 30; presidential powers, 88, 90–92, 94, 105–106, 110; primary elections, 187, 191, 209; public support for democracy, 277–278, 280, 285, 295; supreme audit institutions, 123, 125–126; voter turnout, 249–250, 255–256

Venezuela: attorney general's office, 131, 135, 142; campaign finance regulation, 198, 204–205, 210; candidate selection, 181, 195; direct democracy institutions, 224–225, 233–236; Freedom House 2004 indexes, 275*n4*; legislative electoral system in, 41–42, 48, 54, 57, 63, 69–70, 72, 76; legislature's powers, 94–95, 101–102; ombudsman office, 137–138; party system fragmentation and polarization, 173–175; party system institutionalization, 152, 155–156, 161, 165, 174; presidential electoral system in, 23, 30–31, 33, 35; presidential powers, 88, 91–92, 94, 103, 105–106; primary elections, 187, 192, 209; public support for democracy, 278, 285, 292; supreme audit institutions, 125–126; voter turnout, 250, 252, 254, 256

Verba, Sidney, 248

vertical accountability, 120

vetoes, 88–89, 97

Vicente, Néstor, 192

voter turnout: averages for presidential elections, 252*fig*; and democratic freedoms, 258*fig*; educational levels and, 258, 260–261, 264; evolution in Latin America of, 253*fig*; factors affecting, 262*tab*, 263*tab*; gender and, 260–261; government performance and, 259*fig*, 265*fig*; incentives for, 268; integrity of electoral process, 242,

267*tab*; knowledge and interest in politics and, 260–261, 264*fig*, 265*fig*; in Latin America (by country), 250, 251*tab*, 266–267; low levels of, 243; macro factors affecting, 255–258; micro factors affecting, 258–266; support for democracy and, 261*tab*, 264; in transition vs. subsequent elections, 256*fig*; trends in, 253–255; trust in government/political parties, 260, 264; types of registration and voting systems and, 257*tab*; and voting as instrument of change, 266*fig*; world comparisons of, 249, 250*fig*, 267. *See also* elections; electoral participation

voto cruzado, 20

women, 6, 260–261

World Trade Organization (WTO), 276

World Values Survey, 273, 277

Zamora, Luis, 192